The Bedford Glossary of Critical and Literary Terms

The Bedford Glossary of Critical and Literary Terms

Third Edition

Ross Murfin
Southern Methodist University

Supryia M. Ray

Bedford/St. Martin's   Boston ◆ New York

For Bedford/St. Martin's

Executive Editor: Stephen A. Scipione
Production Editor: Katherine Caruana
Production Supervisor: Andrew Ensor
Marketing Manager: Adrienne Petsick
Editorial Assistant: Marisa Feinstein
Text Design: Maureen Murray
Copyeditor: Jeannine Thibodeau
Indexer: Steve Csipke
Cover Design: Donna Lee Dennison
Composition: Achorn International, Inc.
Printing and Binding: Haddon Craftsmen, Inc., an RR Donnelley & Sons Company

President: Joan E. Feinberg
Editorial Director: Denise B. Wydra
Editor in Chief: Karen S. Henry
Director of Marketing: Karen R. Soeltz
Director of Editing, Design, and Production: Marcia Cohen
Assistant Director of Editing, Design, and Production: Elise S. Kaiser
Managing Editor: Elizabeth M. Schaaf

Library of Congress Control Number: 2008925882

Manufactured in the United States of America.

3   2   1   0   9   8
f   e   d   c   b   a

For information, write: Bedford/St. Martin's, 75 Arlington Street, Boston, MA 02116   (617-399-4000)

ISBN-10: 0-312-46188-7
ISBN-13: 978-0-312-46188-1

Published and distributed outside North America by:

PALGRAVE MACMILLAN
Houndmills, Basingstoke, Hampshire RG21 6XS
Companies and representatives throughout the world.

ISBN-13: 978-0-230-22330-1
ISBN-10: 0-230-22330-3

A catalogue record for this book is available from the British Library.

Contents

Preface

The Bedford Glossary of Critical and Literary Terms grew out of our work on the Bedford/St. Martin's *Case Studies in Contemporary Criticism* series, which presents classic literary works reprinted with editorial material and critical essays designed to introduce college students to current literary theories, concepts, and terms. The success of the series and of our collaboration in helping students grapple with complex literary and critical discourses encouraged us to try our hands at a full-scale glossary.

In undertaking this project, we consulted other available guides, and, although we admired and learned from them, we also concluded that they were not fully attuned to current developments in literary studies or to the needs of contemporary students. Accordingly, we set out to produce a glossary that would not only redefine old terms in a concise and accessible manner but also comprehensibly introduce the newest critical theories, approaches, and terminology. In the process, we sought to incorporate a wide variety of examples reflecting the diversity of the arts and the world itself. Furthermore, we saw the glossary as an opportunity to help students understand how "literariness" figures in their lives, not only in the classroom and in the books they read but also in all the "texts" that shape their experiences, including those of popular culture.

Notable Features of This Glossary

It defines more than 900 important terms. We have sought to define and describe hundreds of traditional, indispensable terms — such as *genre, irony, metaphor, narrative,* and *rhyme* — in a manner that readers would find clear and current, taking into account their changing inflections and possible new applications. For example, we acknowledge the view, increasingly prevalent since the advent of deconstruction, that irony is a figure of speech; identify examples of anagnorisis in films such as M. Night Shyamalan's *The Sixth Sense;* and distinguish between two scenes in Clint Eastwood's film *Million Dollar Baby* by applying the concepts of crisis and climax. We have also included terms from classical rhetoric (e.g., *prolepsis*) and logic (e.g., *aporia*), many of which have been given new currency in contemporary critical discourse, as well as relatively new terms (e.g., *disability studies, hypertext, urban legend*) still emerging in our culture and classrooms.

We have included entries on literary theories and forms of literary criticism ranging from formalism to poststructuralism, dialogic criticism to queer theory, the old historicism to the new, as well as the sometimes daunting concepts associated with these varied approaches, such as carnival, *différance, epistémé, jouissance,* overdetermination, and thick description. Furthermore, we have written entries for numerous periods and movements relevant to literary studies, from the Old English Period to the Postmodern Period, from the Enlightenment to existentialism. Finally, along with our entries describing traditional literary genres such as poetry, prose, and fiction, we have profiled popular, mass-market sub-genres such as detective fiction, fantasy fiction, and science fiction.

Its examples are drawn from both literature and popular culture. We have searched for illustrative examples not only in canonical literature but also in contemporary literature and older literary works that have often been overlooked. We have thus included hundreds of examples from major figures commonly cited in literary glossaries: Homer, Shakespeare, Swift, Wordsworth, Dickens, Dickinson, Joyce, Woolf, and other classic writers. But we also reference previously marginalized writers such as Aphra Behn and Olaudah Equiano, as well as culturally diverse contemporary authors such as Isabelle Allende, Nuruddin Farah, Khaled Hosseini, Rohinton Mistry, Toni Morrison, Octavio Paz, Salman Rushdie, Dai Sijie, Amy Tan, and Yann Martel.

More distinctively, we have included examples from "nonliterary" forms and genres, including art, advertising, architecture, movies, music, television shows, newspaper columns, political speeches, and comic books. In our glossary, students will see literary strategies and devices at work in episodes of *Lost,* hip-hop lyrics, and propaganda posters. Such pop-culture examples acknowledge the theoretical blurring of the boundaries between "high" and "low" culture. They also invite students who find literary studies formidable to discover that traditionally literary concepts pervade all of our arts — and our lives. Similes and flashbacks are as common in the texts students know best as they are in literary works more traditionally defined; literary devices are at work in both *Borat* and *Brokeback Mountain.*

Most distinctively, we have included numerous visual examples that illustrate the principles discussed in the entries. For instance, we use a strip from Garry Trudeau's comic strip *Doonesbury* to show that allusions can be visual as well as verbal and a *Far Side* cartoon to illustrate analepsis and prolepsis, two major types of anachrony. We often hear that images are displacing texts in the cognitive realm of students; with our visual examples, we try to suggest that text and image can be equally "literary."

It is designed to be a straightforward and handy reference. We have aimed to produce a glossary that is accessible and enjoyable. Accordingly, we have tried to keep our definitions succinct and our examples lively. Entries are arranged alphabetically, from *absence* to *zeugma,* and are extensively cross-referenced. Terms defined elsewhere in the glossary appear in boldface within each entry. (For a more detailed explanation of technical matters — the use of boldface and italics, the meaning of the phrases "See" and "See also," and how we handle dates and foreign language titles — turn to "A Note on References and Cross-References," p. xiii.) We have included an index of examples at the back of the book in the event that a reader wants to see if and how the glossary makes use of a particular work.

New to This Edition

A new edition offers an invaluable opportunity to update and improve a book, particularly one that aims to reflect recent developments and incorporate contemporary examples. A nationwide survey of instructors who have used the first and second editions has informed our work on this evolving project.

Thoroughly updated and expanded entries, plus more than 50 new terms defined. Literary glossaries are almost infinitely expandable, and yet no matter how comprehensive, every glossary omits some terms that are important or likely to become important. In seeking a balance between comprehensiveness and concision, we reviewed every term from the second edition, revising and updating entries based on reviews and substantial new research. Furthermore, we added definitions of traditional terms, such as *golden age* and *voice;* terms whose usage and applicability are currently evolving, such as *early modern;* and contemporary terms, such as *blog* and *constructionism.* We also further increased our attention to genres, whether traditional (e.g., *fairy tale, metrical romance*) or contemporary (e.g., *graphic novel, Language poetry*); added or expanded entries pertaining to important cultural movements (e.g., *Enlightenment, Harlem Renaissance*); and substantially expanded our accounts of literary periods (e.g., *Edwardian Age, Middle English Period*) and critical approaches (e.g., *narratology, textual criticism*).

Many more diverse and contemporary examples, including visual examples. To continue to appeal to today's students, we have further diversified illustrative examples, drawing heavily from contemporary and world literature as well as from popular culture. Such examples range from novels such as Zadie Smith's *White Teeth* and Carlos Ruiz Zafón's *The Shadow of the Wind* to J. K. Rowlings's *Harry Potter* series, the *South Park* and *Sopranos* television series, and the lyrics of Rakim and the Cranberries. We have also added new visual examples including Hieronymus Bosch's grotesque depiction of hell; the cover of *Opportunity* magazine, which accompanies a greatly expanded entry on the Harlem Renaissance; and military recruitment posters exhibiting intertextuality.

A complete list of terms defined in the glossary at the front of the book. For ease of reference, and in accordance with reviewer requests, we have added an "at-a-glance" list of all terms defined in the glossary at the front of this edition.

Acknowledgments

Our initial thanks go to the colleagues and friends who helped shape the various editions of the glossary: Tom Arp, Sylvan Barnet, Steven Barney, Susan Belasco, Shari Benstock, Noelle Bowles, Richard Bozorth, Patrick Brantlinger, Brian Buchwitz, William Cain, John Chun, Russ Castronovo, the late Pascal Covici, Michael Demson, Vincenzo DeNardo, Dennis Foster, Paul Fry, Tom Goodman, Rob Hampton, David Hausman, Tracy Helenbrook, Paul Holdengräber, Michael Householder, Carolyn Jeter, Jacques Lezra, John Lewis, Steven Mailloux, J. Hillis Miller, Scott Moss, Audrey Murfin, Jennifer Negrin, Margot Norris, Sylvia O'Sullivan, Brigitte Peucker, John Paul Riquelme, Philip Rollinson, John Paul Russo, Sarah Scofield, Brook Thomas, Rosemary Garland-Thomson, H. Lewis Ulmann, Benjiman Webb, and Bonnie Wheeler.

Our second round of thanks is to those who reviewed the first and second editions and offered their comments and suggestions. These people include Mark Addison Amos, Southern Illinois University at Carbondale; Susan Blake, Lafayette College; Christine Brandel, Bowling Green State University; Richard Braverman, Columbia University; James Brock, Florida Gulf Coast University; William Crenshaw, Erskine College; Susan Cruea, Bowling Green State University; Amie Doughty, Lake Superior State University; Brian Glavey, University of Virginia; J. Bartholomay Grier, Wilkes University; Natalie Grinnell, Wofford College; Julie Haught, Bowling Green State University; Michael Hennessey, Southwest Texas State University; Martin Hipsky, Ohio Wesleyan University; Kristin Jacobson, Richard Stockton College of New Jersey; Carol Kessler, Pennsylvania State University in Delaware County; Peggy Kulesz, University of Texas at Arlington; Lisa Lampert, University of California-San Diego; Daniel T. Lochman, Texas State University at San Marcos; Jeanette McVicker, SUNY Fredonia; Fran Michel, Willamette University; Barry Milligan, Wright State University; W. Jason Nelson, Bowling Green State University; Arthur Robinson, Diablo Valley College; Kenneth M. Roemer, University of Texas at Arlington; Jack Ryan, Gettysburg College; Julie Shaffer, University of Wisconsin Oshkosh; Jason Steed, University of Nevada; Rebecca Steinitz, Ohio Wesleyan University; Zabelle Stodola, University of Arkansas at Little Rock; Brad Sullivan, Florida Gulf Coast University; Lee Upton, Lafayette College;

Stephen Warner, SUNY Fredonia; Nancy Effinger Wilson, Texas State University at San Marcos; and Rebecca Wood, University of California-Santa Barbara.

Thanks also go to the editorial staff at Bedford/St. Martin's: former president Charles H. Christensen, who signed the project; current president Joan E. Feinberg, who continues to believe in it; and executive editor Steve Scipione, for managing the development of all three editions. We remain grateful to Pam Ozaroff for her work developing the first edition and the continuing support of editorial director Denise B. Wydra and editor-in-chief Karen S. Henry. We also thank those on the production end of the process: Marcia Cohen, Elise Kaiser, Elizabeth Schaaf, and Katherine Caruana, the third edition's editor, who guided the book through the production schedule. We appreciate the permissions-clearing work done by Sandy Schechter and the editorial assistance of Marisa Feinstein, as well as the marketing efforts of Adrienne Petsick.

Finally, and most importantly, we would like to acknowledge the support of our spouses: the late Pam Murfin, Heather Flabiano, and Todd Nystul. Todd in particular has served as the sounding board for many of our ideas and obligingly allowed countless evenings, weekends, and even vacations to become occasions for what we came to refer to as "glossarizing."

A Note on References and Cross-References

A glossary is a reference book that inevitably refers not only to authors and works exemplifying literary concepts but also to itself. For information on our cross-referencing system and the way we reference literary examples, particularly with regard to dates and foreign language titles, see below.

1. Our Use of *See* and *See Also*

Where we have felt that the understanding of a specific term is particularly important to understanding the definition at issue, we have emphasized the importance of looking up that other term by using *see* or *see also*. *See* signals the most crucial terms to look up; we have used it infrequently. For instance, the term *vehicle* can hardly be understood without reference to the term *tenor*. *See also* signals other relevant entries that readers might want to consult.

We use *see* in three other contexts as well: (1) to direct readers from a less common term to its most common synonym (e.g., from **paronomasia** to **pun**); (2) to direct readers from a less common spelling of a term to its more common spelling (e.g., from **katharsis** to **catharsis**); and (3) to direct readers to another entry in which the term being looked up is actually (or more fully) defined (e.g., from **absence** to **presence and absence**).

2. Our Use of Boldface

We have defined more than 900 terms in this glossary, and whenever one of these terms is used in the definition of another, we have typically boldfaced that term to signal that it has its own entry. (We say "typically" because we have generally avoided bolding common words that are commonly understood — words like *author* and *play* — even though we define them.) Thus, if you look up **metaphor,** you will see a number of terms printed in boldface type within that definition, including **figure of speech, simile, tenor,** and **vehicle.**

Sometimes when boldfaced words are juxtaposed, they refer the reader to a single term and entry (e.g., **long meter**). At other times, each word is its own term and is defined separately (e.g., **iambic pentameter** refers the reader to our separate definitions of **iamb** and **pentameter**).

Usually we have boldfaced the first appearance of the term in a given entry; occasionally, however, we have chosen to boldface a later usage instead where that seemed more helpful. Moreover, we have typically boldfaced terms in whatever form they first appear. Hence you may see **new historicist** but discover that the term we actually define is **the new historicism.**

3. Our Use of *Italics*

Occasionally, italics is used as part of our cross-referencing system. Specifically, we have italicized, rather than boldfaced, the first appearance of a term that has its own entry elsewhere if that entry is followed by a *see* that would merely refer you back to the term you initially looked up. For instance, if you are reading the definition of **Marxist criticism,** you will come upon the italicized terms *base* and *superstructure*. If you were to look up the latter two terms, you would find boldfaced entries for them, but those entries would send you right back to the definition of Marxist criticism. We want to let you know that italicized terms are important, but we don't want to send you on a wild goose chase that leads you back to where you started. We also, of course, want our cross-referencing system to permit you to come upon these terms boldfaced within other definitions (*base* and *superstructure* appear as **base** and **superstructure** within the definition of **gap,** in which case you will look the terms up and be told to "See **Marxist criticism**").

Usually, however, italics is used for one of four other purposes. The most common is to refer to titles of novels, other long works, or plays. The second most common is in connection with terms that are being used as such — that is, as terms. In essence, if you see the phrase "the term" in front of a term — or if you could insert that phrase without disturbing the flow of the sentence — that term will be italicized (unless it has already been bolded). For instance, witness our italicization of *see, see also, vehicle,* and *tenor* in the second paragraph of this Note.

We have also occasionally italicized terms *purely* for emphasis, as in this sentence. Finally, we have sometimes used italics to highlight a series of some sort, particularly types or classifications. For instance, under **accent** we discuss *word accent, rhetorical accent,* and *metrical accent.*

4. Our Use of Dates

In referring to examples of the literary terms and concepts we define, we have attempted to provide what no other major glossary does — a date for each and every example, whether from traditional or popular culture sources. Note, however, that although we have tried to provide the best dates possible, this glossary is not intended to be a scholarly sourcebook for dates. By "best," we mean that we have tried to provide the date that would be most helpful to our readers. Usually that is the work's original publication date — but not always. Some works were written and became known long before the advent of movable type (Geoffrey Chaucer's *The Canterbury Tales,* for instance). Other works were written early but not published until late in an author's lifetime. (Thomas Hardy, for instance, didn't publish many of the poems he wrote in his twenties until he was in his fifties and had ended his novelistic career.) In such cases, the date of composition, not the date of publication, best places the poem in biographical and historical contexts.

There are other reasons why we have sometimes chosen not to pair a given title with its initial publication date: for instance, when we are quoting the better-known, later version of a work such as D. H. Lawrence's poem "Love on the Farm" or when it makes the most sense to pair a title that has been translated into English (say, Fyodor Dostoyevsky's *Notes from the Underground*) with an original language publication date. The point is that the glossary is by no means a consistent bibliographic tool; we have made subjective judgments to further our aim of defining terms via telling historical examples.

5. Our Use of Foreign Language Titles

As our reference to the dating of *Notes from the Underground* suggests, we have not always cited original foreign language titles along with their English translations. (For practical reasons, we have *never* included original foreign language titles when the work in question was not written in a language using the Roman alphabet.) Whether the original title, the English language title, or both titles appear depends upon what we felt constituted helpful, relevant information within the context of a given definition. Hence you will see the French philosopher Michel Foucault's work *The Archeology of Knowledge* listed using both its original French title, *L'archéologie du savoir,* and the aforementioned English translation. Just keep in mind that, as with dates, the glossary should not be used as a bibliographic reference.

For ease of reference, we have alphabetized foreign language titles in the index according to the first letter of the first word, even if that word is an article like *une* or *la* that translates as "a" or "the." Thus, while you will find *The Archeology of Knowledge* alphabetized under *A* rather than *T*, the corresponding foreign language title, *L'archéologie du savoir,* appears under *L,* not *A.*

List of Terms Defined in *The Bedford Glossary*

A

absence
abstract
absurd, the
accent
accentual verse
accentual-syllabic verse
acrostic
act
action
aesthetic distance
Aestheticism (Aesthetic Movement)
aesthetics
affective fallacy
affective stylistics
Age of Johnson
Age of Sensibility
Agrarians
alba
Alexandrine
allegory
alliteration
allusion
ambiguity
amphibrach
amphimacer
amplification

anachronism
anachrony
Anacreontic poetry
anacrusis
anagnorisis
analepsis
anapest
anaphora
anastrophe
anecdote
Anglo-Saxon Period
antagonist
anticlimax
antihero
antimasque
antinovel
antistrophe
antithesis
antithetical criticism
antonomasia
anxiety of influence
aphorism
Apocalypse, apocalyptic literature
apocryphal
Apollonian
apologue
aporia

ecopoetry
écriture (writing)
écriture féminine
Edwardian Age
ego
Einfühlung
ekphrasis (ecphrasis)
Electra complex
elegy
elision
Elizabethan Age
ellipsis
empathy
encomium
end rhyme
end-stopped line
English sonnet
enjambement (enjambment)
Enlightenment
Entwicklungsroman
envoy (*envoi*)
ephebe
epic
epic simile
epideictic
epigram
epigraph
epilogue
epiphany
episodic structure
epistémé
epistle
epistolary novel
epitaph
epithalamium (epithalamion)
epithet
epochē
epode
Erziehungsroman
eschatology
essay
essentialism
etymology
euphony
euphuism
exegesis
exemplum
existentialism

explication
explication de texte
expressionism
expressive criticism
expressive form
extrametrical
eye rhyme

F

fable
fabliau
fabula
faction
fairy tale
fallacy of expressive form
falling action
fancy
fantastic
fantasy fiction
farce
Federalist Age
feet
feminine ending
feminine rhyme
feminine writing
feminist criticism
fiction
figurative language
figure of speech
figure of thought
fin de siècle
first-person point of view
flashback
flashforward
flat and round characters
foil
folk
folk drama
folklore
folk song
folk tale
foot
foregrounding
foreshadowing
form
formalism
formalism, Russian
fourfold meaning

fourteener
fractured fairy tale
frame story
free indirect discourse
free verse
French Symbolists
Freytag's Pyramid
frozen metaphor
Fugitives
full rhyme

G

gap
gay and lesbian criticism
gender
gender criticism
generative linguistics
Geneva School
genre
Georgian Age
golden age
Gothic, Gothic literature
graphic novel
Graveyard School of Poetry
green criticism
grotesque
gynocriticism

H

hagiography
haiku
half rhyme
hamartia
hard-boiled detective fiction
Harlem Renaissance
Hartford Wits
head rhyme
hegemony
heptameter
hermeneutics, hermeneutic circle
hero/heroine
heroic couplet
heteroglossia
hexameter
hieratic
historical linguistics
historical novel
historical romance

historicism
history play
hokku
Homeric epithet
Homeric simile
Horatian ode
Horatian satire
horror
hubris
Hudibrastic verse
humours
hybridity
hybris
hymn
hyperbaton
hyperbole
hyperlink
hypertext
hypertext fiction
hypotaxis, hypotactic style
hysteron proteron

I

iamb
icon
iconography
id
identical rhyme
ideology
idyll
illisible (unreaderly)
illocutionary act
image
imagery
Imaginary order
imagination
Imagism
imitation
imperfect rhyme
impersonal narrator
implied author
implied reader
impressionism
impressionistic criticism
incremental repetition
index
indirect discourse
influence

initial rhyme
in medias res
intention
intentional fallacy
interior monologue
interlude
internal rhyme
interpretive communities
intertextuality
intrigue
intrusive narrator
invocation
Irish Literary Renaissance
Irish Revival
irony
irony of fate
irregular ode
Italian sonnet

J

Jacobean Age
jouissance
judicial criticism
jump-marker
Jungian criticism
Juvenalian satire

K

katharsis
kenning
Kuleshov effect
Künstlerroman

L

lai
lampoon
Language poetry
langue
lay
lecture (reading)
legend
leitmotif
leonine rhyme
lesbian criticism
lexicography
lexicon
light ending
light verse

limerick
limited point of view
linguistics
link
lisible (readerly)
literariness
literary criticism
literature of sensibility
literature of the absurd
litotes
local color
locution
locutionary act
logocentric, logocentrism
long meter (long measure)
loose sentence
Lost Generation
lyric

M

madrigal
magic(al) realism
malapropism
Marxism
Marxist criticism
masculine ending
masculine rhyme
masque (mask)
maxim
mechanic form
medieval
medievalism
Medieval Period
medieval romance
meiosis
melodrama
memoir
Menippean satire
metafiction
metaphor
metaphysical conceit
metaphysical poets
meter (metre)
metonymy
metrical accent
metrical romance
metrics
Middle Ages

Middle English Period
mimesis
mimetic criticism
miracle play
mirror stage
mise-en-scène
mixed metaphor
mock epic, mock heroic
mode
modernism
Modern Period
monody
monologic
monologue
monometer
monosyllabic
montage
mood
morality play
morpheme
morphology
motif
motivation
muckraker
mummers' play
muses
mystery fiction
mystery play
mysticism
myth
myth(ic) criticism
mythology
mythopoeia (mythopoesis)

N

naive hero
narration
narrative
narratology
narrator
naturalism
Naturalistic Period
nature writing
near rhyme
negative capability
neo-Aristotelianism
Neoclassical Period
neoclassicism

neologism
Neoplatonism
New Criticism, the
new cultural history, the
new historicism, the
new novel
New Wave
Noble Savage
nom de plume
nonfiction
nonfiction novel
nonsense verse
nouveau roman
novel
novelette
novella

O

objective correlative
objective criticism
objective narrator
objectivity
object-relations theory
oblique rhyme
occasional verse
octameter (octometer)
octave (octet)
ode
Oedipus complex
Old English Period
omniscient point of view
onomatopoeia
oppositions
oration, oratory
organic form
orientalism
Other, the
ottava rima
overdetermined
overstatement
oxymoron

P

paeon
palimpsest
palindrome
palinode
pantomine

parable
paradigm
paradox
paralipsis
parallelism
pararhyme
parataxis, paratactic style
Parnassians
parody
parole
paronomasia
pastiche
pastoral
pastoral elegy
pathetic fallacy
pathos
patriarchal
pattern poetry
pen name
pentameter
perfect rhyme
performative
periodicity
periodic sentence
Periods in American literature
Periods in English literature
periphrasis
perlocutionary act
persona
personal criticism
personification
Petrarchan conceit
Petrarchan sonnet
phallocentric
phallus
phenomenological criticism
phenomenology
philology
phoneme
phonetics
phonocentrism
phonology
picaresque narrative
picaresque novel
Pindaric ode
plagiarism
plaisir

Platonic criticism
Platonic love
Platonism
play
plot
plurality
poem
poetaster
poetic diction
poetic justice
poetic license
poetics
poetry
point of view
polyphonic
portmanteau word
positivism
postcolonial literature, postcolonial theory
postmodernism
Postmodern Period
poststructuralism
practical criticism
pragmatic criticism
Prague Linguistic Circle
Pre-Raphaelitism
presence and absence
primitivism
privilege
problem novel
prolepsis
prologue
propositional act
proscenium
prose
prose encomium
prose poem
prosody
prosopopoeia
protagonist
proverb
pseudonym
psychic(al) distance
psychoanalytic criticism
psychological criticism
psychological novel
pulp fiction
pun

Puritan Interregnum
purple patch
pyrrhic

Q

quantitative verse
quatrain
queer theory
quest romance

R

race (and literary studies)
reader-oriented criticism
reader-reception criticism
reader-response criticism
Real, the
realism
realistic novel
Realistic Period
reception theory
refrain
regular ode
Renaissance
Renaissance Period
renga
representation
resolution
Restoration Age
revenge tragedy
Revolutionary Period
rhetoric
rhetorical accent
rhetorical criticism
rhetorical figures
rhetorical irony
rhyme
rhyme royal
rhyme scheme
rhythm
rime riche
rime royal
rising action
roman à clef
romance
romantic
romantic comedy
romantic irony

romanticism
Romantic Period (in American literature)
Romantic Period (in English literature)
rondeau
round character
run-on line
Russian formalism

S

sapphic
sarcasm
satire
scansion
scene
scheme
science fiction
scriptible (writerly)
second-person point of view
semantics
semiology
semiotics
Senecan tragedy
sensibility
sententia
sentimental comedy
sentimentalism
sentimental novel
septenary
sestet
sestina
setting
Seven Cardinal Virtues
Seven Deadly Sins
sextet
sexualities criticism
sexuality
Shakespearean sonnet
shaped verse
she-tragedy
short meter (short measure)
short story
sibilance
sign
significance
signified
signifier
simile

The Bedford Glossary of
Critical and Literary Terms

Glossary of Critical and Literary Terms

A

▶ **absence:** The idea, advanced by French theorist Jacques Derrida, that **authors** are not present in **texts** and that meaning arises in the absence of any authority guaranteeing the correctness of any one interpretation.

See **presence and absence** for a more complete discussion of the concepts of presence and absence.

▶ **abstract:** The opposite of **concrete**. Broadly speaking, abstract terms and statements describe ideas, concepts, or qualities, whereas concrete terms and statements refer to specific people, places, events, or things. "Love" and "hate," for instance, are abstract terms, as are "agony," "ingenuity," "persistence," and "theocracy." By contrast, terms such as "firefighter," "kiss," "mall," "rain," and "spider" are concrete. Likewise, the last two lines of John Keats's "Ode on a Grecian Urn" (1820), spoken by the urn itself, are abstract: "'Beauty is truth, truth beauty, — that is all / Ye know on earth, and all ye need to know.'" By contrast, the first two lines of William Butler Yeats's "The Wild Swans at Coole" (1919), which also include the word "beauty," are concrete: "The trees are in their autumn beauty, / The woodland paths are dry . . . ."

While *abstract* and *concrete* are often viewed as a contrary philosophical and linguistic pair, or **binary opposition,** they may be better understood as end points of a continuum. The more intangible a term or statement, the more general, the more it is associated with the intellect, the more abstract it is likely to be. Likewise, the more tangible a term or statement, the more specific, the more it invokes the five senses, the more concrete it is likely to be.

When applied to literary works, the terms *abstract* and *concrete* also describe the level of detail, **imagery,** and sensory language in a passage or work. Concrete passages are richly detailed and often make use of **figurative language** to create a vivid and immediate experience for the reader. Abstract passages are more general, often taking an intellectual or theoretical approach to the subject being described. The old adage "show, don't tell" reflects a preference for concrete writing.

The term *abstract* is also used to refer to a short summary or overview of a longer work. Abstracts are standard in several fields, particularly in the sciences.

FURTHER EXAMPLES: Robert Burns's most famous poetic statement, "O, my Luve's like a red, red rose / That's newly sprung in June" (1796), is a concrete poetic statement. W. H. Auden's statement on love in "Heavy Date" (1940) is abstract:

> I believed for years that
> Love was the conjunction
> Of two oppositions;
>   That was all untrue. . . .

▶ **Absurd, the (absurd, literature or theater of the):** A phrase referring to works that use absurdity as a device to depict the actual absurdity of the modern human condition, often with implicit reference to humanity's loss or lack of religious, philosophical, or cultural roots. Such works depict the individual as essentially isolated, even when surrounded by others.

Because writers associated with the **genre** believe that the only way to represent the absurdity of the modern human condition is to write in kind, the literature of the Absurd is bizarre in both **style** and subject matter. Familiar **conventions,** governing everything from **plot** to **dialogue,** are routinely flouted, as is the notion that a work of literature should be unified and coherent. The resulting **scenes,** actions, and dialogue are usually disconnected, repetitive, and intentionally nonsensical. Absurdist works might be comic if not for their obviously and grotesquely **tragic** dimensions.

The Absurd has its roots in such movements as **Dadaism** and **surrealism.** Other influences range from **nonsense verse** and silent film comedy to Alfred Jarry's play *Ubu roi* (*Ubu the King*) (1896) to the works of August Strindberg, James Joyce, and Franz Kafka. Key ideas underpinning the genre also developed in France during the 1940s in the **existentialist** works of Jean-Paul Sartre and Albert Camus depicting the lonely, confused, often anguished individual in an utterly bewildering universe. However, unlike existentialist works, which take a deliberative, rational approach to this sense of disconnection, Absurdist works reject logic, devalue language, and convey their sense of absurdity through absurdity itself.

The theater of the Absurd — a phrase attributed to critic Martin Esslin, whose *The Theatre of the Absurd,* originally published in 1961, remains the standard study of the genre — established itself in the 1950s, with Eugène Ionesco's *La cantatrice chauve* (*The Bald Soprano*) (1950), in which, not surprisingly, there is no soprano, let alone a bald one. Equally influential was Samuel Beckett's play *En attendant Godot* (*Waiting for Godot*) (1952), in which two tramps wait in vain for someone who may not even exist — and with whom they are not even sure they have an appointment.

Most Absurdist works have been written as plays, though certain novels, particularly several written during the 1960s, contain Absurdist elements. Harold Pinter was primarily responsible for developing British Absurdist theater; Edward Albee is America's leading Absurdist playwright.

While the genre peaked in the 1960s, Absurdist works continue to be produced today. The Absurdly-named Untitled Theater Company #61, founded by playwright Edward Einhorn, describes itself as "[p]resenting a modern Theater of the Absurd in New York City since 1992."

FURTHER EXAMPLES: Jean Genet's *Le balcon* (*The Balcony*) (1956), Edward Albee's *The Sandbox* (1959), and Harold Pinter's *The Homecoming* (1965). Joseph Heller's *Catch-22* (1961) is at once a popular novel and an Absurdist work. A contemporary example of Absurdist theater is *Linguish* (2006), a one-act play by Einhorn described by *The Village Voice* as "an inspired Absurdist comedy" that "follows four strangers infected with a mysterious form of aphasia [a neurological condition that causes loss of language] who are quarantined in a No Exit bunker. Literally at a loss for words, they must invent a new language in order to communicate — or to keep from going crazy."

▶ **accent:** The **stress,** or emphasis, placed on a syllable (the symbols ´ and ˘ are used for stressed and unstressed syllables, respectively). Three main types of accent exist. *Word accent* refers to the stress (or lack thereof) placed on syllables of words as they are pronounced in ordinary speech. *Rhetorical accent* refers to the stress placed on syllables or words according to their location or importance in a sentence. *Metrical accent* refers to the stress placed on syllables in accordance with the poetic **meter;** when the metrical pattern of a poem "forces" a syllable to be stressed that would not be stressed in ordinary speech, the accent is said to be **wrenched.** In **versification,** accent refers specifically to the meter itself, the more or less regular pattern of stressed and unstressed syllables. Some poets and critics, however, differentiate between *accent* and *stress,* reserving the term *stress* for metrical emphasis and *accent* for the emphasis used in everyday **discourse** (word accent).

Accent may also refer to distinctive regional speech patterns and intonations (for example, a Brooklyn or Texas accent).

EXAMPLES: Accent in the following sentence is different depending on whether word accent, rhetorical accent, or metrical accent is used. Using word accent, you'd probably say it like this:

"I'll do the grocery shopping *later*, Pam." [word accent]

If you wanted to stress the fact that you, and not someone else, were going to do the shopping, you'd probably say the sentence more like this:

"*I'll* do the grocery shopping later, Pam." [rhetorical accent]

As a line in a poem written in **iambic pentameter,** a meter in which every line contains a regular pattern of five alternating unstressed and stressed syllables, the accents would look like this:

"I'll dŏ thĕ grócĕry shŏppĭng látĕr, Pám." [metrical accent]

In the following poem, " 'Faith' is a fine invention" (c. 1860), Emily Dickinson placed a rhetorical accent on the word *see* as well as on the entire word *Microscopes*. Note that the last syllable of the last line (*cy*) carries a metrical accent made evident, in part, by the stress placed on *see* two lines earlier.

"Fáith" ĭs ă fíne ĭnvéntĭon
Whĕn Géntlĕmĕn căn *sée* —
Bŭt *Mícróscópes* ăre prúdĕnt
Ĭn án Ĕmérgĕncý.

▶ **accentual verse:** See **meter.**

▶ **accentual-syllabic verse:** See **meter.**

▶ **acrostic:** A **text** in which certain letters are placed so that they spell out words, phrases, or other significant sequences when read horizontally, vertically, or according to some other specific sequence. Acrostics may be composed using **verse** or **prose** or simply as freestanding puzzles for entertainment or education. Acrostics date back to ancient times, when they may have been used as memory-enabling devices or deemed to have magical or spiritual properties.

There are several different types of acrostics, all of which are defined in terms of the positioning of the letters forming meaningful sequences. The *true acrostic* is the most basic one: the first letter of each line (or paragraph or sentence or other unit) forms part of a word (or words) when read "down," that is, vertically. In the *mesostich,* the middle letters, read vertically, have meaning; in the *telestich* the last letters; and in the *double acrostic* both the first and last letters. *Abecedarian acrostics* follow an alphabetical pattern, such that the first letter of each line or other unit begins with the letters of the alphabet, in order. A still more complicated form is the *cross acrostic,* in which the text is arranged so that the initial letter of the first line or other unit, the second letter of the second, the third letter of the third, and so forth, spell a word. Most complex of all is the *all-around acrostic,* or *acrostic square,* in which the text is arranged in a perfect square with an equal number of letters and lines that read the same way horizontally and vertically whether starting from the top left corner or the bottom right one.

Today, acrostics are often found in newspapers, magazines, and puzzle publications. They are also used as an educational tool to teach the alphabet or creative writing and are still viewed as helpful mnemonic devices.

EXAMPLES: The following Roman acrostic (c. A.D. 500), written in Latin and discovered on an Egyptian papyrus, is an all-around acrostic often translated as "the sower Arepo holds the wheels carefully":

```
S A T O R
A R E P O
T E N E T
O P E R A
R O T A S
```

Edgar Allan Poe's poem "Elizabeth" (1829) is a true acrostic; when read "down," the initial letters of the poem's lines spell out the name "Elizabeth Rebecca." David Mark Hummon's book for children entitled *Animal Acrostics* (1999) includes "vertical" descriptions of animals as well as instructions to help children write acrostics.

Abecedarian acrostics can be found in a number of psalms and in the Dead Sea Scrolls, as well as in Geoffrey Chaucer's "An ABC" (c. 1360s). Recent examples of abecedarian acrostics include Steven Schnur's *Winter: An Alphabet Acrostic* (2002) and his similar publications about the other seasons.

The *New York Times* publishes acrostic puzzles featuring quotations from well-known figures every other week in its Sunday edition. The common crossword puzzle contains acrostic arrangements, though it is not itself a true acrostic.

▶ **act:** A major division of the **action** of a **play** or **drama**. Acts are generally subdivided into **scenes**. Acts and scenes were developed by ancient Roman dramatists, who normally divided their plays into five acts. William Shakespeare followed this Roman tradition; later, playwrights such as Henrik Ibsen and Anton Chekhov wrote plays in four acts. Modern plays typically consist of two or three acts, but some playwrights have dispensed with acts altogether in favor of serial scenes or episodes.

▶ **action:** The events or unfolding of events in a **narrative**. The action is what happens in the **plot** of a literary work, including what the **characters** say or do, to advance the **story**.

▶ **aesthetic distance (distance, psychic[al] distance, dramatic illusion):** A separation between the audience and a work of art that is necessary for the audience to recognize and appreciate the work as an **aesthetic** object. The term has also been used to refer to the relatively **objective** perspective writers may maintain toward their work. Such objectivity, some critics argue, allows the writer to relate the **story** and present its **characters** without recourse to personal, judgmental commentary. Distance, however, does not imply complete detachment. Rather, it allows the writer (and audience) to view the work "free" from overly personal identifications and thus to render (and experience) its contents fully and freely.

In "Literary History as a Challenge to Literary Theory" (1967), German critic Hans Robert Jauss used *aesthetic distance* in a new way. In the context of **reception theory** (a type of **reader-response criticism**), the term refers to the difference between how a work was viewed when it was originally published and how that same work is viewed today.

See also **aesthetics**.

▶ **Aestheticism (Aesthetic Movement):** A movement that developed in Europe in the second half of the nineteenth century and whose proponents insisted on the separation of art from morality, maintaining that art need not be moral to have value. *L'art pour l'art* (**"art for art's sake"**) was the rallying cry for writers who valued art for its inherent **aesthetic** quality rather than for its **didactic** potential.

Literary influences on the movement included French writer Théophile Gautier, who asserted in his preface to *Mademoiselle de Maupin* (1835) that art has no utilitarian value; American writer Edgar Allan Poe, who developed a theory of the supremacy of the "poem *per se*" in an essay entitled "The Poetic Principle" (1850); and the English **Pre-Raphaelites,** whose poems (like Pre-Raphaelite paintings) emphasized sensuous detail. Charles Baudelaire, Gustave Flaubert, J. K. Huysmans, and Stéphane Mallarmé, French writers who were early leaders of the Aesthetic Movement, promoted the idea that art is the supreme human endeavor. In England, the work of painters and illustrators such as Aubrey Beardsley, Max Beerbohm, and James McNeill Whistler complemented the writings of Algernon Swinburne, Walter Pater, and, especially, Oscar Wilde. The **Parnassians,** a group of French and English poets who strove to write **objective** poetry that exalted **form** and minimized authorial **presence,** also played a significant, if lesser known, role in Aestheticism.

FURTHER EXAMPLE: Wilde's *The Decay of Lying* (1889) expresses some of the attitudes of Aestheticism through a **character** named Cyril, who at one point remarks:

> Art never expresses anything but itself. It has an independent life, just as Thought has, and develops purely on its own lines. It is not necessarily realistic in an age of realism, nor spiritual in an age of faith. So far from being the creation of its own time, it is usually in direct opposition to it, and the only history that it preserves for us is the history of its own progress.

▶ **aesthetics:** The study of beauty in nature and the arts. Two approaches to aesthetics exist: (1) the philosophical approach, which poses questions relating to the nature or definition of beauty; and (2) the psychological approach, which examines the perception, origins, and effects of beauty. Aesthetics is relevant to **literary criticism** insofar as it considers the relationship between beauty and other values, such as truth. The study of aesthetics also involves inquiry into the nature of artistic creation and audience appreciation.

In the second half of the nineteenth century, an extreme philosophy of aesthetics emerged that came to be called **Aestheticism.** Advocating **"art for art's sake,"** adherents of Aestheticism valued literature for its inherent or affective qualities and maintained that art need not take moral or practical issues into consideration.

Eighteenth-century German philosopher Immanuel Kant used the term *aesthetic* in another sense, to refer to the effort to relate the material to the spiritual. Aesthetic objects, according to Kant, combine the two realms, simultaneously entailing tangibility and sanctity. This idea that the aesthetic is somehow a locus of universal or even divine truth — a realm where words are somehow not just arbitrary **signifiers** but rather revelatory **signs** with some special status — was debunked in the twentieth century, both by **deconstructors** like Paul de Man and **Marxist critics** like Terry Eagleton. In *Aesthetic Ideology* (1988) and *The Ideology of the Aesthetic* (1990), de Man and Eagleton, respectively, argued that the **privileging** of aesthetic language and the belief that it has transcendental significance are but manifestations of the prevailing Western **ideology** and, to use Eagleton's paraphrase of de Man's argument, "pernicious mystifications."

▶ **affective fallacy:** A term coined by **New Critics** William K. Wimsatt and Monroe C. Beardsley in their essay "The Affective Fallacy" (1946) to refer to what they regarded as the erroneous practice of interpreting **texts** according to the psychological responses of readers. Wimsatt and Beardsley described the affective fallacy as "a confusion between the poem and its *results* (what it *is* and what it *does*). . . . It begins by trying to derive the standard of criticism from the psychological effects of the poem and ends in impressionism and relativism." **Reader-response critics,** who study the way individual readers and **interpretive communities** go about making sense of texts, reject the concept of the affective fallacy.

See also **authorial intention.**

▶ **affective stylistics:** A phrase coined by American **reader-response critic** Stanley Fish in an essay entitled "Literature in the Reader: Affective Stylistics" (1970) to refer to the impact that the **structure** of a given **text** has on the minds of individual readers as they read and, more generally, to a personal and private process of reading that Fish once believed everyone employs. In setting forth his **theory** of affective stylistics, Fish significantly developed the ideas of reader-response critic Louise M. Rosenblatt and **hermeneutical** theorist E. D. Hirsch. He suggested that meaning is an "event" that takes place in the mind of an individual reader during the act of reading; that reading is a temporal process in which each succeeding word, sentence, paragraph, **stanza,** and so forth provides additional information that readers must incorporate into their understanding; and therefore that meaning changes as the reader progresses through the work. At each step, readers reevaluate their interpretations, forming new expectations and perhaps rejecting old ones, recognizing past mistakes and making new ones.

Subsequently, beginning with an essay entitled "Interpreting the Variorum" (1976), Fish shifted his focus away from the individual reader to **interpretive communities,** arguing that members of a given interpretive community tend to share the same reading strategies and that the meaning of a given text may differ significantly from group to group. In making this shift, Fish substantially modified his reader-response theory, coming to view affective stylistics as one of several possible reading strategies.

▶ **Age of Johnson (in English literature):** The last of three literary eras within the **Neoclassical Period** in English literature, an age generally said to range from the middle of the eighteenth century until 1798, the year in which poets William Wordsworth and Samuel Taylor Coleridge published *Lyrical Ballads*, a volume often cited as inaugurating the **Romantic Period** in English Literature. While the Age of Johnson spans the same time period as the *Age of Sensibility*, the two names for this era reflect different literary interests and priorities as well as its transitional status. Critics using the term *Age of Johnson* — the older and more traditional of the two names — focus on the era as the final stage of English **neoclassicism;** those using the term *Age of Sensibility* see it as anticipating **romanticism** in English literature.

The Age of Johnson, named for the influential poet, critic, and writer Samuel Johnson, calls to mind neoclassical **aesthetics** and **Enlightenment** values such as reason, balance, order, and a focus on humanity in general. Major works include Edmund Burke's *A Philosophical Enquiry into the Origins of our Ideas of the Sublime and Beautiful* (1757), Oliver Goldsmith's novel *The Vicar of Wakefield* (1766), Edward Gibbon's *The Decline and Fall of the Roman Empire* (1787), and James Boswell's **biography** *Life of Samuel Johnson* (1791), as well as Johnson's own works, including his essays in *The Rambler* (1750–52), his *Dictionary of the English Language* (1755), and his "Oriental tale" *Rasselas* (1759).

By contrast, the Age of Sensibility evokes an emphasis on feeling and **sensibility** and a shift toward new forms of literary expression including the **sentimental comedy** and **sentimental novel.** Unlike neoclassicists, who looked to **classical** writers for guidance and inspiration, writers associated with the Age of Sensibility (most of whom were poets) developed an interest in **medieval** history, **bardic poetry, folk** literature such as **ballads,** and **primitivism,** trending toward romanticism's emphasis on individualism, **imagination,** and the language of the common people. Such writers included poets Thomas Gray, best known for his "Elegy Written in a Country Churchyard" (1751); Williams Collins; William Cowper; and Christopher Smart. Laurence Sterne's *Tristram Shandy* (9 vols.; 1759–67) and Henry Mackenzie's *The Man of Feeling* (1771) are considered **classic** prose fiction examples of the Age of Sensibility.

See also **neoclassicism, romanticism.**

▶ **Age of Sensibility (in English literature):** See Age of Johnson (in English literature).

▶ **Agrarians:** A group of twelve Southern scholars and writers, most of whom were faculty, students, or alumni of Vanderbilt University, who promoted agrarian regionalism. The Agrarians, who were active from 1928– 1937, developed as an offshoot of the **Fugitives,** a group of Southern poets active from about 1915–1928 who also had major ties to Vanderbilt. Unlike the Agrarians, who pressed for political and economic reform, the Fugitives were a nonpolitical literary group focused on poetry and criticism. Only four Fugitives — Donald Davidson, John Crowe Ransom, Allen Tate, and Robert Penn Warren — were also Agrarians, though all but Warren played leading roles in the movement.

The Agrarians were best known for their controversial manifesto *I'll Take My Stand* (1930), a collection of twelve essays subtitled *The South and the Agrarian Tradition* which opposed industrial capitalism, advocated an agricultural base for the American economy, and provided the philosophical and **ideological** underpinnings of the "back-to-the-land" Agrarian movement. The Agrarians sharply attacked industrialism, criticizing the dehumanizing effects of science and technology as well as mass consumerism. They essentially equated industrialism with communism, arguing that the collectivism inherent in both systems devalued work and that people threatened with redundancy by machines would turn to communism. The manifesto's title, a line from the Confederate song "Dixie," reflected the Agrarians' intense regionalism and strong defense of the Old South.

By 1933, with the ever-deepening Great Depression, the Agrarians' crusade became a larger, more organized movement, and the Agrarians shifted their focus from cultural critique to more practical policies and programs. Critical to the Agrarian vision was a proprietary ideal, involving land reform, property rights, and restoration of the means of production to the control of individuals. The Agrarians also **privileged** traditional Southern sociocultural values, such as family, faith, leisure, and a perceived special tie to the land. They experienced substantial internal tensions, however, especially over race relations and segregation.

Seeking a venue for their work, the Agrarians partnered with New York publisher Seward Collins on his *American Review* (1933–37), a literary journal that gave voice to a variety of political and economic ideas. Despite their disagreement with Seward's own pro-fascist views, the Agrarians provided editorial support for the journal and contributed about seventy essays and reviews. Agrarian Frank Owsley's essay "The Pillars of Agrarianism" (1935), which the group generally endorsed, outlined a set of specific reforms to promote Southern agriculture, including creation of a new homestead program, prohibitions against land speculation, measures to conserve soil and rehabilitate the land, and a constitutional amendment to divide the country into economic regions.

The Agrarians also partnered with the English Distributists, who supported broad distribution of the means of production among individuals and a return to subsistence farming as a "third way" around both capitalism and socialism. Their last book, *Who Owns America?* (1936), a collection of twenty essays, was a joint project with the Distributists.

Members of the Agrarians aside from the four Fugitives and Owsley included John Fletcher, Henry Kline, Lyle Lanier, Andrew Lytle, Herman Nixon, John Wade, and Stark Young. While the Agrarians have often been seen as reactionary, concerns about the environmental and cultural effects of industrialism have sparked renewed interest in agrarian ideals, as seen in the work of writer and critic Wendell Berry.

See also **Fugitives.**

▶ *alba*: See **aubade.**

▶ **Alexandrine:** A line of **verse** with twelve syllables, characterized in French by four **stresses** and a **caesura** after the sixth syllable and in English by the use of **iambic hexameter** (six iambic **feet**). Likely named after **medieval** French **romances** commemorating Alexander the Great, the Alexandrine became the dominant **meter** in French verse from the sixteenth to nineteenth centuries. It was also popular in Dutch and German verse but relatively rare in English, though it appears as the ninth and final line of the **Spenserian stanza** (following eight lines of iambic **pentameter**).

EXAMPLES: The second line of the following **couplet**, which ends one of the Spenserian stanzas in Edmund Spenser's *The Faerie Queene* (1590, 1596):

> A loathly, wrinckled hag, ill-favoured, old,
> Whŏse sé|crĕt fílth |gŏod mán|nĕrs bíd|dĕth nót | bĕ tóld.

▶ **allegory:** The **concrete** presentation of an **abstract** idea, typically in a **narrative** — whether **prose, verse,** or **drama** — with at least two levels of meaning. The first level is the surface story line, which can be summed up by stating who did what to whom when. The second level is typically moral, political, philosophical, or religious. To facilitate recognition of this deeper level of meaning, allegories are often thinly veiled; **personification** is common, and sometimes **characters** bear the names of the qualities or ideas the author wishes to represent. Allegories need not be entire narratives, however, and narratives may contain allegorical elements or figures. Many critics consider the allegory to be an extended **metaphor** and, conversely, consider metaphors — which involve saying one thing but meaning another — to be "verbal allegories."

Allegories generally fall into two major categories: (1) the *political and historical allegory*; and (2) the *allegory of abstract themes*. In the first type, the figures, **settings,** or actions correspond directly and specifically to historical personages, places, and events (Napoleon's defeat at Waterloo, for instance). In the second type, the characters stand for ideas or abstract qualities. (In an allegory warning against laziness, the main character might encounter figures such as Sloth and Perseverance.)

Allegory continues to be used as a narrative device today, although its popularity peaked in the **Middle Ages,** when the **dream vision** was a prevalent form. Types of allegory common in other historical periods include the **fable,** *exemplum,* and **parable.**

EXAMPLES: John Bunyan's *Pilgrim's Progress* (1678), an allegory of abstract themes, is the most famous English allegory. On the surface, it tells the story of a man named Christian who journeys from one city to another, but on a deeper level, the problems he encounters represent obstacles that a good Christian must overcome to live a godly life. Christian encounters such blatantly allegorical figures as Mr. Worldly Wiseman and places such as Vanity Fair and the Slough of Despair.

In "Lend Me Your Light," an **autobiographical** short story from Rohinton Mistry's collection *Swimming Lessons* (1989), the protagonist, an Indian émigré who has returned to Bombay for a visit home, observes the activity at a train station, enacted "with all the subtlety of a sixteenth-century morality play":

> The drama began when the train, Reality, rolled into the station. It was overcrowded because everyone wanted to get on it: Virtue, Vice, Apathy, Corruption, all of them. Someone, probably Poverty, dropped his plastic lunch bag amidst the stampede, nudged on by Fate. Then Reality rolled out of the station with a gnashing and clanking of its metal, leaving in its wake the New Reality. And someone else, probably Hunger, matter-of-factly picked up Poverty's mangled lunch, dusted off a *chapati* which had slipped out of the trampled bag, and went his way. In all of this, was there a lesson for me? To trim my expectations and reactions to things, trim them down to the proper proportions?

The **graphic novelist** Neil Gaiman introduced an allegorical dimension to his *Sandman* series (1991–97) by giving the major recurring characters names such as Dream, Desire, and Destiny.

▶ **alliteration:** The repetition of sounds in a sequence of words. Alliteration generally refers to repeated consonant sounds (often initial consonant sounds or those at the beginning of **stressed** syllables) but has also been used by some critics to refer to repeated vowel sounds. When *s* is the repeated sound, the result is said to be **sibilant**. Alliteration was especially important in **Old English** verse, establishing the **rhythm** and **structure** of the poetic line. Since then, its role has diminished, although poets to this day use alliteration to create powerful musical effects and to highlight and emphasize key words, concepts, and relationships.

Densely alliterative utterances that are difficult to pronounce — such as "Peter Piper picked a peck of pickled peppers" and "She sells seashells by the seashore" — are called *tongue twisters*.

EXAMPLES: The last line of Wallace Stevens's poem "Of Mere Being" (1955):

> The bird's fire-fangled feathers dangle down.

S appears as a sibilant alliterative sound in this passage from Kate Chopin's *The Awakening* (1899):

> The voice of the sea is seductive; never ceasing, whispering, clamoring, murmuring, inviting the soul to wander for a spell in abysses of solitude; to lose itself in mazes of inward contemplation. The voice of the sea speaks to the soul. The touch of the sea is sensuous, enfolding the body in its soft, close embrace.

An example of alliteration gone overboard appears in this description of "progression" by Warren G. Harding, nominating William Howard Taft for president at the 1912 Republican convention, eight years before Harding himself made a successful run at the presidency:

> Progression is not proclamation nor palaver. It is not pretense nor play on prejudice. It is not of personal pronouns, nor perennial

pronouncement. It is not the perturbation of a people passion-wrought, nor a promise proposed.

The following passage from Michael Byers's short story "Blue River, Blue Sun," from his collection *The Coast of Good Intentions* (1998), is packed with *s* and *p* sounds:

> The plastic water vials shifted in his pack like tiny men shifting in sleep, and when he dipped to fill a sample his old knees popped and pinged. Away across the grasses he could see his students advancing one slow step at a time.

Sheryl Crow's rowdy pop song "All I Wanna Do [Is Have Some Fun]" (1993) is heavily alliterative, repeating the letters *b* and *l* in eleven of the twenty-eight words — e.g., *beer, bar, early, Billy, peel, labels, Bud, bottle* — in the two opening lines. Moreover, alliteration is a common device in hip hop — itself an alliterative term. Examples include Nas's "It Ain't Hard to Tell" (*Illmatic*, 1994), which plays on the letter *l*, especially in the second verse, and the opening lines of Pharoahe Monch's "Hell" (*Internal Affairs*, 1999), in which *f* is the repeated sound.

▶ **allusion:** An indirect reference, often to a person, event, statement, **theme**, or work. Allusions enrich meaning through the **connotations** they carry. An **author's** use of this device tends to presuppose that readers in general will possess the knowledge necessary to make the connection, but sometimes allusions are used that only a choice few can understand.

EXAMPLES: Someone who says, "Frankly, my dear . . ." is probably alluding to Rhett Butler's parting words to his mercurial wife Scarlett in the movie version of Margaret Mitchell's *Gone with the Wind* (1936; adapted to film 1939): "Frankly, my dear, I don't give a damn."

When, in T. S. Eliot's *The Waste Land* (1922), a voice says

> I remember
> Those are pearls that were his eyes

some readers will recognize the allusion to William Shakespeare's *The Tempest* (c. 1611), in which the character Ariel sings:

> Full fathom five thy father lies;
> Of his bones are coral made;
> Those are pearls that were his eyes

lines that Caroline Kennedy read at the memorial service for her brother, John F. Kennedy, Jr. But when, in Eliot's "Gerontion" (1920), the speaker says

> I was neither at the hot gates
> Nor fought in the warm rain

only readers of Greek would know that "hot gates" is an allusion to the fifth-century B.C. Battle of Thermopylae (literally, "hot gates") between the Greeks and the Persians.

Allusions to ancient events and literary **classics** may be found even in popular culture. Hot Gates is the name of a porn actress pitted against the superhero Batman in Frank Miller's **graphic novel** *Batman: The Dark Knight Returns* (1986). The Eagles' song "Get Over It" (1994) alludes to William Shakespeare's *Henry VI, Part 2* (c. 1594) by quoting "Old Billy's" famous line "Let's kill all the lawyers" verbatim.

In the *Doonesbury* comic strip shown below, Garry Trudeau visually alludes to Charles M. Schulz's *Peanuts* with an image of Trudeau's lovable hippie, Zonker Harris, who is dressed like Schulz's Charlie Brown and looks addled atop Snoopy's **iconic** doghouse.

(*DOONESBURY* © 1997 G. B. Trudeau. *Reprinted with permission of UNIVERSAL PRESS SYNDICATE. All rights reserved.*)

▶ **ambiguity:** Lack of clarity or uncertainty in meaning. A word, phrase, statement, or passage is ambiguous when it can be understood or interpreted in more than one way. Ambiguity often results from use of pronouns without proper referents, use of words with multiple meanings, unusual **syntax,** and inordinate brevity.

Ambiguity may be intentional or unintentional and, depending on the context, may be a virtue or a flaw. If **denotative** precision is required, as is often the case in speech, ambiguity is a flaw. But if *plurisignation*, or multiple meanings, are intended or desirable, as is often the case in literature, ambiguity is a virtue. The richness and complexity of literary works depend to a great extent on ambiguity, which can be used to create alternate meanings or levels of meaning or to leave meaning indeterminate. In his exploration of ambiguity as a literary device in English poetry, critic William Empson highlighted the importance of **connotation** to meaning and identified various types of ambiguity in his book *Seven Types of Ambiguity* (1930).

EXAMPLES: The following lines of poetry contain verbal ambiguities:

> Piping songs of pleasant glee
> On a cloud I saw a child. . . .
> — William Blake, "Introduction"
> to *Songs of Innocence* (1789)

Who is piping: the speaker or the child? And who is on the cloud?

> The pears are not seen
> As the observer wills.
> — Wallace Stevens,
> "Study of Two Pears" (1938)

What point is Stevens trying to make? That the observer does not want to see the pears and so does not see them? Or that the observer wants the pears to be seen in a certain way, but they have not been depicted in that way by the painter of the "Study"?

Sometimes ambiguity is of a more general nature. Whether the ghosts of Emily Brontë's *Wuthering Heights* (1847) and Henry James's *The Turn of the Screw* (1898) are supernatural beings or hallucinations is left ambiguous. General ambiguity, of course, depends upon an accumulation of verbal ambiguities, as may be seen in the passage from *The Turn of the Screw* in which the **narrator,** a governess, relates the death of her charge Miles. Suspecting that the child has seen the ghost of Peter Quint, the governess asks:

> "Whom do you mean by 'he'?"
> "Peter Quint — you devil!" His face gave again, round the room, its convulsed supplication. "*Where?*"

Is Miles's exclamatory statement an answer to the governess's question (in which case he is calling his governess a "devil"), or is it an address to the ghost of Quint (in which case he is calling Quint a "devil")? And why is Miles asking "*Where?*" The governess's **narrative** continues:

> They are in my ears still, his supreme surrender of the name and his tribute to my devotion. "What does he matter now, my own? — what will he *ever* matter? *I* have you," I launched at the beast, "but he has lost you for ever!" Then for the demonstration of my work, "There, *there!*" I said to Miles.
>
> But he had already jerked straight round, stared, glared again, and seen but the quiet day. With the stroke of the loss I was so proud of he uttered the cry of a creature hurled over an abyss, and the grasp with which I recovered him might have been that of catching him in his fall. I caught him, yes, I held him — it may be imagined with what a passion; but at the end of a minute I began to feel what it truly was that I held. We were alone with the quiet day, and his little heart, dispossessed, had stopped.

Has the governess frightened Miles to death? Murdered him in some more direct way? Is the child the victim of a successful but fatal exorcism? James chose to leave the answer to these and many other questions ambiguous, thereby igniting a century of critical controversy.

▶ **amphibrach:** See foot.

▶ **amphimacer:** See foot.

▶ **amplification:** A **rhetorical figure** involving a dramatic ordering of words, often emphasizing some sort of expansion or progression, whether conceptual, valuative, poetic, or even with regard to word length. Among those who have criticized this once common form of verbal flourish is Alexander Pope, who in *Peri Bathous [On Bathos]: Of the Art of Sinking in Poetry* (1728) derided amplification, calling it "the spinning wheel" of **bathos.**

EXAMPLES: In the following lines from Geoffrey Chaucer's *Troilus and Criseyde* (c. 1383), the narrator amplifies his subject, the sun, using **metaphor** (day's honor), **synecdoche** (heaven's eye), and **personification** (night's foe):

> The daye's honour, and the heven's ye,
> The nyghte's foo — all this clepe° I the sunne.   *call*

A more familiar example of amplification is also an instance of **asyndeton:** "It's a bird, it's a plane, it's *Superman!*"

▶ **anachronism:** Something outside of its proper historical time period. When this "error" occurs, an author places an event, person, or thing during a time when it could not have existed.

EXAMPLES: The clock that strikes in William Shakespeare's *Julius Caesar* (1598), for no such clocks existed in the Rome of Caesar's time. The film *A Knight's Tale* (2001), described by critic David Ansen in *Newsweek* as "wildly anachronistic," includes a scene in which the crowd at a jousting tournament set in **medieval** England not only sings along to "We Will Rock You" (1977), a heavy metal song by Queen, but also does "the wave."

▶ **anachrony:** The literary technique of presenting material out of chronological order; alternatively, the achronological presentation of events. Anachronous **narratives** are characterized by **plots** in which events are recounted in an order different from their chronological sequence. **Narratologist** Mieke Bal therefore described anachrony as "chronological deviation" in *De theorie van vertellen en verhalen (Introduction to the Study of Narrative)* (2nd ed. 1980).

There are three major types of anachrony: (1) **analepsis,** the insertion of **scenes** that have occurred in the past; (2) **prolepsis,** the insertion of scenes that take place in the future; and (3) **ellipsis,** the omission of material in a narrative that creates a chronological **gap.** Analepsis, the most common form of which is **flashback,** usually occurs near the beginning of a work and often recounts an event that occurred before the opening scene. Prolepsis, which includes **flashforward** and other techniques for previewing future events or developments, is commonly used in television and films to create feelings of anticipation, curiosity, and suspense. Sometimes prolepsis takes the form of a **figure of speech** that hints at an eventual outcome. Ellipsis is a form of chronological deviation that enables an author to skip over periods rather than directing the reader or audience backward or forward in time. Some authors use ellipses to invite the reader to "fill in the gap," whereas others use this technique to achieve brevity.

Reader-response critic Gérard Genette further analyzed anachrony in his study *Discours du récit* (*Narrative Discourse*) (1972), where he used the term *portée* ("reach" or "distance") to refer to the "temporal distance" between an anachrony and the "present moment" and *amplitude* ("extent" or "span") to refer to the duration (in story time) of the anachrony. He also classified types of anachrony in greater detail, distinguishing *internal, external, partial, completing,* and *repeating* analepses and prolepses. Internal analepses and prolepses refer to the achronological presentation of events that take place *within* the work's time line, external ones to the anachronous presentation of events occurring *outside* the work's chronological boundaries, that is, before the beginning or after the ending of the time period covered by the **story** proper. Partial analepses or prolepses recount an isolated moment, past or future, in the story; completing ones fill in gaps left by ellipses. Repeating analepses and prolepses flash back or forward to events that have been previously presented or that will be presented later.

EXAMPLES: Thornton Wilder's play *Our Town* (1938) contains an analeptic flashback to the twelfth birthday of Emily Webb, the play's main **character**. "The File on the Mayfair Witches," a lengthy analeptic section of Anne Rice's novel *The Witching Hour* (1990), provides readers with relevant historical background.

Perhaps the most famous example of proleptic anachrony is found in William Shakespeare's *Hamlet* (1602), in which the wounded **protagonist** says, **figuratively,** "Horatio, I am dead." The film *Terminator 2: Judgment Day* (1991) contains a similar, more recent example: the heroine's statement to the disbelieving doctors at a mental institution that "You're already dead. . . . This whole place, everything you see, is gone."

Examples of external prolepsis occur in the TV series *The Simpsons* (1989–), which has occasionally revealed what certain family members will look and be like twenty years in the future. Movies about psychics regularly use internal prolepsis to flashforward to what their prescient protagonists subconsciously know.

The phrase "FOUR YEARS LATER," which fills the screen near the end of the movie *Cast Away* (2000), is an example of elliptic anachrony, indicating the omission of the intervening four years, which are presumably irrelevant to the movie.

The *Far Side* cartoon on page 17 by Gary Larson mixes prolepsis with analepsis, quickly propelling the reader forward from the present, in which a man shoots a werewolf, to the future point at which he will be "ripped to shreds" and then back to a moment "earlier in the day" when he first saw the tie sported by the attacking werewolf.

See also **analepsis, prolepsis.**

THE FAR SIDE® By GARY LARSON

Oh, yes! I guarantee these bullets are pure silver.

Blam! Blam!

© 1994 FarWorks, Inc. All Rights Reserved/Dist. by Creators Syndicate

Moments before he was ripped to shreds, Edgar vaguely recalled having seen that same obnoxious tie earlier in the day.

A cartoon example of **anachrony**.

▶ **Anacreontic poetry: Verse** named for the sixth-century B.C. Greek poet Anacreon. Usually written in **tetrameter** lines consisting of a **pyrrhic foot**, two **trochees**, and a **spondee**, Anacreontic poetry treats the **themes** of eroticism, love, women, and bacchanalian pleasures.

EXAMPLE: Thomas Moore's *Odes of Anacreon* (1800), a translation of Anacreon's poems. "Listen to the Muse's Lyre" follows:

> Master of the pencil's fire
> Sketch'd in painting's bold display,
> Many a city first portray;
> Many a city, revelling free,
> Full of loose festivity.
> Picture then a rosy train,

> Bacchants straying o'er the plain;
> Piping, as they roam along,
> Roundelay or shepherd-song.
> Paint me next, if painting may
> Such a theme as this portray,
> All the earthly heaven of love
> These delighted mortals prove.

▶ **anacrusis:** One or more extra unstressed syllables at the beginning of a line of **verse** that are not counted as part of the **meter.**

EXAMPLE: Samuel Taylor Coleridge's "The Rime of the Ancient Mariner" (1798) is written primarily in four-line **stanzas** that alternate **tetrameter** and **trimeter** lines. The "and" in the first **iambic** tetrameter line of the following stanza exemplifies anacrusis:

> And the bay was white with silent light,
> Till rising from the same,
> Full many shapes, that shadows were,
> In crimson colors came.

▶ **anagnorisis:** A term used by Aristotle in his *Poetics* (c. 330 B.C.) to refer to the moment in a **drama** when the **protagonist** "discovers" something that either leads to or explains a reversal of fortune — that is, the protagonist gains some crucial knowledge that he or she did not have. In a **tragedy,** the revelation is usually closely associated with the protagonist's downfall, whereas in a **comedy** it usually signals his or her success.

EXAMPLES: Sophocles' *Oedipus Rex* (c. 430 B.C.) presents a well-known example of anagnorisis. Having married the widow of the murdered King Laius, Oedipus vows to bring Laius's killer to justice, only to discover that he himself killed Laius and that Laius was his father. This revelation portends a reversal of fortune for Oedipus, who ultimately blinds and banishes himself as punishment for having, however unwittingly, killed his father and married his mother. The term *anagnorisis* might also be loosely applied to the most famous scene in Neil Jordan's film *The Crying Game* (1992), in which the male protagonist's relationship with another **character** is drastically altered by the startling revelation that the character — to all appearances an attractive woman — is actually a man.

More recent examples of anagnorisis occur in two movies directed by M. Night Shyamalan: *The Sixth Sense* (1999), in which the protagonist, a psychologist, discovers he is dead, and *The Village* (2004), a **dystopia** in which the blind protagonist discovers that the horrifying demon-beasts roaming the outskirts of her seemingly **bucolic** world are costumed village elders intent on preventing youth from leaving the community. The revelation allows her to leave in search of help for the dying young man she loves.

▶ **analepsis:** The evocation in a **narrative** of scenes or events that took place at an earlier point in the **story.** One of the three major types of **anachrony,** analepsis is commonly equated with **flashback,** but **reader-response critics**

Gérard Genette and Gerald Prince have argued that it is in fact a broader term (much as its opposite, **prolepsis,** is a broader term than **flashforward**). For instance, analepsis may involve an **image** or **figure of speech** that harks back to something encountered earlier. Sometimes a retrospective thought or meditation disrupts the chronological flow of material being recounted. Occasionally, analepsis even involves a subconscious memory or vision of the past that suddenly manifests itself in the consciousness or dreams of the **narrator** or of a main **character** whose mental processes are recounted by the narrative — for instance, via **free indirect discourse.**

EXAMPLES: The italicized clause in the following sentence: "Carolyn was surprised when she read the exam questions because, although *she had spent the entire weekend studying,* she couldn't answer a single one." In *Interview with the Vampire* (1976), novelist Anne Rice repeatedly used flashback as the narrator-**protagonist** Louis tells a young reporter how he became a vampire.

In Memoriam A. H. H. (1850), the **elegy** Alfred, Lord Tennyson wrote following the death of his friend Arthur Henry Hallam, contains numerous examples of analepsis more broadly defined, including powerful recollective experiences ("The dead man touched me from the past") and various **mystical** experiences and **dream visions,** some of which recall Hallam in aspects and situations more **surreal** than real ("The man we loved was there on deck, / But thrice as large as man").

See also **anachrony, prolepsis.**

▶ **anapest:** A metrical **foot** in **poetry** that consists of two unstressed syllables followed by a **stressed** syllable (˘˘´).

EXAMPLES: contradíct, interfére, in the búff, "are you mád?"

Edgar Allan Poe's poem "Annabel Lee" (1849) contains many anapestic lines, such as:

> For the móon never beáms, without bringing me dréams
>   Of the beáutiful ÁNNABELLÉE;
> And the stárs never ríse, but I sée the bright éyes
>   Of the beáutiful ÁNNABEL LÉE.

"Helter Skelter," a famous and controversial song from the Beatles' *White Album* (1968), is predominantly anapestic.

▶ **anaphora:** A **rhetorical figure** involving the exact repetition of words or phrases at the beginning of successive lines or sentences. Anaphora is a type of **parallelism.**

EXAMPLES: The following **stanza** from Geoffrey Chaucer's *Troilus and Criseyde* (c. 1353):

Swich fin° hath, lo, this Troilus for love;	*Such ending*
Swich fin hath al his grete° worthinesse;	*great*
Swich fin hath his estaat real° above;	*royal*
Swich fin his lust, swich fin hath his nobleness;	
Swich fin hath false worlde's brotelnesse:°	*brittleness*

> And thus bigan his loving of Criseyde,
> As I have told, and in this wise he deide.°   *died*

Martin Luther King employed anaphora in his famous "I Have a Dream" speech (1963), in which several successive sentences begin with the phrase "I have a dream that one day..."

▶ **anastrophe:** See **hyperbaton.**

▶ **anecdote:** A brief account of some interesting or entertaining and often humorous incident. Lacking the complexity of the **short story,** an anecdote simply relates a particular episode or event that makes a single point. Since an anecdote is supposed to be true, the incident described and the point made by the anecdote are typically more important than *how* the anecdote is told — that is, the artistry or **style** of the telling. Anecdotes frequently relate an incident in a particular person's life that reveals a character trait.

EXAMPLES: The story about George Washington and the cherry tree, which reveals Washington's honesty and the importance of telling the truth. When his father asked him who chopped down the cherry tree, Washington supposedly replied "I cannot tell a lie" and told the truth, even though he expected to be punished for his actions.

In Joseph Conrad's *Lord Jim* (1900), a pathetic guano exporter named Chester tells Marlow, the novel's **narrator,** a story about Holy-Terror Robinson, a man once shipwrecked on an island with six other men who was subsequently found alone, "kneeling on the kelp, naked as the day he was born, and chanting some psalm-tune or other." "Cannibal?" Chester asks suggestively. This darkly humorous anecdote suggests that morality and civilized behavior may succumb to the survival instinct.

At the beginning and end of many episodes of his **classic** television show *Seinfeld* (1989–98), comedian Jerry Seinfeld appears on stage in a comedy club, telling anecdotes that relate to the **plot** of the episode. This device makes it difficult to tell whether the comedian's stand-up routine distills "real-life" incidents and situations — or whether his show elaborates dramatically on humorous stories.

▶ **Anglo-Saxon Period (in English Literature):** See **Old English Period (in English literature).**

▶ **antagonist:** The **character** pitted against the **protagonist** — the main character — of a work. An evil or cruel antagonist is a *villain.*

EXAMPLES: Creon is the antagonist in Sophocles' *Antigone* (c. 441 B.C.). Heathcliff, in some ways the young **hero** of the first half of Emily Brontë's *Wuthering Heights* (1847), is the antagonist throughout most of the novel's second half. Darth Vader is the antagonist and villain of the original *Star Wars* trilogy (1977, 1980, 1983). On the lighter side, the devilish Lester Wallace (played by Keith David) is the antagonist and villain of the movie *Barbershop* (2002), in which he schemes to wrest control of the third-generation family business from protagonist and owner Calvin Palmer (played by rapper Ice Cube) in order to turn it into a strip joint. In the docudrama *Good Night,*

and Good Luck (2005), Senator Joseph McCarthy, bent on ferreting out supposed Communists and Communist sympathizers, serves as an antagonist
some would call villainous and others would deem only — if profoundly —
misguided.

By contrast, examples of antagonists who are not remotely villainous —
who simply hinder or block the protagonist — may be found in short stories
like Frank O'Connor's "My Oedipus Complex" (1950), in which the antagonist is the **narrator's** father, whose return from war interferes with the
boy's exclusive relationship with his mother, and Amy Tan's "Two Kinds"
(1989), in which the antagonist is the narrator's mother, whose goals for
her daughter conflict with what Jing-mei wants for herself.

▶ **anticlimax:** **Rhetorical** descent, usually sudden, from a higher to a lower
emotional point — from a topic or **tone** with greater drama or significance
to one with less impact or importance. Anticlimax typically results in the
disappointment or even reversal of expectations.

Anticlimax may be used intentionally, usually for comic effect, or it may
be unintended, the result of **authorial** ineptitude. When an unintentional
descent from the lofty to the trivial or even ridiculous occurs while the writer
is trying to achieve **the sublime,** the effect is known as **bathos.**

EXAMPLES: The last ten chapters of Mark Twain's *Adventures of Huckleberry Finn* (1884) — chapters in which Huck arrives at Aunt Sally Phelps's
place, is joined by Tom Sawyer, and goes along with Tom's ridiculously
and needlessly elaborate plans to rescue the runaway slave Jim — are often
said to be anticlimactic.

In the following passage from Isabel Allende's *La casa de los espiritus*
(*The House of the Spirits*) (1982), Clara's anticlimactic response to her husband's angry tirade reduces his fury to a pathetic and ineffectual outburst:

> He shouted like a madman, pacing up and down the living room and
> slamming his fist against the furniture, arguing that if Clara intended
> to follow in her mother's footsteps she was going to come face to face
> with a real man, who would pull her pants down and give her a good
> spanking so she'd get it out of her damned head to go around ha-
> ranguing people, and that he categorically forbade her to go to prayer
> meetings or any other kind and that he wasn't some ninny whose wife
> could go around making a fool of him. Clara let him scream his head
> off and bang on the furniture until he was exhausted. Then, inatten-
> tive as ever, she asked him if he knew how to wiggle his ears.

By contrast, the following sentence from a Knight Ridder News Service
dispatch (1995) is probably unintentionally anticlimactic: "The crime bill
passed by the Senate would reinstate the Federal death penalty for certain
violent crimes: assassinating the President; hijacking an airliner; and mur-
dering a government poultry inspector."

▶ **antihero:** A **protagonist,** particularly in a modern literary work, who
does not exhibit the qualities of the traditional **hero.** Instead of being a
grand and/or admirable figure — brave, honest, and magnanimous, for

example — an antihero is all too ordinary and may even be petty or criminal.

The term *antihero* should not be confused with **antagonist,** which refers to the **character** pitted against the protagonist in the work, or **villain,** which refers to an evil or cruel antagonist.

EXAMPLES: Willy Loman, the salesman in Arthur Miller's *Death of a Salesman* (1948); Jim Stark, the **character** played by James Dean in the movie *Rebel Without a Cause* (1955); and the rival murderesses in the musical *Chicago* (1975; adapted to film 2002), Roxie Hart and Velma Kelly. More contemporary antiheroes include Ben Sanderson, the suicidal alcoholic in the movie *Leaving Las Vegas* (1995); Nick Guest, the gay postgraduate student in Alan Hollinghurst's novel *The Line of Beauty* (2004); the brooding Batman depicted in the movie *Batman Begins* (2005); mob boss Tony Soprano from *The Sopranos* (1999–2007); and pirate captain Jack Sparrow of the *Pirates of the Caribbean* movie trilogy (2003–07).

▶ **antimasque:** An interlude frequently featuring **grotesque** or bawdy humor that is interspersed between the more serious elements of the **masque.** Whereas the masque was performed by amateur members of the nobility or even royalty, the antimasque generally used the lower class of professional dancers and actors. The invention and development of the antimasque are attributed to Ben Jonson, a seventeenth-century English poet and playwright generally considered one of the greatest writers of masques.

EXAMPLE: Jonson's *The Masque of Queens* (1609), written for Queen Anne, contains an antimasque, "devis'd," as the dramatist explained, "that twelve Women in the habit of *Hags,* or *Witches,* sustaining the Persons of *Ignorance, Suspicion, Credulity, &c.* the Opposites to good *Fame,* should fill that part; not as a *Masque* but a *Spectacle* of strangeness . . . ."

▶ **antinovel:** A type of experimental **novel** that attempts to present the reader with experience itself, unfiltered by **metaphor** or other vehicles of authorial interpretation. The term — or, more specifically, its French counterpart, *anti-roman* — was coined by twentieth-century **existentialist** Jean-Paul Sartre in his introduction to Nathalie Sarraute's *Portrait d'un inconnu* (*Portrait of a Man Unknown*) (1948). Antinovelists attempt to depict reality without recourse to a moral frame of reference; they avoid the kind of subjective **narrative** evaluation that tends to creep into more traditional fiction, including so-called **realistic** and **naturalistic** narratives. Their novels are characterized by the avoidance or minimization of standard narrative elements, including **characterization, dialogue,** and **plot,** as well as by the creation of **ambiguity** and confusion through elements such as dislocations of time and space and inconsistency in **point of view.** Ironically, making sense of the antinovel's achronological and alogical narrative sequences usually requires employing conventional reading strategies.

Antinovel is sometimes used interchangeably with the *nouveau roman,* which arose in France in the mid-twentieth century and reached its height in the 1950s and 1960s. The term may, however, be used more broadly; indeed, works ranging from Laurence Sterne's *Tristram Shandy* (9 vols.; 1759–67) to Uwe Johnson's *Mutmassungen über Jakob* (*Speculations about Jakob*) (1959) to Margaret Drabble's *The Middle Ground* (1980) have been called antinovels. *Antinovel* is sometimes also used interchangeably with **new novel.**

FURTHER EXAMPLES: Alain Robbe-Grillet's *Le voyeur* (*The Voyeur*) (1955); Vladimir Nabokov's *Pale Fire* (1962); John Hawkes's *The Blood Oranges* (1971).

See also *nouveau roman.*

▶ **antistrophe:** (1) The second **stanza** of the **classical** Greek choral **ode.** The antistrophe, which the **chorus** sang while moving from left to right, came between the **strophe,** which the chorus sang while moving from right to left, and the **epode,** which the chorus sang while standing still. The antistrophe served as an "answer" to the strophe, with a corresponding **meter** and movement of the chorus mirroring that of the strophe. (2) The second of three recurrent parts of the **Pindaric ode.**

▶ **antithesis:** A **rhetorical figure** in which two ideas are directly opposed. For a statement to be truly antithetical, the opposing ideas must be presented in a grammatically parallel way, thus creating a perfect rhetorical balance.

EXAMPLES: The following line from Adrienne Rich's "Toward the Solstice" (1977) is antithetical:

I long and dread to close.

This passage from John Lyly's *Euphues* (1579) relies heavily on antithesis:

> So likewise in the disposition of the mind, either virtue is overshadowed with some vice or vice overcast with some virtue: Alexander valiant in war, yet given to wine; Tully eloquent in his glozes [flattering or fine speeches], yet vainglorious; Solomon wise, yet too too wanton; David holy, but yet an homicide; none more witty than Euphues, yet at the first none more wicked.

Former U.S. president Ronald Reagan's speeches made frequent use of antithesis. In a speech given to the British House of Commons on June 8, 1982, Reagan contrasted totalitarianism and freedom, two ideas that are themselves antithetical, asking:

> Who would voluntarily choose not to have a right to vote, decide to purchase government propaganda handouts instead of independent newspapers, prefer government to worker-controlled unions, opt for land to be owned by the state instead of those who till it, want government repression of religious liberty, a single political party instead of a free choice, a rigid cultural orthodoxy instead of democratic tolerance and diversity?

▶ **antithetical criticism:** A method of **literary criticism** proposed and practiced by American critic Harold Bloom in his revisionist phase that involves reading poems as *mis*readings (by the poet) of earlier poems written by powerful and influential precursors. Thus, a critic practicing antithetical criticism might see Percy Bysshe Shelley's *Prometheus Unbound* (1820) as a strong misreading of John Milton's **epic** *Paradise Lost* (1667).

Antithetical criticism is grounded in a **theory** of literary **influence** that Bloom set forth in *The Anxiety of Influence* (1973) and developed in *A Map of Misreading* (1975); in these and several subsequent books, Bloom suggested that the writing of all poets involves the rewriting of earlier poets and that this rewriting always and inevitably involves some form of misreading or "misprision." Bloom also believed that all readers misinterpret works, since they read them "defensively" — that is, with an eye to preserving their own autonomy and creativity. With this in mind, Bloom recognized that the readings of antithetical critics (including his own readings) are necessarily misreadings as well. He justified antithetical criticism, however, by arguing that its strong misreadings culminate in interesting interpretations widely divergent from what the poet may have thought he was saying, as well as from the "weak misreadings" produced by critics taking other critical approaches who purport to ascertain and reveal what a poem really means. Bloom predicted that the inherent difference of antithetical readings from other kinds of readings would secure a place for them along with all the other strong misreadings throughout history.

See also **anxiety of influence**.

▶ **antonomasia:** A **rhetorical figure** involving the regular substitution of an **epithet** for a proper name. The term has also been used to describe the substitution of a proper name for a general idea that the name evokes.

EXAMPLES: John Milton's frequent substitution of "The Great Adversary" for "Satan" in *Paradise Lost* (1667) is an example of antonomasia where an epithet is substituted for a proper name. Other examples include the ship captain's continual use of epithets such as "that absurdly whiskered mate" and "my terrifically whiskered mate" to refer to his second-in-command in Joseph Conrad's **novella** *The Secret Sharer* (1912) and Reuben Land's references to Martin Andreeson, the federal agent on the trail of his fugitive brother, as "the putrid fed" in Leif Enger's novel *Peace Like a River* (2003).

By contrast, use of the name "Judas" or Benedict Arnold" to refer to a traitor is an example of the second usage of antonomasia.

▶ **anxiety of influence:** American literary critic Harold Bloom, who is now best known for his controversial book *The Western Canon* (1994), developed a brand of "revisionist" or **antithetical criticism** in the 1970s that challenged conventional conceptions of **influence**. In *The Anxiety of Influence* (1973), Bloom significantly developed ideas set forth by another American critic, Walter Jackson Bate, in his book *The Burden of the Past and the English Poet* (1970). Whereas Bate had argued that poets inevitably feel that their precursors may have already accomplished all that *can* be accomplished, Bloom discussed the way in which poets deal with this fear, or "anxiety."

He suggested that the writing of all poets involves the rewriting of earlier poets, and that this rewriting always and inevitably involves some form of "misprision," a kind of misreading that allows the later writer's creativity to emerge. Bloom acknowledged the long-standing view that any given poet (particularly since seventeenth-century English poet John Milton) is in fact influenced by a "precursor" poet or poets, but he further contended that the "belated" poet (or *ephebe*) fears that the precursor poet has overshadowed him, encroaching upon his territory and thereby negating his creativity.

Bloom relied heavily on Sigmund Freud's theory of the **Oedipus complex** to explain the anxiety of the belated poet, who jealously regards the precursor poet as a competitor even as he admires that earlier poet's work. The belated poet, or son, respects and learns from the **patriarchal** precursor poet, or father, but also envies and resents his predecessor's precedence and preeminence. In an effort to preserve a sense of autonomy and individual creativity, the belated poet reads the precursor poet's works "defensively," subverting them in accordance with one or more of several "revisionary ratios," which Bloom modeled on Freudian defense mechanisms. The ephebe, for instance, may write a poem that appears to correct or complete a poem by a precursor; he may also write a poem that appears to have influenced an earlier poem by a precursor — a poem that, in fact, influenced his own poem. In composing his own works, the belated poet cannot help but incorporate elements of the precursor's work — many of which are themselves distortions of *his* great precursor's work — even as he ardently seeks to establish his originality.

Since Bloom believed that everyone employs revisionary ratios in reading, he also argued that *all* reading can be considered misreading of sorts; any interpretation inevitably involves some misinterpretation. He thus ultimately asserted that no one can understand a "poem-in-itself."

See also **antithetical criticism.**

▶ **aphorism (*sententia*):** A concise, pointed, **epigrammatic** statement that purports to reveal a truth or principle. Aphorisms can be attributed to a specific person. Once a statement is so generally known that authorship is lost, it is called a *proverb* rather than an aphorism. A statement that gives behavioral advice rather than simply revealing a truth or principle is called a *maxim*.

EXAMPLES: Aphorisms include "A rose by any other name would smell as sweet" (William Shakespeare), "No man is a hero to his valet" (La Rochefoucauld), "Beauty is truth, truth beauty" (John Keats), "Mistrust first impulses; they are always good" (Charles Talleyrand), "All you need is love" (the Beatles), and "Life is like a box of chocolates — you never know what you're going to get" (*Forrest Gump*, 1994).

Proverbs include "Still waters run deep," "A rolling stone gathers no moss," "There are many paths to the top of the mountain, but the view is always the same" (Chinese), "A sandal is not a shoe; a cap is not a turban" (Afghan), "The witness of a rat is another rat" (Ethiopian), "It takes a whole village to raise a child" (Yoruba of Nigeria), and "An ember burns where it falls" (Turkish).

"A stitch in time saves nine" is a maxim, as are "The early bird gets the worm" and "The lawyer who represents himself has a fool for a client."

▶ **Apocalypse, apocalyptic literature:** *Apocalypse,* or *The Apocalypse of John,* is an alternative name for the book of Revelation, the last book of the New Testament of the Bible, which through complex and detailed **symbolism** depicts a catastrophic end to the world. The term also refers to the violent end of the world and subsequent Day of Judgment prophesied in the book of Revelation and Christian theology more generally.

The term *apocalyptic* stems from the word *Apocalypse,* which is in turn derived from the Greek word *apokaluptein,* meaning "to uncover." Literature is called apocalyptic when it purports to uncover, reveal, or prophesy the future. A number of Christian and Jewish writers produced apocalyptic religious works during the period 200 B.C.–A.D. 150. In general, these works as well as subsequent apocalyptic **texts** involve visions of unbridled doom and destruction — predictions of an imminent, often fiery and terrible end to the world.

Recently, some critics have used *apocalyptic* even more generally to refer to visionary or revelatory literature; thus, William Blake's prophecies (*The Book of Thel* [1789], *The Four Zoas* [c. 1800]), John Keats's "Hyperion" poems (1818–19), Percy Bysshe Shelley's *Prometheus Unbound* (1820), and William Butler Yeats's *A Vision* (1925) have all been called apocalyptic. Mary Shelley's novel *The Last Man* (1826), certain stories by Edgar Allan Poe ("Ligea" [1838], "The Fall of the House of Usher" [1839]), James Thomson's poem "The City of Dreadful Night" (1874), and H. G. Wells's *The War of the Worlds* (1898), are also commonly cited as nineteenth-century examples of apocalyptic literature. Twentieth-century apocalyptic novels include Nevil Shute's *On the Beach* (1935) and Walker Percy's *Love in the Ruins* (1971). Mark Waid and Alex Ross's **graphic novel** *Kingdom Come* (1998) builds to an apocalyptic **climax.** Other recent examples of apocalyptic literature include Tim LaHaye and Jerry B. Jenkins's *Left Behind* series of novels (1995–2007).

In giving his 1979 retrospective film about the Vietnam War the title *Apocalypse Now,* director Francis Ford Coppola used the term *apocalypse* somewhat loosely, since an apocalyptic retrospective is something of a contradiction in terms. Moreover, as noted **deconstructor** J. Hillis Miller pointed out in "*Heart of Darkness* Revisited" (1985), "Apocalypse is never now."

See also **eschatology.**

▶ **apocryphal:** See **canon.**

▶ **Apollonian:** An adjective derived from Apollo (the Greek god of music and light and the **symbol** of reason and culture) describing writing that exhibits a serene and orderly quality. In *The Birth of Tragedy* (1872), German philosopher Friedrich Nietzsche used *Apollonian* in conjunction with the term **Dionysian** (signifying impulsiveness and irrationality) to refer to the balance struck by the two sides of Greek **tragedy. Classical** and **neoclassical** writing are often Apollonian, whereas **romantic** writing tends to draw on the more passionate Dionysian tradition.

See also **Dionysian.**

▶ **apologue:** See **fable.**

▶ **aporia:** A term borrowed from logic for use in **literary criticism,** most frequently in **deconstruction,** to indicate an interpretative dilemma or impasse involving some **textual** contradiction that renders — or seems to render — meaning **undecidable.** Deconstructors often speak of the aporic "juncture" or "moment" as the point at which the reader lacks the justification to choose or cannot choose between two meanings.

Aporia can also be used more generally to refer to any indecision or doubt expressed by the speaker of a work, whether actual or voiced with **ironic** intent.

▶ **aposiopesis:** A **rhetorical figure** involving individual sentences left suggestively incomplete or otherwise involving a dramatic breaking off of **discourse,** often suggesting that a speaker has been rendered speechless by a flood of emotions. In written texts, aposiopesis is usually indicated by ellipses (...) or a dash (—).

EXAMPLES: A famous speech by Demogorgon in Percy Bysshe Shelley's *Prometheus Unbound* (1820) employs aposiopesis:

> If the abysm
> Could vomit forth its secrets. . . . But a voice
> Is wanting, the deep truth is imageless.

The following line from Thomas Hardy's "The Temporary the All" (1898) also uses aposiopesis: "Thus I...but lo, me!"

Novelist Henry James, who employed this device regularly, often followed aposiopeses with the three-word sentence "She hung fire," a nineteenth-century idiom meaning that a person is overcome by strong feelings. Zadie Smith's *White Teeth* (2001) uses aposiopesis to convey the gap between Londoners from different cultural backgrounds. Offered an "Indian sweet" that's "half-white, half-pink," a young office staffer named Noel responds to what for him is an "unwelcoming odor" by stammering "that's very . . . But it's really not my cup of . . ."

▶ **apostrophe:** A **rhetorical figure** in which the speaker directly and often emotionally addresses a person who is dead or absent, an imaginary or nonhuman entity, or a place or concept (usually an **abstract** idea or ideal). The object of the apostrophe, if not human, is often **personified.**

The **invocation** is a type of apostrophe involving an explicit request for aid in writing made to a supernatural entity.

EXAMPLES: The biblical lines "O death, I will be thy plagues; / O grave, I will be thy destruction" (Hosea 13:14). George Gordon, Lord Byron, apostrophizes the sea in the following line, taken from the fourth **canto** of his long poem, *Childe Harold's Pilgrimage* (1818): "Roll on, thou deep and dark blue ocean, roll!"

Sixteenth-century French poet Louise Labé addressed her absent lover in *Les délices et les épreuves du corps* (*The Delights and Trials of the Body*), calling on him to "Baise m'encor, rebaise-moi et baise, / . . . Je t'en rendrai quatre plus chauds que braise" ("Kiss me again, kiss me once more and kiss / . . . I will give you four that are hotter than embers").

Thomas Hardy addressed "Love" in his cynical poem "I Said to Love" (1901):

> I said to him,
> "We now know more of thee than then;
> We were but weak in judgment when,
>   With hearts abrim,
> We clamoured thee that thou woulds't please
> Inflict on us thy agonies,"
>   I said to him.

▶ **applied criticism:** See **practical criticism.**

▶ **appropriation:** The tendency of readers to interpret **texts** according to their own cultural presuppositions, regardless of those of the **author** — and even if the author wrote the work from a different cultural or **ideological** perspective.

▶ **approximate rhyme:** See **half rhyme.**

▶ **Arcadia:** A remote, mountainous region of Greece, in the Peloponnesus, that was popularized and idealized in literature in **classical** times, particularly by the Roman poet Virgil, who in his *Eclogues* (c. 40 B.C.) made it the ideal **pastoral** environment, a place where singing shepherds and shepherdesses peacefully watch over their flocks. Subsequently, in the **Renaissance,** poets such as Jacopo Sannazzaro, Edmund Spenser, and Sir Philip Sidney incorporated Arcadian **settings** and **themes.** Today, the word *Arcadia* still suggests this supposed **golden age,** when the virtues of simplicity and harmony reigned supreme in an unchanged and unchanging land uncorrupted by civilization.

FURTHER EXAMPLES: Sannazzaro's *L'Arcadia* (1504), which mixes prose and verse; Sidney's prose romance *Arcadia* (1590). Nicolas Poussin's painting "The Arcadian Shepherds" (1647) features four Arcadians at a tomb inscribed "ET IN ARCADIA EGO."

Tom Stoppard used the term **ironically** in his play *Arcadia* (1993). Arcadia is also a plane of existence in the popular role-playing fantasy game *Dungeons & Dragons*™, first issued in 1973.

▶ **archaism:** A word, expression, or phrase that has become obsolete. Archaisms are sometimes used intentionally to evoke **images,** sensations, and attitudes associated with the past.

EXAMPLES: "Forsooth" for "in fact," "thou" or "thee" for "you," "wherefore" for "why," "bloomers" for "undergarments," "ice box" for "refrigerator," "perpendicular railway" for "elevator," "alienist" for "psychologist." One can also loosely refer to an attitude as archaic. For example, the idea that a girl should not allow herself to be kissed on a first date is widely considered archaic in Western cultures.

▶ **archetypal criticism:** A type of **literary criticism** that emerged in the 1930s focusing on those patterns in a particular literary work that commonly recur in other literary works. Archetypal criticism owes its origin chiefly to the work of the Swiss analytical psychologist Carl Jung, who argued that humanity has a **collective unconscious** that manifests itself in dreams, **myths,** and literature through **archetypes:** persistent **images, figures,** and **story** patterns shared by people across diverse cultures. Archetypal criticism was also influenced by the studies of a group of Cambridge University anthropologists who found that certain myths and rituals recurred in a wide variety of cultures.

Critics taking an archetypal approach to literature seek to identify archetypes within both specific works and literature in general. Some argue that the presence of certain recurrent images, story lines, **character** types, and so forth is ipso facto evidence of their status as memories in the collective unconscious; others refer to persistent elements and patterns in literature (and other forms of **representation**) as archetypes without reference to Jung's theory of the collective unconscious.

Heavily influenced by Maud Bodkins's *Archetypal Patterns in Poetry* (1934), archetypal criticism emerged as a dominant critical practice in the 1950s and 1960s. The influential critic Northrop Frye further explored and refined archetypal criticism in *The Anatomy of Criticism* (1957). Incorporating into archetypal criticism a typological interpretation of the Bible and the visionary poet William Blake's concept of **imagination,** Frye challenged the **conventional** terrain of literary criticism and **theory.** He proposed the existence of four *mythoi* (types of **plots**), which formed the basis of the four major **genres,** each of which has archetypal associations with one of the four seasons: **comedy** (spring), **romance** (summer), **tragedy** (fall), and **satire** (winter). Individual works may, of course, contain other archetypes. Frye viewed the vast corpus of literary works as a "self-contained literary universe," one created by the human imagination to quell fears and fulfill wishes by reducing nature in all its threatening vastness and incomprehensibility to a set of basic, manageable (archetypal) forms.

EXAMPLE: A "Fryed" reading of Alfred, Lord Tennyson's "The Lady of Shalott" (1832), a poem about a virgin who dies after glimpsing Sir Lancelot from the lonely tower in which she lives, would view it as a tragedy whose overall archetypicality is autumnal but that contains other archetypal images as well; for example, the river, the virgin bower/tower, the unrequited lover, and the **phallic** male.

See also **archetype.**

▶ **archetype:** Generally, the original model from which something is developed or made; in literary criticism, those **images**, **figures**, **character** types, **settings**, and **story** patterns that, according to the Swiss analytical psychologist Carl Jung, are universally shared by people across cultures. Archetypes are embedded deep in humanity's **collective unconscious** and involve "racial memories" of situations, events, and relations that have been part of human experience from the beginning. They not only manifest themselves in the subconscious material of dreams but are also persistently expressed in the more consciously constructed material of **myths** and literature. Jung postulated that when an author recounts a **narrative** based on such unconscious memories, the reader's mind is subconsciously stirred, producing a singularly powerful psychological effect because the memories evoke primordial feelings, concerns, and responses that cannot logically be explained.

Literary critics who follow Jung's theory seek to identify archetypes within both specific works and literature in general. Referred to as **archetypal, Jungian,** or (even more commonly) **myth critics,** they look for and analyze certain recurrent images, character types, and story lines under the assumption that their persistence in literature indicates their presence in the memories of the collective unconscious. Some practitioners of archetypal criticism use the term *archetype* in a more limited fashion to refer to recurrent elements and patterns in literature and other **representational** forms and **discourses,** but without reference to Jung's theory of the collective unconscious. Preeminent among archetypal or myth critics was Northrop Frye, whose interest was in images and **symbols** so prevalent in literature as to provide a common thread through the diverse literary experiences of individuals.

EXAMPLES: The snake is an archetypal image (or figure), as is the trickster. The Flood is an archetypal image persistently expressed in the myths and literatures of most of the world's cultures, even as the Savior is an archetypal personage. For instance, the Christian and Hindu observances of Easter and Mahashivarati, respectively, celebrate deliverance from death, with Easter commemorating the resurrection of Jesus and Mahashivarati commemorating the night Shiva drank a poison that threatened the world.

▶ **argument:** An introductory **prose** statement to a long **poetic** work that summarizes its **plot** or its main meaning.

EXAMPLE: Each of the books of John Milton's *Paradise Lost* (1667) is prefaced by an argument.

▶ **arsis:** In Greek **poetry**, the unstressed syllable in a **foot** of **verse** (as opposed to the **thesis**, or **stressed** syllable). In later Latin usage, however, the terms became reversed, with *arsis* referring to the stressed syllable and *thesis* referring to the unstressed syllable. According to Greek usage, the arsis of the word *arsis* falls on the second (the unstressed) syllable, whereas in Latin usage, the arsis of the word *arsis* falls on the first (the stressed) syllable. In **prosody** (the study of **versification**), both usages persist, though the Latin usage is more common.

See also **accent**.

▶ **art for art's sake:** See Aestheticism, aesthetics.

▶ **aside:** A **convention** in **drama** whereby a **character** onstage addresses the audience to reveal some inner thought or feeling that is presumed inaudible to any other characters in earshot. It is as if a character delivering an aside has momentarily stepped outside of the world of the play and into the world of the audience in order to provide illuminating information.

EXAMPLES: In William Shakespeare's *As You Like It* (c. 1600), Touchstone, who is about to be married to "a country wench" named Audrey, informs the audience that:

> I am not in the mind but I were better to be married of [bumbling vicar Sir Oliver Martext] than of another, for he is not like to marry me well, and not being well married, it will be a good excuse for me hereafter to leave my wife.

In John Guare's play *Four Baboons Adoring the Sun* (1991), the following aside is prefaced by the stage direction, "PENNY *turns out to us as if she is in a later time — say, three years hence — relating a story to us, a story she is still puzzling over*":

> Mel had what he wanted. I had what I wanted. Everybody had what they wanted. Their father was a congressman. My leaving had actually helped Mel get reelected. He got the sympathy vote. Mel had found his true constituency. The embittered male.

▶ **assonance:** The repetition of identical or similar vowel sounds, usually in **stressed** syllables, followed by different consonant sounds in proximate words. Assonance is different from **perfect rhyme** in that **rhyming** words also repeat the final consonant sounds.

EXAMPLES: *Fate* and *cave* show assonance; *fate* and *late* show perfect rhyme. In the opening **stanza** of D. H. Lawrence's "Love on the Farm" (1928), *large, dark,* and *are; hands, at,* and *Grasping; those* and *golden; window, in, its,* and *wind; weaves* and *evening;* and the *ing* suffixes are all assonant. Only *light* and *delight* rhyme:

> What large, dark hands are those at the window
> Grasping in the golden light
> Which weaves its way through the evening wind
> At my heart's delight?

Assonance is common in hip-hop music, as in Public Enemy's "Do You Wanna Go Our Way???" (*There's a Poison Goin On*, 1999), in which the long *o* sound is repeated eleven times in four lines — in the words *knows, controls, radios, chose, road, hoes, so, rose, woes, negroes,* and *nose*. Rapper Eminem (Marshall Mathers) relies heavily on assonance, for example in his singles "The Way I Am" (*The Marshall Mathers LP*, 2000) and "Lose Yourself" (*8 Mile Soundtrack*, 2002).

▶ **asyndeton:** A **rhetorical figure** involving the deliberate omission of conjunctions to create a concise, terse, and often memorable statement.

EXAMPLES: Julius Caesar's declaration "Veni, vidi, vici" ("I came, I saw, I conquered"), following his defeat of Pharnaces at Zela in 47 B.C. A more familiar example of asyndeton is also an instance of **amplification:** "It's a bird, it's a plane, it's *Superman!*"

▶ **atmosphere:** The general feeling created for the reader or audience by a work at a given point. Atmosphere is established through elements such as **imagery, setting,** and sound and helps shape the reader's expectations for the work.

Although the terms *atmosphere* and **tone** may both be equated with **mood,** their meanings differ. Unlike *atmosphere,* which refers to the prevailing feeling the **author** creates for the reader or audience, *tone* refers to the author's attitude toward the reader, audience, or subject matter.

▶ **aubade:** A **lyric** or song delivered at dawn, generally involving lovers who must part or, occasionally, one lover who asks the other to wake up. The German equivalent of the aubade is the *Tagelied.*

The aubade is related to the Provençal *alba.* The *alba* laments the end of the lovers' night together, whereas the aubade tends to involve a joyful announcement of the new day.

EXAMPLE: William Shakespeare's "Hark, hark, the lark," from *Cymbeline* (c. 1610):

> Hark, hark, the lark at heaven's gate sings,
>   And Phoebus 'gins arise,
> His steeds to water at those springs
>   On chaliced flowers that lies;
> And winking Mary-buds begin
>   To ope their golden eyes;
> With every thing that pretty is,
>   My lady sweet, arise;
>   Arise, arise!

The best known examples of the *alba* in English are John Donne's "The Good Morrow" (1633) and "The Sun Rising" (1633), which begins:

> Busy old fool, unruly Sun,
> Why dost thou thus,
> Through windows, and through curtains call on us.

▶ **Augustan Age (in English literature):** Once commonly used to refer to the literary age of Virgil, Horace, and Ovid (all of whom wrote during the reign of the ancient Roman Emperor Augustus, 27 B.C.–A.D. 14), a term primarily used now to refer to the second of three literary eras within the **Neoclassical Period** in English literature. Writers most commonly associated with the English Augustan Age, which is generally said to span the first half of the eighteenth century, include Joseph Addison, Alexander Pope, and

Jonathan Swift. These English "Augustans" modelled themselves after their **classical** precursors, emphasizing the importance to society of order, balance, propriety, civility, and **wit**.

See **neoclassicism**.

▶ **author:** In traditional literary usage, the writer of a **text**, or, more broadly, the person deemed responsible for its creation and for controlling its meaning or meanings. In the 1940s, with the advent of **the New Criticism**, the role of the author came under scrutiny, with William K. Wimsatt and Monroe C. Beardsley coining the term **intentional fallacy** to reject the practice of basing textual interpretation on an author's **intentions**. Subsequently, **structuralist** and **poststructuralist** theorists questioned the whole idea of authorship. In "The Death of the Author" (1967), Roland Barthes, a structuralist who was transitioning to poststructuralism, viewed the author not as an original and creative master and manipulator of the linguistic system but, rather, as one of its primary vehicles, a "scriptor" who is "born simultaneously with his text." Dethroning the author in favor of the reader as the focus of writing, Barthes argued that a text "does not consist of a line of words releasing a single 'theological' meaning (the 'message' of the Author-God), but is a space of many dimensions, in which are wedded and contested various kinds of writing, no one of which is original." By contrast, in his essay "What Is an Author?" (1969), Michel Foucault, a French philosophical historian most often associated with **the new historicism**, analyzed the author as "a function of discourse," a "functional principle by which, in our culture, one limits, excludes, and chooses" among "the cancerous and dangerous proliferation of significations."

▶ **authorial intention:** Defined narrowly, an **author's** intention in writing a work, as expressed in letters, diaries, interviews, and conversations. Defined more broadly, authorial intention involves unexpressed motivations, designs, and purposes, some of which may also be unconscious. The debate over whether critics should try to discern an author's intentions (conscious or otherwise) is an old one.

William K. Wimsatt and Monroe C. Beardsley, early pioneers of **the New Criticism**, coined the term **intentional fallacy** to refer to what they viewed as the wrongheaded practice of basing interpretation on a writer's expressed or implied intentions.

▶ **autobiographical criticism:** See **personal criticism**.

▶ **autobiographics:** See **autobiography, feminist criticism, personal criticism**.

▶ **autobiography:** A **narrative** account typically written by an individual that purports to depict his or her life and character. Unlike diaries and journals, which are kept for the **author's** private use, autobiographies are written expressly for a public audience. Autobiographies are distinguished from **memoirs** (also produced for public consumption), whose authors render an account of the people and events they have known and experienced without providing the detailed reflection and introspection characteristic of most autobiographies. Some fiction writers draw so heavily on their own experiences that their works, though not autobiographies in the strict sense of the term, are viewed as being autobiographical in nature or even as thinly disguised autobiographies.

A number of **feminist** literary scholars and critics have argued that traditional **biography** is a **gendered,** "masculinist" **genre,** one whose established **conventions** call for a life-**plot** that turns on action, triumph through **conflict,** intellectual self-discovery, and often public renown. The body, reproduction, children, and intimate interpersonal relationships are generally well in the background and often absent. Arguing that the lived experiences of women and men differ — women's lives, for instance, are often characterized by interruption and deferral to a much greater extent than men's, with many women taking time off from their careers to have and raise children — certain feminists have developed a theory of self-**representation** that Leigh Gilmore termed *autobiographics* in her eponymously titled 1994 book.

EXAMPLES: St. Augustine's *Confessions,* written in the fourth century A.D., is the earliest fully developed example of the genre. Benjamin Franklin's *Autobiography* (1791) is a famous early American example. Trappist monk Thomas Merton's *The Seven Storey Mountain* (1948) is a modern spiritual **classic.** More recent examples of autobiography include poet Maya Angelou's *I Know Why the Caged Bird Sings* (1969), Mel White's *Stranger at the Gate: To Be Gay and Christian in America* (1994), and Katharine Graham's *Personal History* (1997).

Not all autobiographies are written directly or entirely by their subjects. *The Autobiography of Malcolm X,* published in 1965 after the activist and black Muslim leader's assassination, was a collaboration with journalist Alex Haley based on taped interviews from 1963–65. In 1982, Elisabeth Burgos-Debray interviewed Rigoberta Menchú, a 23-year-old Quiché Indian activist from Guatemala, and then transcribed and edited Menchú's oral **narration** of her harrowing life story into a **monologue,** *Me llamo Rigoberta Menchú y así me nació la conciencia* (*I, Rigoberta Menchú*) (1983). Literary commentator and collaborator Digby Diehl has co-written three autobiographies, including *Angel on My Shoulder* (2000) with singer Natalie Cole.

Examples of autobiographical fiction include Philip Roth's *Portnoy's Complaint* (1969), whose protagonist is prone to constant masturbation — an attribute that led novelist Jacqueline Susann to remark, "I'd like to meet him [Roth], but I wouldn't want to shake his hand"; Terry McMillan's *How Stella Got Her Groove Back* (1996), a novel about a middle-aged woman who meets a much younger man in Jamaica and falls passionately in love; and John Grisham's *A Painted House* (2001), which draws on the author's childhood in Arkansas.

▶ *avant-garde:* See **modernism.**

B

▶ **ballad:** A **poem** that recounts a **story**—generally some dramatic episode —
in the form of a song. *Traditional ballads* (also called *popular* or *folk ballads*) are **folk songs** normally sung by common people that typically relate
popular and often **tragic** stories in simple language. The form, which arose in
the later **Middle Ages,** ultimately became popular throughout Europe as
well as in North America. Francis J. Child's *English and Scottish Popular
Ballads* (1882–98) remains the standard compilation of traditional ballads
in English.

"Traditional" ballads are so called because they are passed down orally
from one generation to the next. The tradition of oral transmission results
in ongoing and continuous modifications to the ballad, which accounts for,
among other things, the many variations a ballad is likely to undergo over
time and across geographical space. It also renders traditional ballads common property, their **authorship** long forgotten.

Traditional ballads typically exhibit the following features: (1) simple
stanzas, many of which take the form of the **ballad stanza;** (2) abrupt tran-
sitions between stanzas due to weak verses that have been dropped from
the ballad at some point; (3) **refrains,** which often include a nonsense line
that probably resulted from a mistake or misunderstanding in oral transmission; (4) stock descriptive phrases, often incorporated to make it easier
for the singer to remember the words of the ballad; (5) **incremental repetition,** the restatement of a phrase or line with a variation that adds additional information or meaning; (6) **dialogue** used to advance the story line;
(7) minimal **characterization;** and (8) an impersonal **narrator.** Despite the
"objectivity" of the singer's language, however, ballads typically veil a great
deal of emotion.

Other types of ballads include the *broadside ballad,* the *literary ballad,*
and the various contemporary works we currently refer to as ballads. The
broadside ballad, an English form that arose in the sixteenth century, typically addressed current events and was printed on a broadside (a large sheet
of paper) sold by street vendors. The literary ballad, which arose in the late
eighteenth century with the rise of **romanticism,** is a poem written in **imitation** of the traditional **folk** ballad. (Nineteenth-century poets such as William
Wordsworth, Samuel Taylor Coleridge, and Thomas Hardy wrote literary
ballads in an attempt to reground poetry in the language and emotions of
common people.) Since the 1960s, *ballad* has been used loosely to refer to
lyrics associated with social protest movements and slow love songs as well
as **folk songs.**

FURTHER EXAMPLES: Well-known traditional ballads include "Bonny Barbara Allen," "Danny Boy," and "The Demon Lover"; other more recent
examples include "Alouette," "Camptown Races," and "Michael, Row the

Boat Ashore." Two of the most well-known literary ballads are Samuel Taylor Coleridge's "The Rime of the Ancient Mariner" (1798) and John Keats's "La belle dame sans merci" (1820). Arlo Guthrie's "Alice's Restaurant" (1967) is an example of a late-1960s protest song containing traditional ballad elements. John Mellencamp's "Jack and Diane" (1982) and Billy Joel's "Downeaster Alexa" (1989) are more contemporary ballads, as are many of Bruce Springsteen's songs, such as "Streets of Philadelphia" (1994) and the tracks on *The Ghost of Tom Joad* (1995). The term has also been applied to "slow-dance" love songs such as The Eagles' "Desperado" (1973); Chris de Burgh's "Lady in Red" (1986); Celine Dion's "My Heart Will Go On," featured in the movie *Titanic* (1997); James Blunt's "You're Beautiful" (2004), a song about seeing an "angel" on a crowded subway; and Sheryl Crow and Sting's duet "Always on Your Side" (2006).

▶ **ballade:** A **verse** form that originated in **medieval** France consisting of three long **stanzas** (most commonly eight lines rhyming *ababbcbc*) and a concluding *envoi* (usually four lines rhyming *bcbc*) addressed to a patron or other important person. The last line of each stanza, including the *envoi*, was repeated as a **refrain.** The ballade was especially popular in the fourteenth century; however, its most famous practitioner was the fifteenth-century poet François Villon. The nineteenth-century English **Pre-Raphaelite** poet Dante Gabriel Rossetti loosely translated some of these ballades, his most famous translation being of Villon's "Ballade des dames du temps jadis" ("The Ballad of Dead Ladies") (1489).

▶ **ballad stanza (ballad meter):** A four-line **stanza** used in the traditional **ballad.** The ballad stanza is usually characterized by an *abcb* **rhyme scheme,** although the rhyme may be approximate (**half rhyme**) rather than **perfect rhyme.** The first and third lines typically have four **accented** syllables while the second and fourth lines have three.

The term *ballad stanza* is sometimes used synonymously with **common meter,** but common meter tends to be associated with **hymns** and most often rhymes *abab*.

EXAMPLES: Scottish poet Robert Burns's "Ye Flowery Banks" (1792) is written in ballad stanzas:

> Yĕ flówĕry bánks ŏ' bónnĭe Dúnes,
>   Hŏw cán yĕ blúme săe fáir?
> Hŏw cán yĕ chánt, yĕ líttlĕ bírds,
>   Ănd Í săe fú'° ŏ' cáre?   *full*

Samuel Taylor Coleridge's "The Rime of the Ancient Mariner," published in *Lyrical Ballads* (1798), is composed mainly of traditional, four-line ballad stanzas such as the following:

> All in a hot and copper sky,
> The bloody Sun, at noon,
> Right up above the mast did stand,
> No bigger than the Moon.

▶ **bard:** A term originally used to **denote** early Celtic poets who composed poems glorifying warriors and heroes, now sometimes used to refer to William Shakespeare (the Bard), to any individual poet, or to poets (or the poet) in general.

▶ **bardic poetry:** Declamatory or proclamatory **verse,** often honoring or celebrating a great person, group of people, or place. Nineteenth-century American poet Walt Whitman is sometimes referred to as a bardic poet; Carl Sandburg's "Chicago" (1916) has been called a bardic poem.

▶ **baroque:** From the Portuguese *barroco* for "rough pearl," a term originally used by art historians to malign a style in architecture and art that flourished throughout Europe from about 1600 to 1750 (after the **Renaissance** but before the Rococo period). The term is now used in a more neutral manner to refer to a style characterized by a certain ornate and elaborate flamboyance that threatens to overshadow Renaissance elements of the work. Baroque works inject more picturesque, unusual, "wild," or even **grotesque** elements into the order and balance of Renaissance **aesthetics** to create formal tension and a kind of counterpoint between disquiet and composure. Energy, movement, and the heavy use of the diagonal are characteristic features. After its original application to art and architecture, *baroque* came to be applied to musical works, such as the preludes and fugues of German composer Johann Sebastian Bach.

As a literary term, *baroque* is less common, but it has been used to refer to a period of seventeenth-century post-Renaissance literature as well as to any writing characterized by a consciously elaborate, ornate, and dramatic style. **Conceits** are generally considered baroque, as is much of the writing of the **metaphysical poets.** Most critics regard the work of poets such as Giambattista Marino, Luis de Góngora, and Richard Crashaw (all of whom wrote elaborate, ornate, even fantastic conceits) as baroque. Some would argue that the most elaborately Latinate, **allusive, imaginative,** and **metaphorical** passages of John Milton's *Paradise Lost* (1667) are baroque in style.

FURTHER EXAMPLES: Baroque qualities abound in Crashaw's poem "The Weeper" (1646), in which a speaker addresses the following lines to Mary Magdalene (who washed Christ's feet with her tears and her hair):

> When some new bright guest
> Takes up among the Stars a Roome,
> And Heav'n will make a feast
> Angells with Chrystall Vyalls come,
> And draw from these full eyes of thine,
> Their master's Water; their owne wine.

▶ **base:** See **Marxist criticism.**

▶ **bathos:** Descent into mundane or sentimental language by a writer who is striving for the noble and elevated. Bathos is a stylistic **anticlimax,** the unintended (and therefore ridiculous) result of an unsuccessful attempt to achieve **pathos** or **the sublime.** English **neoclassical** poet and critic Alexander Pope gave prominence to the term in an essay entitled "Peri Bathous [On Bathos]: Of the Art of Sinking in Poetry" (1728), in which he mocked much of the poetry of his time.

EXAMPLES: Pope's generally lofty, philosophical poem entitled "An Essay on Man" (1733) itself sinks into bathos in the following lines:

> The lamb thy riot dooms to bleed today,
> Had he thy reason, would he skip and play?
> Pleased to the last, he crops his flowery food,
> And licks the hand just raised to shed his blood. . . .

The following passage from Robert James Waller's novel *The Bridges of Madison County* (1992), in which itinerant photographer Robert Kincaid tries to control his attraction to a married woman, is a modern example of bathos:

> The old ways struggling against all that is learned, struggling against the propriety drummed in by centuries of culture, the hard rules of civilized man. He tried to think of something else, photography or the road or covered bridges. Anything but how she looked just now.
>
> But he failed and wondered again how it would feel to touch her skin, to put his belly against hers. The questions eternal, and always the same. The goddamned old ways, fighting toward the surface. He pounded them back, pushed them down, lit a Camel, and breathed deeply.

Also bathetic is the anonymous poem "The Handwriting on the Wall," widely circulated as an email "forward." In the poem, a "weary mother," informed that her son has written in crayon on the wall, "rant[s] and rave[s] / About the expensive wallpaper and how she had saved" — only to find, moments later, that "The message she read pierced her soul with a dart. / It said 'I love Mommy,' surrounded by a heart."

▶ **beast fable:** A **fable** in which the principal **characters** are animals. Beast fables may be **didactic** or **satiric.** Noted beast fabulists include seventeenth-century French writer Jean de la Fontaine, nineteenth-century American journalist Joel Chandler Harris, and twentieth-century American humorist James Thurber.

EXAMPLES: Aesop's story of the fox and the grapes (c. 550 B.C.); the story, probably of Russian origin, of the little red hen, whose animal friends don't want to help her plant, water, or harvest the grain but who *do* want to help her eat her bread. Geoffrey Chaucer's "The Nun's Priest's Tale" (1387) warns against the sin of pride through the story of a rooster named Chauntecleer. Challenged by a fox to prove he can sing as well as his father, Chauntecleer nearly loses his neck when he stretches it to sing. Rudyard Kipling's *Just So Stories* (1902) are also beast fables.

George Orwell's beast fable *Animal Farm* (1945) is a political **allegory** of the Russian Revolution in which a rebellion by oppressed farm animals against their human masters devolves into even more brutal totalitarianism when the pigs gain unchecked power.

▶ **Beat writers (Beat Generation):** A group of American poets and novelists who were active and influential in the late 1950s, Beat writers rejected the prevailing social mores. Feeling oppressed by the dominant culture, they held and publicly advocated anti-intellectual, antipolitical, and, in general, antiestablishment views. *Beat* not only referred to feelings of oppression ("beaten down") but also to a desired, "beatific" state of vision or of ecstasy. Beat writers tended to express their alternative values through the form of their writing, which, compared to more conventional modern works, has a very loose structure and uses a great deal of slang.

Beat Generation (like the term *beatnik,* which refers to a member of that generation) applies to those who came of age just after World War II and who revolted against the dominant political and social culture of that complacent and materialistic era by acting in various ways (riding motorcycles, smoking marijuana) that defied the staid and crew-cut **conventions** of the times. The Beat movement of the 1950s had considerable influence on the 1960s' and 1970s' idea of counterculture. During this later era, the **connotations** of *Beat* expanded to include not only oppression and ecstasy but also the rebellious rhythms of rock 'n' roll (The Beatles).

EXAMPLES: Jack Kerouac's novel *On the Road* (1957); the following lines from Allen Ginsberg's "Howl" (1956):

> I saw the best minds of my generation destroyed by madness,
>   starving hysterical naked,
> dragging themselves through the negro streets at dawn looking for
>   an angry fix,
> angelheaded hipsters burning for the ancient heavenly connection
>   to the starry dynamo in the machinery of night. . . .

The character played by James Dean in *Rebel Without a Cause* (1955) typifies the feeling of oppression experienced by the members of the Beat Generation.

More recently, "poetry slams" — readings and recitations of aggressive personal poetry on college campuses and in urban coffeehouses and bars — have signaled a revival of Beat poetry. Henry Rollins, former lead vocalist for the punk rock band Black Flag, figured significantly in this revival.

▶ **beginning rhyme (head rhyme, initial rhyme):** (1) **Rhyme** that occurs at the beginning of two or more lines of **verse.** (2) A synonym for **alliteration.** Beginning rhyme, in the first sense, is rare in English verse.

▶ **bildungsroman (*Bildungsroman*):** A **novel** that recounts the development (psychological and sometimes spiritual) of an individual from childhood or adolescence to maturity, to the point at which the **protagonist** recognizes his or her place and role in the world. Also called an *apprenticeship novel* or *novel of formation* (after the **etymological** meaning of *bildungsroman*), such a work is often **autobiographical** but need not be. The **genre** was heavily influenced by Johann Wolfgang von Goethe's ***Erziehungsroman*** *Wilhelm Meisters Lehrjahre* (*Wilhelm Meister's Apprenticeship*) (1796).

While *bildungsroman* is often used synonymously in English-language **literary criticism** with *Erziehungsroman,* the novel of education or upbringing, *bildungsroman* is a more general term, encompassing *Erziehungsroman* as well as other coming-of-age novels. Other types of bildungsroman include the *Entwicklungsroman,* which recounts the general growth of an individual with an emphasis on life events rather than inner thoughts, and the ***Künstlerroman,*** or "novel of the artist," which specifically explores the development of an artist from childhood to the point when the subject realizes his or her artistic potential.

EXAMPLES: Charles Dickens's *Great Expectations* (1861); Somerset Maugham's *Of Human Bondage* (1915); Zora Neale Hurston's *Their Eyes Were Watching God* (1937); Ralph Ellison's *Invisible Man* (1947); S. E. Hinton's *The Outsiders* (1967) (published during the author's freshman year in college); Chaim Potok's *My Name Is Asher Lev* (1972); Jeanette Winterson's *Oranges Are Not the Only Fruit* (1985); and Romesh Gunesekera's *Reef* (1994), which recounts the development of Triton, a Sri Lankan housekeeper, from dependent servant boy to self-sufficient entrepreneur. The *Spider-Man* story (Marvel Comics, 1962– ; adapted to film 2002–07) has also been characterized as a bildungsroman.

▶ **binary oppositions:** A concept borrowed from **linguistics** by **poststructuralist** theorist Jacques Derrida, a philosopher of language who coined the term **deconstruction,** to suggest that people in Western culture tend to think and express their thoughts in terms of contrary pairs. Something is white but not black, masculine and therefore not feminine, a cause rather than an effect. Other common and mutually exclusive pairs include beginning/end, conscious/unconscious, and **presence/absence.** Derrida suggested that these dichotomies are not simply oppositions but also valuative hierarchies, containing one term that Western culture views as positive or superior and another considered negative or inferior, even if only slightly so.

Derrida deconstructed a number of these binary oppositions, including two — speech/writing and **signifier/signified** — that he believed to be central to linguistics in particular and Western culture in general. He didn't seek to reverse these oppositions, however, because doing so would simply perpetuate the same forms that he sought to deconstruct. He instead aimed to erase the boundary between binary oppositions — and to do so in such a way that the hierarchy implied by the oppositions is thrown into question.

Traditionally, **literary criticism** has entailed choosing between opposed and contradictory meanings and arguing that works support one meaning rather than the other. Derrida and other deconstructors have argued that **texts** contain opposed strands of **discourse,** providing no basis for choosing one reading over another. They may therefore support readings involving *both* reason and passion, life and death, hope and despair.

French **feminist critics** have adapted the ideas of Derrida and other deconstructors in their critique of Western language and culture. They have not only argued that language is structured in accordance with binary oppositions such as male / female, reason / emotion, and active / passive, but that qualities such as reason and activity are associated with masculinity, whereas emotion and passivity are aligned with femininity. Furthermore, they have asserted that (**patriarchal**) Western culture values those qualities associated with masculinity over those associated with femininity; reason, for instance, is valued more highly than emotion. French feminist critics have thus concluded that language is both hierarchically structured and **phallocentric**, or masculine-centered.

▶ **biography:** A written account of the life of a particular person from birth to death that attempts not only to elucidate the facts about that person's life and actions but also to draw a coherent picture of a self, personality, or character. Biographies should be distinguished from **autobiographies** (in which individuals depict their own lives) and **memoirs** (in which individuals render an account of things, people, and events they have experienced without focusing as directly on themselves).

As a **genre**, biography has changed over the centuries. Ancient Greek and Roman biographers, with some exceptions, were more interested in depicting an individual's character than in chronicling the straightforward facts of his life. Greek historian Plutarch's *Parallel Lives* (c. A.D. 100), which pairs accounts of notable Greeks and Romans, reflects this bias: "It is not histories I am writing, but lives; . . . a small thing, like a phrase or a jest, often makes a greater revelation of a character than battles where thousands die." Writers of **medieval** biography, which was mainly *hagiography* (the recounting of saints' lives), often relied on **legend** and were less concerned with detailing the events of a life or even depicting an actual person than with presenting an exemplary model of human piety. Notable exceptions include the Welsh bishop Asser's *Life of King Alfred* (893) and the English historian and theologian Eadmer's *Vita Anselmi* (*Life of Anselm*) (c. 1124), which incorporated **anecdotes** providing insight into the saint's personality. With the **Renaissance** came a new focus on the individual, and it became far less common for biographers to turn their subjects into illustrations, theses, examples, or exaggerated human types. Secular portrayals also gained ground, as exemplified by Florentine painter and architect Giorgio Vasari's popular *Le vite de' più eccellenti pittori, scultori e architettori* (*Lives of the Artists*) (1550, 1568), Englishman William Roper's *Life of Sir Thomas More* (written c. 1558; published 1626), and English writer Izaak Walton's five *Lives* (1640–78). Subsequently, the term *biography* was itself introduced into English, defined as "the history of particular men's lives" in English **neoclassical** poet and critic John Dryden's 1683 translation of Plutarch's *Parallel Lives*.

The complexity and popularity of biography as a genre in England increased most markedly during the eighteenth century. Samuel Johnson wrote fifty-two biographical studies, including lives of Dryden and two other poets, John Milton and Alexander Pope. James Boswell made Johnson, also a poet, critic, and **lexicographer**, the subject of his 1791 *Life of Samuel Johnson*, still thought by many to be the greatest biography of all time. By using **concrete** details and examples to flesh out Johnson's character and ways of thinking and feeling, Boswell helped establish not only the authenticity of biography but also the essential freedom of the biographer to explore anything that might facilitate or deepen the reader's understanding of the subject. This freedom was temporarily curtailed during the **Victorian Period,** when the notion that biography should not shake the public's faith in its great figures resulted in the production of authorized "life and letters" biographies catering more to appearances and politesse than truth.

Biography regained its standing as a revealing and critical endeavor in the twentieth century while also developing in new directions. For instance, English writer Lytton Strachey, who asserted that "Discretion is not the better part of biography," revolutionized the genre with a brief, selective, **witty** approach in works such as *Eminent Victorians* (1918). Other biographers sought to psychoanalyze their subjects, speculating on their inner thoughts and unconscious motivations. Today, most serious modern biographies are dispassionate works, grounded in extensive research and based on the proposition that presenting an accurate view of an individual's life and character requires examining the facts with a critical and neutral eye.

FURTHER EXAMPLES: Catherine Drinker Bowen's *Yankee from Olympus* (1944), detailing the life of the renowned Supreme Court Justice Oliver Wendell Holmes; Irving Stone's *The Agony and the Ecstasy* (1961), a biography of Michelangelo; Fawn Brodie's *Thomas Jefferson, An Intimate History* (1974). Noted twentieth-century literary biographies include Walter Jackson Bate's *John Keats* (1979); Shari Benstock's *No Gifts from Chance* (1994), on Edith Wharton; and Carlos Baker's *Emerson Among the Eccentrics* (1996).

Other noted contemporary biographies include Matthew Stephens's *Hannah Snell: The Secret Life of a Female Marine, 1723–1792* (1997); Sylvia Nasar's *A Beautiful Mind* (1998; adapted to film 2001), on the schizophrenic mathematician and Nobel Laureate John Forbes Nash; Anthony Sampson's *Mandela: The Authorized Biography* (1999); David McCullough's *John Adams* (2001); and Kai Bird and Martin J. Sherwin's *American Prometheus: The Triumph and Tragedy of J. Robert Oppenheimer* (2006), on the man viewed as "the father of the atomic bomb." Noted contemporary film biographies include *Ray* (2004) and *Walk the Line* (2005), which chronicle the lives of pianist and soul-music pioneer Ray Charles and country music singer-songwriter Johnny Cash.

▶ **black humor (black comedy):** A dark, disturbing, and often morbid or **grotesque mode** of **comedy** found in certain, generally **postmodern, texts,** especially **antinovels** and **Absurdist** works. Such humor often concerns death, suffering, or other anxiety-inducing subjects. Black humor usually goes hand in hand with a pessimistic worldview or **tone,** expressing a sense of hopelessness in a wry, sardonic, and grimly humorous way.

EXAMPLES: Joseph Heller's *Catch-22* (1961), Thomas Pynchon's *V* (1963), John Kennedy Toole's novel *A Confederacy of Dunces* (1980), and the works of Kurt Vonnegut contain a great deal of black humor. *Little Shop of Horrors*, originally a Roger Corman film written by Charles B.

Griffith (1960) that was made into a musical (1982) and then remade as a movie (1986), contains many instances of black humor. Other contemporary films utilizing black humor include *Fargo* (1996) and *Bad Santa* (2003). The writer and illustrator Edward Gorey consistently incorporates black humor into children's books; in *The Gashlycrumb Tinies* (1962), Gorey presented each letter of the alphabet via the name of a child who met an untimely death: "A is for Amy, who fell down the stairs. B is for Basil, assaulted by bears. . . ."

▶ **blank:** See **gap.**

▶ **blank verse:** Broadly defined, any unrhymed **verse** but usually referring to unrhymed **iambic pentameter.** Most critics agree that blank verse, as commonly defined, first appeared in English when the Earl of Surrey used it in his translation (c. 1540) of books 2 and 4 of Virgil's *The Aeneid* (c. 15 B.C.). It appeared for the first time in **drama** in Thomas Sackville and Thomas Norton's *Gorboduc* (1562). Over the centuries, blank verse has become the most common English verse form, especially for extended poems, as it is considered the closest form to natural patterns of English speech. Christopher Marlowe, William Shakespeare, and especially John Milton (particularly in his **epic** *Paradise Lost* [1667]) are generally credited with establishing blank verse as the preferred English verse form.

FURTHER EXAMPLES: The following passage from Elizabeth Barrett Browning's "verse novel" *Aurora Leigh* (1857), an extended poem of some eleven thousand lines:

> . . . But poets should
> Exert a double vision; should have eyes
> To see near things as comprehensively
> As if afar they took their point of sight,
> And distant things as intimately deep
> As if they touched them. Let us strive for this.
> I do distrust the poet who discerns
> No character or glory in his times. . . .

The opening lines of Robert Frost's poem "Birches" (1916) are written in blank verse:

> When I see birches bend to left and right
> Across the lines of straighter darker trees,
> I like to think some boy's been swinging them.
> But swinging doesn't bend them down to stay
> As ice-storms do. . . .

▶ **blend:** See **portmanteau word.**

▶ **blog:** As a noun, a website consisting of dated entries open to the public, often focused on a particular topic, and displayed in reverse chronological order, with the most recent postings appearing first; as a verb, to post content on or maintain a blog. The term *blog* is short for "web log"; *blogosphere* is often used specifically to designate an alternative media universe for the dissemination of news, information, and opinion. Blogging, which developed from online diaries in the mid-1990s, expanded substantially beginning in 1999, following the release of blogging software such as blogger and LiveJournal, and took off in the wake of 9/11. As of May 2008, Technorati, a leading blog search engine, tracked 112.8 million blogs <http://technorati.com/about/> (accessed May 15, 2008).

Blogs, which may be **authored** by an individual or a group of contributors, provide commentary and observations on one or more topics; indeed, the ease and speed of publication enables nearly instantaneous reporting. Blogs often take the form of a webzine (online newsletter) or personal journal and have an interactive format, inviting feedback in the form of comments from readers posted after the relevant entry. They generally include **links** to other websites; are updated regularly; and may also contain **images,** video, discussion threads, and search features.

Many well-known blogs are politically oriented, such as Marcos Moulitsas Zúniga's DailyKos; Glenn Reynolds's InstaPundit; and Wonkette, founded by Ana Marie Cox; other popular blogs include Boing Boing, which describes itself as "a directory of wonderful things," and PostSecret, which invites readers to "mail in their secrets anonymously on one side of a homemade postcard." Corporate blogs are on the rise, as is the use of blogging for "real-time" reporting and for literary purposes, such as the publication of short stories and novels. Examples of *blooks* — books based on blogs or other websites — include Colby Buzzell's *My War: Killing Time in Iraq* (2005), based on his 2004 blog detailing his year of service in Iraq, and Andrew Losowsky's *The Doorbells of Florence* (2006), a collection of photographs and short stories.

▶ **blues:** A form of **folk** music, characterized by slow, melancholy **lyrics** and the use of flatted "blue notes," that arose in African American communities in the American South in the late nineteenth century after emancipation from slavery. Blues give voice to feelings of despair, grief, worry, and oppression and often address **themes** of death, hard times, and loss of love. African American blues musician B. B. King famously called the blues "an expression of anger against shame and humiliation."

Tracing the history of "Negro music in white America" in *Blues People* (1963), poet and music critic LeRoi Jones (now known as Amiri Baraka) located the "immediate predecessors of blues" in "the Afro-American/American Negro work songs, which had their musical origins in West Africa," but emphasized that the blues were "a native American music, the product of the black man in this country." Early blues songs, which drew on forms ranging from work songs such as field hollers and shouts to Negro spirituals to the traditional British **ballad,** were generally improvised and sung a cappella. The typical blues form, established around the turn of the twentieth century, is a twelve-bar, three-line **stanza** in which the first and second lines are identical, as exemplified by the following verse:

Gwine lay my head right on de railroad track,
Gwine lay my head right on de railroad track,
'Cause my baby, she won't take me back.

The blues gradually evolved to become a form of entertainment, one that continued to advance an intensely personal account of the African American experience but that changed considerably in style with the addition of musical accompaniment and the infusion of developing elements of popular American music. Noted twentieth-century blues singers included Ida Cox, Sara Martin, Bessie Smith, and Gertrude "Ma" Rainey, who pioneered what is sometimes referred to as "classic blues." The following excerpt from the song "Put It Right Here or Keep It Out There" (1923) is an example of a **classic** blues song written by Porter Grainger and sung by Smith:

I've had a man for fifteen years, give him his room and board;
Once he was like a Cadillac, now he's like an old, worn-out Ford;
He never brought me a lousy dime and put it in my hand;
So there'll be some changes from now on, according to my plan:
He's got to get it, bring it, and put it right here,
Or else he's goin' to keep it out there;
If he must steal it, beg it, or borrow it somewhere,
Long as he gets it, I don't care. . . .

Moreover, during the **Harlem Renaissance,** a literary and cultural movement centered in Harlem in the 1920s, novelists and poets as well as musicians and dance bands began to celebrate and rework this form of artistic expression. Over time, the term *blues* came to refer not just to lyrics or songs recounting the African American experience but also to works by other American writers and musicians exploring the trials and tribulations of growing up outside the confines of established American culture.

FURTHER EXAMPLES: W. C. Handy's "St. Louis Blues" (1914); works by Harlem Renaissance novelists such as Jean Toomer (*Cane* [1923]) and George Schuyler (*Black No More* [1930]), as well as much of the poetry, fiction, and drama of Langston Hughes. Jazz dance bands and orchestras inspired by the blues included those of Duke Ellington, Chick Webb, Luis Russell, and Louis Armstrong.

Examples of contemporary blues literature include Toni Morrison's novels *Song of Solomon* (1977) and *Jazz* (1992), as well as Sheldon Epps's dramatic musical revue *Blues in the Night* (1982). The Robert Cray Band's albums *Bad Influence* (1983) and *False Accusations* (1985) are viewed as inheriting a black blues tradition that has, more recently, spilled over into other **racial** and ethnic tributaries. Notable examples of the blues most widely defined include "Reservation Blues" (1995) by Jim Boyd (a Colville Confederate Tribe member) in collaboration with Sherman Alexie (a Spokane Indian) as well as white blues guitarist Stevie Ray Vaughan's posthumous album *Blues at Sunrise* (2000).

For a humorous take on the blues, see Judith Podell's "How to Sing the Blues," published in *WordWrights Magazine* (Jan. 1997) before being copied and circulated widely on the Internet, often in modified forms. Podell's primer is a series of rules for the blues, ranging from who has the right to sing the blues — e.g., the blind, those who've shot a man in Memphis or can't be satisfied — to acceptable forms of transportation, namely, walkin', Chevies, Cadillacs, Greyhound buses, and southbound trains.

▶ **body criticism:** See **disability studies.**

▶ **bombast:** Inflated, extravagant, often ranting language, particularly common in **Elizabethan** literary works and political speeches.

EXAMPLE: These lines from Christopher Marlowe's *Tamburlaine the Great* (1587), spoken by Tamburlaine himself:

> The host of Xerxes, which by fame is said
> To drink the mighty Parthian Araris,
> Was but a handful to that we will have.
> Our quivering lances, shaking in the air,
> And bullets, like Jove's dreadful thunderbolts,
> Enroll'd in flames and fiery smoldering mists,
> Shall threat the gods more than Cyclopian wars;
> And, with our sun-bright armor as we march,
> We'll chase the stars from Heaven and dim their eyes
> That stand and muse at our admired arms.

Another example of bombast, rife with absurdly **mixed metaphors,** can be found in an 1870 Nebraska newspaper editorial discussing legislative turmoil: "The apple of discord is now fairly in our midst, and if not nipped in the bud it will burst forth in a conflagration which will deluge society in an earthquake of bloody apprehension."

▶ **bourgeois tragedy:** See **domestic tragedy.**

▶ **Breton lay:** See *lai.*

▶ **bucolic (poetry):** From the Greek for "cowherd," a term that has traditionally been used to refer to **pastoral** writings. Bucolic poetry typically concerns itself with the pastoral subjects of shepherds and their country ways and values. The plural (*bucolics*) has been used to refer to the entire corpus of pastoral works by **classical** writers such as the third-century B.C. Greek poet Theocritus and the first-century B.C. Roman poet Virgil. Today, *bucolic* and *bucolics* are used more loosely to refer to works with rural or rustic **settings** or **styles.**

▶ **burlesque:** A type of **comedy** in which distortion and exaggeration are employed to ridicule and deflate, either through the trivialization of a lofty subject or through the glorification of a lowly or commonplace one. Humor results from the disparity between subject and **style.** Some critics distinguish between *high* and *low* burlesque, the former referring to works with an inappropriately heightened style for an inconsequential subject and the latter to works in which a lofty subject is degraded by an inappropriately base style.

Burlesque works may be written purely to entertain, but writers more commonly employ burlesque as an instrument of **satire**. Since burlesque frequently **imitates** another work or aspect of that work in a mocking way, it is often used to deride specific (and often identifiable) works or their **authors,** certain subject matters, or even entire **genres.**

Burlesque is sometimes conflated with **parody** and **travesty.** While critical usage of these terms varies, burlesque may be said to encompass both parody and travesty; in this view, parody is a type of high burlesque (as are the **mock epic** and **mock heroic**) and travesty a type of low burlesque.

The term *burlesque* may also be used to refer to a saucy, satirical form of variety theater that includes acts ranging from mime, novelty performances, and striptease to chorus numbers, bawdy songs, and **slapstick** comedy. The genre flourished in the U.S. in the late nineteenth and early twentieth centuries before becoming the target of various censorship efforts and has recently undergone a revival.

EXAMPLES: Miguel de Cervantes's *Don Quixote* (1605, 1615), which parodies **chivalric romances,** is an example of high burlesque; Monty Python's *Life of Brian* (1979), which makes a travesty of the New Testament story of Jesus, is an example of low burlesque.

See also **parody, travesty.**

C

▶ **cacophony:** Harsh, unpleasant, or discordant sounds. Cacophony is the opposite of **euphony,** pleasing or harmonious sounds. Cacophony can be either unintentional or purposely used for artistic effect.

EXAMPLES: In his long poem *The Bridge* (1930), Hart Crane wrote cacophonously to convey the chaotic energy, the sinister unworldliness, of the modern industrial world:

> The nasal whine of power whips a new universe . . .
> Where spouting pillars spoor the evening sky,
> Under the looming stacks of the gigantic power house
> Stars prick the eyes with sharp ammoniac proverbs,
> New verities, new inklings in the velvet hummed
> Of dynamos, where hearing's leash is strummed . . .
> Power's script, — wound, bobbin-bound, refined —
> Is stopped to the slap of belts on booming spools, spurred
> Into the bulging bouillon, harnessed jelly of the stars.

Pop culture examples of cacophony may be found in Lou Reed's grinding *Metal Machine Music* (1975), in music associated with the industrial rock movement, and in many songs recorded by the rock group Nine Inch Nails.

See also **dissonance.**

▶ **caesura (cesura):** A pause in a line of **poetry.** The caesura is dictated not by **meter** but by natural speaking **rhythm.** Sometimes it coincides with the poet's punctuation, but occasionally it occurs where some pause in speech is inevitable. In **scansion,** the caesura is indicated by the symbol ‖.

EXAMPLE: In the following lines from William Butler Yeats's "The Lake Isle of Innisfree" (1893), the caesura in the first line coincides with Yeats's punctuation, whereas the one in the second is indicated solely by natural rhythms of speech:

> I will arise and go now, ‖ for always night and day
> I hear lake water lapping ‖ with low sounds by the shore. . . .

▶ **canon:** Most generally, a body of written works accepted as authoritative or authentic. As a religious term, *canon* has been used with reference to Christianity since the fourth century A.D. to refer to books of the Bible accepted as Holy Scripture, that is, as being divinely inspired. The term is also used in the phrase *Saints' Canon* to refer to the group of people that the Catholic Church officially recognizes as saints. As a literary term, *canon* may refer to the body of works that scholars generally attribute to a particular **author** or, more broadly, to those literary works that are **privileged** (accorded special status) by a given culture. Thus we speak of the "Shakespearean canon" (thirty-seven or thirty-eight plays that scholars believe can be definitely attributed to William Shakespeare) or the "Western canon" (the fundamental literary **texts** of Western culture). Works widely regarded as **classics**, or "Great Books" — texts that are repeatedly reprinted, anthologized, and taught in classes — constitute the canon in its broader literary sense.

By contrast, the term *apocryphal* generally refers to written works of doubtful or uncertain authenticity or authorship. Books or other works outside of the canon (noncanonical works) that religious bodies consider apocryphal are not viewed as divinely inspired but may still have high status. For instance, while the Book of Judith does not appear in the Hebrew Bible, it is included in the apocrypha of the King James Bible. Literary works are considered apocryphal when their authorship is disputed or otherwise uncertain. For instance, several plays including *Locrine* (1595) and *The Puritan* (1607), both attributed to "W.S.," are included in the "Shakespeare Apocrypha," given insufficient evidence of Shakespeare's authorship as well as evidence suggesting the authorship of another playwright such as Wentworth Smith or Thomas Middleton.

Contemporary **Marxist, feminist,** and **postcolonial** critics have argued that, for political reasons, many excellent works never enter the canon. Canonized works, they claim, are those that reflect — and respect — the culture's dominant **ideology** or perform some socially acceptable or even necessary form of "cultural work." Attempts have been made to broaden or redefine the canon by rediscovering valuable texts, or versions of texts, that were repressed or ignored for political reasons. These have been published in both traditional and nontraditional anthologies. The most outspoken critics of the canon, especially certain critics practicing **cultural criticism,** have called into question the whole concept of canon or "canonicity." These critics, who do not privilege any form of expression, treat cartoons, comic strips, and soap operas with the same cogency and respect they accord novels, poems, and plays.

▶ **canto:** From the Italian for "song," a section, often numbered, of a long **poem.**

EXAMPLES: Dante Alighieri's *Divina commedia* (*The Divine Comedy*) (1321), Edmund Spenser's *The Faerie Queene* (1590, 1596), and George Gordon, Lord Byron's *Childe Harold's Pilgrimage* (1812–18) are divided into cantos.

▶ **caricature:** From the Italian for "to load," an exaggeration or other distortion of an individual's prominent features or characteristics that makes the person appear ridiculous. Caricatures exaggerate distinctive or idiosyncratic traits, such as a large nose or a habit of apologizing frequently. The term *caricature* tends to be applied to graphic rather than written representations, where the term **burlesque** (or sometimes **satire** or **parody**) is usually used.

EXAMPLES: **Victorian** novelist Charles Dickens created many literary caricatures, including Fagin, the **antagonist** in *Oliver Twist* (1837), "whose villanous-looking and repulsive face was obscured by a quantity of matted red hair." Anthony Trollope parodied Dickens's tendency to create caricatures rather than three-dimensional **characters** in his novel *The Warden* (1855), where he described a fictitious novel (*The Almshouse*) written by a fictitious **author** (Mr. Popular Sentiment) as follows:

> The demon of *The Almshouse* was the clerical owner of this comfortable abode. He was a man well stricken in years but still strong to do evil; he was one who looked cruelly out of a hot, passionate, bloodshot eye, who had a huge red nose with a carbuncle, thick lips, and a great double flabby chin which swelled out into solid substance, like a turkey cock's comb, when sudden anger inspired him; he had a hot, furrowed, low brow from which a few grizzled hairs were not yet rubbed off by the friction of his handkerchief; he wore a loose unstarched white handkerchief, black loose ill-made clothes, and huge loose shoes adapted to many corns and various bunions; his husky voice told tales of much daily port wine, and his language was not so decorous as became a clergyman.

Garry Trudeau often caricatures American political figures through the use of **symbols** in his comic strip *Doonesbury* (1970–). He **represented** vice president Dan Quayle as a feather, for instance, Speaker of the House Newt Gingrich as a bomb with a lit fuse, and president George W. Bush as an asterisk wearing a cowboy hat.

▶ **carnival:** In popular parlance, a festival or a traveling amusement show (with rides, clowns, games, etc.). More specifically, the term also refers to the extravagant celebrations held in the Christian world on Mardi Gras, the "Fat Tuesday" that precedes Ash Wednesday, the beginning of Lent. As a literary term, however, *carnival* is associated with Soviet critic Mikhail Bakhtin and with **dialogic criticism,** a method of **literary criticism** based on Bakhtin's **theories.**

   In the book *Rabelais and His World* (1940), Bakhtin used the term *carnival* to refer not only to such festivities as Mardi Gras — celebrations during which not only commoners but also the more privileged classes were temporarily free to transgress all kinds of written and unwritten social and ecclesiastical laws — but also to "low" or popular culture, such as fairs and spontaneous **folk dramas** (including puppet shows). The **discourse** of carnival, as Bakhtin understood it, is infused by the down-to-earth priorities and values held by the underprivileged or plebeian "second world" of commoners, or **folk.** Because that world is necessarily concerned with basic issues of survival, with the sustenance and reproduction of life, the language of carnival is substantially concerned with the body, eating, sex, and death; characteristically playful, it typically involves sensous **imagery.** In carnivalesque discourse, matters of the body are treated with a kind of profound humor — neither simply funny as we might say about a situation comedy, nor serious as we expect a high drama to be, but something in between. This doubleness produces an ambivalent or **grotesque** quality that contrasts starkly with the official discourse, the language of power and propriety. As Bakhtin wrote, "carnival celebrated temporary liberation from the prevailing truth and from the established order; it marked the suspension of all hierarchical rank, privileges, norms, and prohibitions. Carnival was the true feast of time, the feast of becoming, change, and renewal. It was hostile to all that was immortalized and completed."

Both dialogic critics and practitioners of other contemporary approaches have followed and expanded upon Bakhtin's concept of carnival. Michael Bristol, for instance, argued in "Funeral Bak'd Meats: Carnival and the Carnivalesque in *Hamlet*" (1994) that the **scene** in which William Shakespeare's famous gravedigger reminisces about a fool named Yorick (whose skull he has plucked from the site of Ophelia's grave) is a carnivalesque moment in *Hamlet* (1602), a play whose official discourse concerns the usurpation of power and its tragic consequences. Bristol also suggested that King Claudius functions as a carnivalesque Lord of Misrule in *Hamlet* and gave as an example Claudius's statement that he has "taken to wife" his murdered brother's wife, the Queen, "with mirth in funeral, and with dirge in marriage."

▶ **Caroline Age (in English literature):** An age spanning the reign of Charles I (1625–49) that is often classified as the fourth of five literary eras within the **Renaissance Period** in English literature. The Caroline Age, which derives its name from *Carolus* (Latin for Charles), was racked from 1642 to 1651 by civil war between the Cavaliers, royalists who supported the king, and the Roundheads, who supported the Puritan parliamentary opposition. In their **satirical** history of England entitled *1066 and All That* (1931), Walter Carruthers Sellar and Robert Julian Yeatman described this war as the "utterly memorable struggle between the Cavaliers (Wrong but Romantic) and the Roundheads (Right but Repulsive)."

Writers whose careers are closely associated with the Caroline Age include prose writer Sir Thomas Browne and the royalist **Cavalier poets** — Thomas Carew, Robert Herrick, Richard Lovelace, and Sir John Suckling — who sided with the king in the civil war and wrote **lyrics** about love, women, and gallantry. Other authors associated with the Caroline Age began or ended their careers in another era, such as Robert Burton, author of *Anatomy of Melancholy* (1621), who began to write during the preceding **Jacobean Age**; George Herbert, a **metaphysical poet** who also began writing during the Jacobean Age; and John Milton, who did his greatest work in the succeeding **Commonwealth Age** and **Restoration Age**.

While drama flourished throughout most of the Caroline Age, the **genre** was strongly constrained from 1642, the year in which the Puritan-dominated Parliament closed all theaters to suppress stage plays, until 1660, with the end of the Puritan Interregnum and the restoration of the monarchy to power.

See also **Cavalier poets, Renaissance**.

▶ *carpe diem:* Latin for "seize the day," a phrase referring to the age-old literary **theme** (particularly prevalent in **lyric** poetry) that we should enjoy the present before opportunity — and even life itself — slips away.

EXAMPLES: *Carpe diem* is the theme of the movie *Dead Poets Society* (1989). The schoolmaster urges his students to "seize the day" — to live for the moment and for themselves, enjoying life. Robert Herrick's "To the Virgins, to Make Much of Time" (1648) ("Gather ye rosebuds while ye may / Old Time is still a-flying . . .") is a more **classic** example, as is sixteenth-century French poet Pierre de Ronsard's **ode** to Cassandre (c. 1552), the last **stanza** of which follows:

> Donc, si vous me croyez, mignonne,
> Tandis que votre âge fleuronne
> En sa plus verte nouveauté,
> Cueillez, cueillez votre jeunesse:
> Comme à cette fleur la vieillesse
> Fera ternir votre beauté.

> [So, if you believe me, darling,
> While your age is blossoming
> In its green freshness,
> Gather, gather your youth
> While it flowers, for old age
> Will tarnish your beauty.]

▶ **catachresis:** From the Greek for "misuse," a term referring to the incorrect or strained use of a word. Catachresis often involves a mixed or "illogical" **metaphor**. The phrase *tooth of a comb* is a strict example of catachresis since combs do not really have teeth. The meaning of the word *dry* is strained when we refer to a town in which liquor cannot be purchased as "dry." A **classic** literary example involving a mixed and illogical metaphor occurs in John Milton's "Lycidas" (1638):

> Blind mouths! that scarce themselves know how to hold
> A sheep-hook. . . .

▶ **catalexis (truncation):** Omission of one or two un**stressed** syllables in the last **foot** of a line of **verse**.

EXAMPLE: The **trochaic octameter** lines of Edgar Allan Poe's "The Raven" (1849) sometimes lack the last **unaccented** syllable, as in the second line below:

> While I nodded, nearly napping, suddenly there came a tapping,
> As of some one gently rapping, rapping at my chamber door —
> Only this and nothing more.

See also **feminine ending.**

▶ **catastrophe:** The culmination of the **falling action** in the **plot** of a **story** or **drama**. Catastrophe is one of five **structural** elements associated with

Freytag's Pyramid, a model developed by nineteenth-century German writer Gustav Freytag for analyzing five-act plays (**tragedies** in particular). The term *catastrophe* may be applied to the concluding action of any work but is usually reserved for tragedies. The catastrophe often involves the death of the **hero,** but some other tragic outcome may occur instead.

EXAMPLE: In William Shakespeare's tragedy *Macbeth* (1606), the catastrophe occurs in the penultimate scene in which Macbeth dies during a sword fight with Macduff.

See also **Freytag's Pyramid.**

▶ **catharsis (katharsis):** The emotional effect a **tragic drama** has on its audience. Aristotle, an ancient Greek philosopher, introduced this term (which can mean either "purgation" or "purification" in Greek) into **literary criticism** in the *Poetics* (c. 330 B.C.). He sought to explain the feeling of exaltation or relief that playgoers commonly experience during and after the **catastrophe** (which invariably **foregrounds** suffering, defeat, and even death). Aristotle argued that while viewing such a work, the audience experiences a purging or cleansing of emotions, specifically fear and pity, which in turn produces the beneficial sensation of relief or exaltation. The final line of John Milton's long poem *Samson Agonistes* (1671) describes the carthartic state: "Calm of mind, all passions spent."

Two schools of thought exist regarding the nature of catharsis and, more specifically, how it is effected. Some argue that emotions are purged or cleansed though a vicarious identification by the audience with the tragic **hero** and his or her downfall. Others claim that viewers (or readers) are so caught up in emotions of fear and pity for the hero that they forget their own problems and emotional conflicts. Presumably, the expenditure of emotion on the hero engenders the beneficial feelings associated with the carthartic experience.

▶ **Cavalier poets:** Poets who were associated with the reign of Charles I of England (1625–49) and who wrote graceful, polished, **witty,** and even brazen **lyrics** about love, women, and gallantry. The term *Cavalier* refers to royalists who backed the king against the Roundheads, who supported the Puritan parliamentary opposition, during the English civil war. Most of the Cavalier poets were courtiers who wrote casual, lighthearted verse on everyday matters in colloquial language or **occasional verse** commemorating particular events.

The Cavalier poets, who wrote during the **Caroline Age** and were influenced by the polished style of English poet Ben Jonson, are also sometimes called *Caroline poets* (*Caroline* is an adjective derived from *Carolus,* Latin for Charles) or *Sons of Ben.* Noted Cavalier poets included Thomas Carew, Richard Lovelace, Sir John Suckling, and Robert Herrick, who, though not a courtier, often treated **themes** of love and gallantry in the Cavalier manner.

EXAMPLE: Suckling's "Love Turned to Hatred" is an example of Cavalier poetry:

I WILL not love one minute more, I swear,
No, not a minute; not a sigh or tear
Thou get'st from me, or one kind look again,
Though thou shouldst court me to 't and wouldst begin.

I will not think of thee but as men do
Of debts and sins, and then I'll curse thee too:
For thy sake woman shall be now to me
Less welcome, than at midnight ghosts shall be:
I'll hate so perfectly, that it shall be
Treason to love that man that loves a she;
Nay, I will hate the very good, I swear,
That's in thy sex, because it doth lie there;
Their very virtue, grace, discourse, and wit,
And all for thee; what, wilt thou love me yet?

▶ **Celtic Revival (Celtic Renaissance, Irish Literary Renaissance, or Irish Revival):** An Irish movement of the late nineteenth and early twentieth centuries to revive and promote an indigenous Celtic cultural, literary, and artistic tradition to counter centuries of imperial English domination. Writers of the Celtic Revival sought to construct an independent, nationalistic literature based on Irish traditions, **themes,** and subject matter, such as those preserved in Celtic **folklore** and **legend.** In the fine arts, painters and sculptors of the Celtic Revival likewise pursued nationalistic aims, often depicting Irish subject matter.

William Butler Yeats; Isabella Augusta, Lady Gregory; and Edward Martyn, all writers, are often credited with inaugurating the Celtic Revival. Other major literary figures included critic and poet A. E. (George W. Russell), playwrights J. M. Synge and Sean O'Casey, and novelist George Moore. James Joyce, a novelist, short story writer, and poet, is also often classified as a Celtic Revival writer — despite having mocked and disparaged the movement, subverting the phrase "Celtic twilight" into "cultic twalette" — since his writing featured Irish subjects and themes. Artists associated with the Celtic Revival included painter Jack Yeats, the brother of William Butler Yeats, and Oliver Sheppard, a sculptor.

Substantial influences on the Celtic Revival aside from growing Irish nationalism and the corresponding push for independence included Standish O'Grady's *History of Ireland: Heroic Period* (1878); Douglas Hyde's *A Literary History of Ireland* (1899); the Dublin Lodge of the Theosophical Society; and the *Conradh na Gaelige* (Gaelic League), which Hyde, a Gaelic scholar who later became the first president of Ireland, founded in 1893.

The Celtic Revival paralleled another movement, called the Gaelic Movement or Gaelic Revival, to preserve and promote the use of Gaelic, the Irish language, and to encourage a national literature written in Gaelic. Notably, while many of those who participated in the Celtic Revival supported the Gaelic Movement, they chose to write in English rather than Gaelic.

One of the goals of the Celtic Revival was to establish Irish institutions to rival those of England. The Irish Literary Theatre, the Abbey Theatre (home of the Irish National Theatre Society), and literary societies such as the Irish National Literary Society were founded during this period, as was the Gallery of Modern Art, which showcased Irish art as well as contemporary art from other European countries.

The term *Celtic Revival* is sometimes also applied to an earlier literary movement dating back to the second half of the eighteenth century that focused on ancient Celtic literature, **myths,** and traditions. Key figures in this earlier Celtic Revival were the poets Thomas Gray and James Macpherson.

EXAMPLES: William Butler Yeats's *The Celtic Twilight* (1893), a collection of narratives recounting encounters with fairies that Yeats called "this handful of dreams"; Synge's play *The Playboy of the Western World* (1907); James Stephens's novel *The Crock of Gold* (1912), based on Irish **fairy tales.** For an account of the Celtic Revival movement by one of its leaders, see Moore's three-volume **memoir** *Hail and Farewell* (1914).

▶ **center:** An idea, event, or **image** that, once identified or posited, gives apparent structure to a **text** — be it a relatively short utterance, a literary work, or an entire social **discourse** — thereby limiting its possible meaning or meanings. For example, the creation of Eve from Adam's rib has served as a "centering" idea, event, and image in Western culture. Jacques Derrida, the theorist most closely associated with **deconstruction,** suggested that texts have no one determinate and determinable meaning and therefore have no identifiable fixed center or purpose.

Practitioners of deconstruction (as well as many **new historicists** and other **poststructuralist** critics) aim to *decenter* the text, that is, to undermine the text's presumed center and its concomitant structure. By drawing attention to the divergent meanings that arise from the diverse **connotations** of **signifiers** within the text, they challenge the assumption that its "meaning" is either determinate or determinable.

Similarly, poststructuralist **psychoanalytic critics** have deconstructed the subject, or self, suggesting that — like the text as understood by deconstructors — it lacks the defining center and structure typically posited by traditional **theories** regarding personality and character. Psychoanalytic theorist Jacques Lacan contended that the concepts of the subject, self, **ego,** and "I" are merely constructs, fictions of coherence that hide the inconsistency, contradictoriness, and indeterminacy of being.

▶ **cesura:** See **caesura.**

▶ **character, the character, characterization:** In its most general literary sense, a character is a figure in a literary work. That figure need not be human, although most characters are. Characters may be animals or even nonliving entities, provided that the **author** characterizes them by giving them the attributes of a human individual. *Character* also carries the nonliterary **connotations** of personality and morality (or lack thereof) — hence, we speak of persons of good, bad, and "shady" character.

Occasionally **literary critics** use the phrase *the character* in a highly specialized way to refer to a literary **genre** that developed in seventeenth- and eighteenth-century England and France. The character, based on the late-fourth- and early-third-century B.C. Greek philosopher Theophrastus' *Characters,* is a genre in which a character *type,* rather than a truly individual character, is sketched in a brief work written in prose or verse. The particular virtue or vice of the character type being described (such as the braggart soldier or the pedant) is briefly delineated. Modern versions of the character are generally called *character sketches.*

The term *characterization* refers to the various means by which an author describes and develops the characters in a literary work. In discussing depth and complexity of characterization, E. M. Forster made a distinction between **flat and round characters** that is still in use today. He argued that flat characters are types or **caricatures** defined by a single idea or quality, whereas round characters have the three-dimensional complexity of real people. Characterization may also be *static* or *dynamic.* Static characters do not change significantly over the course of a work no matter what occurs, whereas dynamic characters change (whether for better or worse) in response to circumstance and experience.

Characterization is inextricably intertwined with **plot.** In order for a work to be believable, the reader must find the characters convincing; in order to find the characters convincing, the reader must be able to visualize them. Authors must therefore make their characters "come alive" by describing thoughts and emotions as well as physical attributes, actions, conversations, and so forth. The author may employ *direct characterization,* explicitly presenting or commenting on the characters (i.e., *telling* the reader about the characters), or *indirect characterization,* setting forth characters through representations of their actions, statements, thoughts, and feelings (*showing* the reader what the character is like). In either case, for readers to identify with or side against given characters, authors must describe them convincingly and provide compelling **motivation** for their actions and beliefs.

▶ **chiasmus:** A **rhetorical figure** in which certain words, sounds, concepts, or **syntactic** structures are reversed or repeated in reverse order. The term *chiasmus* is derived from the x-shaped Greek letter *chi;* the implication is that the two parts of a chiastic whole mirror each other as do the parts of the letter *x.*

EXAMPLES: William Shakespeare's *Macbeth* (1606) contains the chiastic line, "Fair is foul and foul is fair." James Joyce used chiasmus in "The Dead" (1907) when he wrote, "His soul swooned slowly as he heard the snow falling faintly through the universe and faintly falling...." ("Falling faintly" and "faintly falling" mirror each other in a perfect chiastic design.)

Not all chiasmus is this precise, however. Samuel Taylor Coleridge, for example, wrote that "Flowers are lovely, love is flowerlike." His poem "Kubla Khan" (1816) begins with what some would call a *sonic* chiasmus

(chiasmus effected by sound): "In Xanadu did Kubla Khan . . ." Two of U.S. President John F. Kennedy's most famous statements — "Ask not what your country can do for you; ask what you can do for your country" and "Let us never negotiate out of fear but let us never fear to negotiate" — display chiastic structure.

Chiastic structure may also create or heighten **paradox**. The **protagonist** in Carrie Fisher's *Postcards from the Edge* (1987) tells her diary that "I was into pain reduction and mind expansion, but what I've ended up with is pain expansion and mind reduction. Everything hurts now, and nothing makes sense." Likewise, in Amy Tan's novel *The Joy Luck Club* (1989), a **character** named Lena gorges herself to the point of sickness on strawberry ice cream and wonders why "eating something good could make me feel so terrible, while vomiting something terrible could make me feel so good."

Alexander Pope used a type of chiasmus effected by reversal of a syntactic pattern in his "An Essay on Criticism" (1711), a long poem in which he stated that art "works without show and without pomp presides." Here the syntactic pattern of the quoted line is verb ("works"), prepositional phrase ("without show"), prepositional phrase ("without pomp"), and verb ("presides").

▶ **Chicago school (neo-Aristotelianism):** A type of **literary criticism** that combines an emphasis on **theory** and method with an historical interest in critical approaches and literary **genres** and a practical focus on the **form, structure,** and relations of elements within individual works. Chicago critics are noted for their commitment to pluralism in critical methods and the application of Aristotelian principles to literary analysis (hence the term *neo-Aristotelianism*). The school, which originally included six scholars associated with the University of Chicago, arose in the mid-1930s, particularly with the publication of R. S. Crane's essay "History versus Criticism in the Study of Literature" (1935), in which Crane **privileged** criticism rather than history or **impressionism** in the study of literature. Subsequently, the group published *Critics and Criticism: Ancient and Modern* (1952), a landmark book addressing both the criticism of the day and the history of literary criticism generally. Later generations of critics applying Chicago school methods and theories have also been referred to as Chicago critics, without regard to any association with the University of Chicago.

The original Chicago critics sought to make literary criticism a discipline. To this end, they engaged in two major efforts: a general critique of criticism that embraced pluralism; and the development of one historical system, the poetic method of Aristotle. In the introduction to *Critics and Criticism,* Crane emphasized that criticism is "reasoned discourse" and called for "a general critique of literary criticism . . . such as might yield objective criteria for interpreting the diversities and oppositions among critics and for judging the comparative merits of rival schools." Subsequently, in *The Languages of Criticism and the Structure of Poetry* (1953), he advocated using "various critical languages . . . as tools of our trade — as so many distinct conceptual and logical means, each with its peculiar capacities and limitations, for solving truly the many distinct kinds of problems which poetry . . . presents to our view."

With regard to Aristotle, Chicago critics based their own methodology on his analytical, differentiating approach. In the *Poetics* (c. 330 B.C.), Aristotle, who viewed art as an imitation of nature, treated poetic works as artistic wholes comprised of various elements such as **plot** and structure and explored how poets created such unified works. As Crane explained in *Critics and Criticism,* Aristotle outlined "hypotheses and analytical devices for defining, literally and inductively, and with a maximum degree of differentiation, the multiple causes operative in the construction of poetic wholes of various kinds and the criteria of excellence appropriate to each." Building on Aristotle's method, Chicago critics focused on "the internal causes which account for the peculiar construction and effect of any poem qua artistic whole," which they viewed as separable from external factors such as authorial **intention** and audience tastes.

In analyzing individual works, Chicago critics have focused particularly on form, which they view as the shaping principle of a **text,** and the way in which form is articulated in a work's structure. For Chicago critics, form both enables the **author** to synthesize the elements of a work into a whole and shapes the reader's response; in *The Idea of the Humanities and Other Essays* (1967), Crane described form as the "principle of construction, from which [the artist] infers, however instantaneously, what he must do in constituting and ordering the parts." Chicago critics also speak of the *dynamis,* the "final cause" or "power" of the form, as inhering in and determining the unique form of a work. Moreover, given their interest in works as artistic wholes, many Chicago critics have analyzed the relationship between individual works and categories of works. Notable form and genre studies include Elder Olson's *Tragedy and the Theory of Drama* (1961), Mary Doyle Springer's *Forms of the Modern Novella* (1975), and Austin Wright's *The Formal Principle of the Novel* (1982).

While Chicago critics may be called **formalists** insofar as they focus on textual analysis, their interest in authorial intention and historical matters is decidedly not formalist. Indeed, Chicago critics believed that the approach of the formalist **New Critics,** who focused strictly on textual analysis, was unduly narrow, reductive, and even wrong with regard to concepts such as the **intentional fallacy,** which rejected consideration of authorial intention. As Crane explained in *Critics and Criticism,* "We cannot infer the 'poetic' nature or value of any artistic whole from its antecedents in the poet's life or in contemporary or earlier culture; but, having determined critically what the poem is in itself, we can then replace it in its setting of events and other writings and eventually develop a history of poetry in terms of the interaction of artistic and extra-artistic causes of change."

Original members of the Chicago school aside from Crane included Olson, W. R. Keast, Richard McKeon, Norman Maclean, and Bernard Weinberg.

Members of the second generation — including Springer, Wright, Wayne C. Booth, Ralph Rader, and Sheldon Sacks — further developed theoretical concepts, particularly in form and genre studies, and placed greater emphasis on **ideology, rhetoric,** and the functions of the author and reader. Booth was particularly influential, developing concepts such as the **implied author** in *The Rhetoric of Fiction* (1961) and spurring a more general shift from Aristotelian **poetics** to the communicative and persuasive aspects of fiction. Members of the third, contemporary generation, such as James Phelan, Peter Rabinowitz, Adena Rosmarin, and David Richter, have continued to apply Chicago methods but have often focused on **narratological** issues while also incorporating a variety of contemporary approaches and concerns.

▶ **chivalric romance:** See **medieval romance.**

▶ **choriambus:** See **foot.**

▶ **chorus:** In Greek **drama,** a group of people who sang and danced, commenting on the **action** of the **play.** A chorus was also used to chant **odes.** The chorus has its origins in an ancient Greek religious event and was later used in Greek **tragedies** and Roman plays. The use of such choruses generally declined with the continuing development of drama. By **Elizabethan** times, the chorus, when used, often comprised a single **character** delivering a **prologue** and **epilogue** and occasionally making other explanatory remarks, such as introductions and notes on offstage happenings delivered at the beginning of an **act.** Modern critics have adopted the term *choral character* or *chorus character* to refer to a character in a work who comments on characters and events, thereby providing the audience with an additional perspective. Although choral characters are occasionally used today, few modern or contemporary plays use actual choruses.

As a musical term, *chorus* has two meanings. It can refer to a group that sings pieces composed in at least four parts (soprano, alto, tenor, bass), and it can also refer to the **refrain** in a piece of choral music, such as an anthem. In operas and musicals, choruses often perform the **classical** function of setting the scene and commenting on the action.

EXAMPLES: Plays by the ancient Greek dramatists Sophocles and Aeschylus typically contain choruses with an active role. Algernon Charles Swinburne's *Atalanta in Calydon* (1865), a late Victorian **closet drama** deeply influenced by Greek tragedy, has a chorus, as do two **modernist** works, T. S. Eliot's play *Murder in the Cathedral* (1935) and W. H. Auden's Christmas oratorio *For the Time Being* (1944). Woody Allen's film *Mighty Aphrodite* (1995) is one of the few contemporary works to include a chorus. The Fool in William Shakespeare's *King Lear* (1606) is often cited as an example of a choral character.

In *1876* (1976), Gore Vidal used the term *Greek chorus* **metaphorically** to contrast grand old man and Democratic presidential candidate Samuel Tilden with his supporters as they awaited the result of the 1876 election. Tilden was one of four American presidential candidates, including Al Gore, to lose the presidency while winning the popular vote: "In a room just off the main ballroom, Tilden seated himself comfortably near the ticker-tape machine. Hewitt sat on one side of him; Green on the other. The rest of us served as Greek chorus to the grand single Aeschylean protagonist."

▶ **chronicle play:** A **play** that purports to be based on and to recount historical events. Chronicle plays were at their height in late-sixteenth-century England, particularly after the defeat of the Spanish Armada during the reign of Elizabeth I. The **Elizabethan** chronicle plays, sometimes called **history plays,** were based on the *Chronicles* (1578), **tales** by Raphael Holinshed and others that offered a patriotic version of English history to a largely uneducated public. Early chronicle plays, which often strung together a series of incidents that occurred during a single ruler's reign, exhibited a very loose **structure** and tended to hold audience attention through glitzy displays of pageantry and battle scenes occasionally interrupted by comic interludes. Later chronicle plays showed greater literary sophistication, particularly as manifested in **character** portrayal and development.

EXAMPLE: William Shakespeare's *Henry IV* plays (1597–99), memorable for their portrayals of fat Falstaff and his bad influence on the young Henry, Prince of Wales, the King's son.

▶ **class (and literary studies):** A matter of birth in some older, socially stratified cultures; since the Industrial Revolution, a term more generally used to refer to social and, especially, economic groups. German philosophers Karl Marx and Friedrich Engels, who together wrote *The Communist Manifesto* (1848), divided capitalist societies into two classes — the bourgeoisie and the proletariat — and saw the history and future development of such societies in terms of class struggle. Since then, social theorists from Max Weber (*Economy and Society* [1921]) to Pierre Bourdieu (*Distinction: A Social Critique of the Judgment of Taste* [1979]) have generally agreed that the **Marxist** paradigm, though helpful, does not adequately define the way in which classes are delineated, defined, and constructed in modern societies. Class status depends not only on economic production — whether one produces wealth as do laborers or enjoys surplus wealth as do the bourgeoisie — but also on patterns of consumption; ethnic, political, and national affiliations; social goals, expectations, opportunities, and so on.

Literary **texts** are among the most powerful forms of cultural **discourse,** and as such they may attest to, perpetuate, or critique the class divisions prevalent in a given culture at a given period of history. Indeed, a work of literature may simultaneously perpetuate and critique the class structure because, as Soviet critic Mikhail Bakhtin pointed out in works such as *Rabelais and His World* (1940), a literary text may be **dialogic** or even **polyphonic.** That is, it may contain two or more **voices** or discourses, one of which reinforces or reflects the values of the ruling class or dominant **ideology,** the other(s) of which represent(s) the priorities and values of the underprivileged class(es), the plebeian "second world" of commoners or **folk.** Michael Bristol undertook a Bakhtinian analysis when he argued in

"'Funeral Bak'd Meats': Carnival and the Carnivalesque in *Hamlet*" (1994) that William Shakespeare's *Hamlet* (1602) not only gives voice both to royal figures and to poor gravediggers but also may be seen in light of class consciousness and **conflict.**

Although Marxist critics tend to see literature in terms of class and class conflict, some Marxists have cautioned against an overly simplistic view of class oppression and of literature's role in class struggle. In his *Quaderni del carcere,* written during the period 1929–35 (and partially published in English as *Selections from the Prison Notebooks* [1971]), Italian communist Antonio Gramsci argued that even working-class people have some power to struggle against the dominant ideology and change history. French Marxist Louis Althusser, in works such as *For Marx* (1969) and *Lenin and Philosophy and Other Essays* (1971), saw ideology as being riven with **contradictions** that works of literature reflect but also expose; he followed Marx and Gramsci in believing that although literature must be seen in *relation* to ideology, it also has some independence from it. British **cultural critic** Raymond Williams, in *Culture and Society 1780–1950* (1958) and *The Long Revolution* (1961), warned against viewing working-class people as the "masses," rather than as individuals, and viewed literary texts in the context of dynamically changing and evolving cultures of individuals.

Nonetheless, because class divisions are real — and because they unquestionably result in very different experiences for those they separate — most contemporary critics, particularly those practicing cultural criticism, argue that class, class distinctions, and class differences must be taken into account when we speak or write about literary texts. They hasten to add, however, that matters of class are inevitably intertwined with matters of **race, gender,** ethnicity, and nationality. For instance, the experiences of working-class women differ from those of working-class men, and those differences, compounded by differences of race, ethnicity, and/or nationality, are reflected in literary texts. Thus, a class-based, comparative reading of two novels published in 1989, *The Joy Luck Club*, by the Asian American novelist Amy Tan, and *Como agua para chocolate* (*Like Water for Chocolate*), by the Mexican novelist Laura Esquivel, should address racial and ethnic differences and the impact those differences have on not only the two women novelists but also the female and male **characters** who populate their fictions.

▶ **classic, classical:** The term *classic* refers to works from the ancient Graeco-Roman tradition; those written in **imitation** of it; or, more generally, works that have gained such widespread recognition that readers and critics over time agree that they have merit transcending the particular period in which they were written. Although some would generally define the classics as those frequently anthologized **texts** we associate with the Western **canon,** the word *classic* may be used to define an exceptional work arising out of any cultural tradition.

Classical has also had a number of meanings over the centuries. Its root (like the root of *classic* and **classicism**) is the Latin word *classicus*, referring to a person or thing of the first rank. A *scriptor classicus* was a writer whose audience was upper-**class**; thus, classical literature first referred to works written for the nobility. Over time, however, this term came to signify any Greek or Roman work deemed particularly worthy, and subsequently Graeco-Roman writing in general. Still later it was used to refer to texts that imitated the Graeco-Roman tradition and even to ones that, although not written in imitation of the ancients (and perhaps even written in **thematic** or **stylistic** opposition to them), were deemed particularly worthy. *Classical* can also be used to describe works that exhibit the qualities or characteristics of classicism, a complex set of attitudes and standards that *classicists*, scholars of Graeco-Roman antiquity, believe to be reflected in the art, architecture, history, philosophy, politics, and literature of ancient Greece and Rome. Classicists believe that the ancients achieved a standard of excellence that has seldom been surpassed by more modern writers; as a result, the term *classical* carries the positive **connotations** of excellence and achievement.

EXAMPLES: Classic works from the ancient Graeco-Roman tradition include Homer's Greek **epics** *The Iliad* (c. 850 B.C.) and *The Odyssey* (c. 850 B.C.); Greek **tragedies** including Aeschylus' *Agamemnon* (c. 458 B.C.), Sophocles' *Oedipus Rex* (c. 430 B.C.), and Euripides' *Electra* (c. 413 B.C.); and Virgil's Roman epic *The Aeneid* (c. 15 B.C.). Ancient classics arising out of other cultural traditions include the *Tao Te Ching* (sixth century B.C.), the works of Confucius (sixth–fifth century B.C.), and the *Kama Sutra* (fourth century A.D.). Works written in English that are commonly referred to as "classics" include William Shakespeare's play *Hamlet* (1602) and Charles Dickens's novel *Great Expectations* (1861).

Beatrix Potter's *The Tale of Peter Rabbit* (1902), Kenneth Grahame's *The Wind in the Willows* (1908), A. A. Milne's *Winnie-the-Pooh* (1926), E. B. White's *Charlotte's Web* (1952; illustrated by Garth Williams), and Shel Silverstein's *The Giving Tree* (1964) are widely considered children's classics, while J. K. Rowling's *Harry Potter* novels (1997–2007) are well on their way to achieving this status.

The songs "(I Can't Get No) Satisfaction" (1965) by the Rolling Stones and the Doors' "Light My Fire" (1967) are regularly referred to as "rock classics" or "classic rock." Classic rock albums include The Beatles' *Sgt. Pepper's Lonely Hearts Club Band* (1967) and U2's *The Joshua Tree* (1987). The music of the alternative and grunge band Pearl Jam (1990–), influenced by classic rock of the 1970s, is itself coming to be considered classic rock.

▶ **classicism:** A broad and general term (like **romanticism,** with which it is often contrasted) that refers to a complex set of beliefs, attitudes, and values presumed to be grounded in the cultures of ancient Greece and Rome. Some would even call classicism a doctrine or set of doctrines.

When used in connection with the arts or, more specifically, with literature, the term calls to mind certain characteristics in the critical writings and artistic achievements of the ancient Greeks and Romans. These include qualities such as simplicity, directness, order, clarity, **decorum**, balance, unity, and an emphasis on reason. Today *classicism* is not used exclusively to refer to Greek and Roman works; rather, the term can be used in connection with any work that exhibits some combination of these qualities and that thereby captures something of the spirit of the ancient Graeco-Roman tradition. English literature has been strongly marked by classicism, the ideals and characteristics of which were resurrected most notably in the **Renaissance** and the subsequent movement we refer to as **neoclassicism.**

During the Renaissance, scholars and critics took a particular interest in two ancient **texts:** Aristotle's *Poetics* (c. 330 B.C.) and Horace's *Ars poetica* (*Art of Poetry*) (c. 20 B.C.). Aristotle, a Greek philosopher, set forth rules governing **epic** and **tragedy,** argued that poetry properly **imitates** nature, and maintained that art has a salutary mental and moral effect. Most of the sixteenth-century commentators on Aristotle were Italians; of these, Julius Caesar Scaliger most influenced the emergence of classicism in England through his book *Poetice* (*Poetics*) (1561). Horace, a Roman poet, emphasized the importance of craftsmanship and decorum in poetry; he defined a decorous poetic **style** as one that is appropriate to the character, **setting,** and/or situation depicted in a given work. Sixteenth-century critics responsible for perpetuating Horace's literary theory included the French poet Pierre Ronsard and the English poet Sir Philip Sidney. Ronsard, leader of the Renaissance literary group known as the Pléiade, argued in his *Défense et illustration de la langue française* (*Defense and Illustration of the French Language*) (1549) for the need to adapt French poetic tradition to a **classical** mold. In *An Apology for Poetry* (1595), Sidney maintained that the intellectually and morally formative power of poetry resides in its power to represent truths vividly.

Although classicism was most effectively (re)theorized in the sixteenth century, some of the best-known restatements of classical principles came during the **Neoclassical Period,** which spanned the years 1660–1798. Examples include Pierre Corneille's discussion of the classical **unities** in *Discours* (*Discourses*) (1660), John Dryden's *An Essay of Dramatic Poesy* (1668), Nicolas Boileau's *L'art poétique* (*The Art of Poetry*) (1674), David Hume's *Of Tragedy* (1757), Johann Joachim Winckelmann's *Geschichte der Kunst des Alterthums* (*History of Ancient Art*) (1764), Samuel Johnson's *Preface to Shakespeare* (1765), Gotthold Ephraim Lessing's *Laocoön* (1766), and the *Discourses* (1769–90) of the English portrait painter and founding president of the Royal Academy, Sir Joshua Reynolds.

Classical **aesthetic** principles had substantial impact on **imaginative** literature in Europe from the seventeenth century through the first half of the nineteenth century, particularly during the Neoclassical Period. In England, the influence of classicism was apparent in the plays of Ben Jonson, the poetry of Dryden and Alexander Pope, the **satire** of Jonathan Swift, and the novels of Henry Fielding. In France, classicism most profoundly influenced the theater, as evidenced by the plays of Corneille, Jean Racine, and Molière

(Jean-Baptiste Poquelin). In Germany, the poetry of Friedrich Hölderlin and various works in several **genres** by Johann Wolfgang von Goethe owe a debt to classicism (and Greek classicism in particular).

▶ **cliché:** An expression used so often (and so often out of context) that it has become hackneyed and has lost its original impact. Many clichés were once hailed as striking **metaphors,** only to become denigrated over time.

EXAMPLES: Using "under the weather" to indicate feeling ill. "Don't rock the boat," "just what the doctor ordered," and "have a nice day" are common clichés, as are the more contemporary phrases "get a grip," "don't go there," and "show me the money!," prominently featured in the movie *Jerry Maguire* (1996).

The first line of Robert Burns's poem "A Red, Red Rose" (1796), "O my Luve's like a red, red rose," has become clichéd with overuse and the passage of time. Neil Young's song "Love Is a Rose" (1975) puts a twist on the "love is a rose" cliché by advising listeners not to pick it!

In Khaled Hosseini's novel *The Kite Runner* (2003), Amir, the **protagonist,** observes: "A creative writing teacher at San Jose State used to say about clichés: 'Avoid them like the plague.' Then he'd laugh at his own joke. The class laughed along with him, but I always thought clichés got a bum rap. Because, often, they're dead-on."

▶ **climax:** (1) The point of greatest tension or emotional intensity in a **plot.** (2) A term used synonymously with **crisis** to refer to the turning point in the **action** when the **protagonist's** lot will change decisively, whether for the better or the worse. In this sense, climax, which follows the **rising action** and precedes the **falling action** in the plot of a story or drama, is a **structural** element, one of five associated with **Freytag's Pyramid,** a model developed by nineteenth-century German writer Gustav Freytag for analyzing five-act plays (**tragedies** in particular). (3) As a **rhetorical** term, the last and most important in a series of items or terms ordered progressively based on their importance.

Some critics also apply the terms *climax* and *crisis* to minor peaks in the plot that change or intensify the course of the action. Most critics, however, limit the use of the term *crisis* to the plot's ultimate turning point.

EXAMPLE: In *Million Dollar Baby* (2004), the instant paralysis suffered by female boxer Maggie Fitzgerald as a result of a cheap punch thrown after the bell has rung in a match serves as the crisis, the pivotal moment when Maggie's lot changes decisively for the worse, whereas her request that her trainer euthanize her to end her suffering serves as the climax, the point of greatest emotional intensity.

▶ **closed couplet:** Two successive lines of rhyming **verse** whose meaning is grammatically or logically complete, forming a statement that can stand meaningfully on its own.

EXAMPLES: John Dryden's "Epigram on Milton" (1688), a poem about three poets (Homer of Greece, Virgil of Rome, and John Milton of England), is suggestively composed of three closed couplets (the last of which involves an **eye rhyme**):

Three poets, in three distant ages born,
Greece, Italy, and England did adorn.
The first in loftiness of thought surpassed,
The next in majesty, in both the last:
The force of Nature could no farther go;
To make a third, she joined the former two.

▶ **close reading (explication):** The nuanced and thorough analysis of a literary **text**. Close reading places particular emphasis on the interrelationships among textual elements (such as **allusions, diction, images,** and sound effects) and provides a means of interpreting the text and illuminating its complexities and **ambiguities**. Close reading is often associated with *explication de texte,* a method of **exegesis** that originated in France, and **the New Criticism,** a **formalist** variety of **literary criticism** that arose in the U.S.

▶ **closet drama:** A **drama,** often written in **verse,** that is meant to be read rather than performed, even though it includes **acts, scenes, dialogue,** and sometimes even stage directions. Many closet dramas have been written in **imitation** of dramatic works and **styles** of some earlier literary epoch or period.

Some scholars would include under the umbrella of closet drama other works that were once performed onstage before an audience (or, at least, that were written to be so performed) but that are now viewed strictly as literary **texts** to be read by individuals. Others would include works that, though still occasionally performed, make for better reading than theater, whether because of the staging problems they entail, the type or level of language used, or the antiquated and recondite nature of their **settings** or subjects.

EXAMPLES: John Milton's *Samson Agonistes* (1671), George Gordon, Lord Byron's *Manfred* (1817), Percy Bysshe Shelley's *The Cenci* (1819), Robert Browning's *Pippa Passes* (1841), and W. H. Auden's *The Sea and the Mirror* (1944) and *For the Time Being* (1944).

▶ **closure:** The condition of finality and wholeness established at the end of a literary work or part thereof; alternatively, the process by which a work or part is brought to a fitting conclusion. Closure provides more than an ending; it provides the reader or audience with a sense of completeness. In **narratives,** the kind of ending that provides closure often involves the resolution of a **conflict** or revelations that lay to rest — satisfactorily if sometimes surprisingly — unanswered questions, such that the reader or audience no longer wonders what happens next.

As early as the fourth century B.C., ancient Greek philosopher Aristotle recognized the importance of endings, arguing in the *Poetics* (c. 330 B.C.) that an artistic whole is "that which has a beginning, a middle, and an end," with the end being "that which itself naturally follows some other thing, either by necessity, or as a rule, but has nothing following it." Endings, however, are no simple matter; as novelist Henry James declared in the 1907 preface to his **Künstlerroman** *Roderick Hudson* (1875), "Really, universally, relations stop nowhere, and the exquisite problem of the artist is eternally but to draw, by a geometry of his own, the circle within which they shall happily *appear* to do so." Subsequently, in *Poetic Closure: A Study of How Poems End* (1968), American literary critic Barbara Herrnstein Smith theorized that closure "allows the reader to be satisfied by the failure of continuation or, put another way, it creates in the reader the expectation of nothing."

Notably, not all works induce a sense of closure, or at least not one that most readers agree on. For instance, a meditative poem may end with the restatement of an unanswerable question. Similarly, some "open-ended" works contain linguistic or structural **ambiguities** that lead different readers or **interpretive communities** to different conclusions. Other works, particularly **modernist** and **postmodernist** texts such as **Absurdist** plays and the *nouveau roman,* resist or subvert the traditional imperative to "make sense," deliberately flouting **conventions** including the quest for closure — and inviting the reader's active participation. In *S/Z* (1970), French **structuralist,** later **poststructuralist,** theorist Roland Barthes contrasted *lisible* (readerly) texts, which are more traditional and convention-bound, with experimental, *scriptible* (writerly) ones, which encourage or even demand the reader's cocreative involvement.

In *Closure in the Novel* (1981), **cultural critic** Marianna Torgovnick emphasized that closure is a process, the "effective" test of which is the "honesty and the appropriateness of the ending's relationship to beginning and middle, not the degree of finality or resolution achieved by the ending." Including both traditional and "open" or "anti-closural" works within her study, Torgovnick developed a theoretical framework for describing endings and strategies of closure in the novel, focusing on the relationship of the ending to the beginning and middle (identifying circular, parallel, incomplete, tangential, or linking patterns), the **point of view** in the ending (overview or close-up), the relationship between **author** and reader during closure (congruent, incongruent, or even confrontational), and the author's relationship to his or her own ideas (self-aware or self-deceiving).

While *closure* is typically used with reference to the ending or conclusion of a work, it may also apply to textual segments. Thus, each of the five parts of a **play** identified in **Freytag's Pyramid** — the introduction, **rising action, climax, falling action,** and **catastrophe** — comes to some degree of closure, with the last two parts bringing closure to the work as a whole. Similarly, chapters, paragraphs, and **stanzas** can themselves come to closure, as can sentences and poetic lines; for instance, the **rhyming** syllables in **couplets** create closure at the end of each pair of lines.

EXAMPLES: Percy Bysshe Shelley's **sonnet** "Ozymandias" (1818), about a haughty mocking king of the ancient world who built a monument to his own power, concludes as follows:

> Round the decay
> Of that colossal wreck, boundless and bare
> The lone and level sands stretch far away.

This ending provides imagistic and thematic closure to the poem, suggesting that efforts by tyrants to immortalize themselves are pathetically doomed to failure.

In Jane Austen's novel *Pride and Prejudice* (1813; adapted to film most recently in 2005), the marriage of Elizabeth Bennet to Fitzwilliam D'Arcy brings to closure a **plot** riddled with romantic, familial, and **class**-based differences. The ending of Virginia Woolf's *To the Lighthouse* (1927) is an example of circularity, for it transports Mr. Ramsay and his children to the very lighthouse that the late Mrs. Ramsay had promised to take their son James to at the beginning of the novel. The novel *The Magus* (1966) struck readers as being so open-ended that its author, John Fowles, revised the book in 1978 in part to achieve closure "less ambiguously."

By contrast, Frank Stockton's short story "The Lady or the Tiger?" (1882), in which a king forces his daughter's lover to choose between doors that lead to a hungry tiger and a marriageable lady-in-waiting, invites its readers to provide closure. As the man struggles to make his decision, he spots his lover, the princess, who directs him toward one of the doors. The story ends as the man opens the door, leaving his fate — and whether the princess chose to save him by having him marry another woman — an open question. The children's series "Choose Your Own Adventure" (1979–98; relaunched in 2005) provides a further twist on the idea of closure, situating young readers as **protagonists** who make choices about what actions to take — choices that can result in very different consequences and endings. Today, many digital games allow players to choose their own action figures and adventures.

Serial television dramas such as *24* (2001–) and *Lost* (2004–) build from episode to episode, but each season of *24* covers a 24-hour period in real-time that comes to closure at the end of the season, whereas each season of *Lost* flows into the next in one ongoing story. By contrast, in dramas such as *Law and Order* (1990–) and the first six seasons of *CSI* (2000–), each episode is self-contained.

▶ **codes:** Organizing principles and assumptions underlying a **text** that facilitate (or occasionally resist) interpretation. Although widely used by modern practitioners of **hermeneutics**, the **theory** of interpretation and interpretive methods, as well as by practitioners of various critical approaches, the term *codes* is most often associated with **structuralist critics** such as Roman Jakobson, Claude Lévi-Strauss, and Roland Barthes. **Structuralists** believe that all literary works — indeed, all elements of human culture — can be understood as part of a system of **signs** that includes numerous **conventions**. For instance, audiences aware of the fact that William Shakespeare's *Hamlet* (1602) is a **revenge tragedy** and who understand the conventions of that **genre** know, even without reading or seeing the play, that the story will probably involve a son's or father's quest to avenge the other's death as well as a dramatic and probably violent showdown between the **protagonist** and **villain**. Similarly, **Renaissance comedies** nearly always have a happy ending involving marriage.

Jakobson used the term *code* to refer to language, one of the elements of communication. According to Lévi-Strauss, codes are grounded in the **binary oppositions** that permeate Western **discourse**, including literary works. For instance, the opposition "head / heart" — and all the other dualities it implies — not only underlies countless texts, shaping the structure of their **plots**, the struggles of their **characters**, and the patterns of **symbols** they contain, but also drives our interpretations of those texts.

By contrast, Barthes's *S/Z* (1970) identifies five different types of codes: the *hermeneutic*, which comprises the binary questions and answers that serve to provide suspense in a **narrative**; the *semic*, which allows readers to distinguish characters and understand their behavior; the *symbolic*, which guides the reader's understanding of **figurative language**, including **metaphors** and symbols; the *proairetic*, which governs ideas regarding the work's plot and its likely development; and the *referential*, or *cultural*, which involves social assumptions, such as those concerning the tradeoff between tradition and change. Barthes identified several additional types of codes in his "Textual Analysis: Poe's 'Valdemar'" (1981) — the *metalinguistic*, the *socioethnic*, the *social*, the *narrative*, the *scientific*, and the *scientific-deontological* — but some if not all of these may simply be subsets of the types he previously identified.

In later writings, Barthes acknowledged that codes may not always be sufficient or reliable as interpretive tools. He recognized, for instance, that readers themselves bring to the hermeneutic process assumptions and experiences (including experiences with other texts) that affect reading outcomes. He also argued that experimental (*scriptible*, or "writerly") texts may use language to create **ambiguous** and even contradictory references, thereby flouting conventional associations and expectations. This latter development in Barthes's theory of the interpretive process and ideas about **intertextuality** is one of many indications of his shift from structuralism toward **poststructuralism**.

Jacques Derrida, a leading theorist of poststructuralism closely associated with **deconstruction**, suggested that the dichotomies forming the binary oppositions so firmly embedded in code-rich Western discourse are not simply oppositions but also valuative hierarchies in which one component is viewed as positive or superior while the other is considered negative or inferior, even if only slightly so. For instance, "active" is considered the more positive term in the opposition "active / passive."

Derrida's insight has made the term *code* increasingly useful to **feminist** and **gender critics** interested in the **representation** of **gender** and **sexuality**, as well as to **new historicist** and **cultural critics** interested in the literary representation of **race** and **class**. For instance, recurrent references to characters of one race or gender in terms of physical and emotional traits and to characters of another group in terms of intellectual traits can convey racist or sexist attitudes in cultural "code." That is because words and ideas associated with "body" and "feeling" within the pairs "mind / body" and "thought / feeling" generally carry inferior **connotations**.

These understandings of the term *code*, complex as they may seem, do not differ radically from what people think when they conclude that a statement like "I just want to be friends" is code for some other communication that the speaker wishes to be understood — but would prefer to leave unsaid.

See also **convention, sign, structuralism**.

▶ **collective unconscious:** A term used by Swiss analytic psychologist Carl Jung to refer to a repository of unconscious memories dating back to the origins of human experience that Jung believed are shared by all members of the human race and that are manifested in dreams, **myths,** and literature.

See **archetypal criticism, Jungian criticism.**

▶ **Colonial Period (in American literature):** An era in American literary history spanning the years 1607, when English settlers founded Jamestown, Virginia, to 1765, when the passing of the Stamp Act by the English parliament enraged the colonists in America, sparking opposition that led to the American Revolution some eleven years later in 1776.

To say that an "American" literature existed during the Colonial Period is somewhat misleading. Although the colonists came from a variety of countries, the influence of England on every "American" institution was overwhelming, and most colonial writers modelled themselves after English writers. Furthermore, the very fact that the colonists came from different lands and religious backgrounds with few unifying influences made it difficult to form any "national" literature. The geographic dispersal of the colonists into small, relatively insulated, and generally self-sufficient communities and the limited communication between the thirteen original colonies created additional obstacles.

Some have even suggested that the use of the term *literature* to describe works written during the Colonial Period is inappropriate. Literature as we often conceive of it today — as an artistic medium — was in short supply during the Colonial Period. Indeed, imaginative literature was banned in several colonies until the American Revolution, thanks in large part to the Puritans, who viewed drama and the novel in particular as paths to perdition. Drama was explicitly labeled an evil akin to cockfighting by the Continental Congress as late as 1774. Furthermore, the harsh conditions of frontier life in America also inhibited the development of an artistic literature.

With practical needs and survival as priorities for settlers, colonial works were largely historical and **didactic,** intended to record, instruct, or even warn. Letters, journals, **narratives,** and histories were popular forms of writing. John Smith's *A True Relation of Occurrences and Accidents in Virginia* (1608) is sometimes called the first "American" book, but given that Smith was an Englishman who returned home in 1609, this label is questionable if not dubious. Other writers, however, migrated to America and stayed. Political figures such as William Bradford and John Winthrop kept personal journals recording events in Plymouth and New England, respectively, that became key sources of colonial history. Bradford's journal, written between 1620 and 1647, was published as *History of Plymouth Plantation* in 1856; Winthrop's journal, covering the years 1630–1649, was published in part in 1790 and then in its entirety in 1825 as *The History of New England from 1630 to 1649*. William Byrd's two histories of a border dispute, based on a diary he kept during a surveying expedition in 1728, were also published much later, in 1929, as *Histories of the Dividing Line betwixt Virginia and North Carolina*. By contrast, Mary Rowlandson's account of being captured by "Indians," *A Narrative of the Captivity and Restauration of Mrs. Mary Rowlandson,* was published at the time, in 1682, to wide circulation in both America and England. Many colonial writers, preoccupied with issues of day-to-day survival, expressed hostility and fear toward Native Americans, including a strong opposition to miscegenation (mixing of the races).

Many colonial works were also polemical or religious in nature. *The Bay Psalm Book* (1640), the first book published in America, was a compilation of psalms modified for singing. Sermons, philosophical pieces, and theological tracts were some of the most common forms of written expression; a number of ministers who were members of Massachusetts's famous Mather family delineated the dictates of Puritanism. Calvinist preacher and theologian Jonathan Edwards is perhaps most famous for his awe-inspiring, terrifying sermon "Sinners in the Hands of an Angry God" (1741).

Although poetry was not a major focus of colonial expression, a few poets emerged during the Colonial Period. Anne Bradstreet inaugurated **lyric** poetry in America with the publication of a volume entitled *The Tenth Muse Lately Sprung Up in America* (1650). Edward Taylor wrote a number of religious poems, but his work remained unpublished until 1937. Michael Wigglesworth was perhaps the best-known poet of the time; his poem *The Day of Doom* (1662), which set forth Calvinistic theology, was required reading for most schoolchildren of the day. Finally, toward the end of the period, Jupiter Hammon, a slave in New York, inaugurated the African American literary tradition with the publication of his poem "An Evening Thought: Salvation by Christ, with Penitential Cries" (1760).

Nonreligious and nonhistorical prose was fairly rare, but among prose authors Benjamin Franklin — who incorporated **Enlightenment** ideas into many of his works — stands out. Franklin's *Poor Richard's Almanac* (1732) remains famous today; Richard Saunders is probably the first fully developed fictional **character** in American literature. A very different kind of imaginative prose was produced by John Cleland, author of the early erotic, softcore porn **classic** *The Life of Fanny Hill (or, Memoirs of a Woman of Pleasure)* (1749).

The first **slave narratives** were also written during the Colonial Period. An example is *A Narrative of the Uncommon Sufferings, and Surprizing Deliverance of Briton Hammon, A Negro Man, — Servant to General Winslow of Marshfield, in New England* (1760).

▶ **comedy:** Broadly defined, any amusing and entertaining work; more narrowly defined, an amusing and entertaining **drama.** Comedy is often contrasted with **tragedy,** not only because it ends happily and presents the "lighter side" of life but also because it generally represents the experiences of ordinary people in common or vernacular language, whereas tragedy has traditionally depicted noble **characters** in a loftier literary **style.** Humor (or **wit**) is the essential element of any comedy. Comic effect may be subtle or coarse; it is typically achieved through some incongruity, whether physical, verbal, or conceptual (such as when a character is exaggerating what he has done or would be able to do if a given situation arose). Although comedies aim to evoke laughter, they may also have a serious purpose.

Ancient Greek comedy is typically subdivided into three categories. *Old Comedy*, represented by the works of Aristophanes, was characterized by a combination of political **satire** and **fantastic** elements. *Middle Comedy*, which focused on social concerns, served as a bridge between Old and *New Comedy*. New Comedy, epitomized by the works of Menander, typically depicted two lovers who had to overcome obstacles to live happily ever after.

During the **Middle Ages,** the term *comedy* was applied to any literary work that had a happy ending and a style less exalted than that ascribed to tragedy. Hence Dante Alighieri's great work was named *Divina commedia* (*The Divine Comedy*) (1321) even though it does not make particular use of humor.

Many types of comedy (and ways of classifying comedy) have emerged since the **Renaissance**. Some critics subdivide comedies into three categories: **romantic, satiric,** and *rogue.* Romantic comedies have a pair (or pairs) of lovers as their center of interest. William Shakespeare, who based his comedies on the prose **romances** of his time, is credited with the development of this form. Satiric comedies typically have a critical purpose, attacking philosophical or political notions through ridicule. They may also direct ridicule at those who depart from societal rules and norms, or at meddlesome characters who somehow interfere with a pair of lovers. In rogue comedies, the audience is entertained by the antics of clever but congenial miscreants. Other critics classify comedies as **realistic** (including satiric forms such as the **comedy of manners** and the **comedy of humors**), romantic, or **sentimental**. Still other critics classify the comedy of manners separately rather than subsuming it under the heading of realistic comedy.

Comedies may also be categorized as *low* or *high.* Low comedies typically rely on the crude or the obvious to evoke laughter; they include *situation comedies,* **farces,** and *slapstick* works. Situation comedies (including television "sitcoms") contain characters whose absurdities are revealed through some entertaining machination of the **plot.** Farces are based on ludicrous situations, such as those that develop in cases of mistaken identity. Slapstick comedies are perhaps the least subtle of all types of comedy, relying on physical action (brawls, spectacular but harmless falls, two-fingered pokes in the eyes) to provoke loud guffaws from the audience. High comedies rely heavily on intellectual issues, viewpoints, and the incongruities between them to produce their comic effect. Often satiric in nature and serious in purpose, they tend to emphasize humanity's foibles and seldom appeal to the audience's emotions. Witty repartee is common and is perhaps epitomized in the **Restoration**-era comedy of manners. High comedy of more recent vintage is sometimes referred to as *intellectual comedy* or *comedy of ideas.*

EXAMPLES: Aristophanes's *The Frogs* (c. 405 B.C.) is an example of ancient Greek Old Comedy, whereas Menander's *Dyskolos* (317 B.C.) is an example of New Comedy. Nicholas Udall's *Ralph Roister Doister* (1553) is generally credited with being the first dramatic comedy in English, and the seventeenth-century French playwright Molière (Jean-Baptiste Poquelin) is considered by many to be the greatest of all comic dramatists. Playwright William Shakespeare's *Much Ado About Nothing* (1599) is a romantic comedy, as are movies such as *Annie Hall* (1977), *When Harry Met Sally* (1989), *Groundhog Day* (1993), and *Bridget Jones's Diary* (2001). Twentieth-century playwright George Bernard Shaw wrote intellectual comedies such as *Major Barbara* (1905). The twentieth-century comedy act The Three Stooges and the television sitcom *Three's Company* (1977–84) both relied heavily on slapstick humor. Other popular sitcoms since the advent of television include *I Love Lucy* (1951–57), *The Andy Griffith Show* (1960–68), *All in the Family* (1971–79), *The Cosby Show* (1984–92), *Seinfeld* (1990–98), and *Arrested Development* (2003–06); notable animated sitcoms include *The Simpsons* (1989–) and *South Park* (1997–).

▶ **comedy of humors (comedy of humours):** A **satiric** form of **comedy**, developed in the late sixteenth century by the English playwrights George Chapman and Ben Jonson, that presents **characters** with personality types dominated by one quality that lead them to behave in a ridiculous manner. The word *humor* in the phrase *comedy of humors* does not refer to humor as we understand it today. Rather, the comedy of humors is based on a physiological **theory** of human behavior, current during the **Middle Ages** and the **Renaissance**, that held that personality was determined by the relative amounts of each of the four fluids, or humors, in the body: blood, phlegm, yellow bile, and black bile. According to this theory, as long as the humors were in balance, an individual would exhibit a perfect temperament and no illness, but an imbalance would affect behavior in a very specific way. That is, an excess of blood would produce a sanguine (happy) personality, phlegm a phlegmatic (cowardly, passive) personality, yellow bile a choleric (argumentative, stubborn) personality, and black bile a bilious (melancholy) one. The comedy of humors influenced comedies of the **Restoration Age.**

EXAMPLES: Chapman's *An Humorous Day's Mirth* (1597), Jonson's *Every Man in His Humour* (1598). Molière's (Jean-Baptiste Poquelin's) comedy *Le misanthrope* (1666) features the melancholy Alceste, who continuously rails against humankind. The subtitle of the work — *L'atrabilaire amoureux* — overtly evokes the theory of humors, "*L'atrabilaire*" meaning (according to the *Dictionnaire de l'Académie*), "Qui est plein d'une bile noire et aduste. Visage atrabilaire, humeur atrabilaire" (One who is full of black, burnt bile. Peevish countenance, peevish disposition).

▶ **comedy of manners:** A **satiric** form of **comedy**, most often associated with **Restoration-Age drama**, that **satirizes** the conduct and codes of a social group or **class**, usually sophisticated high society. The comedy of manners generally takes love, especially amorous intrigues, as its subject and frequently satirizes both societal affectations and **stock characters** who fail to conform to societal **conventions**. The **subgenre** is noted for **witty** repartee and a certain cynicism with regard to affairs of the heart. The perceived moral shortcomings of these plays eventually caused a backlash and a consequent upsurge in the number of **sentimental comedies** — relatively upbeat works that were deemed more wholesome by audiences tired of Restoration excesses. The form was revived, however, later in the **Neoclassical Period**, toward the end of the eighteenth century, and subsequently influenced nineteenth-century novels such as Jane Austen's *Emma* (1815) and James Fenimore Cooper's *The Pioneers* (1823).

EXAMPLES: George Etherege's *The Man of Mode, or, Sir Fopling Flutter* (1676), William Congreve's *The Way of the World* (1700), and Richard Brinsley Sheridan's *The School for Scandal* (1777) are early examples. Later comedies of manners include plays such as Oscar Wilde's *The Importance of Being Earnest* (1895) and Noël Coward's *Private Lives* (1930).

Modern comedies of manners include Whit Stillman's film *Metropolitan* (1990); Amy Heckerling's *Clueless* (1995), a contemporary movie version of Jane Austen's *Emma* (1815) set in Beverly Hills; and the television sitcom *Seinfeld* (1990–98).

▶ **comic relief:** A humorous scene or passage inserted into an otherwise serious work. Comic relief is intended to provide an emotional outlet and change of pace for the audience as well as to create a contrast that further emphasizes the seriousness of the work.

EXAMPLES: William Shakespeare used the gravedigger scene in *Hamlet* (1602), the drunken porter in *Macbeth* (1606), and the **character** of Mercutio in *Romeo and Juliet* (1596) to provide comic relief. Ratso Rizzo, played by Dustin Hoffman, provides comic relief in John Schlesinger's darkly disturbing film *Midnight Cowboy* (1969).

Jim Crace's novel *Quarantine* (1998), which chronicles Jesus' forty days in the wilderness, contains numerous scenes that provide comic relief, such as the one in which Musa, a trader whom Jesus has healed, orders that a dead donkey be pushed over a cliff above the cave in which Jesus is awaiting a sign from God.

▶ *commedia dell'arte:* From the Italian for "comedy of the professional actors," a form of **character**-centered, improvisational **comedy** that was performed by professional, traveling groups of actors and that flourished in Europe from the sixteenth through the eighteenth centuries. Performances typically featured scenarios with **stock characters** and situations; incorporated a variety of forms of entertainment, including acrobatics, dance, music, **pantomime, farce,** and clowning or other buffoonery; and **satirized** or ridiculed events, institutions, and personalities of the day. Staging was often minimal, with heavy reliance instead on masks, traditional costumes, and simple props.

Commedia dell'arte developed in Italy in the sixteenth century as popular street theater; major Italian troupes included the Gelosi, Confidenti, and Uniti. As troupes traveled throughout Europe, *commedia dell'arte* gained immense popularity, especially in France, where it was called the *comédie italienne*. Though its origins are difficult to pinpoint, the **genre** is often traced to ancient

Roman works such as comedies by Plautus and Terence. It was banned at numerous times and places in Europe when performances provoked the opposition of powerful figures (e.g., Louis XIV) and institutions (e.g., the Catholic Church).

Commedia dell'arte troupes developed and drew on a stable of basic characters and storylines for their performances, improvising much of the detail and **dialogue** with an eye to local events. Stock characters included figures such as Arlecchino (Harlequin), the illiterate servant of Pantalone, a rich but miserly merchant; il Capitano (the Captain), a braggart soldier; il Dottore (the Doctor), typically an aristocratic and rotund physician or lawyer; and the Inamorati, a pair of lovers. Stock situations included love intrigues such as a young couple outsmarting parents with the help of servants to attain wealth and happiness. Actors rehearsed oft-repeated scenarios in advance and learned elements such as *lazzi*, comic gags or routines, that could be applied to any play.

Commedia dell'arte had a substantial influence on European **drama,** including the plays of English playwright William Shakespeare and French playwright Molière (Jean-Baptiste Poquelin). The genre also influenced English and French pantomime, puppet shows (Punch in "Punch and Judy" is based on the *commedia* character Pulcinella, a hunchback who chases after women), **slapstick** comedy, and vaudeville. Moreover, while *commedia dell'arte* had nearly died out by the nineteenth century, it subsequently experienced periods of revival and continues to be performed today. *Commedia* troupes in the U.S. include Commedia dell'Carte (Dallas), i Sebastiani (Boston), and Tutti Frutti Commedia (San Francisco).

▶ **common meter (common measure):** A four-line **stanza** with an *abab* or *abcb* **rhyme scheme** in which the first and third lines are written in **iambic tetrameter** and the second and fourth in **iambic trimeter**. Common meter, often abbreviated "C.M.," is akin to the **ballad stanza,** or *ballad meter* — indeed, the terms are sometimes used synonymously — but common meter tends to be associated with **hymns** and most often rhymes *abab*, whereas the ballad stanza is associated with the traditional **ballad** and is usually characterized by an *abcb* rhyme scheme.

EXAMPLE: The hymn "Amazing Grace" (1779), written by John Newton, the first stanza of which follows:

> Ămáz | iňg gráce! | (hŏw swéet | thě sóund)
> Thăt sáv'd | ă wrétch | lĭke mé!
> I once was lost, but now am found,
> Was blind, but now I see.

▶ **Commonwealth Age (in English literature):** Also known as the *Puritan Interregnum* (literally, "between reigns"), an age often classified as the last of five literary eras within the **Renaissance Period** in English literature. The Commonwealth Age began with the beheading of King Charles I in 1649 and ended with the restoration of the Stuart monarchy via the coronation of

Charles II in 1660. During the interregnum, England was ruled by a Puritan-dominated Parliament led first by Oliver Cromwell (Lord Protector, 1653–58) and then briefly by his son Richard Cromwell (Lord Protector, 1658–59).

Writers of prose and nondramatic poetry dominated the literary arena during the Commonwealth Age. Prose writers of the epoch include Thomas Hobbes, Jeremy Taylor, Izaac Walton, and John Milton, whose "Tenure of Kings and Magistrates" (1649) attempted to justify the execution of Charles I. Milton, a Puritan, was also one of the greatest poets of the era, although his major works (*Paradise Lost* [1667] and *Paradise Regained* [1671]) were published during the subsequent **Restoration Age**. Other noted poets of the interregnum include Abraham Cowley, Andrew Marvell, and Henry Vaughan.

Playwrights were constrained during the Commonwealth Age, due in part to the Parliament's decision to close all theaters in 1642. Interregnum playwrights lacked the support that had enabled great dramatists — such as Sir Francis Beaumont, John Fletcher, Ben Jonson, Christopher Marlowe, Thomas Middleton, William Shakespeare, and John Webster — to flourish in the first half of the seventeenth century, during the **Elizabethan, Jacobean,** and **Caroline Ages.**

See also **Renaissance.**

▶ **communicative presumption:** See **discourse analysis, speech-act theory.**

▶ **conceit:** From the Italian for "idea" or "concept," a **figure of speech** involving an elaborate and often surprising comparison between two apparently highly dissimilar things, often in the form of an extended **metaphor.** Whether it involves strikingly original **images** or an unusual take on the familiar, the conceit is most notable for its ingenuity. Although the term acquired a derogatory **connotation** in the eighteenth and nineteenth centuries, it is generally used today in a more neutral, descriptive sense and can thus be applied to effective comparisons as well as to overbearing or strained ones.

There are two major types of conceits. The **metaphysical conceit** frequently uses esoteric or, alternatively, commonplace objects or references in a previously unthought-of or entirely unfamiliar way; it sometimes functions as the controlling image for an entire poem. The **Petrarchan conceit** (following the example of the fourteenth-century Italian poet Petrarch) typically employs analogy, **hyperbole,** or **oxymoron** to portray one or both lovers in an unequal love relationship, exaggerating the beauty and cruelty of the beloved woman while rendering as unjust or pathetic the suffering of the lovestricken man who worships her.

EXAMPLES: Emily Dickinson frequently used conceits, as in her poems "I taste a liquor never brewed" (c. 1860), in which she characterizes the elating effect of nature as drunken intoxication, and "I dwell in possibility" (c. 1862), the text of which follows:

> I dwell in Possibility —
> A fairer House than Prose —

More numerous of Windows —
Superior — for Doors —

Of Chambers as the Cedars —
Impregnable of Eye —
And for an Everlasting Roof
The Gambrels of the Sky —

Of Visitors — the fairest —
For Occupation — This —
The spreading wide my narrow Hands
To gather Paradise —

Metaphysical and Petrarchan conceits can be found, respectively, in John Donne's "The Flea" (1635), in which a flea is used to represent the sexual union the speaker desires, and the thirtieth sonnet of Edmund Spenser's *Amoretti* (1595), in which the poet compared a frustrated lover to fire and the object of his love to ice.

See **metaphysical conceit** and **Petrarchan conceit** for additional examples of these terms.

▶ **concrete:** See **abstract**.

▶ **concrete poetry:** A modern term for *pattern poetry*, or *shaped verse*, a type of poetry that has existed since the time of the ancient Greeks but that is most often associated with the **Renaissance**, the seventeenth century, and the **Modern Period**. A concrete poem is meant to be perceived as a visual object and is at least as notable for its graphic design as for its verbal meaning. Thus, concrete poems are not meant simply to be read; in fact, many cannot be read at all in the way we think of reading. Concrete poems rarely employ conventional sentence **structure** and are often made up of a single word or phrase, parts of which may be repeated, strategically placed on the page, or otherwise highlighted by the use of different colors, fonts, or sizes.

EXAMPLES: A poem about fish might be shaped like a fish; a poem about motion might place the letters in the word *motion* in a wavy pattern on the page. George Herbert's poem "Easter Wings" (1633), when printed, visually suggests the wings of an angel. A more recent example by e. e. cummings follows:

l(a

le
af
fa

ll

s)
one
l

iness

The poem characterizes loneliness by visually depicting the slow downward flutter of a single leaf in the phrase "(a / le / af / fa / ll / s)."

▶ **confessional poetry:** A contemporary poetic **mode** in which poets discuss matters relating to their private lives. Confessional poets go beyond **romanticism's** emphasis on individual experience in their use of intimate detail and often **psychoanalytic** terms to describe even their most painful experiences. The reader is often addressed directly by the confessional poet, who typically expresses some very private confusion or sorrow.

EXAMPLES: Anne Sexton's *To Bedlam and Partway Back* (1960) and *Live or Die* (1960), as well as Sylvia Plath's *Ariel* (1965), are volumes of confessional poetry by pioneers of this poetic mode. The following excerpt is from Plath's poem "Daddy," included in the *Ariel* collection:

> You stand at the blackboard, daddy,
> In the picture I have of you,
> A cleft in your chin instead of your foot
> But no less a devil for that, no not
>
> Any less the black man who
> Bit my pretty red heart in two.
> I was ten when they buried you.
> At twenty I tried to die
> And get back, back, back to you.

Jane Kenyon's "Having It Out with Melancholy" (from *Constance: Poems* [1993]) is also an example of confessional poetry. The first **stanza** reads as follows:

> When I was born, you waited
> behind a pile of linen in the nursery,
> and when we were alone, you lay down
> on top of me, pressing
> the bile of desolation into every pore.

▶ **conflict:** A confrontation or struggle between opposing **characters** or forces in the **plot** of a **narrative** work, from which the **action** emanates and around which it revolves.

Conflict is usually broken down into three major categories: *physical, social,* and *internal* (or *psychological*) conflict. Physical conflict generally involves the "elemental" clash between a character and nature or the physical world. Social conflict takes place between humans competing or struggling against one another or against that overarching entity called society. Opposing forces are typically represented or embodied by the **protagonist** and the **antagonist,** but conflict need not involve two distinct people, entities, or institutions, as demonstrated by the third type of conflict. Internal, or psychological, conflict involves the inner divisions or turmoil of a single character. Conflicts of this sort may result from the character's attempt to decide between multiple alternatives for action or between opposing attitudes or beliefs. Some critics have spoken of a fourth kind of conflict — *metaphysical conflict* — involving the clash between a human character and fate or some type of deity. In general, literary works employ more than one type of conflict in order to enrich the plot and avoid oversimplification.

EXAMPLE: In Herman Melville's *Moby-Dick* (1851), Captain Ahab's psychological conflict is played out in his metaphysical conflict with God or fate, his physical conflict with the whale, and his social conflict with an endangered crew.

▶ **connotation:** The association(s) evoked by a word beyond its **denotation,** or literal meaning. A connotation may be perceived and understood by almost everyone if it reflects broad cultural associations, or it may be recognized by comparatively few readers or listeners who have certain knowledge or experience. A connotation may even be unique to a particular individual, whose personal experiences have led him or her to associate a given word with some idea or thing in a way that would not be familiar to others.

EXAMPLES: The word *water* might commonly evoke thoughts or images of an ocean, a fountain, thirst, or even a water balloon. Less common would be thoughts of the Wicked Witch of the West (from L. Frank Baum's *The Wizard of Oz* [1900]), who melted when Dorothy threw a bucket of water on her, or of Samuel Taylor Coleridge's "The Rime of the Ancient Mariner" (1798), which includes the famous lines "Water, water, everywhere, / And all the boards did shrink; / Water, water, everywhere, / Nor any drop to drink." A near-drowning victim might associate water with sheer terror, as would someone who was hydrophobic. A woman whose husband had proposed to her on a canoeing trip might associate water with her engagement ring or, more broadly, her personal happiness.

A passage from Alice Munro's story "Boys and Girls" (1968) explains *connotation* without explicitly using the term:

> The word *girl* had formerly seemed to me innocent and unburdened, like the word *child;* now it appeared that it was no such thing. A girl was not, as I had supposed, simply what I was; it was what I had to become. It was a definition, always touched with reproach and disappointment.

▶ **consonance:** The repetition of a final consonant sound or sounds following *different* vowel sounds in proximate words (*made / wood*). Most scholars maintain that the repetition of initial or intermediate consonant sounds, when occurring in *addition* to repeated final consonant sounds, also constitutes consonance (*litter / letter, wade / wood*).

EXAMPLES: Emily Dickinson's poem #214 (c. 1860) uses consonance rather than **perfect rhyme** in the words *Pearl* and *Alcohol* as well as in the words *brewed, scooped,* and *Yield.*

> I taste a liquor never brewed —
> From Tankards scooped in Pearl —
> Not all the Vats upon the Rhine
> Yield such an Alcohol!

Wilfred Owen's "Arms and the Boy" (1920) provides an example of consonance in which initial as well as final consonant sounds are repeated (in the words *blade* and *blood, flash* and *flesh*):

Let the boy try along this bayonet-blade
How cold steel is, and keen with hunger of blood;
Blue with all malice, like a madman's flash;
And thinly drawn with famishing for flesh.

▶ **constative:** See **performative.**

▶ **constructionism:** In **literary criticism,** the view that **gender** and/or sexuality are culturally constructed and determined, not biologically based; the opposite of *essentialism.* Broadly speaking, constructionists believe that gender and/or sexuality — particularly the dichotomies *masculine/feminine* and *homosexual/heterosexual* — are social artifacts, learned behaviors, products of language and culture, whereas essentialists believe that they are natural or innate. French feminist Simone de Beauvoir's **classic** assertion in *Le deuxième sexe (The Second Sex)* (1949), "One is not born a woman: one becomes one," reflects a constructionist perspective. So does queer theorist David Halperin's claim in *Saint Foucault: Towards a Gay Hagiography* (1995) that "homosexual" is "a discursive, and homophobic, construction" rather than a natural category. By contrast, French feminist critic Hélène Cixous posited an essential connection between the female body and writing in "The Laugh of the Medusa" (1976) when she exhorted women to "Write your self. Your body must be heard."

Debates about constructionism and essentialism — culture or nurture versus biology or nature — have occurred both among and within various critical schools, particularly **feminist criticism, gender criticism, gay and lesbian criticism,** and **queer theory.** Thus, while many feminist critics have viewed (and celebrated) gender differences between men and women as a product of nature, other feminist critics have joined gender critics and queer theorists in seeing them as cultural (and often destructive) artifacts. Likewise, while many gay and lesbian critics take an essentialist view of sexuality, some join with queer theorists in contending that sexuality is as much a social construct as gender. Moreover, while constructionism and essentialism are often seen as a contrary philosophical pair, or **binary opposition,** they encompass a range of viewpoints. The most essentialist feminists, for instance, write as if no amount of enculturation or nurture could alter female nature and female difference. Extreme constructionists (also called *postfeminists*), on the other hand, argue that even **sex** and nature are cultural constructs; in *Gender Trouble: Feminism and the Subversion of Identity* (1990), gender critic Judith Butler argued that all sexual difference is culturally produced rather than natural, that "sex, by definition, will be shown to have been gender all along." And there are also, of course, a whole range of views between these purist poles. Most constructionists, for instance, distinguish gender from sex, viewing only gender as a cultural construct.

▶ **contextual criticism:** A revolutionary offshoot of **the New Criticism** that incorporated and modified the basic analytical methods and underlying outlook of its parent form. Eliseo Vivas and Murray Krieger shaped and defined this mode of **literary criticism,** which emphasizes **close readings** of individual **texts** and evaluations of those texts based on their internal **structure** and **aesthetic** impact. Although by the late 1960s contextual criticism was no longer in vogue, some of its assumptions and analytical methods persist in more contemporary critical approaches, such as **deconstruction.**

▶ **convention:** A literary device, **form, style,** situation, or usage so widely employed that, however unrealistic, it has become accepted and even expected by knowledgeable readers or audiences. Conventions create a framework within which an **author** operates, entailing both restrictions and a certain freedom; the conventions of **science fiction,** for instance, vary from those of the **romance,** and within the latter **genre,** the conventions of a bodice-ripping Harlequin romance differ from other subtypes, such as **medieval romances** and **Gothic** ones. Some conventions gain acceptance because they facilitate the presentation of material or enhance the quality of the **aesthetic** experience. For instance, onstage in a play a single set of large *papier-mâché* cylinders may represent tree trunks in one **scene** and architectural columns in the next, and **flashbacks** may interrupt the present **action** of a **narrative** to depict an earlier event. Sometimes an original story (the **medieval** damsel in distress), **character** type (the mustachioed **villain** of **Victorian melodrama**), or **theme** (the **romantic** idea that we should "get back to Nature") will so speak to the fears, fantasies, or preoccupations of an age that it will be repeated in a variety of different works, remaining conventional as long as new writers rework it and new audiences accept it.

In the twentieth century, convention took on an even broader meaning, thanks in part to **structuralist critics** who considered every literary work to include a plethora of **codes.** The reader or viewer, structuralists argued, "naturalizes" these codes by squaring them with his or her culturally determined assumptions and perceptions.

EXAMPLES: William Shakespeare's frequent use of **asides, soliloquies,** and **stock characters** (such as the fool) are conventions. Equally conventional, in Shakespeare's day, was the practice of using male actors for all the women's parts (and, therefore, the parts of women pretending to be men, like Viola in *Twelfth Night* [1599] and Rosalind in *As You Like It* [c. 1600]). **Renaissance** audiences thus accepted that Juliet in *Romeo and Juliet* [1596] was female, even though the actor playing her would have been a boy. In our own day, it is conventional for women to play women's roles in plays — including plays by Shakespeare. Nonetheless, our appreciation of a play like *Twelfth Night* or *As You Like It* still depends upon conventions. Audiences accept that the **heroines** of these two plays are mistaken for the men they pretend to be, even though the parts are played by women who look like women, masculine garb and hairstyle notwithstanding.

In *Eats, Shoots & Leaves* (2003), semi-comically subtitled *The Zero Tolerance Approach to Punctuation,* Lynne Truss makes the case for punctuation as follows:

> Isn't it the case, in the end, that punctuation is just a set of conventions, and that conventions have no intrinsic worth? One can't help

remembering the moment in Lewis Carroll's *The Hunting of the Snark* [1876] when the Bellman exhibits his blank map and asks the crew how they feel about it:

> "What use are Mercator's North Poles and Equators,
> Tropics, Zones and Meridian Lines?"
> So the Bellman would cry: and the crew would reply,
> "They are merely conventional signs!"

▶ **corona (crown of sonnets):** See **sonnet sequence.**

▶ **Corpus Christi play:** See **mystery play.**

▶ **cosmic irony:** See **irony.**

▶ **couplet:** Two successive lines of rhyming **verse,** often of the same **meter** and generally either octosyllabic or decasyllabic.

EXAMPLE: The following **stanza** from Robert Lowell's "Waking Early Sunday Morning" (1967) contains four successive couplets:

> No weekends for the gods now. Wars
> flicker, earth licks its open sores,
> fresh breakage, fresh promotions, chance
> assassinations, no advance.
> Only man thinning out his kind
> sounds through the Sabbath noon, the blind
> swipe of the pruner and his knife
> busy about the tree of life . . .

See also **closed couplet.**

▶ **courtesy book:** See **Renaissance.**

▶ **courtly love:** A philosophy of love prevalent in **medieval** literature that purported to describe — but more truly prescribed — certain codes of behavior between aristocratic men and women. Although courtly love has come to suggest an ideal, spiritual love beyond physical pleasure, the term still refers to a specific method of courtship and specific manner of amorous conduct.

Courtly love **conventions** are often traced to the **lyrics** of the **troubadours** of eleventh- and twelfth-century Provence (now part of France). Important influences included the Roman poet Ovid, who wrote *Ars amatoris* (*The Art of Love*) (c. 1 B.C.) and *Remedia amoris* (*The Remedies for Love*) (c. A.D. 1), and traditions involving the veneration of the Virgin Mary.

As its name suggests, courtly love refers to love as practiced among the nobility. It involves a nobleman (often a knight) meeting a lady with such striking beauty that he instantly falls in love and begins to exhibit wretched symptoms of ill health and anxiety (such as pallor, loss of appetite, and fits of weeping). If the lady who is the object of his veneration accepts him as her lover, however, the man regains his health and well-being. He then subjects himself to her every caprice and obsequiously serves her. Courtly love does not lead to marriage, which for medieval aristocrats was generally arranged and based on political and economic considerations. Indeed, the lady involved in a courtly love relationship is usually a married woman who depends upon the discretion of her lover to keep their relationship a secret.

With regard to adultery, two traditions of courtly love exist. In the early days of the courtly love tradition, adultery was glorified to the point that it was represented as an almost religious experience; of course, the two lovers had to remain completely — and eternally — faithful to each other. The man was also inspired to perform great deeds and to follow rigorously Christian and chivalrous tradition in every other respect in order to be worthy of his lady's love. Beginning particularly with Italian **epic** poet Dante Alighieri, however, courtly love often meant a **Platonic** (unconsummated) **love,** one in which the lady inspired her lover to achieve a higher spiritual state rather than to perform noble deeds.

Whether courtly love was purely a literary convention or whether it actually reflected aristocratic practice to any significant extent is still debated. Although **representations** of courtly love became less common toward the end of the **Medieval Period,** the influence of the courtly love tradition persisted in the literature of subsequent eras, particularly in **Renaissance** love poetry influenced by the **sonnets** of Petrarch, a fourteenth-century Italian poet. The special spiritual status accorded to women and the **theme** of love's ennobling power are two aspects of the courtly love tradition that have continued to influence Western thought, perhaps even to this day.

EXAMPLES: Courtly love traditions are represented in "Le rossignol" by the twelfth-century Anglo-Norman poet Marie de France, "La mort de Tristan et d'Yseult" (from *Les romans de Tristan*) by the twelfth-century Anglo-Norman poet known simply as Thomas, "The Knight's Tale" (c. 1387) by Geoffrey Chaucer, and *Le morte d'Arthur* (1485) by Sir Thomas Malory.

▶ **Cowleyan ode:** See **irregular ode.**

▶ **creolization:** See **postcolonial literature, postcolonial theory.**

▶ **crime novel:** See **detective fiction.**

▶ **crisis:** The point in a **plot** when the **conflict** has intensified to a level at which the **protagonist's** lot will change decisively, whether for the better or for the worse. The crisis is sometimes called the *turning point* because it represents the pivotal moment when the protagonist's fortunes begin to turn. The term *crisis,* which refers to a purely **structural** element of plot, is sometimes but not always synonymous with **climax,** which also (and perhaps especially) signifies the point of greatest tension or emotional intensity in a plot. Thus, though the crisis and climax of a work often occur together, this need not be the case.

Some critics also apply the terms *crisis* and *climax* to minor peaks in the plot that change or intensify the course of the **action.** Most critics, however, limit the use of the term *crisis* to the plot's ultimate turning point.

EXAMPLE: In the movie *Dead Poets Society* (1989), the main character, Neil, decides to perform in a play even though his father has forbidden him to do so. When the father finds out and shows up at the play, the crisis occurs. From this point, Neil's fortunes decline progressively, ending with his suicide.

▶ **criticism:** See **literary criticism.**

▶ **critics of consciousness:** See **Geneva School.**

▶ **cultural criticism, cultural studies:** Critical approaches with roots in the British cultural studies movement of the 1960s. A movement that reflected and contributed to the unrest of that decade, it both fueled and was fueled by the challenges to tradition and authority apparent in everything from the antiwar movement to the emergence of "hard rock" music. Birmingham University's Centre for Contemporary Cultural Studies, founded by Stuart Hall and Richard Hoggart in 1964, quickly became the locus of the movement, which both critiqued elitist definitions of culture and drew upon a wide variety of disciplines and perspectives.

In Great Britain, the terms *cultural criticism* and *cultural studies* have been used more or less interchangeably, and, to add to the confusion, both terms have been used to refer to two different things. On one hand, they have been used to refer to the analysis of literature (including popular literature) and other art forms in their social, political, or economic contexts; on the other hand, they have been used to refer to the much broader interdisciplinary study of the relationships between a variety of cultural **discourses** and practices (such as advertising, gift-giving, and racial categorization). In North America, the term *cultural studies* is usually reserved for this broader type of analysis, whereas *cultural criticism* typically refers to work with a predominantly literary or artistic focus. In this entry, we adhere to North American usage and focus mainly on cultural criticism.

Examples of cultural studies include various analyses of consumerism indebted to the work of Hall, Michel de Certeau, and Dick Hebdige, whose 1979 book *Subculture: The Meaning of Style* paved the way for critics like John Fiske (*Television Culture* [1987]), Greil Marcus (*Dead Elvis* [1991]), and Rachel Bowlby (*Shopping with Freud* [1993]). These analyses have addressed topics such as the resistance tactics employed by television viewers, the influence of consumers on rock music styles, and the psychology of consumer choice. Examples of cultural criticism include Mary Poovey's book *The Proper Lady and the Woman Writer* (1984) and Patrick Brantlinger's *Rule of Darkness* (1988). Poovey viewed eighteenth-century novels by women in light of conduct manuals, ladies' magazines, and the **patriarchal** system governing the ownership and inheritance of property. Brantlinger read Joseph Conrad's *Heart of Darkness* (1899) in the context of late-nineteenth-century imperialism, racism, the goals of the Congo Reform Association, **impressionism,** popular **romances** concerning love and adventure, and "exposé literature" (mis)representing cannibalism in Africa.

Cultural critics examine how literature emerges from, influences, and competes with other forms of discourse (such as religion, science, or advertising) within a given culture. They analyze the social contexts in which a given text was written, and under what conditions it was — and is — produced, disseminated, and read. Like practitioners of cultural studies, they oppose the view that culture refers exclusively to high culture, culture with a capital C, seeking to make the term refer to popular, folk, urban, and mass (mass-produced, -disseminated, -mediated, and -consumed) culture, as well as to that culture we associate with so-called great literature. In other words, cultural critics argue that what we refer to as culture is in fact a set of interactive *cultures*, alive and changing, rather than static or monolithic. They favor analyzing literary works not as aesthetic objects complete in themselves but as works to be seen in terms of their relationships to other works, to economic conditions, or to broad social discourses (about childbirth, women's education, rural decay, etc.). Cultural critics have emphasized what de Certeau, a French theorist, called "the practice of everyday life" in *L'invention du quotidien* (*The Practice of Everyday Life*) (1980), approaching literature more as an anthropologist than as a traditional "elitist" literary critic.

Cultural critics are as willing to write about *Star Trek* as they are to analyze James Joyce's *Ulysses* (1922), a modern literary classic full of allusions to Homer's *Odyssey* (c. 850 B.C.). When they do write about *Ulysses*, they are likely to emphasize how it reflects and represents cultural forms common to Joyce's Dublin, such as advertising, journalism, film, and pub life. They also typically demonstrate how the boundary between high and low culture is transgressed in innumerable ways within works on both sides of the putative cultural divide.

Hence, a cultural critic might compare a revered literary classic with a movie or even a comic strip version. The classic might also be seen in light of some more common form of reading material (a novel by Jane Austen might be compared to Gothic romances). Alternatively, it might be seen as the reflection of common cultural myths or concerns (Mark Twain's *Adventures of Huckleberry Finn* [1884] might be shown to reflect and shape American myths about race and concerns about juvenile delinquency). Finally, a cultural critic might use a work to demonstrate the permeable nature of the alleged boundary between low and high culture. For instance, some cultural critics have noted that although William Shakespeare's plays began as popular works enjoyed by working people, they were later considered "highbrow" plays that only the privileged and educated could appreciate. With the advent of film production, however, they have regained an increasingly popular audience. In the 1990s, cultural critics, responding to a spate of Shakespeare plays turned into movies, analyzed the "cultural work" accomplished by Mel Gibson and Franco Zeffirelli in the latter's 1990 film production of Shakespeare's *Hamlet* (1602) and by Baz Luhrman's 1996 resetting of *Romeo and Juliet* (1596) in contemporary, crime-ridden America.

In combatting traditional definitions of what constitutes culture, cultural critics sometimes contest traditional definitions of what constitutes the literary canon, that is, those literary works given special status by a given culture (classics or "Great Books"). Indeed, these critics generally critique the very idea of canon, rather than seeking to substitute a counterculture canon for the traditional one or to add books (or movies or sitcoms) to the old list of texts that every "culturally literate" person should supposedly know.

Cultural critics eschew the notion that certain works are the "best" ones produced by a given culture. They seek to be more descriptive and less evaluative; they seek to relate, rather than rate, cultural products and events. They also aim to discover the (often political) reasons why one aesthetic or cultural product is more highly valued than another. This is particularly true when the product has been produced since 1945, for most cultural critics follow Jean Baudrillard (*Simulations* [1981]) and Andreas Huyssen (*The Great Divide* [1986]) in arguing that any distinctions that may have existed between "high," popular, and mass culture collapsed after World War II.

Cultural critics have also questioned other value hierarchies. Many have criticized the institution of the university, for it is in universities that the old definition of culture as high Culture (and as something formed, finished, and canonized) has been most vigorously defended and preserved. Cultural critics have been especially critical of the departmental structure of universities, which has kept the study of the "arts" relatively distinct from the study of history, not to mention television, advertising, journalism, **folklore**, current affairs, and gossip. By maintaining artificial boundaries, universities reassert the high / low culture distinction. By implicitly associating **aesthetics** with literature and propaganda with advertising, for instance, they impede recognition of the propagandistic aspects of a literary work and the aesthetic aspects of an ad. Cultural critics have consequently mixed and matched the analytical procedures developed in numerous disciplines, focusing on human consciousness rather than a body of works assumed to reflect a given culture. They seek to understand and demonstrate that consciousness is itself largely forged by cultural forces.

In attempting to understand this process, cultural critics have drawn on **structuralist** thought. Using a scientific approach and the **linguistic** theory of Swiss linguist Ferdinand de Saussure, structuralists such as Roland Barthes and Claude Lévi-Strauss suggested that *all* elements of human culture, including literature, may be understood as parts of a system of **signs**. The ideas of French structuralist **psychoanalytic** theorist Jacques Lacan have been particularly influential, serving as the theoretical underpinning for cultural critics who have sought to show how **subjectivities**, that is, our very identities, are produced by social discourses and practices.

Poststructuralist French philosopher Jacques Derrida has also influenced the development of cultural criticism and cultural studies. In *De la grammatologie (Of Grammatology)* (1967), Derrida provocatively asserted that "*there is nothing outside the text.*" In making this statement, Derrida refused to categorically distinguish world and text, simultaneously asserting that every human (worldly) product can be viewed as a text and that every text reflects and shapes the world we perceive. Cultural critics have used Derrida's **deconstruction** of the world / text distinction, like his deconstruction of so many of the hierarchical **binary oppositions** we habitually use to interpret and evaluate reality, to erase the boundaries between high and low culture, classic and popular literary texts, and literature and other cultural discourses.

Several thinkers influenced by **Marxism** have also powerfully affected the development of cultural criticism and cultural studies. The French philosophical historian Michel Foucault perhaps had the strongest influence on North American cultural criticism and **the new historicism,** a type of **literary criticism** whose evolution has often paralleled that of North American cultural criticism. In works such as *Surveiller et punir* (*Discipline and Punish*) (1975) and *Histoire de la sexualité* (*The History of Sexuality*) (1976), Foucault studied cultures in terms of power relationships, a focus typical of Marxist thought. Unlike Marxists, however, Foucault did not see power as something exerted by a dominant **class** over a subservient one but, rather, as a complex of forces generated by the confluence — or conflict — of discourses. This approach led him to examine texts that most traditional historians and literary critics overlooked, such as diaries, court records, and doctors' reports. Foucault sought to pinpoint the crossroads at which discourses and social practices were contravened and transformed. His interdisciplinary work acknowledged the viewpoints and histories of women and of racial, ethnic, and sexual minorities, groups seldom studied by those interested in culture with a capital C.

Prominent British — as opposed to Continental — influences include E. P. Thompson and Raymond Williams. Thompson, a Marxist historian and author of *The Making of the English Working Class* (1963), revolutionized study of the Industrial Revolution by writing about its impact on human attitudes, even human consciousness. He showed how a shared cultural view, specifically that of what constitutes a fair price, influenced crowd behavior, causing disturbances like the "food riots" of the eighteenth and nineteenth centuries. Williams, best known for his book *Culture and Society: 1780–1950* (1958), argued that culture is living and evolving rather than fixed and finished, further stating in *The Long Revolution* (1961) that "art and culture are ordinary."

Although Williams did not define himself as a Marxist throughout his entire career, he always followed the Marxist practice of viewing culture in relation to **ideologies,** which he defined as the "residual," "dominant," or "emerging" ways in which classes or individuals holding power in a given social group view the world. He avoided dwelling on class conflict and class oppression, however, focusing on people and the way they experience the conditions in which they find themselves and creatively respond to those conditions through their social practices.

Because cultural criticism and cultural studies have been heavily influenced by Marxism (some contemporary cultural critics even consider themselves **Marxist critics** as well), it is important to be familiar with certain

Marxist concepts, particularly those advanced by Mikhail Bakhtin, Walter Benjamin, Antonio Gramsci, and Louis Althusser. Bakhtin was a Soviet critic so original in his thinking and wide-ranging in his influence that some would say he was never a Marxist at all. He viewed literary works in terms of discourses and **dialogues** *between* discourses. The **narrative** of a novel written in a society in flux, for instance, may include not only an official, legitimate discourse but also others that challenge that official viewpoint. In *Problems of Dostoevsky's Poetics* (1929) and *Rabelais and His World* (1940), Bakhtin examined what he called **polyphonic** novels, each characterized by several **voices** or discourses. In works by Rabelais, for instance, Bakhtin found that the (profane) discourses of the **carnival** and of other popular festivities play against and **parody** the more official discourses of churches and magistrates.

Benjamin, a German Marxist best known for his essay "The Work of Art in the Age of Mechanical Reproduction" (1936), questioned the superior value placed on certain traditional literary forms that he felt conveyed a stultifying "aura" of culture and hailed the development of new art forms involving mechanical production and reproduction. He thus anticipated by decades the work of those cultural critics interested in mass-produced, massmediated, and mass-consumed culture, in forms such as photography, radio, and film that could render the arts a more democratic, less exclusive domain.

Gramsci, an Italian Marxist whose 1929–35 *Quaderni del carcere* were partially published in English as *Selections from the Prison Notebooks* (1971), argued that all intellectual or cultural work is fundamentally political, relating literature to the ideologies — the prevailing ideas and beliefs — of the culture in which it was produced. He developed the concept of **hegemony,** which refers both to the process of consensus formation and the authority of ideologies to shape the way things look, what they mean, and, therefore, what reality *is* for most people. However, Gramsci did not see people, even poor people, as the helpless victims of hegemony, as ideology's hapless robots but, rather, as having the power to break out of the weblike system of prevailing assumptions and to form a new consensus.

Louis Althusser, a French Marxist, also explored the relationship between literature and ideology, in works such as *For Marx* (1969) and *Lenin and Philosophy and Other Essays* (1971). But unlike Gramsci, Althusser tended to portray ideology as controlling people, and not vice versa. He argued that ideology serves to reproduce the society's existing relations of production, even in literary texts and especially in popular works — a view many cultural critics reject. For instance, in "Marxism and Popular Fiction" (1986), Marxist cultural critic Tony Bennett used *Monty Python's Flying Circus* (1969–74) and another British television show, *Not the 9 O'clock News* (1979–82), to reject the Althusserian notion that all forms of culture are manifestations of capitalist ideology. Indeed, Bennett argued that "popular fiction" (books, films, television, etc.) often has the effect of "distancing" or separating the audience from — rather than rebinding the audience to — prevailing ideologies.

Most practitioners of cultural criticism and cultural studies, however, are not Marxists in any strict sense. Anne Beezer, who has analyzed advertisements and women's magazines, gives both the media she is concerned with and their audiences more credit than Althusserian Marxists presumably would. Beezer points out that the same magazines that tell women how to please their men also offer women liberating advice about how to preserve their independence. And, she suggests, many advertisements advertise their status as ads, just as many people see them as advertising and interpret them accordingly.

Tania Modleski and Janice Radway undertook similarly complex analyses of paperback romance novels in *Loving with a Vengeance: Mass-Produced Fantasies for Women* (1982) and *Reading the Romance: Women, Patriarchy, and Popular Literature* (1984), respectively. Radway, a **feminist** cultural critic who incorporates some Marxist ideas, pointed out that many women read romances in order to carve out a time and space that is wholly their own. Although many such novels end in marriage, the marriage is usually between a feisty **heroine** and a powerful man she has "tamed." Radway's reading is typical of feminist cultural criticism in that it is political but not exclusively about oppression. Although the thinking of romance readers may be governed to some extent by what they read, these women also affect what is published, thus performing "cultural work" of their own. Romances in which heroines are degraded are not popular among romance readers and, therefore, are rarely produced.

The overlap between feminist and cultural criticism is hardly surprising, especially given the recent evolution of feminism into various femin*isms*. These typically focus on "majority" women of European descent, minority women in Western culture, and women living in Third World (preferably called postcolonial) societies. The culturalist analysis of value hierarchies has focused on **class, race, gender, sexuality,** and national origin; the terms of its critique have proved useful to contemporary feminists, many of whom differ from their predecessors insofar as they see *woman* not as an overarching category but rather as one of several contributing to identity, or "subject," formation. The influence of cultural criticism (and, in some cases, Marxist class analysis) can be seen in the work of contemporary feminist critics such as Gayatri Chakravorty Spivak, Trinh T. Minh-ha, and Gloria Anzaldúa, who stress that although all women are female, they are something else as well (e.g., working-class, lesbian, Native American), a facet that must be considered in analyzing their writings.

The expansion of feminism and feminist literary criticism to include multicultural analysis parallels a transformation of education in general. African American studies, a form of cultural studies, has grown and flourished; African American critics have pointed out that the North American white cultural elite has tended to view the oral-musical traditions of African Americans (jazz, the **blues,** sermons, **folk tales,** etc.) as entertaining but nonetheless inferior. In order not to be similarly marginalized, black writers have produced texts that, as scholar and critc Henry Louis Gates has noted, fuse the language and traditions of the white Western canon with a black vernacular and tradition derived from African and Caribbean cultures.

Interest in race and ethnicity has accompanied a new, interdisciplinary focus on colonial and postcolonial societies, in which issues of race, class, and ethnicity loom large. As Homi K. Bhabha pointed out in an essay entitled "Postcolonial Criticism" (1992), **postcolonial theorists** analyze the way in which certain cultures (mis)represent others in order to achieve and extend political and social domination in the modern world order. Thanks to the work of scholars like Edward Said, who inaugurated postcolonial theory with his book *Orientalism* (1978), Anzaldúa, Bhabha, Gates, and Spivak, education in general and literary study in particular is becoming more democratic, multicultural, and **decentered** (less patriarchal and Eurocentric) in its interests and emphases.

▶ **cultural materialism:** An approach to the analysis and understanding of culture developed by **Marxist critic** Raymond Williams in works such as *Culture and Society* (1958) and *Marxism and Literature* (1977) and grounded in the belief that economic forces and modes of production inevitably affect cultures and cultural products, such as literature. Cultural materialists have often argued that literary **texts** perform a "subversive" or otherwise politically charged function — not only in their own historical eras but also in subsequent epochs, when they take on different meanings and become the **sites** of new kinds of debate. This view of literature as persistently subversive is in keeping with the broader interest of most cultural materialists in transforming the existing sociopolitical order, which they tend to view as being exploitative along the lines of **class, gender,** and **race.** A number of British and American **new historicist** and **cultural critics** have borrowed the terminology of cultural materialists, either to emphasize their **Marxism** or as a means of relating their descriptions of the past to the politics of present-day **discourses** and institutions.

▶ **cultural poetics:** See **new historicism, the.**

▶ **cultural studies:** See **cultural criticism, cultural studies.**

▶ **curtal sonnet:** See **sonnet.**

▶ **cyberfiction:** A word coined in the late twentieth century that is used interchangeably with *cyberpunk* and *hypertext fiction* but that may also refer more broadly to any fictional **text,** whether **classic** or contemporary, published (in some cases exclusively) on the Internet. The term *cyberfiction* acknowledges the increasing influence of computer technology on literature, whether manifested in terms of **plot** (e.g., computer-oriented **science fiction**), medium of publication (e.g., any work of fiction now available on the World Wide Web), reader participation (e.g., interactive novels that invite the reader's creative involvement), or in some other way.

Cyberpunk refers to a type of science fiction that emerged in the mid-1970s and that gained popularity in 1984 with the publication of William

Gibson's novel *Neuromancer*. The prefix "cyber" is taken from *cybernetics*, the study of the control systems of the human brain and nervous system and of analogous mechanical and electronic technology, and invokes the idea of the *cyborg*, a hybrid of human and machine. The "punk" component of the term refers to a counterculture movement that began in the 1970s and that is especially associated with a form of rock music characterized by extreme and even offensive expressions of anger and alienation.

Cyberpunk authors such as Gibson, Bruce Sterling, Rudy Rucker, and Neal Stephenson write novels and short stories about near-future societies populated by characters who are totally immersed in a "cyborg world" in which the distinction between human and machine has been blurred, if not erased. Life is experienced only through the virtual reality of *cyberspace*, a term coined by Gibson in 1984 to describe a linked network called the "matrix." Characters are usually technologically proficient, self-serving loners, computer "console cowboys" who have no loyalty to governments, nations, or politics and who may also be violent and unethical. Human bodies are routinely injected with drugs, hormones, and serums, as well as surgically implanted with advanced microprocessors, prostheses, and memory-enhancing components such as silicon-based storage. In Gibson's novels, these hybrids, or cyborgs, see "life in the flesh" as dull and are satisfied only when freed from bondage to "the meat," their term for the human body.

Cyberpunk fiction sometimes deals with religious beliefs and the nature of divinity, and some commentators believe it may forewarn of the negative effects of society's increasing dependence on technology. Unlike most classic science fiction of the 1930s and 1940s, however, cyberpunk does not present a view of the future that is either overtly positive or negative; rather, it presupposes that ethics and integrity have become irrelevant in a computer-dominated world. Cyberpunk is also characterized by a mix of conventional language and "cyberjargon," terms such as ICE ("intrusion countermeasure electronics," i.e., security programs), A.I. (artificial intelligence), and ROM (technically meaning "read only memory," but as cyberfiction jargon referring to recordings preserving a personality after death). Cyberpunk fiction, which has inspired movies such as *Universal Soldier* (1992) and the *Matrix* trilogy (1999–2003), typically appears in traditional print media but may also be published online and even written as hypertext fiction.

Hypertext fiction generally refers to interactive novels, short stories, and poems that are available on the Internet, CD-ROMs, and floppy disks and that often include sound and graphic art. This type of nonlinear, fragmented text is said to be **decentered,** because readers are allowed to leave the primary document through **links** that provide access to additional texts. As Jay Bolter stated in *Writing Spaces: The Computer, Hypertext, and the History of Writing* (1991), "the fluidity of the electronic medium allows the texts to be in a perpetual state of reorganization." Unlike traditional books printed on paper that compel the reader to follow a linear route through the text, hypertext fiction greatly expands the universe of possible perceptions and conclusions by allowing readers to navigate the text, to choose which paths to follow — and when. As a result, readers become active participants, and their relationship to the text changes significantly. Indeed, they may even become authors if asked to solve a problem or mystery encountered along the way — or to contribute to the plot by submitting their own writings.

The continuing use of *cyberfiction* to refer to classic or contemporary literature published or republished on the Internet ensures that this term will, for the foreseeable future, be broad in its applicability, meaning different things to different users.

FURTHER EXAMPLES: Cyberpunk novels by Sterling include *Islands in the Net* (1988), *The Difference Engine* (1990) (coauthored with Gibson), and *Holy Fire* (1996). Other cyberpunk titles include Stephenson's *Snowcrash* (1992), *The Diamond Age* (1995), and *Cryptonomicon* (1999).

Examples of hypertext fiction include Michael Joyce's *afternoon, a story* (1989), which is about a writer who suspects that the accident he saw earlier in the day involved his ex-wife, and an interactive novel entitled *The Patchwork Girl* (1995), a post**feminist** revision of Mary Shelley's *Frankenstein* (1818) by Shelley Jackson that considers the possibility that Mary Shelley, rather than Dr. Frankenstein, could have created a female monster. (Both of these works are available, at this writing, through the website of Eastgate Systems, Inc., <www.eastgate.com>.) In 1997, Internet retailer Amazon.com sponsored an interactive writing contest in which it invited visitors to contribute to a collaborative hypertext story, "Murder Makes the Magazine." After posting the first paragraph, written by novelist John Updike, Amazon chose one paragraph a day for forty-four days from viewer submissions to advance the story, which Updike then ended with a final paragraph.

An example of cyberfiction broadly defined is Stephen King's Web novel *Riding the Bullet* (2000), initially available only as an e-book but republished on audiocassettes in 2002.

See also **hypertext**.

▶ **cyberpunk:** See **cyberfiction**.

D

▶ **dactyl:** A metrical **foot** in **poetry** that consists of one **stressed** syllable followed by two unstressed ones (˘˘).

The *double dactyl* is a **form** of **light verse** consisting of eight lines, each composed of two dactyls. The first double dactyl must be a nonsense phrase, the second a person's name, and the seventh a single word.

EXAMPLES: pórtăblĕ, márgĭnăl, écstăsў. Numerous nursery rhymes contain dactyls ("Hígglĕdў pígglĕdў," "Pát-ă-cakĕ, pát-ă-cakĕ," "Ríngs ŏn hĕr fíngĕrs ănd bĕlls ŏn hĕr tóes," etc.).

Alfred, Lord Tennyson's poem "The Charge of the Light Brigade" (1854) is dactylic:

> Cánnŏn tŏ ríght ŏf thĕm,
> Cánnŏn tŏ léft ŏf thĕm,
> Cánnŏn ĭn frónt ŏf thĕm
>   Vólleyĕd ănd thúnderĕd;
> Stórmed ăt wĭth shŏt ănd shĕll,
> Bóldlў thĕy róde ănd wĕll,
> Íntŏ thĕ jáws ŏf Dĕath,
> Íntŏ thĕ móuth ŏf hĕll
>   Róde thĕ síx húndrĕd.

The following poem by C. Webster Wheelock, from *History Gistory,* his unpublished history of the world, is a double dactyl:

> Monocle-bonocle
> Theodore Roosevelt
> Bullied his way to the
> Top of San Juan:
> Muscular buster of
> Trusts and a booster of,
> Incontrovertibly,
> Brains under brawn.

The **classic** rock song "Lucy in the Sky with Diamonds" (1967) by The Beatles has a predominantly dactylic **rhythm.**

▶ **Dadaism:** A movement founded by Romanian writer Tristan Tzara in Zurich, Switzerland, in 1916 to rebel against the "civilization" that produced World War I, a war seen by members of this movement as insane. Dadaism rapidly spread to other European countries, where its adherents sought to destabilize the art and philosophy of the time, offering in their place seemingly insane, nihilistic works designed to protest the madness of war. The movement was particularly well received in Paris, which became its capital. Dadaists self-consciously insisted on absolute artistic freedom, ignored standard logic and restraint, and made a point of making shocking statements and doing outrageous things.

Many Dadaists claimed that the term *Dadaism* was chosen arbitrarily. Some students of the movement accept this explanation, noting that *dada* means "hobbyhorse" in French and pointing out that it would be in keeping with the spirit of the movement to defy traditions and **conventions** by picking a name with no apparent relevance. Others, however, see greater significance in the name, arguing that the *dada* in *Dadaism* involves an **allusion** to fatherhood (*dada* rather than *mama*) and reflects the desire of Dadaists to inject masculinity rather than femininity into literature.

As a movement, Dadaism was fairly short-lived. It was, however, the immediate forerunner of the **surrealist** movement of the mid-1920s and an influence on other subsequent **genres,** such as **Absurdist theater** and the **antinovel.**

▶ **dead metaphor (frozen metaphor):** A word or phrase once used as a **metaphor** (a direct comparison between two distinct things without *like* or *as*) that has become so familiar it is no longer perceived as one. Because the **vehicle** of a dead metaphor is no longer recognized as an **image** used to illustrate the **tenor,** or subject, the word or phrase is treated literally rather than **figuratively.** The term *dormant metaphor* is sometimes used to refer to a word or phrase that is in the process of dying as a metaphor; dormant metaphors are typically used literally, without regard to their figurative value, but can still be readily recognized as metaphors.

EXAMPLES: Keel over, toe the line, know the ropes, the foot of the bed. In "Renovations" (1977), a poem about the everyday business of taking a shower, Robert B. Shaw used a dead metaphor ("fiddling") to strike an appropriately casual tone: "A twist, a little fiddling / With temperature, then in." When we use the term *fiddled* ("I fiddled with the color on my TV set"), no one thinks of the activity in terms of playing the violin!

▶ **decadence:** Broadly defined, moral decline or the decline of a great artistic or literary period. The literary application of decadence **denotes** a lapse in the quality of works associated with a particular literary era or movement. Decadent phases tend to be characterized by bizarre or esoteric subject matter as well as a self-consciously refined **style** that emphasizes polish and ornamentation, elevating technique — even artifice — over substance. For instance, "silver age" Latin literature written during the reign of Trajan (A.D. 98–117) is often considered decadent in comparison to the **golden age** literature produced during the reign of Augustus (27 B.C.–A.D. 14).

When capitalized, *Decadence* refers to a literary movement strongest in France but also prevalent in England and America toward the end of the nineteenth century. The Decadence is closely associated with the Aesthetic Movement; indeed, the term is often used to refer to the last phase or the decline (depending on the user's perspective) of **Aestheticism.** Like members of the Aesthetic Movement, Decadents extolled *l'art pour l'art* (**art for art's sake**). In addition to rejecting traditional artistic and **aesthetic** norms, they sought to flout conventional morality in their dress, behavior, and sexual practices. Decadence is also closely associated with *fin de siècle* ("end of the century"), a term **connoting** the boredom and indolence that so many of the Decadent writers expressed. The Decadents published a short-lived journal entitled *Le décadent* (1886); French writer and critic Théophile Gautier outlined many of the tenets of Decadence in his preface to an edition of Charles Baudelaire's volume of poems, *Les fleurs du mal* (*The Flowers of Evil*) (1868). Prominent French Decadents included Baudelaire, Arthur Rimbaud, and Paul Verlaine; English adherents included Aubrey Beardsley, Algernon Charles Swinburne, and Oscar Wilde, who was noted for **epigrammatic** statements reflecting both the **wit** and dissatisfaction of the movement. Examples include "When the gods wish to punish us, they answer our prayers" and "In this world there are only two tragedies. One is not getting what one wants, and the other is getting it."

▶ **decenter:** See **center.**

▶ **deconstruction:** A **poststructuralist** approach to **literary criticism** involving the **close reading** of **texts** in order to demonstrate that any given text has irreconcilably contradictory meanings, rather than being a unified, logical whole. As J. Hillis Miller, the preeminent American deconstructor, explained in an essay entitled "Stevens' Rock and Criticism as Cure" (1976), "Deconstruction is not a dismantling of the structure of a text, but a demonstration that it has already dismantled itself. Its apparently solid ground is no rock but thin air." Deconstructing a text involves showing that it — like DNA with its double helix — can and does have intertwined yet opposite **discourses,** multiple and conflicting strands of **narrative,** threads of meaning that cross and contradict one another.

Deconstruction was both created and profoundly influenced by Jacques Derrida, an Algerian-born French philosopher of language. Derrida, who coined the term *deconstruction,* argued that in Western culture people tend to think and express their thoughts in terms of **binary oppositions.** Something is white but not black, masculine and therefore not feminine, a cause rather than an effect. Other common and mutually exclusive pairs include beginning / end, conscious / unconscious, **presence / absence,** and speech / writing. Derrida suggested these dichotomies are not simply oppositions but also hierarchies in miniature, containing one term that Western culture views as positive or superior and another considered negative or inferior, even if only slightly so. (Presence, for instance, is more clearly preferable to absence than speech is preferable to writing.) Derrida didn't seek to reverse these oppositions, however, because doing so would mean falling into the trap of perpetuating the same forms that he sought to deconstruct. He instead aimed to erase the boundary between binary oppositions — and to do so in such a way that the hierarchy implied by the oppositions is thrown into question.

Of particular interest to Derrida, perhaps because it involves the language in which all the other dichotomies are expressed, was the speech / writing opposition. Derrida argued that the **privileging** of speech, that is, the tendency to regard speech in positive terms and writing in negative terms, cannot be disentangled from the privileging of presence. (Postcards are written by absent friends; we read Plato because he cannot speak from beyond the grave.) Furthermore, the tendency to privilege both speech and presence is part of the Western tradition of **logocentrism,** the belief that a creative Beginning requires spoken words announced by an ideal, present God. Derrida also used the word *phallogocentrism* to point out the connection between logocentrism and the **phallocentrism** (**patriarchal** structure) of a culture whose God created light, the world, and man before creating woman — from Adam's rib.

Derrida used the theories of Swiss linguist Ferdinand de Saussure, who invented the modern science of **linguistics,** to remind us that associating speech with present, obvious, and ideal meaning and writing with absent, merely pictured, and therefore less reliable meaning is suspect, to say the least. As Saussure demonstrated, words are not the things they name and, indeed, are only arbitrarily associated with those things. A tiger, for instance, need not be represented by the word *tiger;* any other word would do just as well. A word, like any **sign,** is what Derrida called a "deferred presence" in an essay entitled "Différance" (1973); that is to say, the thing being **signified** is never actually present, and every signified concept invokes others in an endless string of **connotations.** Thus, neither spoken nor written words have positive, identifiable attributes in and of themselves. Indeed, they have meaning only by virtue of their *difference* from other words and, at the same time, their contextual relationship to those words. When reading, to know whether the word *read,* for example, is the present or past tense of the verb — that is, whether it rhymes with *reed* or *red* — we need to see it in relation to some other word or words (for example, *yesterday*).

Derrida argued that all language is constituted by **différance,** a word he coined that **puns** on the French verb *différer,* which can mean either "to differ" or "to defer." He used the term to demonstrate that words are only the deferred presences of the things they "mean," and that the meaning of words is grounded in their difference from other words. The word *différance* also suggests the French noun *différence,* meaning "difference"; changing the second *e* in *différence* to an *a* in *différance* is itself a playful, witty challenge to the notion that writing is inferior or "fallen" speech, for this change can be seen in written French but cannot be heard in the spoken language.

In *De la grammatologie* (*Of Grammatology*) (1967), Derrida began to redefine writing by deconstructing some of the ways in which it was defined.

Using Swiss philosopher Jean-Jacques Rousseau's *Confessions* (1783) to expose Rousseau's conflicting attitudes and behavior with respect to speech and writing, he demonstrated the contradiction between writing as a secondary, even treacherous supplement to speech and writing as necessary to (effective) communication. Although Rousseau condemned writing as mere **representation**, a corruption of the more natural, childlike, direct, and supposedly undevious speech, he admitted that he often blurted out exactly the wrong thing in public and expressed himself better in writing.

Although Derrida deconstructed numerous texts, he did not claim to have explained or revealed their true meaning, at least not in any traditional sense. In fact, Derrida would have denied that any one "true" meaning could be found, arguing that those who seek to find a single, homogeneous, or universal meaning in a text are imprisoned by the structure of thought that insists only one of various readings can be "right." Deconstructors believe that all works defy the laws of Western logic, the laws of opposition and noncontradiction. Texts don't say *A* and not *B* (or *B* and not *A*). They say *A* and not *A* (or *B* and not *B*). As Barbara Johnson noted in her translator's introduction to *Dissémination* (*Dissemination*) (1972), Derrida made a typical deconstructive move to show that a text dismantles itself when he unearthed "dimensions of Plato's *text* that work against the grain of (Plato's own) Platonism." Johnson also pointed out in *A World of Difference* (1987) that the word *deconstruction* is itself intended to "undermine the either / or logic of the opposition 'construction / destruction.' " Deconstruction is both, it is neither, and it reveals the way in which both construction and destruction are themselves not what they appear to be.

Although its ultimate aim may be to criticize Western idealism and logic, deconstruction arose as a response to **structuralism** and to **formalism**, two **structure**-oriented theories of reading. Structuralists believe that all elements of human culture, including literature, may be understood as parts of a system of signs. Using Saussure's linguistic theory, they attempted to develop a **semiology**, or science of signs, arguing that anything people do or use to communicate information of any type constitutes a sign. For instance, Roland Barthes — who later turned to poststructuralism — tried to recover literary language from the isolation in which it had been studied and to show that the same laws govern all signs, from road signs to handshakes to articles of clothing. In "The Structural Study of Myth" (1955) and other works, Claude Lévi-Strauss, a structural anthropologist, found in **myths** what he called "mythemes," or building blocks (such as basic **plot** elements) that occur in similar myths from different cultures.

Derrida did not believe that structuralists could explain the laws governing human signification and thus provide the key to understanding the **form** and meaning of everything from an African village to Greek myth to Rousseau's *Confessions*. In his view, the scientific search by structural anthropologists for what unifies humankind amounted to a new version of the old search for the lost ideal. Derrida also rejected the structuralist belief that texts have **centers** of meaning, classifying it as a derivative of the logocentric belief that there is a reading of the text that accords with "the book as seen by God."

Deconstruction questions assumptions made about literature by formalists as well, although deconstruction and formalism are superficially similar. Formalist critics, such as **the New Critics,** assume that a work of literature is a freestanding, self-contained object whose meaning can be found in the complex network of relations between its parts (**allusions, images, rhythms,** sounds). Like deconstruction, formalism is a text-oriented approach whose practitioners often focus on **figurative language.** And formalists, long before deconstructors, discovered counterpatterns of meaning in the same text. But here, the similarities end.

Formalists, who associated literary with figurative language, ranked some figures above others in a valuative hierarchy. They preferred **symbols** and **metaphors** to **metonyms,** for instance, arguing that the former are less arbitrary figures than the latter. For formalists, metonyms involve associations that, however common in a given culture, are purely arbitrary; liquor may be referred to as "the bottle," but there is no inherent relationship between the two. A metaphor ("I'm feeling blue"), by contrast, supposedly involves a special, intrinsic, even "natural" relationship between **tenor** (the subject of the figure, the thing being represented, here the feeling of melancholy) and **vehicle** (the **image** used to represent the tenor, here the color blue); a symbol ("the river of life") involves a unique fusion of image and idea.

Deconstructors have questioned the formalist hierarchy of figures and the distinctions upon which hierarchical valuations are based. In "The Rhetoric of Temporality" (1969), Belgian-born theorist and critic Paul de Man deconstructed the distinction between symbol and **allegory;** elsewhere, he, Derrida, and Miller questioned the distinction between metaphor and metonymy, arguing that all figuration is a process of linguistic substitution. In the case of a metaphor (or symbol), they claimed, we have simply forgotten what juxtaposition or contiguity gave rise to the association that now seems mysteriously special. In an essay and book entitled, respectively, "La mythologie blanche: la métaphore dans le texte philosophique" ("White Mythology: Metaphor in the Text of Philosophy") (1971) and *Allegories of Reading* (1979), Derrida and de Man also challenged the priority of literal over figurative language; Miller even denied the validity of the literal / figurative distinction, arguing in *Ariadne's Thread: Story Lines* (1992) that all words are figures.

Deconstructors also differ from formalists in evaluating the counterpatterns of meaning that can be found in any text. Formalists conceded that the resulting **ambiguity** is characteristic of literary texts, but they also believed that a complete understanding of the literary work was possible pending the objective resolution of ambiguities by the reader. Deconstructors, by contrast, argue that the conflicts are irreconcilable or "undecidable," embedded as they are within the text itself. *Undecidability,* as de Man came to define it, is a complex notion easily misunderstood. Many people (incorrectly) assume that it refers to readers who, when forced to decide between two or more equally plausible and conflicting readings, give up and decide that the choice can't be made. Undecidability, however, actually debunks the whole notion of reading as a decision-making process by readers. To say that we are forced to choose or decide — or that we are unable to do so — is falsely to locate undecidability within ourselves, rather than recognizing it as an intrinsic feature of the text.

Undecidability thus differs from the formalist concept of ambiguity. Deconstructors reject the formalist view that a literary work is demonstrably unified from beginning to end, in one certain way, or that it is organized around a single center that ultimately can be identified. As a result, deconstructors see texts as more radically heterogeneous than do formalists. Formalists ultimately make sense of ambiguity, even if only by recognizing that it serves a definite, meaningful function; undecidability, by contrast, is never reduced, let alone mastered. Though a deconstructive reading can reveal the incompatible possibilities generated by the text, it is impossible for the reader to decide among them.

Deconstruction, then, is not really interpretation, the act of choosing between or among possible meanings. It is more accurately defined as reading, as long as reading is defined as de Man defined it: a process involving moments of **aporia** (irreconcilable uncertainty) and an act performed with the awareness that all texts are ultimately unreadable (that is, irreducible to a single, homogeneous meaning). In *The Ethics of Reading* (1987), Miller explained unreadability by saying that although moments of great lucidity in reading exist, each such moment itself contains a "blind spot" that must be elucidated, and so on. Miller's reservations concerning moments of lucidity suggest that critics practicing deconstruction know that their own insights — even their insights into what is or isn't contradictory, undecidable, or unreadable in a text — are hardly sacrosanct.

For deconstructors, the boundaries between any given text and that larger text we call language are always shifting. It was this larger text that Derrida was referring to in *Of Grammatology* when he said *"there is nothing outside the text."* In making this statement, Derrida refused to categorically distinguish world and text, simultaneously asserting that every human (worldly) product can be viewed as a text and that every text reflects and shapes the world we perceive. It is through language that we express ourselves and understand the world; the acts that constitute the "real world" (the Oklahoma City bombing and 9/11 attacks, and the decision to marry) are both inseparable from the discourses out of which they arise and as open to interpretation as any work of literature. If no language or discourse existed, neither would tradition nor even disagreement. Terrorist acts likely would not occur were there no newspapers to report them and no clash between competing philosophies to incite them in the first place.

Since a text is always open to being seen in the light of new contexts, any given text can be different each time it is read. Furthermore, as Miller showed in *Ariadne's Thread*, the various terms and families of terms we use in reading invariably affect the results. Whether we choose to focus on a novel's **characters** or its **realism,** for instance, leads us to view the same text differently; no single thread, as Miller put it, serves to control and unify the whole. Even the individual words of narratives — words used to compose a mental picture of a character or place — usually have several (and often conflicting) meanings.

Notably, deconstruction has been the target of considerable opposition, expressed not only in academic books and journals but also in popular magazines such as *Newsweek*. Indeed, some of the movement's harshest critics, pointing to articles de Man wrote during World War II for Nazi-controlled or collaborationist newspapers, have charged that deconstruction is morally as well as intellectually flawed. In *The Ethics of Reading*, Miller identified and refuted two notions commonly repeated by deconstruction's detractors. First, critics of deconstruction often claim that deconstructors believe a text means nothing insofar as it means whatever the playful reader wants it to mean. Miller responded by pointing out that both Derrida and de Man consistently argued that readers cannot make texts mean anything they want them to mean because texts do not support a single meaning or interpretation.

Second, Miller noted that deconstruction has been criticized as "immoral" insofar as it refuses to view literature traditionally, that is, "as the foundation and embodiment, the means of preserving and transmitting, the basic humanistic values of our culture." Miller rejected the notion that deconstructors shirk an ethical responsibility because they do not seek to (re)discover and (re)assert the values contained in the Western **canon,** finding it contingent upon "a basic misunderstanding of the way the ethical moment enters into the act of reading." For Miller, reading is an act that leads to further ethical acts, decisions, and behavior, for which the reader must take responsibility, as for any other ethical act.

Foes of deconstruction also object to the attitude of pleasurable playfulness, or *jouissance,* that practitioners exhibit in teasing out the contradictory interpretive possibilities generated by the words in a text, their **etymologies** and contexts, and their potential to be read figuratively or even **ironically.** In *The Post Card: From Socrates to Freud and Beyond* (1987), Derrida associated deconstruction with pleasure; in an interview published in his *Acts of Literature* (1992), he speculated that "it is perhaps that *jouissance* which most irritates the all-out adversaries of deconstruction." According to Derrida, however, the pleasure of deconstruction arises from dismantling repressive ideas, not from playing delightfully useless little word games with texts.

Perhaps the most common charge levelled at deconstructors is a claim that they divorce literary texts from historical, political, and legal institutions. Derek Attridge countered this charge in his introduction to *Acts of Literature* by noting that deconstructors like Derrida view literature not as a word-playground but, rather, as discourse "brought into being by processes that are social, legal, and political, and that can be mapped historically and geographically." Derrida also pointed out in *Memoires for Paul de Man* (1986) that deconstructors have pointedly questioned the tendency of historians to view the past as the source of (lost) truth and value, to look for explanations in origins, and to view as unified epochs (for example, the **Victorian Period,** 1837–1901) what are in fact complex and heterogeneous times in history. Derrida further noted that de Man's commentaries acknowledge that conflicting interpretations reflect and are reflected in the policies of institutions.

In addition to history and politics, deconstructors have focused on the law. In an essay on Franz Kafka's "Before the Law," Derrida showed that for Kafka the law as such existed but could never actually be confronted. Miller pointed out in *The Ethics of Reading* that the law "may only be confronted in its delegates or representatives or by its effects on us or others." The law's presence is continually deferred by narrative, that is, writing about the law which constantly reinterprets it in the attempt to reveal what it really is and means. This very act of (re)interpretation, however, serves to "defer" or distance the law even further from the case at hand, since the (re)interpretation takes precedence (and assumes prominence) over the law itself.

A number of contemporary thinkers have adapted and applied deconstruction in their work. For instance, a deconstructive theology has been developed, as has a deconstructive architectural theory. In the area of law, scholars associated with the Critical Legal Studies movement, such as Gerald Frug, David Kennedy, and Pierre Schlag, used deconstruction (among a number of other nonlegal methodologies) in the early to mid-1980s. These scholars sought to critique the claims to rational coherence made by judicial and legal discourse and to criticize the way in which particular legal regimes affect justice between groups by highlighting the **gaps,** conflicts, and ambiguities in the law and legal discourse. Although Derridean concepts were not invoked by name until the 1980s, American legal theory had developed a practice of internal critique of legal concepts during the Realist movement of the 1930s that anticipated deconstructive methodologies.

In the field of literary studies, deconstruction's influence is apparent in the work of critics ostensibly taking some other, more "political" approach. In *The Critical Difference: Essays in the Contemporary Rhetoric of Reading* (1980), Johnson put deconstruction to work for the **feminist** cause, arguing that chief among those binary oppositions "based on a repression of differences *within* entities" is the opposition man / woman. Johnson, Shoshana Felman, and Gayatri Spivak combined Derrida's theories with the **psychoanalytic** theory of Jacques Lacan to analyze the way in which **gender** and **sexuality** are ultimately textual, grounded in language and **rhetoric. Gay and lesbian critics** have followed their lead, hence Eve Kosofsky Sedgwick's recognition in *Epistemology of the Closet* (1990) that the "categories presented in a culture as symmetrical binary oppositions — actually subsist in a more unsettled and dynamic tacit relation." For instance, although most people think of sexual preference in terms of the binary opposition heterosexual / homosexual, sexuality is more accurately represented along a continuum.

In "Telling the Story of Deconstruction" (*The Pleasure of Babel: Contemporary American Literature and Theory* [1993]), Jay Clayton suggested that what began as theory in the late 1960s and 1970s has, over time, developed into a method employed by critics taking a wide range of approaches to literature — ethnic, feminist, **new historicist, Marxist** — and even by critics whose focus is broader than literary studies, such as critical race theorists and **postcolonial theorists.** Edward Said, a scholar who inaugurated **postcolonial criticism,** is just one of many who have imported deconstruction from the literary to the nonliterary arena. In *Orientalism* (1978), Said deconstructed the East / West, Orient / Occident opposition and the stereotypes entailed, arguing that they not only facilitated colonization but still govern Western relations with Arab and Eastern countries today.

▶ **decorum:** (1) Generally, propriety of conduct in accordance with societal conventions. (2) In **rhetoric,** propriety in argument matching subject and words. (3) In literature, propriety of the elements in a literary work (particularly **poetry**) such that **style, character, setting,** subject, **action,** language, and situation are compatible and fitting. The idea of literary decorum dates back to **classical** times; in the *Poetics* (c. 330 B.C.), for instance, the Greek philosopher Aristotle asserted the dual importance of choosing the appropriate and avoiding the inconsistent in areas such as **characterization** and **genre,** and in *Ars poetica* (*Art of Poetry*) (c. 20 B.C.) the Roman poet Horace stressed the need for appropriateness and consistency among elements such as characterization, language, subject, and style to maintain a work's unity. Literary decorum was also championed by **Renaissance** and **neoclassical** critics, who drew heavily on their classical predecessors and emphasized the importance both of choosing an appropriate style and using "correct" language. Notably, while decorum has remained a locus of critical attention since classical times, many writers have adapted or even disregarded the prevailing decorum of their time to suit their particular needs and goals.

EXAMPLE: Literary decorum dictates that a young chimney sweeper depicted in a **Victorian** novel should not speak in the elevated, high-mannered, and grammatically precise style of an Oxford don. In *Oliver Twist* (1837), Charles Dickens deliberately broke the rules of decorum by giving the workhouse orphan Oliver Twist the speech of a young gentleman.

▶ **deep ecology:** See **ecocriticism.**

▶ **deictic(s):** A word that refers to another word or element in a **text** or passage and relies on that word or element for its meaning. Deictics are often pronouns, adjectives, or adverbs, although any word that directly refers to and is contingent upon something else is a deictic.

EXAMPLE: The sentence, "Jack was shot here yesterday; he was a drug dealer, so it came as no surprise," contains four deictics: *here, yesterday, he,* and *it. He* and *it* are pronouns that clearly refer to *Jack* and the shooting, respectively. *Here* could refer to a location (such as Chicago or a subterranean garage) or to the part of Jack's body the bullet entered (such as the head). If we are given the referent for *here* before we read or hear this sentence, we can easily understand what *here* refers to. If we are not given this information, *here* is a deictic that brings us into the narrative *in medias res* ("in the middle of things"); despite the lack of a named referent, *here* is a deictic because it refers to something specific even if we do not know what that something is. The meaning of *yesterday* is similarly determined by whatever information, if any, we are given.

▶ **demotic:** From the Greek for "commoner," a term originally used with reference to a simplified form of ancient Egyptian **hieratic** writing, itself a stylized but simplified form of hieroglyphic writing. As adapted to **literary criticism** by the Canadian **archetypal critic** Northrop Frye, the term refers to an unpretentious **style** of literature that employs the **connotations, diction, rhythms,** and **syntax** of everyday speech, in contrast to hieratic style, which uses devices and **conventions** associated with **literariness** to elevate language above the level of ordinary speech. Frye also used the term *demotic* to **denote** a populist linguistic phase, one of three linguistic phases through which he argued cultures cycle.

For further discussion, see **hieratic.**

▶ **denotation:** A word's literal meaning(s), independent of any **connotations** — associations evoked by the word — that a given individual might attach to it; the "dictionary definition" of a word.

▶ *dénouement:* From the French for "unknotting," a term that both refers to the events following the **climax** of a **plot** and implies some ingenious resolution of the dramatic **conflict** and explanation of the plot's mysteries or misunderstandings. Although *dénouement* may be applied to both **tragedy** and **comedy,** the term **catastrophe** is typically used with reference to tragedy.

EXAMPLE: The *dénouement* of the film *Finding Forrester* (2000) provides literary **closure** as well as a sense of **poetic justice** when Jamal Wallace — a poor African American student recruited by a fancy New York prep school to play basketball and then falsely accused of plagiarism — inherits the house, furniture, and books of his mentor, elderly New York writer William Forrester.

▶ **descriptive linguistics:** The branch of **linguistics** concerned with classifying the characteristics of a given language. Descriptive linguistics is different from *historical linguistics,* which concentrates on studying the development of a language over time.

▶ **detective fiction:** A type of **fiction** featuring a crime (in most cases, a murder) that is solved by the **protagonist,** a detective, through the use of deductive reasoning from a series of clues. **Characterization, setting,** and description have often taken a backseat in detective fiction to the twists and turns of the **plot,** in which clues and "red herrings" alike are introduced to the reader as the detective comes across them. Although the **genre** has evolved through the years, allowing writers to stray from the strict principles established by the London Detection Club (founded in 1928), the basic elements of detective fiction have remained the same: a baffling crime that usually occurs at the beginning of the story, an often-eccentric sleuth who solves the case through an impressive display of logic, several suspects, and an unexpected conclusion. The poet W. H. Auden concisely defined detective fiction in "The Guilty Vicarage: Notes on the Detective Story, by an Addict" (1948) when he wrote: "A murder occurs; many are suspected; all but one suspect, who is the murderer, are eliminated; the murderer is arrested or dies."

Detective fiction should be distinguished from **mysteries** more generally, which are fictional works concerning any type of perplexing mystery, criminal or otherwise, and which may or may not involve a detective, deductive reasoning, or the other hallmarks of detective fiction. Thus, while detective fiction is a subset of mystery fiction, the terms are not coextensive.

Detective fiction should also be distinguished more specifically from the *crime novel,* another type of mystery fiction that was heavily influenced by detective fiction. While both detective fiction and crime novels involve crime, the focus of the crime novel is on the criminal and his or her psychological state, rather than on investigative efforts to solve the crime through logical, deductive reasoning. Dorothy Sayers's *The Omnibus of Crime* (1929) provides a **classic** overview of the genre; Tony Hillerman and Rosemary Herbert's *A New Omnibus of Crime* (2005) picks up where Sayers left off, compiling notable crime fiction from the 1930s to the present.

Detective fiction may have its roots in works involving crime and criminal apprehension written as early as the mid-1700s. Such precursors include Voltaire's *Zadig* (1747), Tobias Smollett's *The Adventures of Ferdinand Count Fathom* (1753), William Godwin's *The Adventures of Caleb Williams* (1794), and Eugène François Vidocq's **autobiography,** *Les mémoires de Vidocq* (1828). The many editions of *The Newgate Calendar* — a collection of true crime stories first published in London in 1773, updated and reprinted for more than a century — are also viewed as forerunners of detective fiction. Two attorneys, Andrew Knapp and William Baldwin, produced an 1809 edition of *The Newgate Calendar* that was a best-seller for its day, but what became known as "Newgate Fiction" did not reach the height of its popularity until the 1830s.

Most scholars agree that the first true example of detective fiction is American writer Edgar Allan Poe's "Murders in the Rue Morgue" (1841), a watershed work that both established the **codes** and **conventions** of the genre and introduced one of the first fictional detectives, Le Chevalier C. Auguste Dupin. Consequently, Sir Arthur Conan Doyle, a British master of detective fiction, called Poe "the father of the detective tale." Other early detective stories by Poe include "The Purloined Letter" (1845) and "The Mystery of Marie Roget" (1850).

Other notable writers of nineteenth-century detective fiction include Wilkie Collins, an Englishman, and Frenchman Émile Gaboriau. In 1868, Collins published *The Moonstone,* a novel involving a diamond heist that is said to have influenced all subsequent detective fiction. The twentieth-century poet T. S. Eliot referred to Collins's work as "the first and greatest of English detective novels" in his essay "Wilkie Collins and Dickens" (1927). Sayers, a contemporary of Eliot's and herself an important detective novelist, wrote: "Taking everything into consideration, *The Moonstone* is probably the very finest detective story ever written." Gaboriau, author of the first full-length French detective novel (*Le crime d'Orcival* [1867]) and the first to make his detective, Lecoq, a policeman, is credited with establishing the *roman policier,* a French form of detective and crime fiction.

It was Doyle's short stories and novels, though, that made detective fiction a popular form of literary entertainment. When he introduced the extraordinarily observant and astute Sherlock Holmes in his first two **novellas,** *A Study in Scarlet* (1887) and *The Sign of the Four* (1890), he created the prototype for countless fictional detectives to come. (In Dr. James Watson, he also created the model confidant, or sidekick, another common element of detective fiction.) In 1891, short stories he published in the magazine *The Strand* vastly increased the market for detective fiction by appealing to a broad range of readers. Two collections of stories — *The Adventures of Sherlock Holmes* (1892) and *The Memoirs of Sherlock Holmes* (1894) — were followed by a novel, *The Hound of the Baskervilles* (1902), and several other Sherlock Holmes works. Doyle inspired a generation of British authors including Ernest Bramah, who created the first blind detective (Max Carrados); Arthur Morrison, whose Investigator Martin Hewitt is a man of extraordinary technical and statistical knowledge; and R. Austin Freeman, who introduced the first scientific detective (Dr. John Thorndyke) and anticipated the *inverted detective story,* a form of detective fiction in which the reader is aware of the killer's identity from the beginning of the story although the detective is not.

In America, the most prominent — and prolific — detective fiction authors following Poe were women. Anna Katherine Green, the first American female author of detective fiction, published her first novel, *The Leavensworth Case,* in 1878; Mary Rinehart published one of her best-known works, *The Circular Staircase,* thirty years later. Perhaps the most popular male author was S. S. Van Dine (a **pseudonym** for Willard Huntington Wright), whose *The Benson Murder Case* (1926) launched a series of similarly titled novels.

The period between World War I and World War II (1918–39) is generally considered to be both the **golden age** of detective fiction and its *classic* period. In 1928, G. K. Chesterton, a well-respected English poet and author of the Father Brown series of detective stories, became the first president of the London Detection Club, whose guiding principles may have been influenced by Van Dine's "Twenty Rules for Writing Detective Stories" (1928) and Monsignor Ronald Knox's "A Detective Story Decalogue" (1929). One of these principles, which prohibited authors from concealing any vital clue from readers, became part of the solemn oath taken by club members. Particularly important during the interwar period were four women — Sayers, Agatha Christie, Ngaio Marsh, and Margery Allingham — referred to as the "Big Four." Christie, the creator of the mustachioed Belgian detective Hercule Poirot and the dauntless English spinster Miss Jane Marple, became the best-known detective novelist of the twentieth century. Her eighty-plus novels, perhaps the most famous of which is *Murder on the Orient Express* (1934; adapted to film in 1974) have been translated into dozens of languages.

Other respected classic detective writers include E. C. Bentley; Anthony Berkeley (a pseudonym for Anthony Cox, who also wrote as Frances Iles), a key figure in developing the inverted detective story; Nicholas Blake (pseudonym for C. Day Lewis, who is said to have based his detective on W. H. Auden); John Dickson Carr; Erle Stanley Gardner, the creator of lawyer-detective Perry Mason; Michael Innes (pseudonym for J. I. M. Stewart); A. E. W. Mason; and Ellery Queen (pseudonym for two writers, Frederic Dannay and Manfred Lee). Widely noted post–World War II authors in the classic tradition include Stanley Ellin, Kenneth Fearing, Elizabeth Ferrars, P. D. James, Simon Nash, Ellis Peters, Ruth Rendell, Rex Stout, and Patricia Highsmith, whose novels *Strangers on a Train* (1949) and *The Talented Mr. Ripley* (1957) were both later adapted to film: *Strangers* in 1951 and *Ripley* first in 1960 (under the title *Plein Soleil*, or *Purple Noon*) and then again in 1999.

As popular as classic detective writing became, however, it had to contend with a powerful competitor. In the 1920s, a new, decidedly American subgenre called *hard-boiled detective fiction* emerged, gaining adherents so rapidly that it began to eclipse the classic tradition in the 1940s. Unlike classic detective fiction, in which the world is depicted as an orderly place in which crimes are aberrations and order is restored by the crime-solving detective, the hard-boiled world is one in which gangsters reign, chaos and violence are the norm, and the detective only temporarily provides relief from dysfunction. **Black humor** and **grotesque** scenes and situations are common. Moreover, hard-boiled stories, typically set on mean city streets patrolled by corrupt cops, take a different view of law enforcement than classic *whodunits*, in which honest if inept police are apt to bumble around plush country estates, as in the 2001 film *Gosford Park*.

Practitioners of hard-boiled stories found it difficult to gain recognition in part because such stories were not initially considered to be literature. Indeed, hard-boiled stories were first published in magazines printed on cheap paper made from wood pulp. *Black Mask*, one popular pulp magazine founded in 1920 by H. L. Mencken and George Nathan, offered writers like Raymond Chandler, Carroll John Daly, and Dashiell Hammett a penny per word to publish their stories. Daly's Race Williams was the prototype of the new American detective, but Chandler's Philip Marlowe and

Hammett's Continental Op and Sam Spade were the best-known private eyes, or "dicks," of the hard-boiled subgenre. Also notable are Raoul Whitfield's stories, first published in *Black Mask* in 1930, about a tough Filipino "Island Investigator" named Jo Garr.

Writers James M. Cain, Mickey Spillane, and Jim Thompson continued the hard-boiled tradition in the ensuing decades. Ross Macdonald, who was first published in the 1940s and continued writing into the 1970s, patterned his novels after the fiction of Chandler, Daly, and Hammett but softened the violence and took a psychological approach to characters in order to attract sophisticated upper-middle-class readers. Subsequent popular writers who further modified the hard-boiled style include Andrew Bergman, James Crumley, James Ellroy, Arthur Lyons, Robert B. Parker, and Roger L. Simon.

Hard-boiled detective fiction was introduced primarily by male authors and, perhaps for that reason, generally portrayed women as either good housewives or femmes fatales. Exceptions included the works of a few female authors who published in this style during its early years. In 1928 Katherine Brocklebank's "Tex of the Border Service," featuring a female detective, was published in *Black Mask*. Other early female "hard-boiled" writers included Leigh Brackett, Dolores Hitchens (who sometimes published under male pseudonyms), and Dorothy B. Hughes. Contemporary women who write hard-boiled detective fiction include Sara Paretsky, whose private eye Victoria Iphigenia ("V.I.") Warshawski first appeared in *Indemnity Only* (1982); Sue Grafton, who publishes a series of novels with alphabetical titles such as *"A" is for Alibi* (1983); and Janet Evanovich, who writes about a sassy and irreverent bail enforcer in a series of novels with numbered titles such as *Hot Six* (2000) and *Twelve Strong* (2006).

In addition to presenting a darker, grittier world than their classic counterparts, contemporary hard-boiled detective writers have often woven hard-hitting social and **racial** issues into their stories, leading the way in resurrecting social **realism**. As writer Dennis Lehane, using the term "crime novel" broadly, said, "Today's social novel *is* the crime novel." Novelist Walter Mosley is generally credited with starting this trend through his *Easy Rawlins* mystery series (1990–), which chronicles several decades of black life in Los Angeles. Paula L. Woods has likewise incorporated black experience into her *Charlotte Justice* novels, in which the **protagonist** is a black woman in the mostly white, mostly male LAPD. In *Inner City Blues* (1999), Woods's debut novel, Justice comments, "I learned from my mother's experiences that life in America was a game called Pigmentocracy, color a card you played."

Notably, although female writers of detective fiction played prominent roles throughout the history and development of the genre, there were few black practitioners until well after World War II. Hughes Allison's story "Corollary" (1948), a police procedural featuring a black detective named Joe Hill, broke new ground as the first African American detective story published in the prestigious *Ellery Queen's Mystery Magazine*. African

American writers subsequently gained a solid foothold on the terrain of detective fiction with the popularity of Chester Himes, who wrote several hard-boiled detective novels set in Harlem in the late 1950s and 1960s, and John Ball, whose novel *In the Heat of the Night* (1965) was adapted to film in 1967 (with Sidney Poitier playing Detective Virgil Tibbs).

Whether classic, hard-boiled, or hybrid in their approach, contemporary authors have tended to situate many or all of their stories in a particular historical period, professional environment, geographical setting, or cultural or religious context. For instance, the *Brother Cadfael* novels (1977–94) of Ellis Peters (Edith Pargeter), who followed a classic approach, are set in a medieval English monastery, with the "detective" being a monk, whereas murders committed in the *Kate Fansler* novels (1964–2002) of Amanda Cross (literary critic Carolyn Heilbrun) always occur in an academic setting. Nevada Barr's female park ranger, in novel after novel, solves murders that occurred in a national park (*Anna Pigeon* series, 1993–); Robert B. Parker's Spenser works out of Boston (novel series 1973– ; adapted to television 1985–88); John Sandford's Lucas Davenport is a Twin Cities detective in the *Prey* series (1989–); and Julie Smith's policewoman Skip Langdon and lawyer Rebecca Schwarz solve crimes in New Orleans and San Francisco, respectively.

Hillerman's detective novels are defined by a culture as well as a location, centered as they are in a Southwest reservation and featuring Native American detectives Jim Chee and Joe Leaphorn (1970–). Other novelists who highlight culture and/or religion include Sandra Scoppetone, who wrote about gay culture and lesbian detective Lauren Laurano (1991–99), and Harry Kemelman, whose novels had a religious context and featured the detective Rabbi David Small (1964–96).

The works of Patricia Cornwell and Jeffery Deaver, as well as the television series *Quincy, M.E.* (1976–83) and the more recent *CSI* series (2000–), reflect the growing interest in sophisticated professional crime scene investigators who use forensics and physical evidence found at the site of the murder. Cornwell's **heroine** Kay Scarpetta, like Quincy, is a medical examiner (series 1990–), and Deaver's **hero** Lincoln Rhyme is a quadriplegic who once headed the NYPD forensics unit (series 1997–). On the lighter side, the popular *Cat Who* series (1966–) by best-selling author Lillian Jackson Braun features a mystery-solving cat, K'ao Ko Kung, better known as Koko by readers and by his mustachioed owner Jim Qwilleran, a former reporter-turned-mystery-solver who has been transplanted up north to Moose County from "Down Below."

Detective fiction for children is also popular, though it generally involves nonviolent crimes or at least not murders. Classic examples include the *Hardy Boys* (1927–29, 1979–) and *Nancy Drew* (1930–) mystery series, created by Edward Stratemeyer and written by various authors under the **pseudonyms** Franklin W. Dixon and Carolyn Keene, respectively, and Donald J. Sobol's *Encyclopedia Brown* books (1963–).

See also **mystery fiction.**

▶ **deus ex machina:** From the Latin for "god from a machine," a phrase referring specifically to the intervention of a nonhuman force to resolve a seemingly unresolvable **conflict** in a literary work. It also refers more generally to improbable or artificial resolutions of conflicts, such as those provided by unbelievable coincidences or unexpected strokes of good luck.

EXAMPLES: Toward the end of Molière's (Jean-Baptiste Poquelin's) *Tartuffe* (1667), Orgon has lost all his property to the dissembling Tartuffe and, thanks to Tartuffe's treachery, has been arrested for disloyalty to the King (who, in Molière's day, would have been seen as God's representative on earth). Suddenly, an officer of the Crown appears, forgives Orgon, and restores his property, saying:

> Sir, all is well; rest easy, and be grateful.
> We serve a Prince to whom all sham is hateful,
> A Prince who sees into our inmost hearts,
> And can't be fooled by any trickster's arts.

In George Eliot's novel *Adam Bede* (1859), Hetty Sorrell — about to be hanged for infanticide — suddenly hears a shout in the street:

> It was a shout of sudden excitement at the appearance of a horseman cleaving the crowd at full gallop. The horse is hot and distressed, but answers to the desperate spurring; the rider looks as if his eyes were glazed by madness, and he saw nothing but what was unseen by the others. See, he has something in his hand — he is holding it up as if it were a signal.
> The Sheriff knows him: it is Arthur Donnithorne, carrying in his hand a hard-won release from death.

The arrival of Donnithorne with a document officially ordering that Hetty is to be deported, rather than hanged, amounts to something like *deus ex machina*. It is worth pointing out, however, that this **convention** has its limits in **realistic** fiction. Donnithorne is, after all, an interested party; he is the father of the baby Hetty abandoned to die of exposure. Moreover, the reader subsequently learns that Hetty herself has died during an attempt to return to England.

Bertolt Brecht parodied the use of *deus ex machina* in *The Threepenny Opera* (1928), a play with music by Kurt Weill, in a **scene** in which Macheath, a **villain**, is saved from hanging by a pardon from the king.

▶ **diachronic:** A term used in **linguistics** to refer to historical linguists' study of the evolution of a language or family of languages over time, that is to say, of changes in language(s) over time.

▶ **dialect:** As traditionally defined, a way of speaking or using a language that is particular to a geographic region or social group and that varies considerably from the speech and usage patterns predominant within that language. In modern **linguistics**, *dialect* is defined more broadly, referring to any form of a language whose grammar differs systematically from other forms of the language. So used, *dialect* includes the dominant form of any language, often called the "standard" or "prestige" dialect, as well as other forms based on regional or social factors. Linguists emphasize that no dialect is superior or inferior to any other; each dialect simply uses a different set of rules.

Dialect involves not only pronunciation but also vocabulary and **syntax** that may be entirely unfamiliar to speakers of other dialects. Thus, it is distinguishable from **accent,** which refers to distinctive but generally comprehensible regional speech patterns and intonations. When a person with a pronounced East Texas accent says, "That gah might could help you," native speakers of American English readily understand this to mean "that guy might be able to help you." By contrast, the Yorkshire dialect spoken by the character Joseph in Emily Brontë's *Wuthering Heights* (1848) proved extremely difficult even for nineteenth-century British readers to understand — as when he scolds the children Catherine and Heathcliff, "T' maister nubbut [only] just buried, and Sabbath nut oe'red [over], und t'sahnd [sound] uh't gospel still i' yer lungs, and yah darr [you dare] be laiking [playing]!"

Some "dialects" differ so dramatically from the dominant form of the language that they are, in effect, separate languages. For example, what is commonly spoken in Sicily, though often referred to as a dialect of Italian, is virtually incomprehensible to a native of Florence, whose version of the language is the one taught in schools throughout the nation, including Sicily. Indeed, the "standard" version of any language is inevitably the one viewed as "correct" and "proper" and supported by most institutions, including schools, the government, and the media. While linguists tend to distinguish between dialect and language based on mutual intelligibility, they recognize that other factors, including political boundaries, influence classification. The often questionable boundary between dialect and language is pointed up by an **aphorism** attributed to twentieth-century Yiddish linguist Max Weinrich: "a language is a dialect with an army and a navy."

In any given language, the earliest literary productions were typically popular **lyrics** and **narratives** in **verse** that were spoken or sung in regional dialects; passed down orally from one generation to the next; and, in many cases, later committed to writing. The best-known poems written in what we now call Middle English were composed in different dialects, with the anonymous fourteenth-century **romance** *Sir Gawain and the Green Knight* and William Langland's *Piers Plowman* (1366–87) both written in West Midland dialect and Geoffrey Chaucer's *The Canterbury Tales* (c. 1387) written in the East Midland dialect spoken in London. Both because London was the capital and largest city in England and because Chaucer's works became so popular and influential, the East Midland dialect eventually evolved into the nation's predominant dialect, sometimes referred to as *Standard English*. During the **Renaissance** and subsequent periods, regional dialect poetry became less common, partially due to the advent of the printing press and the related, continuing standardization of English, but did not completely disappear.

FURTHER EXAMPLES: Nineteenth-century English writer William Barnes wrote poetry in the Dorset dialect, and Thomas Hardy — who came from the Dorset region and admired Barnes — occasionally used it in his novels (*Far from the Madding Crowd* [1874]) and poems (*Wessex Poems* [1898]). In D. H. Lawrence's *Sons and Lovers* (1913), Walter Morel, a character based on the author's own coal-miner father, speaks in a Nottinghamshire dialect that readers today, even in England, strain to understand. Told by his abused wife Gertrude "The house is filthy with you," Morel drunkenly responds, "Then ger out on't."

Other dialect writers include turn-of-the-century poet Paul Lawrence Dunbar, noted for his African American dialect poetry, including "An Ante-Bellum Sermon" (1895); **Harlem Renaissance** poet Claude McKay, whose *Songs of Jamaica* (1912) depicted black life in Jamaica; and many twentieth-century Italian poets, such as Pier Paolo Passolini (*La meglio gioventù* [*The Best of Youth*] [1954]). *The Full Monty* (1997) and the Coen brothers' *O Brother Where Are Thou?* (2000), which employ dialects from Northern England and the Southern U.S., respectively, are examples of contemporary films that many English-speaking audiences — on both sides of the Atlantic — find difficult to understand.

▶ **dialectic:** Originally developed by Greek philosophers, mainly Socrates and Plato (in *The Republic* and *Phaedrus* [both c. 360 B.C.]), a form and method of logical argumentation that typically addresses conflicting ideas or positions. When used in the plural, *dialectics* refers to any mode of argumentation that attempts to resolve the contradictions between opposing ideas.

The early-nineteenth-century German philosopher G. W. F. Hegel described dialectic as a process whereby a **thesis**, when countered by an *antithesis*, leads to the *synthesis* of a new idea. Karl Marx and Friedrich Engels, adapting Hegel's idealist theory, used the phrase *dialectical materialism* to discuss the way in which a revolutionary **class** war might lead to the synthesis of a new socioeconomic order.

In **literary criticism**, *dialectic* typically refers to the oppositional ideas and/or mediatory reasoning that pervade and unify a given work or group of works. Critics may thus speak of the dialectic of head and heart (reason and passion) in William Shakespeare's plays. American **Marxist critic** Fredric Jameson coined the phrase *dialectical criticism* to refer to a Marxist critical approach that synthesizes **structuralist** and **poststructuralist** methodologies.

▶ **dialectical criticism:** See **dialectic**.

▶ **dialectical irony (Socratic irony):** See **irony**.

▶ **dialectical materialism:** See **dialectic**.

▶ **dialogic:** See **dialogic criticism, monologic**.

▶ **dialogic criticism:** A method of **literary criticism** based on theories developed by Soviet critic Mikhail Bakhtin. Bakhtin developed his theories in the 1920s and 1930s, but they did not enter the mainstream of Western literary criticism until the 1980s, when they were translated from Russian.

In *Problems of Dostoevsky's Poetics* (1929), Bakhtin spoke of works as being either comparatively **monologic** or *dialogic,* using Leo Tolstoy, whom he criticized, and Fyodor Dostoevsky, whom he praised, as exemplars of the two approaches, respectively. A monologic work, according to Bakhtin, is one that is clearly dominated by a single, controlling **voice** or **discourse,** even though it may contain **characters** representing a multitude of viewpoints. Contrary voices are subordinated to the **authorial** (and authoritative) voice, which is usually, though not always, representative of the dominant or "official" **ideology** of the author's culture. A dialogic work, by contrast, is one that permits numerous voices or discourses to emerge and to engage in **dialogue** with one another. In dialogic works, the culture's dominant social or cultural ideology may vie with the discourses of popular culture. In *Rabelais and His World* (1940), Bakhtin associated these discourses with **carnival,** a term he used to refer not only to such festivities as the extravagant Mardi Gras celebrations held in the Christian world before Lent but also to "low" or popular culture in the more general sense, as exemplified by fairs and spontaneous **folk dramas** (including puppet shows).

Having made the distinction between monologic and dialogic works, Bakhtin argued that no work can be completely monologic. That is because the **narrator,** no matter how authorial and representative of the "official" culture, cannot avoid **representing** differing and even contrary viewpoints in the process of relating the thoughts and remarks of the diverse group of literary characters that populate a credible fictional world. These other voices, which make any work **polyphonic,** or *polyvocalic,* to some degree, inevitably disrupt the authoritative voice, even though it may remain dominant. Thus, for Bakhtin, the monologic / dialogic opposition was not an absolute; some works are more monologic, others more dialogic.

In a later essay, "Discourse in the Novel" (1934–35), Bakhtin further developed his concept of the novel as a primarily dialogic literary form. Contravening the Greek philosopher Aristotle's **privileging** of **plot** in the *Poetics* (c. 330 B.C.), Bakhtin argued that discourse is the main element of a **narrative** work. According to Bakhtin, the multiple voices contained in any narrative work invariably represent diverse and often conflicting attitudes, philosophies, and ideologies. Regardless of the efforts of the author to establish an uncontroverted (or incontrovertible) narrative voice, any work thus remains open and indeterminate to some extent.

Contemporary dialogic critics base their interpretations of literary works on Bakhtin's argument that no work can be completely monologic, for every work contains myriad voices that contend for recognition and disrupt the authorial voice and the dominant or official ideology. Following Bakhtin, these critics view the concurrence of numerous and often contrary voices as the definitive feature of literary narratives, celebrating the diversity of viewpoints these voices inevitably engender. In keeping with their own outlook, dialogic critics openly acknowledge that their perspective is only one possible approach that must compete with many other view-points and theories.

Practitioners of other modes of contemporary criticism have also drawn on Bakhtin's ideas. A few **deconstructors** have relied on Bakhtin's theory that a single work contains contending and conflicting discourses in their effort to show the contradictions in — and the **undecidability** of — literary **texts. Marxist critics** have applied Bakhtin's notion that even those works dedicated to perpetuating the existing power structure may be seen, on closer inspection, to contain subversive "carnivalesque" elements and perspectives. But Bakhtin's theory may have had its greatest impact on **cultural criticism,** whose practitioners argue that the boundary we tend to envision between "high" and "low" forms of culture is transgressed in numerous ways within works on both sides of the putative cultural divide. Thus, a cultural critic might ground in Bakhtinian theory the argument that James Joyce's novel *Ulysses* (1922) reflects not only the **influence** of Homer's **epic** *The Odyssey* (c. 850 B.C.) but also the diverse cultural forms common to Joyce's Dublin, such as advertising, journalism, film, and pub life.

See also **discourse analysis.**

▶ **dialogue:** Conversation between two or more **characters** in a literary work.

▶ **dibrach:** See **pyrrhic.**

▶ **diction:** (1) Narrowly defined, a speaker's (or author's) word choice. (2) More broadly defined, the general type or character of language used in speech or in a work of literature. (3) With reference to pronunciation and enunciation, the perceived accuracy and clarity with which someone pronounces words.

In the second, broader sense, diction is typically divided into two components: *vocabulary* and **syntax.** *Vocabulary* encompasses the degree of difficulty, complexity, abstractness, formality, and currency of words used, as well as their **etymology** or origin (native or foreign, Latinate or Germanic, and so forth). *Syntax* refers to the arrangement — the ordering, grouping, and placement — of words within a phrase, clause, or sentence. The term may also be extended to encompass such things as the complexity or completeness of a given arrangement of words. In **critical** circles, vocabulary is often described in terms of the "level" of the language used, whereas syntax tends to be discussed in terms of its "texture."

Poetic diction refers specifically to the choice and phrasing of words suitable for **verse.**

▶ **didactic:** Instructive or providing information for a particular purpose. Literature is considered didactic when its primary aim is to teach readers some lesson — whether moral, political, religious, ethical, or practical. It might be argued that most literary works are didactic, insofar as they have some purpose or idea that the **author** seeks to convey. However, works that are essentially imaginative rather than instructive are usually not considered didactic.

EXAMPLES: Religious works such as the New Testament letters of Paul to early Christians and the Muslim holy book the *Qur'an* (Koran) are primarily didactic, as are the following works: the *Kama Sutra* (a fourth-century A.D. ancient Indian erotic manual), Geoffrey Chaucer's "The Parson's Tale" (c. 1387), Alexander Pope's "An Essay on Criticism" (1711), and eighteenth-century English ladies' conduct manuals. Many people would say that William Bennett's anthology of moral tales entitled *The Book of Virtues* (1994) is a didactic work.

▶ *différance:* A term coined by the Algerian-born French theorist of **deconstruction** Jacques Derrida to show that words are only the deferred presences of the things they "mean"; that every meaning invokes others in a never-ending string of **connotations;** and that the meaning of words is grounded in both their difference from and relationship to other words. *Différance* is a **neologism** that **puns** on the French verb *différer,* which can mean either "to differ" or "to defer," a double meaning Derrida used to demonstrate the impossibility of arriving at a determinate — that is, single and definitive — interpretation of language, particularly literary language. Derrida first introduced the term in his book *La voix et le phénomène* (*Speech and Phenomena*) (1967) and subsequently elaborated on it in a lecture and essay titled *"Différance"* (1968).

Drawing on the theories of Swiss linguist Ferdinand de Saussure, Derrida argued that the quest for meaning — an effort we undertake whenever we read or listen to something — is endless. As Saussure pointed out, the relationship between a word (the **signifier**) and what it signifies (the **signified**) is always arbitrary, and a single word, or signifier, can connote any number of different signifieds. Moreover, each signifier has connotations that themselves have connotations, making every signified another signifier. As a result, according to Derrida, meaning is continually deferred as we seek to differentiate among an array of interpretive choices and to negotiate the **gap** between an ever increasing number of signifiers and signifieds.

The term *différance* also suggests the French noun *différence,* meaning "difference." The distinction between the homonyms *différance* and *différence* is one that can be seen in written French but not heard in the spoken language, a point that Derrida used to subvert, or "deconstruct," the **privileging** of speech and **presence** over writing and **absence** in **logocentric** Western metaphysics, which understands Creation to have taken place when a present God spoke the words "Let there be light."

See also **deconstruction.**

▶ **dimeter:** A line of **verse** consisting of two **metrical feet.**
EXAMPLES: The lines "The clock struck one / And down he ran" from the nursery rhyme "Hickory, Dickory, Dock." Thomas Hardy wrote a number of poems entirely in dimeter, such as "To Lizbie Browne" (1901):

> Dear Liz|bie Browne,
> Where are | you now?
> In sun, | in rain? —
> Or is | your brow
> Past joy, | past pain,
> Dear Liz|bie Browne?

▶ **Dionysian:** An adjective derived from Dionysus (the Greek god of wine) describing writing that exhibits an impulsive or even frenzied quality. Dionysian writing involves imaginative and sensual expression rather than rational, critical **discourse.** In *The Birth of Tragedy* (1872), German philosopher Friedrich Nietzsche used *Dionysian* in conjunction with the term **Apollonian** (signifying reason and order) to refer to the balance struck by the two sides of Greek **tragedy.** **Romantic** writing tends to draw on the passionate Dionysian tradition, whereas **classical** and **neoclassical** writing are often Apollonian.

See also **Apollonian.**

▶ **direct discourse:** See **discourse.**

▶ **dirge:** A song or **poem** of mourning, typically intended for a funeral, that is written to commemorate and lament someone's death. Dirges should be distinguished from **elegies,** which may lament loss or death more generally as well as the death of a particular person; are typically longer, more formal, and more reflective in character; and are intended to be read rather than sung.

EXAMPLES: Ariel's song in William Shakespeare's *The Tempest* (c. 1611), lamenting the death of Ferdinand's father; Peter Gabriel's song "Biko" (1980), lamenting the murder of South African civil rights leader Stephen Biko.

▶ **disability:** See **disability studies.**

▶ **disability studies:** A movement within **literary criticism** and the humanities more generally that focuses on and critiques *disability* as it is commonly conceived, applying cultural, historical, social, and other sociohumanistic approaches to the study of disability in society. Many people associate disability with *in*ability—with physical or mental defects that abnormally define and limit—and with personal misfortune. Proponents of disability studies seek to transform these commonly held perceptions, to show that disability is a matter of identity, an ordinary human variation like **race** or **gender.**

Disability studies, which emerged in the latter half of the 1990s, builds upon a **cultural-studies** approach that examines the nature of stigma and draws heavily on disciplines involving other types of identity studies, such as women's studies and African American studies. The movement also benefited from the work of Michel Foucault, a French philosophical historian whose recognition of the power dynamics implicit in medicine and a medicalized approach to people laid the groundwork for *body criticism,* which identifies and analyzes the imposition of cultural messages regarding the human body.

Disability studies seeks to overturn the medicalized understanding of disability and to replace it with a social model. Its proponents define disability not as a physical, mental, or developmental defect — a medical perspective they believe has had the effect of segregating people with disabilities — but, rather, as a social construct, a way of interpreting human differences.

Disability studies examines the historical formation of the social identity "disabled," pointing out that it covers a wide range of physical, mental, and emotional variations such that it encompasses a large and diverse group of people who actually have little in common. Disability studies also considers the history of how disability influences and is influenced by power, status, and distribution of resources; changes in the way disability has been interpreted over time and within varying cultural contexts; the impact of institutionalizing disabled persons versus integrating them into the community; the political and material implications for *all* people of the practice of assigning value to bodies; and how disability affects artistic production.

In assessing **sites** where a given culture defines and interprets disability, disability studies ranges across art and literature, religion and philosophy, history and politics, linking these fields with others as diverse as **aesthetics,** epistemology, and ethnic studies. Its practitioners have shown that **representations** of disability abound in the seminal **texts** of Western culture, from Sophocles' *Oedipus Rex* (c. 430 B.C.) to the Human Genome Project and beyond. These representations provide a **narrative** about human differences, an interpretation of physiological and mental traits, that can be critically examined and charted over time. Countering false constructs of disability — "disability fictions," as it were — is important because these narratives shape the material world, inform human relations, and mold our sense of who we and our fellow human beings are.

Literary analyses of disability often focus on how disability influenced the **author** and operates **thematically** in the text. (Interestingly, the works of many disabled authors are taught in the classroom without reference to the author's disability.) Proponents of disability studies have examined the role of disability in works ranging from those of the ancient Greeks, who made lame Hephaestus the butt of jokes, to the eighteenth-century English writers Samuel Johnson and Alexander Pope, to the twentieth-century American writers Audre Lorde and William Styron. Practitioners have focused repeatedly on the works of **canonical** European writers such as William Shakespeare, Charles Dickens, and Gustave Flaubert. They have also pointed out the pervasiveness of disability in **classic** American literature: in "The Author to Her Book" (1678), Anne Bradstreet imagined her book of poetry as a deformed child; Nathaniel Hawthorne **symbolized** human imperfections through the marked bodies of the wife in the short story "The Birthmark" (1843) and of Roger Chillingworth in the novel *The Scarlet Letter* (1850); Ralph Waldo Emerson elaborated the ideal of the

American individual in opposition to the figure of the "invalid"; Herman Melville figured human excess as disability through **characters** such as the one-legged Captain Ahab in *Moby-Dick* (1851); Mark Twain used deafness for humorous effect; and Toni Morrison constructs female characters whose disabilities ultimately enable them to avoid the subservient roles women often play in society and to find other, more independent paths. Likewise, disabled figures and the concept of disability are central to American **sentimental** literature; abolitionist **discourse**; religious devotional literature; writings about philanthropy; and the **modernist** Southern literature of the **grotesque** as developed by writers such as William Faulkner, Carson McCullers, and Flannery O'Connor.

A number of seminal texts and collections **theorizing** disability were published in the 1990s: Lennard J. Davis's *Enforcing Normalcy: Disability, Deafness, and the Body* (1995); *The Disability Studies Reader* (1997), edited by Davis; Thomas Couser's *Recovering Bodies: Illness, Disability and Life Writing* (1997); Rosemarie Garland-Thomson's *Extraordinary Bodies: Figuring Physical Disability in American Culture and Literature* (1997); Simi Linton's *Claiming Disability: Knowledge and Identity* (1998); Brenda Jo Brueggemann's *Lend Me Your Ear: Rhetorical Constructions of Deafness* (1999); and David T. Mitchell and Sharon L. Snyder's *Narrative Prosthesis: Disability and the Dependencies of Discourse* (2000). Snyder, Brueggemann, and Garland-Thomson subsequently published a collection of critical essays conducting literary analyses entitled *Disability Studies: Enabling the Humanities* (2002). Disability studies is also proliferating in the form of special issues of journals such as *Hypatia, Gay and Lesbian Studies*, and *The National Women's Studies Association Journal*.

Theorizing disability responds not only to the recent emphasis on **discourse analysis**, social **constructionism**, and the politics of inclusion but also to an increasing scholarly interest in representations of the body and the relationship of those representations to **subjectivity** and identity. Efforts to recover the history of disabled people are part of the shift in the practice of social history from studying the powerful and the elite to focusing on the previously marginalized. Political activism, as embodied by the rallying cry "nothing about us without us," and bids to reclaim old derogatory terms such as "cripple" and "gimp" likewise aim to empower the disabled. Finally, emphasis on the importance of integrating disability and the disabled into society at large and into the curriculum and the classroom more specifically furthers the commitment to acknowledging and serving underrepresented populations.

▶ **discourse:** Used specifically, (1) the thoughts, statements, or **dialogue** of individuals, especially of **characters** in a literary work; (2) the words in, or **text** of, a **narrative** as opposed to its story line; or (3) a "strand" within a given narrative that promotes a certain point or value system. Discourse of the first type is sometimes categorized as *direct, indirect,* or *free indirect.* In direct discourse, the **narrator** relates the thoughts and utterances of others in an unfiltered way, typically by using quotes. (She thought, "Maybe I should take an umbrella.") In indirect discourse, the narrator takes a more independent approach, reporting — and sometimes paraphrasing — what characters think or say. (She thought that it might be a good idea to take an umbrella.) Free indirect discourse combines elements of direct discourse and indirect discourse, giving the reader a sense of being inside a character's head without actually quoting his or her thoughts or statements. (She thought that perhaps she should take an umbrella.)

More generally, *discourse* refers to the terms, methods, and **conventions** employed in discussing a subject or area of knowledge or transacting a certain kind of business. Human knowledge is collected and structured in discourses. Theology, law, and medicine are defined by their discourses, as are politics, **sexuality**, and **literary criticism.**

Contemporary literary critics have maintained that society is generally made up of a number of different discourses or *discourse communities,* one or more of which may be dominant or serve the dominant **ideology.** Each discourse has its own **vocabulary**, concepts, and rules — knowledge of which constitutes power. The French **psychoanalytic** theorist Jacques Lacan treated the unconscious as a form of discourse, the patterns of which are repeated in literature. **Cultural critics,** following Soviet critic Mikhail Bakhtin, use the word **dialogic** to analyze the dialogue between discourses that takes place within language or, more specifically, a literary text.

Some **poststructuralists** have used *discourse* in lieu of *text* to refer to any verbal structure, whether literary or not. Poststructuralists who emphasize discourse often do so in an attack on the **deconstructive** concept of the *general text,* Algerian-born French deconstructor Jacques Derrida's idea that *"there is nothing outside the text."* Discourse, they argue, is influenced by specific historical circumstances, including social and cultural factors.

▶ **discourse analysis:** An approach to literature developed in the 1970s that examines how language is used in more-or-less continuous **discourse,** that is, in a running spoken or written conversation or **dialogue.** Practitioners of discourse analysis, unlike critics using conventional **linguistics** or **stylistics,** concentrate on the larger pattern of discourse (the language, or totality of words, used in a given passage or conversation), rather than on smaller linguistic units such as individual words or phrases.

Speech-act theorist H. P. Grice played a major role in the development of discourse analysis. In his 1975 essay "Logic and Conversation," Grice coined the phrase **communicative presumption** to refer to the set of assumptions that he claimed are shared by speakers of any given language. These assumptions, Grice argued, form the baseline from and the framework within which we interpret what we read and hear. How we interpret any given statement depends on how it conforms — or fails to conform — to our expectations. Other language theorists have further explored Grice's **theory** of the communicative presumption, identifying a number of shared assumptions that function to make discourse comprehensible and meaningful. Such assumptions include the supposition that the speaker or writer seeks to communicate with others and thus employs language in a deliberate manner in accordance with commonly accepted rules and **conventions,** as well as the supposition that the meaning of any given statement can vary and must be examined in light of the situation at hand. What is a threat in one circumstance ("You're going to get it") may be a promise in another.

Discourse analysis has influenced the practice of stylistics as well as critical examination of dialogue in literary works. Those who analyze dialogue often seek to demonstrate how **characters** and readers alike infer meanings from utterances when those meanings are not directly revealed. Such critics typically draw on Grice's theory, arguing that these inferences also depend on a set of shared assumptions, the agreement with or breach of which determines how a given phrase is interpreted. Discourse analysis has had particular impact on **dialogic criticism,** whose practitioners examine the way in which contrary **voices** representing opposed social, political, and cultural viewpoints or perspectives often compete within **polyphonic** works. The multiple voices of a polyphonic work include those of the characters and, of course, the narrator's "authoritative" voice (which often, but not always, represents the prevailing or "official" **ideology** of the **author's** culture).

Influential discourse analysts include Malcolm Coulthard, Teun A. van Dijk, and Walter Kintsch.

▶ **discursive formation:** See *epistémé.*

▶ **dissemination:** Literally, "the sowing of seeds," usually used more generally to refer to other forms of scattering or dispersal, such as in the expression "the dissemination of ideas." In traditional **literary criticism,** the term *dissemination* has sometimes been used to refer to the way in which earlier works **influence** later ones across the generations, almost as if words were seeds carried by the winds of time from one literary era to the next.

More recently, *dissemination* has been used quite differently to refer to the way in which the meaning of a given word scatters, spreads, or disperses. This usage implies that any word or word-cluster inevitably means different things to different readers, in part because every word has a complex **etymology** and is embedded in a web of diverse (and often contradictory) **connotations.** Jacques Derrida, the Algerian-born French theorist of **deconstruction,** wrote about this kind of linguistic dissemination, arguing that competing linguistic forces render the meaning of any utterance indeterminable. According to Derrida, the act of using language inevitably produces a "surplus" and "spilling" of meaning that preclude the definite ascension of any one meaning over another. For this reason, deconstructors have spoken of the **undecidability** of the **text.**

▶ **dissociation of sensibility:** A phrase used by poet and critic T. S. Eliot in his essay "The Metaphysical Poets" (1921) to refer to a divergence of thought and feeling that he claimed emerged in seventeenth-century En-

glish literature (particularly poetry) after the era of the **metaphysical poets.**
Eliot maintained that earlier writers, especially **Elizabethan** dramatists and
the **Jacobean** poet John Donne, possessed a "direct sensuous apprehension
of thought," a "unification of sensibility" that enabled them to fuse heterogeneous ideas into a whole. As Eliot explained:

> When a poet's mind is perfectly equipped for its work, it is con-
> stantly amalgamating disparate experience; the ordinary man's expe-
> rience is chaotic, irregular, fragmentary. The latter falls in love, or
> reads Spinoza, and these two experiences have nothing to do with
> each other, or with the noise of the typewriter or the smell of cooking;
> in the mind of the poet these experiences are always forming new
> wholes.

Eliot traced the dissociation of sensibility in part to John Milton and John
Dryden, whom he claimed "performed certain poetic functions so magnifi-
cently well that the magnitude of the effect concealed the absence of others." According to Eliot, few subsequent poets attained the unified poetic
sensibility characteristic of the metaphysical poets and their predecessors.
They thought or felt but were unable to fuse intellect and emotion, and for
many "while the language became more refined, the feeling became more
crude." Alfred, Lord Tennyson, and Robert Browning, Eliot wrote, "are
poets, and they think; but they do not feel their thought as immediately as
the odour of a rose." By contrast, Eliot viewed **modernist** poets as heirs returning to the unified tradition.

Following Eliot, the **New Critics** borrowed the term *dissociation of sensibility* and used it widely, but since the 1950s, this notion has come under
attack. Those who still agree with Eliot's theory point not to Milton and
Dryden but, rather, to the advent of scientific rationalism as the cause of
the dissociation of sensibility. Less sympathetic critics claim that Eliot manufactured the doctrine to justify his own literary tastes and sociopolitical
views (namely, his dissatisfaction with the course of English history since
the mid-seventeenth century). Some critics also argue that dissociation of
sensibility can be found in the works of poets who wrote long before the
metaphysical poets and that other unified sensibilities have existed since
their time.

▶ **dissonance:** Harsh, discordant sounds. Some scholars use the terms *dissonance* and **cacophony** synonymously, but others differentiate them, using
the latter to refer to harsh or discordant sounds themselves and the former
to refer to the use of cacophony to achieve a specific effect.

EXAMPLE: Dissonance in "The Lay of Ike," the twenty-third of John
Berryman's *77 Dream Songs* (1964), signals political opposition to President
Dwight D. Eisenhower:

> This is the lay of Ike.
> Here's to the glory of the Great White — awk —
> who has been running — er — er — things in recent — ech —

in the United — If your screen is black,
ladies & gentlemen, we — I like —
at the Point he was already terrific — sick

to a second term, having done no wrong —
no right — no right — having let the Army — bang —
defend itself from Joe, let venom' Strauss
bile Oppenheimer out of use — use Robb,
who'll later fend for Goldfine — Breaking no laws,
he lay in the White House — sob!! — . . .

See also **cacophony**.

▶ **distance:** See **aesthetic distance**.

▶ **dithyramb:** Originally a wild **hymn** sung by a **chorus** in honor of Dionysus (the Greek god of wine); now a term applied to any highly spirited,
zealous, or frenzied speech or writing. While its origins are debated, the
dithyramb appeared in ancient Greece around the seventh century B.C., was
given its traditional literary form by the poet Arion (c. 600 B.C.), and became the subject of competitions during festivals around the fifth century
B.C. Many scholars trace the development of Greek **tragedy** to the dithyramb, which continued as a form in its own right.
  EXAMPLES: John Dryden's *Alexander's Feast* (1697), a **stanza** of which
follows:

> The praise of Bacchus then the sweet musician sung,
> Of Bacchus ever fair and ever young:
> The jolly god in triumph comes;
> Sound the trumpets, beat the drums;
> Flushed with a purple grace
> He shows his honest face;
> Now give the hautboys° breath; he comes, he comes!   *oboes*
> Bacchus, ever fair and young
> Drinking joys did first ordain;
> Bacchus' blessings are a treasure,
> Drinking is a soldier's pleasure;
> Rich the treasure,
> Sweet the pleasure
> Sweet is pleasure after pain.

The opening lines of "Jazz to Jackson to John" (1988), by Jerry W.
Ward, Jr., provide a more modern (but similarly musical) example of
dithyrambic verse:

> it must have been something like
> sheets of sound wrinkled
> with riffs and scats,
> the aftermath of a fierce night
> breezing through the grits and gravy;
> or something like a blind leviathan
> squeezing through solid rock,

marking chaos in the water
when his lady of graveyard love went
turning tricks on the ocean's bottom;
or something like a vision
so blazing basic, so gutbucket, so blessed
the lowdown blues flew out: jazz

▶ **doggerel:** Poorly written or crude **verse** that usually has a humorous quality, a rough or irregular **style,** and a **sentimental** or trite subject. Doggerel may be intentional (for comic effect) or unintentional (due to the poet's ineptitude).

EXAMPLE: The following **stanza** from James Whitcomb Riley's "The Doctor" (1907) is unintentional doggerel:

He is the master of emotions — he
Is likewise certain of that mastery, —
Or dare he face contagion in its ire,
Or scathing fever in its leaping fire?
He needs must smile upon the ghastly face
That yearns up toward him in that warded place
Where even the Saint-like Sisters' lips grow dumb.
Why not idealize the Doctor some?

Today, doggerel routinely circulates on the Internet, such as through email "forwards."

▶ **domesticity:** An aspect of the **patriarchal,** nineteenth-century doctrine of separate spheres, according to which a woman's place was in the privacy of the home whereas a man's place was in the wider, public world. Domesticity implied a wide range of "feminine" attitudes, behaviors, and character traits that were especially expected of middle- and upper-class women and that stood in stark contrast to the attitudes and activities (such as adventure, commerce, and intellectual inquiry) associated with "masculine" life.

In **Victorian** England, the phrase "angel in the house" was used to refer to the domestic ideal of womanhood. The phrase conjured up the image of a dutiful young wife and mother who embodied the virtues of marital fidelity, patience, kindness, self-control, submissiveness, and Christian charity. This ideal, domestic woman not only provided her children with a moral and religious education but also sought to make the family home a cheerful refuge for her hardworking husband. Sarah Stickney Ellis described this latter aspect of a woman's domestic duty in her book *The Women of England: Their Social Duties and Domestic Habits* (1858), in which she explained that women should provide a "relief from the severer duties of life" so that men can "pursue the necessary avocation of the day" while "keep[ing] as it were a separate soul for his family, his social duty, and his God."

Domesticity and the larger doctrine of separate spheres for men and women implied by the domestic ideal are relevant to literature and literary study for a number of reasons, many of which have been identified by practitioners of **feminist** and **gender criticism.** For one thing, the ideal of domestic femininity made it extremely difficult for women to become writers. Young women being prepared for a life of nurturing others within the home received a very different kind of education than young men preparing for life outside its confines, and women who *did* manage to read widely and hone their writing skills were discouraged from pursuing writing careers, since writing was understood to be a public, and therefore masculine, activity. Furthermore, because writers tend to draw on their own knowledge and experience, many women who managed to write and publish in spite of societal discouragement confined themselves to domestic subjects and were careful to conform to stylistic proprieties. More ambitious women writers, such as the Brontë sisters, chose to publish their works under male **pseudonyms.**

In addition to having affected women's careers as writers, the values associated with domesticity are evident in the content of nineteenth-century fiction and poetry. Nineteenth-century novels such as Jane Austen's *Emma* (1815) and Charlotte Brontë's *Jane Eyre* (1847) reflect the prevailing social view that, for a proper young woman, one of the few acceptable alternatives to being a wife and mother was the undesirable job of governess — a mother and teacher rolled into one, a kind of substitute angel in some rich person's great house. Poets, as well as novelists of the period, tended to depict women who were *not* wives, mothers, dutiful daughters, or good governesses as evil homewreckers (or even nation-wreckers). As Nina Auerbach argued in *Woman and the Demon: The Life of a Victorian Myth* (1982), "women exist only as spiritual extremes: there is no human norm of womanhood, for she has no home on earth, but only among divine or demonic essences." Thus, the "loose woman" — as depicted by William Makepeace Thackeray (in *Vanity Fair* [1848]), Alfred, Lord Tennyson (in *Idylls of the King* [1859]), and Dante Gabriel Rossetti (in his poem "Jenny" [1870]) is only the flip side of the angel in the house, a dark manifestation of the **ideology** governing the doctrine of separate spheres and the ideal of domesticity.

The cult of domesticity, however, was not just manifested in literary works; it pervaded nineteenth-century political **discourse** more broadly, as exemplified in the Supreme Court's 1876 majority opinion that one Myra Bradwell, though qualified in every way except sex, should not be allowed to practice law in the state of Illinois. "The civil law," Justice Bradley wrote,

> as well as nature herself, has always recognized a wide difference in the respective spheres and destinies of man and woman. Man is, or should be, woman's protector and defender. The natural and proper timidity and delicacy which belongs to the female sex evidently unfits it for many of the occupations of civil life. The constitution of the family organization, which is founded in the divine ordinance, as well as the nature of things, indicates the domestic sphere as that which properly belongs to the domain and functions of womanhood. The harmony, not to say identity, of interests and views which belong or should belong to the family institution, is repugnant to the idea of a woman adopting a distinct and independent career from that of her

husband. . . . The paramount destiny and mission of woman are to fulfill the noble and benign offices of wife and mother. This is the law of the Creator.

▶ **domestic tragedy:** A type of **tragedy,** a **play** concerning an ordinary person facing a domestic disaster. Domestic tragedy differs from traditional **classical** and **Renaissance** tragedies, which depicted a high-born **hero** facing an extraordinary challenge and falling from a great height. The **genre** is sometimes called *bourgeois tragedy,* although this term is a misnomer, since the **protagonist** can come from the lower as well as middle **class.**

Domestic tragedy emerged during the **Renaissance Period** in English literature, particularly the **Elizabethan** and Jacobean Ages, with dramas written in **verse** such as the anonymous *Arden of Faversham* (1592); Thomas Heywood's *A Woman Killed with Kindness* (1603); and *A Yorkshire Tragedy* (1608), likely written by Thomas Middleton. It was later developed by eighteenth-century writers, most notably George Lillo, an English dramatist whose play *The London Merchant* (1731) was written in **prose** and concerned the seduction, exploitation, and moral destruction of a naive apprentice by a greedy prostitute. Domestic tragedies of the period exhibited considerable **sentimentalism,** playing on the emotions of pity and sympathy to a degree that modern audiences find excessive. Nonetheless, the basic vision of domestic tragedy — the painful, unsuccessful struggle of common people against the vicissitudes of daily domestic or social situations — persisted well into the twentieth century.

FURTHER EXAMPLES: Henrik Ibsen's *A Doll's House* (1897); Eugene O'Neill's *The Iceman Cometh* (1939); Tennessee Williams's *The Glass Menagerie* (1944); Arthur Miller's *Death of a Salesman* (1948), featuring **antihero** Willy Loman, whose name reflects both his social class and personal situation.

▶ **dormant metaphor:** See **dead metaphor.**

▶ **double dactyl:** See **dactyl.**

▶ **double rhyme: Feminine rhyme** involving two syllables in which the rhyming **stressed** syllable of each word is followed by an identical unstressed syllable. *Double rhyme* is often used as a synonym for *feminine rhyme* but is better classified as a type of feminine rhyme.

EXAMPLES: *Daughter/slaughter* and *rowing/showing* are double rhymes, as is *glider/divider,* since each pair of words has a rhyming stressed syllable followed by an identical unstressed syllable that ends the word. The first and third lines and the second and fourth lines of George Dillon's poem "The World Goes Turning" (1926) exemplify double rhyme:

> The world goes turning,
> Slowly lunging,
> Wrapped in churning
> Winds and plunging
> Rains.

▶ **drama:** In today's usage, a serious literary work usually intended for performance before an audience. From the Greek *dran*, meaning "to do," drama as we know it is generally believed to have arisen from unrelated ancient Greek and **medieval** Christian religious ceremonies. Greek **comedy** originated in fertility rites, Greek **tragedy** (the word means "goat song") in rites of sacrifice. Following the decline of Rome, which had adopted the Greek dramatic tradition (but not its religious associations), drama virtually disappeared in the West, although miming and other ceremonies influenced by Greek comedy and tragedy may have kept a certain consciousness of drama alive. Medieval drama appears to have arisen independently in Western Europe from Christian rituals commemorating the birth, death, and resurrection of Jesus. With the advent of the **Renaissance** came the rediscovery of **classical** works and a fusion of classical and medieval traditions and **conventions.**

The term *drama* originally encompassed all works, whether **prose** or **verse,** written to be performed onstage. Beginning with mid-eighteenth-century French productions of plays by Denis Diderot, however, the term came to be applied specifically to serious (as opposed to comic) plays that, whether they end happily or unhappily, treat some important (nontrivial) issue or difficulty. This usage is common today, although tragedy and comedy are still often defined as the two major divisions of drama. In addition, contemporary usage permits the term *drama* to be applied to a wide range of serious works. Thus the movies *The Shawshank Redemption* (1994), *A Beautiful Mind* (2001), and *Mystic River* (2003) are typically classified in the drama section of video stores.

Although **play** is the most common synonym for *drama,* a play is a drama intended for performance. Thus, although all plays are, broadly speaking, dramas, not all dramas are plays. W. H. Auden's *The Sea and the Mirror* (1944) and *For the Time Being* (1944) — though they involve **acts, characters,** and **dialogue** — are correctly referred to as **closet dramas,** not as plays, because they are meant to be read as poems rather than to be seen in a theater by an audience.

See also **play.**

▶ **drama of sensibility:** See **sentimental comedy.**

▶ **dramatic illusion:** See **aesthetic distance.**

▶ **dramatic irony:** See **irony.**

▶ **dramatic monologue:** A **lyric poem** in which the speaker addresses a silent listener, revealing himself or herself in the context of a dramatic situation. The speaker provides information not only about his or her personality but also about the time, the **setting,** key events, and any other **characters** involved in the situation at hand.

EXAMPLES: Robert Browning's "The Bishop Orders His Tomb" (1845), T. S. Eliot's "The Love Song of J. Alfred Prufrock" (1917).

▶ **dramatis personae:** The cast of **characters**. In a play (and sometimes in other works such as novels), a listing of all the characters generally precedes the **text** and is included in the programs passed out at live performances. Sometimes the list also includes short descriptions of the characters and their relationship to other characters in the work.

▶ **dream allegory:** See **dream vision**.

▶ **dream vision (dream allegory):** A type of **narrative** in which the **narrator** falls asleep, dreams, and relates the contents of the dream. Dream visions have an **allegorical** aspect (the narrator may meet figures bearing names like Hope or Remembrance, for instance), hence the generally equivalent term *dream allegory*. Dream visions were a popular form of storytelling in the **Middle Ages;** they are less common today.

EXAMPLES: *Le roman de la rose* (*The Romance of the Rose*), initially composed by Guillaume de Lorris around 1230 and expanded by Jean de Meung around 1270, and Dante Alighieri's *Divina commedia* (*The Divine Comedy*) (1321) are famous **medieval** examples. John Keats's "The Fall of Hyperion: A Dream" (1819) and "La belle dame sans merci" (1820) offer **romantic** variations on the form. Lewis Carroll's *Alice's Adventures in Wonderland* (1865) and James Joyce's *Finnegans Wake* (1939) exemplify more modern developments, as does the 1939 movie version of L. Frank Baum's *The Wizard of Oz* (1900). A more recent movie that experiments with the **conventions** of the dream vision is Adrian Lyne's *Jacob's Ladder* (1990). The *Nightmare on Elm Street* series (1984–) of "slasher" movies also toys with many of the allegorical and narrative conventions of the dream vision.

▶ **dumb show:** See **pantomime**.

▶ **dynamic cutting:** See **montage**.

▶ **dystopia:** From the Greek for "bad place," the opposite of a **utopia**. A dystopia is usually set at some point in the author's future and describes a nightmarish society in which few would want to live. Writers presenting dystopias generally want to alert readers to the potential pitfalls and dangers of society's present course or of a course society might conceivably take one day. Accounts of dystopias inevitably conclude by depicting unpleasant, disastrous, or otherwise terrifying consequences for the **protagonists** as well as for humanity as a whole.

EXAMPLES: George Orwell's *1984*, written in 1948, describes a society in which "Big Brother" is always watching and in which one party not only governs a territory called Oceania (presumably North America, South America, and at least part of Europe) but also attempts to control everyone and everything within it. The government tries to monitor thought using organizations such as "thinkpol" (the Thought Police) and tortures and brainwashes anyone who exhibits even a shred of independent thought or hostility to the Party.

Margaret Atwood's novel *The Handmaid's Tale* (1985), in which women of the future have lost their personal freedoms, also depicts a dystopia. Women are slotted into male-controlled categories: wives, servants (Marthas), breeders (handmaids), and women who enforce the repression of their peers (Aunts). They are denied access to printed material to enforce their mental as well as physical repression, and those who won't cooperate are shipped off to the Colonies to perform hazardous labor (cleaning up after nuclear accidents or toxic spills).

E

▶ **early modern:** A term that began to be used, with considerable variation, in the latter half of the twentieth century by some historians, linguists, and literary scholars to refer to a period beginning around the latter half of the fifteenth century in Western Europe and extending to some point between the mid-seventeenth century and the end of the eighteenth century. Significant developments in the early modern period, which roughly bridged the Middle Ages and the Industrial Revolution, included the decline of feudalism; the invention of the printing press; the discovery of the Americas; the Protestant Reformation; the rise of modern science; the establishment of nation states, often with associated empires; and the emergence of modern capitalism, through the protectionist economic system of mercantilism. With capitalism came a non-aristocratic merchant class able to patronize the arts, literature, and other realms that had earlier been financially supported and controlled by the aristocracy and the Church.

The term *early modern period* is often used to refer to the **Renaissance,** but this usage is misleading. *Renaissance* is a cultural marker **denoting** the rebirth of learning, literature, and the other arts that began at different times in different regions of Europe, whereas *early modern* is a term more appropriately applied to: (1) a global historical period spanning some three centuries, from about 1500–1800; (2) language as it evolved and became standardized following the **Middle Ages,** with Early Modern English and Early Modern French, for instance, succeeding the **Middle English** and Middle French **linguistic** stages of the late **Medieval Period;** and (3) literature produced in early modern languages, including Niccolò Machiavelli's *Il Principe* (*The Prince*) (written 1513; published 1532), Michel de Montaigne's *Essais* (1580), and Miguel de Cervantes's *Don Quixote* (1605, 1615).

As applied to English literature, the early modern period generally coincides with the **Renaissance Period** in English literature, which extended from 1500–1660, a time of unprecedented and, some would say, unparalleled literary production. The period gave rise to **prose** works such as William Tyndale's translation of the Bible (1525), the **poetry** of Edmund Spenser (1552–99), the **plays** of Christopher Marlowe (1564–93), the poems and plays of William Shakespeare (1564–1616), and the poems and prose of John Donne (1573–1631) and John Milton (1608–1674).

▶ **Early National Period (in American literature):** An era in American literary history roughly spanning the years 1790–1828 that was significantly shaped by the work of building the United States as a new nation. The Early National Period is sometimes referred to as the *Federalist Age* for the conservative federalists who dominated American government from 1789, when the federal government was formed, to 1828, when Andrew Jackson won the presidential election (an event often called the "second revolution").

Jackson, a slaveholder who implemented some brutal policies affecting Native Americans, was widely characterized as a populist, a proponent of frontier individualism, and a champion of the common people.

While writers of the preceding **Colonial** and **Revolutionary Periods** tended to **imitate** English precursors, more distinctively American voices began to emerge in most **genres** during the Early National Period. Except in **drama,** a relatively independent and **imaginative** literature began to arise as the nation developed, marking a shift from the **didactic** or polemical character of much prior "American" writing. William Cullen Bryant is perhaps the best-known poet of the time; Edgar Allan Poe began his literary career toward the end of the period, with *Tamerlane and Other Poems* (1827). Washington Irving, an essayist and storyteller, is perhaps the best-known prose writer, with works such as *A History of New-York* (1809), published under the **pseudonym** Diedrich Knickerbocker, and *The Sketch-Book of Geoffrey Crayon* (1819–20), which included "The Legend of Sleepy Hollow" and "Rip Van Winkle." Moreover, in 1815, the first long-running American magazine, the *North American Review* (1815–1940; 1964–), was established.

Novels, most of which were **sentimental** or **Gothic**, also began to flourish during the Early National Period. Sentimental novels generally claimed to set forth a "true" story for the purpose of moral instruction in general and for warning young ladies of the perils of seduction in particular. Examples include Susanna Rowson's *Charlotte: A Tale of Truth* (1791), later retitled *Charlotte Temple;* Hannah Webster Foster's *The Coquette* (1797); and Catharine Maria Sedgwick's *Hope Leslie: or, Early Times in the Massachusetts* (1827). Gothic novels, such as Charles Brockden Brown's *Wieland* (1798), were characterized by their focus on the **grotesque** or supernatural and their preoccupation with doom, **horror, mystery,** passion, and **suspense.** James Fenimore Cooper took a different path, inaugurating **spy fiction** with *The Spy* (1821) and beginning his Leatherstocking Tales, a series of five novels featuring frontiersman Natty Bumppo, with *The Pioneers* (1823) and *The Last of the Mohicans* (1826).

Other notable works of the period included descriptive accounts of life on the frontier and Noah Webster's *An American Dictionary of the English Language* (1828).

▶ **Early Tudor Age (in English literature):** The first of five literary eras within the **Renaissance Period** in English literature, an age generally said to have begun in 1500 and ended in 1558 with the coronation of Elizabeth I. The Early Tudor Age is best known for its poetry and nonfiction prose, although Nicholas Udall's *Ralph Roister Doister,* often referred to as the first dramatic comedy in English, was initially performed in 1553.

John Skelton, the first major poet of the age, began his career **imitating** the work of **medieval** poet Geoffrey Chaucer but later developed an original, **satirical** style that he turned on both church and state. Later poets of note include Sir Thomas Wyatt — who imitated and translated poems (especially **sonnets**) he read while on diplomatic missions to Italy, France, and Spain — and Henry Howard, the Earl of Surrey. Surrey is generally credited with being the first English poet to: (1) write in **blank verse,** which he encountered in an Italian translation of Virgil's *The Aeneid* and used in his own English translation (c. 1540) of that ancient Roman **epic**; and (2) adapt the **Italian,** or **Petrarchan, sonnet** to the English language, turning it from a poem consisting of an (eight-line) **octave** followed by a (six-line) **sestet** into a form characterized by three (four-line) **quatrains** plus one (two-line) **couplet.** (This **English sonnet,** first developed by Surrey during the Early Tudor Age, came to be called the **Shakespearean sonnet** during the **Elizabethan Age.**) Important prose works of the Early Tudor Age include Sir Thomas Elyot's *The Boke Named the Governour* (1531), which describes the cultivation of a gentleman (highlighting especially the essential role of Greek and Roman **classics** in a proper education), and Sir Thomas More's *Utopia,* written in Latin in 1516 but not published in English until 1551. More's work, which depicts life in a **utopian** land where reason and justice prevail, shows the **influence** of Plato's *The Republic* (c. 360 B.C.).

Writers of the Early Tudor Age characteristically focused on the relationship between the individual and the state, respected and used **classical** works, and tended to import and adapt classically influenced literary forms from other countries, as did those of the Renaissance Period in English literature and the **Renaissance** in general.

See also **Renaissance.**

▶ **eclogue:** From the Greek for "selection," a short, formal, typically **pastoral poem** written as a **monologue** or **dialogue.** The term *eclogue* originally referred more broadly to any choice poem or extract but came to have a more limited meaning with its application to the Roman poet Virgil's *Bucolics* (c. 40 B.C.), a collection of pastoral poems featuring shepherds conversing or singing alone or in pairs. Virgil modeled his poems after the *Idylls* of Theocritus, a third-century B.C. Greek poet who romanticized rustic life in the Sicilian countryside; he adapted elements including the idealized rural setting, singing contests, and the use of **refrains,** thereby establishing several **conventions** of the **genre.** Traditional eclogues **privilege** sentiment, **form,** and **setting** over **action** and **characterization** and often concern love or death. Common forms include the singing contest between two shepherds, the shepherd's song of courtship, the shepherd's song of frustrated or distressed love, and the lament for a dead shepherd.

The eclogue declined after ancient Roman times until the **Renaissance,** when the poets Dante Alighieri, Petrarch, and Boccaccio renewed interest in the genre. The *Eclogues* (1498) of Mantuan (Baptista Mantuanus Spagnuoli), written in Latin, were particularly influential. Other noted writers of eclogues were the Spanish poet Garcilaso de la Vega and English poets Edmund Spenser and John Milton, both of whom wrote "golden-age eclogues," a messianic form that typically features a child who brings about a regeneration of nature and the return of a **golden age.** Over time, the eclogue was extended to nonpastoral subjects, such as fishermen and city life, and the term came to be distinguished from *pastoral,* the former indicating the **dramatic** form of a poem and the latter referring to its **sentimental** content.

Since the eighteenth century, nonpastoral eclogues have been written on a variety of subjects to express social and political commentary, but the form has generally been in decline since the **Romantic Period.**

EXAMPLES: Edmund Spenser's *The Shepheardes Calendar* (1579) contains twelve pastoral eclogues, one for each month of the year. Perhaps the best-known nonpastoral eclogue is Jonathan Swift's "A Town Eclogue. 1710. Scene, The Royal Exchange" (1710). Percy Bysshe Shelley introduced "Rosalind and Helen: A Modern Eclogue" (1819) by advising readers that "[t]he story of *Rosalind and Helen* is, undoubtedly, not an attempt in the highest style of poetry. It is in no degree calculated to excite profound meditation; and if by interesting affections and amusing the imagination, it awakens a certain ideal melancholy favorable to the reception of more important impressions, it will produce in the reader all that the writer experienced in the composition."

W. H. Auden's long poem *The Age of Anxiety: A Baroque Eclogue* (1947) describes four **characters** representing diverse personality types (or, perhaps, mental faculties) seeking to journey from the modern condition of alienation, decay, and despair to a state of rejuvenation and harmonious reconciliation. Instead of traversing **conventionally** pastoral rural scenery, they pass through landscapes **symbolically** suggestive of human anatomy.

▶ **ecocriticism:** A type of **literary criticism,** sometimes popularly referred to as *green criticism,* that focuses on the relationship between nature and literature. Ecocriticism, which arose in the U.S. and is grounded in ecology, natural history, and environmental studies, examines how people interact with nature and how these interactions inform and are forged by symbolic **representations** of nature. Ecocriticism often involves the study of *nature writing,* which, as a **genre,** refers to American and European nature-oriented literature dating back to Henry David Thoreau's *Walden* (1854). Ecocritics frequently analyze: (1) the relationship between literary representations of nature and human interactions with the natural world; and (2) the role of literature and language in furthering or hindering agendas for changing humanity's relationship with the natural environment. Unlike other approaches to literary criticism, ecocriticism addresses the relationship between writers, **texts,** and the world from a truly global perspective — one in which the "world" is the entire ecosphere, not just human society.

The term *ecocriticism,* coined by William Rueckert in 1978 in an essay entitled "Literature and Ecology: An Experiment in Ecocriticism," did not gain currency in critical **discourse** until 1989, when Cheryll Glotfelty, a leading theorist in the field, suggested referring to all ecologically informed literary criticism as ecocriticism. Because ecocriticism involves a shared frame of reference rather than a particular methodology or **theoretical** perspective, some practitioners refer to their work as "ecological literary criticism," "the study of nature-oriented literature," or "literature-and-environment studies." Most, however, use the term *ecocriticism*. To ecocritics, who are motivated by the conviction that the earth's ecology is precarious — as former U.S. vice president Albert Gore posited in *Earth in the Balance* (1992) — values matter in the most fundamental way.

Several early examples of ecocriticism, dating back to the 1970s, emphasize scientific concepts and employ relatively direct applications of ecological science to literature. Rueckert, for example, used biological concepts to construct what he termed "literary ecology," arguing, for instance, that "poems can be studied as models for energy flow, community building, and ecosystems." Similarly, Joseph Meeker employed physical models of ecosystems to analyze literary **modes** in his book *The Comedy of Survival: Studies in Literary Ecology* (1972).

Ecocritical works from the 1970s and early 1980s that focused on representations of the land, wilderness, and women's relationship to nature, however, ultimately had a greater impact on contemporary ecocriticism than explicitly scientific applications. Influential examples include Annette Kolodny's *The Lay of the Land: Metaphor as Experience and History in American Life and Letters* (1975) and *The Land Before Her: Fantasy and Experience of the American Frontiers, 1630–1860* (1984), both of which discuss representations of land in American culture; Carolyn Merchant's *The Death of Nature: Women, Ecology, and the Scientific Revolution* (1980), which investigates the interplay between representations of women and nature; and Roderick Nash's *Wilderness and the American Mind* (1982), which traces the concept of the wilderness throughout American intellectual and cultural history. Subsequently, in the late 1980s and early 1990s, several anthologies of American nature writing came out, including Thomas J. Lyons's *This Incomperable Lande: A Book of American Nature Writing* (1989), which was prefaced with a piece entitled "A Taxonomy of Nature Writing" that detailed questions about the purpose of the genre.

In 1992, following the emergence of ecocriticism as a movement in literary studies, a group of American scholars established the Association for the Study of Literature and Environment (ASLE) to encourage the exploration of both literary and other cultural representations of human relationships to nature, an aim advanced in part through ASLE's journal *ISLE: Interdisciplinary Studies in Literature and Environment*. Two highly influential works of ecocriticism followed in 1996: *The Ecocriticism Reader: Landmarks in Literary Ecology,* in which Glotfelty and coeditor Harold Fromm mapped the lineage and landscape of ecocriticism, then still largely focused on American nonfiction nature writing or on explicitly nature-oriented fiction and poetry; and Lawrence Buell's *The Environmental Imagination: Thoreau, Nature Writing, and the Formation of American Culture,* which examined Thoreau's influence on American attitudes and writing about the natural world.

Many ecocritics work within one of two related but contrasting theoretical frameworks: *deep ecology* and *ecofeminism*. Deep ecology, first outlined by Norwegian philosopher Arne Naess in his book *Ecology, Community and Lifestyle* (1989), locates the source of contemporary environmental crises in Western **ideologies** characterized by *anthropocentrism,* the tendency to conceive of nonhuman nature primarily in terms of human interests. Deep ecologists advocate a complete return to nature, in contrast to more moderate environmentalists, who emphasize conservation. Deep ecologists, who contend that nature has value in and of itself, should thus be distinguished from social ecologists, who believe that nature must ultimately be approached in light of human needs.

Ecofeminists take an explicitly **feminist** approach to ecocriticism. While ecofeminists, like deep ecologists, locate the source of environmental problems in the tendency to **privilege** human interests, many argue more specifically that *androcentrism,* the tendency to conceive of nonhuman nature in terms of human *male* interests, has led **patriarchal** cultures, particularly in the West, to associate and exploit women and nature. For essays relating environmental problems to androcentric ideologies, see Greta Gaard and Patrick D. Murphy's *Ecofeminist Literary Criticism: Theory, Interpretation, Pedagogy* (1998). For an ecofeminist identification and analysis of women's contributions to natural history and nature writing, see Very Norwood's *Made from This Earth: American Women and Nature* (1993).

Some ecocritics incorporate **poststructuralism,** which addresses the relationship between our experience of the material world and the language we use to describe that world, into their analyses. For instance, SueEllen Campbell's 1989 essay "The Land and Language of Desire: Where Deep Ecology and Post-Structuralism Meet" describes the inherent tension between ecocritics' concern with the material effects of the relationship between language and the natural environment and poststructuralist views on how language mediates and even creates all of our experiences (including our experience of the material world). Neil Evernden's book *The Social Creation of Nature* (1992), as well as the essays collected in Michael E. Soule and Gary Lease's *Reinventing Nature?: Responses to Postmodern Deconstruction* (1995), likewise deal with issues involving nature, language, and poststructuralist theory.

Ecocritics also draw on **rhetorical** theory and on ideas and attitudes growing out of the global environmental justice movement to study political and literary discourse in the context of public debate about environmental problems. M. Jimmie Killingsworth and Jacqueline S. Palmer's *Ecospeak: Rhetoric and Environmental Politics in America* (1992), like many of the essays in Carl Herndl and Stuart C. Brown's *Green Culture: Environmental Rhetoric in Contemporary America* (1996), analyzes public debate about environmental issues such as the spotted owl controversy in the Pacific Northwest.

Some ecocritics, influenced by the personal style of much nature writing, also employ **personal criticism** in analyzing literature. They may extensively discuss their own experiences, and they tend to exhibit the same kind of heightened appreciation of place and community that is the defining feature of many of the works they study. (Indeed, some ecocritics have argued that "place" should be a critical category akin to **race, class,** and **gender.**) For instance, in *Reading the Mountains of Home* (1998), John Elder alternated interpretations of Robert Frost's poem "Directive" with **first-person** accounts of his own life and exploration in Vermont's Green Mountains, where Frost once also lived. Likewise, in *American Indian Literature, Environmental Justice, and Ecocriticism: The Middle Place* (2001), Joni Adamson's **narrative** scholarship places her examination of Native American literature in the context of her personal experience in natural and human communities that have borne the brunt of environmental degradation.

Ecocritics aim to raise environmental consciousness and to remind us of our dependence on the earth and its resources. Aldo Leopold's concept of the "land ethic" — that is, of nature as a part of the community rather than as a commodity — has been particularly influential. Moreover, ecocritics highlight nature's **aesthetic** and **symbolic** value, seeking to show that nature is far more than the object of scientific scrutiny. Many ecocritics even regard science as something of an enemy, particularly insofar as technology has contributed to environmental degradation. Common **themes** in ecocritical analyses include the interrelation of all elements in an ecosystem (from natural phenomena to social and political factors), the need to monitor technologies and to pursue sustainable means of living, the quest for environmental justice, and the interconnections between nature and culture. As Glotfelty explains in the introduction to *The Ecocriticism Reader,* "all ecological criticism shares the fundamental premise that human culture is connected to the physical world, affecting it and affected by it." While some practitioners of **cultural studies** have reduced nature to little more than a linguistic construct, one among many texts for analysis, ecocritics counter that all human culture exists in the natural world and that any human act affecting nature ultimately affects culture.

Ecocritics also aim to establish a "green" **canon,** so to speak, by identifying the **classics** of nature writing, offering ecological readings of these texts, and explaining why the texts and readings matter. Aside from Thoreau's *Walden,* which offers an intensely personal take on living in harmony with nature, key works of nature writing often studied by ecocritics include Mary Austin's *Land of Little Rain* (1903), Aldo Leopold's *A Sand County Almanac* (1949), Rachel Carson's *Silent Spring* (1962), Edward Abbey's *Desert Solitaire* (1968), Annie Dillard's *Pilgrim at Tinker Creek* (1974), Barry Lopez's *Arctic Dreams* (1986), Gary Snyder's *Practice of the Wild* (1990), and Terry Tempest Williams's *Refuge* (1991). Several nature poets, including Snyder, Wendell Berry, W. S. Merwin, and Mary Oliver, have also been the subject of ecocritical attention. Notably, all of these writers are American, a focus likely due both to ecocriticism's American origins and to the perception that *Walden* launched nature writing as a genre.

Recently, ecocritics have recognized the need for ecocritical studies of works both in other literary arenas and in other art forms and national and cultural contexts. Nature has played a key role in the art, literature, and culture of many peoples around the world since ancient times; **pastoral** works dating back to the ancient Greeks, for instance, glorified rural environments, and **Romantic** works from the late 1700s and early 1800s extolled nature's divinity and deplored the mechanization of society associated with the Industrial Revolution. Karla Armbruster and Kathleen R. Wallace's *Beyond Nature Writing: Expanding the Boundaries of Ecocriticism* (2001) features essays discussing works dating from **medieval** Europe to the present day and ranging from traditionally canonical texts to virtual/cyber landscapes. J. Scott Bruson's *Ecopoetry: A Critical Introduction* (2002) examines the role of nature in Western poetry and assembles scholarly inquiries into the roots of *ecopoetry* (a type of nature poetry that addresses environmental issues and concerns) as well as into recurrent themes such as extinction, genocide, **postcolonialism,** and the female and lesbian body. Murphy's *Farther Afield in the Study of Nature-Oriented Literature* (2000) looks beyond Euro-American literary traditions to survey African, Asian, Australian, and South American works, and Terrell Dixon highlights urban environments in *City Wilds: Essays and Stories about Urban Nature* (2002).

Chicano and Chicana literature has been a particularly fertile ground for nature writing and ecocriticism. In *Borderlands/La Frontera: The New Mestiza* (1987), Gloria Anzaldúa testified to the exploitative and destructive effect of patriarchal values on the land and on Mexicans living on both sides of the United States–Mexico border. In *The Brushlands* (1997), Arturo Longoria discussed the devastation of brushlands along the border, as well as the effects of this destruction on the human spirit. Other Chicano and Chicana texts that highlight the link between environmental degradation and marginalization along economic, ethnic, and class lines include Rudolfo Anaya's novel *Bless Me, Ultima* (1971) and the works of two ecofeminists: Ana Castillo's *So Far from God* (1993) and Helena María Viramontes's *Under the Feet of Jesus* (1995).

▶ **ecofeminism:** See **ecocriticism.**

▶ **ecopoetry:** See **ecocriticism.**

▶ *écriture* **(writing):** See **text.**

▶ *écriture féminine:* See **feminist criticism.**

▶ **Edwardian Age (in English literature):** A brief era in English literary history spanning the years 1901–1914 and named for Edward VII, whose reign began with the death of Queen Victoria in 1901 and ended in 1910, four years before the outbreak of World War I. The Edwardian Age is often seen as a "long sunlit afternoon," a **golden age** of innocence, leisure, style, and opulence that bridged the gap between the **Victorian Period,** when England reached the height of its power and influence, as reflected by the phrase "the sun never sets on the British Empire," and the **Modern Period**, which was born in the ensuing chaos, death, and destruction of the Great War. Yet the era was also one in which people began to question the existing social order, including the "upstairs downstairs" system of rigid **class** distinctions, the stark gap between rich and poor, and the unequal standing of women.

Like Victorian literature, the literature of the Edwardian Age encompassed virtually all **forms, genres,** and **styles,** but many writers of the era reacted against what they viewed as the staid attitudes and **conventions** of Victorianism. Prose was dominant, especially prose fiction in the form of novels and short stories. Major prose fiction writers included J. M. Barrie, Arnold Bennett, Joseph Conrad, Ford Madox Ford, John Galsworthy, Thomas Hardy, and H. G. Wells. Barrie and Galsworthy were also playwrights, and notable poets included Hardy, Rudyard Kipling, Alfred Noyes, and Arthur Symons.

Chronological boundaries notwithstanding, the Edwardian Age is relatively unhelpful as a literary category. For one thing, the brevity of the era means that many of the authors associated with it are also associated with the preceding Victorian era or either of two subsequent and overlapping eras, the **Georgian Age** and the Modern Period. (Hardy, whose career extended from 1865 to 1928, is a case in point.) In addition, except for the general reaction against Victorianism, works said to represent the Edwardian Age seem less united by an underlying worldview and **aesthetic** than the works generally affiliated with many other literary eras or movements. Finally, the term *Edwardian* is sometimes also used with reference to American **realist** contemporaries (such as Henry James) as well as Irish writers (such as Isabella Augusta, Lady Gregory; J. M. Synge; and W. B. Yeats) associated with the **Celtic Revival,** a movement intended to revive and promote an indigenous Celtic cultural, literary, and artistic tradition to counter centuries of imperial English domination.

▶ **ego:** See **id.**

▶ *Einfühlung:* See **empathy.**

▶ **ekphrasis (ecphrasis):** The literary, especially poetic, **representation** of or response to a visual work of art, such as a painting or sculpture. A **rhetorical** device, ekphrasis may involve description or analysis of the work itself or may focus on the writer's encounter with and experience of the work. If the work in question is imaginary, the ekphrasis is *notional.*

Ekphrasis was particularly popular among **romantic** and **Pre-Raphaelite** poets, but its use dates back at least to **classical** times, as exemplified by Homer's description of Achilles' shield in the *Iliad* (c. 850 B.C.). Common **conventions** include giving the work of art a "voice," speaking to the work, using a museum as the **setting,** and focusing on the artist's studio.

FURTHER EXAMPLES: John Keats's "Ode on a Grecian Urn" (1820); William Butler Yeats's "Leda and the Swan" (1928), which represents the

Greek **myth** of the seduction of Leda by Zeus in the guise of a swan as rape; John Ashbery's "Self Portrait in a Convex Mirror" (1974), describing sixteenth-century Italian artist Il Parmigianino's use of a convex mirror to paint his own portrait. In his poem "In Santa Maria del Popolo" (1958), poet Thom Gunn described his encounter with Caravaggio's painting *Conversione de San Paolo* (*The Conversion of St. Paul*) (c. 1523–24), asking "what is it you mean / In that wide gesture of the lifting arms?" By contrast, W. H. Auden, responding to Pieter Brueghel's painting *Landscape with the Fall of Icarus* (c. 1554–55) — which itself depicts the Greek myth of Icarus, who fashioned a pair of wings with wax and fell to his death in the sea after flying too close to the sun — mused in "Musée des Beaux-Arts" (1938):

> In Brueghel's *Icarus,* for instance: how everything turns away
> Quite leisurely from the disaster; the ploughman may
> Have heard the splash, the forsaken cry,
> But for him it was not an important failure. . . .

▶ **Electra complex:** See **Oedipus complex.**

▶ **elegy:** In ancient Greek and Roman times, any **poem** composed in elegiac **meter** (pairs of **hexameter** and **pentameter** lines composed primarily of **dactyls**). In **Elizabethan** times, *elegy* was often used to refer to love poems. Since the seventeenth century, the term has typically referred to reflective poems that lament the loss of someone or something (or loss or death more generally) but may also be used even more broadly to refer to any serious, reflective poem. Elegies written in English frequently take the **form** of the **pastoral elegy.**

EXAMPLES: Thomas Gray's "Elegy Written in a Country Churchyard" (1751) is a famous English elegy, as is Alfred, Lord Tennyson's *In Memoriam A. H. H.* (1850). A more modern example is W. H. Auden's "In Memory of W. B. Yeats" (1940). In "A Refusal to Mourn the Death, by Fire, of a Child in London" (1946), Dylan Thomas struggled to resist the temptation to write an "elegy of innocence and youth," concluding his poem with a **stanza** that is, nonetheless, eloquently elegiac in spirit and **tone:**

> Deep with the first dead lies London's daughter,
> Robed in the long friends,
> The grains beyond age, the dark veins of her mother,
> Secret by the unmourning water
> Of the riding Thames.
> After the first death, there is no other.

The following lines by Theodor Seuss Geisel, better known as Dr. Seuss, are likewise elegiac:

> How did it get so late so soon?
> It's night before it's afternoon.
> December is here before it's June.
> My goodness how the time has flewn.
> How did it get so late so soon?

Although *elegy* is not generally used with reference to songs, Don McLean's "American Pie" (1971), which associates the death of singer Buddy Holly with the end of an idealistic and optimistic era, is elegiac in its subject and tone.

▶ **elision:** The omission of part of a word (typically a letter). Elision most commonly involves replacing a word-ending vowel with an apostrophe when it is followed by another word that begins with a vowel. Elision is often employed to make verse more **rhythmic** or to conform to a **metrical** pattern but may also be used in prose.

EXAMPLES: *E'er, o'er*. The line in John Milton's *Paradise Lost* (1667) in which the angel Michael tells Adam "All th'earth he gave thee to possess and rule" involves the omission of the first of two adjacent vowels.

In the first **stanza** of "Beauty" (1656), Abraham Cowley elides (omits) the letter *e* on numerous occasions:

> Beauty, thou wild fantastic ape,
> > Who dost in ev'ry country change thy shape!
> Here black, there brown, here tawny, and there white;
> Thou flatt'rer which compli'st with every sight!
> > Thou Babel which confound'st the eye
> With unintelligible variety!
> > Who hast no certan What, nor Where,
> But vari'st still, and dost thy self declare
> Inconstant, as thy she-possessors are.

▶ **Elizabethan Age:** The second of five literary eras within the **Renaissance Period** in English literature, an age spanning the reign of Elizabeth I (1558–1603) that is often considered the height of the **Renaissance** in England. The Elizabethan Age, which reached its pinnacle with the English navy's victory over the Spanish Armada in 1588, is closely associated with the transnational and transcultural Renaissance, or "rebirth," of Western culture following the **Medieval Period**, the so-called "Dark Ages" of European history. The era is widely viewed as the **golden age** of English drama, having produced playwrights including Christopher Marlowe and William Shakespeare. Poetry and prose also flourished thanks to poets such as Sir Philip Sidney and Edmund Spenser and prose writers such as Francis Bacon and Sir Walter Raleigh.

The term *Elizabethan* is sometimes extended beyond Elizabeth I's reign to include literature, particularly drama, of the **Jacobean Age** or even the **Caroline Age**. Indeed, the phrase *Elizabethan drama* is commonly used to refer to English drama from 1558 to 1642, the year in which the Puritan-dominated Parliament closed all theaters to suppress stage plays. As applied to **authors**, extended use of the term *Elizabethan* may cover both Elizabethan writers (Shakespeare and Bacon included) who also wrote during the subsequent Jacobean Age and authors whose careers were not fully established until the Jacobean era (such as the poet John Donne and the playwright Ben Jonson).

See also **Renaissance**.

▶ **ellipsis:** See **anachrony.**

▶ **empathy (*Einfühlung*):** From the German *Einfühlung*, literally a "feeling into," an involuntary projection of self into an external object, whether animate or inanimate (e.g., a person, animal, place, natural force, or thing), that entails identification with the object. Empathy involves participation in an object's existence to the point of feeling what the object senses or undergoes.

The concept of *Einfühlung*, which entered English-language **literary criticism** in the twentieth century, was initially developed by nineteenth-century German theorists. Some scholars credit German philosopher Rudolf Hermann Lotze with formulating the idea as early as 1858, in the second volume of *Mikrokosmos*. Others trace it to German psychologist Robert Vischer, who developed a psychological **theory** of art, set forth in *Über das optische Formgefühl* (*On the Optical Sense of Form*) (1873), holding that the viewer of a work of art experiences physical and emotional sensations suggested by the work and derives pleasure from the fusion of object and self. Another German psychologist, Theodor Lipps, subsequently elaborated on Vischer's theory of **aesthetic** response in *Ästhetik* (2 vols., 1903–06), an extensive analysis of empathy with examples from the visual arts. A few years later, the concept was imported into English by British-American psychologist Edward Titchener, who translated *Einfühlung* as "empathy" and defined it as "the process of humanizing objects, of feeling ourselves or reading ourselves into them" in *Lectures in Experimental Psychology* (1909).

Empathy should be distinguished from *sympathy,* a term that **connotes** affinity with or compassion for an external object but not identification with it. While most critics distinguish between the "feeling into" of empathy and the "feeling along" of sympathy, some consider the terms to be essentially synonymous.

EXAMPLES: To feel terrified and cower, shoulders hunched, like the hunted **character** in a movie, is to experience empathy, whereas to feel sorry or afraid for the intended victim (but not personally fearful) is to experience sympathy. The many **images** from 9/11 of onlookers holding up their hands as if to keep the World Trade Center towers from collapsing after the terrorist attacks reflect the experience of empathy.

Philip K. Dick's **science-fiction** novel *Do Androids Dream of Electric Sheep?* (1968; adapted to film as *Blade Runner* in 1982) explores empathy as a central **theme,** asking whether empathy is uniquely a human trait. **Protagonist** Rick Deckard, a bounty-hunter tasked with finding and "retiring" rogue androids, uses a "Voigt-Kampff machine," intended to measure the subject's empathic response, to distinguish real humans from their cyborg counterparts. He has to wonder, though, whether he has ever erroneously "retired" a real human, especially once he discovers that some androids are capable of learning empathy.

▶ **encomium (encomiastic):** Originally, a **choral hymn** developed in ancient Greece praising victorious athletes of the Olympic games; later, any ancient Greek work written to glorify people, events, or objects. Today encomiums may take two forms: eulogies for the dead, often delivered at funerals; or **odes** or other types of verse written to celebrate individuals, objects, or **abstract** ideas. Essays or speeches written in praise of a person or group of people are usually referred to as **epideictics** but are sometimes called **prose encomiums.**

EXAMPLES: Pindar's victory odes, such as *Olympian 1* and *2* (476 B.C.); Gorgias's epideictic speech *Encomium of Helen* (late-fifth-century B.C.); Desiderius Erasmus's **satiric** *Encomium moriae* (*In Praise of Folly*) (1509). *Encomium: A Tribute to Led Zeppelin* (1995), a tribute album by bands and artists ranging from Duran Duran to Stone Temple Pilots to Sheryl Crow, offers a contemporary musical twist on the encomium.

▶ **end rhyme:** **Rhyme** that occurs at the end of lines in **verse.** In end rhyme, the most common type of rhyme, the last word of a line rhymes with the last word of another line. End rhyme is distinguished from **internal rhyme,** which occurs within a line of verse.

▶ **end-stopped line:** A line of **poetry** whose meaning is complete in itself and that ends with a grammatical pause marked by punctuation. End-stopped lines are distinguished from *run-on lines,* which exhibit *enjambement.*

EXAMPLES: Each of the four lines of this **stanza** from William Blake's "A Poison Tree" (1794) is end-stopped:

> I was angry with my friend:
> I told my wrath, my wrath did end.
> I was angry with my foe:
> I told it not, my wrath did grow.

In the first stanza of the poem "Oread" (1924) by H. D. (Hilda Doolittle), all but the third and fourth lines (which demonstrate *enjambement*) are end-stopped. The third line is not end-stopped because there is no grammatical pause after the word *pines;* the fourth line is not end-stopped because the meaning of the line is not complete in itself:

> Whirl up, sea, —
> whirl your pointed pines,
> splash your great pines
> on our rocks,
> hurl your green over us,
> cover us with your pools of fir.

▶ **English sonnet (Shakespearean sonnet):** A fourteen-line **sonnet** consisting of three **quatrains** with the **rhyme scheme** *abab cdcd efef,* followed by a **couplet** rhyming *gg.* The **Spenserian sonnet,** developed by English poet Edmund Spenser, follows the same basic **stanzaic** form — three quatrains followed by a couplet — but links the quatrains together by its rhyme scheme: *abab bcbc cdcd ee.*

EXAMPLE: In Sonnet 118 (1609), William Shakespeare approximated the standard rhyme scheme by using **eye rhyme** and **half rhyme**:

> Let me not to the marriage of true minds
> Admit impediments. Love is not love
> Which alters when it alteration finds,
> Or bends with the remover to remove:
> Oh, no! It is an ever-fixèd mark,
> That looks on tempests and is never shaken;
> It is the star to every wandering bark,
> Whose worth's unknown, although his height be taken.
> Love's not Time's fool, though rosy lips and cheeks
> Within his bending sickle's compass come;
> Love alters not with his brief hours and weeks,
> But bears it out even to the edge of doom.
> If this be error and upon me proved,
> I never writ, nor no man ever loved.

▶ *enjambement* (enjambment): French for "striding over," a **poetic** statement that spans more than one line. Lines exhibiting *enjambement* do not end with grammatical breaks, and their sense is not complete without the following line(s). Such lines are also commonly referred to as *run-on lines* and are distinguished from **end-stopped lines**. The meaning of an endstopped line, in which a grammatical pause marked by punctuation and the physical end of the line coincide, is complete in itself.

EXAMPLES: The second, third, and fourth lines of the following passage from an untitled **sonnet** published in 1807 by William Wordsworth exemplify *enjambement*, whereas the first line is end-stopped:

> It is a beauteous evening, calm and free,
> The holy time is quiet as a Nun
> Breathless with adoration; the broad sun
> Is sinking down in its tranquility.

The following lines from Thom Gunn's "Considering the Snail" (1956) also exhibit *enjambement*:

> The snail pushes through a green
> night, for the grass is heavy
> with water and meets over
> the bright path he makes, where rain
> has darkened the earth's dark. He
> moves in a wood of desire,
>
> pale antlers barely stirring
> as he hunts. I cannot tell . . .

Amiri Baraka (LeRoi Jones) used *enjambement* in his poem "An Agony. As Now" (1964), the first **stanza** of which follows:

> I am inside someone
> who hates me. I look

out from his eyes. Smell
what fouled tunes come in
to his breath. Love his
wretched women.

▶ **Enlightenment:** An eighteenth-century philosophical movement in Europe and America that critically examined traditional ideas and institutions, **privileged** reason, and championed progress. Thinkers associated with the Enlightenment sought to uncover fundamental principles governing humanity and nature and believed in universal order and the perfectability of the individual and society. As rationalists and empiricists, they advocated use of the scientific method, observation, and experience to understand — and modify — both the natural world and human society. Notably, proponents themselves used the term *Enlightenment* in reference to the movement and their worldview, believing that reason could overcome ignorance, intolerance, superstition, and tyranny with the light of truth. As German philosopher Immanuel Kant asserted in his essay "Was ist Aufklärung?" ("What Is Enlightenment?") (1784):

> If it is asked whether we at present live in an *enlightened* age, the answer is: No, but we do live in an age of *enlightenment*. As things are at present, we still have a long way to go before men as a whole can be in a position (or can even be put in a position) of using their own understanding confidently and well in religious matters, without outside guidance. But we do have distinct indications that the way is now being cleared for them to work freely in this direction, and that the obstacles to universal enlightenment, to man's emergence from his self-incurred immaturity are gradually becoming fewer.

Kant also invoked the Enlightenment motto, "*sapere dare*," often translated as "have courage to use your own understanding" or, more briefly, as "dare to know" or "dare to think."

Enlightenment thinkers were particularly concerned with religion and governance. They sought to humanize religion, rejecting religious dogma and promoting tolerance, and opposed religious interference with science, arguing that religion had nothing to do with inquiries into the natural and human worlds. In search of a universal "natural religion," many rejected organized religion and embraced deism, belief in the existence of God based on reason and experience rather than revelation. Deists viewed God as an impersonal deity, the source of the universe, and linked reverence and worship with a rational moral code. Regarding governance, Enlightenment thinkers explored the relationship between the individual and the state, developing the idea of the social contract, an implicit agreement forming the basis for society that sets forth the rights and responsibilities of individuals and the state. They also viewed the state as a tool for progress, supporting centralization and standardization. Notably, given the widespread chaos and violence stemming in large part from religious wars in the sixteenth and seventeenth centuries, most supported monarchical government and even absolute monarchy, though many called for enlightened absolutism as a means of imposing Enlightenment reforms. Ultimately, however, the thinking of absolutists such as seventeenth-century French bishop Jacques-Bénigne Bossuet, who asserted the divine right of kings as rulers enthroned by and accountable only to God, gave way to the competing concept of natural law and its corollary, natural rights.

While the Enlightenment is often dated to the eighteenth century, many scholars argue that the movement began in the mid-seventeenth century or even earlier. In either event, René Descartes, a French philosopher, mathematician, and scientist who used reason to support faith and viewed the universe in mechanistic, "clockwork" terms, was a seminal influence. Exploring the acquisition of knowledge in *Discours de la méthode* (*Discourse on Method*) (1637), he privileged **subjectivity** and the individual over **objectivity** and tradition in his search for a certain truth, concluding *Cogito, ergo sum* ("I think, therefore I am"). Other major seventeenth-century influences on or manifestations of Enlightenment thinking include English mathematician and philosopher Sir Isaac Newton's discoveries of natural laws concerning gravitation and motion; English philosopher Thomas Hobbes's political **classic** *Leviathan* (1651), which set forth the concept of the social contract as the basis for society and posited the need for a strong sovereign to enforce the contract; French mathematician and philosopher Blaise Pascal's *Pensées* (*Thoughts*) (1669), an unfinished work intended as a defense of Christianity; Jewish rationalist philosopher Benedictus de Spinoza's *Ethics* (c. 1677), which expressed the pantheistic view that God and nature are one; and the skepticism of French philosopher Pierre Bayle, embodied in his *Dictionnaire historique et critique* (*Historical and Critical Dictionary*) (1697). Also important was English philosopher John Locke's empirical theory of the human mind and political theories involving natural law. In "An Essay Concerning Human Understanding" (1690), Locke argued that the human mind begins as a *tabula rasa*, or blank slate; that all knowledge comes from sensory experience; and that changing the human environment can change society. Politically, he posited natural law as the basis for government in *Two Treatises on Government* (1690), argued that people are equal, and framed the social contract as a means of furthering equality and freedom.

Subsequently, the *philosophes*, French philosophers active in the mid-eighteenth century, championed the tenets of the Enlightenment, embracing deism, religious tolerance, and rational progress. The most influential *philosophes* were Jean-Jacques Rousseau, who focused on liberty and the relationship between the individual and the state, and Voltaire (François Marie Arouet), who promoted empiricism and religious tolerance. In works such as "*Discours sur l'origine et les fondements de l'inégalité parmi les hommes*" ("A Discourse on Inequality") (1754) and *Le contrat social* (*The Social Contract*) (1762), Rousseau developed the idea of the "noble savage," a non-civilized but innately good human, and argued that the social contract should be based on rights and equality for all. Voltaire, unlike most French philosophers, rejected rationalism, insisted on verification through the senses, and advocated for the primacy of secular values, arguing in works such as *Traité sur la tolérance* (*A Treatise on Tolerance*) (1763) that the worst crimes against humanity were committed in the name of religion. Also important in the political realm was Baron de Montesquieu's *De l'esprit des lois* (*The Spirit of the Laws*) (1748), which called for independent legislative, executive, and judicial branches in government, a separation of powers creating a system of checks and balances. Other notable *philosophes* included Denis Diderot and Jean le Rond d'Alembert, who spearheaded an *Encyclopédie, ou dictionnaire raisonnée des sciences, des arts et des métiers* (*Encyclopedia*) (28 vols., 1751–72) meant to secularize learning and serve as a manifesto of the *philosophe* movement.

Major figures associated with the Enlightenment in Britain — English, Irish, and Scottish *philosophes,* so to speak — included George Berkeley, Edward Gibbon, David Hume, and Adam Smith. Hume, an empiricist and skeptic, argued in *An Enquiry Concerning Human Understanding* (1748) that impressions (sensations or emotions) are the source of all human ideas, denied that humans can know anything with certainty, and sanctioned moral relativism. Smith, who posited the existence of an invisible, guiding hand in free markets and advocated *laissez-faire* economics, theorized capitalism in *An Inquiry into the Nature and Causes of the Wealth of Nations* (1776).

In Germany, noted Enlightenment philosophers aside from Kant included Gotthold Ephraim Lessing and Moses Mendelssohn. Lessing advocated religious tolerance in works such as his play *Nathan der Weise* (*Nathan the Wise*) (1779) and further argued in *Die Erziehung des Menschengeschlechts* (*The Education of the Human Race*) (1780) that the history of world religions showed evolving moral awareness. Mendelssohn promoted rational progress and spurred the *Haskalah,* or Jewish Enlightenment. In Italy, Cesare Beccaria's *Dei delitti e delle pene* (*On Crimes and Punishments*) (1764), which opposed corporal and capital punishment and advocated incarceration as a way to protect society and rehabilitate convicts, revolutionized European penal systems. In America, leading figures such as Benjamin Franklin, Thomas Jefferson, and Thomas Paine, all deists, based the American Revolution and founding documents such as the Declaration of Independence and the Constitution on Enlightenment ideas, putting concepts such as inalienable rights, natural law, self-determination, and self-evident truths into practice. The same concepts subsequently influenced the French Revolution, which broke out in 1789 and ended following the Reign of Terror engendered by Maximilien Robespierre.

▶ *Entwicklungsroman:* See bildungsroman.

▶ envoy (*envoi*): A brief, concluding stanza of a poem. Envoys are often addressed to a patron, an important person, or an abstract entity but may also be used to comment on or summarize the poem as a whole. In addition, envoys may include a line used as a **refrain** in the body of the poem. Major **forms** of **verse** with an envoy include the **ballade,** which ends with a four-line stanza (a **quatrain**) that often has a *bcbc* **rhyme scheme;** the *chant royal,* a form related to the ballade that typically ends with a five-line stanza rhyming *ddede;* and the **sestina,** which ends with a three-line stanza that incorporates the last word of each of the preceding six stanzas in a specific pattern.

EXAMPLES: The envoy of François Villon's "Ballade des dames du temps jadis" (1498), quoted here in the original, fifteenth-century French:

> Prince, n'enquerez de sepmaine
> Ou elles sont, ne de cest an,
> Que ce refrain ne vous remaine:
> Mais ou sont les neiges d'antan?

Two nineteenth-century English poets, Algernon Charles Swinburne and Dante Gabriel Rossetti, creatively translated Villon's **ballades.** What follows is Rossetti's translation, in what he calls "The Ballad of Dead Ladies" (1870), of the envoy by Villon quoted above:

> Nay, never ask this week, fair lord,
>   Where they are gone, nor yet this year,
> Except with this for an overword, —
>   But where are the snows of yester-year?

▶ **ephebe:** See **anxiety of influence.**

▶ **epic:** A long and formal **narrative poem** written in an elevated **style** that recounts the adventures of a **hero** of almost **mythic** proportions who often embodies the traits of a nation or people. A distinction is generally made between *traditional* (**folk** or primary) epics and *literary* (art or secondary) epics. Traditional epics are derived from oral tradition, whereas literary epics are the work of a single poet, written in conscious **imitation** of the traditional style.

Epics typically share a wide variety of characteristics: (1) the **protagonist** is a hero of great stature and significance (whether historical or mythic) with the two traditional virtues of bravery (*fortitudo*) and wisdom (*sapientia*); (2) the **setting** is on a grand and vast scale, often encompassing the known world at the time of the epic's composition; (3) the **plot** entails noble, fantastic, and even superhuman efforts; (4) supernatural entities usually involve themselves in the **action** and in the affairs of the hero, who often must descend into some kind of underworld before he can claim victory; and (5) the writing exhibits an elevated style designed to complement and heighten the already mythic stature of the **characters** and their actions.

Epics also generally involve certain **conventions.** These include: (1) invoking a **muse's** aid during the **argument** and posing a question to her; (2) starting the narrative *in medias res;* (3) introducing the roster of characters in a formal manner and giving them speeches revealing their principal characteristics and attitudes; and (4) using **epic similes.**

Today, the term *epic* may also be used more generally to refer to any event involving heroic actions taken in broadly significant situations.

EXAMPLES: Homer's *The Iliad* and *The Odyssey* (both c. 850 B.C.) are traditional epics, as are *Beowulf* (c. A.D. 700), an epic in Old English, and *La chanson de Roland* (*The Song of Roland* [c. 1100]), an epic in Old French. Virgil's *The Aeneid* (c. 15 B.C.), Dante Alighieri's *Divina commedia* (*The Divine Comedy*) (1321), and Ludovico Ariosto's *Orlando furioso* (*Orlando Enraged*) (1516) are literary epics. James Joyce's novel *Ulysses* (1922) and Derek Walcott's long poem *Omeros* (1990) are twentieth-century works in the epic tradition. Both are based on *The Odyssey*, as is Francis Ford Coppola's lavish television movie by the same name (1997).

An example of *epic* in its broadest sense appeared in "Recording Replays Flight 93's Fight to the Death," an April 13, 2006, *Washington Post* story on the Zacarias Moussaoui trial in which Jerry Markon and Timothy Dwyer reported that "The 32-minute tape [from the voice recorder of United Flight 93, one of the planes hijacked on 9/11] captures an epic struggle as passengers surged forward to retake the plane, using whatever low-tech weapons they could find."

▶ **epic simile (Homeric simile):** An extended and elaborate **simile** (comparison) in which the **vehicle** (the **image** used to describe or define the subject, or **tenor**, of a **figure of speech**) is itself described at such length that it nearly obscures the tenor. The epic simile is sometimes called the *Homeric simile* because writers ranging from the Roman poet Virgil to the English poet John Milton consciously patterned their similes after the ornate similes used by the ancient Greek poet Homer in his **epics.**

EXAMPLE: The following **Spenserian stanza** from Edmund Spenser's *The Faerie Queene* (1590, 1596) uses an epic simile to describe two knights who have broken their weapons in combat:

> As when two rams, stird with ambitious pride,
> Fight for the rule of the rich fleeced flocke,
> Their horned fronts so fierce on either side
> Doe meete, that, with the terror of the schocke,
> Astonied,° both stand senceless as a blocke,   *Astonished*
> Forgetfull of the hanging victorie:
> So stood these twaine, unmoved as a rocke,
> Both staring fierce, and holding idely
> The broken reliques of their former cruelty.

▶ **epideictic:** From the Greek for "display," a term referring to **poems** (*epideictic poetry*), speeches (*epideictic rhetoric*), and **essays** (*epideictic prose*) meant to edify an audience by demonstrating the strengths (or, on rare occasions, the weaknesses) of some person or persons through praise (or blame). Works of epideictic prose are sometimes referred to as **prose encomiums.**

EXAMPLES: Statius's *Silvae* (c. A.D. 75) is a famous, **classical** example of epideictic poetry; a more recent instance is Robert Hayden's poem "Frederick

Douglass" (1962). Abraham Lincoln's "Gettysburg Address" (1863) is perhaps the best-known piece of epideictic rhetoric, whereas Samuel Johnson's *Preface to Shakespeare* (1765), a prose encomium, exemplifies epidiectic prose.

▶ **epigram:** From the Greek for "inscription," originally an inscription on a monument, then simply a short **poem;** now either a short poem with a brief, pointedly humorous, quotable ending or simply a **witty,** terse **prose** statement.

EXAMPLES: Martial's *Epigrams* (12 books; A.D. 86–103); Ben Jonson's *Epigrams* (1616). Persian poet Omar Khayyám's *Rubáiyát* (c. eleventh–twelfth century), translated into English by Edward Fitzgerald and published in 1859 as the *Rubáiyát of Omar Khayyám*, contains about 500 epigrams.

W. H. Auden's volume of poetry *About the House* (1965) is full of witty little epigrams:

> Money cannot buy
> The fuel of Love:
> But is excellent kindling.

Equally epigrammatic is John Lennon's disingenuously innocent statement "All these financial takeovers and things — it's just like Monopoly" and the statement "Like sands through the hourglass, so are the days of our lives," which begins every episode of the long-running soap opera *Days of Our Lives* (1965–).

▶ **epigraph:** (1) An inscription on a coin, stone, statue, or building. (2) A passage printed on the title page or first page of a literary work or at the beginning of a section of such a work. Epigraphs, which tend to set the **tone** or establish the **theme** of what follows, are generally taken from earlier, influential **texts** by other **authors.** Some **modernist** and **postmodernist** authors, however, have written their own epigraphs, presumably in an attempt to wrest control from the past of the way in which contemporary texts are read.

EXAMPLES: Two epigraphs precede T. S. Eliot's poem "The Hollow Men" (1925): "Mistuh Kurtz — he dead" and "A penny for the Old Guy." The first epigraph is taken from Joseph Conrad's **novella** *Heart of Darkness* (1899) and refers to the death of Kurtz, the morally hollow **antihero** of the work. The second epigraph refers to a line commonly heard in London on Guy Fawkes Day, when children go door-to-door for money and older revellers burn straw effigies of the man who plotted to blow up King James I and the Houses of Parliament in 1605. The two epigraphs are thematically connected; in concert, they suggest that Kurtz has become a hollow man, a man of straw, an effigy, and they set the tone for a poem about "stuffed men" without morals, without even the will to act shown by Kurtz or Guy Fawkes.

Postmodernist novelist Kathy Acker wrote her own epigraph to part 2 of *Don Quixote: Which Was a Dream* (1986), her radical reimagining of

Miguel de Cervantes's **classic** narrative: "Being born into and part of a male world, she had no speech of her own. All she could do was read male texts, which weren't hers."

In *We wish to inform you that tomorrow we will be killed with our families* (1998), an account of the 1994 Rwandan genocide in which 800,000 minority Tutsis were killed in three months by the Hutu majority, journalist Philip Gourevitch incorporated epigraphs throughout the **narrative,** including an original passage introducing the work as a whole and quotations from other works that preface various parts and chapters of the book. Gourevitch drew on Plato's *Republic* (c. 360 B.C.), John Milton's *Paradise Lost* (1667), George Eliot's *Daniel Deronda* (1876), Ralph Ellison's *Invisible Man* (1947), and Primo Levi's *Survival in Auschwitz* (1958) and *The Drowned and the Saved* (1986) to bring home the idea that genocide can happen again — and happen anywhere.

▶ **epilogue:** (1) The concluding section of a work. (2) A speech that comes at the end of a **play,** often requesting the appreciation of the audience and kind reviews from critics.

EXAMPLE: The epilogue to William Shakespeare's *The Tempest* (c. 1611) is spoken by Prospero, who begins by saying:

> Now my charms are all o'erthrown
> And what strength I have's all my own

and ends by subtly suggesting that the audience applaud:

> As you from crimes would pardoned be,
> Let your indulgence set me free.

Contemporary works that contain epilogues include Paulo Coelho's **fable** *O alquimista* (*The Alchemist*) (1988), Jane Smiley's novel *A Thousand Acres* (1991), and Charles Frazier's novel *Cold Mountain* (1997).

▶ **epiphany:** From the Greek for "manifestation" or "showing-forth," a term traditionally used to refer to the incarnation or manifestation of a divine being (in Christian circles, Jesus Christ in particular); used more specifically in reference to literature, a sudden revelatory experience or a work in which such an experience occurs. The term was introduced into **literary criticism** by Irish writer James Joyce, who in *Stephen Hero* (an early version, not published until 1944, of *A Portrait of the Artist as a Young Man* [1916]) used *epiphany* **figuratively** to describe the insight or revelation gained when one suddenly understands the essence of an object, gesture, statement, situation, moment, or mentality, seeing the commonplace for what it really is beneath the surface and perceiving its inner workings, its nature. By *epiphany,* Joyce's **protagonist** "meant a sudden spiritual manifestation, whether in the vulgarity of speech or of gesture or in a memorable phase of the mind itself. He believed that it was for the man of letters to record these epiphanies with extreme care, seeing that they themselves are the most delicate and evanescent of moments."

Although the term can describe secular experience, epiphany retains a **mystical**, almost religious, **connotation** due to the emphasis on the intuitive connections made during the epiphanic moment — associations so surprising and unusual as to seem almost unworldly. As Joyce wrote of the epiphanic object: "Its soul, its whatness, leaps to us from the vestment of its appearance. The soul of the commonest object . . . seems to us radiant. The object achieves its epiphany."

FURTHER EXAMPLES: Virginia Woolf's novel *Mrs. Dalloway* (1925) ends with a party at which a doctor attributes his late arrival to the need to care for a young, former soldier who had committed suicide by throwing himself from a window onto a railing below. The doctor's story triggers an epiphanic moment for Clarissa Dalloway, the hostess. She retreats from her guests to an empty room, where she envisions the young man's death and suddenly has the strange and surprising sense that he may have preserved something by throwing his life away:

> He had thrown himself from a window. Up had flashed the ground; through him, blundering, bruising, went the rusty spikes. There he lay with a thud, thud, thud in his brain, and then a suffocation of blackness. So she saw it. But why had he done it? And the Bradshaws talked of it at her party!
>
> She had once thrown a shilling into the Serpentine, never anything more. But he had flung it away. . . . A thing there was that mattered; a thing wreathed about with chatter, defaced, obscured in her own life, let drop every day in corruption, lies, chatter. This he had preserved. Death was defiance. Death was an attempt to communicate; people feeling the impossibility of reaching the centre which, mystically, evaded them; closeness drew apart; rapture faded; one was alone. There was an embrace in death.

In Leif Enger's novel *Peace Like a River* (2001), the **protagonist**, Reuben Land, describes his father's "whispered tornado story," an experience that led the elder Land to abandon his medical studies for plumbing and janitorial work:

> Dad, he himself would say, was baptized by that tornado into a life of new ambitions — interpreted by many, including my mother, as a life of no ambitions. . . . Having been whisked though four miles of debris-cluttered sky, having been swallowed by the wrath of God and been kept not just safe but unbruised inside it, having been awakened mid-morning in a fallow field by a face-licking retriever — Dad's response was to leave his prosperous track and plunge his hands joyfully into the sewer.

▶ **episodic structure:** The **form** of a work containing a series of incidents or episodes that are loosely connected by a larger subject matter or **thematic structure** but that could stand on their own. A **text** that has a sustained story line or that would not be complete without one of its parts does not exhibit episodic structure.

EXAMPLES: Tobias Smollett's **picaresque novel** *Roderick Random* (1748); Laurence Sterne's **sentimental novel** *A Sentimental Journey* (1768); the *Sleeping Beauty* trilogy (1983–85) by Anne Rice, writing under the *nom de plume* A. N. Roquelaure; Bill Bryson's travel **narrative** *Notes from a Small Island* (1995). *Crash* (2004), which explores **themes** of racism and stereotyping, involves a number of separate story lines, some of which ultimately interweave or converge; the connections in *Babel* (2006), which features four major story lines, are even more tenuous.

▶ *epistémé* (discursive formation): From the Greek for "knowledge," a term used by twentieth-century French philosophical historian Michel Foucault to refer to: (1) a network of discursive practices — of thoughts, concepts, and cultural **codes** — dominant during a given historical period; and (2) the rules governing the transformation of those practices. In *Les mots et les choses* (*The Order of Things*) (1970), Foucault himself defined *epistémé* as a "historical a priori, [which] . . . in a given period, delimits in the totality of experience a field of knowledge, defines the mode of being of the objects that appear in that field, provides everyday perception with theoretical powers, and defines the conditions in which one can sustain a discourse about things which is recognized to be true." Foucault subsequently substituted the term *discursive formation* for *epistémé* in *L'archéologie du savoir* (*The Archaeology of Knowledge*) (1969).

An *epistémé* governs the way that people perceive and approach the world at any given time. It is analogous to *paradigm*, as used by American historian of science Thomas Kuhn, since both are conceptual frameworks that govern systems of knowledge until they shift, break down, and are replaced by new frameworks. According to Foucault, only one *epistémé* can exist at any given time, and each is unique. Over time, a new *epistémé* develops that replaces the last one, ushering in a new era in which people think differently than they did before. So long as any given *epistémé* is in place, however, it governs the boundaries within which people think and the ways in which they gain, process, and pass on knowledge. Insofar as *epistémés* entail universally accepted positions, they also preclude challenges to those positions.

Foucault identified a number of successive *epistémés* in his body of work. The **Renaissance** *epistémé* of the sixteenth century was based on the concept of similitude between things and on uncovering such resemblances, whereas the subsequent **neoclassical** *epistémé* of the seventeenth and eighteenth centuries was based on the quite opposite concept of differences and distinctions. Instead of thinking of words and things as inextricably and reliably linked, as was common in the Renaissance, the connection between them was severed in the **Neoclassical Period.** During the nineteenth century, the neoclassical *epistémé* was displaced by the concept of historical development and of history as a way to trace language, which was in turn displaced by the present *epistémé,* in which the human being is the center for knowledge. The next *epistémé*, Foucault predicted, will involve a diminution and **decentering** of the human being's role.

Epistémé should be distinguished from **ideology,** the frequently unrecognized set of beliefs underlying the customs, habits, and practices of a given social group. *Epistémé* refers to an even more dominant and deterministic system than ideology. Whereas the **gaps, conflicts,** and contradictions in ideologies can be exposed through creative and critical **texts,** there is simply no vantage point outside an *epistémé*, which sets the boundaries within which people think, and thus no way to critique its rules or suggest alternative **discourses.**

Foucault's concept of *epistémé* has been criticized on several grounds. First, critics contend that Foucault ignored relevant contradictory evidence in his quest to identify particular *epistémés*. Second, proponents of the concept cannot account for why discursive practices *do* change over time. Third, they cannot explain why the very concept of *epistémé* and all the commentary it has generated are not themselves products of the current *epistémé* and its all-governing, or "totalizing," laws of transformation.

FURTHER EXAMPLES: In *Surveiller et punir: Naissance de la prison (Discipline and Punish: The Birth of the Prison)* (1975), Foucault discussed the shift in the understanding of the human "subject," or self. He argued that in Europe, prior to the eighteenth century, a subject was a *body* subject to the power of a monarch — and subject to being physically punished by that power. Later, however, the subject became the internalized sense of individual self, a *psychological* entity punished through incarceration. Likewise, in *Naissance de la clinique (The Birth of the Clinic)* (1963), Foucault focused on the shift in perception of the human body due to shifts in the "medical gaze" from one *epistémé* to the next.

▶ **epistle:** A letter. As a literary form, an epistle is generally restricted to a formal (not conversational), thoughtfully composed letter that is intended for a distant individual or group of people. Although some of the most famous epistles come from the New Testament of the Bible, any such formal letter, regardless of religious or moral intent, is an epistle. Nearly all epistles are written in **prose,** but a few have been composed in **verse,** including a number by English poet Alexander Pope.

▶ **epistolary novel:** A **novel** whose **plot** is entirely developed through letters, whether through an exchange of letters among multiple **characters** or through the correspondence of only one character. The epistolary form enables **authors** to directly reveal the intimate private thoughts of characters and lends immediacy to **narratives** in permitting events to be recounted just after — and occasionally even during — the moment of their occurrence. Samuel Richardson's *Pamela; or, Virtue Rewarded* (1740) and *Clarissa Harlowe* (1748) are early examples that are generally considered to have established the **genre,** which was extremely popular during the eighteenth century but fell out of fashion thereafter.

EXAMPLES: Tobias Smollett's *The Expedition of Humphry Clinker* (1771), Johann Wolfgang von Goethe's *The Sorrows of Young Werther* (1774), Isabelle de Charrière's *Les lettres de Mistriss Henley* (1784), Choderlos de Laclos's *Les liaisons dangereuses* (*Dangerous Liaisons*) (1784), Hannah Foster's *The Coquette: or, The History of Eliza Wharton* (1797). Contemporary examples include Mariama Bâ's *Une si longue lettre* (*So Long a Letter*) (1981) and Kalisha Buckhanon's *Upstate* (2005), an exchange of letters between two Harlem teenagers, seventeen-year-old Antonio, jailed for murder, and his sixteen-year-old girlfriend Natasha, that begins: "Baby, the first thing I need to know from you is do you believe I killed my father?" Nick Bantock adapted the epistolary form in *Griffin and Sabine* (1991) and *Sabine's Notebook* (1992), popular short works that include actual envelopes, removable letters, and postcards by two correspondents, one of whom may be the invention of the other.

▶ **epitaph:** An inscription on a tomb to commemorate the deceased. Epitaphs often contain basic **biographical** information as well as memorial phrases. The term *epitaph* can also refer to a **poem**, whether serious or humorous, that commemorates the deceased.

EXAMPLES: Ben Jonson's "Epitaph on Elizabeth, L. H." (1616), quoted here in part:

> Underneath this stone doth lie
> As much beauty as could die;
> Which in life did harbor give
> To more virtue than could live.
> If at all she had a fault,
> Leave it buried in this vault.

George Gordon, Lord Byron's 1808 epitaph for his dog Botswain, next to whom he intended to be buried, reads:

> To mark a friend's remains these stones arise;
> I never knew but one — and here he lies.

▶ **epithalamium (epithalamion):** From the Greek for "at the bridal chamber," a **poem** written to celebrate a specific marriage, to celebrate the bride and groom. An epithalamium was originally sung just outside the room to which the bride and groom retired on their wedding night.

EXAMPLES: Edmund Spenser's *Epithalamion* (1595), written to celebrate his own marriage; John Donne's "Epithalamion, or Marriage Song, On the Lady Elizabeth, and Count Palatine Being Married on St. Valentine's Day" (1613).

▶ **epithet:** An adjective or phrase applied to a noun to accentuate a certain characteristic.

EXAMPLES: The Founding Fathers; Elizabeth, the Virgin Queen; blundering fool; male chauvinist pig. In H. G. Wells's **science fiction** novel *The*

Time Machine (1895), the **narrator** uses epithets to refer to all but one of the **characters** who frequent the Time Traveller's — itself an epithet — house every Thursday evening: the Medical Man, the Provincial Mayor, the Editor, the Psychologist, the Very Young Man, and so forth. Tom Brokaw's book *The Greatest Generation* (1998) takes as its title the well-known epithet for the generation that came of age in the Great Depression and World War II.

Professional athletes are commonly referred to epithetically, as are political figures. Examples include "Wilt the Stilt" Chamberlain, "Magic" Johnson, "Give 'em Hell" Harry (Truman), "Tricky Dick" (Richard Nixon), and the "Teflon President" (Ronald Reagan). President George W. Bush created an epithet for himself in 2006 when he declared, in response to calls for the resignation of Defense Secretary Donald Rumsfeld, "I'm the decider, and I decide what's best." Examples of political epithets applied more generally to individuals or groups include the "Bible Belt," "Blue Dog Democrat," and "compassionate conservative," as well as derogatory terms such as "crony capitalist," "feminazi," and "Uncle Tom." Zealous fans of conservative talk radio host Rush Limbaugh even call themselves "Dittoheads."

▶ **epoché:** See **phenomenology.**

▶ **epode:** (1) The third **stanza** of the **classical** Greek choral **ode.** After the **strophe** and the **antistrophe,** which involve movement, the **chorus** sang the epode while standing still. (2) The third of three recurrent parts of the **Pindaric ode.** (3) A poem in which a short stanza or line follows a long one.

▶ *Erziehungsroman:* German for "novel of upbringing," a **novel** that recounts the education, training, or upbringing of the **protagonist.** While *Erziehungsroman* is often used synonymously in English-language **literary criticism** with **bildungsroman,** the more general novel of formation, it is better classified as a type of bildungsroman. Both the *Erziehungsroman* and bildungsroman examine the growth and development of a central **character** from childhood to maturity, but the *Erziehungsroman* focuses on the educational process and often addresses the protagonist's relationship with one or more mentors who offer guidance and training.

EXAMPLES: Johann Wolfgang von Goethe's *Wilhelm Meister's Apprenticeship* (1796), George Eliot's *The Mill on the Floss* (1860), Evelyn Waugh's *Brideshead Revisited* (1946). J. K. Rowling's *Harry Potter* series of **fantasy** novels (1997–2007), set largely at Hogwarts, a school for the education and training of witches and wizards, is a contemporary example of *Erziehungsroman.*

▶ **eschatology:** Thought or belief concerning "ultimate" questions, last things, "end times" — that is, what happens after death or the end of the world and life as we know it. Christian eschatology includes such concepts as heaven and hell, salvation and damnation, and God's judgment and forgiveness. **Medieval** Christian eschatologists developed the concept of Purgatory, one still espoused by the Roman Catholic Church but rejected by Protestants after the **Reformation.** Eschatology is generally relevant to the study of literature, which has often been concerned with first and last things, ultimate questions.

EXAMPLES: The biblical book of Revelation, medieval **mystery plays** about Creation and the Day of Judgment, Dante Alighieri's *Divina commedia* (*The Divine Comedy*) (1321), Mary Shelley's *The Last Man* (1826). Contemporary examples of eschatological literature include Piers Anthony's **fantasy** series *Incarnations of Immortality* (1983–89) and the **apocalyptic** *Left Behind* series of novels (1995–2007) by Tim LaHaye and Jerry B. Jenkins.

See also **Apocalypse, apocalyptic literature.**

▶ **essay:** A **nonfiction** composition that usually explores a single **theme** or topic. While essays may range from less than a single page to novel length, most are relatively brief. Most are also written in **prose,** but a few have been composed in **verse,** such as Alexander Pope's "An Essay on Criticism" (1711) and "An Essay on Man" (1733). The form developed in **classical** times, but the term itself derives from the French *essai* (meaning "attempt"), first applied by the French writer Michel de Montaigne to his 1580 collection of informal compositions. Montaigne's use of the term *essai* was meant to reflect the uncertain and inquiring quality of his ruminations. The term entered English in 1597, when philosopher Francis Bacon applied it to the first edition of his famous work *Essays.* The **etymology** of the term reminds us that essayists make no claim to an exhaustive and technical examination of a subject, seeking instead to record their thoughts and ruminations for a general audience.

Essays are often classified as *argumentative, descriptive, expository,* or **narrative,** although the categories overlap. They may also be categorized as *formal* or *informal.* Formal essays, which are designed to declaim and instruct, are characterized by an impersonal, analytical examination of their subject matter and a dignified or solemn **tone.** Informal essays tend to be shorter, lighter, funnier, and more conversational than their formal counterparts and to make greater use of **anecdotes** and **aphorisms.**

Until the eighteenth century, most essays were published as collections in books. The development of the periodical in the early eighteenth century, however, made essay writing a more prevalent and popular form. It also had a standardizing effect, particularly on the informal essay, elevating the role of humor and restricting maximum length. In the nineteenth century, the formal essay was chiefly found in a handful of important literary magazines, and the *personal essay,* a type of informal essay stressing **autobiographical** content and often written in an urbane and intimate manner, emerged. The proliferation of periodicals — whether literary or popular, from the eighteenth-century *Tatler* to the present day *New Yorker* — has kept the essay in the forefront of literary **genres.**

FURTHER EXAMPLES: Ralph Waldo Emerson, a formal essayist, is generally considered the dean of American essayists; Henry David Thoreau's "Civil Disobedience" is perhaps the best-known formal American essay. Noted exponents of the personal essay include three nineteenth-century Englishmen: Thomas De Quincey, William Hazlitt, and Charles Lamb.

Notable twentieth-century collections of formal essays by American essayists include Susan Sontag's *Against Interpretation, and Other Essays* (1966) and Joan Didion's *Slouching Towards Bethlehem* (1967). Journalist Calvin Trillin has published several collections of informal essays drawn from columns written for *The Nation* and *Time* including *Uncivil Liberties* (1982) and *Too Soon to Tell* (1995). Humorist David Sedaris is perhaps the best-known personal essayist, with collections including *Dress Your Family in Corduroy and Denim* (2004).

Contemporary writers who are not primarily essayists have also turned their attention to this form. American poet Nikki Giovanni has written three collections of essays, including *Racism 101* (1994), and British novelist Julian Barnes recently published *Something to Declare* (2002), a series of essays on France and French culture.

▶ **essentialism:** See **constructionism.**

▶ **etymology:** See **linguistics.**

▶ **euphony:** Pleasing, harmonious sounds. Euphony is the opposite of **cacophony,** or discordant sounds. The pleasurable impression achieved may be due as much or more to the **images** evoked as to any inherent musicality in the sounds; terming a passage euphonious thus necessarily involves a subjective judgment.

EXAMPLES: The first **stanza** of Christina Rossetti's "Song" (1862):

> When I am dead, my dearest,
> Sing no sad songs for me;
> Plant thou no roses at my head,
> Nor shady cypress tree.
> Be the green grass above me
> With showers and dewdrops wet;
> And if thou wilt, remember,
> And if thou wilt, forget.

Trumbull Stickney's poem "Mnemosyne" (1902) alternates matter-of-fact, one-line stanzas with euphonious **tercets:**

> It's autumn in the country I remember.
>
> How warm a wind blew here about the ways!
> And shadows on the hillside lay to slumber
> During the long sun-sweetened summer days.
>
> It's cold abroad the country I remember.
>
> The swallows veering skimmed the golden grain
> At midday with a wing aslant and limber;
> And yellow cattle browsed upon the plain.

Prose can also be euphonious, as in the description of snow in the concluding sentences of James Joyce's story "The Dead" (1907):

> It lay thickly drifted on the crooked crosses and headstones, on the spears of the little gate, on the barren thorns. His soul swooned slowly as he heard the snow falling faintly through the universe and faintly falling, like the descent of their last end, upon all the living and the dead.

▶ **euphuism:** An artificial literary **style**, particularly popular in late-sixteenth-century and seventeenth-century England, that made frequent use of **alliteration;** elaborate and extended **figures of speech; neologisms;** rhetorical questions; and **parallel** or balanced constructs, including **antitheses.** The term is derived from the extended prose **narrative** *Euphues* (1579) by John Lyly, who broadened the appeal of euphuistic writing by combining and elaborating on features developed by several predecessors. Although viewed as extravagant and thoroughly affected today, euphuism positively affected the development of English **prose,** which had previously been ponderously Latinate in style and sentence structure and consequently thick and tedious to follow. Euphuistic writing, although artificial, brought **imagination, wit,** and greater clarity to English prose.

EXAMPLE: The following passage from Lyly's *Euphues:*

> But this grieveth me most, that thou art almost vowed to the vain order of the vestal virgins, despising, or at the least not desiring, the sacred bands of Juno her bed. If thy mother had been of that mind when she was a maiden, thou hadst not now been born to be of this mind to be a virgin. Weigh with thyself what slender profit they bring to the commonwealth, what slight pleasure to themselves, what great grief to their parents, which joy most in their offspring and desire most to enjoy the noble and blessed name of a grandfather. Thou knowest that the tallest ash is cut down for fuel because it beareth no good fruit, that the cow that gives no milk is brought to the slaughter, that the drone that gathereth no honey is contemned, that the woman that maketh herself barren by not marrying is accounted among the Grecian ladies worse than a carrion, as Homer reporteth. Therefore, Lucilla, if thou have any care to be a comfort to my hoary hairs or a commodity to thy commonweal, frame thyself to that honourable estate of matrimony which was sanctified in Paradise, allowed of the Patriarchs, hallowed of the old Prophets, and commended of all persons.

▶ **exegesis:** Most specifically, the interpretation (and, by implication, the explanation) of passages from sacred writings such as the Bible. When applied more generally to the study of literature, *exegesis* refers to the elucidation of a **text,** typically by **close reading.**

▶ *exemplum:* A **story,** often an **anecdote,** told to illustrate a moral point or lesson; a type of **allegory. Medieval** preachers made frequent use of this device — so much so, in fact, that they occasionally lost sight of their moral point while recounting their *exempla,* or "examples." This tendency was criticized by contemporaries such as Florentine **epic** poet Dante Alighieri.

Although *exempla* seem rather ridiculous to modern readers, they held wide appeal for medieval audiences, who appreciated their **concreteness** and applicability to daily life.

EXAMPLES: *Exempla* can be found throughout Geoffrey Chaucer's *Canterbury Tales* (c. 1387). The "Nun's Priest's Tale," a **beast fable**, contains several *exempla,* and "The Pardoner's Tale" is itself an *exemplum.*

▶ **existentialism:** A philosophical school concerned with the human condition, particularly with questions of existence and meaning for human beings, and with the individual's perpetual, anguished struggle to navigate a complex and perplexing world. Existentialists emphasize the individual, asking what it means to exist as a human being and highlighting individual freedom, choice, and **subjectivity.** Whether theistic or atheistic, existentialists deny that human reason can adequately explain the universe and deny notions of immutable or absolute value systems. Moreover, they reject deterministic systems of fate or predestination, maintaining that individuals have free will and are thus entirely responsible for their actions. Individuals must create morality and meaning in a world without defined guideposts or rules, an anxiety-provoking situation that often leads to denial and self-deception.

Existentialism, which arose in the twentieth century and gained global eminence in the aftermath of World War II, particularly in Europe, has its roots in the philosophy of nineteenth-century Danish theologian Søren Kierkegaard, who examined the individual's relationship to God and argued that only through God could one escape despair. Kierkegaard maintained that most people live on an **aesthetic** level ruled by appearances and **conventions** and that movement to the second, ethical stage involves a "leap," as does movement to the third and highest stage, the religious stage. According to Kierkegaard, who emphasized the importance of individual decision, the leap is not rational but a conscious choice to embrace meaning; faith is a matter of choice, not logic. Notable works by Kierkegaard include *Fear and Trembling* (1843), *The Concept of Dread* (1844), *Concluding Unscientific Postscript to the Philosophical Fragments* (1846), and *Sickness Unto Death* (1848).

Other important influences on existentialism include two German philosophers, Friedrich Nietzsche, an individualist, anti-Christian thinker who rejected religion as a crutch, and Edmund Husserl, who founded **phenomenology.** Nietzsche argued that people must accept that they exist in a material world; claimed that the "will to power," rather than sympathy or socialization, is the main human instinct; and set forth the idea of the *Übermensch,* an "overman" or "superman" who overcomes nihilism by rejecting religious and social coventions, accepting complete responsiblity for himself, and developing his own morality. Key works expounding these ideas include *Thus Spake Zarathustra* (1883–85) and *The Will to Power* (1888). Husserl, who emphasized the psychical realm of awareness and sought to describe experience in order to reach "the things themselves," argued that objects attain meaning only as they are perceived in an individual's consciousness, rejecting the idea that objects have inherent meaning.

Existentialists typically fall into two major camps: theistic and atheistic. Theistic existentialists focus on the relationship between human beings and God and, following Kierkegaard, emphasize that faith is an individual, conscious choice that must be made without objective proof. Christian existentialists such as German-American theologian Paul Tillich and French philosopher Gabriel Marcel have emphasized that true freedom — including freedom from conflict and despair — may be found in God. Tillich, for instance, maintained that individuals, as finite beings, experience existential anguish (dread of non-being, or death) and are alienated from God, the infinite "Ground of Being"; human existence is dependent upon but estranged from the creating and sustaining essence, a gap that Christ, a "New Being," heals by bridging the finite and the infinite and thereby revealing the essence inherent in existence. Much of Tillich's existentialist thinking is set forth in *The Courage to Be* (1952). Major works by Marcel, who is often credited with coining the term *existentialism* but considered his own thought neo-Socratic, include *Être et avoir* (*Being and Having*) (1935) and *Le mystère de l'être* (*The Mystery of Being*) (1949–50). Other noted theistic existentialists include Swiss theologian Karl Barth, Jewish philosopher Martin Buber, German philosopher Karl Jaspers, and German theologian Karl Rahner.

Atheistic existentialists, rejecting the idea of a supreme being, maintain that existence precedes essence and assert that the universe is an absurd, irrational place without purpose or meaning. Drawing on Nietzsche, they argue that individuals must define themselves and create meaning through their exercise of free will. They emphasize the importance of facing up to the human situation and living authentically by accepting and exercising the attendant freedom and responsibility. The two major figures associated with atheistic existentialism are Martin Heidegger, a German philosopher, and Jean-Paul Sartre, a French philosopher and writer.

Heidegger, a student of Husserl who rejected the existentialist label, referred to his seminal work *Sein und Zeit* (*Being and Time*) (1927) as phenomenological ontology. Focused on the meaning of being, he began by asking, "Why is there something, rather than nothing?" Then, highlighting the contrast between being (existence), and nothing, he argued that to be human was to find oneself "thrown" into the world and that existence necessarily involved participation in the world (*dasein*, or "being there"). He also grounded being in time, maintaining that one's possibilities and potential change over time, and distinguished between two ways of living in the world: a banal, passive, uncritical mode he deemed "inauthentic" and an "authentic" mode involving recognition of the human condition and active self-analysis.

In *L'être et le néant: Essai d'ontologie phénoménologique* (*Being and Nothingness: An Essay in Phenomenological Ontology*) (1943), Sartre, who was influenced by both Heidegger and Husserl, emphasized that "[e]xistence precedes and rules essence" and that "man makes himself." He advocated dragging oneself out of the slimy *visqueux*, out of a passive existence; imbuing existence with essence, or meaning, by the exercise of choice and free will;

and living an authentic life as an individual by asserting total freedom and accepting total responsibility. Moreover, unlike many other existentialists, Sartre accepted the characterization of his work as existentialist and adopted the term in a 1945 lecture, published as *L'existentialisme est un humanisme* (*Existentialism Is a Humanism*) (1946), which introduced his philosophy and responded to Chistian and **Marxist** charges of quietism, negativity, subjectivism, isolationism, and relativism or permissiveness. Describing man as "condemned to be free," Sartre reiterated the importance of emerging from a passive existence and becoming *engagé* — engaged or committed in the social sphere, including political struggles against repressive institutions, laws, and conventions. In the literary arena, he commonly focused on the anxiety and alienation of the individual in an absurd and meaningless world, with major works including the play *Huis Clos* (*No Exit*) (1943) and the novel *La nausée* (*Nausea*) (1938). Other influential existentialist writers include Albert Camus, Simone de Beauvoir, Fyodor Dostoyevsky, and Franz Kafka.

Existentialist **literary criticism,** as pioneered by Sartre in works such as *Qu'est-ce que la littérature?* (*What Is Literature?*) (1947), evaluates literary works based on how well they represent the modern condition in general and, in particular, the struggle of individuals to define themselves through responsible individual action and social engagement in spite (or perhaps because) of their isolation and alienation.

▶ **explication:** See **close reading,** *explication de texte.*

▶ *explication de texte:* French for "explanation of text," a method of literary analysis that originated in late-nineteenth-century France involving **close reading** of the text. *Explication de texte,* which features a detailed examination of a short poem or passage as a means of elucidating the work as a whole, was once the chief method and remains a prominent mode of **exegesis** in French literary study. Only elements that bear directly on the interpretation of the text and a further understanding of its meaning are considered; hence practitioners of this method concentrate on **diction, imagery, style, symbolism, tone,** and so forth.

The **New Critics, formalist** literary critics who emphasized a text-only approach as the one valid method of analysis, helped popularize *explication de texte* in English-language **literary criticism** through works such as Robert Penn Warren and Cleanth Brooks's *Understanding Poetry* (1939). As a critical term in English, *explication* is synonymous with *close reading.*

▶ **expressionism:** An artistic and literary movement, which was born in Germany in the late nineteenth century and which reached its zenith in the 1920s, whose proponents believed that objective depictions of circumstances and thoughts cannot accurately render an individual's subjective experience. Expressionists reject **realism** and share (although perhaps with more intensity) the **impressionist** intention to present a personal vision through art. To render this personal vision artistically, expressionists depict their subjects as they feel or sense or experience them, rather than as those subjects appear from an external viewpoint. To expose the idiosyncratic and often extreme states of human consciousness and emotion, expressionist works tend to oversimplify and distort. In addition, the singularly "unreal" or even nightmarish **atmosphere** of these works accentuates the gulf between personal perception and objective reality.

Literary expressionism originated in Germany in the plays of Carl Sternheim and Frank Wedekind. However, it quickly influenced poets (such as Franz Werful) and fiction writers (such as Franz Kafka). In time, literary critics began to apply the term to virtually any twentieth-century **text** in which reality is purposely distorted. For these reasons, it has become as difficult to define literary expressionism exactly as it is to associate it with a single school or period. Some critics do limit the term's application, however, using it to describe the early-twentieth-century German literary movement (especially as manifested in **drama**) that sought to explore the recesses of the human mind and to divulge its secrets, an interest inaugurated by the work of **psychoanalytic** theorists such as Sigmund Freud.

Although the German expressionist movement was suppressed in Nazi Germany in the 1930s, it continued to **influence** other European and American writers, as evidenced by the tendency of many critics to label any twentieth-century work exhibiting purposeful distortion of reality expressionist. Inheritors of the expressionist tradition include the **Beat writers** as well as Tennessee Williams, Joseph Heller, and Thomas Pynchon.

Expressionism has a more precise meaning in art criticism, where it most often refers to an early-twentieth-century German school of painters who believed that human consciousness or essence could not be represented adequately by simulating external reality. Noted practitioners include Max Beckmann, Georg Grosz, Wassily Kandinsky, Oskar Kokoschka, and Käthe Kollwitz.

EXAMPLES: August Strindberg's *A Dream Play* (1902), Eugene O'Neill's *The Emperor Jones* (1921), and Elmer Rice's *The Adding Machine* (1923) exemplify expressionist drama; T. S. Eliot's poem *The Waste Land* (1922) and James Joyce's novel *Finnegans Wake* (1939) show the strong influence of expressionism. Henri Matisse's paintings contain expressionist elements; Edvard Munch's postimpressionist painting *The Scream* (1893) anticipates and heavily influenced the expressionist movement.

▶ **expressive criticism:** See **pragmatic criticism, rhetorical criticism.**

▶ **expressive form, fallacy of expressive form:** The phrase *expressive form* refers to a literary **convention** holding that an **author's** (especially a poet's) **form** or **style** should derive from the idea or feeling being expressed. American poet and critic Yvor Winters and **New Critics** such as R. P. Blackmur rejected this concept, hence the phrase *fallacy of expressive form*. Winters, perhaps the first critic to attack the convention of expressive form, asserted in his essay "The Influence of Meter on Poetic Convention" (from *Primitivism and Decadence* [1937]) that:

To say that a poet is justified in employing a disintegrating form in order to express a feeling of disintegration is merely a sophistical justification for bad poetry, akin to the Whitmanian notion that one must write loose and sprawling poetry to "express" the loose and sprawling American continent. In fact, all feeling, if one gives oneself (that is, one's form) up to it, is a way of disintegration; poetic form is by definition a means to arrest the disintegration and order the feeling; and in so far as any poetry tends toward the formless, it fails to be expressive of anything.

Indeed, as Winters wrote to Blackmur in 1933, he viewed this "relaxation, or giving way to one's material" as "the central vice of modern poetry."

New Critics, who **privileged** craftsmanship, further developed the critique of expressive form by suggesting that poets relying solely on inspiration and the intensity of personal emotion are unable to accurately judge the effects of their work because they lack objective standards. As Blackmur explained in a 1935 essay entitled "D. H. Lawrence and Expressive Form," reprinted in *Language as Gesture: Essays in Poetry* (1952):

When you depend entirely on the demon of inspiration, the inner voice, the inner light, you deprive yourself of any external criterion to show whether the demon is working or not. Because he is yours and you willfully depend on him, he will seem to be operating with equal intensity at every level of imagination. That is the fallacy of the faith in expressive form — the faith . . . that if a thing is only intensely enough felt its mere expression in words will give it satisfactory form, the dogma, in short, that once material becomes words it is its own best form.

For Blackmur, expressive form was a "plague affecting the poetry of the last hundred and fifty years," Lawrence its "extreme victim." Without an objective form, carefully chosen and crafted, substance would suffer; "the chaos of private experience cannot be known or understood until it is projected and ordered in a form external to the consciousness that entertained it in flux."

▶ **extrametrical:** See **meter.**

▶ **eye rhyme:** Words that appear to **rhyme** due to their spelling but that do not actually rhyme given their pronunciation. Most eye rhymes fall into the category of **half rhyme.**

EXAMPLES: *Laughter* and *slaughter, bough* and *cough* and *dough, demon* and *lemon.* Anne Bradstreet used eye rhyme in these lines from "A Letter to Her Husband, Absent upon Public Employment" (1678):

> Flesh of thy flesh, bone of thy bone,
> I here, thou there, yet both but one.

William Blake used eye rhyme in the second and fourth lines of the first **stanza** of "The Sick Rose" (1794):

O Rose, thou art sick.
The invisible worm
That flies in the night
In the howling storm

Has found out thy bed
Of crimson joy,
And his dark secret love
Does thy life destroy.

F

▶ **fable (apologue):** A short, fictional **story** in **prose** or **verse** told to illustrate a moral point or lesson; a type of **allegory**. The moral of a fable is often expressed at the end of the **tale** via an **aphorism, epigram,** or **maxim.** Fables often feature **personified** animals as their principal **characters;** animal-centered or animal-dominant fables may also be called **beast fables.** (The term *apologue,* generally used synonymously with *fable,* is sometimes used more specifically to designate the *beast fable.*) While often considered to be children's literature today, fables typically originated in **folklore** told by, for, and to adults; the **genre** dates back to ancient times in both the East and West.

Legends, myths, lies, and unbelievable stories may also be loosely referred to as fables. Furthermore, in **literary criticism,** *fable* has sometimes been used synonymously with **plot,** particularly by **neoclassical critics.**

EXAMPLES: Aesop's *Fables* (c. 550 B.C.), including the story of the tortoise and the hare, the moral of which may be summed up: "Slow and steady wins the race." Paulo Coelho's *O alquimista* (*The Alchemist*) (1988), a magical story about an Andalusian shepherd boy who seeks a worldly treasure, is subtitled *A Fable about Following Your Dream.* Ian McEwan described his novel *Amsterdam* (1998), in which three men meet at the funeral of their former lover, as a "contemporary fable."

▶ *fabliau:* A short, **comic,** often cynical or **satiric** verse **narrative** generally composed in octosyllabic **couplets.** *Fabliaux,* which were particularly popular in **medieval** France in the twelfth and thirteenth centuries, spread to England and Italy but essentially disappeared as a **genre** around the sixteenth century. The **tales,** which commonly involve trickery and were designed to entertain rather than to make a moral point, featured human **characters,** especially middle- and lower-class people, and portrayed their concerns in a **realistic** manner. *Fabliaux* frequently took humor to the point of ridicule and ribaldry, often targeting clergy, women, and cuckolded husbands.

EXAMPLES: French *fabliaux* include the thirteenth-century poet Rutebeuf's *Frère Denyse* and *La Vengeance de Charlot. Dame Siriz* (c. 1275), an early English *fabliau* based on the "weeping bitch" **motif,** involves a young wife who is duped into sleeping with a man she has previously refused when a trickster shows her a weeping dog whom she says was her daughter — transformed by a clerk whose advances she had refused. Geoffrey Chaucer's *Canterbury Tales* (c. 1387) includes such *fabliaux* as "The Miller's Tale" and "The Reeve's Tale."

▶ *fabula:* See **Russian formalism.**

▶ **faction:** See **fiction.**

▶ **fairy tale:** A prose **narrative** intended to entertain or instruct that typically relates **fantastic** or magical occurrences involving a **hero** or **heroine**. While the term *fairy tale*, a translation of the French *conte de fée*, is sometimes used to refer specifically to a **story** about fairies, this usage is uncommon. As writer J. R. R. Tolkien explained in his essay "On Fairy-Stories" (1938), "fairy-stories are not in normal English usage stories about fairies or elves, but stories about Fairy, that is Faërie, the realm or state in which fairies have their being." Indeed, many fairy tales contain no fairies at all. Accordingly, many scholars prefer the term *Märchen*, a German word meaning "tale."

Fairy tales are characterized by a number of elements. They often begin "once upon a time" in an unspecified **setting** (in terms of place and time); feature **flat characters**; and involve magic, talking animals, disguises or physical transformations, and prohibitions or taboos. Fairy tales also employ **motifs** such as cruel stepmothers, fairy godmothers, and prolonged sleeps and address the **theme** of good versus evil. Modern versions usually end "happily ever after."

There are two types of fairy tales: folk fairy tales (or *wonder tales*) and literary fairy tales. Folk fairy tales, oral **tales** verbally transmitted through successive generations within a given community, tend to evolve over time and to emphasize **plot** and repetition as memory aids. Literary fairy tales, written by a specific, identified person, may be original stories or may retell, draw on, or adapt stories from folk fairy tales or other sources such as **myths**. Many folk fairy tales are eventually committed to writing; examples include Cinderella, Puss in Boots, Sleeping Beauty, and Snow White, perhaps the earliest written versions of which are in Italian courtier Giambattista Basile's *Lo cunto de li cunti* (*The Tale of Tales*) (2 vols., 1634, 1636), also known as *Il Pentamerone*.

While fairy tales are commonly considered children's literature today — a view firmly established since the mid-nineteenth century — in the past they were composed by and for adults; many incorporated social or political critique, a subversive subtext disguised by the fairy tale form. Several women in late-seventeenth-century France, for instance, used the **genre** to resist and critique social constraints on women, reworking tales first in salons (in oral retellings) and then in writing, as exemplified by Marie-Catherine d'Aulnoy's *Contes de fées* (*Fairy Tales*) (1697). As oral versions began to be written down in the seventeenth to nineteenth centuries, however, many stories were recast as morality tales and sanitized for children's consumption by the removal of violence, the punishment of **villains**, and the addition of happy endings. Recently, many writers have sought to reinvigorate the fairy tale, for both children and adults, by putting new and often comic twists on traditional stories. *Fractured fairy tales*, as these stories are often called, are usually designed to be funny but may also provide multicultural or **feminist** critiques of Western or **patriarchal** bias.

FURTHER EXAMPLES: The "Cinderella" story appears in cultures the world over; the earliest known version, "Yeh-Shen," is Chinese and was first put in writing in the mid-ninth century by Tuan Ch'eng-shih. Other versions include the Algonquin Indians' "The Rough-Face Girl"; England's "Tattercoats"; Germany's "Aschenputtel," or "Ash-Girl"; and Zimbabwe's "Nyasha." There are also Caribbean, Egyptian, Hmong, Korean, Persian, Philippine, and Zuni Cinderellas, among others. Major collections of fairy tales include Charles Perrault's *Contes de ma mère l'Oye* (*Tales of Mother Goose*) (1697), also known as *Histoires ou contes du temps passé*; *Kinder- und Hausmärchen* (*Nursery and Household Tales*) (2 vols., 1812, 1814), by the Brothers Grimm; Hans Christian Andersen's *Eventyr* (*Fairy Tales*) (1835); and Andrew Lang's *Fairy Book* series starting with *The Blue Fairy Book* in 1889 and ending with *The Lilac Fairy Book* in 1910. Contemporary fractured fairy tales for children include Robert Munsch's *The Paper Bag Princess* (1982), about a princess who saves a prince; Fiona French's *Snow White in New York* (1986); and Jon Scieszka's *The True Story of the 3 Little Pigs* (1989), which tells the tale from the wolf's **point of view.** Fractured fairy tales for an adult audience include Angela Carter's *The Bloody Chamber* (1979), a dark feminist reworking of traditional tales, and *Black Thorn/White Rose* (1994), a collection edited by Ellen Datlow and Terri Windling. The tagline of *Shrek* (2001), a twisted fairy tale that **lampoons** the fairy-tale formula, was "[t]he greatest fairy tale never told."

▶ **fallacy of expressive form:** See **expressive form.**

▶ **falling action:** In a **tragedy,** that portion of the **plot** that follows the **climax** or the **crisis** and that leads to and culminates in the **catastrophe.** (In other **genres** — fiction, for example — the falling action leads to and culminates in the **resolution** of the plot.) Falling action is one of five **structural** elements associated with **Freytag's Pyramid,** a model developed by nineteenth-century German writer Gustav Freytag for analyzing five-act plays (tragedies in particular).

▶ **fancy:** A term generally used synonymously with **imagination** and in opposition to *reason* until the publication of *Biographia Literaria* (1817), by **romantic** poet Samuel Taylor Coleridge, who assigned a much higher value to imagination than to fancy. Coleridge saw fancy as a mode of memory "emancipated" from the normal constraints of time and space and assigned to it the function of reordering the sensory **images** it receives. He thus denied fancy any creative capability, limiting its effects to a rearrangement of what already exists. He credited imagination with the loftier function of creation, arguing that it is the **organic** imagination that can dissolve and remake sensory images — essentially "re-birth" them — into something completely new and different. Imagination alone, unlike the **mechanical** fancy, has the ability to unify disparate and even contradictory elements into a vital and interdependent whole. William Wordsworth, also a romantic poet, had drawn a similar (though by no means identical) distinction between imagination and fancy two years before Coleridge in his preface to the 1815 edition of *Lyrical Ballads;* nonetheless, it is Coleridge who usually is credited with making the distinction because of his extensive and in-depth discussion in the *Biographia Literaria.*

Subsequent critics have continued to differentiate fancy from imagination, but most do not delineate the two in as judgmental a manner as Coleridge. Instead, they typically claim that fancy produces a lesser, lighter verse while imagination generates the higher, more serious work we attribute to greater artists.

EXAMPLES: Coleridge considered John Milton an imaginative writer and Abraham Cowley a fanciful one. Since Coleridge, most critics have assumed that **light verse**, such as **limericks**, results from the workings of fancy, whereas a poem like Walt Whitman's "Song of Myself" (1881) is the work of imagination.

▶ **fantastic:** See **fantasy fiction.**

▶ **fantasy fiction:** A type of **fiction** set wholly or in part in a vaguely **medieval** Arthurian or imaginary land populated by inhabitants subject to magic, as well as by magical figures, creatures, or beasts. Attempts to define the term more broadly are complicated by the overlap between fantasy fiction and other **genres,** such as **science fiction** and **horror,** and further compounded by the tendency of fantasy authors to import and mix elements of different genres. Examples of hybrid works include Piers Anthony's fantasy–science fiction *Apprentice Adept* series (1980–90), Clive Barker's fantasy-horror novel *Weaveworld* (1987), and television's animated *He-Man* (1983–85, 2002–) and *She-Ra* (1985–88) cartoon series, which combine fantasy, science fiction, and action / adventure.

Fantasy should not be confused with *fantastic,* a related term applicable not only to fantasy fiction but also to other literary **forms,** such as **magic realism** and **cyberfiction,** that contain fanciful, supernatural, or otherwise incredible elements. As defined by theorist Tzvetan Todorov in *Introduction à la littérature fantastique (The Fantastic)* (1970), the fantastic mingles the marvelous (which concerns magical events and locales) with the uncanny (which can be explained as delusion), thereby creating "hesitation" (i.e., **ambiguity** and uncertainty) as to whether a natural or supernatural explanation accounts for events in a **narrative.** It is this uncertainty that distinguishes fantastic **plots** from horror plots, which typically involve an unquestionably supernatural actor or element. Fantastic **texts** discussed by Todorov include works ranging from *The Arabian Nights* (also known as *The Thousand and One Nights* [c. 1450]) to Edgar Allan Poe's short stories (c. 1840s) to Henry James's *The Turn of the Screw* (1898).

Fantasy fiction, which has roots in **folk tales** and **fairy tales,** emerged as a modern literary **mode** in the mid-nineteenth century, during the **Victorian Period. Tales** translated into English in the first half of the nineteenth century from sources including *The Arabian Nights* and the **classic** stories of Hans Christian Andersen and the Brothers Grimm proved particularly influential, as evidenced by works such as Charles Dickens's *A Christmas Carol* (1843), John Ruskin's *The King of the Golden River* (1851), George MacDonald's *Phantastes* (1858), Lewis Carroll's *Alice's Adventures in Wonderland* (1865), Oscar Wilde's *The Happy Prince and Other Stories* (1888), Arthur Machen's *Fantastic Tales* (1890), and William Morris's *The*

Roots of the Mountains (1890). Illustrations of many fantasy narratives produced by these writers anticipate the extravagant visual aspects of some forms of present-day fantasy fiction.

Other important influences on the development of fantasy fiction as a genre include **Romantic** poetry, **medievalism,** and Arthurian **legends.** Romantic poetry, which **privileged** the **imagination** and incorporated fantastic elements, as exemplified by Samuel Taylor Coleridge's "The Rime of the Ancient Mariner" (1798) and Percy Bysshe Shelley's "The Witch of Atlas" (1824), helped set the stage for the emergence of fantasy fiction, which by its very nature eschews "believable" events and **settings.** Medievalism — an interest in the art, history, and thought of the **Middle Ages** exhibited by several Romantic poets as well as writers and painters associated with the Victorian movement of **Pre-Raphaelitism,** such as Morris — provided fantasy writers with a source of **images, themes,** and settings that remain popular to this day. In this regard, the genre is especially indebted to Alfred, Lord Tennyson, whose influential narrative poem *Idylls of the King* (1859) repopularized traditional Arthurian legends, that is, tales of King Arthur and the Knights of the Round Table. Fantasies attesting to continuing interest in Arthurian lore throughout the twentieth century and beyond include T. H. White's *The Once and Future King* (1958), which compiles *The Sword in the Stone* (1938) and the three other novels comprising White's Arthurian tetrology; Mary Stewart's *Merlin* trilogy (1970–79); movies such as John Boorman's *Excalibur* (1981) and Jerry Zucker's *First Knight* (1995); and the 2001 TNT television production of Marion Zimmer Bradley's novel *The Mists of Avalon* (1982), which presents Arthurian materials from the perspective of female **characters.**

Nineteenth-century fantasy narratives were frequently meant primarily for children and young adults, but early in the twentieth century fantasy emerged as a form of popular literature with a more diverse audience. Influential fantasies from the first half of the twentieth century include E. R. Eddison's *The Worm Ourobouros* (1922); **Celtic Revival** novelist Edward Plunkett, Lord Dunsany's *The King of Elfland's Daughter* (1924); J. R. R. Tolkien's *The Hobbit* (1937); and Mervyn Peake's **Gothic, grotesque** *Gormenghast* trilogy (1946–59), adapted to television by the BBC and aired by PBS in 2001. Notable short stories, published in the American magazine *Weird Tales,* include H. P. Lovecraft's "The Call of Cthulhu" (1928); Clark Ashton Smith's "A Rendezvous in Averoigne" (1931); and Robert E. Howard's "The Phoenix on the Sword" (1932), the first of the *Conan the Cimmerian* (better known as *Conan the Barbarian*) stories.

Ironically, it was two Oxford University scholars of the **Medieval Period** — Tolkien and C. S. Lewis — who contributed significantly to the expansion of fantasy fiction beyond medieval settings and Arthurian lore. Both writers sought to produce literary works distinct not only from **realism** but also from the **allusive,** complex **modernism** of writers such as T. S. Eliot and James Joyce, who drew heavily on **classical mythology.** The characters in Lewis's seven-volume *Narnia* series (1950–56), an example of theological fantasy fiction, shift back and forth between the middle-class world of twentieth-century England and the alternative, imaginary world of Narnia. The characters in Tolkien's *The Hobbit* and his *Lord of the Rings* trilogy (1954–55; adapted to film 2001–03), by contrast, exist solely in a second world, called "Middle Earth," that is heavily influenced by Scandinavian and Anglo-Saxon myths.

There are two basic narrative strategies typical of non-Arthurian fantasy fiction. The first, exemplified by Lewis, is to have characters shuttle back and forth between a "real" and a fantasy realm. The second, exemplified by Tolkien, is to set stories entirely in a "second world," one that is separate and different from historical reality, though it may contain familiar elements. (Responding to charges of escapism, Tolkien defended the creation of second worlds as a way to loosen the constraints of conventional thinking.) In either case, the fantasy narrative is generally linear, proceeding in a logical, chronological fashion.

Today, Tolkien is commonly regarded as the fountainhead of contemporary fantasy fiction. His essay "On Fairy-Stories" (1938) has figured significantly in discussions of fantasy's **aesthetic** and social value, and his *Lord of the Rings* trilogy, more than any other work, continues to define the **conventions** of the genre. Key among these conventions is a focus on the struggle between good and evil, often conceptualized as light and dark. Several scholars have characterized Tolkien's description of this tension as ethnocentric, arguing that the struggle in Middle Earth is culturally twofold, with "good" characters — men, elves, dwarves, and hobbits — being identified with Western (and, more specifically, Anglo-Saxon) values, and "bad" ones — including subhuman trolls and goblins, as well as corrupted or mutated elves (orcs), humans (e.g., Nazgul), and hobbits (e.g., Gollum) — representing the nonwhite, non-Western **Other**. Other scholars, however, have argued that Tolkien's world is not so clearly delineated, pointing out, for instance, that it is Gollum's fateful intervention, not that of the hobbit **hero** Frodo Baggins, that ultimately results in the destruction of the terrible Ring of Power.

Also conventional in fantasy fiction is the use of a male **protagonist** with traditional, **patriarchal** Western values and attitudes. The **archetypal** hero is typically unaware, at first, of his true identity and/or abilities, but his coming fulfills some prophecy, and his actions ultimately save his life, love, and community from the depredations of evil, magical, and often foreign enemies. Fantasy fiction involving heroic triumph of such magnitude is sometimes called **epic**, or "high," fantasy.

Although religion and religious faith are seldom a focus of fantasy fiction, the protagonist's conduct rarely strays far from that prescribed by the Ten Commandments, and his battles are grounded in Judeo-Christian moral precepts. Archetypal heroes invariably strive to do the right thing, assiduously avoiding self-serving, decadent behavior and often avoiding intimate, sexual relationships as well. When such relationships do occur, they tend to be implied rather than expressly acknowledged and are almost always monogamous, or at least serially monogamous, like those of Conan, a typical "sword and sorcery" hero. Infidelity is almost always the result of bewitchment, and profanity usually takes the form of archaic English expressions or of words coined by gods. Violent action, although often described graphically, mainly affects the story's **antagonists;** the protagonist and his companions generally emerge relatively unscathed, though they may suffer greatly in the course of achieving their quests. Notably, when good characters do die, they are often resurrected in the final scene or scenes.

Fantasy fiction, while privileging magic, tends to de-emphasize technology and science and to emphasize sociopolitical structures characteristic of preindustrial societies. Unlike science fiction and cyberfiction, which feature computers, spaceships, and a variety of as-yet-only-imagined technological marvels, fantasy fiction is more likely to incorporate agrarian inventions such as aqueducts, catapults, and windmills. Where issues of politics and government are concerned, fantasy fiction tends to rely on feudal models involving peasants and kings, slaves and serfs, knights and lords.

Several additional fantasy conventions derive from the work of Ursula K. Le Guin, a popular writer of both fantasy and science fiction. For instance, the training of wizards, a fantasy **motif** extensively developed in J. K. Rowling's *Harry Potter* series (1997–2007), harks back to Le Guin's novel *A Wizard of Earthsea* (1968). Le Guin is also credited with creating an "economy" and "ecology" of magic, for her magicians pay a physical price for using their arcane powers. As one of the teachers at the wizardry school on the island of Roke explains in *A Wizard of Earthsea*, every act has its consequence: "To light a candle is to cast a shadow." These concepts of physical costs and consequences later came literally into play with the development of *Dungeons & Dragons™*, the ongoing role-playing fantasy game initially developed in 1973 in which players earn the ability to perform tasks and must recover after casting a spell.

Le Guin, who, like Tolkien, is a theorist as well as a novelist, has written extensively on fantasy and science fiction. In her 1973 essay, "Dreams Must Explain Themselves," she pointed out that fantasy is circular: "The snake devours its tail. Dreams must explain themselves." In a 1974 essay entitled "The Child and the Shadow," she characterized fantasy as "the language of the inner self," a vehicle for depicting and exploring the psychic and moral journey of self-knowledge.

In the last decades of the twentieth century, authors began to break with some of the long-standing conventions of fantasy fiction. One major shift has been in the **representation** of women in a genre that, given its tendency toward patriarchal models and male protagonists, has historically had few female writers and few powerful or good female characters. Women's roles within Tolkien's works, as Noelle Bowles and other **feminist** scholars have pointed out, were limited to those of peacekeepers and prizes for men's heroic efforts. Even Le Guin, a leader in feminist fantasy fiction, began her foray into the genre by implicitly accepting its patriarchal assumptions. In her first novel, *A Wizard of Earthsea,* for instance, men dominate not only the magical and mundane arenas but also the entire story line. More recently, however, Le Guin and some of her contemporaries have made a concerted effort to give the women of fantasy fiction a voice and a place of substance. Thus, while "weak [or wicked] as women's magic" are common sayings among the **folk** in the patriarchal world of Earthsea, women have emerged both as supporting and central characters in subsequent books of the *Earthsea* cycle (1968–2001). Likewise, Angela Carter's **burlesque** (and **picaresque**) novel *Nights at the Circus* (1984) features a nineteenth-century woman whose career is based on her wings and her ability to fly. Even computer and video games, traditionally male-oriented, have begun to incorporate female characters in meaningful ways. For example, the computer game *Diablo II: Lord of Destruction* (2001), a role-playing game, permits players to choose among seven roles, including three female roles (sorceress, amazon, and assassin). Perhaps in recognition of changing social values, the film version of *The Lord of the Rings: The Fellowship of the Ring* (2001) attempts to give women a larger, more influential part than they actually played in Tolkien's original.

Several contemporary authors have inverted the usual theme of the formulaically good hero succeeding on a conventionally moral quest. For instance, Stephen Donaldson's six-volume *Chronicles of Thomas Covenant* series (1977–83) involves a psychologically dysfunctional **antihero** who dies horribly without benefit of divine intervention, wrongs that are not magically righted, and characters who bear the scars of their hasty decisions. Unlike traditional fantasy heroes, Covenant doubts not only the goodness but even the reality of the second world he visits, where he brutally rapes a young woman he thinks is only a figment of his imagination. Ultimately, he becomes the unwilling savior of the very realm in which he never fully believes. In Robert Jordan's *Wheel of Time* series (1990–), the hero's exposure to and use of magic drives him insane; in *Final Fantasy VII* (1997), a video and computer game, the line between good and evil is complicated by the hero's apparent delusions; and in Terry Goodkind's *Wizard's First Rule* (1994), the hero is subjected to sexual torture. Yet such variations on the fantasy formula remain the exception rather than the rule.

FURTHER EXAMPLES: Mark Twain's **satirical** fantasy novel *A Connecticut Yankee in King Arthur's Court* (1889) draws on Arthurian legends. Madeleine L'Engle's science fiction fantasy *A Wrinkle in Time* (1962), Julie Andrews's fantasy *The Last of the Really Great Whangdoodles* (1974), and Piers Anthony's seven-volume *Incarnations of Immortality* fantasy series (1983–89) are examples of non-Arthurian fantasy novels.

The Princess Bride (1987), directed by Rob Reiner, is a well-known, lighthearted fantasy-fairy-tale film. By contrast, *The Company of Wolves* (1984), a film directed by Neil Jordan and written by Angela Carter, presents a much darker take on a traditional fairy tale — specifically, the story of Little Red Riding Hood — in casting a Freudian eye on the wolf-girl relationship.

Fantasy elements also play a significant role in magic realism and neo-Gothic works such as Anne Rice's *Interview with the Vampire* (1976), Salman Rushdie's *Midnight's Children* (1981), and Toni Morrison's *Beloved* (1987). The permeable nature of the boundary between forms of fantasy fiction is further demonstrated by the fact that *Dungeons & Dragons*™, a game influenced by Le Guin's novels, has in turn influenced later works of published fiction, such as those in the multiauthored *Dragonlance* novel series (1984–) — which has itself spawned several new games while also serving as a campaign setting for *Dungeons & Dragons*.

Fantasy, particularly medieval fantasy, is also popular in the online gaming world, as exemplified by massively multiplayer online role-playing games such as *EverQuest* (1999), the Arthurian *Dark Age of Camelot* (2001), and *World of Warcraft* (2004).

▶ **farce:** From the Latin for "to stuff," a type of low **comedy** that employs improbable or otherwise ridiculous situations and mix-ups, **slapstick** and horseplay, and crude or even bawdy **dialogue**. The humor in a farce is anything but subtle, aiming simply to entertain and evoke guffaws. Comedies or dramas may contain farcical elements without being farcical themselves.

EXAMPLES: Brandon Thomas's play *Charley's Aunt* (1892); the movie *One, Two, Three* (1961), a cold war farce set in West Berlin; Joe Orton's **black comedy** *Loot* (1965); the movie *Airplane!* (1980), which spoofs disaster films; Michael Frayn's play *Noises Off* (1982; adapted to film 1992), a backstage farce including a play-within-a-play, *Nothing On*, that is itself a sex farce; Ray Cooney's bedroom stage farce *Run for Your Wife!* (1984); the *Home Alone* movies (1990, 1992, 1997); Roger Boylan's **satirical** novel *Killoyle: An Irish Farce* (1997); Neil Simon's play *Rumors* (1998); Steve Martin's play *The Underpants* (2002), an adaptation of Carl Sternheim's 1910 satire on the bourgeoisie involving the attentions paid to a young wife (and the fears of her uptight husband) after her underpants unaccountably fall to her feet during a parade. The actor Leslie Nielsen has made a career of starring in farces, including *The Naked Gun* (1988) and *Spy Hard* (1996). *A Knight's Tale* (2001), in which Geoffrey Chaucer, **author** of *The Canterbury Tales* (c. 1387), is a **character,** is an action-packed film farce set in **medieval** times.

Sitcoms often make use of farce, whether as a mainstay or an element of a given episode. *Seinfeld* (1990–98), a contemporary **comedy of manners,** drew heavily on farce. Other sitcoms that frequently used farce include *Cheers* (1982–93, e.g., the "Dinner at Eightish" episode from season 5) and *Frasier* (1993–2004, e.g., the season 4 episode "The Two Mrs. Cranes"). The long-running television show *Saturday Night Live* (1975–) routinely features farcical skits.

▶ **Federalist Age:** See Early National Period (in American literature).

▶ **feet:** See foot.

▶ **feminine ending (light ending):** A line of **verse** ending with an extra, un-stressed syllable is said to have a feminine ending. This **extrametrical** sylla-ble, which usually concludes an **iambic** or **anapestic** line, often provides **rhythmical** variety and movement.

EXAMPLE: The following humorous, **half-rhymed,** generally anapestic lines in *A Fable for Critics* (1848), James Russell Lowell's long poem about the mid-nineteenth-century American artistic scene, have feminine endings:

> Whў, thĕre's scárce|lў ă húd|dlĕ ŏf lóg-|hŭts ănd shán|tiĕs
> Thăt hás| nŏt brŏught fórth| ĭts ŏwn Míl|tŏns ănd Dán|tĕs;
> Ĭ mўsélf| knŏw tĕn Bý| rŏns, ŏne Cóle|rĭdge, thrĕe Shél|leўs,
> Two Raphaels, six Titians, (I think) one Apelles,
> Leonardos and Rubenses plenty as lichens,
> One (but that one is plenty) American Dickens. . . .

See also **catalexis.**

▶ **feminine rhyme:** **Rhyme** in which rhyming **stressed** syllables are fol-lowed by one or more unstressed syllables. A feminine rhyme that extends over two syllables is called **double rhyme,** and one extending over three syl-lables is called **triple rhyme.** Feminine rhyme extending over four or more syllables (*quadruple rhyme, quintuple rhyme,* etc.) is rare in English.

EXAMPLES: *Banter/canter* is a double rhyme, as is *glider/divider,* since each pair of words has a rhyming stressed syllable followed by an identical unstressed syllable. *Bantering/cantering* and *insidious/perfidious* are triple rhymes. *Indicated/syndicated* is an example of quadruple rhyme. In the first **stanza** of "The Violin" (1902), Trumbull Stickney alternated double feminine rhyme (*fingers/lingers*) with an **eye rhyme** that is **masculine** (*how* and *bow*):

> You came to teach me how the hardened fingers
> Must drop and nail the music down, and how
> The sound then drags and nettled cries, then lingers
> After the dying bow. —

▶ **feminine writing:** See **feminist criticism.**

▶ **feminist criticism:** A type of **literary criticism** that became a dominant force in Western literary studies in the late 1970s, when feminist theory more broadly conceived was applied to **linguistic** and literary matters. Since the early 1980s, feminist literary criticism has developed and diversi-fied in a number of ways and is now characterized by a global perspective. It is nonetheless important to understand differences among the interests and assumptions of French, British, and North American (used in this entry to refer to the United States and Canada) feminist critics writing during the 1970s and early 1980s, given the extent to which their works shaped the evolution of contemporary feminist critical **discourse.**

French feminist criticism garnered much of its inspiration from Simone de Beauvoir's seminal book, *Le deuxième sexe* (*The Second Sex*) (1949).

Beauvoir argued that associating men with humanity more generally (as many cultures do) relegates women to an inferior position in society. Subsequent French feminist critics writing during the 1970s not only acknowledged Beauvoir's critique but focused on language as a tool of male domination, analyzing the ways in which it represents the world from the male point of view.

Drawing on the ideas of French **psychoanalytic** theorist Jacques Lacan, French feminist critics argued that language is a realm of public discourse. Children enter the linguistic realm just as they begin to understand that they are individuals, distinct from their mothers; boys also begin to identify with their fathers, the family representative of culture. All children then learn to speak a language structured in accordance with **binary oppositions** (dichotomous terms), such as masculine / feminine, father / mother, son / daughter, phallus / vagina, head / heart, active / passive, reason / emotion, and light / dark. French feminist critics pointed out that terms listed first in these binary sets tend to be aligned, as are terms listed second. Hence masculinity is associated with qualities such as light, reason, and activity, whereas femininity recalls passivity and emotion. They also argued that these two sets of terms are hierarchically structured; reason, for instance, is valued over emotion by the masculine-dominated culture. They thus concluded that language is **phallocentric, privileging** the **phallus** and masculinity.

Many French feminist critics argued that language systematically forces women to choose between adopting the male-dominated discourse or opting out — and thereby remaining silent. Women may either imagine and **represent** themselves as men imagine and represent them (in which case they may speak but will speak as men) or they can choose "silence," becoming in the process "the invisible and unheard sex," as Ann Rosalind Jones argued in her essay "Inscribing Femininity: French Theories of the Feminine" (1985).

Some French feminist critics, however, maintained that language only seems to give women a narrow range of choices. These feminists suggested that women not only have different life experiences than men but also write differently, which led them to advocate embracing and developing a feminine language. Early French feminists such as Annie Leclerc, Xavière Gauthier, and Marguerite Duras spoke of this special, feminine language as *l'écriture féminine: feminine writing,* or women's writing. Julia Kristeva, commonly considered a pioneer of French feminist thought even though she eschews the feminist label, characterized feminine language as **semiotic,** not **symbolic,** as the male-dominated **canon** of "Great Books" is said to be in works such as *Séméiôtiké: recherches pour une sémanalyse (Desire in Language: A Semiotic Approach to Literature and Art)* (1969) and *La révolution du language poétique (Revolution in Poetic Language)* (1974). By *semiotic,* she meant that feminine language is rhythmic and unifying; it does not rigidly oppose and rank qualities or elements of reality, nor does it symbolize one thing but not another in terms of a third. If from the male perspective it seems fluid to the point of being chaotic, that is a fault of the male perspective.

According to Kristeva, feminine language is derived from the pre**oedipal** period of fusion between mother and child, the period during which children do not recognize that they are separate from their mothers. Since feminine language is associated with the maternal rather than the paternal, it poses a threat to **patriarchal** culture. Kristeva's central claim — that truly feminist innovation in all fields requires an understanding of the relation between maternity and feminine creation — came paired with a warning, however: feminine or feminist writing that resists or refuses participation in "masculine" discourse risks being politically marginalized in a society that still is, after all, patriarchal. Like Kristeva, other leading French feminist critics also associated feminine writing with the female body. Hélène Cixous, for instance, posited an **essential** (natural rather than socially constructed) connection between women's bodies and women's writing: "Write your self. Your body must be heard," Cixous urged in an essay entitled "The Laugh of the Medusa" (1976). Luce Irigaray explored the connection between women's sexuality and women's language through the following analogy in a book entitled *Ce sexe qui n'en est pas un* (*This Sex Which Is Not One*) (1977): Just as women's *jouissance* (sexual pleasure) is more multiple than men's unitary, phallic pleasure ("woman has sex organs just about everywhere"), so "feminine" language is more diffusive than its "masculine" counterpart.

This emphasis on feminine writing as an expression of the female body drew criticism from other French feminists, many of whom argued that emphasizing the body either reduces "the feminine" to a biological essence or elevates it in a way that shifts the valuation of masculine and feminine but retains the binary categories. Christine Fauré, for instance, argued in "La crépuscule des déesses, ou la crise intellectuelle en France en milieu féministe" ("The Twilight of the Goddesses, or the Intellectual Crisis of French Feminism") (1981) that Irigaray's celebration of women's difference failed to address the issue of masculine dominance. Marxist-feminist Catherine Clément warned that "poetic" descriptions of the feminine do not challenge masculine dominance in the realm of production; the boys will still make the toys and decide who gets to use them. Monique Wittig even called for the abolition of sexual categories in "The Category of Sex" (1976/1982) so that women could be redefined as political rather than sexual beings.

North American feminist critics of the 1970s and early 1980s shared with French critics both an interest in and a cautious distrust of the concept of feminine writing. In "Some Notes on Defining a 'Feminist Literary Criticism'" (1975), Annette Kolodny worried that the "richness and variety of women's writing" could be overlooked in the effort to celebrate only its "feminine mode" or "style." And yet Kolodny proceeded to point out that women do have their own **style,** which includes reflexive constructions ("she found herself crying") and particular, recurring **themes** (Kolodny mentioned clothing and self-fashioning; other North American feminists have focused on madness, disease, and the demonic).

Interested as they became in the "French" subject of feminine language and writing, North American feminist critics began by analyzing literary texts — not by abstractly discussing language — via **close reading** and historical scholarship. Critics like Carolyn Heilbrun, Judith Fetterley, and Kate Millett developed a model for American feminist criticism that Elaine Showalter called the *feminist critique* of "male-constructed literary history" in an essay entitled "Toward a Feminist Poetics" (1985). Critics undertaking the feminist critique reviewed canonical works by male writers, embarking on a revisionist rereading of Western literary tradition. They examined how female **characters** are portrayed, exposing the patriarchal **ideology** implicit in the so-called **classics** and demonstrating that attitudes and traditions reinforcing systematic masculine dominance are inscribed in the literary canon. In *The Resisting Reader: A Feminist Approach to American Fiction* (1978), Fetterley urged women to become "resisting readers"; to notice how biased most male-authored texts are in their language, subjects, and attitudes; and to actively reject this bias so as to render reading a less "immasculating" experience.

Another group of North American feminist critics, including Sandra Gilbert, Susan Gubar, Patricia Meyer Spacks, and Showalter herself, created a different model, which Showalter dubbed **gynocriticism**. Whereas feminists writing feminist critique analyzed works written by men, gynocritics studied the writings of women who produced what Showalter called "a literature of their own," in a book by the same name (1977). In *The Female Imagination* (1975), Spacks examined the female literary tradition to find out how women writers across the ages have perceived themselves and imagined reality. In *The Madwoman in the Attic* (1979), Gilbert and Gubar focused on nineteenth-century women writers, arguing that similar concerns, **images,** and themes recur in their works because they lived "in a culture whose fundamental definitions of literary authority were both overtly and covertly patriarchal."

If one of the purposes of gynocriticism was to (re)study well-known women authors, another was to rediscover women's history and culture, particularly women's communities that nurtured female creativity. Another related purpose was to discover neglected or forgotten women writers and thus to forge an alternative literary tradition, a canon that better represents the female perspective. In *A Literature of Their Own*, Showalter outlined just such a tradition by providing a comprehensive overview of women's writing through three of its phases. She defined these as the "Feminine, Feminist, and Female" phases, phases during which women imitated a masculine tradition (1840–80), protested against its standards and values (1880–1920), and advocated their own autonomous, female perspective (1920–present).

With the recovery of a body of women's texts, attention returned to a question raised by North American feminist critic Lillian Robinson in *Sex, Class, and Culture* (1978): shouldn't feminist criticism formulate a **theory** of its own practice, since without one feminist critics must rely on critical discourses that are themselves part of the patriarchal tradition? Some feminist critics worried that using approaches such as psychoanalytic theory, **formalism,** and **Marxism** would prevent feminist theory from being accepted as an equal; others denied the need for a special or unifying theory of feminist practice. Kolodny, for instance, advocated a "playful pluralism" encompassing a variety of critical schools and methods. Nevertheless, critics such as Jane Marcus feared that if feminists incorporated too many approaches, they might relax the tensions between feminists and the educational establishment that spur political activism.

While it gradually became customary to refer to an Anglo-American tradition of feminist criticism, British feminist critics of the 1970s and early 1980s criticized the tendency of some North American critics to find universal feminine attributes, arguing that differences of **race, class,** and culture gave rise to crucial differences among women. Taking a more political approach, British feminist critics emphasized an engagement with historical process in order to promote social change. They asserted that North American celebrations of individual **heroines** falsely suggest that certain individuals may be immune to repressive, patriarchal conditions and may even imply that *any* individual can go through life unconditioned by the culture in which he or she lives. Similarly, British critics like Judith Newton and Deborah Rosenfelt viewed the North American effort to recover women's history as an endeavor that obscured male oppression, implying that it created special opportunities for women. Most importantly, British feminist critics rejected the universalizing and essentializing tendencies of much North American practice and most French theory; they feared that celebrating sexual difference disguised women's oppression and enabled patriarchy to survive and thrive.

By the early 1990s, the French, American, and British approaches had so thoroughly critiqued, influenced, and assimilated one another that nationality no longer automatically signaled a practitioner's approach. Today's critics seldom focus on "woman" as a relatively monolithic category; rather, they view "women" as members of different societies with different concerns. Feminists of color, **postcolonial** feminists, and lesbian feminists ask whether the universal category of woman constructed during the 1970s and early 1980s by certain French and North American critics is appropriate to describe women in minority groups or non-Western cultures. They stress that women are not defined solely by the fact that they are female; other attributes (such as religion, class, and **sexuality**) are also important, making the problems and goals of one group of women different from those of another. For instance, in *Borderlands/La Frontera: The New Mestiza* (1987), Gloria Anzaldúa, who grew up under the influence of both the Mexican and Anglo cultures, discussed the experience of many women living on the margins of Eurocentric North American culture.

Instead of being divisive, this evolution of feminism into femin*isms* fostered a more inclusive, global perspective, a recognition that feminism comes in many forms and that feminist critics have a variety of goals. The emphasis on recovering women's texts — especially texts by white Western women — has been supplanted by an effort to recover entire cultures of women. In works such as *In Other Worlds: Essays in Cultural Politics* (1987) and *Outside in the Teaching Machine* (1993), Indian feminist critic Gayatri Chakravorty Spivak demonstrated that national political independence for postcolonial countries is not the simple and beneficial change metropolitan Westerners commonly assume it to be; rather, independence has complex implications for "subaltern" and "subproletarian" women (women with an inferior position, rank, or caste and nonwage-earning women whose material conditions are substantially inferior to those we associate with working-class life), who may end up worse off than they were under colonial rule.

With the shifting understanding of woman as the nexus of diverse experiences, some white, Western, "majority" feminists like Jane Tompkins and Nancy K. Miller have advocated and practiced **personal** or **autobiographical criticism,** incorporating their personal reactions and even histories in their readings of literary texts. And with the advent of more personal feminist critical styles has come a new interest in women's autobiographical writings. Some feminist critics have characterized traditional **autobiography** as a gendered, "masculinist" **genre,** given that its established **conventions** emphasize action, triumph through **conflict,** intellectual self-discovery, and public renown and downplay or even ignore the body, reproduction, children, and intimate interpersonal relationships. Arguing that the lived experience of women and men differ, with women's lives being characterized by interruption and deferral to a much greater extent than men's, Leigh Gilmore developed a theory of women's self-representation in her book *Autobiographics* (1994).

Other developments in feminist criticism include feminist performance theory, feminist film theory, and **lesbian criticism.** Building on Joan Riviere's insight in "Womanliness as Masquerade" (1929) that all femininity involves masquerade, feminist performance theorists argue that femininity is a social construct rather than a natural quality. Feminist film theorists analyze films as vehicles that perpetuate and enshrine the perception of women as sex objects. As Teresa de Lauretis argued in *Alice Doesn't: Feminism, Semiotics, Cinema* (1986), movies represent "woman as spectacle — body to be looked at, place of sexuality, and object of desire." Lesbian critics have focused on sexuality by arguing that most critics (including some of their feminist counterparts) proceed from heterosexual and even heterosexist assumptions and by reinterpreting works by authors ranging from Emily Dickinson to Toni Morrison. All three of these approaches, however, have been as often associated — if not more often associated — with **gender criticism** as with feminist criticism.

Gender criticism, an approach to literary criticism that focuses on — and critiques — **gender** as it is commonly conceived in order to expose its insufficiency as a category, has grown considerably since the mid-1980s. Feminist criticism, which arose before gender criticism and heavily influenced its development, is now sometimes viewed as a form of gender criticism because of its focus on the feminine gender. Nonetheless, several distinctions can be made between adherents of the two approaches, even as practitioners of each continue to critique and influence those in the other. First, feminist critics tend to focus on women and women's issues, whereas gender critics have focused as much on men as women. Second, many feminist critics tend to equate gender with sex and gender difference with sexual difference, treating both gender and sex as natural or innate, whereas gender critics typically take a **constructionist** position, viewing gender as a social artifact, a product of language and culture distinct from biological sex. Third, many feminist critics have spoken of a feminine language grounded in sexual difference, a concept many gender critics reject, positing a relationship only between gender and writing, not biological sex and writing.

▶ **fiction:** In the broadest sense of the word, any writing that relates imagined **characters** and occurrences rather than recounting real ones. Defined more narrowly, *fiction* refers to prose **narratives** (specifically the **short story** and the **novel**), rather than to **verse** or nonnarrative **prose.**

The boundary between fiction and **nonfiction** is porous, as the movie *Capote* (2005) suggests referencing Truman Capote's description of his book *In Cold Blood* (1965), about the murder of a Kansas family, as "nonfiction fiction." **Autobiographical** fiction, in which the **author** passes off as inventions events that actually occurred, and the **historical novel,** in which the author makes use of real people or events in an invented **plot,** are types of fiction that border on fact. Conversely, nonfictional works such as *creative nonfiction* and the **nonfiction novel** make extensive use of techniques associated with fiction. The term *faction,* a **portmanteau word** often credited to American writer Norman Mailer, refers to works that blur the boundary between fact and fiction. For example, Frances Sherwood's *Vindication* (1993), which Sherwood characterized as a "biographical novel," is a heavily researched but fictionalized account of the life of Mary Wollstonecraft, author of the groundbreaking work *A Vindication of the Rights of Women* (1792).

▶ **figurative language:** Language that employs one or more **figures of speech** to supplement or modify the literal, **denotative** meanings of words with additional **connotations.** Figurative language adds color, immediacy, and richness to **narratives.**

EXAMPLES: The following passage from E. Annie Proulx's *The Shipping News* (1993):

> It began with his parents. First the father, diagnosed with liver cancer, a blush of wild cells diffusing. A month later a tumor fastened in the mother's brain like a burr, crowding her thoughts to one side. The father blamed the power station. Two hundred yards from their house sizzling wires, thick as eels, came down from northern towers.

In Geraldine Brooks's **historical novel** *Year of Wonders* (2001), set in a plague-ridden seventeenth-century English village, herbalist Anys Gowdie insists on her freedom, telling Anna, the **protagonist,** "I'm not made to be any man's chattel. . . . And besides, . . . sometimes a woman needs a draught of nettle beer to wake her up, and sometimes she needs a dish of valerian to calm her down. Why cultivate a garden with only one plant in it?"

For a humorous take on the difference between literal and figurative interpretations of a statement — in this case, a witch's declaration that she has a baby "in the oven" — see the *Far Side* cartoon below.

See also **figure of speech.**

THE FAR SIDE® BY GARY LARSON

© 1990 FarWorks, Inc. All Rights Reserved/Dist. by Creators Syndicate

The Far Side® by Gary Larson © 1990 FarWorks, Inc. All Rights Reserved. The Far Side® and the Larson® signature are registered trademarks of FarWorks, Inc. Used with permission.

"Oh, Helen! You're pregnant? That's wonderful! ...
At first, I was taking you quite literally when you
said you had one in the oven!"

▶ **figure of speech:** A literary device involving unusual use of language, often to associate or compare distinct things. Figures of speech typically depart from the usual order of words or from their literal meaning to create an **image** in the reader's mind. Language that uses figures of speech is called **figurative language.**

Numerous figures of speech exist, and they are commonly divided into two general categories: **rhetorical figures** and **tropes.** Rhetorical figures, also called **schemes,** use words in some special way to create an unexpected effect without significantly altering the words' meanings. (If your mother asks you to "Trot on down to the video store and check out *The Da Vinci Code,*" she doesn't change the meaning of the word *trot,* but she may cause you to picture yourself as a horse.) Tropes, also called *figures of thought,* fundamentally change the meanings of words. (If you say that someone is "hot to trot," or if you tell someone that you "plowed through Dan Brown's novel *The Da Vinci Code* before watching the DVD," you change the meaning of the words *trot* and *plow.*)

Figures of speech have also been categorized in other ways, for instance by dividing them into three classes, depending on whether they **foreground** imagined similarities (e.g., **conceit, simile**), associations (e.g., **metonymy, synecdoche**), or appeals to the ear and eye (e.g., **alliteration, onomatopoeia**). Most critics, however, do not recognize devices in the third category as figures of speech, instead referring to them as *figures of sound.*

Perhaps the best-known and therefore most readily recognizable figures of speech are the five principal tropes: **metaphor,** metonymy, **personification,** simile, and synecdoche. Major rhetorical figures include **antithesis, apostrophe, chiasmus, parallelism, syllepsis,** and **zeugma. Deconstructive** critic Paul de Man also viewed **irony** as a figure of speech.

▶ **figure of thought:** See **figure of speech, trope.**

▶ *fin de siècle:* French for "end of the century," a phrase referring generally to works produced in the last years of any century and specifically to the transitional 1890s, when French, English, and American writers were beginning to break free from the constraints and polite **conventions** associated with **Victorianism** in favor of bold techniques and bolder subjects. When used as a chronological marker for the period 1890–1900, *fin de siècle* encompasses works written by darkly **realistic** writers, members of the **Aesthetic Movement,** and authors of radical or revolutionary works envisioning an **apocalyptic** end to the old social order. The phrase is most often used, however, with reference to late-nineteenth-century French writers associated with the **Decadence,** a literary movement characterized by works that conveyed a sense of lassitude and boredom, rejected conventional social mores, and reflected the view that art is independent of morality. The term has also come to signify a period of literary decline or confusion.

▶ **first-person point of view:** See **point of view.**

▶ **flashback:** A **scene** that interrupts the present **action** of a **narrative** work to depict some earlier event — often one that occurred before the opening scene of the work — via reverie, remembrance, dreaming, or some other mechanism. The term may be used to refer to the scene itself or to its presentation.

Flashback is a form of **analepsis,** one of the three major types of **anachrony.** The device has its origins in the ancient **epic** tradition of beginning a work *in medias res* ("in the middle of things") and then moving back in time to tell the beginning of the story.

EXAMPLES: The entire narrative of Daphne du Maurier's *Rebecca* (1938), which begins "Last night I dreamt I went to Manderley again," is a flashback imbued wih uncertainty and **ambiguity.** In *The Naked and the Dead* (1948), a novel of World War II that depends upon the interplay between past and present, author Norman Mailer identified flashback sequences via the indented, boldfaced phrase "The Time Machine." Movies with flashbacks include *Casablanca* (1942), in which the song "As Time Goes By" signals a flashback to happier times, Rick and Ilsa's whirlwind romance prior to the Nazi occupation of Paris; *The Accused* (1988), which flashes back to the scene of a gang-rape near the end of the movie, as a witness is testifying at trial; Quentin Tarantino's *Reservoir Dogs* (1992) and *Pulp Fiction* (1994), both of which weave flashbacks throughout the **action;** and *Eternal Sunshine of the Spotless Mind* (2004), which begins with the main **characters,** former lovers Joel and Clementine, meeting again and most of which involves a flashback to their first relationship and subsequent effort to literally erase one other from their memories. The television show *Lost* (2004–), in which victims of a plane crash struggle to survive under mysterious and threatening conditions on a tropical island, incorporates multiple flashbacks in nearly every episode to provide characters' backstories and shed light on their motivations, secrets, and pre-crash connections with others on the island.

▶ **flashforward:** See **anachrony, prolepsis.**

▶ **flat and round characters:** Terms coined by English writer E. M. Forster in *Aspects of the Novel* (1927) to refer to the depth and complexity of **characterization.** *Flat characters* lack depth and complexity. They tend to be **caricatures** defined by a single idea or quality whose essences can be summed up in a sentence. *Round characters,* by contrast, are fully developed, with the complexity and depth associated with real people. They can surprise readers convincingly, for they have full-blown personalities complete with contradictions and quirks that make it difficult to describe them reductively. Forster argued that works need a mixture of flat and round characters in order to represent the world as readers perceive it, so he did not automatically assign a pejorative **connotation** to flat characters.

EXAMPLE: Minor characters in the *Sweet Valley High* adolescent novel series (1983–98), created by Francine Pascal, tend to be flat characters; consistently described in the same way, they can be depended on to behave predictably, thereby fulfilling specific **plot** functions. Examples include Bruce Patman, an arrogant rich snob; Lila Fowler, a daddy's girl obsessed with her wealth and looks; and Enid Rollins, Elizabeth Wakefield's devoted, loyal, studious — and mousy — best friend. These characters become round characters in the books devoted to them; thus, the rare book featuring Bruce Patman as the **protagonist** can be counted on to reveal good qualities underlying and complicating his trademark snootiness.

▶ **foil:** A **character** whose contrast with the main character (**protagonist**) serves to accentuate the latter's distinctive qualities or characteristics.

EXAMPLES: Fortinbras is a foil to Hamlet in William Shakespeare's play *Hamlet* (1602), taking decisive action while Hamlet, the protagonist, vacillates. "Slasher movies" often use a less subtle foil. In films such as the *Halloween* (1978–95) and *Friday the 13th* (1980–) series, promiscuous teenagers are murdered, often while they are having sex, thus highlighting the virginal purity of the **heroine**, who survives the killer's attacks.

▶ **folk:** See **folklore**.

▶ **folk drama:** Originally, theatrical performances by ordinary people, or **folk**. Folk drama encompasses a wide variety of forms, such as **plays**, renditions of religious stories, and traditional ceremonies and activities (such as sword dances) associated with seasonal festivals. Folk drama originated in the fertility rites of ancient communities as a way to pay tribute to agricultural gods. Performances honoring Dionysus — the Greek god of fertility, vegetation, and, more specifically, wine — may have been forerunners of Greek **tragedy**. Some English folk dramas grounded in **medieval** traditions and dating from the **Renaissance** — for example, *The Plough Monday Play* — are still performed today.

In the twentieth century, the term *folk drama* was defined more broadly to include works written by playwrights and performed by professional actors, so long as the works express the beliefs, culture, language, and traditions of the folk. Accordingly, the plays of J. M. Synge; Isabella Augusta, Lady Gregory; William Butler Yeats; and other writers of the **Celtic Revival** are considered to be folk drama.

FURTHER EXAMPLES: Forms of folk drama from around the world include *mummers' plays* (England), which feature **fantastic** situations, masked actors, **pantomimes**, and sword fights; Yangge (China); Ta'ziyeh (Iran); Apidán (Nigeria); and Karagöz (Turkey). **Victorian** children's author Juliana Horatia Ewing's story *The Peace Egg* (1871) features the performance of a Christmas folk drama; Ewing later assembled a script from five versions of the folk drama and published it as *A Christmas Mumming Play* (1884). Thomas Hardy's novel *The Return of the Native* (1878) also incorporates a folk drama, a mummers' play known as *The Play of St. George*, into Book 2, Chapters 4–6. In a 1901 interview with critic William Archer, published in *Pall Mall Magazine* (1901) and *Real Conversations* (1904), Hardy described the play and its performance, which continued until about 1880 in some areas, as follows:

> Oh, our mummers hereabouts gave a regular performance — *The Play of St George* it was called. It contained quite a number of traditional characters: the Valiant Soldier, the Turkish Knight, St George himself, the Saracen, Father Christmas, the Fair Sabra, and so on. . . .

The performers used to carry a long staff in one hand and a wooden sword in the other, and pace monotonously round, intoning their parts on one note, and punctuating them by nicking the sword against the staff — something like this: — "Here come I, the Valiant Soldier (*nick*), Slasher is my name (*nick*)".

. . . [I]t ended in a series of mortal combats in which all the characters but St George were killed. And then the curious thing was that they were invariably brought to life again. A personage was introduced for the purpose — the Doctor of Physic, wearing a cloak and a broad-brimmed beaver.

. . . Sometimes a large village would furnish forth two sets of mummers. They would go to the farmhouses round, between Christmas and Twelfth Night, doing some four or five performances each evening, and getting ale and money at every house. Sometimes the mummers of one village would encroach on the traditional "sphere of influence" of another village, and then there would be a battle in good earnest.

Hardy later published a version of the play in 1928.

Twentieth-century playwright Paul Green's **history plays** reflect the regional experiences, values, and culture of ordinary people who settled in the U.S. *The Common Glory*, Green's "symphonic drama" of the Revolutionary War "with music, commentary, English folksong, and dance," was performed by the Jamestown Corporation in Williamsburg, Virginia, from 1947–76; *The Lost Colony* (1937), a symphonic drama about the mysterious fate of the Roanoke Island colony in North Carolina, is still put on every summer by the local historical association. Folk dramas based on "Old World" religious drama still being performed today as part of Hispanic Christmas celebrations along the Rio Grande in Texas include *Pastorela* (also called *Los pastores*), an often-comedic account of the shepherds' journey to see the Christ child, and *Las Posadas,* a serious account, performed over nine nights, of Joseph and Mary's search for lodging prior to Jesus's birth. The Mummers Parade in Philadelphia, held on New Year's Day since 1901, is organized by local clubs; draws about 15,000 performers annually; and features spectacular costumes, dance routines, and portable scenery. Troupes compete in one of four categories: Comics, skits often based on current events; Fancies, costume spectaculars; String Bands, marching bands with costumes, dancers, and portable scenery; and Fancy Brigades, costumed dancers who perform with scenery and prerecorded music at a set point.

See also **folklore.**

▶ **folklore:** The beliefs, traditions, rituals, stories, and other creative expressions of ordinary people, or *folk,* that have been transmitted orally or shared by example through successive generations. Folklore encompasses a wide range of community traditions that tend to evolve over time and that may be articulated through **ballads, tales, epics, dramas, legends,** and **myths,** as well as through less "literary" forms such as **folk tales, folk dramas, folk** songs, folk dances, **proverbs, maxims,** riddles, nursery rhymes, superstitions, spells, and plant and animal lore. Social customs and rituals regarding key life events such as birth, death, courtship, and marriage are also aspects of folklore, as are the traditions associated with the communal construction of quilts, houses, and barns.

Scholars today differ in their definitions of *folklore,* perhaps in large part because various individuals and groups have assigned the term different meanings over time. W. J. Thoms, a nineteenth-century English scholar, coined the word in 1646 as an Anglo-Saxon alternative to the Latinate phrase "popular antiquities," which referred to the intellectual heritage of the peasant **class.** Subsequently, in the late 1800s, the Folklore Society of London treated folklore as a means as well as subject of study, asserting that folklore involves "the comparison and identification of the survivals of archaic beliefs, customs, and traditions in modern ages." Later, Alexander H. Krappe, who like the Folklore Society approached folklore as a discipline and not merely as a subject of study, asserted in *The Science of Folklore* (1930) that folklore allows us to understand the unwritten "spiritual history" of past civilizations by focusing on the sayings of common people rather than on histories written by intellectuals.

With the expansion over time of the term **folk** to all people who lived before the industrial age, the scope of the term *folklore* has likewise been broadened. Increasingly, it is not limited to the traditions of earlier cultures but encompasses the distinctive traditions of any community, past or present, with widely shared interests, purposes, and attitudes toward everyday life. In addition, although these attitudes and their expression have generally been recognized as folklore only when conveyed orally, some scholars have recognized as "folkloric" certain traditions and customs transmitted in writing.

Although experts do not agree upon any one definition, most have acknowledged that folklore has five basic characteristics, the first three being the most important. Folklore must be: (1) primarily transmitted orally; (2) rooted in tradition; (3) available in different versions or **texts;** (4) anonymous; and (5) eventually standardized. Most scholars also agree that folklore is shared and passed on at the grass-roots level of society rather than being formally taught via societal institutions such as the government, schools, churches, and so on. **Privileging** its **aesthetic** aspect, scholar Dan Ben-Amos summarized folklore as "artistic communication in small groups" in his essay "Toward a Definition of Folklore in Context" (1971).

Although folkloric **genres** and traditions have customarily been distinguished from the literary, musical, and dance forms associated with so-called high culture, folk **conventions, motifs,** and lore are commonly incorporated into these more "sophisticated" forms.

EXAMPLES: Eliot Wigginton's *Foxfire* books — especially *The Foxfire Book* (1972) and *Foxfire 2* (1973) — extensively collected and preserved Appalachian folklore including ghost stories, snake lore, burial customs, and information about planting various crops in accordance with astrological cycles. **Urban legends** — a much more recent phenomenon — have been similarly collected by folklore professor Jan Brunvand in ten compilations including the *Encyclopedia of Urban Legends* (2002) and *Be Afraid, Be Very Afraid* (2004).

As noted above, folklore comes in many forms. Folkloric superstitions include the beliefs that walking under a ladder, breaking a mirror, and crossing paths with a black cat bring bad luck, as well as the belief that throwing spilled salt over your shoulder will counter the bad luck entailed by the spill. Proverbs include such contradictory standbys as "absence makes the heart grow fonder" and "out of sight, out of mind." Maxims include the advice that "people who live in glass houses shouldn't throw stones" and "an apple a day keeps the doctor away." Folklore also comes in the form of scary campfire stories, such as the tale about a babysitter receiving a phone call from inside the house and the one about two people who, after parking in a locked car, find the hook of a one-armed convict hanging on the door handle. Children's folklore includes the sidewalk superstition "Step on a crack, break your mother's back" and nursery rhymes such as "Ring Around the Rosy," which is often said to reference a very serious subject: the bubonic plague, also called the Black Death, that swept across China, West Asia, and Europe in the fourteenth century and broke out again in London in 1665.

The influence of ancient folklore traditions on **classical** literature is evident in works such as William Shakespeare's *King Lear* (1606), in which the **tragic hero** disinherits his honest daughter for saying she loves him only as a daughter should. With regard to more contemporary works, the Coen brothers' film *O Brother, Where Art Thou?* (2000) reflects the ancient folkloric **theme** of men bewitched by fairy women.

See also **folk drama, folk song, folk tale.**

▶ **folk song:** A song of unidentified origin that has been orally transmitted through successive generations within a given community. Folk songs, which are usually accompanied by acoustic instruments, typically recount stories about everyday life and express the hopes and beliefs of ordinary people. Common types of folk songs include **ballads,** carols, lullabies, spirituals, work songs, hobo songs, drinking songs, songs of the sea, and songs of unrequited love.

In North America, the definition of folk song broadened in the twentieth century to include folksy lyrics written or popularized by musical artists such as Woody Guthrie; Pete Seeger; Peter, Paul, and Mary; Joan Baez; Judy Collins; Joni Mitchell; Bob Dylan; and Arlo Guthrie.

EXAMPLES: Anonymous religious songs such as "Kumbaya My Lord," a slave song with African roots, and "Have-Na Gila," a popular Jewish folk song and dance. Folk songs that began as written compositions attributable to a specific person include works by Stephen Foster (1826–64) such as "Camptown Races" and "Oh! Susanna." *The Long Road to Freedom: An Anthology of Black Music,* a multi-artist recording project spearheaded by Harry Belafonte from 1961–71 and released in 2001, documents three hundred years of black American folk music, from the early 1600s to the early twentieth century.

Well-known twentieth-century folk songs include Woody Guthrie's "This Land Is Your Land" (1940); Belafonte's version of the Jamaican "Banana Boat Song" from his album *Calypso* (1956); Pete Seeger's "We Shall Overcome" (1963), his version of a union labor song that was itself based on a gospel **hymn;** Bob Dylan's "Blowin' in the Wind" (1963); and Steve Goodman's "City of New Orleans" (1970), a song popularized by Arlo Guthrie in 1972 about ordinary people on a lightly loaded passenger train by that name. Contemporary folk singers include Catie Curtis, Ani Difranco, and Nanci Griffith.

See also **ballad, folklore.**

▶ **folk tale:** A short **narrative** that has been orally transmitted through successive generations within a given community and that typically evolves over time. Although folk tales usually begin as oral **tales** of unidentified origin, they are generally committed to writing at some point. Occasionally, the reverse happens: an original, published story by a specific, identified person comes to be thought of as a folk tale and thus enters the realm of **folklore.**

Folk tales may include **fables, fairy tales, legends, myths,** tall tales, ghost stories, stories about giants, stories about saints, and humorous **anecdotes.**

EXAMPLES: Stories about Annie Oakley, Casey Jones, Daniel Boone, Davy Crockett, Jesse James, Johnny Appleseed, Paul Bunyan, Pecos Bill, and Sacajawea are staples of American frontier folklore, as are stories about former slave John Henry, who was said to be the strongest steel-driver working the railroads. As the folk tale goes, Henry beat out a steam-powered drill in a contest of man against machine, only to die immediately thereafter of an aneurysm. People say that Henry's image can be seen — and his hammering heard — in the tunnel where he worked.

Many African American and Native American folk tales feature animals and recount stories of trickery or the origin of certain animal characteristics. Anansi (a spider), Brer Rabbit, and the tortoise are often clever tricksters in African American lore, whereas Coyote is one of the major tricksters in Native American tradition. Stories explaining particular animal characteristics include the African American tale that pigs have short, square noses because God cut off the pig's nose to punish it for eating all of the food given to the animals and the Native American Caddo tale that dogs have long tongues because a hunter pulled on his talkative dog's tongue as punishment for gossiping about a hunt. For a collection of African American folk tales arranged by subject — such as fool tales, mistaken identity tales, and preacher tales — see Zora Neale Hurston's posthumously published *Every Tongue Got to Confess: Negro Folk-Tales from the Gulf States* (published 2001; collected in the 1920s).

The Grimm brothers' fairy tales, or *Märchen,* have been widely translated from German and include such favorites as Cinderella, Little Red Riding Hood, and Hansel and Gretel. In *The Tales of Uncle Remus* (1880), Joel

Chandler Harris claimed to have recorded accurately the dialect and **plot** of tales told by slaves he encountered during his childhood in Georgia.

Washington Irving's "The Legend of Sleepy Hollow" (1819) is an example of a folk tale that began as a published literary work.

See also **folklore, tale.**

▶ **foot:** A **rhythmic** unit containing two or more syllables in a line of **verse.** Feet are classified according to a combination of two elements: (1) the number of syllables; and (2) the relative **stress** or duration of the syllables. In **accentual-syllabic verse,** the most common **metrical** form in English, a foot may have any of several combinations of stressed and unstressed syllables but usually consists of one stressed syllable (´) and one or two unstressed syllables (˘). Some theorists also contend that a single stressed syllable may qualify as a foot (the **monosyllabic**). By contrast, in **quantitative verse,** a metrical form most often associated with **classical** Greek and Roman poetry, a foot may consist of any of several combinations of long and short syllables ("long" and "short" referring to the duration of the syllables, i.e., the time needed to pronounce them).

Five types of feet are particularly common in English-language verse: the **iamb** (˘´), **trochee** (´˘), **anapest** (˘˘´), **dactyl** (´˘˘), and **spondee** (´´). Other less common metrical feet are the **pyrrhic** (˘˘), *amphibrach* (˘´˘), *amphimacer* (´˘´), **choriambus** (´˘˘´), and *paeon*, which has four forms (´˘˘˘, ˘´˘˘, ˘˘´˘, and ˘˘˘´).

EXAMPLE: Samuel Taylor Coleridge's poem "Metrical Feet — Lesson for a Boy" (1834) exemplifies seven forms of metrical feet:

> Tróchĕe trĭps frŏm lóng tŏ shórt;
>
> From long to long in solemn sort
>
> Slów Spóndĕe stálks; stróng fóot! yea ill able.
>
> Évĕr tŏ cóme ŭp wĭth Dáctўl trĭsýllăblĕ.
>
> Ĭambĭcs márch frŏm shórt tŏ lóng; —
>
> Wĭth ă leáp ănd ă boúnd thĕ swĭft Ánapæsts thróng;
>
> One syllable long, with one short at each side,
>
> Ămphĭbrăchўs hástes wĭth ă státelў stríde; —
>
> Fírst ănd lást beĭng lóng, mĭddlĕ shórt, Ămphĭmácer
>
> Strĭkes hĭs thúndĕrĭng hoófs líke ă proúd hĭgh-brĕd Rácer. . . .

▶ **foregrounding:** Giving prominence to something in a literary work that would not be accentuated in ordinary **discourse.** The notion of foregrounding comes primarily from the work of **Russian formalist** critics, who deemed foregrounding a necessary component of "**literariness**," the highly wrought, carefully crafted quality that charaterizes literary works. When Russian formalists spoke of foregrounding, they referred in particular to the foregrounding of "device," that is, all those aspects of verbal expression that are present in the literary work but are not functionally necessary to communication. Literary critics practice foregrounding as well, **privileging** those aspects of the **text** that they believe to be important.

EXAMPLES: In Laurence Sterne's *Tristram Shandy* (9 vols; 1759–67), the foregrounding of literary device is manifested in constant digressions and temporal discontinuities that violate the **conventions** of ordinary discourse. In his foreword to Zora Neale Hurston's *Every Tongue Got to Confess* (2001), a posthumously published collection of African American **folk tales** from the Gulf States, novelist John Edgar Wideman stated that Hurston "foregrounds creolized language and culture in her fiction and nonfiction, dramatizing vernacular ways of speaking that are so independent, dynamic, self-assertive and expressive that they cross over, challenge and transform mainstream dialects."

▶ **foreshadowing:** The technique of introducing into a **narrative** material that prepares the reader or audience for future events, actions, or revelations. Foreshadowing often involves the creation of a **mood** or **atmosphere** that suggests an eventual outcome; the introduction of objects, facts, events, or **characters** that hint at or otherwise prefigure a developing situation or **conflict**; or the exposition of significant character traits allowing the reader or audience to anticipate that character's actions or fate. Occasionally the **theme** or conclusion of a work is foreshadowed by its title. **Prolepsis,** the evocation in narrative of scenes or events that take place at a later point in the **story,** necessarily foreshadows that future event or action.

Foreshadowing is found in all narrative **genres** but is especially common in **suspense fiction,** including **mysteries, Gothic novels,** and **detective fiction.** Although there are many methods of foreshadowing and many reasons to use this technique, its effect is to unify the **plot** by making its development and **structure** seem logical and perhaps even inevitable. As nineteenth-century Russian playwright Anton Chekhov once said, "if there is a gun hanging on the wall in the first act, it must fire in the last."

EXAMPLES: The mood created in the first few sentences of Edgar Allan Poe's *The Fall of the House of Usher* (1839) forewarns the reader of horrible events to come:

> During the whole of a dull, dark, and soundless day in the autumn of the year, when the clouds hung oppressively low in the heavens, I had been passing alone, on horseback, through a singularly dreary tract of country, and at length found myself, as the shades of the evening drew on, within view of the melancholy House of Usher.

Similarly, the discordant music prior to the shower scene in Alfred Hitchcock's *Psycho* (1960) prepares the audience for the grisly stabbing of the character played by Janet Leigh.

The titles of Thomas Mann's *Death in Venice* (1912) and Willa Cather's *Death Comes for the Archbishop* (1926) foreshadow the eventual demise of their respective **protagonists,** Gustav von Aschenbach and Archbishop Jean Marie Latour. The early presentation in *Death in Venice* of a minor character who, though old, from a distance looks young — thanks to rouge, cheap dentures, a bad wig, and a fake mustache — foreshadows Aschenbach's own, later, hopelessly self-destructive pursuit of youth in the form of a beautiful young stranger.

Early in his novel *Kingsblood Royal* (1947), Sinclair Lewis used the technique of foreshadowing by character trait. By revealing the racism of Neil Kingsblood, a Minnesota banker researching his family's genealogy in hopes of discovering that he is descended from British royalty, Sinclair ironically foreshadowed Kingsblood's eventual discovery of an African American ancestor. Likewise, in Charlotte Brontë's *Jane Eyre* (1847), the revelation that Mr. Rochester's mentally ill wife lives in the attic of Thornfield Hall is foreshadowed by the "demoniac laughter" that governess Jane Eyre hears in her room late one evening.

Carlos Ruiz Zafón's *La sombra del viento* (*The Shadow of the Wind*) (2001) makes use of foreshadowing when the protagonist Daniel Sempere proleptically announces "In seven days' time I would be dead." So does *Attack of the Clones* (2002), the second episode of the *Star Wars* series, when Obi-wan Kenobi tells his young Jedi apprentice Anakin Skywalker, "You'll be the death of me."

See also **prolepsis**.

▶ **form:** Either the general type or the unique **structure** of a literary work. In the sense of "general type," *form* refers to the categories according to which literary works are commonly classified (e.g., **ballads, novellas, sonnets**) and may imply a set of **conventions** related to a particular **genre**. It may also refer to **metrical** arrangements, **rhyme** patterns, and so forth (**blank verse,** the **heroic couplet** form, **quatrain** forms). The term is often used more specifically, however, to refer to the structure of a particular work; in this case, form involves the arrangement of component parts by some organizational principle, such as **parallelism** or the chronological sequence of events.

Some theorists (such as those associated with **the New Criticism**) have equated form and structure, whereas others (such as those associated with the **Chicago school**) have distinguished between the terms, arguing that form is the emotional force or shaping principle that gives rise to the mechanics of structure. Others have debated whether or not form and **style** are the same, separate, or overlapping features of the work — and whether or not style and content are separable. Still others have challenged the oft-made distinction between form and content — traditionally manifested in the view that form is the structure devised by the **author** to contain the content (and ultimately the meaning) conveyed by a work — as misleading and even inaccurate. Most contemporary critics argue that form, structure, style, and content are intertwined and that distinctions among them, though useful tools of literary analysis, tend to obscure the intimate interrelationships that are essential to the effectiveness of the literary **text** as a whole. Such a critic might speak of concepts like **aesthetic** form, extending consideration to the integration of internal structural elements as well as to the external organizational qualities of form.

See **organic form** for the distinction between *organic form* and *mechanic form*.

▶ **formalism:** A general term covering several similar types of **literary criticism** that arose in the 1920s and 1930s, flourished during the 1940s and 1950s, and are still in evidence today. Formalists see the literary work as an object in its own right. Thus, they tend to devote their attention to its intrinsic nature, concentrating their analyses on the interplay and relationships between the text's essential verbal elements. They study the **form** of the work (as opposed to its content), although *form* to a formalist can connote anything from **genre** (for example, one may speak of "the **sonnet** form") to grammatical or rhetorical **structure** to the "emotional imperative" that engenders the work's (more mechanical) structure. No matter which **connotation** of *form* pertains, however, formalists seek to be **objective** in their analysis, focusing on the work itself and eschewing external considerations. They pay particular attention to literary devices used in the work and to the patterns these devices establish.

Formalism developed largely in reaction to the practice of interpreting literary **texts** by relating them to "extrinsic" issues, such as the historical circumstances and politics of the era in which the work was written, its philosophical or theological *milieu,* or the experiences and frame of mind of its **author.** Although the term *formalism* was coined by critics to disparage the movement, it is now used simply as a descriptive term.

Formalists have generally suggested that everyday language, which serves simply to communicate information, is stale and unimaginative. They argue that **literariness** has the capacity to overturn common and expected patterns (of grammar, of story line), thereby rejuvenating language. Such novel uses of language supposedly enable readers to experience not only language but also the world in an entirely new way.

A number of schools of literary criticism have adopted a formalist orientation, or at least make use of formalist concepts. **The New Criticism,** an approach to literature that reached its height in the U.S. in the 1940s and 1950s, is perhaps the most famous type of formalism. But **Russian formalism** was the first major formalist movement; after the Stalinist regime suppressed it in the early 1930s, the **Prague Linguistic Circle** adopted its analytical methods. The **Chicago school** has also been classified as formalist insofar as Chicago critics focus on textual analysis, but their interest in authorial **intention** and historical material is decidedly not formalist.

▶ **formalism, Russian:** See **Russian formalism.**

▶ **fourfold meaning (four levels of meaning / of interpretation):** A method of analysis generally applied to biblical works (or **allegories,** particularly religious ones) in which meaning is found on four levels: (1) the literal level, that is, the surface story; (2) the moral or tropological level, at which generally applicable principles of human behavior are revealed; (3) the allegorical level, at which the reader understands the religious (usually New

Testament) truth signified by the literal level; and (4) the anagogical level, which contains the highest spiritual, often **eschatological,** meanings of the work (those having to do with questions about what happens to the individual after death and, even more generally, at the end of time, on the Day of Judgment). This method of **exegesis** was common in the **Medieval Period** and continued to be widely used well into the eighteenth century. It has also been applied to, and adapted for, secular material, particularly secular poetry.

Some authors, such as Florentine **epic** poet Dante Alighieri, have implied that their works have not four but two levels of meaning: the literal and allegorical. However, they have gone on to subdivide the latter category of meaning into three levels: the allegorical, moral, and anagogical.

▶ **fourteener:** A line of **verse** that has fourteen syllables; such a line is usually written in **iambic heptameter.**

   EXAMPLE: George Chapman's 1616 translation of Homer's *The Iliad* (c. 850 B.C.) was done in fourteeners.

▶ **fractured fairy tale:** See **fairy tale.**

▶ **frame story:** A **story** that contains another story or stories. Usually, the frame story explains why the interior story or stories are being told. For example, the frame story in *The Thousand and One Nights* (c. 1450) (also known as *The Arabian Nights*) explains that Queen Shahrazad tells her husband, King Shahryar, a story every night — each one ending with a reference to or preview of the story to be told the following night — because the King has had over a thousand previous wives executed the morning after the wedding night in order to ensure that they would never be unfaithful to him, as was his first wife.

   The degree to which the frame story has its own **plot** varies; that is, the frame story may be extremely sketchy or fairly well developed. The interior stories are likely to be fully developed **tales,** usually completely separate from one another (except insofar as they are linked by the **narrative** frame and sometimes by **theme** or subject matter).

   FURTHER EXAMPLES: *Panchatantra* (c. A.D. 500; anonymous), Boccaccio's *Decameron* (1348–53), Geoffrey Chaucer's *Canterbury Tales* (c. 1387), Marguerite de Navarre's *Heptaméron* (1548), and Joseph Conrad's *Heart of Darkness* (1899). Movies such as *Invasion of the Body Snatchers* (1956) and *The Princess Bride* (1987) also make use of frame stories.

▶ **free indirect discourse:** A **mode** of presenting **discourse,** the thoughts or statements of **characters** in a work, that blends **third-person narration** with the **first person point-of-view.** Free indirect discourse combines elements of **direct discourse** and **indirect discourse** to give the reader a sense of being inside a character's head without actually quoting his or her thoughts or statements. Describing the mode in *The Dual Voice: Free Indirect Speech and Its Functioning* (1977), Roy Pascal wrote: "On the one hand it evokes the person, through his words, tone of voice, and gesture, with incomparable vivacity. On the other, it embeds the character's statement or thought in the narrative flow, and even more importantly in the narrator's interpretation, communicating also his way of seeing and feeling."

In direct discourse, the **narrator** relates a character's thoughts and utterances in an unfiltered way, conveying precisely what the character thinks or says. (She thought, "I'll demand the money from him, or else!") In indirect discourse, the narrator takes a more independent approach, reporting — and sometimes paraphrasing — what characters think or say. (She planned to demand the money from him, coupling it with a threat.) Free indirect discourse infuses the reportorial approach with the character's perceptions and language, giving rise to a "dual voice" that may interweave or even merge the **voices** of narrator and character. (She would demand the money from him, or else!)

Pioneers of free indirect discourse include nineteenth-century English novelist Jane Austen and French novelist Gustave Flaubert, who used it extensively in *Madame Bovary* (1857). In the twentieth century, **modernist** writers made particular use of the mode, which remains common today.

EXAMPLES: The following passage from Austen's *Emma* (1815), which relates Emma's impressions of the orphaned, illegitimate Harriet Smith, whom she decides to take on as a protégé:

> She was not struck by anything remarkably clever in Miss Smith's conversation, but she found her altogether engaging — not inconveniently shy, not unwilling to talk — and yet so far from pushing, shewing so proper and becoming a deference, seeming so pleasantly grateful for being admitted to Hartfield, and so artlessly impressed by the appearance of every thing in so superior a style to what she had been used to, that she must have good sense and deserve encouragement. Encouragement should be given. Those soft blue eyes and all those natural graces should not be wasted on the inferior society of Highbury and its connections. The acquaintance she had already formed were unworthy of her. The friends from whom she had just parted, though very good sort of people, must be doing her harm.

Virginia Woolf's *Mrs. Dalloway* (1925) relies heavily on free indirect discourse, beginning "Mrs. Dalloway said she would buy the flowers herself. For Lucy had her work cut out for her."

▶ **free verse:** From the French *vers libre*, literally meaning "free verse," **poetry** that lacks a regular **meter**, does not **rhyme**, and uses irregular (and sometimes very short) line lengths. Writers of free verse disregard traditional poetic **conventions** of rhyme and meter, relying instead on **parallelism**, repetition, and the ordinary cadences and **stresses** of everyday **discourse**. In English, notable use of free verse dates back to the 1611 King James translation of the Psalms and Song of Solomon, but it was not really recognized as an important new form until the American poet Walt Whitman's *Leaves* *of Grass* (1855). Since World War I, nonrhyming and nonmetrical forms of verse have become the norm.

EXAMPLES: Carl Sandburg's "Grass" (1918), the first half of which follows:

> Pile the bodies high at Austerlitz and Waterloo.
> Shovel them under and let me work —
> I am the grass; I cover all.
>
> And pile them high at Gettysburg
> And pile them high at Ypres and Verdun.
> Shovel them under and let me work. . . .

Other examples of free verse include Whitman's "When Lilacs Last in the Dooryard Bloom'd" (1865) and W. S. Merwin's "The Judgment of Paris" (1967).

▶ **French Symbolists:** See **symbolism.**

▶ **Freytag's Pyramid:** German writer Gustav Freytag's conception of the **structure** of a typical five-act **play**, introduced in *Die Technik des Dramas* (*Technique of the Drama*) (1863). According to Freytag's analysis, such plays are divisible into five parts: the introduction (containing an "inciting moment" or "force"), **rising action, climax, falling action,** and **catastrophe.** These parts loosely correspond with the five **acts** of the drama, although rising action can occur during the first act and falling action usually includes the catastrophe or "closing action," which typically takes place in the fifth and last act. Freytag referred to the five acts — as opposed to the five parts — of a drama as "the act of introduction," "the act of the ascent" (in which the play's action intensifies as **conflicts** develop), "the act of the climax" (containing the play's most important **scene,** the one in which the rising action culminates), "the act of the return" (in which new **characters** are introduced and "fate wins control over the hero"), and "the act of the catastrophe."

Although Freytag confined his analysis to five-act plays (**tragedies** in particular, and especially William Shakespeare's), Freytag's Pyramid has been applied to other dramatic forms and even to fiction, including prose. In these applications, the term **resolution** is used instead of *catastrophe.*

▶ **frozen metaphor:** See **dead metaphor.**

▶ **Fugitives:** A group of sixteen Southern poets, most of whom were faculty, students, or alumni of Vanderbilt University, who met in Nashville, Tennessee, to discuss their work and who were best known for *The Fugitive* (1922–1925), an amateur journal of poetry and criticism.

Members of the Fugitives began meeting regularly in 1915 to discuss philosophy, aesthetics, and literature; following World War I, they shifted their focus to poetry, using the meetings to read and critique their own work. Key figures included Donald Davidson, Sidney Hirsch, Merrill Moore, John Crowe Ransom, Allen Tate, and Robert Penn Warren. In 1922, the group began publishing *The Fugitive,* managing the journal collectively and contributing their work under **pseudonyms**. With reference to the moniker "Fugitive," Ransom wrote in the inaugural issue that "THE FUGITIVE flees from nothing faster than the high-caste Brahmins of the Old South."

While *The Fugitive* was short-lived as a literary journal, many would say it inaugurated the Southern literary renaissance, especially the development of the modern Southern novel, as exemplified by William Faulkner. Fugitive poetry and criticism emphasized **form** (especially **allegorical** form), technique (with particular attention to **prosody**), and language, placing intellect on an equal level with emotion and eschewing sentimentality. The Fugitives also drew on **classical** humanism and Southern traditions of gentility. After their Fugitive period, Ransom, Tate, and Warren contributed significantly to the development of **the New Criticism,** a type of **formalist** (**text**-based) literary **criticism** that reached its height in the 1940s and 1950s.

While there is some overlap between the Fugitives and the **Agrarians,** another group of Southern writers with major ties to Vanderbilt University, it is a mistake to conflate the two groups. The Fugitives, active from about 1915–1928, were a nonpolitical, nonideological, tightly knit literary group focused on poetry and criticism and concerned chiefly with poetry as a carefully crafted literary form. The Agrarians, by contrast, came together around an **ideology** of agrarian regionalism, were active from about 1928–1937, and pressed for political and economic reform. Their controversial manifesto, *I'll Take My Stand* (1930) attacked industrial capitalism and promoted an agricultural base for the American economy. Only four Fugitives — Davidson, Ransom, Tate, and Warren—were also Agrarians.

The last work published by the Fugitives was *Fugitives: An Anthology of Verse* (1928), a volume of poems about half of which were reprinted from *The Fugitive* journal. Although the group continued to meet sporadically up to 1962, it did not engage in any further collaborative literary efforts.

See also **Agrarians.**

▶ **full rhyme:** See **perfect rhyme.**

G

▶**gap (blank):** As used by **reader-response critics** influenced by German critic Wolfgang Iser, an indeterminate element or section of a literary **text**. A gap may be said to exist wherever a reader perceives something to be missing or uncertain and may be found at various levels of the text, whether pragmatic (relating to the intention of the text), **semantic,** or **syntactic.** Readers respond to gaps actively and creatively, reconciling apparent inconsistencies in **point of view,** accounting for jumps in chronology, speculatively supplying information missing from **plots,** and resolving **ambiguities.**

Naturally, gaps are to some extent a product of readers' perceptions. One reader may find a given text to be riddled with gaps while another may find it comparatively consistent and complete; different readers may find different gaps in the same text. Moreover, different readers may fill in the same gap differently. Indeed, for a reader-response critic, the very variety of responses helps explain why works are interpreted in different ways.

Notably, reader-response critics see gaps not as textual defects but as "the fundamental precondition for reader participation," as Iser explained in his essay "Indeterminacy and the Reader's Response in Prose Fiction" (1971). According to Iser, gaps "give the reader a chance to build his own bridges, relating the different aspects of the object which have thus far been revealed to him." The gap-filling process is also guided, however, as Iser argued in "Interaction Between Text and Reader" (1980), with gaps, or blanks, "initiating structured operations in the reader." Blanks, Iser explained, "are the unseen joints of the text," "empty spaces" that "trigger and simultaneously control the reader's activity," indicating that "the different segments and patterns of the text are to be connected even though the text itself does not say so."

Practitioners of other approaches to **literary criticism** have also made use of the concept of the gap. **Deconstructors,** for instance, have used the term to explain that every text contains contradictory **discourses** that cannot be reconciled. **Psychoanalytic critics** have applied it in several contexts, for instance: (1) to describe the manifestation or nature of the unconscious as a gap, or absence; and (2) to reference the idea that the **ego,** which is ensnared in the **Symbolic order** of law, language, and society and desires the (false) sense of wholeness and unity experienced in the **Imaginary order,** senses an incompleteness that it cannot remedy. **Marxist critics** have applied the term to the divide that opens up between economic **base** and cultural **superstructure** as well as to textual **conflicts.** One kind of conflict or contradiction, they would argue, results from the fact that all texts reflect an **ideology** that precludes the **representation** or even recognition of certain subjects and attitudes. As a result, readers at the edge or outside of that ideology perceive something missing. Another kind of conflict or contradiction results from the fact that works do more than reflect ideology; they are also fictions that, consciously or unconsciously, distance themselves from that ideology.

▶ **gay and lesbian criticism (sexualities criticism):** Forms of **literary criticism** focused on textual **representations** of and readings responsive to issues of homo- (and hetero-) sexuality. Since gay and lesbian criticism both feature **sexuality** as the issue that troubles **gender** as a category, the approaches are typically classified more specifically as types of **gender criticism,** though not all gay and lesbian critics would so categorize their work. Gay and lesbian criticism emerged in the mid-1980s with the publication of Eve Kosofsky Sedgwick's *Between Men: English Literature and Male Homosocial Desire* (1985). In this pioneering work, Sedgwick adapted **feminist** critical theory to analyze relationships between men; between male **characters** in literary works; and, most importantly, between gender and sexuality.

Some practitioners of gay and lesbian criticism have extended a debate between feminist and gender critics about whether there is such a thing as "reading like a woman" (or man) by arguing that there are gay and lesbian ways of reading. In *On Lies, Secrets, and Silence: Selected Prose, 1966–1979* (1979), lesbian poet-critic Adrienne Rich read Emily Dickinson's poetry as a lesbian, thereby revealing a poet quite different from the one heterosexual critics have made familiar. In "Wilde's Hard Labor and the Birth of Gay Reading" (1990), Wayne Koestenbaum defined the gay reader as one who "reads resistantly for inscriptions of his condition, for texts that will confirm a social and private identity founded on a desire for other men."

The question of whether distinct gay and lesbian ways of reading exist corresponds with broader debates in feminist, gender, and gay and lesbian criticism over whether gender and sexuality are biologically or socially determined. **Essentialists** maintain that gender and sexuality are natural or innate, whereas **constructionists** contend that they are cultural artifacts. Following the lead of French theorist Michel Foucault, constructionist gay and lesbian critics view sexuality not as a fixed set of **binary oppositions** (heterosexual/homosexual) but as a continuum encompassing a range of behaviors and responses. They emphasize, for instance, that sexuality is not restricted to homosexuality and heterosexuality but also includes practices such as bondage, sadomasochism, and transvestism. They also note that many people have felt attracted to members of both sexes even if they are predominantly hetero- or homosexual.

Lesbian critics have taken some of their feminist counterparts to task on the grounds that the latter proceed from fundamentally heterosexual and even heterosexist assumptions. Particularly offensive to lesbians have been those feminists who, following British writer Doris Lessing, have implied that to affirm a lesbian identity is to act out feminist hostility against men. In an essay entitled "Compulsory Heterosexuality and Lesbian Existence" (1983), Rich rejected this assertion, noting that women from diverse cultures and historical eras have "undertaken the task of independent, nonheterosexual,

women-centered existence" even in the face of economic uncertainty and social disapproval. Rich further suggested that "heterosexuality [is] a beachhead of male dominance," which, "like motherhood, needs to be recognized
and studied as a political institution."

Lesbian critics have produced a number of controversial reinterpreta-
tions of works by authors as diverse as Dickinson, Virginia Woolf, and
Toni Morrison. For example, both Rich and Barbara Smith have claimed
that Morrison's novel *Sula* (1973) can be read as a lesbian **text**. In an essay
entitled "Toward a Black Feminist Criticism" (1985), Smith pointed to Nel
and Sula's close friendship and what she identified as Morrison's critique
of heterosexual institutions such as marriage to support her claim, even
though Morrison previously had rejected such claims in Claudia Tate's
Black Women Writers at Work (1983).

Gay male critics have produced a body of readings no less revisionist
and controversial, focusing on writers as staidly **classic** as Henry James and
Wallace Stevens. In *Hero, Captain, and Stranger* (1986), Robert K. Martin
suggested that triangles of homosexual desire exist in Herman Melville's
Moby-Dick (1851) and *Billy Budd* (written 1891, published 1924). In
Moby-Dick, for instance, the **narrator-hero** must choose between a captain
who represents the "imposition of the male on the female" and a "Dark
Stranger" (Queequeg) who represents an "alternate sexuality," one less
grounded in "performance and conquest." More recently, Richard Bozorth
argued in *Auden's Games of Knowledge: Poetry and the Meanings of Homosexuality* (2001) that the poetry of W. H. Auden addresses and reflects the
psychology and politics of same-sex desire.

The work of gay and lesbian critics who are more theoretically oriented
than text-centered has come to be called **queer theory,** an approach to literature and culture that assumes sexual identities are flexible, not fixed, and
that critiques gender and sexuality as they are commonly conceived in
Western culture. Queer theorists, constructionists who view sexuality as
performative, a process involving signifying acts rather than a "normative"
identity, argue that textual representations have defined the contours of
sexual identity in society. They also proudly and defiantly embrace the
term *queer*. As Judith Butler pointed out in *Bodies That Matter: On the
Discursive Limits of Sex* (1993), *queer* may be a "discursive rallying point
for younger lesbians and gays . . . and for bisexuals and straights for whom
the term expresses an affiliation with antihomophobic politics." Other notable contributions to the field of queer theory include Sedgwick's *Epistemology of the Closet* (1991) and *Tendencies* (1993), a special "Issue on
Queer Theory" edited by Teresa de Lauretis and published by the journal
differences (1993), and Alan Sinfield's *Cultural Politics — Queer Reading*
(1994).

See also **gender criticism, queer theory.**

▶ **gender:** A term referring to the perceived identities *man* and *woman* and
the range of characteristics commonly associated with masculinity and

femininity. Some contemporary **gender critics** also use the term to refer to various **sexualities,** perceived identities such as *heterosexual, bisexual,* and *transgendered.* While some critics, particularly certain **feminist critics,** tend to equate gender with *sex,* the biological designation of male or female, most critics distinguish the two, viewing gender as a social construct. Thus, gender is widely held to be a product of the mores, expectations, and stereotypes of a particular culture, and what it means to be "masculine" or "feminine" (rather than "male" or "female") may vary from one culture to the next. Whether **essentialists** or **constructionists,** however, most critics agree that Western civilization has been predominantly **patriarchal** and has thus tended to extol the masculine and devalue the feminine, associating masculinity with "positive" traits such as activity and rationality and femininity with "negative" traits such as passivity and emotionality.

▶ **gender criticism:** A type of **literary criticism** that focuses on — and critiques — **gender** as it is commonly conceived, seeking to expose its insufficiency as a categorizing device. Gender critics draw a distinction between *gender,* the identities and characteristics commonly associated with men, women, masculinity, and femininity, and *sex,* the biological designation of male or female. They typically reject the **essentialist** view that gender is natural or innate and instead take the **constructionist** position that gender is a social artifact, a learned behavior, a product of language and culture. Teresa de Lauretis, for instance, argued in *Technologies of Gender: Essays on Theory, Film, and Fiction* (1987) that gender is "the product of various social technologies, such as cinema," not "a property of bodies or something originally existent in human beings."

Some gender critics have extended the term *gender* to reference **sexuality** as well, questioning the distinction between heterosexuality and homosexuality and arguing that these terms are social constructs, too. These critics, including **queer theorists,** view sexuality not as a fixed set of **binary oppositions** limited to hetero- and homosexuality but as a continuum encompassing behaviors and responses ranging from bestiality to bondage. Other gender critics, especially many **gay and lesbian critics,** take an essentialist position, arguing that sexuality is innate rather than culturally produced.

As an approach to literary criticism, gender criticism arose out of **feminist criticism,** with gender critics both drawing on feminist **theory** and practice and attacking feminist concepts and claims. Notably, although feminist criticism preceded gender criticism by a decade, many commentators have argued that feminist criticism should be classified as a form of gender criticism insofar as it focuses on the feminine — and even though many gender theorists identify with the feminist perspective. Others maintain that gender criticism has overshadowed the feminist approach. For instance, in an essay entitled "Feminist and Gender Studies" (1992), Naomi Schor estimated that gender studies began to prevail over feminist criticism around 1985, the same year that Eve Kosofsky Sedgwick's *Between Men: English Literature and Male Homosocial Desire* was published. In *Between*

Men, which substantially influenced gender criticism generally, and gay and lesbian criticism more specifically, Sedgwick adapted feminist theory to analyze relationships between men, between male **characters** in literary works, and between gender and sexuality — a subject she took up again in *Epistemology of the Closet* (1990), where she argued that "the question of gender and the question of sexuality, inextricable from one another though they are . . . are nonetheless not the same question."

Unlike feminist critics, who have tended to focus on women and women's issues, gender critics have focused as much on men as women. They have analyzed masculinity as a complex construct that produces and reproduces a host of behaviors and goals such as performance and conquest, many of them destructive and most of them harmful to women. For example, in an article entitled "Anti-Porn: Soft Issue, Hard World" (1983), B. Ruby Rich challenged the "legions of feminist men" who deplore the effects of pornography on women to find out "why men like porn (not, piously, why this or that exceptional man does *not*)." In an essay entitled "Testing the Razor" (1989), Stephen H. Clark analyzed T. S. Eliot's address in *The Waste Land* (1920) to a specifically masculine audience — "'You! hypocrite lecteur! — mon semblable, — mon *frère!*'" — by concluding that many of Eliot's poems articulate a masculine "psychology of sexual fear and desired retaliation." Other analyses of masculinity have examined boyhood, the fear men have that artistry is unmasculine, and the **representation** in literature and film of subtly erotic male disciple-patron relationships.

Gender critics have reacted most strongly, however, against essentialist strains of feminist criticism that ground "female difference" in the female body, i.e., "nature." In the 1970s, French feminist critics argued that the female body gives rise to a special feminine language, writing (*écriture féminine*), and **style,** and French-influenced North American feminist critics, such as Toril Moi and Nancy K. Miller, subsequently posited an essential relationship between sex and **text.** Miller, for instance, suggested in *Subject to Change: Reading Feminist Writing* (1988) that no man could write the "female anger, desire, and selfhood" that Emily Brontë inscribed in her poetry and in *Wuthering Heights* (1847). Such critics equated gender with sex, gender difference with sexual difference, and thus viewed gender differences as natural.

As constructionists, gender critics attribute differences between men and women in language, writing, and style to cultural influences, not sexual difference. For instance, Peggy Kamuf, one of the first critics to attack the notion of **feminine writing,** posited a relationship only between gender and text, not sex and text, and therefore focused less on whether an **author** was a woman than on whether the author was "Writing Like a Woman" (1980), as the name of one of her essays suggests. If gender differences are social constructs, men can read and write like women, women like men.

Many gender theorists have found especially disturbing the inclination of some *avant-garde* French feminists to equate the female body with the maternal body, an association they worry may play into the hands of fundamentalists seeking to reestablish **patriarchal** family values. For instance, in *The Reproduction of Mothering: Psychoanalysis and the Sociology of Gender* (1978), Nancy Chodorow examined what we call "mothering" — not just the ability to give birth and nurse but to nurture more generally — and challenged the assumption that it is in women's nature or biological destiny to "mother" in the broader sense. Instead of linking mothering with sex, Chodorow argued that the separation of home and workplace engendered by capitalism and the Industrial Revolution made mothering appear to be a woman's job in modern Western society.

Some extreme constructionists (also called *postfeminists*) have further complicated the sex-gender debate by arguing that even nature is in some sense a cultural construct. For instance, in *Gender Trouble: Feminism and the Subversion of Identity* (1990), gender theorist Judith Butler argued that sexual difference, like gender, is culturally produced rather than natural, with notions about sex created as a byproduct of the cultural construction of gender. As a result, no one can really know how the body functions apart from the culture in which it lives. Or, as Schor explained in "Feminist and Gender Studies": "there is nothing outside or before culture, no nature that is not already enculturated."

As provocative as such claims about nature have been, however, it is sexuality that has played the biggest role in distinguishing gender criticism from feminist criticism and raising its profile in literary studies. Drawing on French theorist Michel Foucault's critique of the homosexual/heterosexual dichotomy, many gender critics have focused on sexuality as the topic that most confounds traditional notions of gender. In *Histoire de la sexualité* (*The History of Sexuality*) (1976), Foucault distinguished sexuality from sex, calling sexuality a "technology of sex." He also suggested that the Western concept of homosexuality — and heterosexuality, as its binary opposite — is a relatively recent invention. Prior to the nineteenth century, people spoke of "acts of sodomy" and of people who committed them as "sodomites," but the sodomite was a "temporary aberration," not the "species" he became in the nineteenth century.

Gender critics, particularly queer theorists, who follow Foucault's lead have argued that the homosexual/heterosexual distinction is as much a cultural construct as the masculine/feminine dichotomy. Indeed, these critics have used the very variety of sexual identifications, behaviors, and responses to expose the inadequacy of gender as a category. With bisexuality and bondage, swinging and sadomasochism, transsexualism and transvestism, it is "an astonishing simplification," as Sedgwick noted in "Gender Criticism" (1992), that "if I ask you what your sexual orientation or sexual preference is, you will understand me to be asking precisely one thing: whether you are homosexual or heterosexual." The range of sexualities notwithstanding, however, other gender critics have argued that sexuality is inherent or innate. For instance, many gay and lesbian critics have celebrated homosexual difference, much as many feminist critics postulated the existence of and embraced female difference. Moreover, like essentialist feminists, many essentialists on sexuality have argued that gay and lesbian ways of reading exist and have reinterpreted works by authors such as Henry James, Herman Melville, Emily Dickinson, Virginia Woolf, and Toni Morrison.

With the growing interest in sexuality in literary studies, gay and lesbian criticism and queer theory have become increasingly prominent approaches, and their relationship to gender criticism has been the subject of some debate. Gay and lesbian criticism, whether constructionist or essentialist, has focused on textual representations of and readings responsive to homo- and heterosexuality; queer theory, an outgrowth of gay and lesbian criticism, has taken a strongly constructionist, more theoretical, and less text-oriented approach to both literature and culture, viewing sexual identities as flexible, not fixed. In either case, though, the approaches have focused on sexuality as the issue that "troubles" gender as a category, making them classifiable as gender criticism, though not all gay and lesbian critics and queer theorists would so categorize their work.

The critique of gender as a category of analysis continues to evolve and expand. Joan Riviere's essay "Womanliness as Masquerade" (1929), in which Riviere argued that all femininity involves masquerade, has sparked an interest in performance theory in both the feminist and gender approaches. In *Vested Interests: Cross-Dressing and Cultural Anxiety* (1992), Marjorie Garber, a **cultural critic,** analyzed the constructed nature of gender by focusing on people who have apparently achieved gender identity through transvestism, transsexualism, and sexual role-playing or reversal — **themes** that surface in or even pervade cultural productions ranging from the works of Shakespeare, Elvis Presley, and Liberace to **folk tales** such as "Little Red Riding Hood" to movies such as *La cage aux folles* (1979), *The Birdcage* (1996), and *Hedwig and the Angry Inch* (2001).

Moreover, gender critics have established the significance of gender, however defined, not only in poems and novels but also in areas such as advertising, television, and everyday life. For instance, Sedgwick's book *Tendencies* (1993) begins with commentary on subjects as diverse — and connected — as the suicide rate among gay teenagers, American Christmas traditions, AIDS, queer reading, and contemporary journalism. Other gender critics have focused on film, arguing that it plays a primary role in gender construction. *Rebel Without a Cause* (1955), *Tootsie* (1982), and *Million Dollar Baby* (2004) are among the many movies that reflect, perpetuate, and even challenge stereotypical gender roles and characteristics.

See also **feminist criticism, gay and lesbian criticism, queer theory.**

▶ **generative linguistics:** One of the two components of Noam Chomsky's theory of **linguistics** postulated in *Syntactic Structures* (1957). Chomsky attempted to account for what he called the "rule-bound creativity" of any given language — that is, the fact that a native speaker who is speaking to another native speaker can utter an original sentence, a series of words that neither has heard in that exact form and order before, but that both of them nonetheless easily understand due to their linguistic competence.

Chomsky argued that competence in a given language follows from mastery of a certain set of generative and transformational rules. Thus his theory is termed "generative" in its attempt to determine the set of rules that accounts for all the possible **syntactically** correct sentences in any given language. His theory is termed "transformational" in its belief that a certain set of transformative rules produces a plethora of variations on "kernel sentences" (basic sentences) in the "deep structure" of any given language.

See also **transformational linguistics.**

▶ **Geneva School:** A mid-twentieth-century group of **literary critics,** many of whom were professors at the University of Geneva in Switzerland, who practiced a type of **expressive criticism** called **phenomenological criticism** with the aim of experiencing an **author's** consciousness and reflecting it in their analysis. Geneva critics, also called *critics of consciousness,* sought to achieve an intuitive understanding of the author's **subjective** mindset and worldview, to get inside the author's head, so to speak. As Georges Poulet explained in "Criticism and the Experience of Interiority" (1970): "I am aware of a rational being, of a consciousness; the consciousness of another, . . . [that] allows me, with unheard-of license, to think what it thinks and feel what it feels." In seeking such "consciousness of the consciousness of another," Geneva critics endeavored to set aside all references external to the **text,** including their own mindset and worldview, to become a better vessel for the author's **intentionality,** or awareness.

Geneva critics believed that an author's consciousness is unique and fundamentally consistent through time. For instance, prior to his turn to **deconstruction,** J. Hillis Miller asserted in *Charles Dickens: The World of His Novels* (1959) that "all works of a single writer form a unity, a unity in which a thousand paths radiate from the same center." Accordingly, Geneva School analyses often ranged over the whole of an author's writings in search of this unity or center, relating textual elements such as **imagery** and **figurative language** to the author's personal development. Since Geneva critics believed that early writings, like late ones, reveal the same consciousness, they could discuss an adolescent love letter, a poem written during a midlife crisis, and a late novel side by side; when concentrating on a single work, they often sought to reconcile a variety of passages. They also sought to identify what Poulet termed the "point of departure" — the defining, organizing principle of the author's work, or, as Miller described it in "The Literary Criticism of Georges Poulet" (1963), the "act from which each imaginary universe opens out."

In their emphasis on the unique consciousness of the author, Geneva critics recall nineteenth-century **romantics,** who considered insight into the author's personality and creative genius a chief objective of literary analysis. Rejecting **objective** approaches to literary criticism, the Geneva School flourished in the 1950s and 1960s, influencing other approaches including **reception theory** and **reader-response criticism.** By the early 1970s, however, the school came under attack from both **structuralists** and **poststructuralist** deconstructors. Structuralists found the Geneva critics' approach unscientific and unduly subjective; deconstructors, who view texts as riven by irreconcilable contradictions, called into question the very notion of the unified psyche or self on which the Geneva School and phenomenological criticism rest. With deconstruction itself on the wane, however, David Lavery called for a revival of Geneva School criticism in "The Geneva School Revisited" (2003).

Members of the Geneva School aside from Miller and Poulet included Albert Béguin, founder Marcel Raymond, Jean-Pierre Richard, Jean Rousset, and Jean Starobinski. Influential works include Poulet's *Studies in Human Time* (4 vols., 1949–68) and "Phenomenology of Reading" (1969) as well as Miller's *Thomas Hardy: Distance and Desire* (1970).

▶ **genre:** From the French for "kind" or "type," the classification of literary works on the basis of their content, **form**, or technique. For centuries works have been grouped according to a number of classificatory schemes and distinctions, such as **prose / poem, epic / drama / lyric,** and the traditional **classical** divisions **comedy / tragedy / lyric / pastoral / epic / satire.** Current usage is broad enough to permit umbrella categories of literature (e.g., **fiction,** the **novel**) as well as subcategories (e.g., **science fiction,** the **sentimental novel**) to be **denoted** by the term *genre.*

Scholars and critics of the **Renaissance** and **Neoclassical Period** tended to take a rigid approach to genre, ranking genres hierarchically, advocating strict boundaries between genres, identifying "laws of kind" for each genre, and judging works accordingly. The emphasis on generic purity generated critical controversies over works that did not "fit," such as the hybrid **tragicomedy,** and sometimes even led to formal proceedings against noncompliant **authors.** For instance, in seventeenth-century France, Pierre Corneille had to defend himself before the Académie Française against charges of breaking the classical rule of the three **unities** in his play *Le Cid* (1636).

With the advent of **romanticism,** which emphasized innovation, **imagination,** and the individual, as well as the emergence of new categories such as the novel, the genre system began to decline. A few critics have proposed new classificatory schemes; **archetypal critic** Northrop Frye, for instance, argued in *The Anatomy of Criticism* (1957) that literary works may be associated with one of four *mythoi* (types of **plots**) that are in turn associated with the four seasons, yielding four main genre classifications: comedy (spring), **romance** (summer), tragedy (fall), and satire (winter). Most critics, however, have roundly criticized traditional thinking about genre, especially the underlying idea that literary works can be classified according to set, specific categories. Those who still employ rigid genre distinctions are often accused of overgeneralizing and of obscuring aspects of works that "cross" or "mix" genres.

Contemporary theorists of genre tend to follow the lead of Austrian philosopher Ludwig Wittgenstein, who in *Philosophische Untersuchungen*

(*Philosophical Investigations*) (1953) characterized genre in terms of "family resemblances," a set of similarities some (but by no means all) of which are shared by works classified together. Viewed this way, genre is a helpful, though arguably loose and arbitrary, categorizing and descriptive device that provides a basic vantage point for examining most historical and many modern and contemporary works. Genre classifications also remain a staple of everyday **discourse**. Bookstores and libraries organize their collections on the basis of genre; movies are marketed as documentaries, dramas, or even docudramas; television shows are classified as educational programming, reality TV, **sitcoms,** and so forth.

In art criticism, the term *genre* has a specific (and nonliterary) application, referring to paintings that depict ordinary life in a **realistic** manner. Notable genre painters include seventeenth-century Dutch painter Johannes Vermeer and twentieth-century American painter Norman Rockwell.

Genres defined in this glossary include the Absurd, acrostic, alba, allegory, Anacreontic poetry, anecdote, antinovel, apocalyptic literature, aubade, autobiography, ballad, ballade, bardic poetry, the baroque, beast fable, bildungsroman, biography, blank verse, blues, Breton lai, bucolic poetry, burlesque, the character, chronicle play, closet drama, comedy, comedy of humors, comedy of manners, *commedia dell'arte,* concrete poetry, confessional poetry, courtesy book, crime novel, curtal sonnet, cyberfiction, detective fiction, didactic literature, dirge, dithyramb, domestic tragedy, drama, dramatic monologue, dream vision, eclogue, ecopoetry, elegy, encomium, *Entwicklungsroman,* epic, epigram, epistolary novel, epithalamium, *Erziehungsroman,* essay, *exemplum,* fable, *fabliau,* faction, fairy tale, fantasy fiction, farce, fiction, folk drama, folk song, folk tale, free verse, Gothic literature, the grotesque, graphic novel, hagiography, haiku, hard-boiled detective fiction, historical novel, historical romance, history play, Homeric ode, Horatian satire, horror, Hudibrastic verse, hymn, idyll, interlude, irregular ode, Italian sonnet, Juvenalian satire, *Künstlerroman, lai,* lampoon, Language poetry, legend, light verse, limerick, literature of sensibility, local color writing, lyric, madrigal, magic realism, masque, medieval romance, metrical romance, melodrama, memoir, Menippean satire, metafiction, metaphysical poetry, miracle play, mock epic, mock heroic, monody, morality play, mummers' play, mystery fiction, mystery play, myth, nature writing, New Wave, nonfiction, nonfiction novel, nonsense verse, *nouveau roman,* novel, novella, occasional verse, ode, *ottava rima,* palinode, pantomime, parable, parody, *pastiche,* pastoral, pastoral elegy, picaresque novel, Pindaric ode, play, poetry, postcolonial literature, problem novel, prose, prose poem, psychological novel, pulp fiction, quest romance, realistic novel, renga, revenge tragedy, *roman à clef,* romance, romantic comedy, rondeau, rondel, roundel, sapphic, satire, science fiction, Senecan tragedy, sentimental comedy, sentimental novel, sestina, Shakespearean sonnet, short story, situation comedy, slapstick, slave narrative, socialist realism, sociological novel, sonnet, sonnet redoublé, Spenserian sonnet, spoof, spy fiction, stream-of-consciousness narrative, suspense fiction, tale, *terza rima,* thesis novel, threnody, thriller, tragedy, tragedy of blood, tragicomedy, travesty, triolet, urban legend, utopian literature, *vers de société*, verse, villanelle, whodunit, and wonder tale.

▶ **Georgian Age (in English literature):** (1) An era in English literary history spanning the years 1714–1830 and named for kings George I, George II, George III, and George IV, who reigned successively. (2) An era in English literary history spanning the years 1910–36, during which George V was king. Both Georgian ages overlap with other literary eras, the first with the **Neoclassical Period** and **Romantic Period,** and the second with the **Edwardian Age** and the **Modern Period.** This entry focuses on the twentieth-century Georgian Age since use of the term *Georgian* in **literary criticism** is most common with respect to poetry from this era.

Georgian poetry, showcased in Edward Marsh's five *Georgian Poetry* anthologies (1911–22), is characterized by quiet, formal, often **elegiac** and **pastoral lyrics.** Georgian poets sought to widen the audience for poetry by writing simply and directly; using colloquial language; and featuring the individual, often in a rural **setting** in keeping with the traditions of **romanticism.** Significant Georgian poets included Richard Aldington, Rupert Brooke, W. H. Davies, Walter de la Mare, and John Masefield, although Aldington and Brooke also wrote passionately about the war experience, as did lesser-known Georgians Wilfred Owen, Isaac Rosenberg, and Siegfried Sassoon. Notably, the term *Georgian* is not generally used to describe **modernist** contemporaries, whose poetry was more fragmented, **allusive,** and unconventional. Thus, although T. S. Eliot, William Butler Yeats, and American expatriate Ezra Pound all lived in Britain and wrote during the Georgian Age, they are rarely called Georgian poets.

At the outset, Georgian poets were viewed as "Young Turks" challenging the status quo, reacting against imperialism, nationalistic **verse,** and the **didacticism** and **conventions** of **Victorianism.** Marsh characterized the shift in the preface to the first *Georgian Poetry* anthology, covering the years 1911–12, by writing that "English poetry is now once again putting on new strength and beauty." With the advent of the more radical, experimental modernism, however, particularly the publication of Eliot's *The Waste Land* (1922), Georgian poetry was eclipsed and frequently denigrated as conservative, simplistic, and escapist, negative **connotations** that persist to some extent today.

By contrast, when applied to other **genres,** such as prose and drama, the term *Georgian* is used neutrally and covers a wide range of works. Many novelists of the earlier Edwardian Age, such as Arnold Bennett, Joseph Conrad, and H. G. Wells, wrote well into the Georgian Age and are sometimes called Georgian novelists. Modernist novelists who wrote during the Georgian Age include James Joyce, D. H. Lawrence, Dorothy Richardson, and Virginia Woolf. In theater, George Bernard Shaw further developed the kind of serious, intellectual drama pioneered by the nineteenth-century playwright Henrik Ibsen, and Noël Coward helped revive the lighter genre known as the **comedy of manners.** John Galsworthy, whose career spanned most of the Edwardian and Georgian Ages, addressed issues of **class** both in novels (*The Forsyte Saga* [1906–21]) and plays (*The Skin Game* [1920]).

▶ **golden age:** A term variously used to refer to a **mythical** age of abundance and happiness, the historical epoch in which a given civilization reached prominence, and a particularly notable period in the history of a national literature or a literary **genre.**

In **classical** Greek and Roman mythology, *golden age* refers to an original period of human felicity, an idyllic state of ease, harmony, peace, and plenty first described by the Greek poet Hesiod in *Works and Days* (c. 700 B.C.). Later, Christian **pastoralists** associated the golden age with life in Eden before the Fall, viewing Christ as the Good Shepherd who would restore humanity to Paradise. Similar concepts of an ideal first age also exist in Eastern cultures; for instance, Hindu teachings, set forth in works such as the ancient Sanskrit **epic** *Mahābhārata,* posit a cycle of four ages, each associated with a color (much as the Greeks spoke of golden, silver, bronze, and iron ages), beginning with an enlightened, "white" era and subsequently descending into want, wickedness, and strife.

When used with regard to a historical era, *golden age* can reference any past period, however recent ("the golden age of air travel"). Usually, however, the term is reserved for epochs associated with achievements that have defined our understanding of a civilization; for example, the period of the Tang dynasty (618–906) and the reign of Elizabeth I (1588–1603) are commonly referred to as the golden ages of Chinese and English history, respectively. The Islamic golden age, noted particularly for achievements in science, mathematics, and medicine, is generally said to have lasted from the eighth to the thirteenth centuries.

In connection with literary history, the term often refers specifically to sixteenth- and seventeenth-century Spanish literature, the *Siglo de Oro,* or "Century of Gold," whose leading figures included **lyric** poet Luis de Góngora; playwrights Lope de Vega and Pedro Calderón de la Barca; and Miguel de Cervantes, author of *Don Quixote* (1605, 1615). It may also, however, be applied to other literatures or genres, as when the **Elizabethan Age** is called the golden age of English drama.

▶ **Gothic, Gothic literature:** The term *Gothic,* which originally referred to a Germanic tribe, the Goths, is often used more generally today to mean Germanic, **medieval,** or uncouth, as well as to refer more specifically to a style of architecture that originated in France and flourished during the **Medieval Period,** particularly during the thirteenth through fifteenth centuries. Gothic buildings are characterized by ornamental detail, flying buttresses, pointed arches and vaults, narrow spires, stained glass windows, and prominent verticality; cathedrals are often adorned with **grotesque** carvings of people, monsters, or devils known as gargoyles. As a result, Gothic architecture can seem flamboyant, mysterious, or even frightening.

When applied to literature, *Gothic* has been used both positively and pejoratively to refer to a **genre** characterized by a general **mood** of decay, suspense, and terror; action that is dramatic and generally violent or otherwise disturbing; loves that are destructively passionate; and landscapes that are grandiose, if gloomy or bleak. To eighteenth-century **neoclassicists,** who valued simplicity and unity, the appellation *Gothic* signified the barbaric or crude. For them, "Gothic" writing was untutored, unrestrained, and ridiculously extravagant. **Romantics**, however, found in the Gothic a freedom of spirit, variety, mystery, and instinctual authenticity (as opposed to reasoned and therefore artificial **discourse**) that meshed well with their own emphasis on individuality, **imagination,** and **the sublime.**

Gothic literature arose in England in the 1760s with the publication of Horace Walpole's novel *The Castle of Otranto: A Gothic Story* (1764), a seminal work that inaugurated a tradition of Gothic novels, short stories, poems, and plays that peaked around 1820. The Gothic novel, the most prominent manifestation of Gothic literature, is a **romance** typically written as a long prose **narrative** pervaded by a sense of doom and gloom and featuring horror and mystery, chivalry and **villainy.** Dark medieval castles chock full of secret passageways and (apparently) supernatural phenomena are common elements used to thrill the reader. Gothic **heroes** and **heroines** tend to be equally mysterious, with dark histories and secrets of their own. The Gothic hero is typically a man characterized more by power and charisma than personal goodness; the Gothic heroine's challenge is to win the hero's love without being destroyed in the process. Exaggeration and emotional language are frequently employed by Gothic writers, who typically emphasize **plot** and **setting** over **character** and **characterization.**

Gothic literature, especially the Gothic novel, which rose to literary eminence with Ann Radcliffe's *The Italian* (1797), has had tremendous impact both on the development of other genres and on individual authors. Genres **influenced** by Gothic literature, which was itself influenced by the **Graveyard School of Poetry,** include the *ghost story,* **horror, mystery fiction,** and **suspense fiction;** Gothic drama, including dramatized versions of Gothic novels, is also said to have influenced the development of **melodrama.** Gothic novels have also had particular influence on the works of many late-nineteenth- and early-twentieth-century writers. Novelists ranging from the Brontë sisters to Henry James to Daphne du Maurier are so indebted to the Gothic novel that some critics have even applied the term *Gothic* to their own works, such as Charlotte Brontë's *Jane Eyre* (1847), Emily Brontë's *Wuthering Heights* (1847), James's *The Turn of the Screw* (1898), and du Maurier's *Rebecca* (1938). Even today, Gothic elements are common in literature (especially but not exclusively in the popular **historical romances** sometimes referred to as "bodice rippers") and in other art forms such as film, music, and television. The number of contemporary works falling into the "Gothic" category is even larger if we follow the current trend of using the term to refer to any work that evokes a brooding, ominous atmosphere.

FURTHER EXAMPLES: Radcliffe's novel *The Mysteries of Udolpho* (1794), Charles Brockden Brown's novel *Wieland* (1798), Samuel Taylor Coleridge's long poem *Christabel* (1816), Edgar Allan Poe's short story "The Fall of the House of Usher" (1839); Bram Stoker's novel *Dracula* (1897). Matthew ("Monk") Lewis authored several Gothic works, including *The Monk*

(1796), a novel he wrote as a teenager; "Alonzo the Brave and the Fair Imogine," a poem from *The Monk* featuring the "spectre bridegroom" motif; *The Castle Spectre* (1796), a play; and "The Anaconda," a short story published in his collection *Romantic Tales* (1808). E. T. A. Hoffmann's **tales**, perhaps the most famous of which is "The Sand-man" (1817), are also often described as Gothic. Jane Austen's novel *Northanger Abbey* (1818) gently **parodies** the Gothic tradition. Twentieth-century examples of Gothic literature include the Gothic romances of Victoria Holt (*Mistress of Mellyn* [1960]) and Phyllis A. Whitney (*Thunder Heights* [1960]), much of Stephen King's fiction (*The Shining* [1977], *It* [1986]), and the novels of Anne Rice (*Interview with the Vampire* [1976], *The Witching Hour* [1990]).

Popular culture continues to feature the Gothic and Gothic horror. Ken Russell's *Gothic* (1987) luridly retells the episode in the lives of Mary Shelley; Percy Bysshe Shelley; and George Gordon, Lord Byron that inspired Mary's **classic** Gothic novel *Frankenstein* (1818). Indeed, *Frankenstein* has been the source of numerous retellings and adaptations, including the movies *Mary Shelley's Frankenstein* (1994) and *Frankenstein* (2004). The WB series *Buffy the Vampire Slayer* (1997–2003) and *Charmed* (1998–2006) also drew on the Gothic tradition. In music, "Goth Rock" enjoyed a vogue in the 1980s, when groups such as The Cure forged a series of majestic, foreboding rock albums awash with morbid sounds and **themes.** An extreme version of Goth Rock with a particularly provocative, even blasphemous, edge is purveyed by Marilyn Manson.

▶ **graphic novel:** Often described as an extended form of comics, a visual **narrative**, published as a book, that tells a **story** through a combination of words and illustrations. Like a **novel**, a graphic novel tells a story via a **plot**, but the design, layout, and artwork are as integral to the story as the text. The term was coined in 1964 by American comics critic Richard Kyle, who used it to distinguish longer, more sophisticated works from short, simple comics.

The graphic novel's origins lie primarily in Europe, the United States, and Japan. In Europe, Belgian artist Frans Masereel used woodcuts to compose wordless, novel-length narratives such as *Mon livre d'heures* (*Passionate Journey*) (1926). Subsequently, fellow Belgian Hergé (George Remi) developed the long-format and long-running comic book series *Les Aventures de Tintin* (1929–83), which were bound into hardcover "albums," as were the similarly popular and durable adventures of *Astérix* (1959–), authored by the French writer-illustrator team René Goscinny and Albert Uderzo. In the United States, drugstore comic books (e.g., the *Classics Illustrated* series [1941–76], which adapted **canonical** literature to graphic form), newspaper "funnies," and superhero stories are often viewed as the principal precursors. In Japan, *emaki* picture scrolls and the caricatures of painter and printmaker Katsushika Hokusai (1760–1849) are often cited as precedents.

Many scholars link the emergence of the graphic novel as a **genre** in the West to the publication of American writer Will Eisner's *A Contract with*

God (1978), a collection of graphically depicted short stories that prominently featured the term "graphic novel" on its cover. While other such texts had appeared earlier, such as Gil Kane's *Blackmark* (1971) and Robert Corben's *Bloodstar* (1976), Eisner's work, which looked like a novel and dealt with serious existential issues (including death and faith) among immigrant cultures, was particularly influential. Contemporaneous examples include Wendy and Richard Pini's *Elfquest* and Don McGregor and Paul Gulacy's *Sabre* (both 1978). Subsequently, in the mid-1980s, graphic novels entered the mainstream in the United States with the success of Alan Moore and Dave Gibbons's *Watchmen* (1986–87); Frank Miller's revisionist four-part Batman miniseries *The Dark Knight Returns* (1986); and Art Spiegelman's *Maus* (1986), a two-volume **memoir** of the Holocaust that melds some **fiction** with fact.

In the United States, the best-selling graphic novelist to date is Neil Gaiman, whose *Sandman* series (1989–96) has been collected in ten volumes totaling more than 2,000 pages. More recent examples of the form include Daniel Clowes's *Ghost World* (1997; adapted to film 2001) and Chris Ware's *Jimmy Corrigan: The Smartest Kid on Earth* (2000), both of which examine issues of disaffection and alienation in the lives of their young **protagonists,** and Gilbert Hernandez's *Palomar: The Heartbreak Soup Stories* (2003).

In Japan, the graphic novel emerged from demand for reprints of serialized comic strips, popularized by Osamu Tezuka, the father of Japanese *manga* (comics) and *anime* (animation). *Manga*, translated into more than a dozen languages, encompasses a wide range of subjects and target audiences: some are subject-specific, such as *jidaimono* (history), *mecha* (robots), and *shōjo-ai* or *yuri* (lesbian romances); others are demographically oriented, such as *kodomo* (for children), *shōjo* (for teenage girls), and *shōnen* (for teenage boys). Noted examples include Tezuka's *Tetsuwan Atomu* (*Astro Boy*) series (1951–81), which has been called the first **science-fiction** graphic novel; Kazuo Koike's cult **classic** about samurai culture, *Lone Wolf and Cub* (1970–76); Keiji Nakazawa's *Barefoot Gen* (1973–74) a loosely **autobiographical** story of surviving the bombing of Hiroshima; Ōtomo Katsuhiro's post-**apocalyptic, cyberpunk** epic *Akira* (1982–90), which brought American attention to *manga*; Hayao Miyazaki's *Nausicaä of the Valley of the Wind* (1982–94; adapted to film 1984) and *anime* film *Spirited Away* (2001); and Tsugumi Ohba's *Death Note* series (2003–06).

Despite the association of *novel* and *fiction,* the term *graphic novel* is also used to refer to **nonfiction** works that fall into categories such as memoir, historical reportage, and journalism. Examples include *Maus*, which set the precedent for the nonfiction graphic novel; Marjane Satrapi's *Persepolis: The Story of a Childhood* (2000; adapted to film 2007), about growing up in Iran following the Islamic Revolution; Joe Sacco's *Palestine* (2001), about the Arab-Israeli conflict; and Alison Bechdel's *Fun Home: A Family Tragicomic* (2006), the author's memoir of coming out as a lesbian while coming to terms with the suicide of her closeted gay father.

Notably, many graphic novelists reject the term *graphic novel*. Some find it unduly broad, given its application to works ranging from the truly novel-like to nonfiction and short story collections; others believe it obscures the genre's character as a form of comics. Moore derided *graphic novel* in an interview in 2000 as "a marketing term . . . . The term 'comic' does just as well for me." Spiegelman called it "an arguably misguided bid for respectability where graphics are respectable and novels are respectable so you get double respectability." Even Eisner himself preferred the terms *graphic literature* and *graphic story*.

As the form has developed, so has a body of commentary, much of which is itself written in graphic novel form. Examples include Scott McCloud's *Understanding Comics* (1994) and Eisner's *Graphic Storytelling* (1996), a guide to writing graphic fiction.

▶ **Graveyard School of Poetry:** A group of eighteenth-century poets who, unlike their "rational" **neoclassical** contemporaries, emphasized (im)mortality, melancholy, **mystery,** and **subjectivity.** The Graveyard School, which arose in England in the first half of the century, spread to continental Europe, where it enjoyed an even greater vogue, in the second half of the century. Graveyard poets typically reflected on death and bereavement in their poems, many of which were actually set in graveyards, and often incorporated ghosts, ruins, and the physical horrors of the grave, using graphic and gloomy **imagery** for spiritual ends. The Graveyard School influenced the development of **Gothic literature** and is often said to have laid the groundwork for English **romanticism.** Notable British Graveyard poets include Robert Blair, Thomas Gray, Thomas Parnell, and Edward Young.

EXAMPLES: Gray's "Elegy Written in a Country Churchyard" (1751) is the most famous Graveyard poem. Other examples include Parnell's "A Night-Piece on Death" (1722), Young's *The complaint; or, Night-thoughts on life, death, & immortality* (1742); and Blair's *The Grave* (1743), the first **stanza** of which follows:

> WHILST some affect the Sun, and some the Shade,
> Some flee the City, some the Hermitage;
> Their Aims as various, as the Roads they take
> In Journeying thro' Life; the Task be mine
> To paint the gloomy Horrors of the *Tomb;*
> Th' appointed Place of Rendezvous, where all
> These Travellers meet. Thy Succours I implore,
> Eternal King! whose potent Arm sustains
> The Keys of Hell and Death. THE GRAVE, dread Thing!
> Men shiver, when thou'rt nam'd: Nature appall'd
> Shakes off her wonted Firmness. Ah! how dark
> Thy long-extended Realms, and rueful Wastes!
> Where nought but Silence reigns, and Night, dark Night,
> Dark as was *Chaos,* 'ere the Infant Sun
> Was roll'd together, or had try'd his Beams
> Athwart the Gloom profound! The sickly Taper

By glimmering thro' thy low-brow'd misty Vaults,
(Furr'd round with mouldy Damps, and ropy Slime,)
Lets fall a supernumerary Horror,
And only serves to make thy Night more irksome.
Well do I know thee by thy trusty *Yew,*
Chearless, unsocial Plant! that loves to dwell
'Midst Sculls and Coffins, Epitaphs and Worms:
Where light-heel'd Ghosts, and visionary Shades,
Beneath the wan cold Moon (as Fame reports)
Embody'd thick, perform their mystick Rounds.
No other Merriment, Dull Tree! is thine.

▶ **green criticism:** See **ecocriticism.**

▶ **grotesque:** From the Italian word for "grottoes" or "caves," a term first used in English in the sixteenth century to refer to decorative paintings or sculptures mixing human, animal, and supernatural figures (such as griffins) in designs found in or **imitating** those discovered in excavated rooms of ancient Roman houses. Such rooms, which were popularly referred to during the **Renaissance** as *grotte,* were literally "grotto-esque," since they were open spaces long buried under more recent buildings and even ruins.

In the seventeenth century, *grotesque* came to be used more broadly to refer to strangely unusual things or artistic **representations,** particularly ones involving bizarre or unnatural combinations of characteristics or **images.** English poet John Milton's representation of Paradise in *Paradise Lost* (1667) as a "steep wilderness" with "hairy sides / With thicket overgrown, grotesque and wild" is itself, properly speaking, a grotesque description, combining images of hair and plant material. With this broader application, the term came to be used as an adjective describing gargoyles, statues combining human, animal, and monstrous features designed to protect buildings, particularly **Gothic** churches and cathedrals. Today, in art and **literary criticism,** the term refers to an **aesthetic** category involving but also **parodying** Gothic elements and **themes.** In literature, it also refers to **characters** who are in some way twisted or deformed, evoking a combination of antipathy and **empathy,** such as the monster in Mary Shelley's novel *Frankenstein* (1818).

The humorous aspect of the grotesque is often grounded in extreme physicality and fascination with sexuality. In *Rabelais and His World* (1940), Russian critic Mikhail Bakhtin maintained that the grotesque is characterized by bodily descriptions and the theme of procreation. The grotesque, however, also elicits fear of those same characteristics that evoke laughter. Wolfgang Kayser, in his book *The Grotesque in Art and Literature* (1957), defined the grotesque as "the estranged world," insisting that unlike **tragedy** or the **fairy tale,** both of which are composed of elements that are distanced from the everyday reality of the reader, the grotesque necessarily evolves out of humorous representations of a world familiar to the reader, resulting both in alienation from that world and in an unwilling participation in it.

Hieronymus Bosch's *Hell:* An example of the **grotesque**.

EXAMPLES: The paintings of Hieronymus Bosch and the writings of François Rabelais have long been considered grotesque, as are numerous short stories by Edgar Allan Poe, whose first collection was titled *Tales of the Grotesque and Arabesque* (1840). See page 211 for an example of the grotesque in Bosch's art, the *Hell* panel of the triptych *The Garden of Earthly Delights*. Twentieth-century literary works containing grotesque elements include Franz Kafka's "The Metamorphosis" (1915), Erskine Caldwell's *Poor Fool* (1930), William Faulkner's *As I Lay Dying* (1930), and Pär Lagerkvist's *The Dwarf* (1945). Contemporary popular works that incorporate the grotesque include Gary Larson's *The Far Side* cartoons (1981–95); the animated television cartoon *South Park* (1997–); the claymation television cartoon *Celebrity Deathmatch* (1998–); and G. E. Graven's illustrated, self-published online novel *Grotesque, A Gothic Epic* (2006), a story set in **medieval** times whose **protagonist**, Squire Lazarus Gogu, is a winged grotesque who must stop the unfolding of Armageddon.

▶ **gynocriticism:** A term adapted from the French *la gynocritique* by Elaine Showalter in *A Literature of Their Own* (1977) to refer to a type of **feminist criticism** that arose in the U.S. in the 1970s and that focuses on literary works written by women. Showalter separated women's writing since 1840 into three phases, which she referred to as "Feminine," "Feminist," and "Female." During these phases, women first imitated a masculine tradition (1840–80); then protested against its standards and values (1880–1920); and finally advocated their own autonomous, female perspective (1920 to the present).

Gynocritics devised a framework for analyzing all varieties of female-**authored** works, whether diaries or letters, poems or novels. As Showalter explained in "Toward a Feminist Poetics" (1979), "the program of gynocritics is to construct a female framework for the analysis of women's literature, to develop new models based on the study of female experience, rather than to adapt male models and theories." Thus, instead of critiquing male-authored works or studying women as readers who must resist the **patriarchal ideology** that most **texts** reinforce, gynocritics sought to demonstrate that a special and explicitly female tradition exists in literature, a tradition too often ignored or denigrated. In so doing, they broadened the literary **canon** to include long-overlooked works such as Aphra Benn's *Oroonoko* (1688) and Kate Chopin's *The Awakening* (1899) and examined the ways in which female writers have formed and benefited from their own communities and traditions.

Gynocritics focused on so-called feminine subjects **privileged** by female authors (such as domestic life, intimate experiences, and personal and family relationships) that are usually excluded from or marginalized in works by male authors, who tend to privilege adventure, achievement, work outside the home, voyages of self-discovery, and other endeavors deemed active, and therefore "masculine." Gynocritics also often sought to demonstrate the existence of a special feminine **subjectivity,** or way of thinking about and experiencing the world. Some gynocritics expanded this view to argue that women's special mode of perception leads them to speak and, especially, to write in a way different from men. These gynocritics asserted the existence of a distinctive **feminine writing,** which in French feminist criticism is referred to as *écriture féminine.*

Some critics, including some feminist critics, have objected to gynocriticism insofar as its emphasis on a special feminine language, writing, and aesthetic reflects an **essentialist** perspective, namely, the view that **gender** differences are natural or innate. Others have criticized the approach for neglecting issues of **class** and **race** in focusing primarily on the works and experiences of white, middle-class women. Influential gynocritics include Showalter, Patricia Meyer Spacks, Sandra Gilbert, and Susan Gubar.

H

▶ **hagiography:** See **biography.**

▶ **haiku:** A Japanese **verse** form consisting of three un**rhymed** lines that traditionally contain a total of seventeen syllables in a five-seven-five pattern. A haiku typically presents **images** of nature, using association and suggestion to appeal to emotion and generate a moment of spiritual awareness or discovery. The haiku, which initially developed in the thirteenth and fourteenth centuries as the opening section, or *hokku,* of the *renga,* a form of multi-authored, linked verse, subsequently evolved into a freestanding form, a development accelerated by the popularity of the *haikai,* a lighter type of renga that emerged in the sixteenth century. In the late nineteenth century, Japanese poet Masaoka Shiki coined the term *haiku* to refer to the hokku as an independent poem, thereby distinguishing it from the hokku as the opening verse of the haikai or traditional renga. In contemporary English usage, however, *haiku* and *hokku* are often used synonymously.

As a self-contained poem, the haiku came to be printed in the nineteenth century in a single, vertical line, hence the common description of haiku as "one-line poems." Some poets also experimented or even dispensed with the two main hokku **conventions:** the five-seven-five syllabic pattern and the *kigo,* traditionally a word or phrase that functions as a **code** signaling the season of composition. In Western poetry, where the three-line format has remained popular but the number of syllables is often reduced and the *kigo* omitted, the haiku debuted around 1900 and had particular **influence** on the development of **Imagism.**

Noted Japanese haiku poets aside from Shiki include seventeenth-century Edo-period poet Matsuo Bashō, Yosa Buson, Kobayashi Issa, and Konishi Raizan. Twentieth-century American poets who experimented with the form include Imagist poets Amy Lowell, Ezra Pound, and William Carlos Williams; Gary Snyder; and Richard Wright, who wrote thousands of haiku using the classic seventeen-syllable, five-seven-five pattern in the year and a half prior to his death in 1960.

EXAMPLES: The following **classic** hokku (1686) by Bashō, commonly considered the most famous of all haiku:

> furuike ya
> kawazu tobikomu
> mizu no oto

As translated into English by Makoto Ueda in *Bashō and His Interpreters* (1991), Bashō's hokku reads:

> the old pond—
> a frog jumps in,
> water's sound

Wright's collection *HAIKU: This Other World,* published posthumously in 1998, contains 817 haiku that he selected for publication. Michael Mc-Clintock, by contrast, departs from the classic syllabic pattern in his work, such as the following haiku published in *Tundra* in 2001:

> the candle
> flares, darkening
> the basilica

▶ **half rhyme:** A form of **rhyme** in which words contain similar sounds but do not rhyme perfectly. Most half rhyme (also called *approximate rhyme, imperfect rhyme, near rhyme, oblique rhyme, pararhyme,* and *slant rhyme*) is the result of **assonance, consonance,** or a combination of the two. Half rhyme may be unintentional or intentional. Unintentional half rhyme results from the poet's lack of rhyming skills; intentional half rhyme is usually the product of **poetic license,** liberties taken by the poet to create specific sound effects.

EXAMPLES: *Rhyme / writhe, horse / hearse, summer / humble,* and *thin / slim.* Emily Dickinson made frequent use of half rhyme; the following passage from "In Winter in my Room" (c. 1860), uses half rhyme in the words *Room / Worm / warm* and *pink / lank*:

> In Winter in my Room
> I came upon a Worm
> Pink lank and warm.

Wilfred Owen also relied heavily on half rhyme in his poetry. In "Strange Meeting" (1920), *hall / Hell, friend / frowned,* and *killed / cold* are examples:

> And by his smile, I knew that sullen hall, —
> By his dead smile I knew we stood in Hell. . . .
>
> "I am the enemy you killed, my friend.
> I knew you in this dark; for so you frowned
> Yesterday through me as you jabbed and killed.
> I parried; but my hands were loath and cold.
> Let us sleep now. . . ."

Philip Larkin's "Toads" (1954) strikes a lighter note. The pair *life / off* constitutes a half rhyme, whereas the pair *work / pitchfork* constitutes an **eye rhyme** as well as a half rhyme:

> Why should I let the toad *work*
> Squat on my life?
> Can't I use my wit as a pitchfork
> And drive the brute off?

Selena's soft-rock **ballad** "I Could Fall in Love with You" (1996) alternates **perfect rhymes** (*how / now*) and half rhymes (e.g., *feel / still*).

▶ **hamartia:** From the Greek for "error," an error in judgment made by a **tragic hero** that brings about the suffering, downfall, and often death of that hero. The term is often used synonymously with **tragic flaw,** but this usage is not strictly correct; the error involved in hamartia need not stem from an inherent character trait, whether conventionally negative (e.g., **hubris**) or positive (e.g., courage), but may instead result from other sources, such as an accident or a lack of crucial knowledge regarding a situation. Thus, although the hamartia may and often does result from a tragic flaw, the two terms are not technically equivalent.

EXAMPLE: Oedipus's hubris — apparent to the reader from the **prologue** of Sophocles' *Oedipus Rex* (c. 430 B.C.), where he crows "Here I am myself — / you all know me, the world knows my fame: / I am Oedipus" — leads to his downfall, in which he blinds and banishes himself after realizing that he unwittingly killed his father and married his mother.

▶ **hard-boiled detective fiction:** See **detective fiction**. See also **mystery fiction**.

▶ **Harlem Renaissance:** An intellectual and cultural movement of the 1920s centered in Harlem, then a predominantly African American section of New York City, and focusing on the arts — literature in particular but also visual art, music, theater, and dance. The movement was originally called the "New Negro Renaissance," reflecting the aspirations and expectations of participants who sought to build racial consciousness, celebrate black heritage, and gain recognition and acceptance. It is commonly dated to 1919, following the end of World War I, and reached its zenith in the latter half of the 1920s. The decline of the movement is often linked to the crash of the stock market in 1929 and the onset of the Great Depression, with an end date ranging from 1929 to the mid-1930s.

The Harlem Renaissance, which presented black life from a black point of view, was fueled by a mass migration of African Americans out of the South and into northern cities during the teens and in the aftermath of the war as well as by the emergence of a cadre of bold black intellectuals. Harlem, often called the "Negro Mecca," grew tremendously during this period and served as a crossroads for urban diversity and rural roots, as exemplified by **folklore** and spirituals. The area became not only the nexus of black literature, theater, music, and dance but also an intellectual and artistic nerve center for the nation, highlighting African American culture for a diverse national audience for the first time. The movement embraced both traditional and new means of expression, employing **classical** as well as **modernist** forms and techniques, producing **sonnets** as well as jazz. Underlying the diversity of **form** and **style**, however, were common goals of race-building and integration. W. E. B. Du Bois, an educator and activist who devoted his life to "the problem of the color line," took this view to an extreme, declaring in his essay "Criteria of Negro Art" (1926) that "all art is propaganda and ever must be, despite the wailing of the purists." Art in an organized, self-conscious movement was a means of building pride, highlighting black heroes and traditions, and changing the way white Americans viewed their black compatriots.

As the leading African American intellectual of his time, Du Bois was a major influence on the Harlem Renaissance, though most of the movement's rising stars would reject his dogmatic insistence on portraying blacks in a positive light. Particularly influential was Du Bois's concept of "twoness," or dual identity; as he explained in *The Souls of Black Folk* (1903), a collection of essays on the plight of black Americans: "One ever feels his two-ness — an American, a Negro; two souls, two thoughts, two unreconciled stirrings: two warring ideals in one dark body, whose dogged strength alone keeps it from being torn asunder." Also influential was his concept of the "Talented Tenth," an educated black elite to achieve social change. In his essay "The Talented Tenth" (1903), Du Bois advocated higher education for "[t]he best and most capable [black] youth" to make them "leaders of thought and missionaries of culture among their people"; he believed in "developing the Best of this race that they may guide the Mass away from the contamination and death of the Worst, in their own and other races." Du Bois's editorship of the NAACP journal *The Crisis* (1910–), a position he held from the founding of the journal until 1934, was also critical in providing an outlet for the work of black writers.

Other significant "elders" of the Harlem Renaissance included Jessie Fauset James Weldon Johnson, and Alain Locke. Fauset, a writer and teacher, served as literary editor of *The Crisis* from 1919–26, cultivating young writers including Countee Cullen, Langston Hughes, Claude McKay, and Jean Toomer in addition to producing several novels, poems, and essays of her own. James Weldon Johnson, already admired for his novel *The Autobiography of an Ex-Colored Man* (1912), compiled two anthologies, *The Book of American Negro Poetry* (1922) and *The Book of American Negro Spirituals* (1925), providing a literary foundation for the movement he called the "flowering of Negro literature." Locke, a firm believer in the power of culture to further black advancement, produced the movement's first manifesto, *The New Negro*, published first as a special issue of the magazine *Survey Graphic* (March 1925) and then in expanded form as an anthology the same year. The anthology, which included portrait drawings by Winold Reiss of movement participants, featured essays, fiction, and poems by emerging writers such as Hughes, Zora Neale Hurston, and McKay. In his introduction, Locke proclaimed that "Negro life is seizing upon its first chances for group expression and self-determination."

With black writers generally shut out of the white publishing world, black periodicals provided virtually the only outlet for African American literature in the teens and the first half of the 1920s. In addition to *The Crisis*, the leading periodical of the Harlem Renaissance was the National Urban League's *Opportunity* (1923–49), edited by sociologist Charles S. Johnson from 1923–28. Johnson, like Fauset, nurtured a generation of young black writers, publishing works including Hughes's poem "The Weary Blues" (1923). Indeed, Johnson is often credited with launching the "New Negro" movement by bringing black writers and white publishers together at a dinner sponsored by *Opportunity* in 1924. *Fire!!* (1926), an **avant-garde** literary magazine founded by artist Richard Bruce Nugent and Hughes and edited by writer Wallace Thurman, took a different approach. As a radical alternative manifesto to *The New Negro*, *Fire!!* featured many of the same leading young writers while presenting the rough, vernacular, even decadent and debauched side of Harlem that the cultural elite sought to hide.

Patrons also played an important role in the Harlem Renaissance, providing support for young participants as well as connections to the publishing world. In 1928, A'Lelia Walker, a black heiress whom Hughes called the "joy-goddess of Harlem's 1920s," founded "The Dark Tower," a salon named for Cullen's column in *Opportunity*, to support Harlem culture. White writer Carl Van Vechten, author of *Nigger Heaven* (1926), a controversial bestseller that described both the unseemly and the Talented Tenth life in Harlem and helped fuel a wave of "Harlemania," provided financial support to Hughes and Hurston, and served as a bridge to the white publishing world. "Godmother" Charlotte Mason, a white **primitivist**, provided financial support to protégés including visual artist Aaron Douglas, Hughes, Hurston, and Locke, funding, among other things, Hurston's two-year expedition to the South to collect Negro folklore. Other white supporters — known as "Negrotarians," a term coined by Hurston — included Jewish capitalists who made common cause with oppressed blacks and authors (such as Waldo Frank and Eugene O'Neill) who wrote black **characters** into their works and provided links to publishers.

Over the course of the 1920s, tensions began to emerge among participants in the Harlem Renaissance, particularly over the literary portrayal of black people. *Fire!!* flaunted its rejection of image-based race-building, the divided response to *Nigger Heaven* highlighted the rift, and the issue was openly debated in *The Crisis,* where Du Bois invited responses to "The Negro in Art: How Shall He Be Portrayed?" (1926). Du Bois and his followers, such as Fauset, Locke, and Cullen, favored dignified, uplifting portrayals focused on the Talented Tenth, which they saw as the engine of liberation. But another faction, dominated by younger artists and writers associated with "Niggerati Manor" — as Hurston referred to a rooming house where many members lived and gathered — sought more freedom of expression, including the freedom to depict "low," popular culture and the "debauched tenth," so to speak, of black society. This faction, which viewed the genteel ethos of the Talented Tenth (derogatorily termed "dicties") as elitist and stultifying, included Douglas, Hurston, Nugent, Thurman, and Hughes, whose landmark essay "The Negro Artist and the Racial Mountain," published in *The Nation* in 1926, addressed the issue of black artistic identity, proclaiming:

Let the blare of Negro jazz bands and the bellowing voice of Bessie Smith singing the Blues penetrate the closed ears of the colored near-intellectuals until they listen and perhaps understand. Let Paul Robeson singing "Water Boy," and Rudolph Fisher writing about the streets of Harlem, and Jean Toomer holding the heart of Georgia in his hands, and Aaron Douglas's drawing strange black fantasies cause the smug Negro middle class to turn from their white, respectable, ordinary books and papers to catch a glimmer of their own beauty. We younger Negro artists who create now intend to express our individual dark-skinned selves without fear or shame.

Publication of McKay's *Home to Harlem* (1928), a **picaresque novel** about Harlem street life written while McKay was living abroad, showed up the rift as never before: Hughes called the book, which became the first best-selling novel in America by a black author, "the finest thing 'we've' done yet"; Du Bois said "I feel distinctly like taking a bath."

While literature was important to the Harlem Renaissance, music, dance, and theater did as much if not more to fuel "Harlemania" and the "vogue of the Negro," white fascination with "exotic" Harlem life and culture. During the era of Prohibition, Harlem was the place to go for jazz, **blues,** speakeasies, and booze. Many were also drawn by an interest in primitivist and African **themes,** by the perception of black Americans as **Noble Savages,** both sensual and spiritual. Musicians and singers such as Louis Armstrong, Duke Ellington, Bessie Smith, Fats Waller, and Ethel Waters played clubs and cabarets including the famous (and famously segregated) Cotton Club, which strictly enforced its whites-only audience policy. Fletcher Henderson, whose orchestra was the leading black society dance band, pioneered the "big band" sound. Musical revues and vaudeville were staples of Harlem Renaissance theater; Noble Sissle and Eubie Blake's *Shuffle Along* (1921) was a breakthrough musical revue written and performed entirely by African Americans. Dance was also popular, with leading performers including Josephine Baker, renowned for "le jazz hot" as an expatriate in Paris; tap dancer Bill "Bojangles" Robinson; and the gyrating Earl "Snakehips" Tucker. The lindy hop, a trendy new dance step, was developed at the Savoy Ballroom in the late 1920s.

While the Harlem Renaissance had ended by the mid-1930s, when **class** concerns began to overshadow **race,** the movement is often cited as an influence on the subsequent civil rights movement. Racial consciousness, integration, interracial cooperation, and the importance of positive **images** of black Americans arose again as major themes in the struggle for equality.

FURTHER EXAMPLES: Hughes's poem "The Negro Speaks of Rivers," written in 1920 and published in *The Crisis* in 1921:

> I've known rivers:
> I've known rivers ancient as the world and older than the flow
> of human blood in human veins.

My soul has grown deep like the rivers.

I bathed in the Euphrates when dawns were young.
I built my hut near the Congo and it lulled me to sleep.
I looked upon the Nile and raised the pyramids above it.
I heard the singing of the Mississippi when Abe Lincoln went
    down to New Orleans, and I've seen its muddy bosom turn
    all golden in the sunset.

I've known rivers:
Ancient, dusky rivers.

My soul has grown deep like rivers.

Other notable works of the Harlem Renaissance include McKay's *Harlem Shadows* (1922), a collection of 70 poems; Toomer's *Cane* (1923), a **modernist** yet **elegiac montage** of poems, sketches, stories, and a **novelette**-drama depicting the black South; Fauset's *There Is Confusion* (1924), the first female-authored novel of the movement; W. C. Handy's *Blues: An Anthology* (1926); Nella Larsen's short novels *Quicksand* (1928) and *Passing*

Opportunity: A periodical of the **Harlem Renaissance**.

(1929); Cullen's *The Black Christ and Other Poems* (1929); Thurman's play *Harlem* (1929), coauthored with William Rapp, a white friend; and Rudolph Fisher's novels *The Walls of Jericho* (1928) and *The Conjure-Man Dies* (1932), generally considered the first African American **detective novel**. Arna Bontemps, a participant in the movement, chronicled its history years later in a collection of essays he edited entitled *The Harlem Renaissance Remembered* (1972).

Amiri Baraka (LeRoi Jones) would later write of Harlem in "Return of the Native" (1969):

> Harlem is vicious
> modernism. BangClash.
> Vicious the way its made.
> Can you stand such beauty?
> So violent and transforming.

▶ **Hartford Wits:** See **Revolutionary Period** (in American literature).

▶ **head rhyme:** See **beginning rhyme**.

▶ **hegemony:** From the Greek for "to lead," the dominance or dominant influence of one nation, group, or **class** over another or others. In **literary criticism**, most notably **Marxist criticism** and **cultural criticism**, *hegemony* refers especially to **ideological** and cultural manipulation and control. The term was adapted by the Italian Marxist critic Antonio Gramsci to refer to the process of consensus formation and to the pervasive system of assumptions, meanings, and values — the web of ideologies, in other words — that shapes the way things look, what they mean, and therefore what reality is for the majority of people within a given culture. Although Gramsci viewed hegemony as a potent force, he did not believe that extant systems were immune to change; rather, he encouraged people to resist the prevailing consciousness, to form a new consensus, and thereby to alter hegemony.

▶ **heptameter (septenary):** A line of **verse** consisting of seven **metrical feet**.
   EXAMPLE: The following lines from Rudyard Kipling's "Tommy" (1890) are **fourteeners** written in **iambic** heptameter:

> Ĭ wént | ĭntó | ă púb|lĭc-'óuse | tŏ gét | ă pínt | ŏ' béer,|
> The pub|lican | 'e up | an' sez, | "We serve | no red|-coats here."|
> The girls | be'ind | the bar | they laughed | an' gig|gled fit | to die, |
> I outs | into | the street | again | an' to | myself | sez I. . . . |

▶ **hermeneutics, hermeneutic circle:** Originally, *hermeneutics* was reserved for principles used in interpreting religious writings (often specifically the Bible), but since the nineteenth century the term has been used to refer to the **theory** of interpretation in general. Modern hermeneutics — which considers the interpretive methods leading to the perception and understanding of **texts** and their underlying organizing principles, or **codes** —

is grounded in the terminology and strategies of modern **linguistics** and philosophy.

In 1819, German theologian Friedrich Schleiermacher first developed a theory of hermeneutics in the general sense of textual interpretation. Wilhelm Dilthey, a German philosopher, built upon and expanded Schleiermacher's views in the 1890s, coining the term *hermeneutic circle* to refer to Schleiermacher's idea that to understand the parts of a whole, one must begin with some general conception of that whole and vice versa. Dilthey argued that our perception and, therefore, our interpretation of both the whole and its component parts are modified as we move through the work. Because of the interdependent relationship between our retrospective comprehension of a work's constituent parts and an evolving concept of the constituted whole, we can ultimately develop a legitimate interpretation of that work.

Hermeneutics came back into critical fashion during the mid-twentieth century, thanks to a renewed interest in language and meaning, an interest expressed not only by philosophers but also by various **formalists**, including **the New Critics**. In the latter half of the century, two major developments in hermeneutics occurred. First, German philosopher Hans Georg Gadamer, a student of the philosopher Martin Heidegger, argued in *Truth and Method* (1960) that language and the interpretive act pervade and characterize all aspects of living, not just the study of literary texts. For Gadamer, our being (what Heidegger called *Dasein,* or "being in the world") involves a sense of time — a history that is past and a future yet to come — that each person individually possesses. That sense, or "pre-understanding," forms the "horizons" within which we interpret. Gadamer further believed that readers can interact with the text, produced as it is by another person operating and communicating from the common baseline of language and temporality. By interacting with the text almost as if it were another person — a "Thou" whom the reader may approach as an "I" — the reader can work with the text, so to speak, cooperatively producing meaning rather than tagging the text as a freestanding, independent, fixed object with a specific, predetermined meaning that the reader must uncover.

Second, American educator and literary critic E. D. Hirsch revived the view that an author's meaning may be **objectively** determined, arguing in *Validity in Interpretation* (1967) and *The Aims of Interpretation* (1976) that a text means what its author intended it to mean and that the search for the author's "verbal intention" appropriately limits the otherwise inexhaustible supply of interpretations that may be derived from a single text. In making this argument, Hirsch distinguished between the "verbal meaning" of the text (which he believed *can* be determined and therefore properly falls in the provenance of hermeneutics) and the "significance" of a text (which depends upon the reader's **subjective,** culturally determined response and which he therefore believed *cannot* be determined and is *not* the proper subject of hermeneutic analysis).

Gadamer's theory, which Hirsch attacked in "Gadamer's Theory of Interpretation" (1965), differs not only from Hirsch's insofar as it denies the possibility of establishing verbal intentions and determinate interpretations but also from hermeneutics as understood by traditional theorists and practitioners. The New Critics, for instance, believed that the text of a poem contains within it an intended meaning; in warning against the pitfalls of the **intentional fallacy,** they warned readers not to assume that an author's intentions can be known by studying things external to the text (the author's letters, for instance). American "ordinary language" philosopher John Searle's **speech-act theory** similarly held out the possibility of determinable, determinate interpretation; Searle's point was that in order for a speaker's intention to be known, his or her **"locution"** must conform to the rules and **conventions** governing **locutionary, illocutionary,** and **perlocutionary acts.**

Gadamer's theory is closer to that espoused by those **reader-response critics** who have viewed the meaning-making process as one carried out by the reader under the guidance of the text. It is also closer to the thinking of **deconstructors,** for whom the text consists of words inscribed in and inextricable from the myriad **discourses** that inform it. From the point of view of deconstruction, the text can hardly "contain" a single determinable and determinate meaning because the boundaries between any given text and that larger text we call language are constantly shifting and uncertain.

▶ **hero/heroine:** Often considered synonymous with **protagonist,** a term referring to the main **character** of a work. Sometimes a work is said to have both a hero and a heroine, even if there is a wide discrepancy in their importance. When this is the case, the main character is the protagonist; the other may be either a major or minor character.

The term **antihero** refers to a protagonist who does not exhibit the qualities of a traditional hero and who may be pathetically ordinary or even criminal.

EXAMPLES: Governess Jane Eyre is the heroine and protagonist of Charlotte Brontë's *Jane Eyre* (1847); her employer and future husband, Mr. Rochester, is the hero. In the movie *Walk the Line* (2005), singer June Carter is the heroine, but her troubled lover Johnny Cash is the hero and protagonist.

▶ **heroic couplet:** A pair of **rhymed** lines written in **iambic pentameter.** Fourteenth-century poet Geoffrey Chaucer, the first English poet to use the heroic couplet extensively, is sometimes also credited with introducing or even developing the form. In the mid-seventeenth century, the heroic couplet became the dominant form of English **verse,** the principal **meter** for poems and plays throughout the **Neoclassical Period;** indeed, the appellation *heroic* stems from use of the couplet in **epic** poetry of the time. Neoclassical heroic couplets were typically **closed,** meaning that each pair of lines comprised a discrete grammatical unit and expressed a complete thought. Beginning with the **Romantic Period,** use of the heroic couplet declined substantially; today, the form is all but extinct.

EXAMPLE: The following lines from Alexander Pope's "The Rape of the Lock" (1712, 1714):

> Meanwhile, declining from the noon of day,
> The sun obliquely shoots his burning ray;
> The hungry judges soon the sentence sign,
> And wretches hang that jurymen may dine. . . .

▶ **heteroglossia:** Translated from the Russian *raznorechie*, meaning "different speech-ness," a term used by Soviet critic Mikhail Bakhtin to refer to the plurality of **voices** present in a literary work — including those of the **author, narrator,** and **characters** — as well as to the **dialogue** between these often competing voices. According to Bakhtin, all novels are somewhat **polyphonic,** or *polyvocalic,* since the speech, **ideology,** and **discourse** of certain characters will inevitably compete against the authorial voice. For instance, a novel may contain explicit or implicit disputes between: (1) characters (especially different groups or classes of characters); (2) certain characters or character groups and the sometimes **monologic** (i.e., singular and controlling) author and/or narrator; (3) the "official" ideology of the author's culture and the subversive ideology that authors may directly or indirectly represent or express; and (4) the traditional mores of the literary **genre** in which the work is written and those exhibited by a given text.

As Bakhtin argued in *The Dialogic Imagination,* a compilation of four essays published in English in 1981 but substantially composed during the 1930s and 1940s, heteroglossia "permits a multiplicity of social voices and a wide variety of their links and interrelationships (always more or less dialogized)." Moreover, the term "conceptualizes" the "place," or "locus," where "centripetal" (e.g., official monologic) and "centrifugal" (e.g., unofficial **dialogic**) forces collide. At these crossroads, or in this "matrix," new viewpoints form in language, almost of their own impetus, as a range of voices interrelate and sometimes override the monologic voice of an author or the predominant ideology of his or her culture. Such interactive diversity provides a means of moving around or beyond **codes, conventions,** and the dominant social discourse.

See also **dialogic criticism, monologic, polyphonic.**

▶ **hexameter:** A line of **verse** consisting of six **metrical feet.** In **classical** (ancient Greek or Latin) hexameter, this verse pattern was rigidly constructed; it consisted of four **dactyls** (´ˇˇ) or **spondees** (´´) followed by a dactyl and then a spondee or **trochee** (´ˇ). Since true spondees are fairly rare in English, the classical hexameter is infrequently used by English-language poets.

EXAMPLE: The following lines from William Butler Yeats's "The Lake Isle of Innisfree" (1893):

> Í wĭll ă|ríse ănd | gó nŏw, | ănd gó | tŏ Ínn| ĭsfrĕe,|
> And a small | cabin | build there, | of clay | and wat|tles made. . . . |

▶ **hieratic:** From the Greek for "priestly," a term originally used with reference to a stylized, cursive form of ancient Egyptian writing based on hieroglyphs. As adapted to **literary criticism** by the Canadian **archetypal critic** Northrop Frye, the term refers to a style of literature that employs devices and **conventions** associated with **literariness,** such as **rhetorical figures** and **figures of speech,** to elevate language above the level of ordinary speech. Frye contrasted hieratic style with **demotic** style, which employs the **connotations, diction, rhythms,** and **syntax** of everyday speech. He associated hieratic style with **aesthetic,** formalist, centripetal tendencies and demotic style with oratorical, populist, centrifugal ones but viewed both styles as essential, writing in *The Well-Tempered Critic* (1963) that:

> If we think of literature in purely esthetic and hieratic terms, we think of the end of criticism as a vision of beauty; if we think of it in purely oratorical and demotic terms, we think of the end of criticism as a possession of some form of imaginative truth. Beauty and truth are certainly relevant to the study of literature, but if either is separated from the other and made an end in itself, something goes wrong.

Frye also distinguished three categories — *high, middle,* and *low* — in both the hieratic and demotic styles, arguing that the high style in each is the "authentic speech" of "the world that man exists and participates in through his imagination," "the language of humanity itself."

Subsequently, Frye extended the terms *hieratic* and *demotic* to refer to aristocratic and populist ages, respectively, two of three linguistic phases he discussed in *The Great Code: The Bible and Literature* (1982), the first phase being the *hieroglyphic,* a divine or **mythical** age. Frye associated the hieroglyphic phase with **metaphoric** language, the hieratic phase with **metonymic** language, and the demotic phase with descriptive language.

▶ **historical linguistics:** See **descriptive linguistics.**

▶ **historical novel:** A **novel** that makes use of historical events or figures in a fictitious **narrative.** While Sir Walter Scott is often credited with inaugurating the historical novel in England, Maria Edgeworth pioneered the **genre** in *Castle Rackrent* (1800), a **satire** on Anglo-Irish landlords that is also frequently considered to be the first *regional novel;* Scott, who corresponded with Edgeworth for years, acknowledged her work in an 1829 preface to his Waverley novels. Significant **influences** on the historical novel include Madame de Lafayette's *La princesse de Clèves* (1678) — sometimes itself called the first historical novel — and **Gothic literature.**

Historical novels reflect varying degrees of research, including into details such as the customs, dress, localities, and speech patterns of the time. True-to-life elements may be added to lend a sense of authenticity to the novel, but in serious examples of this genre, historical matter is central to the story line rather than peripheral or decorative. Historical novels are often vehicles for **authorial** insights into historical figures or into the causes and consequences of historical events.

EXAMPLES: Luó Guànzhōng's *Romance of the Three Kingdoms* (c. fourteenth century); William Makepeace Thackeray's *The History of Henry Esmond* (1852); Henryk Sienkiewicz's *Quo Vadis* (1895); Baroness Emma Orczy's *The Scarlet Pimpernel* (1905); Aleksandr Solzhenitsyn's *August 1914* (1971); Gore Vidal's *Lincoln* (1984). Contemporary novelist Patrick O'Brian's *Aubrey-Maturin* series (1970–2004) features British naval history during the Napoleonic wars and also incorporates Incan history; *Master and Commander: The Far Side of the World* (2003), a film based on the series, draws on several of the novels, including the first, *Master and Commander* (1970). Writer and jazz musician James McBride's novel *Miracle at St. Anna* (2002), set in Italy during World War II and inspired by the African-American "Buffalo Soldiers" of the 92nd Division, addresses a Nazi massacre that occurred in the Tuscan village of Sant'Anna di Stazzema. Novelist Bernard Cromwell has written several series of historical novels, including his most recent *Saxon Stories* (2004–06), a trilogy set during the Viking raids on British kingdoms in the ninth century.

▶ **historical romance:** See **romance.**

▶ **historicism:** Forms of **literary criticism** that examine the relationship between a literary work and its historical milieu. Historicist analyses consider the cultural and social factors that **influenced** and are revealed through the **text.** They may also assess the impact of a literary work on readers in subsequent eras in order to understand how the perceived meaning, reception, and significance of a work evolve over time.

Historicism, which is rooted in **aesthetics** and **romanticism,** initially developed in the nineteenth century as a reaction to the eighteenth-century **Enlightenment** emphasis on reason. Conflicting tendencies toward historical relativism and subjectivism soon emerged, however, and application of the term has varied greatly over time in history, philosophy, and literary criticism. Broadly speaking, however, historicists have **privileged** history as the basis for understanding and evaluation and have sought to identify meaningful historical continuity, a unifying principle that links the present and the past. Philosopher Morris R. Cohen, for instance, described historicism in *The Meaning of Human History* (1947) as "a faith that history is the main road to wisdom in human affairs." Notably, as Dwight E. Lee and Robert N. Beck pointed out in "The Meaning of 'Historicism'" (1954), the concepts associated with historicism "have mainly been concerned with epistemology, with the meaning of history, and the meaningfulness of historiography" and are unrelated to "the basic historical methodology of the search for documents and their critical examination in order to determine such facts as the author, date, and provenance."

In *Toward a New Historicism* (1972), Wesley Morris advocated a historicist aesthetics (unrelated to **the new historicism** that developed in the 1980s) for "explaining the *aesthetic* relationship between the work and its cultural-historical environment." Challenging historicists to make the **paradoxical** argument "that the individual work stands free of its historical context while it simultaneously draws its audience toward that context," Morris outlined four forms of traditional historicism: the *aesthetic, metaphysical, nationalistic,* and *naturalistic.* The aesthetic approach, taken by historian and philosopher R. G. Collingwood, emphasizes the creative act of **author** and critic alike, treating the work as "a key to that imaginative vision which restructures our conception of reality." The *metaphysical* approach, espoused by German philosopher G. W. F. Hegel and American theologian Reinhold Niebuhr, treats the work as part of a transcendent historical continuum; "the aim is to arrive at an understanding of the final fulfillment of historical progress and thereby to have available the criterion of meaning for every individual moment in history." The *nationalistic* approach, exemplified by American historian Frederick Jackson Turner and Danish critic Georg Brandes, "locates the meaning of historical expressions within the confines of national interests," taking "the political or racial unit as the key to all larger evolutions." Finally, the *naturalistic* (or *positivistic* or *scientific*) approach, exemplified by French critic Hippolyte Taine, focuses on observable facts, treating "all human expressions as mere documents, keys to sociological understanding" and viewing the literary work as "wholly transparent; having no substance of its own, it merely reveals the conditions which produced it." Other influential historicists include nineteenth-century English writer and socialist William Morris; twentieth-century American literary scholar and critic Roy Harvey Pearce; and twentieth-century German historian Friedrich Meinecke, who urged the historicist in "Historicism and Its Problems" (1956) "to enter into the very souls of those who acted, to consider their works and cultural contributions in terms of their own premises and, in the last analysis, through artistic intuition to give new life to life gone by — which cannot be done without a transfusion of one's own life blood."

Historicism in Anglo-American literary criticism flourished particularly in the early twentieth century, with the majority of critics focusing on a work's historical content and basing their interpretations on the interplay between the text and historical contexts, such as the author's life or **intentions** in writing the work. By mid-century, however, historicism had given way to **the New Criticism,** a **formalist,** text-oriented approach to literature in which works were treated as self-contained, self-referential objects. Then, in the 1980s, a new form of historical criticism arose whose practitioners analyzed texts with an eye to history but who took a broader, more general approach than their predecessors; among other things, the new historicists incorporated diverse **discourses** such as **Marxism** and **reader-response theory** and were less inclined to see history as linear and progressive.

See **the new historicism** for further discussion of the differences between this approach and more traditional forms of historicism.

▶ **history play:** A **drama** that makes use of historical events, personages, places, or times. Such plays have a greater tendency than **historical novels** to "document" a particular event or the life of a particular person. Sometimes the term *history play* is used more specifically to refer to Elizabethan chronicle plays.

EXAMPLES: Christopher Marlowe's *Edward II* (1593); William Shakespeare's *Henry V* (1599). *Unto These Hills*, a play about the history of the Cherokee Indians and their forced relocation from Georgia to Oklahoma in the 1830s along the "Trail of Tears," was originally written by Kermit Hunter and substantially revised by Hanay Geiogamah in 2005. It has been performed annually by the Eastern Band of Cherokee in Cherokee, North Carolina, since 1950. Stephen Sondheim and John Weidman's musical *Assassins* (1990; revived on Broadway 2004) tells the story of nine people who have assassinated or tried to assassinate a U.S. president.

▶ **hokku:** See **haiku.**

▶ **Homeric epithet:** A short descriptive phrase, often involving compound adjectives, repeated so often that a more or less permanent association between the phrase and noun it was originally meant to modify is created.

EXAMPLES: Examples from Homer include "swift-footed Achilles" and "Odysseus, sacker of cities." Patrick O'Brian, author of the **epic** *Aubrey-Maturin* series of **historical novels** (1970–2004), made Homer's "the wine-dark sea" the title of the sixteenth novel (1993). Western media routinely refer to contemporary musician and songwriter Cui Jian, a Korean who grew up in Beijing, as "the godfather of Chinese rock."

See also **epithet.**

▶ **Homeric simile:** See **epic simile.**

▶ **Horatian ode:** Named for the first-century B.C. Roman **lyric** poet Horace, an **ode** composed of homostrophic **stanzas,** that is, stanzas with the same **rhyme scheme, meter,** and number of lines. The term *Horatian* is sometimes also applied to writing with a meditative, quiet, and informal **tone** like that found in Horace's odes.

EXAMPLE: Andrew Marvell's "An Horatian Ode" (1650), **occasional verse** written upon Oliver Cromwell's triumphant return from the conquest of Ireland; John Keats's "To Autumn" (1820).

▶ **Horatian satire:** A type of formal **satire** that pokes fun at human foibles with a **witty,** even indulgent, **tone.** Horatian satire is named for the first-century B.C. Roman **lyric** poet and satirist Horace (Quintus Horatius Flaccus), who sought to "laugh people out of their vices and follies." It is distinguished from **Juvenalian satire,** the other major type of formal satire, by the latter's denunciatory approach, which is aimed at evoking contempt or indignation from the reader.

EXAMPLES: Ben Jonson's **epigrammatic** poem "On the Famous Voyage" (c. 1612); Alexander Pope's *Four Ethic Epistles,* initially published separately in 1731, 1733, 1734, and 1735. Today, political cartoons are a common vehicle for Horatian satire; examples include Garry Trudeau's

Doonesbury comic strip (1970–) and editorial cartoons by Bob Englehart, who poked fun both at himself and at "literary types" in the *Hartford Courant* on September 27, 2006, when he wrote that:

> Every day, even after 25 years, I continue to learn something new about my craft.
> Textbook publishers regularly reprint my cartoons in their books. I just learned in one of those textbooks that I practice Horatian satire. As proof, one of my cartoons is used as an example.
> It turns out there are two different kinds of satire. Who knew? Not me. I would've known had I gone to college, but I'm an art school dropout. I might not know the different forms of satire but I'll bet not many English Lit majors know how to make tracing paper from scratch.

▶ **horror:** See **fantasy fiction, mystery fiction.**

▶ **hubris (hybris):** Greek for "insolence," excessive pride that brings about the **protagonist's** downfall. Disastrous consequences result when hubris, perhaps the quintessential **tragic flaw,** causes the protagonist to ignore a warning from a god or other important figure, to violate a moral rule, or to try to transcend ordinary limits.

EXAMPLES: In William Shakespeare's play *Macbeth* (1606), the protagonist Macbeth, spurred by proud ambition, murders King Duncan in order to ascend to the throne, an act in flagrant violation of divine and moral rules that ultimately results in Macbeth's own death. Other protagonists taken down by hubris include the title **character** in Werner Herzog's movie *Aguirre: Wrath of God* (1972) and the idealist father in Paul Theroux's novel *The Mosquito Coast* (1982; adapted to film 1986). The sinking of the *Titanic* — a ship billed as "unsinkable," with lifeboat capacity for only half of its passengers — epitomizes the dangers of hubris, as does the collapse of the Enron Corporation, chronicled in Bethany McLean and Peter Elkind's *Enron: The Smartest Guys in the Room* (2003; adapted to film 2005).

On a lighter note, comedian Al Franken took a humorous approach to the term in the introduction to his book *Lies (and the Lying Liars Who Tell Them): A Fair and Balanced Look at the Right* (2003):

> **God** chose me to write this book. . . . This isn't hubris. I'm not saying this in an egotistical way. God didn't choose me because I'm the greatest writer who ever lived. That was William Shakespeare, whose work I have a passing familiarity with. No. I just happened to be the right vessel at the right time.

▶ **Hudibrastic verse:** A humorous, typically **satiric** form of **verse** modeled on seventeenth-century English satirist Samuel Butler's **mock heroic** poem *Hudibras* (1662–77), which ridiculed the Puritans. Following Butler,

Hudibrastic verse takes the form of octosyllabic **couplets** composed in **iambic tetrameter** and is deliberately awkward or even **cacophonous**. As intentional **doggerel**, it pushes the boundaries of **rhyme** for comic effect, deploying an arsenal of unlikely and even absurd **half, double,** and **triple rhymes.**

EXAMPLE: A passage from Butler's *Hudibras* follows:

> Beside 'tis known he could speak *Greek,*
> As naturally as Pigs squeek:
> That *Latin* was no more difficile,
> Then to a Blackbird 'tis to whistle.
> Being rich in both he never scanted
> His Bounty unto such as wanted;
> But much of either would afford
> To many that had not one word.
> For *Hebrew* Roots, although th' are found
> To flourish most in barren ground,
> He had plenty, as suffic'd
> To make some think him circumcis'd. . . .

In "The Sot-weed Factor" (1708), Ebenezer Cook used an **unreliable narrator**, a tobacco agent, to satirize English elitism vis-à-vis Americans; visiting the colony of Maryland, the agent finds:

> These *Sot-weed* Planters Crowd the Shoar,
> In Hue as Tawny as a Moor:
> Figures so strange, no God design'd,
> To be a part of Humane Kind:
> But wanton Nature, void of Rest.
> Moulded the brittle Clay in Jest.

▶ **humours:** A physiological **theory** subscribed to during ancient times, the **Medieval Period,** and the **Renaissance** that held that the relative amounts of or balance between the four main fluids (humours) of the body — blood, phlegm, yellow bile, and black bile — determined an individual's state of health and even general personality. The four humours were also associated with what were then considered to be the four elements: blood with air (hot and moist), phlegm with water (cold and moist), yellow bile with fire (hot and dry), and black bile with earth (cold and dry). The term *humour* comes from the Latin *humor,* meaning "moisture."

Adherents of this theory believed that the humours emitted vapors that rose to the brain, thus affecting both behavior and health. As long as the humours were in balance, the individual supposedly exhibited a perfect temperament and no illness, but an imbalance affected behavior in a very specific way. That is, an excess of blood produced a sanguine (happy) personality, phlegm a phlegmatic (cowardly, passive) personality, yellow bile a choleric (argumentative, stubborn) personality, and black bile a bilious (melancholy) one. Just as an imbalance produced a distinct behavioral effect, so would it produce illness and disease.

This theory was so commonly accepted that it made its way into popular culture and literature. Individuals (or literary **characters**) came to be classified according to their humour, and the word *humour* itself came to signify a variety of things, from disposition or mood to peculiarity or affectation, particularly in **Elizabethan** times. Many works of literature even relied on this theory for **characterization** and to provide convincing **motivation** for the characters' actions.

See also **comedy of humours.**

▶ **hybridity:** See **postcolonial literature, postcolonial theory.**

▶ **hybris:** See **hubris.**

▶ **hymn:** A song of praise, usually written in **verse.** The word *hymn* comes from the Greek *hymnos,* meaning a song of praise to a god, human hero, or idea. Religious hymns praise God or another deity. Literary hymns may make religious references or employ religious terminology but are frequently written solely in praise of some secular ideal, attitude, person, figure, or object. They are often very similar to **odes** and are meant to be read rather than sung. The widespread use and popularity of hymns had a significant impact on **versification,** particularly in English, German, and the Romance languages.

EXAMPLES: "Onward Christian Soldiers" (1871) is a religious hymn, whereas Algernon Charles Swinburne's "Hymn to Proserpine" (1866) is a literary hymn, even though it is ostensibly addressed to a goddess.

▶ **hyperbaton:** A **rhetorical figure** involving a reversal of word order to make a point. The term *anastrophe* is often used synonymously with *hyperbaton* but has also been classified in various ways as a type of hyperbaton, for instance, as hyperbaton in which in the position of a single word is changed, two words are reversed, or an adjective follows rather than precedes the noun it modifies.

EXAMPLES: The most famous example is Sir Winston Churchill's **witty** reminder that grammatical propriety — in this case, the rule that says sentences should never end with prepositions — can produce terrible results: "This is the sort of English up with which I will not put!" The speech of the *Star Wars* Jedi Master Yoda is rife with hyperbaton, such as "Luminous beings are we, not this crude matter" and "Named must your fear be, before banish it you can," both from *Episode V: The Empire Strikes Back* (1980).

▶ **hyperbole:** A **trope** employing deliberate, emphatic exaggeration, usually for **comic** or **ironic** effect. Some critics refer to hyperbole as *overstatement.*

EXAMPLES: Lady Macbeth's guilty musing in William Shakespeare's **tragedy** *Macbeth* (1606), after her husband Macbeth executes her plan to murder King Duncan: "Here's the smell of blood still; / All the perfumes of Arabia / Will not sweeten this little hand." Oscar Wilde commented hyperbolically on Walter Pater's *The Renaissance* (1873) when he said, "the last trumpet should have sounded the moment it was written." John Self, the protagonist of Martin Amis's *Money* (1984), aims his hyperbolic commentary toward the city of Los Angeles: "In LA, you can't do anything unless you drive. . . . The only way to get across the road is to be born there. All the ped-xing signs say DON'T WALK, all of them, all the time." Hyperbole is also common in pop culture, as exemplified by the titles of Bruce Springsteen's song "57 Channels (And Nothin' On)" (1992) and Diane Stafford's *50,001+ Best Baby Names* (2004), whose cover also screams "More Names! More Lists! Better than ever!" and whose spine asserts "the very BEST baby-naming book ever."

▶ **hyperlink:** See **link.**

▶ **hypertext:** In computing, a document retrieval network or database system that permits the user to access any of a group of documents by clicking on a **link,** also called a *hyperlink* or *jump marker.* In a hypertext system, documents may be static or generated in accordance with user input; once accessed, they appear in full-text form on the screen. Links in the link structure of the system may connect to other places within a given document or to other documents, allowing the user to jump within and among linked documents at will. American information technology pioneer Ted Nelson and inventor Douglas Engelbart developed the first hypertext systems in the 1960s. Today, the World Wide Web is the best-known hypertext system.

Adapted to the literary arena, *hypertext* refers to writing that is nonsequential. Nelson coined the term in 1963 to emphasize that linked documents represent ideas in a nonlinear way, contrasting hypertext with the **authorially**-organized linear mode of presentation typically used in other media, such as books, movies, and speeches. As Nelson explained in his seminal paper "A File Structure for the Complex, the Changing, and the Indeterminate" (1965): "Let me introduce the word 'hypertext' to mean a body of written or pictorial material interconnected in such a complex way that it could not conveniently be presented or represented on paper." In diminishing the author's position, the nonlinear format of hypertext invests the reader with a much more active role. Nevertheless, the author retains some modicum of control, if only because someone must set up the links that the reader will use.

Contemporary **literary critics** have explored the connection between hypertext and literary theory generally, as well as between hypertext and specific theoretical approaches, such as **cultural criticism, deconstruction, narratology,** and **the new historicism.** Most agree that the very existence and concept of hypertext alters our conception of the **text,** which traditionally has been thought of as a linear construct with a beginning, middle, and end determined by the author. As digital media scholar Gunnar Liestøl wrote in an essay entitled "Wittgenstein, Genette, and the Reader's Narrative" (1994), the "facilities of manipulation, individual navigation, and freedom from given, authoritative structures provide us with new practices of reading and writing." The development of hypertext has also had a tremendous and growing impact on the study of many literary texts, enabling literary scholars to store and link textual editions and variants, not only with one another but also with contextual (including visual) materials. Jerome J. McGann's "hypermedia environment" archival edition of *The Complete Writings and Pictures of Dante Gabriel Rossetti,* initially available over the World Wide Web and subsequently published on CD-ROM by the University of Michigan Press, is a good example of hypertextual scholarship.

A distinction is sometimes made between hypertext and *hypermedia,* another term coined by Nelson, with the former referring specifically to text formats and the latter also encompassing audio, graphics, and video formats.

See also **cyberfiction.**

▶ **hypertext fiction:** See **cyberfiction.**

▶ **hypotaxis, hypotactic style:** See **style.**

▶ **hysteron proteron:** Greek for "latter earlier" or "latter first," a **rhetorical figure** involving a chronological reversal or other inversion of the normal or expected order of things.

EXAMPLE: In William Shakespeare's *Antony and Cleopatra* (1607), Mark Antony's friend Enobarbus says that retreating ships "fly and turn the rudder." Presumably, the ships turned around before retreating.

▶ **iamb:** A **metrical foot** in **poetry** that consists of one unstressed syllable followed by one **stressed** syllable (˘´). The iamb is the most common metrical foot in English poetry; **unrhymed** iambic **pentameter**, also called **blank verse**, is perhaps the most common form of metrical verse in English.

EXAMPLES: afloat, respect, in love. In "A Slumber Did My Spirit Seal" (1800), one of his "Lucy" poems, William Wordsworth alternated iambic **tetrameter** and iambic **trimeter**:

> Ă slŭmbĕr dĭd mў spírĭt séal;
> Ĭ hád nŏ húmăn fears:
> Shĕ seémed ă thĭng thăt cóuld nŏt feel
> Thĕ tóuch ŏf eárthlў yeárs.
> Nŏ mótiŏn hás shĕ nów, nŏ fórce;
> Shĕ néithĕr heárs nŏr sées;
> Rólled róund ĭn eárth's diúrnăl cóurse,
> Wĭth rócks, ănd stónes, ănd trées.

Harlem Renaissance poet Countee Cullen's "Yet Do I Marvel" (1925), a **sonnet** written in rhymed iambic pentameter, ends with the lines "Yet do I marvel at this curious thing: / To make a poet black, and bid him sing!"

▶ **icon:** In **semiotics**, a type of **sign** that has a likeness or similarity to what it **represents**. Examples include a drawing of a fire, a miniature model ship, a map of Antarctica, a diagram of the structure of the federal court system, and floor plans for a house. The icon is distinguished from the *index*, another type of sign that is directly and regularly connected, physically or through a cause-effect relationship, to what it represents. Examples include smoke, which indicates fire; sundials, which indicate the time of day; and thermometers, which indicate temperature.

The term *icon* also has a specialized religious application, one that refers to a depiction of a religious figure, such as the wooden devotional panels featuring **conventional** portraits of the Virgin Mary in Eastern Christianity. In computing, icons are pictorial signs in a graphical user interface that indicate files, programs, commands, folders, directories, or other resources.

▶ **iconography:** The **representation** of biblical (or, more broadly, any religious) figures in painting and sculpture with an eye to **symbolic** significance. Iconography in most religions encompasses a set of established **conventions** to which the artist must adhere in the portrayal of the subject matter. Iconography can also refer to the study of any subject represented in the visual arts, the conventions governing its representation, and the symbolic significance of the resulting work of art.

▶ **id:** According to Austrian psychoanalyst Sigmund Freud, the inborn, unconscious component of the psyche that generates our instinctual physical, especially libidinal, desires. The id is often described as insatiable; ruled by the pleasure principle, it does not consider the consequences or implications of its desires or the actions involved in satisfying them.

Freud believed the psyche also has two other components: the superego and the ego. The superego, which internalizes social mores and norms, is the opposite of the id. The superego is often subdivided into the ego ideal, an ideal self to which the individual aspires, and the conscience, which distinguishes right from wrong. The ego, which is based on the reality principle, attempts to mediate between the id and the superego in the context of reality and the demands and possibilities it creates for the individual. *Ego strength* refers to how well the ego deals with the conflicting demands of the id and superego.

▶ **identical rhyme:** See **perfect rhyme.**

▶ **ideology:** A set of beliefs underlying the customs, habits, and practices common to a given social group. To members of that group, the beliefs seem obviously true, natural, and even universally applicable. They may seem just as obviously arbitrary, idiosyncratic, and even false to those who adhere to another ideology. Within a society, several ideologies may coexist; one or more of these may be dominant.

Ideologies may be forcefully imposed or willingly subscribed to. Their component beliefs may be held consciously or unconsciously. In either case, they come to form what Johanna M. Smith, in " 'Too Beautiful Altogether': Patriarchal Ideology in *Heart of Darkness*" (1989), called "the unexamined ground of our experience." Ideology governs our perceptions, judgments, and prejudices — our sense of what is acceptable, normal, and deviant. It may cause a revolution; it may also allow discrimination and even exploitation.

Ideologies are of special interest to politically oriented critics of literature because of the way in which **authors** reflect or resist prevailing views in their **texts.** Some **Marxist critics** have argued that literary texts reflect and reproduce the ideologies that produced them; most, however, have shown how ideologies are riven with contradictions that works of literature manage to expose and widen. Other Marxist critics have focused on the ways in which texts themselves are characterized by **gaps,** conflicts, and contradictions between their ideological and anti-ideological functions. Fredric Jameson, an American Marxist critic, argued that all thought is ideological, but that ideological thought that knows itself as such stands the chance of seeing through and transcending ideology.

Not all of the politically oriented critics interested in ideology have been **Marxists.** Certain non-Marxist **feminist critics** have addressed the question of ideology by seeking to expose (and thereby call into question) the **patriarchal** ideology mirrored or inscribed in works written by men — even men who have sought to counter sexism and break down sexual stereotypes. **New historicists** have been interested in demonstrating the ideological underpinnings not only of literary **representations** but also of our interpretations of them.

▶ **idyll:** From the Greek for "little picture," a **narrative** work — usually short, descriptive, and composed in **verse** — that depicts and exalts **pastoral** scenes and **themes.** Idylls often have a formal or artificial quality because they tend to be composed from the viewpoint of a "civilized" society that longs for some more primal, natural, or innocent place untouched by the pace and stresses of civilized life. The simple shepherd's life is a typical subject.

The term *idyll* derives from the *Idylls* of Theocritus, a third-century B.C. Greek poet who romanticized rustic life in the Sicilian countryside. **Renaissance** writers **imitated** the **conventions** of **classical** tradition, but several poets of the **Romantic Period** introduced elements that more **realistically** depicted rural life. **Victorian** poet Alfred, Lord Tennyson, went even further in *Idylls of the King* (1859), a long narrative poem based on Arthurian lore, rejecting the idyll's traditional pastoral mode but retaining the concept of an ideal life away (in time as well as place) from the hustle and bustle of a complex contemporary society. Movies in which the idyllic setting is thematically important include Frank Capra's *Lost Horizon* (1937), Joshua Logan's *South Pacific* (1958), Mark Rydell's *On Golden Pond* (1981), and Ang Lee's *Brokeback Mountain* (2005).

▶ *illisible* (**unreaderly**): See **poststructuralism, text.**

▶ **illocutionary act:** A **speech act** involving a **locution,** or utterance, that performs a particular function. Introducing the term in *How to Do Things with Words* (1962), British "ordinary-language" philosopher John L. Austin characterized it as the "performance of an act *in* saying something as opposed to performance of an act *of* saying something." Thus, an illocutionary act may assert something, or it may order, promise, question, threaten, and so forth.

EXAMPLE: The locution "I'll take the children with me" has multiple illocutionary possibilities. It could be a simple assertion of truth, a promise, or even a threat.

▶ **image:** Most commonly, a visual, physical **representation** (such as a photograph) of something or a mental picture of some visible thing or things. Images can also involve senses other than sight and sensations such as movement and pressure; however, for instance, the sound of musical chords, the smell of freshly cut grass, or the heat of the sun can contribute as much to an image of playing the guitar outside on a hot summer's day as the shape of the guitar or the color of the grass. As an artistic term, *image* usually refers to an artistic representation of the visible world (for example,

"Monet painted images of water lilies") and to the mental impressions conjured up by such a representation. In literature, it most often **denotes** descriptive terms or **figurative language** used to produce mental impressions in the mind of the reader as well as the impressions themselves. Finally, the term may also be used to mean "idea" or "vision." A slave living in the antebellum American South, for instance, likely had an image of Canada related not to appearance but to an intellectual and emotional perception of the country as a place of freedom; similarly, one can speak of an artist's or **author's** image of life or suffering to mean his or her conception of it.

FURTHER EXAMPLES: Iconic images include J. Howard Miller's "Rosie the Riveter" poster (1942) proclaiming "We Can Do It!"; the 1963 photo of John F. Kennedy, Jr. saluting his father's coffin as it passed by; the June 1985 *National Geographic* cover photo by Steve McCurry of a young Afghan girl with piercing green eyes, finally identified in 2002 as Sharbat Gula; and several images of abuse and torture at Abu Ghraib prison in Iraq, such as the photo of a hooded man forced to stand atop a box, his arms outstretched, with electrical wires attached to his hands (2003).

The following **stanza** from John Keats's "Ode to a Nightingale" (1819) demonstrates that images can involve a wide range of sensory perceptions and sensations:

> I cannot see what flowers are at my feet,
>   Nor what soft incense hangs upon the boughs,
> But, in embalmèd darkness, guess each sweet
>   Wherewith the seasonable month endows
> The grass, the thicket, and the fruit-tree wild;
>   White hawthorn, and the pastoral eglantine;
>   Fast fading violets cover'd up in leaves;
>   And mid-May's eldest child,
>   The coming musk-rose, full of dewy wine,
>   The murmurous haunt of flies on summer eves.

Likewise, in her novel *Shelter* (1994), Jayne Anne Phillips used figurative language to produce both visual and non-visual images. Her description of a group of girls at a summer camp walking "double time" is primarily visual: "Alma watched from the rear as her compatriots hit the clearing and swung into action. The line of girls resembled a giant centipede in electroshock." By contrast, the descriptive sentence, "She felt the tug of memory, an image that pulled at her consciousness like a fish on a line," relies primarily on movement, pressure, and touch.

In Dai Sijie's short novel *Balzac et la petite tailleuse chinoise* (*Balzac and the Little Chinese Seamstress*) (2000), the **protagonist,** sent as a teenager to a remote village during China's Cultural Revolution with his best friend Luo, recalls, "It was all such a long time ago, but one particular image from our stint of re-education is still etched in my memory with extraordinary precision: a red-beaked raven keeping watch as Luo crawled along a narrow track with a yawning chasm on either side."

▶ **imagery:** A term used to refer to: (1) the corpus of **images** or in a **text**; (2) the language used to convey a visual picture (or, most critics would add, to **represent** any sensory experience); and (3) the use of **figurative language**, often to express **abstract** ideas in a vivid and innovative way. Imagery of this third type makes use of **figures of speech** such as **simile, personification,** and **metonymy.**

Imagery is a central component of almost all **imaginative** literature and is often said to be the chief element in poetry. Literal imagery is purely descriptive, representing an object or event with words that draw on or appeal to the kinds of experiences gained through the five senses (sight, sound, touch, taste, and smell). Figurative imagery may call sensory experience to mind but does so as a way of describing something else — often some abstract idea that cannot be depicted literally or directly (for example, Emily Dickinson's " 'Hope' is the thing with feathers" [1861]). Whether literal or figurative, however, imagery is generally intended to make whatever the author is describing **concrete** in the reader's mind, to give it some tangible and real existence rather than a purely intellectual one. Imagery also provides the reader with a sense of vividness and immediacy.

Imagery has a specific and special relation to **symbolism.** All **symbols** depend on images, often repeated to give the symbol cogency and depth. In Toni Morrison's novel *Beloved* (1987), the repeated description of Sethe's scarred back as wrought iron or as a tree serves to make her a symbol of the slave's extraordinary physical and spiritual suffering and strength. Some critics have suggested that the key to unlocking the meaning of a work lies in identifying its image patterns and understanding how they work together to suggest or symbolize larger meanings or **themes.** These critics believe that the pattern of imagery in a work more truly reveals its meaning than an **author's, character's** or **narrator's** assertions. **The New Critics,** in particular, examined and analyzed the interrelation among images and their relevance to interpretation.

FURTHER EXAMPLES: In his poem "Fish" (1922), D. H. Lawrence used striking imagery to create the visual picture (and tactile sensation) of a fish on a line. The speaker says that he has:

> Unhooked his gorping, water-horny mouth,
> And seen his horror-tilted eye,
> His red-gold, water-precious, mirror-flat bright eye;
> And felt him beat in my hand, with his mucous, leaping
>   life-throb.

In her poem "The Fish" (1946), Elizabeth Bishop also used imagery to describe a hooked fish. However, whereas Lawrence almost humanized his subject with the image of the "horror-tilted eye," Bishop invoked inanimate objects in the world above the surface:

> I looked into his eyes
> which were far larger than mine

but shallower, and yellowed,
the irises backed and packed
with tarnished tinfoil
seen through the lenses
of old scratched isinglass.
They shifted a little, but not
to return my stare.

Contemporary architect Frank Gehry makes use of fish imagery in his work; in Barcelona, Spain, he incorporated "Fish" (1992), a giant copper-colored fish made of steel lattice, into the Olympic Port complex at the base of two landmark skyscrapers. Fish imagery likewise runs through the work of Japanese sculptural glass artist Hiroshi Yamano; discussing the "Fish Hanger" pieces in his ongoing series *From East to West* (1988–), he explained: "The hanging pieces give me more freedom to deal with space. Still, my concept is the same: a fish, like a tuna or a mackerel, has to swim for its entire life, otherwise it dies. So, I think of the fish as myself. I have to keep doing, keep working, keep going, keep jumping into life" (2006).

▶ **Imaginary order:** Along with **the Real** and the **Symbolic order,** one of the three orders of **subjectivity** according to French **psychoanalytic** theorist and critic Jacques Lacan. The Imaginary order is most closely associated with the five senses (sight, sound, touch, taste, and smell). The human infant, who is wholly dependent on others for a prolonged period, enters the Imaginary order when it begins to experience a unity of body parts and motor control that is empowering. This change, in which the child anticipates mastery of its body, occurs between the ages of six and eighteen months, during what Lacan called the "mirror stage," or "mirror phase," of human development. At the onset of the mirror stage — that is, upon entering the Imaginary order — the child identifies with the image of wholeness (seeing its own image in the mirror, experiencing its mother as a whole body, and so on). This sense of oneness, and also of difference from others (especially the mother or primary caretaker), is established through an **image** or a vision of harmony that is both a mirroring and a "mirage of maturation" (a false sense of individuality and independence).

The Imaginary is a **metaphor** for unity, is related to the visual order, and is always part of human **subjectivity.** Because the subject is fundamentally separate from others and also internally divided (conscious / unconscious), the apparent coherence of the Imaginary, its fullness and grandiosity, is always false, a *mis*recognition that the ego (or "me") tries to deny by imagining itself as coherent and empowered.

The Imaginary, which operates in conjunction with the Real and Symbolic, is not a stage of development equivalent to Freud's pre**oedipal** stage, nor is it prelinguistic. The concept of the Imaginary — like Lacan's "schema" and terminology more generally — has proved useful to psychoanalytic and **poststructuralist** critics analyzing the unities and disunities within **texts.**

See also **the Real, Symbolic order.**

▶ **imagination:** A term that has meant different things at different times, *imagination* was associated in the **Renaissance** with poetry and was understood to be the opposite of *reason.* In the later, **Neoclassical Period** the term was used simply to refer to the mind's power to call up **images** (especially visual images). Then, in the late eighteenth century, imagination once again came to be seen primarily in opposition to reason and as a source of **aesthetic** pleasure. **Romantic** theorists such as William Wordsworth and Samuel Taylor Coleridge gave imagination a much greater value, however, **privileging** it above **fancy** as the creative and unifying faculty of the mind that reveals higher truths through **organic** rather than **mechanical** processes.

See **fancy** for Coleridge's distinction between imagination and fancy.

▶ **Imagism:** An *avant-garde,* Anglo-American movement in **poetry** from 1909–17 that originated in London and emphasized concise, direct expression and the presentation of clear, precise **images.** Key Imagist tenets, as outlined in an anthology of Imagist poetry titled *Some Imagist Poems* (1915), included: (1) using everyday speech and the *"exact* word, not the nearly-exact"; (2) creating new **rhythms;** (3) absolute freedom in choice of subject; (4) presenting an image and "render[ing] particulars exactly"; (5) producing poetry that is "hard and clear, never blurred nor indefinite"; and (6) writing concentrated poetry. Imagists generally employed **free verse** and prized economy of language, seeking to render the poet's response to a visual impression as concisely and precisely as possible.

Imagism drew upon the poetic theory of English writer T. E. Hulme, who championed free verse in "A Lecture on Modern Poetry" (1908) and argued that poetry should be based on accurate presentation of a precise image with no excess verbiage. Starting in 1909, Hulme and other poets began an organized effort to reform the poetry of the time, rejecting **sentimentalism** and embracing concentrated poetic forms such as the Japanese **haiku** and *tanka;* members of the London-based "Eiffel Tower" group aside from Hulme included English poets F. S. Flint and Richard Aldington and American poets Ezra Pound and H. D. (Hilda Doolittle), among others. Pound, who emerged as the leader, coined the term *Imagism* (or, more precisely, *Imagiste*), publicly launching the movement in 1912 when he submitted poems by H. D. and Aldington for publication in *Poetry* magazine as *Imagiste* works. Following the publication of the first Imagist anthology, *Des Imagistes* (1914), leadership of the movement shifted to American poet Amy Lowell, leading the displaced Pound to refer derogatorily to the movement as "Amygism." Three additional anthologies of Imagist poetry followed, each titled *Some Imagist Poets* (1915–17). Years later, after the movement had ended, Aldington edited the *Imagist Anthology 1930* (1930), which included original work from most of the contributors to the prior anthologies.

While Imagism was relatively short-lived as a movement, it signaled the onset of **modernism** and, unlike the more traditional **Georgian poetry** of the time, had wide-ranging **influence** on subsequent poetry, which continues to emphasize the use and juxtaposition of clear, **concrete** images. Imagism had particular influence on free verse, the Objectivist Poets of the 1930s, and the **Beat writers** of the 1950s.

EXAMPLES: Pound's **classic,** haiku-influenced poem "In a Station of the Metro" (1913):

> The apparition of these faces in the crowd;
> Petals on a wet, black bough.

Other poets who published as Imagists include John Gould Fletcher, Ford Madox Ford, James Joyce, D. H. Lawrence, and William Carlos Williams; Carl Sandburg has also been called an Imagist. Williams's "The Red Wheelbarrow" (1923) presents a single concrete image that exemplifies his edict about poetry, "No ideas but in things":

> so much depends
> upon
>
> a red wheel
> barrow
>
> glazed with rain
> water
>
> beside the white
> chickens.

▶ **imitation:** As a literary term, (1) a synonym for *mimesis,* a Greek term used by literary critics to refer to the **representation** of reality in literature; (2) the practice of modeling one's writing after the established **forms** and **styles** of a particular **genre.**

The mimetic sense of imitation derives from the *Poetics* (c. 330 B.C.), in which Greek philosopher Aristotle discussed the representation of human action through the vehicle of poetry, which he subdivided into categories such as **comedy, tragedy,** and **epic.** Aristotle also discussed what types of actions ought to be "imitated," as well as how and in what form, noting especially that the poet should present actions that show the relationship between life and art. Briefly put, Aristotle argued that art imitates nature but that it should do so selectively, with the poet carefully choosing and arranging the events and elements to be **narrated.** This view of poetry as a special imitation of human actions prevailed from **classical** times through the **Neoclassical Period,** although critics disagreed about matters such as which actions were worthy of being represented. With the advent of **romanticism,** however, a new view of poetry emerged not as a translation or record of human actions but rather as the personal, private expression of a poet's feelings and imaginings.

Imitation in the sense of modeling was a common and acceptable practice that likewise persisted until the **Romantic Period,** which championed originality and individual expression. Writers were encouraged to imitate

Graeco-Roman **classics** and the **conventional** forms and styles of a given genre in order to learn the art of composition. Our romantic heritage and attendant definitions of plagiarism incline us to disparage this practice today, but it was regarded throughout most of literary history as proper and useful in cultivating talent.

▶ **imperfect rhyme:** See **half rhyme.**

▶ **impersonal narrator:** See **unintrusive narrator.**

▶ **implied author:** A term coined by **reader-oriented** critic Wayne C. Booth in place of the term **voice** to refer to the unique and pervasive human presence that the reader senses is the driving force behind a literary work and the source of its ethical norms and values. In *The Rhetoric of Fiction* (1961), Booth distinguished the implied author from the real **author,** arguing that the implied author is an "ideal, literary, created version" of the real author, "an implicit picture of an author who stands behind the scenes, ... always distinct from the 'real man' — whatever we may take him to be — who creates a superior version of himself, a 'second self,' as he creates his work." Booth developed the concept of the implied author partly as a response to the **intentional fallacy,** enabling critics to acknowledge authorial presence in a **text** without basing interpretation on the author's expressed or implied intentions, a practice that **New Critics** judged erroneous.

Several critics have further developed or adapted the concept of the implied author. In *Story and Discourse* (1978), for instance, Seymour Chatman treated the implied author as a **structural** principle of **narration** and shifted the focus to the reader, arguing that the implied author is "reconstructed by the reader from the narrative. He is not the narrator, but rather the principle that invented the narrator, along with everything else in the narrative." Subsequently, in *Coming to Terms* (1990), Chatman equated the implied author with "the text itself." Other critics have questioned the utility of Booth's concept; Gérard Genette, for instance, found little cause for distinguishing between an implied and real author in most works, arguing in *Nouveau discours du récit* (*Narrative Discourse Revisited*) (1983) that "a narrative of fiction is produced fictively by its narrator and actually by its (real) author. No one is toiling away between them."

▶ **implied reader:** A phrase coined by **reader-response critic** Wolfgang Iser in *The Implied Reader* (1974) in contradistinction to the "real" or "actual" reader. Whereas the real or actual reader could be any individual who happens to have read or to be reading the **text,** the implied reader is the reader intended, even created, by the text. In *The Act of Reading* (1978), Iser called this implied reader a "construct" of the text who "embodies all those predispositions necessary for a literary work to exercise its effect." Unlike the implied reader, real readers bring their own experiences and preconceptions to the text — and thus their own idiosyncratic modes of perception and interpretation. Some reader-response critics have defined the reader differently. For instance, as a proponent of **affective stylistics,** Stanley Fish spoke of the "informed reader" in *Self-Consuming Artifacts* (1972), whereas Gérard Genette and Gerald Prince discussed the "narratee" in works including *Figures III* (*Narrative Discourse*) (1972) and "Introduction à l'étude du narrative" ("Introduction to the Study of the Narrative") (1973), respectively.

▶ **impressionism:** As a literary term, writing that seeks to capture transitory, **subjective** impressions of **characters, settings,** and events. Literary impressionism took its name from the French Impressionist movement in painting, which reached its height in the 1870s and 1880s. The Impressionists believed that subjective impressions of objects, people, and scenery were legitimate artistic subjects, indeed, that it was more important for painters to render such impressions than to produce technically precise **representations.** Impressionist painters often used bright colors and worked directly from nature, seeking to capture fleeting moments on canvas and to depict the ephemeral effects of light. Leading Impressionists included French painters Édouard Manet, Claude Monet, and Pierre-Auguste Renoir; American painter Mary Cassatt; French sculptor Auguste Rodin; and Polish painter Władysław Podkowiński.

Impressionist literary works emphasize sensory **images** and characters' emotions, thoughts, and perceptions, tending to disregard the type of **objective, concrete** details associated with conventional **plots.** The **French Symbolists,** such as Charles Baudelaire and Stéphane Mallarmé; other writers active in the **Aesthetic Movement,** such as Oscar Wilde; and **stream-of-consciousness** novelists, such as James Joyce and Virginia Woolf, have all been called impressionists or, at least, impressionistic in their writing. Impressionism also **influenced** the early-twentieth-century poetic movement of **Imagism;** indeed, English writer T. E. Hulme, the movement's theorist, declared in "A Lecture on Modern Poetry" (1908) that "[w]hat has found expression in painting as Impressionism will soon find expression in poetry as free verse."

▶ **impressionistic criticism:** A type of **practical criticism** that centers on the critic's **subjective** impressions of a literary work, particularly the feelings and associations elicited in experiencing it. Impressionistic critics deny the possibility of absolute, **objective** judgment and instead view **literary criticism** as a means of explaining and appreciating a given work. They often take a sympathetic approach, glorifying the artistic temperament and employing **anecdotes** and personal reminiscences to engage the reader. As English critic William Hazlitt declared in *An Essay on the Principles of Human Action* (1805), "I say what I think: I think what I feel. I cannot help receiving certain impressions from things; and I have sufficient courage to declare (somewhat abruptly) what they are."

Impressionistic criticism arose with the advent of **romanticism,** which **privileged** the individual and subjective experience, eclipsing **judicial criticism,** the dominant mode during the **Renaissance** and **Neoclassical** periods, over the course of the eighteenth century. Noted impressionistic critics aside from Hazlitt include English critics Walter Pater and George Saintsbury, French writer Anatole France, and American music critic James Gibbons Huneker. France expressed the impressionistic viewpoint in *La vie littéraire* (4 vols.; 1888–92) when he described the "good critic" as "he who relates the adventures of his soul among masterpieces" and asserted that "[t]here is no such thing as objective criticism any more than there is objective art, and all who flatter themselves that they put aught but themselves into their work are dupes of the most fallacious illusion. The truth is that one never gets out of oneself." Impressionistic criticism came under increasing attack in the twentieth century, particularly by **the New Critics,** who viewed it as superficial and arbitrary and believed that it was erroneous to interpret **texts** according to the psychological responses of readers, a practice they termed the **affective fallacy.**

▶ **incremental repetition:** A poetic device involving the repetition of lines or phrases, whether in successive **stanzas** or within a stanza, with subtle modifications or additions to advance the story line. Incremental repetition is commonly used in **ballads,** sometimes employs a question-and-answer format, and often occurs in the last line of each stanza.

EXAMPLES: The **refrain** of each stanza of Emily Brontë's poem "November, 1837" exhibits incremental repetition:

> The night is darkening round me,
> The wild winds coldly blow;
> But a tyrant spell has bound me
> And I cannot, cannot go.
>
> The giant trees are bending
> Their bare boughs weighed with snow,
> And the storm is fast descending
> And yet I cannot go.
>
> Clouds beyond clouds above me,
> Wastes beyond wastes below;
> But nothing drear can move me;
> I will not, cannot go.

Pop music examples include "Day of the Locust" (1970), where Bob Dylan recounted his acceptance of an honorary degree from Princeton and used incremental repetition in the **chorus,** which describes locusts singing, and Sting's "The Hounds of Winter" (1998), in which hounds of winter howl, follow the singer, and ultimately harry him down.

▶ **index:** See icon.

▶ **indirect discourse:** See **discourse.**

▶ **influence:** As a literary term, the effect of a writer or writers (whether disparately or as part of a school) on subsequent writers and their work.

The later writer typically adopts some of the features (**style**, subject matter, etc.) characteristic of the influential, earlier writer's work while slightly or radically modifying others. American literary critic Walter Jackson Bate's *The Burden of the Past in English Poetry* (1970) revitalized the study of literary influence. Subsequently, in his revisionist phase, American critic Harold Bloom challenged conventional conceptions of influence in his book *The Anxiety of Influence* (1973), in which he argued that the writing of all strong poets involves the rewriting of earlier strong poets and that this rewriting always and inevitably involves some form of "misprision," a kind of misreading that allows the later writer's creativity to emerge.

See also **anxiety of influence**.

▶ **initial rhyme:** See **beginning rhyme**.

▶ *in medias res:* Latin for "into the midst of things," the literary technique of beginning a **narrative** in the middle of the **action**. Crucial events that occurred before the point at which the narrative starts are related at a later time, generally through one or more **flashbacks**. Beginning *in medias res* is a **convention** associated primarily with the **epic**, but the technique has also been used in other types of literary works to "hook" the reader or audience.

EXAMPLES: Homer's Greek epics *The Iliad* (c. 850 B.C.) and *The Odyssey* (c. 850 B.C.) both begin *in medias res*, as does John Milton's epic *Paradise Lost* (1667), which opens with Satan and the other fallen angels in hell, following the civil war between Satan's forces and those of God, which is not described until Book 6.

James Bond movies routinely begin *in medias res*, as does the film noir *The Usual Suspects* (1995), which opens with a man being shot twice in the head and an act of arson at the scene of the crime, then cuts to the interrogation of Verbal Kint, the rather **ironically** named **narrator**, who recounts an incredible story involving the elusive criminal mastermind Keyser Söze. As Verbal tells the story, the movie flashes back to the events themselves — as the **unreliable** Verbal describes them. *Mission Impossible III* (2006) likewise begins *in medias res*, with agent Ethan Hunt and his fiancée Julia held captive by the psychopathic international arms dealer Owen Davian, before going back five days to the inception of Hunt's latest "impossible" mission.

▶ **intention:** Long used by literary scholars and critics to refer to an **author's** stated or unstated purpose in writing a work, a term given particular meaning by the German philosopher Edmund Husserl and **hermeneutical theorists** of interpretation such as E. D. Hirsch.

Husserl used *intention* in connection with **phenomenology**, a philosophical school of thought and method of analysis that holds that objects attain meaning only as they are perceived in someone's consciousness. Husserl argued that consciousness is intentional, that is, directed toward an object; as long as we are conscious, we are perceiving something. Husserl's use of *intentional* does not accord with the traditional dictionary definition, "deliberate." Rather, intentionality in phenomenology refers to awareness of an object that brings us into a reciprocal relationship with it.

Hirsch used *intention* differently in his books *Validity in Interpretation* (1967) and *The Aims of Interpretation* (1976). He related what he called the author's "verbal intention" to the interpretation of a work, building his argument that "a text means what its author meant" on the nineteenth-century philosopher Wilhelm Dilthey's assertion that readers can in fact arrive at **objective** and valid interpretations of expressed authorial meaning. He did not equate intention with the author's mental state while writing but rather with the fundamental goal of creating something out of words that will mean a certain thing or things to readers familiar with the extant rules, **conventions,** and norms of reading and interpretation. In determining an author's verbal intentions, readers must gather evidence from a variety of sources. Biographical, historical, and cultural contexts are important, as are other works by the same author. Knowledge of the conventions governing the **genre** in which the work is written is essential. Without reference to intentions and conventions, Hirsch argued, meanings remain elusive or even indeterminate, since no justifiable grounds exist for choosing one meaning over another. The Italian theorist Emilio Betti followed a similar line of argument.

See also **hermeneutics.**

▶ **intentional fallacy:** A term coined by **New Critics** William K. Wimsatt and Monroe C. Beardsley in their essay "The Intentional Fallacy" (1946) to refer to the practice of basing interpretations on the expressed or implied **intentions** of **authors,** a practice they judged to be erroneous. Wimsatt and Beardsley argued that "the design or intention of the author is neither available nor desirable as a standard for judging the success of a work of literary art." As **formalists,** they viewed literary works as objects in their own right and maintained that the critic's task is to show what is actually in the **text,** not what an author intended to put there.

See also **authorial intention.**

▶ **interior monologue:** A literary technique for rendering **stream of consciousness** by reproducing a **character's** mental flow. Interior monologue presents thoughts, emotions, and sensations as experienced by the character, revealing the operation of the psyche at a pre- or sublinguistic level, where **images** and the **connotations** they evoke may supplant the literal **denotative** meanings of words. French writer Édouard Dujardin is usually credited with the first sustained use of the technique, which he relied upon heavily in his pioneering novel *Les lauriers sont coupés* (*We'll to the Woods No More*) (1888).

While *interior monologue* and *stream of consciousness* are often used interchangeably, the latter is more general, encompassing a variety of techniques including interior monologue, which may be *direct* or *indirect*. In the direct, or "quoted," form, the **author** approximates or mimics the character's mental flow, plugging the reader straight into the character's mind.

Direct interior monologue entails presentation of consciousness in a seemingly transparent, uninterrupted way, from the **first-person point of view,** without apparent guidance. By contrast, in the indirect form — classified by some critics as *narrated monologue* rather than interior monologue — the author combines direct interior monologue with **third-person narration,** providing some context for the character's mental flow through commentary and description. The character's consciousness still comes through directly, but it is framed by the **narrator** and often presented through **free indirect discourse.**

FURTHER EXAMPLES: William Faulkner's *As I Lay Dying* (1930), which consists of direct interior monologues by fifteen different characters; the sperm whale passage of Douglas Adams's *The Hitchhiker's Guide to the Galaxy* (1979), which uses direct interior monologue to convey "the complete record" of the newborn whale's thought "from the moment it began its [short] life till the moment it ended it." James Joyce's *Ulysses* (1922) ends with a direct interior monologue representing the consciousness of Molly Bloom, who is lying awake in bed with her husband asleep beside her; the section begins:

> Yes because he never did a thing like that before as ask to get his breakfast in bed with a couple of eggs since the City Arms hotel when he used to be pretending to be laid up with a sick voice doing his highness to make himself interesting for that old faggot Mrs Riordan that he thought he had a great leg of and she never left us a farthing all for masses for herself and her soul greatest miser ever . . . .

Virginia Woolf's *To the Lighthouse* (1927) relies heavily on indirect interior monologue, as in the following, final paragraph, when Lily Briscoe, an artist who has struggled to finish a portrait of Mrs. Ramsay, turns to her canvas:

> . . . There it was — her picture. Yes, with all its green and blues, its lines running up and across, its attempt at something. It would be hung in the attics, she thought; it would be destroyed. But what did that matter? she asked herself, taking up her brush again. She looked at the steps; they were empty; she looked at her canvas; it was blurred. With a sudden intensity, as if she saw it clear for a second, she drew a line there, in the centre. It was done; it was finished. Yes, she thought, laying down her brush in extreme fatigue, I have had my vision.

Contemporary writer Susan Minot used alternating indirect interior monologues to tell the story of two former lovers who hook up again one afternoon a year later in her **novella** *Rapture* (2002).

▶ **interlude:** From the Latin for "between play," a short **play** or other brief **dramatic** entertainment performed in an interval between the **acts** of a longer play or the courses of a banquet. The interlude, which flourished in England during the late fifteenth and early sixteenth centuries, when it was performed by professional acting troupes, was also popular in continental

Europe, where it was known as the *entremet* in France, the *intermezzo* in Italy, and the *entremes* in Spain. The **genre** is often viewed as a transitional form between religious and secular drama, in particular the **morality play** and **realistic comedy.** Some interludes were **allegorical** or **didactic,** some emphasized intellect and **wit,** and some were **comic** or even **farcical.**

EXAMPLES: Henry Medwall's *Fulgens and Lucres* (1497); John Heywood's *The playe called the foure PP; a newe and very mery enterlude of a palmer, a pardoner, a potycary, a pedler* (c. 1520–1545), which features a lying contest among four men denominated by their respective trades.

▶ **internal rhyme:** **Rhyme** that occurs within a line of **verse.**

EXAMPLES: Edward Lear used internal rhyme for comic effect in the following lines from his poem "The Owl and the Pussycat" (1942): "They took some honey, and plenty of money / Wrapped in a five pound note."

The following **stanza** from William Wordsworth's "We Are Seven" (1798), in which a child describes the graves of her brother and sister, has three internal rhymes (*green/seen, more/door,* and *side/side*) in addition to one **end rhyme** (*replied/side*):

> "Their graves are green, they may be seen,"
> The little maid replied,
> "Twelve steps or more from my mother's door,
> And they are side by side."

Internal rhyme also often appears in music. The popular show tune "Bewitched, Bothered, and Bewildered" (1940), written for the musical *Pal Joey* by Lorenz Hart and later recorded by artists ranging from Ella Fitzgerald (1956) and Frank Sinatra (1957) to Sinéad O'Connor (1993) and Rufus Wainwright (2006), pairs *wild* and *beguiled* in one line and *simpering* and *whimpering* in another. Hip-hop duo Rakim and Eric B.'s introduction to "Eric B. Is President" (1986) is rife with internal rhyme, with examples including *door/before, biting/fighting/inviting, esteem/seem,* and *prepared/scared.*

▶ **interpretive communities:** A term used by **reader-response critic** Stanley Fish to acknowledge the existence of multiple and diverse reading groups within any large reading population. Beginning with his essay "Interpreting the Variorum" (1976), Fish argued that the meaning of a given **text** may differ significantly from group to group. (For instance, college students reading novels in academic courses form an interpretive community that is likely to read a famous work of **detective fiction** differently from the way it would be read by retirees living in adult communities.) Different interpretive communities, Fish argued, share different reading goals and strategies; whether a given interpretation appears correct or logical to members of an interpretive community depends greatly on whether it fits in with their shared assumptions, motives, and methods. Thus, Fish suggested, no interpretation is likely to be considered valid by everyone, but certain interpretations are likely to be shared by most members of a given interpretive community.

In formulating this concept, Fish substantially moderated a stand he had taken earlier while developing his **theory** of **affective stylistics.** At that time, Fish had suggested that meaning is an "event" that takes place in the mind of an individual reader during the act of reading and that reading is a temporal process that forces readers to reevaluate their interpretations at every step. In developing the theory of interpretive communities, Fish came to view affective stylistics as one of several possible reading strategies.

▶ **intertextuality:** The condition of interconnectedness among **texts,** or the concept that any text is an amalgam of others, either because it exhibits signs of **influence** or because its language inevitably contains common points of reference with other texts through such things as **allusion,** quotation, **genre, style,** and even revisions. French critic Julia Kristeva, who popularized and is often credited with coining the term *intertextuality,* views any given work as part of a larger fabric of literary **discourse,** part of a continuum including the future as well as the past. Other critics have argued for an even broader use of the term, maintaining that literary history per se is too narrow a context within which to read and understand a literary text. So viewed, *intertextuality* has been used by **new historicists** and **cultural critics** to refer to the significant interconnectedness between literary texts and contemporary, nonliterary discussions of issues represented in those texts. It has also been used by **poststructuralists** to suggest that works of literature can only be recognized and read within a world of **signs** and **tropes** that is itself like a text and that makes any single text self-contradictory and **undecidable.**

EXAMPLES: In his article "Ben Okri's *The Landscapes Within:* A Metaphor for Personal and National Development" (1988), Abioseh Michael Porter explored how Nigerian writer Ben Okri drew on and played off a variety of other sources, including Ayi Kwei Armah's *The Beautiful Ones Are Not Yet Born* (1968) and James Joyce's *A Portrait of the Artist as a Young Man* (1916), in his **Künstlerroman** *The Landscapes Within* (1981).

The television drama *Lost* (2004–) also draws on and plays off other sources. For instance, con-man Sawyer is regularly shown reading books — both real (such as John Steinbeck's *Of Mice and Men* [1937] and Judy Blume's *Are You There, God? It's Me, Margaret* [1970]) and imagined (*Bad Twin,* said in the show to have been written by Gary Troup, a passenger on the doomed plane, and subsequently written in reality by Laurence Shames, using Troup's name, and published in 2006) — many of which are later referenced in the **action.** Likewise, the show incorporates both pop culture (music from the 1960s band The Mamas and the Papas plays in one of the hatches; the movie *Pulp Fiction* [1994] is invoked as an "Other" plunges a huge needle into a Sawyer's chest) and real events, such as the 2004 presidential election and World Series ("Other" Juliet shows an incredulous Jack Shephard a clip of the victorious Boston Red Sox and informs him of George W. Bush's win). It also spawned an interactive, alternate reality game, *The Lost Experience,* that played out from May–September 2006 through ads, a novel, voicemail, and websites. Indeed, *Lost* has become such an icon that references to the series in other media are common. *Mad* magazine spoofed *Lost* in "Lots" (2005), the comic strip *Monty* **parodied** it in 2006, and

characters from television shows such as *South Park* (1997–), *Will & Grace* (1998–2006), and *The Office* (2005–) all discuss the series.

Covers from *The New Yorker* magazine frequently exhibit intertextuality. An example is the February 27, 2006, cover, which featured Vice President Dick Cheney and President George W. Bush dressed in cowboy attire with Cheney calmly blowing the smoke from the end of a just-fired rifle and Bush looking unhappily over Cheney's shoulder with snow-capped mountains in the background; the **image** alludes both to the movie *Brokeback Mountain* (2005), based on Annie E. Proulx's short story, which was first published in *The New Yorker* in 1997, and to the incident on February 11, 2006, in which Cheney accidentally shot a fellow hunter during a weekend quail hunt.

Posters and ads likewise often exhibit intertextuality. For example, numerous military recruitment posters have featured an image of a person pointing at the viewer, imitating an iconic British poster from World War I featuring Lord Horatio Herbert Kitchener, the Secretary of State for War, calling on Britons to join the army. The "Lord Kitchener Wants You" poster (1914), designed by Alfred Leete, is shown below, along with **imitations** including an Uncle Sam "I Want You" U.S. Army poster from 1917 and a Red Army poster from the 1920s. Ads for Absolut Vodka routinely feature the shape of the bottle and pair the word "Absolut" with a noun that ties in to the image — important knowledge to have in understanding any individual ad. For instance, "Absolut Brooklyn" puts an outline of the bottle inside the Brooklyn Bridge, "Absolut Citron" replaces the seeds in a lemon slice with bottles, and "Absolut Rice" shows a bottle with double red marks around the neck, alluding to Anne Rice's *Interview with the Vampire* (1976). Each ad thus refers not only to its particular subject but also connects to the larger series of "Absolut Whatever" ads.

Examples of **intertextual** posters.

▶ **intrigue:** See **plot.**

▶ **intrusive narrator:** An **omniscient, third-person narrator** who provides personal commentary or observation in addition to relating a **story.** The intrusive narrator is opinionated, not detached and impersonal, and makes valuative judgments on the **action** and **characters** in a work. By **convention,** an intrusive narrator's assertions are intended to be authoritative. The term *intrusive* is sometimes also applied to **first-person** narrators, particularly when they interrupt the **narrative** with a personal digression or directly address the reader.

EXAMPLES: Works featuring intrusive narrators include Henry Fielding's *Tom Jones* (1749), whose narrator declares that he "intend[s] to digress, through this whole history, as often as I see occasion, of which I am myself a better judge than any pitiful critic whatever"; Leo Tolstoi's *War and Peace* (1864–66); Halldór Laxness's *Paradísarheimt* (*Paradise Reclaimed*) (1960); Milan Kundera's *The Unbearable Lightness of Being* (1984); and Francisco Goldman's *The Divine Husband* (2004), which begins: "When María de las Nieves Moran crossed from convent school to cloister to become a novice nun, it was to prevent Paquita Aparicio, her beloved childhood companion, from marrying the man both girls called 'El Anticristo.' Of course that is not the version known to history." An example of intrusive first-person **narration** is Jane's announcement in Charlotte Brontë's *Jane Eyre* (1847): "Reader, I married him."

▶ **invocation:** A type of **apostrophe** in which a direct and explicit request for help in writing (usually **verse**) is made to a divine or supernatural entity. **Classical convention** called for such an address to the **muses;** in the **epic,** the address was typically directed to Calliope, the muse of epic poetry, or to Clio, the muse of history. Invocations remained relatively common through the **Neoclassical Period** but are rare today.

EXAMPLE: At the beginning of his cosmic seventeenth-century epic *Paradise Lost* (1667), John Milton invoked Urania, the muse of astronomy in antiquity, remade by Christian writers of the **Renaissance** into a heavenly, Christian muse.

▶ **Irish Literary Renaissance, Irish Revival:** See **Celtic Revival.**

▶ **irony:** A contradiction or incongruity between appearance or expectation and reality. This disparity may be manifested in a variety of ways. A discrepancy may exist between what someone says and what he or she actually means, between what someone expects to happen and what really happens, or between what appears to be true and what actually is true. The term may be applied to events, situations, and structural elements of a work, not just to statements. Irony may even be used as a general **mode** of expression, in which case one might describe an **author's** very **tone** as ironic.

Irony comes from the Greek *eiron*, which derives from *eironeia*, meaning "dissembling." In Greek **drama,** the *eiron* was a **character** who, although weaker than his opponent, the braggart *alazon*, nevertheless defeated him by misrepresenting himself in some way, for instance by acting foolish or stupid. **Meiosis,** or understatement, was perhaps the *eiron*'s most potent — and, to the audience, humorous — weapon.

Irony has been called the subtlest **comic** and **rhetorical** form. Instead of flatly stating a point, the ironist's speech is often tongue-in-cheek, deliberately polished and refined, leaving the impression of intentional restraint. The ironist's approach to a subject may even seem unemotional, a wry illustration of a point. Notably, the success of any irony is subject to a **paradox:** the ironist wears a mask that must be perceived as such. The audience must recognize the discrepancy at issue, or the irony fails to achieve its effect.

Irony should not be confused with either **sarcasm** or **satire.** Sarcasm is intentional derision that usually involves an obvious, even exaggerated form of verbal irony, such as false praise, and is generally directed at a specific person with a hurtful aim. Irony is more restrained, may employ false blame as well as false praise, is often directed toward a situation rather than a person, and generally lacks hurtful intent. Satire is a literary **genre** in which irony, **wit,** and sometimes sarcasm are used to expose human weaknesses, spurring reform through ridicule. Irony is a device or mode, not a genre, and typically lacks satire's ameliorative aim.

Several types of irony exist, all of which may be classified under one of three rubrics: *verbal irony* (also called *rhetorical irony*), *situational irony* (also called *irony of situation*), and *structural irony*. Verbal irony, the most common kind of irony, is characterized by a discrepancy between what a speaker or writer says and what he or she means or believes to be true. In fact, a speaker or writer using verbal irony frequently says the opposite of what he or she actually means. For instance, imagine that you have come home after a day on which you failed a test, wrecked your car, and had a fight with your best friend. If your roommate were to ask you how your day went and you replied, "Great day. Best ever," you would be using verbal irony, just as the **narrator** of Charles Dickens's *Oliver Twist* (1837) did when he said that "the parish authorities magnanimously and humanely resolved that Oliver should be 'farmed,' or, in other words, dispatched to a branch workhouse some three miles off."

Verbal irony is sometimes viewed as a **trope,** one of the two major divisions of **figures of speech,** since it involves saying one thing but meaning another. Balancing the characteristic restraint of irony with the need for recognition makes verbal irony a particularly difficult device to master. Tone probably keys the listener in to the irony more than any other element, but knowledge of the circumstances surrounding the statement may also spur recognition of the speaker's true meaning. Taking the aforementioned example, your roommate might pick up on the irony either through your tone or by knowing that you had suffered one or more calamities that day. Since readers do not have the benefit of hearing a particular speaker's tone, knowledge of circumstances and the general tone of the work play a greater role in accurately identifying ironic statements.

Situational irony, the second type of irony, typically involves a discrepancy between expectation and reality and derives primarily from events or situations themselves, as opposed to statements made by individuals, whether or not they understand the situation as ironic. For instance, situational irony existed when college-bound men in the Vietnam War era celebrated their avoidance of the draft, unaware that their exemption as college students was about to be revoked by Congress. Situational irony continued to exist even after the men learned about the revocation, provided that their college applications had been motivated solely by a desire to avoid the draft, the exemption was revoked after they went through the trouble of applying, and they actually got drafted. The scenarios described by Alanis Morissette in her song "Ironic" (1995) also exemplify situational irony: dying the day after you win the lottery; working up the courage to take your first airplane flight and then crashing; finding the man of your dreams only to discover that he has a beautiful wife; and so forth.

Literary examples of situational irony include O. Henry's short story "The Gift of the Magi" and the **mythic** story of King Midas. In "The Gift of the Magi," both husband and wife give up their most prized possession in order to give something to complement the other's most prized possession. The woman sells her beautiful long hair to buy a platinum fob chain for the man's watch; the man sells his watch to buy the woman tortoiseshell combs to hold up her hair. In the story of King Midas, Bacchus grants the king's wish that everything he touch be turned to gold; much to his chagrin, the king finds that this power does anything but enhance his *true* wealth when he hugs his beloved daughter, thereby (inadvertently) turning her to gold as well. A poetic example of situational irony is Percy Bysshe Shelley's "Ozymandias" (1818), in which "a traveller from an antique land" tells of coming upon a ruined statue, the pedestal of which reads "My name is Ozymandias, King of Kings: /Look on my Works, ye Mighty, and despair!"

Subsets of situational irony include *dramatic irony*, *tragic irony*, and *Socratic irony* (also called *dialectical irony*). Dramatic irony may involve a situation in which a character's words come back to haunt him or her but more commonly involves a discrepancy between a character's perception and what the reader or audience knows to be true. Lacking some material information that the reader or audience possesses, the character responds to a statement or situation in a discordant fashion, whether in the form of an inappropriate statement, expectation, or action. A verbal response involves dramatic irony when a character fails to recognize the true import of his or her words; characters with partial information may thus assign meanings to their words that differ from the meanings assigned by the reader or audience. Expectation and action involve dramatic irony when they are inappropriate under the circumstances that actually exist. Characters may even accurately assess a situation without realizing it, attributing to someone or something a truth that they do not recognize as such.

Dramatic irony has often been used synonymously with *tragic irony*, but this usage is incorrect. Dramatic irony occurs in a wide variety of works, ranging from the **comic** to the **tragic**. Tragic irony is a type of dramatic irony marked by a sense of foreboding. As with all dramatic irony, tragic irony involves imperfect information, but the consequences of this ignorance are **catastrophic**, leading to the character's tragic downfall. In Sophocles' *Oedipus Rex* (430 B.C.), for instance, Oedipus, the King of Thebes, vows to find the murderer of the prior king, only to find out something the audience knew all along: that he himself is the guilty party.

Socratic irony, named for the fifth-century B.C. Greek philosopher Socrates, is, loosely speaking, situational in nature. Plato's dialogues (early fourth century B.C.), describe Socrates as assuming the role of the *eiron*, acting foolish or naive in questioning fellow citizens and drawing out the irrationality or preposterous implications of their positions. For instance, when Euthyphro, an Athenian who is about to turn his father in for murder, says that this is obviously the right thing to do, Socrates pretends to be impressed by Euthyphro's moral certainty, asking a series of seemingly naive questions demonstrating not that Euthyphro is wrong to turn his father in but, rather, that his grounds for doing so are irrational and self-contradictory.

Works that exhibit structural irony, the third major type of irony, contain an internal feature that creates or promotes a discrepancy that typically operates throughout the entire work. Some element of the work's **structure** (or perhaps even its **form**), unrelated to the **plot** per se, invites the audience or reader to probe beneath surface statements or appearances. **Narration** is the most common vehicle for structural irony, especially the use of a **naive** or otherwise **unreliable narrator** whose flaw the audience or reader readily recognizes. A naive narrator means what he or she says, but the audience or reader mistrusts the narrator's perceptions or version of events and thus seeks a different meaning that reflects the author's **intention**. For instance, the reader of Jonathan Swift's "A Modest Proposal" (1729) quickly recognizes that its narrator — an economist who advocates cannibalism, specifically, selling poor Irish infants to "persons of quality and fortune through the kingdom" as "wholesome food" to solve Ireland's perpetual, cyclic problems of poverty, overpopulation, and starvation — is fallible. Since no reasonable reader would take this work at face value, discovering why Swift used a fallible narrator becomes the reader's task. (Swift's title can also be seen as an example of verbal irony, since he most certainly did not consider the proposal "modest.")

Structural irony should not be confused with situational irony. The former involves a sustained feature in the frame of the work, whereas the latter involves an event or comment keyed to the plot. Granted, this difference sometimes seems more one of degree than absolute, as in the case where a plot element underlies the entire work. Examples include *Oedipus Rex* and Oscar Wilde's *The Importance of Being Earnest* (1895), where lack of knowledge about identity serves as the basis of the plots. Nevertheless, both works involve situational rather than structural irony, for the ironic discrepancies arise from the story lines rather than the structure or form of the works themselves.

Subsets of structural irony include *cosmic irony* (also called *irony of fate*) and *romantic irony*. Cosmic irony arises from the disparity between a character's (incorrect) belief in his or her ability to shape his or her destiny and the audience's recognition that an external, supernatural force has power over that character's fate. Just as the unreliable narrator serves as a structural device giving rise to structural irony, so the supernatural force of cosmic irony makes the irony structural rather than situational in nature. The use of cosmic irony is more than a matter of plot.

Cosmic irony is characterized by four elements. First, it typically involves a powerful deity (or, sometimes, fate itself) with the ability and desire to manipulate or even control events in a character's life. Second, the character subject to this irony believes — erroneously — in free will. Whether or not the character acknowledges the deity's existence, he or she persists in attempting to affect events. Third, the deity toys with the character much as a cat might with a mouse; the outcome is clear to the disinterested observer, but the mouse hopes desperately for escape. Fourth, cosmic irony involves a tragic outcome; ultimately, the character's struggle against destiny will be for naught. Cosmic irony is notably apparent in Thomas Hardy's *Tess of the d'Urbervilles* (1891), the last chapter of which contains the statement "the President of the Immortals . . . had ended his sport with Tess."

Romantic irony, as defined by nineteenth-century German philosopher Friedrich Schlegel, is present in poems and prose works whose authors or speakers at some point reveal their narration to be the capricious fabrication of an idiosyncratic and highly self-conscious creator. Romantic ironists typically "give up the game" only after they have carefully constructed some vision of "reality," however. They may reveal their narrator to be a liar, for instance, or they may speak directly to the reader as an author. As a result, they wreak havoc with the reader's or audience's usual **suspension of disbelief,** debunking as illusion the normal operating assumption that the narration is a believable **representation** of reality. Romantic ironists *want* their readers or audiences to "see through" them, that is, to appreciate the manipulative nature of their art and the slightly comic quality of even their most serious artistic endeavors. In Henrik Ibsen's *Peer Gynt* (1875), for example, one of the characters says, "One cannot die in the middle of Act Five." Other examples of romantic irony include Steven Millhauser's *Edwin Mullhouse: The Life and Death of an American Writer, 1943–1954, by Jeffrey Cartwright* (1972) — the fictional **biography** of a cartoon-crazy preteen supposedly written by his best friend — and David Leavitt's *The Term Paper Artist* (1997). This **novella** blurs the line between **fiction** and **autobiography** by giving its **protagonist** the same name, profession, publishers, and written works as the author and by making the protagonist the subject of a plagiarism charge and lawsuit by an English poet, just as the author was in his own life. As Leavitt the character notes at the end of the novella, "Writers often disguise their lives as fiction. The thing they almost never do is disguise fiction as their lives."

FURTHER EXAMPLES: Sometimes different types of irony come into play at once, as in the following passage from Euripides' *Iphigenia at Aulis* (c. 405 B.C.). Agamemnon has brought his daughter Iphigenia to Aulis to be sacrificed to the gods; Iphigenia thinks a marriage has been arranged for her at Aulis with Achilles. Agamemnon's comments exemplify rhetorical irony, given the discrepancy between his literal words and what he really means, whereas Iphigenia's failure to understand the true import of her words exemplifies dramatic irony:

> Iphigenia: It's a long journey then; and you're leaving me behind!
> Agamemnon: Yours is a long journey too, like mine.
> Iphigenia: We could travel together then. You could arrange it.
> Agamemnon: No, your journey is different. You must remember me.
> Iphigenia: Will my mother sail with me? Or must I travel alone?
> Agamemnon: You'll sail alone . . . without father or mother.
> Iphigenia: Have you found me a new home, Father? Where is it?
> Agamemnon: That's enough . . . There are some things young girls
>   shouldn't know.
> Iphigenia: Sort the Phrygians out quickly, Daddy, and come back to me.
> Agamemnon: I must perform a sacrifice, before I go.
> Iphigenia: Of course you must! The right sacred rituals.
> Agamemnon: You'll be there too. By the holy water.
> Iphigenia: Shall I be part of the ceremonies at the altar?

▶ **irony of fate:** See **irony.**

▶ **irregular ode (Cowleyan ode):** Named for its inventor, seventeenth-century English poet Abraham Cowley, an **ode** with an irregular **stanzaic** structure and form. Unlike the recurrent, triadic structure of a **Pindaric ode** and the homostrophic structure of a **Horatian ode,** the structure and form of an irregular ode are flexible; the irregular ode may be any number of stanzas, and the line length, number of lines, and **rhyme scheme** of individual stanzas may vary widely, providing the poet with more freedom in composition.

EXAMPLES: Cowley's rather inaptly named *Pindarique Odes* (1656); William Wordsworth's "Ode: Intimations of Immortality" (1807).

▶ **Italian sonnet (Petrarchan sonnet):** A fourteen-line **sonnet** consisting of two parts: the **octave,** eight lines with the **rhyme scheme** *abbaabba;* and the **sestet,** six lines usually following the rhyme scheme *cdecde* (or sometimes *cdcdcd*). The octave often poses a question or dilemma that the sestet answers or resolves.

The Italian sonnet originated in Italy in the thirteenth century, but its best-known proponent is the fourteenth-century poet Petrarch, hence its alternative name. English poets who have used this form have tended to take greater liberties with the rhyme scheme.

EXAMPLES: Dante Gabriel Rossetti's "Vain Virtues" (1870), which scandalously assaulted **Victorian** mores:

> What is the sorriest thing that enters Hell?
>   None of the sins, — but this and that fair deed
>   Which a soul's sin at length could supersede.

These yet are virgins, whom death's timely knell
Might once have sainted; whom the fiends compel
    Together now, in snake-bound shuddering sheaves
    Of anguish, while the pit's pollution leaves
Their refuse maidenhood abominable.
Night sucks them down, the tribute of the pit,
    Whose names, half entered in the book of Life,
    Were God's desire at noon. And as their hair
And eyes sink last, the Torturer deigns no whit
    To gaze, but, yearning, waits his destined wife,
    The Sin still blithe on earth that sent them there.

Harlem Renaissance poet Claude McKay's poem "The Lynching" (1920) follows the **classic** Italian sonnet form in the octave, which speaks sympathetically of the body and soul of a man lynched in the night, but uses a *cddcee* pattern in the sestet, which details the unsympathetic reaction of the crowds who come to see the body the next day. Donald Justice also tweaked the sestet rhyme scheme in his "The Poet at Seven" (1960), using a *ccddee* pattern with an **eye rhyme** in the final **couplet**.

J

▶ **Jacobean Age (in English literature):** An age spanning the reign of James I (1603–25) that is often classified as the third of five literary eras within the **Renaissance Period** in English literature. The Jacobean Age, which was nearly cut short by the failed Gunpowder Plot to blow up the king and the parliament in 1605, derives its names from *Jacobus* (Latin for James). Many of the most significant Jacobean authors, including playwrights Ben Jonson and William Shakespeare, **metaphysical poet** John Donne and poet Michael Drayton, and philosopher and essayist Francis Bacon, began writing during the preceding **Elizabethan Age.** Noted writers who began their careers during the Jacobean Age include George Herbert, another of the metaphysical poets; playwrights Sir Francis Beaumont and John Fletcher, who are generally credited with developing the hybrid **genre** of **tragicomedy;** and two other dramatists, Thomas Middleton and John Webster. Major prose works of the Jacobean Age include the King James translation of the Bible (1611), Robert Burton's *Anatomy of Melancholy* (1621), and Donne's sermons (published posthumously in various collections including *Six Sermons* [1634]). The king himself also produced several works, including one of the first invectives against tobacco, *A Counterblaste to Tobacco* (1604).

See also **Renaissance.**

▶ *jouissance:* A term used in several approaches to **literary criticism,** including **psychoanalytic criticism, deconstruction,** and **feminist criticism,** to refer in various ways to the enjoyment of language and literary **texts.** Beginning with his seminar *The Ethics of Psychoanalysis* (1959–60), French psychoanalytic theorist Jacques Lacan developed the concept of *jouissance* as a **paradox,** going back to Austrian psychoanalyst Sigmund Freud's argument in *Civilization and Its Discontents* (1930) that the quest for happiness is two-fold, involving both the avoidance of pain and the pursuit of pleasure. Lacan distinguished *jouissance* from simple *plaisir*, or pleasure, arguing that *jouissance* entails sensation verging on discomfort — pleasure to the point of pain, so to speak — experienced upon union with **the Other,** which the subject desires in order to overcome a sense of absence or lack and achieve wholeness. Subsequently, in his seminar *On Feminine Sexuality* (1972–73), Lacan spoke of a *"jouissance au-delà du phallus,"* a *jouissance* beyond the **phallic,** a feminine, supplementary *jouissance* that could be spoken but not written.

Drawing on these psychoanalytic concepts, **poststructuralist** theorist Roland Barthes characterized *plaisir* and *jouissance* as a **binary opposition** in *Le plaisir du texte* (*The Pleasure of the Text*) (1973). While acknowledging that "there is always a vacillation," Barthes contrasted the *"texte de plaisir"* with the *"texte de jouissance"*:

> Text of pleasure [*plaisir*]: the text that contents, fills, grants eupho-
> ria; the text that comes from culture and does not break with it, is
> linked to a *comfortable* practice of reading. Text of bliss [*jouis-
> sance*]: the text that imposes a state of loss, the text that discomforts
> (perhaps to the point of a certain boredom), unsettles the reader's his-
> torical, cultural, psychological assumptions, the consistency of his
> tastes, values, memories, brings to a crisis his relation with language.

For Barthes, *plaisir* was associated with culture, criticism, and the **canon,**
jouissance with "the untenable text, the impossible text," a "text outside
pleasure, outside criticism," for "pleasure can be expressed in words, bliss
cannot."

Practitioners of deconstruction, led by French philosopher of language
Jacques Derrida, have used the term *jouissance* differently to refer to the
attitude of pleasurable playfulness with which they approach literary texts.
Deconstructors seek to show that every text dismantles itself because each
text contains opposed strands of meaning or conflicting **discourses** that
cannot be reconciled, making it impossible to discern or establish any one,
"true" meaning. In *Acts of Literature* (1992), Derrida claimed that the
"subtle and intense pleasure" deconstructors experience arises from the
"dismantl[ing] of repressive assumptions, representations, and ideas — in
short, from the lifting of repression" that occurs during this reading
process. Foes of deconstruction have often objected to its playfulness, to
the pleasure its practitioners take in teasing out the contradictory interpretive possibilities generated by the words in a text, their **etymologies** and
contexts, and their potential to be read **figuratively** or even **ironically.**

Jouissance has also been used in **feminist criticism** to refer to sexual as
well as textual pleasure or, more precisely, to a feminine, linguistic *jouissance* grounded in women's sexual potential and pleasure. As French feminist critic Luce Irigaray argued in *Ce sexe qui n'en est pas un* (*This Sex
Which Is Not One*) (1977), not only is a woman's *jouissance* more diffusive and diverse than a man's unitary phallic pleasure, it cannot be expressed by the dominant, masculine language. Irigaray, like many other
feminist critics, connected this difference in bodily sensation and experience to a difference in the way women and men write, postulating and celebrating the existence of a "feminine language," or **feminine writing,** that is
more diffusive and fluid than its "masculine" counterpart.

▶ **judicial criticism:** A type of **practical criticism** that regards judgment as
the goal of **literary criticism** and aims to assess literary works in accordance
with a set of external principles and rules that are viewed as objective and
unchanging. Judicial criticism is often characterized as prescriptive, legislative, or even absolutist. Seeking a firm ground for judgment, judicial critics
generally eschew individual sensibility and impressions in favor of analyzing
an author's **style,** subject matter, and technique in light of traditional — usually **classical** and **canonical** — standards. As French literary critic Julien-
Louis Geoffroy asserted in the *Journal des débats*, judicial criticism serves

"good taste, sound morals and the eternal foundations of the social order" (1805).

Judicial criticism was the dominant mode of criticism during the **Renaissance** and **Neoclassical** periods, which emphasized adherence to classical **conventions** and rules. With the advent of **romanticism,** which emphasized the individual and **subjective** experience, judicial criticism began to give way to **impressionistic criticism,** and by the latter half of the nineteenth century the rejection of criticism as judgment (with its correlative rules) was nearly complete. A few critics continued to defend or advocate a judicial approach, however, including nineteenth-century French critic Charles Augustin Sainte-Beuve, who moved from impressionism to a judicial approach over the course of his career; nineteenth-century English poet and critic Matthew Arnold, who spoke of a "real estimate, the only true one," as opposed to "historic" and "personal" estimates in "The Study of Poetry" (1888); and twentieth-century American critic Irving Babbitt, who sought to "temper with judgment the all-pervading impressionism of contemporary literature and life" in "Impressionist *Versus* Judicial Criticism" (1906).

Noted judicial critics include seventeenth-century French poet and critic Nicolas Boileau and eighteenth-century English writer and critic Samuel Johnson. English poet Alexander Pope expressed the judicial belief in unchanging principles and rules in *An Essay on Criticism* (1711) when he wrote:

> First follow NATURE, and your Judgment frame
> By her just Standard, which is still the same:
> Unerring NATURE, still divinely bright,
> One clear, unchang'd, and Universal Light.

▶ **jump marker:** See **link.**

▶ **Jungian criticism:** A type of **literary criticism** based on the **theories** of Carl Jung, a Swiss psychiatrist who was originally a disciple of Sigmund Freud. Jung later developed his own theory of analytical psychology, a theory that differs markedly from the **psychoanalytic** theory of Freud. Consequently, it has had an effect on literary criticism quite distinct from that of Freud's psychoanalytic theory. Freud focused on the individual unconscious and its manifestations; Jung identified and concentrated on a **collective unconscious** that, he claimed, is universally shared by people across cultures. According to Jung, this collective unconscious contains racial memories and **archetypes,** primordial **images** and patterns, that reflect the elemental content of human experience from its earliest beginnings.

Like Freud, Jung applied his psychoanalytic theory to literature, suggesting that the works that speak to generation after generation express the archetypes and racial memories contained in the collective unconscious; thus, great authors are great largely because they can tap into the elemental grounds of the human psyche and transcribe its contents for the reader.

Texts that have become **classics** have universal appeal; their universality lies in the fact that they harness the collective unconscious much as do those **myths** that transcend individual cultures. Jungian criticism has influenced **myth criticism** and **archetypal criticism** in substantial ways.

▶ **Juvenalian satire:** A type of formal **satire**, characterized by its harshness and pointed **realism**, that denounces human vice and error in caustic, often scornful **tones**. Juvenalian satire is named for the early-second-century A.D. Roman satirist Juvenal (Decimus Junius Juvenalis), who sought to evoke contempt or indignation from the reader. It is distinguished from **Horatian satire**, the other major type of formal satire, by the latter's **witty**, even indulgent, tone, which is aimed at evoking laughter rather than derision.

EXAMPLES: Juvenal's sixteen *Saturae (Satires)* (c. A.D. 100–128), the sixth of which, a diatribe against women and marriage often entitled *Against Women*, poses a question long since removed from its original context regarding eunuchs and women: "*sed quis custodiet ipsos custodes?*" — "but who will guard the guardians themselves?" Other examples of Juvenalian satire include Jonathan Swift's *A Modest Proposal* (1729), in which Swift "proposes" that the starving Irish sell their children as "wholesome food" to "persons of quality and fortune through the kingdom"; Samuel Johnson's "London" (1738), an **imitation** of Juvenal's third satire; and Anthony Burgess's *A Clockwork Orange* (1962).

K

▶ **katharsis:** See **catharsis**.

▶ **kenning:** A type of **periphrasis**, or circumlocution, in which a **figurative**, often compound phrase is used in place of a simpler or more common term. Kennings, which tend to be both **allusive** and **conventional**, were particularly common in Old English and Old Norse poetry.

EXAMPLES: The hyphenated nouns "whale-road" and "swan-road," used to refer to the sea in *Beowulf* (c. A.D. 700), are kennings, as are the phrases "storm of swords" (for "battle") and "oar-steed" (for "ship"). Contemporary kennings include phrases such as "chicken of the sea," "gas guzzler," and "pencil-pusher."

▶ **Kuleshov effect:** See **montage**.

▶ ***Künstlerroman:*** German for "novel of the artist," a **novel** that examines the development of an artist, typically from childhood to a point of maturity where the **protagonist** realizes his or her artistic potential and mission; a type of **bildungsroman**, the more general novel of formation. *Künstlerroman* typically depict the struggles of sensitive protagonists to overcome bourgeois values and other obstacles, thereby realizing their creative potential.

EXAMPLES: Charles Dickens's *David Copperfield* (1868), James Joyce's *A Portrait of the Artist as a Young Man* (1916), Zelda Fitzgerald's **autobiographical** novel *Save Me the Waltz* (1932), Brian Moore's *An Answer from Limbo* (1962), Ben Okri's *The Landscapes Within* (1981), Shelley Jackson's **hypertext** work *My Body: A Wunderkammer* (1997). Elizabeth Barrett Browning's *Aurora Leigh* (1857), a novel-length **epic lyric** written in **blank verse**, has been called the first female *Künstlerroman*.

Maxine Hong Kingston's *Tripmaster Monkey: His Fake Book* (1987), the story of a fifth-generation Chinese-American, redefines the traditional *Künstlerroman*, which emphasizes the artist's estrangement from society, by focusing on the protagonist's efforts to establish his place as an artist within the mainstream of American society.

L

▶ *lai* (lay): As a literary form, a short **lyric** or **narrative poem**, typically relating a **tale** of love and adventure, that flourished in **medieval** France and England and often drew on Celtic **folklore**. *Narrative lais*, which began to develop in the latter half of the twelfth century, were usually written and recited in Old French in octosyllabic **couplets**. *Lyric lais* had a more varied poetic **form** and **structure**, were sung rather than read or recited, and were typically addressed to a lady or to the Virgin Mary.

The *Breton lai*, a narrative form, drew mainly on Celtic **legends**, such as Arthurian lore. Fairies or other supernatural agents often played a role, and faithful love — as opposed to **courtly love**, which sanctioned adultery — was extolled. Marie de France, who wrote in Old French at the English court toward the end of the twelfth century, pioneered the Breton *lai*.

The fourteenth-century English lay, which **imitated** the Breton *lai* with a few changes, came to be called the *Breton lay*. Over time, as this Anglicized term was applied to any short English verse narrative in the vein of a Breton *lai*, the meaning of *lay* expanded. Increasingly, the subject matter for Breton lays ranged beyond Celtic legends to those of other traditions (even the "Oriental"), and the use of the **tail-rhyme stanza** outpaced octosyllabic couplets. Since the sixteenth century, the English word *lay* has been still more generally employed to describe any song or comparatively short verse narrative. For instance, in the nineteenth century, it was occasionally used to refer to short historical **ballads.**

EXAMPLES: Marie de France's "Le rossignol" ("The Nightingale"), "Le lai des deux amants" ("The *Lai* of Two Lovers"), and "Chèvrefeuille" ("Honeysuckle") are Breton *lais* dating from approximately 1175. Notable fourteenth-century Breton lays include Thomas Chestre's *Lay of Launfal,* the anonymous *Sir Orfeo,* and Geoffrey Chaucer's "The Franklin's Tale" (c. 1387). The oldest extant lyric *lais* were composed by French *trouvère* Gautier de Dargiès in the early thirteenth century. Sir Walter Scott's *Lay of the Last Minstrel* (1805) and Thomas Macaulay's *Lays of Ancient Rome* (1842) are nineteenth-century examples of historical ballads referred to as lays.

An example of a lay from a non-European tradition is Yi Kyu-bo's *The Lay of King Tongmyông* (1193), which recounts an ancient Korean legend regarding the birth of Tongmyông and the founding of his kingdom.

▶ **lampoon:** A **satiric**, often vicious, attack on an individual (or occasionally an institution or society in general). Lampoons were common — and popular — in seventeenth- and eighteenth-century England, but with the development of libel laws became legally risky for their composers and thus waned as the vehicle of choice for satirizing specific people. However, public figures have remained vulnerable to lampoons.

EXAMPLES: In his poetic "Epistle to Dr. Arbuthnot" (1735), Alexander Pope satirized Joseph Addison and Bubb Doddington in the fictional guises of Atticus and Bufo respectively; by contrast, he lampooned John, Lord Hervey, effeminate courtier and confidant of Queen Caroline, through an attack far more personally derogatory than his treatments of Addison and Doddington. He portrayed Hervey through the character of Sporus, whom he called a "thing of silk," a "mere white curd of ass's milk," a "painted child of dirt that stinks and stings," and a "vile antithesis" (presumably a reference to Hervey's allegedly androgynous qualities).

The television show *Saturday Night Live* (1975–) has lampooned political figures throughout its history. Comedian Stephen Colbert, in character as the over-the-top conservative pundit of his mock-news television show *The Colbert Report* (2005–), lampooned George W. Bush at the 2006 White House Correspondents' Association Dinner, targeting the president as well as the press with the following remarks: "I stand by this man. I stand by this man because he stands for things. Not only for things, he stands *on* things. Things like aircraft carriers and rubble and recently flooded city squares. And that sends a strong message, that no matter what happens to America, she will always rebound — with the most powerfully staged photo ops in the world." In the comic strip shown below, Garry Trudeau, who has long satirized the American political landscape in his cartoon series *Doonesbury* (1970–), lampooned the speech of teenagers in the 1990s.

(*DOONESBURY* © 1997 G. B. Trudeau. *Reprinted with permission of UNIVERSAL PRESS SYNDICATE. All rights reserved.*)

The *National Lampoon* series of films (1983–97) lampooned the American family. The movie *Shrek* (2001), in which Shrek, an ogre, saves Princess Fiona, a human by day and an ogre by night, lampooned the **fairy-tale** formula.

▶ **Language poetry:** A school of **postmodern**, *avant-garde* American poetry that arose in the 1970s and that **foregrounds** language rather than expression or meaning. As Language poet and theorist Ron Silliman explained in "The Dwelling Place: 9 Poets" (1975), a selection of Language poems accompanied by notes, Language poets are linked by "concern for language as the center of whatever activity poems might be." The name itself has been subject to debate, with some practitioners preferring L=A=N=G=U=A=G=E P=O=E=T=R=Y and others "language writing" or "language-centered writing." See, for instance, Michael Greer's "Ideology and Theory in Recent Experimental Writing or, The Naming of 'Language Poetry'" (1989).

Language poetry, which emphasizes process or method and embraces collaborative creative activity, is characterized by the use of nontraditional, non**narrative** forms. Notably, Language poets reject the conception of poetry as a communicative mode. Questioning the referentiality of language, they emphasize that writing is based on **codes** and **conventions** and stress the reader's role in making meaning. They also reject the narrative model, embracing disjunction, fragmentation, and incoherence. Indeed, in "Experiments" (1984), Bernadette Mayer recommended that poets "systematically derange the language" — for instance, by using only prepositional phrases — or turn a list of random words into a poem. Journals associated with the movement include *This* (1971–82), edited by Robert Grenier and Barrett Watten, and *L=A=N=G=U=A=G=E* (1978–82), edited by Charles Bernstein and Bruce Andrews. (Grenier's pronouncement "I HATE SPEECH," in his essay "On Speech" from the inaugural issue of *This* [1971], has served as a rallying cry for the school.) Andrews and Bernstein also edited a collection of theoretical writings on Language poetry, *The L=A=N=G=U=A=G=E Book* (1984).

Significant influences on Language poetry include twentieth-century Austrian philosopher Ludwig Wittgenstein's concept of language-games, **modernist** poets Gertrude Stein and Louis Zakofsky, the **Beat writers**, and poets John Ashberry and Robert Creeley.

EXAMPLES: *In the American Tree* (1986), an anthology of Language poetry edited by Silliman; Lyn Hejinian's *My Life* (1987), originally a collection of thirty-seven poems composed of thirty-seven sentences, one for each year of her life, later revised at the age of forty-five to include forty-five poems of forty-five sentences each; *The Grand Piano* (2006–), a collaborative, serial work by ten Language poets who describe it as "an experiment in collective autobiography." One of Grenier's poems, published in "The Dwelling Place," follows:

s o m e o l d g u y s w i t h s c y t h e s

Carla Harryman's "For She" (*Under the Bridge*, 1980) takes the form of a **prose poem**:

> The back of the head resting on the pillow was not wasted. We couldn't hear each other speak. The puddle in the bathroom, the sassy one. There were many years between us. I stared the stranger into facing

up to Maxine, who had come out of the forest bad from wet nights. I came from an odd bed, a vermilion riot attracted to loud dogs. Nonetheless, I could pay my rent and provide for him. On this occasion she apologized.

▶ *langue:* See **semiotics**.

▶ **lay:** See *lai*.

▶ *lecture* (**reading**): See **text**.

▶ **legend:** Originally, a written account of the life of a saint; now, a story, often handed down through oral tradition, typically detailing the adventures of a human cultural **hero** but sometimes addressing the allegedly remarkable attributes of a place. Legends are distinguished from **myths**, traditional anonymous stories, originally religious in nature, told by a particular cultural group to explain a natural or cosmic phenomenon. Although a legend may exaggerate — perhaps even wildly — the exploits of its hero, it is likely to be grounded in historical fact and to rely less on the supernatural. Legends often grow up around figures such as national founders, outlaws, and warriors.

The term *legend* is also used in connection with **urban legend,** a type of contemporary **folklore** typically involving an **apocryphal,** often cautionary **tale** that varies locally and is frequently circulated widely on the Internet. Finally, the term may be used to refer to a caption; an explanatory list of symbols on a map, chart, or graph; or an inscription on an object, such as a coin.

EXAMPLES: Ancient Greek legend has it that the sixth-century B.C. poet Sappho, who taught girls the arts on the island of Lesbos, threw herself into the sea due to unrequited love. Countless legends surround quasi-historical figures such as King Arthur, the Knights of the Round Table, and Robin Hood, as well as clearly historical figures such as Rob Roy MacGregor, a seventeenth-century Scottish **folk** hero; George Washington, an American founding father and the country's first president; Annie Oakley, a late-nineteenth- and early-twentieth-century American sharpshooter; and Ernesto ("Che") Guevara, a twentieth-century Latin-American **Marxist** revolutionary. Place-related legends include those surrounding the lost continent and city of Atlantis, the golden city of El Dorado, and the Bermuda Triangle.

▶ **leitmotif:** German for "leading motive," an **image** or phrase that recurs throughout a work, each time evoking past associations in such a way as to serve as a subtly unifying element of the work as a whole. The term comes from music criticism, where it refers to a brief melodic phrase associated with a particular **character,** idea, object, or situation; the first four notes of Beethoven's Fifth Symphony, for instance, provide the leitmotif of the entire work. The leitmotif is not necessarily the predominant feature of a work, whether literary or musical, rather, it is a repeated element of the work that casts a revealing light on central **themes** and issues.

EXAMPLES: Mr. Brooke's recurring comment in George Eliot's novel *Middlemarch* (1872): "I looked into that at one time but found you could go too far." Examples of verbal and visual leitmotifs in film include "Rosebud" as a word and image in *Citizen Kane* (1941) and the image of a vortex in *Vertigo* (1958), visible both in the swirl of Kim Novak's hair and in the effect created by a camera tracking back quickly while zooming forward. Film score composer John Williams has created numerous leitmotifs, including the two-note musical phrase in *Jaws* (1975), which signals a shark attack; themes associated with various characters in the *Star Wars* saga (1977–2005), such as Darth Vader's "Imperial March"; and the mysterious "Hedwig's Theme" that recurs throughout the *Harry Potter* movies (2001–).

See also **motif**.

▶ **leonine rhyme:** A type of **internal rhyme** in which the last **stressed** syllable before the **caesura,** or pause in a line of poetry, **rhymes** with the last stressed syllable at the end of the line. Leonine rhyme is likely named for Leoninus, a twelfth-century poet and clergyman at St. Victor in Paris, who frequently employed this type of rhyme in his **verse.**

EXAMPLE: The following **stanza** from Samuel Taylor Coleridge's "The Rime of the Ancient Mariner" (1798) exhibits leonine rhyme in the first and third lines:

> "Fly, brother, fly! ‖ more high, more high!
> Or we shall be belated:
> For slow and slow ‖ that ship will go,
> When the mariner's trance is abated."

The first stanza of hip-hop group Run-D.M.C.'s "My Adidas" (1986) exhibits leonine rhyme in four lines, pairing *sand* and *land, hand* and *command, me* and *be,* and *together* and *forever.* Rakim and Eric B.'s "Juice (Know the Ledge)" (1992) pairs both individual words and phrases, such as *clout* and *about, y'all* and *fall, work with these* and *Hercules,* and *southpaw* and *right jaw.*

▶ **lesbian criticism:** See gay and lesbian criticism.

▶ **lexicography:** The writing of dictionaries, or **lexicons.** The practice of lexicography, which dates back to ancient times in cultures ranging from the Mesopotamian to the Chinese to the Roman, has evolved over time, its focus shifting from the explanation of difficult words in specific disciplines to more general coverage in the sixteenth century, and then to the complex system in place today, in which a host of elements including **etymology,** pronunciation, quotations, spelling, and usage may be included along with the definition of the word.

EXAMPLES: The Chinese *Erya* (third century B.C.) and the Homeric glossary (c. first century A.D.) of Apollonius the Sophist are early examples of lexicography. Influential dictionaries in English include English writer

Samuel Johnson's *Dictionary of the English Language* (1755) and American lexicographer Noah Webster's *An American Dictionary of the English Language* (1828). Simon Winchester's *The Professor and the Madman: A Tale of Murder, Insanity, and the Making of the Oxford English Dictionary* (1999), recounts the colossal undertaking of the *Oxford English Dictionary*, focusing on its editor, a professor named James Murray, and one of its major contributors, Dr. W. C. Minor, a delusional American Civil War veteran committed to the Broadmoor Criminal Lunatic Asylum in England for murder.

▶ **lexicon:** A list or book of words and their corresponding **denotative** meanings; a dictionary. The term may also be used to refer to the vocabulary of a particular **class**, profession, subject, and so on (for example, the lexicon of the upper class, sailing, or literature — as in this glossary).

EXAMPLES: The *Oxford English Dictionary*, first published in 1928 and now available online; *Black's Law Dictionary*, first published in 1891 and now in its eighth edition (2004).

▶ **light ending:** See **feminine ending**.

▶ **light verse:** **Verse** aimed at entertaining the reader, whether through **satiric, witty,** or simply playful humor. Light verse is often brief and is distinguished from other verse by its **tone** rather than by its subject matter. Common types include the **double dactyl, epigram, limerick, nonsense verse,** nursery rhyme, **parody,** and *vers de société*.

EXAMPLES: Ogden Nash's short poem "Reflections on Ice-Breaking" (1945):

> Candy
> Is dandy
> But liquor
> Is quicker.

Dorothy Parker, perhaps best known for her statement "I'd rather have a bottle in front of me than a frontal lobotomy," wrote light verse on a topic usually considered "heavy" in a poem entitled "Résumé" (1926):

> Razors pain you;
> Rivers are damp;
> Acids stain you;
> And drugs cause cramp.
> Guns aren't lawful;
> Nooses give;
> Gas smells awful;
> You might as well live.

Shel Silverstein wrote numerous illustrated collections of light verse including *Where the Sidewalk Ends* (1974), *A Light in the Attic* (1981), and *Runny Babbit: A Billy Sook* (published posthumously in 2005). Examples from *A Light in the Attic* include "Reflection," in which a child looks at his reflection in a puddle of water, sees an "Upside-Down Man," and wonders who is really upside down and right side up; "The Meehoo with an Exactlywatt," a take-off on the "knock, knock, who's there?" jokes; and "The Man in the Iron Pail Mask," which **alludes** to Alexandre Dumas's story *The Man in the Iron Mask* (1846; adapted to film 1998).

Asinine Love Poetry (2005), compiled by the editors of the online journal *asinine poetry*, <www.asininepoetry.com>, is a collection of light verse on the subject of love.

▶ **limerick:** A type of **light verse** consisting of five lines that are composed primarily of **amphibrachs** (˘´˘) or **anapests** (˘˘´) and that exhibit an *aabba* **rhyme scheme** in which the *a* lines are **trimeter** and the *b* lines **dimeter.** The two dimeter lines are sometimes combined into one, generating an **internal rhyme.** The humor in limericks, which are often untitled, anonymous, and composed extemporaneously, frequently crosses over into the bawdy and absurd. Edward Lear, an English writer and illustrator of **nonsense verse,** helped popularize the form with his *A Book of Nonsense* (1846), which contained seventy-two illustrated limericks.

EXAMPLES: The following 1903 limerick by G. K. Chesterton, in which the **meter** is amphibrachic and the first, second, and fifth lines have a **feminine ending:**

Thĕre wás ăn | ŏld scúlptŏr | nămed Phídĭ | ăs
Whŏse knówlĕdge | ŏf árt wăs | ĭnvídĭ | oŭs.
Hĕ cárved Ăph | rŏdítĕ
Wĭthóut ăn | ў níghtĭe—
Whĭch stártlĕd | thĕ púrelў | făstídĭ | oŭs.

Countless off-color limericks have been inspired by a famous one about Nantucket Island, printed in the Princeton *Tiger* in 1924 as follows:

There once was a man from Nantucket,
Who kept all his cash in a bucket,
But his daughter, named Nan,
Ran away with a man,
And as for the bucket, Nantucket.

Some limericks toy humorously with the form itself, as in the following anonymous example:

There was a young man from Peru
Whose limericks stopped at line two.

▶ **limited point of view:** See **point of view.**

▶ **linguistics:** The application of scientific principles to the study of language. Linguistics has several divisions, which include *etymology* (the derivation of words), *semantics* (the meaning of words), **syntax** (the arrangement of words), **morphology** (the study of the form of words and their smallest meaningful parts, called **morphemes**), and **phonology** (the study of basic sounds, called **phonemes**).

▶ **link:** An automated cross-reference in a source document to a target, whether another document or another part of the same document. In **hypertext** systems, such as the World Wide Web, links (also called *hyperlinks* or *jump markers*) permit users to jump within and among linked documents by clicking on the link, which may be displayed as an image or as text. When displayed as text, links are normally distinguished from the surrounding text by the use of underlining and color or by other stylistic elements. Major types of links include *internal links,* the links within a given website; *inbound links,* links from an external source to a given website; and *outbound links,* links from a given website to an external target.

▶ *lisible* (readerly): See **poststructuralism, text.**

▶ **literariness:** A term used by **Russian formalists** and their followers in the **Prague Linguistic Circle** to refer to what distinguishes a literary work from other spoken or written **discourse.** Roman Jakobson, a leading **theorist** of Russian formalism, coined the term in *Recent Russian Poetry* (1921), asserting that "the subject of literary study is not literature, but literariness, that which makes a given verbal work a literary work." Formalists such as Jakobson, Viktor Shklovsky and Jan Mukařovský claimed that literariness requires the **foregrounding** of language, particularly through the use of literary devices, in order to separate, or "estrange," the reader not only from the familiar language of everyday speech but also from the world as ordinarily perceived. For instance, in "Art as Device" (1917), Shklovsky, another leading Russian formalist, argued that "the purpose of art, then, is to lead us to a knowledge of a thing through the organ of sight instead of recognition. By 'estranging' objects and complicating form, the device of art makes perception long and 'laborious.' . . . *Art is a means of experiencing the process of creativity; the artifact itself is quite unimportant.*" Mukařovský, a Czech theorist of the Prague Linguistic Circle, asserted in "Standard Language and Poetic Language" (1932) that "the function of poetic language consists in the maximum foregrounding of the utterance. Foregrounding is the opposite of automization . . . . It is not used in the services of communication but in order to place in the foreground the act of expression, the act of speech itself." By overturning common and expected patterns in language, literariness was seen as freeing readers to experience language and the world in a fresh way.

The concept of literariness has been challenged by a variety of **literary critics,** particularly **postmodernists** and **poststructuralists** who deny that literary **texts** differ from other texts in any special way. Other critics have embraced the concept but defined it differently. French critic Michael Riffaterre, for instance, characterized literariness in *La production du texte (Text Production)* (1979) as the "uniqueness" of the text, which "is always one of a kind." David Miall and Don Kuiken, pioneers in the empirical study of literature, reconceptualized literariness as "the product of a distinctive mode of reading" in "What is Literariness? Three Components of Literary Reading" (1999); analyzing readers' responses to several literary texts, they concluded that "literariness is constituted when stylistic or narrative variations strikingly defamiliarize conventionally understood referents and prompt reinterpretive transformations of a conventional concept or feeling."

▶ **literary criticism:** Reflective, attentive consideration and analysis of a literary work. The term *criticism* comes from the Greek *kritikos,* which refers to the ability to discern or judge. Given the **etymology** of the term, many critics assert that an evaluation of the work is an essential element of literary criticism, though others maintain that examination and analysis are sufficient. In popular parlance, criticism refers to the practice of pointing out faults or shortcomings; as a result, it has a somewhat negative **connotation.** Literary criticism refers to a more balanced analysis. Even when literary critics supplement analysis with appraisal, the merits as well as the faults of a work are discussed in order to arrive at a sound, deliberate assessment. If a critic approves of the work he or she is analyzing, the resulting appraisal may be far from critical, at least in the popular sense of the word.

Many schools or types of literary criticism exist; in fact, some might argue that as many kinds of criticism exist as there are critics, especially given the proliferation of **theories** of criticism in Europe and North America since the 1970s. Some kinds of literary criticism involve close and detailed analysis of the **text,** others the biographical background of the writer or the historical contexts within which the work was written, and still others the reader's subjective response to the work. Each school or type of literary criticism **privileges** some aspect or aspects of the work over others, as well as particular strategies of reading or interpretation.

Types of criticism include **antithetical criticism, archetypal criticism, autobiographical criticism, Chicago school, contextual criticism, cultural criticism, deconstruction, dialectical criticism, dialogic criticism, disability studies, discourse analysis, ecocriticism, expressive criticism, feminist criticism, formalism, gay and lesbian criticism, gender criticism, Geneva School, gynocriticism, historicism, impressionistic criticism, judicial criticism, Jungian criticism, Marxist criticism, mimetic criticism, myth(ic) criticism, the New Criticism, the new historicism, objective criticism, personal criticism, phenomenological criticism, Platonic criticism, postcolonial theory, poststructuralism criticism, practical (applied) criticism, pragmatic criticism, psychoanalytic criticism, psychological criticism, queer theory, reader-response criticism, rhetorical criticism, Russian formalism, structuralist criticism, stylistics,** and **theoretical criticism.**

▶ **literature of sensibility:** A term most commonly used to refer to eighteenth-century literature that emphasized emotional sensitivity and charitable feelings, particularly as manifested in the **sentimental comedy** and the **sentimental novel**. The literature of sensibility, which drew on the thought of philosophers such as Anthony Ashley Cooper, the third earl of Shaftesbury, who asserted the natural benevolence of humankind in *Characteristicks of Men, Manners, Opinions, Times* (1711), arose largely in reaction to two seventeenth-century philosophical currents: Stoic rationalism and English philosopher Thomas Hobbes's characterization of humanity in *Leviathan* (1651) as inherently selfish and self-interested. Sentimental comedies, novels, and poems exalted benevolence, sympathy, and **sensibility** as inherent human traits, depicting situations designed to demonstrate the exquisite sensibility of **characters** as well as to elicit pity, joy, and other emotions from readers. Thus, deathbed scenes, fainting virgins, reformed prostitutes, and blushing brides are common.

While most critics confine the term *literature of sensibility* to sentimental works from the eighteenth century, some use it to refer to any work following in this tradition. What was once celebrated as sensibility is often derided today as **sentimentalism.**

EXAMPLES: Eighteenth-century examples include Laurence Sterne's *A Sentimental Journey* (1768), Henry Mackenzie's *The Man of Feeling* (1771), and Fanny Burney's *Evelina* (1778). A typical passage from *The Man of Feeling* follows:

> Had you seen us, Mr. Harley, when we were turned out of South-hill, I am sure you would have wept at the sight. You remember old Trusty, my shag house-dog; I shall never forget it while I live; the poor creature was blind with age, and could scarce crawl after us to the door; he went however as far as the gooseberry-bush; which you may remember stood on the left side of the yard; he was wont to bask in the sun there; when he had reached that spot, he stopped; we went on: I called to him; he wagged his tail, but did not stir: I called again; he lay down: I whistled, and cried 'Trusty'; he gave a short howl, and died! I could have laid down and died too; but God gave me strength to live for my children.

Movies such as *Old Yeller* (1957), *Terms of Endearment* (1983), and *My Girl* (1991) follow in the tradition of literature of sensibility; many would include *Ghost* (1990) and *Titanic* (1997) as well.

See **sensibility.** See also **Age of Johnson.**

▶ **literature of the absurd:** See **Absurd, the.**

▶ **litotes:** From the Greek for "simple" or "meager," a **trope** that involves making an affirmative point by negating its opposite. For instance, the statement "that's not bad" typically means "that's good." Likewise, to say "he's no liberal" does not literally mean "he is not a liberal," nor does it mean "he is a moderate"; rather, it means "he is conservative," perhaps even very conservative. Litotes, a type of **meiosis,** or *understatement,* often used for **ironic** effect, is a common device in both literature and everyday speech.

EXAMPLES: Aphra Behn used litotes in *Oroonoko* (1688) to stress the great melancholy Prince Oroonoko feels on being invited to return to the Court after the death of his beloved Imoinda: "He obeyed, tho' with no little Reluctancy." Other examples of litotes include "She was nat undergrowe," Geoffrey Chaucer's description of the Prioress in the General Prologue to *The Canterbury Tales* (c. 1387), meaning that she was fat; the Biblical lines "I will multiply them, and they shall not be few; I will make them honoured, and they shall not be small" (Jer. 30:19); and **protagonist** Holden Caulfield's false assertion in J. D. Salinger's *The Catcher in the Rye* (1951): "It isn't very serious. I have this tiny little tumor on the brain."

▶ **local color:** The depiction of the distinctive characteristics (**dialect**, dress, mannerisms, culture, etc.) of a particular region, usually in **prose** writing. Though many writers use local color to lend charm or authenticity to a story, others, particularly **realists**, have used it to develop **character**, such as by depicting the breeding grounds of vice and temptation. **Fiction** in which local color, rather than **plot** or character, is the focus is called *local color writing*.

Local color writing typically involves a rural and often remote **setting** that may feature more prominently in the story than its characters, who may be **stock** or **flat** types rather than fully developed individuals. Much local color writing, especially of the less serious kind, takes the form of sketches and **short stories**, often for magazines with a mass, urban audience, and features idealized, nostalgic, or **sentimental** depictions of rural life. Common **narrative** devices include the use of a **frame story** and a sophisticated **narrator** from the outside world.

Local color writing is sometimes equated with or classified as a type of *regionalism*, writing that focuses on the detailed **representation** of a particular area. Critics who distinguish between the two often treat regionalism as having a broader scope, namely, in incorporating the idea of sectional differences among regions rather than simply focusing on the distinctive characteristics of a particular region.

The use of local color was particularly popular in the United States in the period following the Civil War through the turn of the century. Bret Harte, whose stories depicted frontier California, and Sarah Orne Jewett, who set her works in rural and coastal Maine, played leading roles in the rise of local color writing. Indeed, many women figured prominently in the local color movement, including Mary E. Wilkins Freeman and Harriet Beecher Stowe (New England); Mary N. Murfree (Tennessee); Ruth McEnery Stuart (Arkansas); Alice Dunbar Nelson (Creole New Orleans); and Kate Chopin, who was identified mainly as a local colorist for her representations of Creole life in New Orleans until the (re)discovery of her novel *The Awakening* (1899). Other notable local color writers of the time were George Washington Cable, who portrayed Creole life in Louisiana; Hamlin Garland, who focused on Midwestern farm life; and Joel Chandler

Harris, who based his "Uncle Remus" stories on African-American **folklore** and also wrote other stories about rural Georgia.

EXAMPLES: Harte's short story "The Luck of Roaring Camp" (1868); Stowe's *Oldtown Fireside Stories* (1871); Jewett's short-story collections *Deephaven* (1877) and *The Country of the Pointed Firs* (1896); Cable's novel *The Grandissimes: A Story of Creole Life* (1880); Harris's *Uncle Remus, His Songs and His Sayings: The Folk-Lore of the Old Plantation* (1880), a collection of animal **folk tales** featuring Brer Rabbit. Thomas Nelson Page's *In Ole Virginia: Or, Marse Chan and Other Stories* (1887) is a **classic** of the "plantation tradition" that romanticized slavery; Charles W. Chesnutt's "The Goophered Grapevine" (1887) **satirized** such plantation tales. Twentieth-century poet Robert Frost has also been linked to the local color tradition by an epithet commonly used to describe him: "a poet of New England."

▶ **locution:** In **speech-act theory,** an utterance. British "ordinary-language" philosopher John L. Austin characterized locutions as "full units of speech" in *How to Do Things with Words* (1962).

▶ **locutionary act:** The utterance of a statement; a type of **speech act.** Introducing the term in *How to Do Things with Words* (1962), British "ordinary-language" philosopher John L. Austin defined it as "an act *of* saying something" and characterized it as "roughly equivalent to uttering a certain sentence with a certain sense and reference, which again is roughly equivalent to 'meaning' in the traditional sense." He thus emphasized that a locutionary act "has a *meaning.*"

See **speech-act theory.**

▶ **logocentric, logocentrism:** French theorist Jacques Derrida used the term *logocentric* in *De la grammatologie (of Grammatology)* (1967) and other works to describe and characterize Western thought, language, and culture since the time of Plato, a Greek philosopher of the late fourth century B.C. To understand what Derrida meant by *logocentric,* it is important to know that the root word, *logos* (which in Greek means "word," "speech," and "reason"), has in Western philosophical and theological tradition come to signify law, truth, and even ultimate Truth. The suffix *-centric* is generally used to suggest the **privileged** status of that to which the root refers. Thus, defined narrowly, *logocentric* means centered on and revolving around the word (or speech or reason). More broadly, the term implies a belief in the centrality and, more important, the determinability of ultimate Truth. It is this broader meaning that Derrida used when he characterized and critiqued Western traditions as hung up on the notion that words contain Truth.

It is difficult to disentangle Derrida's use of *logocentric* from his concept of **presence.** (In biblical tradition, *logos* refers to the creating, spoken word of a present God who, "In the beginning," said "Let there be light.") In arguing that the Western conception of language is logocentric, Derrida also argued that it is grounded in "the metaphysics of presence," the tendency to believe that **linguistic** systems are grounded in "ultimate referents" (such as God, some **Platonic** or otherwise foundational "Idea," or deep **etymological** word "roots") that make it possible to identify a correct meaning or meanings for any potential statement that can be made within a given system. Rather than supporting this view of language, however, Derrida argued that there are no ultimate referents and thus that presence is an arbitrary, rather than an inherent or true, foundation for language that cannot guarantee determinable (much less determinate) meaning. In other words, presence no more makes it possible to determine meaning than it makes it possible to select one particular meaning with confidence in its correctness.

According to Derrida, Western *logocentrism* is due in part to Western *phonocentrism,* the tendency to privilege the spoken over the written, that is, to regard speech in positive terms and writing as comparatively negative. Derrida argued that the privileging of speech cannot be disentangled from the privileging of presence. (We write postcards, for instance, when the people with whom we wish to communicate are **absent;** similarly, we read Plato because he cannot speak from beyond the grave.) Just as Derrida debunked logocentrism, so he interrogated the privileged status granted to speech in Western metaphysics and culture.

▶ **long meter (long measure):** A four-line **stanza** typically written in **iambic tetrameter** with an *abab* or *abcb* **rhyme scheme.** Long meter, often abbreviated "L.M.," is often used in **hymns.**

EXAMPLE: The first stanza of the hymn "O God, Beneath Thy Guiding Hand" (1793):

> Ŏ Gód, | bĕneáth | thў guíd | ĭng hánd
> Our exiled parents crossed the sea
> And when they trod the wintry strand,
> With prayer and psalm they worshiped thee.

▶ **loose sentence:** A complex sentence in which an independent clause is followed by one or more other elements; the opposite of a **periodic sentence,** which is not **syntactically** complete before its very end. A loose sentence typically contains independent clauses connected by coordinating conjunctions (*and, or, but*) or an independent clause followed by one or more dependent clauses. Loose sentences are less formal, more conversational, and more common in English than periodic sentences. Works predominantly containing loose sentences usually exhibit **paratactic style.**

EXAMPLES: The following sentence from Eleanor Roosevelt's speech on V-J Day, August 14, 1945, marking the surrender of Japan and thus the end of World War II, is loose:

> Today we have a mixture of emotions, joy that our men are freed of constant danger, hope that those whom we love will soon be home among us, awe at what man's intelligence can compass, and a realization that that intelligence uncontrolled by great spiritual forces, can be man's destruction instead of his salvation.

So are the opening sentences from Khaled Hosseini's *The Kite Runner* (2003):

> I became what I am today at the age of twelve, on a frigid overcast day in the winter of 1975. I remember the precise moment, crouching behind a crumbling mud wall, peeking into the alley near the frozen creek. That was a long time ago, but it's wrong what they say about the past, I've learned, about how you can bury it.

▶ **Lost Generation:** A phrase used to describe the generation of young American writers disillusioned by the senseless death and destruction of World War I. As a group, these writers rejected what they viewed as a materialistic, hypocritical society that falsely espoused puritanical **Victorian** mores; many became expatriates in the 1920s, clustering especially in Paris and London. Bohemian and cosmopolitan, they embraced **modernism** and the *avant-garde.* Most of these expatriates returned in the 1930s, during the social and political upheavals caused by the Depression.

The phrase *Lost Generation* entered literary and popular circles with the publication of Ernest Hemingway's novel *The Sun Also Rises* (1926), which began with an **epigraph** that states, "You are all a lost generation." Hemingway borrowed the phrase from American expatriate writer Gertrude Stein, who had previously remarked to him that "All of you young people who served in the war. You are all a lost generation." Hemingway later declared in *A Moveable Feast* (1964), a **memoir** of his life in Paris, that he considered the phrase to be merely "splendid bombast" and that Stein had picked it up from the owner of a Parisian garage.

Notable writers of the Lost Generation, aside from Hemingway, have traditionally been said to include Sherwood Anderson, Hart Crane, John Dos Passos, and F. Scott Fitzgerald. Important female writers of the era rediscovered by Shari Benstock in *Women of the Left Bank* (1986) include Sylvia Beach, Djuna Barnes, Janet Flanner, and Jean Rhys. Fitzgerald expressed the view of the Lost Generation toward the Great War in *Tender Is the Night* (1933) through his **protagonist** Dick Diver, who says of the Battle of the Somme:

> "This land here cost twenty lives a foot that summer. . . . See that little stream — we could walk to it in two minutes. It took the British a month to walk to it — a whole empire walking very slowly, dying in front and pushing forward behind. And another empire walked very slowly backward a few inches a day, leaving the dead like a million bloody rugs. No Europeans will ever do that again in this generation."

▶ **lyric:** From the Greek for "lyre," originally any **poem** designed to be sung while accompanied by a lyre; now a brief **imaginative** and melodic poem characterized by the fervent but structured expression of the personal thoughts and emotions of a single, **first-person** speaker. Lyrics are non-**narrative** poems; they do not tell a story. During ancient Roman times, poets such as Horace wrote lyrics meant to be read, unaccompanied by music, as remains common today.

The lyric, a popular form of **verse** for millennia in the East and West alike, is one of the oldest, most enduring forms of literary expression in English. Common manifestations include the **ballad, hymn, ode,** and **sonnet.** Today, the plural form of the term (*lyrics*) also refers to the words of any song.

EXAMPLES: Noted lyric poets from across the ages include Sappho (Greece, seventh–sixth century B.C.), Ono no Komachi (Japan, ninth century A.D.), Li Qingzhao (China, twelfth century), Hafez (Persia, fourteenth century), Teresa of Ávila (Spain, sixteenth century), Paul Verlaine (France, nineteenth century), Bengali poet Rabindranath Tagore (India, nineteenth–twentieth centuries), and Czesław Miłosz (Poland, twentieth century). American examples of the **genre** include Ralph Waldo Emerson's "Two Rivers" (1858), Emily Dickinson's "Because I could not stop for Death" (1863), Robert Frost's "Stopping by Woods on a Snowy Evening" (1923), and Sara Teasdale's "Wisdom" (1916), which follows:

> It was a night of early spring,
>   The winter-sleep was scarcely broken;
> Around us shadows and the wind
>   Listened for what was never spoken.
>
> Though half a score of years are gone,
>   Spring comes as sharply now as then —
> But if we had it all to do
>   It would be done the same again.
>
> It was a spring that never came;
>   But we have lived enough to know
> That what we never have, remains;
>   It is the things we have that go.

Mexican poet and essayist Octavio Paz's short poem "Escritura" ("Writing"), from his *Ladera Este* collection (1962–68) — *Yo dibujo estas letras / como el día dibuja sus imágenes / y sopla sobre ellas y no vuelve* — is also a lyric; the English translation follows:

> I draw these letters
> as the day draws its images
> and blows over them
>   and does not return.

M

▶ **madrigal:** A short, polyphonic **lyric** that is written in everyday speech, commonly treats a **pastoral** or amatory **theme**, and is usually sung *a cappella* (i.e., without instrumental accompaniment). The madrigal first arose in fourteenth-century Italy as a poetic and musical form, with the text typically comprised of two or three **tercets** followed by a **couplet** and the music composed for two or three voices. Noted composers included Giovanni da Cascia and Jacopo da Bologna. Subsequently, in the sixteenth century, the madrigal enjoyed a revival in Italy, becoming the main form of **Renaissance** secular music and spreading to England, France, Germany, and Spain. Noted composers included the Franco-Flemish Orlande de Lassus, the Italian Claudio Monteverdi, and Englishmen Thomas Morley and Thomas Weelkes.

Unlike its predecessor, the sixteenth-century madrigal was composed as vocal chamber music, typically for four to six voices with the voice parts sometimes performed or doubled by instruments. Moreover, it showed greater structural freedom poetically, particularly with regard to overall length, line length, and the number and arrangement of **rhymes,** though it still tended to end with a couplet. In England, where the form developed in the **Elizabethan Age** and flourished from about 1590 to the 1620s, madrigals tended to be lighthearted love songs with short, rhyming lines and were generally composed for *a cappella* ensembles of five or six voices. In the early seventeenth century, the madrigal began to decline and soon nearly disappeared, first in Continental Europe and then in England, displaced by opera and the lute-song.

EXAMPLES: Jacopo da Bologna's "Non al suo amante" (c. 1350), which uses a poem by Petrarch (Francesco Petrarca); *Musica Transalpina* (1588), a collection of Italian madrigals translated into English by Nicholas Yonge; Morley's *The Triumphes of Oriana* (1601), a collection of twenty-five madrigals by twenty-three composers in honor of Elizabeth I, each of which ends with the **refrain** "Then sang the shepherds and nymphs of Diana: / Long live fair Oriana." The first madrigal in Morley's collection, composed by Michael East, follows:

> Hence stars, too dim of light,
> You dazzle but the sight,
> You teach to grope by night.
> See here the shepherds' star,
> Excelling you so far,
> Then Phoebus wiped his eyes,
> And Zephyr cleared the skies,
> In sweet accented cries.
> Then sang the shepherds and nymphs of Diana:
> Long live fair Oriana.

▶ **magic(al) realism:** In literature, a mode or **genre** in **prose fiction** often associated with **postmodernism** and characterized by a mixture of **realistic** and **fantastic** elements. Works of magic realism are set in the real world and treat the magical or supernatural as an inherent, even mundane part of reality requiring no explanation. They typically feature complex, tangled **plots**; abrupt chronological shifts and distortions of time; and a wealth of **images, symbols,** and emotional and sensory details. Dreamlike sequences are common, as is incorporation of the **carnivalesque, folklore,** and **myths.** Many magic realist works also address cultural **hybridity** and **postcolonial** themes, exploring the intersection of colonizers and the colonized, rural and urban folk, Western and indigenous peoples. Columbian novelist Gabriel García Márquez's *Cien años de soledad (One Hundred Years of Solitude)* (1967), which proclaims in the first paragraph "[t]he world was so recent that many things lacked names, and in order to indicate them it was necessary to point," is often said to be the prototypical magic realist text.

Notably, the phrase *magic realism,* a translation of the German *magischer Realismus,* was first used with regard to visual art — and with a different meaning. German art critic Franz Roh coined it in his essay "Magic Realism: Post-Expressionism" (1925) to describe the work of certain German and other European painters of the time, which featured hyperrealistic **representations** of figures, objects, and scenes that he viewed as revealing the magic inherent in the everyday. As Roh explained, "[i]t seems to us that this fantastic dreamscape [**expressionism**] has completely vanished and that our real world re-emerges before our eyes — bathed in the clarity of a new day"; the "new style . . . is thoroughly of this world . . . . It employs new techniques that endow all things with a deeper meaning," with "the magic of being."

While the phrase quickly entered literary circles, it came to be associated particularly with Latin-American literature beginning in the late 1940s. Venezuelan writer Arturo Uslar-Pietri, whose novel *Las lanzas coloradas (The Red Lances)* (1931) is sometimes considered an early example of magic realism, first applied it to Latin-American literature in *Letras y hombres de Venezuela (Venezuelan Men and Letters)* (1948); subsequently, Puerto Rican literary critic Ángel Flores treated magic realism as an "authentic" Latin-American form in his essay "Magical Realism in Spanish American Fiction" (1955), writing that the "novelty . . . consisted in the amalgamation of realism and fantasy." Much Latin-American magic realism is also marked by the peoples and practices of indigenous cultures and by the enormous economic, political, and social turmoil in the region.

At the same time, Cuban writer Alejo Carpentier introduced a parallel concept, *lo maravilloso real* (the marvelous real), in the prologue to his novel *El reino de este mundo (The Kingdom of This World)* (1949), which he explained in "Lo barroco y lo real maravilloso" ("The Baroque and the Marvelous Real") (1975) as follows: "The marvelous real that I defend and that is our own marvelous real is encountered in its raw state, latent and omnipresent, in all that is Latin American. Here the strange is commonplace and always was commonplace." Some critics equated Carpentier's concept with magic realism; others, however, following Carpentier's own lead, distinguished the two. For instance, in *Carpentier's Baroque Fiction: Returning Medusa's Gaze* (2004), Steve Wakefield argued that it reflected an interest "in depicting the reality of his native continent as *inherently* marvellous, without recourse to the supernatural."

While primarily associated with Latin America, magic realism has gained popularity worldwide. Major Latin-American practitioners aside from Márquez include Chilean writer Isabel Allende, Guatemalan novelist Miguel Ángel Asturias, and the Argentine writers Jorge Luis Borges and Julio Cortázar. Noted practitioners outside the region include Italo Calvino (Italian), John Fowles (English), Günter Grass (German), Haruki Murakami (Japanese), Toni Morrison (American), Ben Okri (Nigerian), and Salman Rushdie (British-Indian).

FURTHER EXAMPLES: Leslie Marmon Silko's *Ceremony* (1977); Rushdie's *Midnight's Children* (1981); Angela Carter's *Nights at the Circus* (1984); Laura Esquivel's *Como agua para chocolate (Like Water for Chocolate)* (1989); Okri's *The Famished Road* (1991); Yann Martel's *Life of Pi* (2001). The **protagonist** of Ian McEwan's novel *Saturday* (2005), a London neurosurgeon, takes a critical view of "the so-called magical realists," whose works he views as "irksome confections . . . written for adults, not children," musing:

> What were these authors of reputation doing—grown men and women of the twentieth century—granting supernatural powers to their characters? . . . In more than one, heroes and heroines were born with or sprouted wings . . . . Others were granted a magical sense of smell, or tumbled unharmed out of high-flying aircraft. One visionary saw through a pub window his parents as they had been some weeks after his conception, discussing the possibility of aborting him.

The 2001 movie *Amélie*, set in Paris, is imbued with magic realism, incorporating talking lamps, paintings, and photographs as well as a winking statue. Other contemporary examples of magic realism in film include *Gabbeh* (1996); *Being John Malkovich* (1999); *Donnie Darko* (2001); and *Crouching Tiger, Hidden Dragon* (2003), which features martial arts fighters in nineteenth-century China who walk on water, float through treetops, and glide from rooftop to rooftop.

▶ **malapropism:** A form of **catachresis**, or misuse of a word, in which a word similar in sound but different in meaning is used in place of the correct word, often to ludicrous effect. The term is named for Mrs. Malaprop, a **character** in Richard Sheridan's play *The Rivals* (1775), who regularly uses words incorrectly, as when she asserts that she would "by no means wish a daughter of mine to be a progeny [prodigy] of learning." Sheridan may have derived his verbally blundering character's name from the French phrase "*mal à propos*," which roughly translates as "bad for the purpose."

FURTHER EXAMPLES: Mrs. Slipslop's address to Joseph in Henry Fielding's *Joseph Andrews* (1741) is rife with malapropisms: "Do you intend to *result* my passion . . . ? Must you treat me with *ironing?* Barbarous monster! how have I deserved that my passion should be *resulted* and treated with *ironing.* . . . Do you *assinuate* that I am old enough to be your mother?" (emphasis added). The character Rachel, in Barbara Kingsolver's novel *The Poisonwood Bible* (1998), is also wildly malapropistic, referring to her "feminine wilds" and making comments such as "I revert my eyes," "I prefer to remain anomolous," and "we Christians have [a] system of marriage called monotony."

Television characters prone to malapropisms include Archie Bunker, who decreed "Case closed. Ipso fatso," on *All in the Family* (1971–79); Latka, from *Taxi* (1978–83); and Ali G of *Da Ali G Show* (2003–04), who, like Rachel, bungled the word *monogamy* when he ungrammatically inquired, "With men and women, does you think that men should marry only one woman? Does you believe in mahogany?" The former Negro League ballplayer of Ruben Santiago-Hudson's one-man show *Lackawanna Blues* (2001; adapted by HBO 2005) also frequently uses malapropisms, referring to the "Statue of Delivery" and the "Entire State Building" and explaining that he has "de roaches of the liver," for which his doctor wrote him a "description."

▶ **Marxism:** A school of thought founded by Karl Marx, a German philosopher known for works such as *Das Kapital* (*Capital*) (1867) and two works he wrote with fellow philosopher Friedrich Engels, *The German Ideology* (1846) and *The Communist Manifesto* (1848).

Marx believed that historical change was primarily the result of **class** struggle and that the State, for as long as it has existed, has used its power to oppress and exploit the laboring masses for the benefit of a wealthy elite. He thus posited an oppositional relationship between the proletariat (the working class) and the capitalist bourgeoisie (those who own the means of production). In Marx's view, economic factors and the class divisions they reflect and reinforce play a primary role in determining social institutions and actions.

Marx believed that the capitalist-run system would eventually and inevitably break down, due to the chasm of inequalities it engenders between the privileged few and the deprived, overworked many. He thought that a dictatorship of the proletariat would temporarily emerge in the wake of capitalism and ultimately be succeeded by a socialist, classless society without need or use for any such government.

Marx, who was himself a **literary critic,** wrote **theoretically** about the relationship between economics, politics, and the arts. In *The German Ideology,* he and Engels argued that economics provides the **base** of society, from which emerges a **superstructure** consisting of law, politics, philosophy, religion, and art (including literature).

Marx's ideas have had a profound effect upon a range of subsequent thinkers, from political philosophers to literary critics. In all corners of the globe, adherents have greatly expanded on and modified them in various (and sometimes contradictory) ways. For instance, Russian revolutionary Nikolai Lenin and Chinese leader Mao Zedong developed quite different forms of political organization that drew upon the heritage of Marxist thought. Marx's ideas about literature and the other arts have powerfully informed the work of leading critics in Western Europe and the United States as well as in the former Soviet Union. As a result, Marxism has played a distinct and important role not only in the development of governments as different as China's and Cuba's, but also in the development of critical methodologies as different as those we associate with **cultural studies, dialogic criticism, the new historicism,** and **Marxist criticism.** What Marxist approaches to literature have in common is the tendency to view the literary work as the product *of* work, as being ultimately rooted or based in the realm of economics and production.

See also **Marxist criticism.**

▶ **Marxist criticism:** A type of **literary criticism** in which literary works are viewed as the product of work and whose practitioners emphasize the role of **class** and **ideology** in reflecting, propagating, and even challenging the prevailing social order. In light of the rapid reform of Soviet-style communism in the former USSR and throughout Eastern Europe, one might suppose that Marxist literary criticism would have become an **anachronism** in a world turning toward market capitalism. In fact, however, Marxist criticism has persisted. It is, after all, a phenomenon distinct from Soviet and Eastern European communism; Marxist literary analysis originated nearly eighty years before the Bolshevik revolution. Furthermore, since the 1940s, the approach has thrived mainly in the West — not as a form of communist propaganda but rather as a form of critique, a **discourse** for interrogating *all* societies and their **texts.**

Rather than viewing texts as repositories for hidden meanings, Marxist critics view them as material products to be understood in broadly historical terms. In short, literary works are seen as products *of* work (and hence of the realm of production and consumption we call economics). For instance, in *Criticism and Ideology* (1978), Marxist critic Terry Eagleton outlined the complex relationship between the soaring cost of books in the nineteenth century, the growth of lending libraries, the practice of publishing "three-decker" novels, and the changing content of those novels. Other Marxist critics have examined the way in which literary works do identifiable work of their own — work that usually enforces and reinforces the prevailing ideology, the network of **conventions,** values, and opinions to which the majority of people uncritically subscribe.

Marxism began with Karl Marx, the nineteenth-century German philosopher best known for writing *Das Kapital* (*Capital*) (1867), the seminal work of the communist movement. Marx was also the first Marxist literary critic, writing critical essays in the 1830s on writers such as Johann

Wolfgang von Goethe and William Shakespeare (whose **tragic** vision of **Elizabethan** disintegration he praised). Even after Marx met Friedrich Engels in 1843 and began collaborating on overtly political works such as *The German Ideology* (1846) and *The Communist Manifesto* (1848), he maintained a keen interest in literature. He and Engels argued about the poetry of Heinrich Heine, admired Hermann Freiligrath (a poet critical of the German aristocracy), and faulted playwright Ferdinand Lassalle for writing about a reactionary knight in the Peasants' War rather than about more progressive aspects of German history.

As these examples suggest, Marx and Engels seldom thought of **aesthetic** matters as being distinct and independent from politics, economics, and history. In fact, they believed the alienation of the worker in industrialized, capitalist societies had grave consequences for the arts. Mechanized and assembly-line production not only resulted in mass-produced identical products bearing no relation to the people who produced them but also served to "reify" those producers (in essence, to turn them into things themselves). Marx and Engels wondered how such workers could possibly be expected to recognize, produce, or even consume things of beauty.

In *The German Ideology*, Marx and Engels discussed the relationship between the arts, politics, and economics in terms of a general social theory. Economics, they argued, provides the *base*, or infrastructure, of society, from which a *superstructure* consisting of law, politics, philosophy, religion, and art emerges. Although Marx later modified his view of the interplay between base and superstructure, admitting that changes in economics may not be reflected by immediate changes in ethics or literature and that **gaps** sometimes open up between economic forms and those produced by the creative mind, he retained his emphasis on economics and its relationship to superstructural elements of society. Central to Marxism and Marxist literary criticism was and is the following "materialist" concept: superstructural elements such as art owe their existence to consciousness, but consciousness is the product rather than the source of social forms and economic conditions.

Marx and Engels drew upon the early-nineteenth-century German philosopher G. W. F. Hegel's theories about the **dialectical** synthesis of ideas from **theses** and **antitheses.** But they rejected the Hegelian dialectic insofar as it anticipated divine intervention, embracing instead a theory of **dialectical materialism** which envisioned a political revolution that could bring about the secular and material salvation of humanity. They believed that a revolutionary class war (pitting the capitalist class against an antithetical, proletarian class) would lead to the synthesis of a new economic order, new forms of consciousness and belief, and, ultimately, great art.

The revolution anticipated by Marx and Engels did not occur in their century, let alone in their lifetime. When it did occur, in 1917, it did so in a place unimagined by either theorist: Russia, a country long ruled by despotic czars but also home to noted novelists and playwrights, including Anton Chekhov; Alexander Pushkin; Fyodor Dostoyevsky; and Leo Tolstoi, author of *War and Peace* (1864–66) and *Anna Karenina* (1866–67). Perhaps because of its significant literary tradition, Russia produced revolutionaries like Nikolai Lenin, who shared not only Marx's interest in literature but also his belief in its ultimate importance. Examining the relationship between a society undergoing revolution and the literature of its bourgeois past in a series of essays on Tolstoi written between 1908 and 1911, Lenin reasoned that continuing interest in Tolstoi, an important nineteenth-century writer whose views did not always accord with those of the revolutionaries, was justified given the primitive and unenlightened economic order of the society that produced him. Nonetheless, in essays like "Party Organization and Party Literature" (1905), he looked forward to the day in which new artistic forms would be produced by progressive writers with revolutionary political views and agendas.

Leon Trotsky, Lenin's comrade in revolution, took a strong interest in literary matters as well, publishing a book called *Literature and Revolution* (1924) that is still viewed as a **classic** of Marxist literary criticism. Trotsky also worried about the future of Marxist aesthetic theory, responding skeptically to groups like Proletkult, which opposed tolerance toward pre- and nonrevolutionary writers and sought to establish a new, proletarian culture. He warned of the danger of cultural sterility, pointing out that there is no necessary connection between the quality of a literary work and its author's politics.

In 1927, a few years after Lenin's death, Trotsky lost a power struggle with Josef Stalin, a man who asserted that writers should be "engineers of human souls." After Trotsky's expulsion from the Soviet Union, the views of groups like Proletkult and the Left Front of Art (LEF) and theorists such as Nikolai Bukharin and Andrei Zhdanov gained ascendancy. **Socialist realism**, a mode of **representation** characterized by an emphasis on class struggle and the glorification of communism, became the official literary form of the USSR in the 1930s, adopted by the Party Central Committee as well as the First Congress of the Union of Soviet Writers, at which Russian author Maxim Gorky called for writing that would "make labor the principal hero of our books." Under the Stalinist regime, the Soviet literary scene degenerated to the point that the works of writers like Franz Kafka were no longer read, either because they were viewed as **decadent, formalist** experiments or because they "engineered souls" in "nonprogressive" directions. Officially sanctioned works were generally ones in which artistry lagged far behind politics.

Of those critics active in the USSR after the expulsion of Trotsky and the triumph of Stalin, two stand out: Mikhail Bakhtin and Georg Lukács. Many of Bakhtin's essays were written in the 1930s and 1940s but were not translated or published in the West until the 1980s. His work reflects an engagement with the Marxist intellectual tradition as well as an indirect, even hidden, resistance to the Soviet government. Bakhtin viewed language — especially literary texts — in terms of discourses and **dialogues.** A novel written in a society in flux, for instance, might include an official, legitimate discourse, as well as one infiltrated by challenging comments. In *Problems of Dostoyevsky's Poetics* (1929) and *Rabelais and His World* (1940), Bakhtin examined what he called **polyphonic** novels, characterized by many **voices** or discourses. Marxist critics writing in the West have used Bakhtin's theories to decode submerged social critique, especially in **early modern** texts; other critics have used his theories as the basis for a method of literary criticism called **dialogic criticism.** Bakhtin has also influenced modern **cultural criticism,** showing that the conflict between "high" and "low" culture occurs between classic and popular texts as well as between the **dialogic** voices that exist within them and is accentuated in works containing **carnivalesque** elements.

Lukács, a Hungarian who began his career as an "idealist" Hegelian critic and converted to Marxism in 1919, was more flexible in his views than the strident Stalinist Soviet critics of the 1930s and 1940s, as reflected in works such as *The Historical Novel* (1937). He disliked much socialist realism and appreciated prerevolutionary, **realistic novels** that broadly reflected cultural "totalities" and were populated with **characters** representing human "types" of the author's place and time. But like his more censorious contemporaries, he refused to accept nonrevolutionary, **modernist** works like James Joyce's *Ulysses* (1922). He condemned movements like **expressionism** and **Symbolism,** preferring works with content over more **decadent,** experimental works characterized mainly by **form.**

Perhaps because Lukács was the best of the Soviet communists writing Marxist criticism in the 1930s and 1940s, non-Soviet Marxists tended to develop their ideas by publicly opposing his. German dramatist and critic Bertolt Brecht countered Lukács by arguing that art ought to be viewed as a field of production, not as a container of content. Brecht also criticized Lukács for his attempt to enshrine realism at the expense not only of the other "isms" but also of poetry and drama, which Lukács had largely ignored.

Even more outspoken was Brecht's critical champion Walter Benjamin, a German Marxist who, in the 1930s, attacked conventional and traditional literary forms for conveying a stultifying "aura" of culture. In a noted essay, "The Work of Art in the Age of Mechanical Reproduction" (1936), Benjamin praised new art forms ushered in by the age of mechanical reproduction. Forms such as radio and film offered hope, he felt, for liberation from capitalist culture, for they were too new to be part of its ritualistic traditions.

Of all the anti-Lukácsians outside of the USSR who contributed to the development of Marxist criticism, the most important was probably Theodor Adorno, leader since the early 1950s of the Frankfurt school of Marxist criticism. Adorno attacked Lukács for his dogmatic rejection of nonrealist modern literature and for his elevation of content over form and argued that the **interior monologues** of modernist works reflect modern alienation in a way that Marxist criticism ought to find compelling.

Non-Soviet Marxists also took advantage of insights generated by non-Marxist critical theories being developed in post-World War II Europe. Lucien Goldmann, a Romanian critic living in Paris, combined **structuralist** principles with Marx's base-superstructure model in works such as *Le dieu caché* (*The Hidden God*) (1955) in order to show how economics determines the mental structures of social groups, which are reflected in literary texts. French Marxist Louis Althusser drew on the ideas of French **psychoanalytic** theorist Jacques Lacan and Italian communist Antonio Gramsci, who discussed the relationship between ideology and **hegemony,** the pervasive system of assumptions and values that shapes the perception of reality for people in a given culture, in works such as his *Quaderni del carcere* (*Prison Notebooks*) (1929–35). Like Gramsci, Althusser viewed literary works primarily in terms of their relationship to ideology; in "Ideology and Ideological State Apparatuses" (1969), for instance, he associated literature with ideological state apparatuses, which he argued served to reproduce the existing relations of production in a given society and, hence, to ensure that the proletariat remains subordinate to the dominant class.

Subsequently, in *A Theory of Literary Production* (1966), French critic Pierre Macherey further developed Althusser's concept of the relationship between literature and ideology. A realistic novelist, he argued, attempts to produce a unified, coherent text but instead ends up producing a work containing lapses, omissions, and gaps. Why? Because within any ideology there are subjects that cannot be covered, things that cannot be said, contradictory views that aren't recognized as contradictory. Furthermore, works don't simply reflect ideology; they are also "fictions," works of art, products of ideology that offer a world-view.

A follower of Althusser, Macherey is sometimes called a *post-Althusserian Marxist*. Eagleton, too, is often described that way, as is his American contemporary Fredric Jameson. Jameson and Eagleton, both post-Althusserians, are also among the few contemporary Anglo-American critics who have closely followed and significantly developed Marxist thought. Previously, Marxist interpretation in English was limited to the work of a handful of critics who generally eschewed Continental Marxist thinkers like Althusser: Christopher Caudwell, Christopher Hill, Arnold Kettle, E. P. Thompson, and Raymond Williams. Of these, Williams — a critic often associated with **cultural criticism** — was the most influential and perhaps the least Marxist in orientation. He felt that Marxist critics unduly isolated economics from culture; that they undervalued individualism, opting instead to see people as "masses"; and that they had become an elitist group. Williams preferred to talk about "culture" instead of ideology; he argued in works such as *Culture and Society: 1780–1950* (1958) that culture is "lived experience" and, as such, an interconnected set of social properties, all grounded in and influencing history.

Eagleton's *Criticism and Ideology* was in many ways a response to the work of Williams. Eagleton proposed an elaborate theory about how history — in the form of "general," "authorial," and "aesthetic" ideology —

enters texts, which in turn may revivify, open up, or critique those same ideologies, setting in motion a process that may alter history. He showed how
texts by Jane Austen, Matthew Arnold, Charles Dickens, George Eliot,
Joseph Conrad, and T. S. Eliot address **conflicts** at the heart of the ideologies behind them: conflicts between morality and individualism, individualism and social organicism.

In *Marxism and Form* (1971), Jameson took up the question of form and
content, arguing that the former is "but the working out" of the latter "in
the realm of superstructure." In *The Political Unconscious* (1981), he used
what in *Marxism and Form* he had called a **dialectical criticism** — a criticism
aware of its own status as ideology — to synthesize a set of complex arguments out of structuralism and **poststructuralism,** Freud and Lacan, Althusser and Adorno. The fractured state of societies and the isolated condition of individuals, Jameson argued, could be seen as indications that an
unfallen state of "primitive communism" originally existed. History —
which records the subsequent divisions and alienations — limits awareness
of its own contradictions and of that lost, Better State via ideologies and
their manifestation in texts, which essentially contain and repress desire,
especially revolutionary desire, into the **collective unconscious.** In Joseph
Conrad's *Lord Jim* (1900), for instance, the knowledge that governing
classes don't deserve their power is contained and repressed by an ending
that metaphysically blames Nature for Jim's tragedy and that **melodramati-
cally** blames wicked Gentleman Brown. All thought, Jameson concluded, is
ideological, and only through ideological thought that knows itself as such
can we eventually transcend ideology itself.

▶ **masculine ending:** A line of **verse** ending with a **stressed** syllable is said
to have a masculine ending.

EXAMPLE: Each of the alternating **iambic tetrameter** and iambic **trimeter**
lines in the opening **stanza** of Stevie Smith's "Our Bog is Dood" (1950) has
a masculine ending:

> Oŭr Bóg | ĭs dóod, | oŭr Bóg | ĭs dóod,
> Thĕy lísped | ĭn ác | cĕnts míld,
> But when I asked them to explain
> They grew a little wild.
> How do you know your Bog is dood
> My darling little child?

▶ **masculine rhyme:** **Rhyme** involving single, **stressed** syllables. Masculine
rhyme frequently involves single-syllable words, such as *meek/sleek,* but
may also occur in a polysyllabic context, such as *show/below* and
deride/subside, provided the stress is on the final syllable.

EXAMPLE: The old adage "An apple a day keeps the doctor away" includes the masculine — and **internal** — rhyme *day/away.* Masculine rhyme
is common in nursery rhymes, such as "Hickory Dickory Dock," which begins "Hickory dickory dock / The mouse ran up the clock," and "Jack and

Jill," which contains two sets of masculine rhyme in the first **stanza,** *Jill/hill* and *down/crown*. Langston Hughes's poem "Harlem" (1951) contains three masculine rhyme pairs, *sun/run*, *meat/sweet*, and *load/explode*:

> What happens to a dream deferred?
>
> Does it dry up
> like a raisin in the sun?
> Or fester like a sore —
> And then run?
> Does it stink like rotten meat?
> Or crust and sugar over —
> Like a syrupy sweet?
>
> Maybe it just sags
> like a heavy load.
>
> *Or does it explode?*

▶ **mask:** See **masque.**

▶ **masque (mask):** A lavish form of courtly entertainment that flourished in England during the **Elizabethan, Jacobean,** and **Caroline** ages until it was brought to an abrupt halt by the Puritan Revolution in 1642. The masque generally had a very thin **plot** line, typically dealing with **mythological** or **allegorical** figures, which served only to provide a framework (or excuse) for the dancing, music, elaborate costumes, and general spectacle that were its main features. The dancers and speaking **characters** wore masks, hence the name *masque*. Noble or even royal amateurs were the actors and dancers in these productions; commoners were only permitted to perform in the **antimasque,** a **grotesque** or bawdy interlude developed by Ben Jonson, a noted masque writer, as a **foil** to the elegant masque. Many Elizabethan playwrights also used the masque as an element of their popular dramas.

Over time, the masque developed from pure spectacle to spectacle with a more artistic or literary purpose. The essential masque, the early form, placed the greatest emphasis on astounding the eye and ear with its parade of beautiful and fabulous figures and rapidly changing **scenes,** all accompanied by appropriate music. With the development of the antimasque, the literary and dramatic qualities of the performance increased significantly, to the point that poetic effect and significant action became elements of the masque. The masque achieved its greatest height under Jonson and the architect Inigo Jones, who designed the visual aspects (sets, stage machinery, costumes, etc.) for performances of Jonson's plays.

EXAMPLES: John Milton's *Comus* (1634) is a masque. William Shakespeare's *The Tempest* (1610–11) includes a masque in Act 4. Peter Greenaway's movie *Prospero's Books* (1991) also includes a masque.

▶ **maxim:** See **aphorism.** See also **folklore.**

▶ **mechanic form:** See **organic form.**

▶ **medieval:** From the Latin for "middle age," an adjective now used broadly to refer to a period of European history ranging from about the fifth to fifteenth centuries A.D. and alternatively called the *Middle Ages* or, more specifically, to aspects and products of the period. Thus one may refer not only to the *Medieval Period* but also to medieval art, architecture, attitudes, history, literature, philosophy, and theology. The term *Middle Ages* — or its equivalent in languages other than English — was first used during the **Renaissance** by writers who felt more artistic, intellectual, and spiritual affinity with the **classical** world of ancient Greece and Rome than with Europe as it had evolved, after the fall of the Roman Empire, under the control of what we now call the Catholic Church. The term *medieval* (originally spelled *mediaeval*) was not introduced into English until the nineteenth century, a period of heightened interest in the art, history, and thought of the Middle Ages. This interest, exhibited in the work of certain **romantic** poets and furthered by the **Victorian** poets and painters associated with **Pre-Raphaelitism**, came to be called *medievalism.*

There is some disagreement about whether the Medieval Period, or Middle Ages, began in the third, fourth, or fifth century A.D. Most scholars, however, associate its onset with the Roman Empire's collapse, which began in A.D. 410 as tribes of Germanic "Visigoths" advanced southward through Italy and into Rome, and was complete by A.D. 476, when the Emperor Romulus was swept out of power by a German tribal chief named Odoacer. Scholars also debate when the Medieval Period ended. Some pinpoint the year 1453, when Turkish forces conquered Constantinople, triggering the migration of Greek scholars into Western Europe. Others take the more general view that the Middle Ages ended with the rise of the Renaissance, which spread beyond Italy throughout Europe during the fifteenth century. Scholars generally agree, however, that the persistent popular assumption that centuries associated with the Medieval Period can be accurately represented by the phrase *Dark Ages* is misleading at best and grossly inaccurate at worst.

The tribes of Visigoths, or Goths (the source of the word **Gothic**), that defeated the armies of Rome also penetrated westward into Gaul (now France) and Spain. Later, the Goths were themselves defeated by Moorish Africans who invaded Spain in 711 and subsequently introduced sophisticated elements of Arabic civilization throughout Spain and other parts of southern Europe. In the meantime, from Italy northward to Germany — under the influence of a Church that, though centered in Rome, had survived and then thrived following the empire's collapse — medieval societies developed that were anything but barbaric and chaotic, artless and ignorant. The Church successfully conveyed to a diverse group of peoples (many of whom had lived in wandering tribes) the value of a stable moral and civil order.

Notably, the foundations of several modern European nations were laid during medieval times. Charlemagne ("Charles the Great") not only conquered vast areas of what is now France but also set out to organize, educate, and unify the people living in the areas he ruled as King of the Franks beginning in 768 and as Emperor of the West from 800 until his death in 814. In England, a group of noblemen united in 1215 to dilute the power of King John, forcing the autocratic monarch to sign a list of rights and provisions guaranteeing, among other things, that taxes could only be "levied with the consent of a council of prelates and greater barons" and that "no freeman shall be arrested, imprisoned, or deprived of property except by judgment of his equals or the law of the land." This list, known as the Magna Carta, or "Great Charter," limited the power of King John and subsequent English monarchs over their subjects and pointed the way toward more democratic government.

Certain historical developments identified with medieval history were unquestionably uncivilized; bloody Inquisitions designed to root heretics out of the Church are among the reasons the Middle Ages have been labeled "dark." However, chivalric ideals (such as courtesy) and highly "civilized" courtly love traditions and conventions were also developed during the Middle Ages. Furthermore, some of the imperialistic military initiatives, such as the Crusades, led to new markets and some degree of cultural cross-fertilization between Western Europe on the one hand and Arabic, Jewish, and Byzantine civilizations on the other. Perhaps as a result, medieval romances paint a portrait of Western Europe delicately marked by Eastern influences, such as those of the Persian tale.

Medieval literature encompassed a variety of religious and secular works, with verse predominating over prose. Common manifestations of religious literature included exempla, hagiography, hymns, medieval dramas such as miracle plays and mystery plays, and theological treatises. Common secular forms included chronicle plays, courtly love lyrics, epics, fabliaux, lais, medieval romances, and travel literature. Noted medieval works include Roman philosopher Boethius's Consolation of Philosophy (524), written while he was in prison; the Anglo-Saxon epic Beowulf (c. 700); the Middle High German epic poem Niebelungenlied (c. 1200); Icelandic sagas including the Völsunga saga (c. 1270) and Grettis saga (c. 1320); the dream vision Le roman de la rose (The Romance of the Rose), initially composed by Guillaume de Lorris around 1230 and expanded by Jean de Meung around 1270; Dante Alighieri's Divina commedia (The Divine Comedy) (1321); Petrarch's (Francesco Petrarca) sonnets (c. 1350); and Geoffrey Chaucer's The Canterbury Tales (c. 1387). When referring specifically to medieval literature in English, scholars typically divide the Medieval Period into the Old English Period, covering the first half of the fifth century to the Norman conquest of England in 1066, and the Middle English Period, usually said to span the years 1100–1500.

Medieval art showed similar variety, encompassing media ranging from architecture, painting, sculpture, and stained glass to jewelry, metalwork, manuscripts, and tapestries. Noted works include lavishly colored "illuminated" manuscripts produced from the seventh through the fifteenth centuries throughout Europe, including in the British Isles, France, Spain, and the Low Countries; cathedrals such as those at Chartres (France) and Cologne (Germany), begun in the 1100s and 1200s, respectively; the paintings of Giotto, including a fresco cycle in the Arena Chapel at Padua (Italy) portraying scenes from the lives of the Virgin Mary and Jesus Christ (completed c. 1305); and the sculptures of Claus Sluter, such as the *Well of Moses* (1395–1403), a fountain commissioned for a monastery near Dijon (France).

See also **Middle English Period (in English literature), Old English Period (in English literature)**.

▶ **medievalism:** See medieval.

▶ **Medieval Period:** See medieval.

▶ **medieval romance (chivalric romance):** A **narrative**, written in **prose** or **verse** and concerned with adventure, chivalry, and **courtly love;** the first manifestation of the **romance**. Common elements include idealization of the hero, whose identity may be shrouded in mystery; the hero's love for his lady and willingness to do anything she requests; use of the supernatural to generate suspense; and an emphasis on exciting events charged with danger and drama, such as encounters with dragons, jousting tournaments, and magical enchantments. A typical story line might involve a brave young knight who takes up an honorable quest but whose progress is impeded by a variety of **fantastic** obstacles and **antagonists**. Some medieval romances are more religious in story line, **motivation, symbolism,** and **theme** than others; all, however, champion both religious and chivalric ideals, particularly courage, manners, piety, loyalty, honor, and mercy.

The medieval romance arose as a narrative verse form in twelfth-century France before spreading throughout Western Europe. The era of the **epic,** with its emphasis on the heroic (matters associated with tribal warfare), ended with the birth of the romance, which stressed the chivalric (matters associated with courtly traditions). Stories steeped in history and **legend** from four traditions were recycled as subject matter: Celtic **folklore,** especially stories involving Arthurian legend (*Matter of Britain*), to which French works added figures not originally included such as Tristan and Lancelot; stories of Germanic/English **heroes** such as King Horn (*Matter of England*); stories of **classical** times, especially of Troy, Thebes, and Alexander the Great (called the *Matter of Rome*, despite the Greek emphasis); and material involving Charlemagne and his era (*Matter of France*). English medieval romances, which appeared in the thirteenth century, drew on all of these traditions and sometimes also on "Oriental" (Arabian or Persian) legend.

EXAMPLES: Medieval **metrical romances** include Chrétien de Troyes's twelfth-century French romances *Lancelot* and *Perceval,* the anonymous thirteenth-century English romance *King Horn,* Wolfram von Eschenbach's thirteenth-century German romance *Parzifal,* and the anonymous fourteenth-century

English romance *Sir Gawain and the Green Knight.* Sir Thomas Malory's fifteenth-century English medieval romance *Le morte d'Arthur* is an example of prose romance.

▶ **meiosis:** From the Greek for "lessening," a **trope** employing deliberate understatement, usually for **comic, ironic,** or **satiric** effect. Meiosis typically involves characterizing something in a way that, taken literally, minimizes its evident significance or gravity. **Litotes,** a type of meiosis, involves making an affirmative point by negating its opposite.

EXAMPLES: The statement "One nuclear bomb can ruin your whole day," popularized by bumper stickers in the 1980s. Mercutio describes his fatal wound as "a scratch, a scratch" in William Shakespeare's *Romeo and*

A cartoon example of **meosis.** (*From* The Big Book of Hell © *1990 by Matt Groening. All Rights Reserved. Reprinted by permission of Pantheon Books, a division of Random House, Inc., NY. Courtesy of Acme Features Syndicate.*)

Juliet (1596); similarly, the Black Knight in *Monty Python and the Holy Grail* (1975) asserts "'Tis but a scratch" and "I've had worse" after King Arthur chops his left arm off, then says "Just a flesh wound" after the king cuts off his right arm as well.

The passive phrase "mistakes were made" often understates the import of an action or situation, as in the 1987 cartoon on page 292 from Matt Groening's *The Big Book of Hell* (1990). The cartoon, in which the little bunny attempts to distance himself from the mess he created, **alludes** to a political scandal of the mid-1980s, when President Ronald Reagan used the phrase to refer to his administration's involvement in the Iran-Contra arms-for-hostages deal. More recently, GM chairman and CEO Rick Wagoner employed the phrase (in a *Newsweek* interview "Fighting Back," Apr. 10, 2006) in connection with major accounting errors that sparked several federal investigations of the company's accounting practices, as did U.S. President George W. Bush and Attorney General Alberto Gonzales, who in March 2007 used it in connection with the administration's politically motivated dismissal of eight U.S. Attorneys.

▶ **melodrama:** Originally, any **drama** accompanied by music used to enhance the emotional impact and **mood** of the performance (for instance, opera); today, any work that relies on the improbable and sensational for dramatic effect and emotional appeal. Melodramas typically feature implausible **plots** emphasizing romance and thrilling, often violent **action**; **stock** or **flat characters**; extravagant emotion; and a happy ending in which virtue prevails.

Melodrama began to develop as a literary **mode** or **genre** in the late eighteenth century, particularly in France, and became the main theatrical form in Europe and the United States in the nineteenth century. In early-nineteenth-century London, melodramas became increasingly popular as a means of circumventing the Licensing Act of 1737, a law requiring government preapproval of plays and authorizing only the Drury Lane and Covent Garden theaters to present them; as musical entertainments, melodramas could be performed elsewhere — and reduce the threat of censorship.

In the **Victorian Period**, melodrama came to emphasize the **conflict** between pure good and evil, pitting **heroes** and **heroines** of impeccable morality against thoroughly despicable **villains** engaged in malevolent **intrigue**. Romantic **plots** twisted by a scheming villain were typical, as were unbelievably happy endings in which **poetic justice** required that evil be punished and good rewarded.

Today, *melodrama* and *melodramatic* are generally used pejoratively.

EXAMPLES: Jean-Jacques Rousseau's *Pygmalion* (1762; first performed 1770); Thomas Holcroft's *A Tale of Mystery* (1802), often considered the first English melodrama; Alexandre Dumas's *The Count of Monte Cristo* (1844); Dion Boucicault's *The Corsican Brothers: A Dramatic Romance* (1852); Harriet Beecher Stowe's *Uncle Tom's Cabin* (1852).

Although Charles Dickens poked fun at "modern melodramas" in *Oliver Twist* (1837), contemporary critics would say that his novel is itself a Victorian melodrama, thanks to scenes like the one in which Oliver finishes his gruel, extends his empty bowl to the workhouse master, and says, "Please, sir, I want some more." Jean Cocteau's play *Les parents terribles* (*Intimate Relations*) (1938) simultaneously exemplifies and **parodies** the excesses of melodramatic **convention.**

The television series *Lassie* (1954–74) was a long-running canine melodrama. Examples of contemporary melodramas include most made-for-TV movies; Spanish-language *telenovelas;* and Danielle Steel's novels, such as *Palomino* (1981) and *H.R.H.* (2006), which typically feature an embattled, faultless heroine, improbable plot twists that provoke **stock responses** of anger and compassion from the reader, and a traditionally happy ending involving marriage and the birth of a child.

▶ **memoir:** A **narrative, nonfiction** account typically written by an individual that depicts things, persons, or events he or she has known or experienced. Memoirs combine elements of **autobiography** and **biography** but are nonetheless distinguishable from both of these **genres** in scope and focus. Unlike autobiographies and biographies, both of which typically cover an individual's life (at least up to the point of writing), memoirs often cover a much shorter or longer timespan, addressing a particularly important or memorable period in the writer's life or extending back into the past, for instance by recounting family history. Memoirs further differ from autobiographies, which concentrate on the writer's unfolding life and character, in their degree of outward focus and from biographies, which are typically the product of extensive research, in their focus on **subjective,** personal recollection.

Some **novels** purport to be or to include the memoirs of **characters** or other **fictional** persons whose writings have been discovered, recorded, or otherwise preserved.

EXAMPLES: William Godwin's *Memoirs of Mary Wollstonecraft* (1798) (a memoir about the life and loss of Wollstonecraft, author of *A Vindication of the Rights of Woman* [1792], by her anarchist husband); Władysław Szpilman's *Śmierć Miasta (Death of a City)* (1946; first published in English as *The Pianist* in 1999 and adapted to film in 2002) (a Holocaust memoir describing the German occupation of Warsaw in World War II and how Szpilman, a Jewish classical pianist, survived); John Edgar Wideman's *Brothers and Keepers* (1984) (a memoir exploring how Wideman and his brother Robby came to lead such different lives, Wideman as an accomplished novelist and Robby as a convict jailed for life); Jung Chang's *Wild Swans: Three Daughters of China* (1991) (an **epic** account of three generations of Chang family women); Frank McCourt's *Angela's Ashes* (1996) (an account of the McCourt family — especially McCourt's mother, Angela — and of growing up poor in Ireland); James McBride's *The Color of Water* (1996) (a book that focuses on McBride's mother, a Polish Jew who married a black Baptist minister and raised twelve children); Joan Didion's *The Year of Magical Thinking* (2005) (an account of Didion's experience with grief in the year following her husband's sudden death from a heart attack, as her daughter struggled with a life-threatening illness herself); and Mukhtar Mai's *Déshonorée (In the Name of Homor)* (2006) (an account, authored in collaboration with Marie-Thérèse Cuny, of Mai's experience as a woman in Pakistan subjected to gang-rape and her subsequent efforts to obtain justice and promote education and women's rights). That the boundary between memoirs, biographies, and autobiographies can be blurry is demonstrated by works such as *The Color of Water* and *Angela's Ashes,* which have also been categorized, respectively, as biography and autobiography.

Arthur Golden's *Memoirs of a Geisha* (1997; adapted to film 2005), a **historical novel** that purports to be a memoir, includes a fictive "Translator's Note" by one Jakob Haarhuis informing the reader that Haarhuis has been granted permission to record the memoirs of a renowned geisha known as Sayuri and opining that "[a] memoir provides a record not so much of the memoirist as of the memoirist's world. It must differ from biography in that a memoirist can never achieve the perspective that a biographer possesses as a matter of course. Autobiography, if there really is such a thing, is like asking a rabbit to tell us what he looks like hopping through the grasses of the field. How would he know?"

James Frey's *A Million Little Pieces* (2003), marketed as a memoir, ignited both outrage and discussion about what constitutes a memoir when The Smoking Gun website charged in "A Million Little Lies" (Jan. 8, 2006) that Frey had "wholly fabricated or wildly embellished details of his purported criminal career, jail terms, and status as an outlaw" and "invented a role for himself in a deadly train accident that cost the lives of two female high school students." Frey subsequently apologized for fabricating parts of the book and for misrepresenting himself, and future editions of the book will contain a corresponding note to the reader.

▶ **Menippean satire:** A type of **satire** that often blends **prose** with **verse** in a loose **narrative** framework, named for the third-century B.C. Greek Cynic philosopher Menippus. Menippean satire is also called *Varronian satire* for the first-century B.C. Roman practitioner Marcus Terentius Varro.

Menippean satires frequently feaure banquets or other **settings** in which **characters** engage in protracted and ridiculous intellectual debates. **Characterization** is subordinated to the attitudes or ideas the satirist seeks to confront, so characters tend to be **flat** rather than **round, caricatures** serving primarily to represent particular viewpoints. Focusing on Menippean satire's philosophic **discourse, archetypal critic** Northrop Frye asserted in *The Anatomy of Criticism* (1957) that the **genre,** at "its most concentrated," presents "a vision of the world in terms of a single intellectual pattern." By contrast, in *Menippean Satire Reconsidered* (2005), theorist Howard Weinbrot argued that its "dominant thrust is to resist or protest events in a dangerous world," characterizing it as "a form that uses at least two other genres, languages, cultures, or changes of voice to oppose a dangerous, false, or specious and threatening orthodoxy," whether in "severe" or "muted" **tones.**

EXAMPLES: *Apocolocyntosis divi Claudii (The Pumpkinification of the Divine Claudius),* generally attributed to first-century A.D. Roman writer Seneca, ridiculing the deification of the emperor upon his death; the *Satyre Ménippée* (1594), an anonymous pamphlet written by supporters of Henry of Navarre's claim to the French throne against their opponents, the conservative Catholic League; Robert Burton's *Anatomy of Melancholy* (1621), written as an exhaustive medical analysis of melancholy; Lewis Carroll's *Alice's Adventures in Wonderland* (1865) and *Through the Looking Glass* (1872). Citing Frye's description of Menippean satire as "deal[ing] less with people as such than with mental attitudes," film critic Stuart Klawans classified Spike Lee's *Bamboozled* (2000) as a Menippean satire in his review in *The Nation* (Nov. 6, 2000).

▶ **metafiction:** Self-reflexive **fiction** that examines the nature and status of fiction itself and often seeks to test fiction as a **form.** (As a word, *metafiction* means something like "fiction about fiction.") The term, coined by American writer and critic William H. Gass in "Philosophy and the Form of Fiction" (1970), was popularized by American literary critic Robert Scholes, who characterized it in his essay "Metafiction" (1970) as "assimilat[ing] all the perspectives of criticism into the fictional process itself" and "tend[ing] toward brevity because it attempts, among other things, to assault or transcend the laws of fiction." Subsequent critics have tended either to emphasize self-awareness as key to metafiction or to characterize it in connection with **literary criticism.** For instance, in *Metafiction: The Theory and Practice of Self-Conscious Fiction* (1984), theorist Patricia Waugh described metafiction as "fictional writing which self-consciously and systematically draws attention to its status as an artifact in order to pose questions about the relationship between fiction and reality"; Mark Currie, by contrast, described it in *Metafiction* (1995) as "writing which places itself on the border between fiction and criticism, and which takes that border as its subject."

Most metafictions cannot be easily classified as **realism** or **romance** and in fact flout the rules and **conventions** of these **genres.** Common techniques include writing about someone who is writing or reading a story, making the **author** a **character** in the **narrative,** making characters aware of their status as such, incorporating another piece of writing within the narrative, and directly addressing the reader. Metafiction is heavily associated with — but not limited to — **postmodernist** works.

EXAMPLES: Miguel de Cervantes's *Don Quixote* (part 1, 1605; part 2, 1615); Laurence Sterne's *Tristram Shandy* (9 vols.; 1759–67); John Barth's *Lost in the Funhouse* (1967); John Fowles's *The French Lieutenant's Woman* (1969); Yasutaka Tsutsui's *Samba of Escape and Pursuit* (1971);

Umberto Eco's *Il nome della rosa* (*The Name of the Rose*) (1980); and Salman Rushdie's *The Moor's Last Sigh* (1995). Fowles's *Mantissa* (1982) is a metafictional **parody** of metaficiton.

Nathaniel Hawthorne's "Feathertop" (1852), in which a witch transforms a scarecrow into a man, contains the metafictional commentary: "Shall I confess the truth? At its present point of vivification, the scarecrow reminds me of some of the lukewarm and abortive characters, composed of heterogeneous materials, used for the thousandth time, and never worth using, with which romance writers (and myself, no doubt, among the rest) have so overpeopled the world of fiction." Vladimir Nabokov's novel *Pale Fire* (1962) consists of a 999-line poem written by a fictional poet, John Francis Shade, and accompanied by a 200-page commentary written by his equally fictional friend Charles Kinbote, who advises the reader in a foreward to consult his commentary and index first since "without my notes Shade's text simply has no human reality at all." Haruki Murakami's *The Wind-Up Bird Chronicles* (1994–95) contains a chapter titled "No Good News in This Chapter." Michael Faber's *The Crimson Petal and the White* (2002) features characters who are writing books of their own.

▶**metaphor:** From the Greek for "to transfer," a **figure of speech** (more specifically a **trope**) that associates two distinct things without using a connective word to link the **vehicle** and the **tenor**. Metaphor is distinguished from **simile,** another trope that associates two distinct things by using a connector such as *like* or *as*. To say "That child is a mouse" is to use a metaphor, whereas to say "That child is like a mouse" is to use a simile. In either case, the mouse is the vehicle, the **image** being used to represent the child, which is the tenor, or subject of the figure.

Theorists ranging from the fourth-century B.C. Greek philosopher Aristotle to the twentieth-century English literary critic I. A. Richards have argued that metaphors equate the vehicle with the tenor instead of simply comparing the two. This identification of vehicle and tenor can provide both linguistic punch and enhanced meaning. For instance, by saying "Last night I plowed through a book" rather than "Last night I read a book," you convey not only *that* you read a book but also *how* you read it, for to read a book in the way that a plow rips through earth is surely to read in a relentless, unreflective way. Note that, in the sentence above, a new metaphor — "rips through" — has been used to explain an old one, demonstrating just how thick (another metaphor) language is with metaphors.

Metaphors may be classified as *direct* or *implied*. A direct metaphor, such as "That child is a mouse," expressly identifies both tenor and vehicle. An implied metaphor, by contrast, specifies only the vehicle, leaving the tenor to be inferred from the context of the sentence or passage. For instance, in the sentence "Last night I plowed through a book," the tenor — the act of reading — is implied. A *mixed metaphor* exists when multiple, very different — and sometimes incongruous — vehicles are used to represent the same tenor. In his essay "Politics and the English Language"

(1946), George Orwell gave as an example of mixed metaphor the sentence "The fascist octopus has sung its swan song."

Metaphors may also be classified as *living, dead,* or *dormant.* A **dead metaphor,** also called a *frozen metaphor,* is a word or phrase that is no longer recognized as a metaphor because it has become so familiar. A **dormant metaphor** is a word or phrase in the process of dying as a metaphor.

Traditionally, metaphor has been viewed as the most significant of the five principal tropes, the others being simile, **metonymy, personification,** and **synecdoche.**

FURTHER EXAMPLES: Common legal metaphors include "black-letter law," calling a long-standing constitutional principle a "fixed star," and seeking to "square" judicial precedents. **Victorian** poet Matthew Arnold rather obviously makes the sea a metaphor for religious faith in his poem "Dover Beach" (1867):

> The Sea of Faith
> Was once, too, at the full, and round earth's shore. . . .

Modernist poet D. H. Lawrence uses metaphor less obtrusively in his poem "Cypresses" (1923), in which the tall, thin, blackish-green trees so familiar in European paintings are metaphorically transformed into "supple, brooding, softly-swaying pillars of dark flame." In John Updike's novel Rabbit, Run (1960), metaphors reveal the anxieties and obsessions of protagonist Henry "Rabbit" Angstrom, who thinks of his car as "a sheath for the knife of himself" and of Chinese food as "Candy. Heaped on a smoking breast of rice." In Carrie Fisher's Postcards from the Edge (1987), the protagonist is told that

> "In India they say that the body is the envelope of the spirit, and the spirit, I guess, is essentially who you are. Well, we live in a city of envelopes. The thing that's terrific about you is that *you* are a *letter.* I mean, it takes a letter to know a letter, and I can see we're really two letters in a town of envelopes. . . ."

In *We Wish to Inform You That Tomorrow We Will Be Killed with Our Families* (1998), an account by journalist Philip Gourevitch of the 1994 Rwandan genocide in which 800,000 minority Tutsis were killed in three months by the Hutu majority, a dispirited American military intelligence officer tells Gourevitch, "Do you know what genocide is? A cheese sandwich. Write it down. Genocide is a cheese sandwich." Puzzled, Gourevitch asks for an explanation, and the officer replies, referring to the apparent lack of international interest in or response to the killings, "What does anyone care about a cheese sandwich?" Asking Gourevitch whether he has ever heard of the Genocide Convention, the officer concludes, "That convention makes a nice wrapping for a cheese sandwich."

Tom Petty's song title "Love Is a Long, Long Road" (1989) is metaphorical, as is the Rolling Stones' "She's So Cold" (1980), in which a reference to a bleeding volcano mixes two vehicles (wound and eruption) to represent one tenor (emotional overflow). Rapper Mos Def used mining metaphors in the first verse of "Travellin' Man" (1998) to discuss **rhyming,** comparing the search for the perfect rhyme to coal mining and finding a diamond.

See **metonymy** for a discussion of the relationship between metaphor and metonymy.

▶ **metaphysical conceit:** A type of **conceit** most commonly associated with seventeenth-century **metaphysical poetry.** The metaphysical conceit involves the use of **paradox, imagery** drawn from arcane sources, and an original and usually complex comparison between two highly dissimilar things. Its originality often derives from the new or startling use of ordinary or esoteric materials. A single metaphysical conceit may function as the controlling **image** for an entire poem.

After the seventeenth century, the metaphysical conceit fell into disuse. It regained popularity in the twentieth century, however, thanks to the revival of interest in the metaphysical poets for their intellectualism and psychological analysis. Scottish literary critic H. J. C. Grierson, poet T. S. Eliot, and **the New Critics** were largely responsible for this revaluation.

EXAMPLE: The following comparison between lovers' souls and a compass in John Donne's "A Valediction: Forbidding Mourning" (1640), a poem about lovers parting:

> If they be two, they are two so
>   As stiff twin compasses are two;
> Thy soul, the fixed foot, makes no show
>   To move, but doth, if th' other do.
>
> And though it in the center sit,
>   Yet when the other far doth roam,
> It leans and hearkens after it,
>   And grows erect, as that comes home.

▶ **metaphysical poets:** A group of seventeenth-century English poets who wrote **lyrics,** often in the form of an argument, characterized by their analytical approach, originality, **wit,** and intellectual **tone.** The metaphysical poets were linked less by a common worldview than by a **style** or **mode** of writing stemming from their reaction against idealized **Elizabethan** love poetry. Common elements included the use of colloquial language; rough or irregular **rhythmic** patterns; and the **metaphysical conceit,** an elaborate, original comparison between two highly dissimilar things that presents the esoteric or commonplace in an unfamiliar way. Poets widely considered part of the group include John Donne, the leading figure; John Cleveland; Abraham Cowley; Richard Crashaw; George Herbert; Andrew Marvell; Thomas Traherne; and Henry Vaughan.

The term *metaphysical* is something of a misnomer, since the metaphysical poets tended to be more concerned with how to regard God and women than the essence of reality. Moreover, as initially used, the term was critical or even derogatory. **Neoclassical** writer John Dryden, the most noted critic of the **Restoration Age,** disparaged Donne's poetry in "A Discourse concerning the Original and Progress of Satire" (1693), writing that he "affects the metaphysics . . . in his amorous verse, where nature only should reign; and perplexes the minds of the fair sex with nice speculations of philosophy, when he should engage their hearts." Subsequently, neoclassical writer and critic Samuel Johnson applied the term *metaphysical* in *Life of Cowley* (in *Lives of the Poets* [1779–81]) to the broader group of poets, criticizing their use of wit: "The most heterogeneous ideas are yoked by violence together; nature and art are ransacked for illustrations, comparisons, and allusions; their learning instructs, and their subtlety surprises; but the reader commonly thinks his improvement dearly bought."

Following a long period of critical disregard and obscurity, interest in the metaphysical poets was revived in the twentieth century with the publication of Scottish literary critic H. J. C. Grierson's anthology *Metaphysical Lyrics and Poems of the Seventeenth Century: Donne to Butler* (1921) and poet T. S. Eliot's essay "The Metaphysical Poets" (1921), in which Eliot contrasted what he regarded as the unified poetic sensibility of the metaphysical poets with the **dissociation of sensibility,** or divergence of thought and feeling, that he claimed subsequently emerged in English literature.

EXAMPLE: Donne's "The Dissolution" (published posthumously in *Songs and Sonnets* [1633]), which ends by comparing two souls with two bullets:

SHE's dead; and all which die
To their first elements resolve;
And we were mutual elements to us,
And made of one another.
My body then doth hers involve,
And those things whereof I consist hereby
In me abundant grow, and burdenous,
And nourish not, but smother.
My fire of passion, sighs of air,
Water of tears, and earthly sad despair,
Which my materials be,
But near worn out by love's security,
She, to my loss, doth by her death repair.
And I might live long wretched so,
But that my fire doth with my fuel grow.
Now, as those active kings
Whose foreign conquest treasure brings,
Receive more, and spend more, and soonest break,
This — which I am amazed that I can speak —
This death, hath with my store
My use increased.
And so my soul, more earnestly released,

Will outstrip hers; as bullets flown before
A latter bullet may o'ertake, the powder being more.

▶ **meter (metre):** The more or less regular **rhythmic** pattern of **stressed** and unstressed syllables in **verse.** Four basic types of meter exist: (1) **quantitative,** which is based on the amount of time it takes to pronounce a particular syllable (long or short) in a poetic line (standard in Sanskrit and **classical** Greek and Roman verse, but rare in English due to the strongly accented nature of English and the difficulty of determining the duration of its syllables); (2) *accentual,* which is based on the number of stressed syllables per line (typical of Germanic verse, Old English verse included); (3) *syllabic,* which is based on the total number of syllables per line (common in Japanese and Romance-language verse but fairly uncommon in English); and (4) **accentual-syllabic,** in which both the total number of syllables and the number of stressed and unstressed syllables are relatively consistent from line to line (standard in English).

Meter is typically described by the dominant type of **foot,** the rhythmic unit of a line of verse; the number of feet per line; or a combination of these two factors. Standard English feet include the **iamb** (˘ ´), **trochee** (´ ˘), **anapest** (˘˘ ´), **dactyl** (´ ˘˘), **spondee** (´ ´), and **pyrrhic** (˘ ˘). **Light verse** excepted, few poems are written using only one type of foot — poets generally vary the metrical pattern to avoid sounding singsongy or like a metronome — so meter is identified based on the prevailing foot. Standard English lines range from one to eight feet per line and include **monometer, dimeter, trimeter, tetrameter, pentameter, hexameter, heptameter,** and **octameter** (though monometer and octameter are rare). Common metrical combinations in English include iambic pentameter, iambic tetrameter, and trochaic tetrameter. Additional syllables, whether stressed or unstressed, exceeding the meter of a line of verse are called *extrametrical.*

▶ **metonymy:** From the Greek for "change of name," a **figure of speech** (more specifically a **trope**) in which one thing is **represented** by another that is commonly and often physically associated with it. In metonymy, the **vehicle** (the **image** used to represent something else) substitutes for the **tenor** (the thing being represented). Metonymy is distinguished from **synecdoche,** a trope in which a part of something is used to represent the whole (or, occasionally, the whole is used to represent a part). Referring to someone's handwriting as his or her "hand," or calling a monarch "the crown," involves metonymy, whereas referring to a boat as a "sail" involves synecdoche.

Certain **structuralists,** such as Roman Jakobson (e.g., *Fundamentals of Language,* coauthored with Morris Halle [1956]), have emphasized the difference between metonymy and **metaphor,** a trope in which two distinct things are associated or equated (for example, silence and gold in the phrase "silence is golden"). Such theorists argue that metonymy entails a contiguous association between tenor and vehicle, whereas metaphor involves a perceived similarity.

Other contemporary critics, particularly those associated with **deconstruction,** deny that metonymy involves an intrinsic association between vehicle and tenor. Deconstructors, who maintain that *all* figuration is arbitrary, contend that the vehicles of metonyms and metaphors alike are arbitrarily (rather than intrinsically) associated with their tenors. For instance, they would say that there is no special relationship between crowns and monarchs; it's just that crowns traditionally sit on monarchs' heads and not on the heads of university professors. In addition, deconstructors including Paul de Man and J. Hillis Miller, have questioned the **privilege** that structuralists grant to metaphor — commonly viewed as the most significant of the five principle tropes — and have challenged the metaphor / metonymy distinction or "opposition," suggesting that all metaphors are really metonyms.

FURTHER EXAMPLES: The opening line of the Pledge of Allegiance, "I pledge allegiance to the flag," exhibits metonymy, given that the flag is used to represent the United States of America. "The pen is mightier than the sword," an **aphorism** from Edward Bulwer-Lytton's play *Richelieu* (1839), metonymically uses "pen" to represent the power of writing and "sword" to represent military force. The first sentence of George Eliot's *Adam Bede* (1859), in which a "drop of ink" represents the **author's** words, similarly involves metonymy:

> With this drop of ink at the end of my pen, I will show you the roomy workshop of Mr. Jonathan Burge, carpenter and builder, in the village of Hayslope, as it appeared on the eighteenth of June, in the year of our Lord 1799.

Likewise, in Joseph Conrad's *Lord Jim* (1900), the alcoholic chief engineer of the ill-fated ship *Patna* is said to have been "shut . . . up with a supply of bottles in an upstairs room" of "Mariani's billiard-room and grog shop." Here, "bottles" is a metonym for "booze," for what the engineer is really "shut up with" is a supply of "grog," which is stored in bottles in most cultures.

In Shirley Hazzard's *The Transit of Venus* (1980), a **character** remarks, "Paul Ivory is marrying that castle," by which he means that Paul — engaged to a daughter of an English lord — is marrying neither a building nor a woman but, rather, the British aristocracy, with all the rights and liabilities that pertain.

▶ **metre:** See **meter.**

▶ **metrical accent:** See **accent.**

▶ **metrical romance:** A **romance** composed in **verse.** The term is sometimes associated specifically with verse romances of the **Middle Ages,** perhaps because the first metrical romances were **medieval romances,** which arose in twelfth-century France and then spread throughout Western Europe. More broadly defined, however, the metrical romance persisted into the nineteenth century, when it was eclipsed by romances written in **prose.**

EXAMPLES: The anonymous fourteenth-century English medieval romance *Sir Gawain and the Green Knight*; George Gordon, Lord Byron's *The Giaour* (1813).

▶ **metrics:** The study of **rhythmic** patterns in **verse.** Metrics is sometimes used synonymously with **prosody** but is better defined as a branch of prosody.

▶ **Middle Ages:** See **medieval, Middle English Period (in English literature).**

▶ **Middle English Period (in English literature):** A period in English literary history often said to span the years 1100–1500 but sometimes dated to 1066, the year of the Norman (French) conquest of England. The Middle English Period was punctuated by war, including the four Crusades (late eleventh–early thirteenth centuries), the French-English conflicts during the Hundred Years' War (1337–1453), and the civil war known as the War of the Roses (1455–85), but also encompassed the signing of the Magna Carta (1215), which limited the power of the monarchy, and the introduction of printing into England by William Caxton in the 1470s. It is often divided into two parts: an Anglo-Norman phase particularly dominated by French influence and ending around 1300 or 1350, and a later phase in which Middle English prevailed. Much of the literature of the period was anonymous; much was religious in nature, particularly in **drama,** and forms such as **hagiography,** sermons making use of **exempla,** and devotional manuals were also popular. But secular **genres** also thrived, ranging from **ballads, legends,** and **tales** to chronicles (histories), **dream visions,** and **medieval romances.**

During the Anglo-Norman phase of the Middle English Period, a transitional form of English, bridging **Old English** and Middle English, competed with Anglo-Norman, a **dialect** of French. Thus, Middle English literature cannot properly be said to have existed before 1200. Moreover, scholarly works of the Anglo-Norman phase were often written in Latin, which was also the language of the Church, and works of "high" literature were written in Anglo-Norman, the language of the royal court and aristocracy. For instance, Geoffrey of Monmouth's prose chronicle *Historia regum Britanniae* (*History of the Kings of Britain*) (c. 1135–39), which included legends of the Arthurian court, was written in Latin, and Marie de France's *lais* (c. 1160–78), **narrative** poems that drew on Celtic **folklore,** were composed in Anglo-Norman. The native English vernacular, by contrast, surfaced primarily in popular works, including drama; **folk** literature; **lyrics,** such as the mid-thirteenth-century song "Sumer Is Icumen In" ("Summer Has Arrived"); and **metrical romances,** such as *King Horn* (thirteenth century) and *Havelok the Dane* (c. 1300).

Middle English verse drew on both foreign and native literary forms and traditions. Layamon's *Brut* (c. 1205), an early example, is a verse chronicle based on an Anglo-Norman version of Geoffrey's *Historia.* "The Owl and the Nightingale," a poem from the twelfth or thirteenth century, employed a French form, the *débat,* which featured a debate between two **characters.** In the thirteenth and fourteenth centuries, poets imitating Marie de France and writing in Middle English developed the **Breton lay,** which drew on **classical** and Oriental lore as well as Celtic **themes.** In the latter half of the fourteenth century, a revival of verse written in **alliterative meter,** as was common in Old English literature, produced works including the dream vision *Pearl* and medieval romance *Sir Gawain and the Green Knight,* both attributed to the same, anonymous poet, and William Langland's dream vision *Piers Plowman* (c. 1362–95). At the same time, Middle English poetry flourished in different **dialects.** For instance, each of the aforementioned alliterative poems was written in the West Midlands dialect, whereas Geoffrey Chaucer's *Canterbury Tales* (c. 1387) was written in the East Midlands dialect. Chaucer, who was influenced heavily by Italian poets, particularly Boccaccio, and who experimented with a variety of genres and **end-rhymed** verse forms including **rhyme royal,** is also credited with the first efforts at humor based on dialect, particularly in the *Reeve's Tale.* Other noted works include John Gower's *Confessio Amantis, or, Tales of the Seven Deadly Sins* (1386–90), concerning **courtly love,** and James I's dream vision in rhyme royal, *The Kingis Quair* (*The King's Book*) (c. 1424).

Drama also began to develop in the Middle English Period. **Miracle plays** and **mystery plays,** forms of religious drama that arose within the Christian Church as dramatized parts of the liturgy, were subsequently sponsored by towns and religious and trade guilds, which often staged productions on festival days. **Morality plays,** which arose in the second half of the period and used **allegory** to make a moral point, portrayed the quest for salvation, featuring a **protagonist** who represented humanity as well as a cast of other **characters** vying for the protagonist's soul. The **interlude,** a transitional form between religious and secular drama, arose toward the end of the Middle English Period.

In prose, Middle English came into its own in the latter half of the period and was the vehicle of the earliest known efforts of women writers in English. Noted religious works include *Ancrene Wisse* (c. 1200), a guide for anchoresses (female religious recluses); the fourteenth-century prose of **mystic** Richard Rolle, such as *The Form of Perfect Living,* which also offered advice to an anchoress; the "Wycliffe Bible" (c. 1380–82), the first complete translation of the Bible into English, led by theologian John Wycliffe; the *Showings* of female religious recluse Julian of Norwich (c. 1393); and the spiritual **autobiography** of Margery Kempe (c. 1436–38), recorded by two scribes and now known as *The Book of Margery Kempe.* Secular works include the correspondence of the landowning Paston family of Norfolk, England, commonly referred to as the "Paston Letters" (1422–1509), and Sir Thomas Malory's medieval romance *Le morte d'Arthur,* an encyclopedic synthesis of almost three hundred years of the Arthurian literary tradition completed in 1470 and printed by Caxton in 1485.

▶ **mimesis:** See **imitation.**

▶ **mimetic criticism:** A type of **literary criticism** inaugurated by fourth-century B.C. Greek philosopher Plato that assumes literary works to be reflections or **representations** of life and the world in general. Mimetic critics evaluate works based on whether they accurately portray their subject matter. Representations of the subject should be "true," according to this school of thought; consequently, **realism** would be among the more modern **genres** meeting with the approval of mimetic critics.

▶ **miracle play:** Broadly defined, a **medieval** religious **drama** presenting the life of a saint, the performance of a miracle, or a story from the Bible. Some scholars make a distinction between miracle plays and **mystery plays,** limiting the former to nonbiblical material, such as stories of St. Nicholas and miraculous intercessions of the Virgin Mary, and reserving the latter for biblical material, stories from the Old or New Testament. Others use the term *miracle play* to refer to a drama featuring any miracle, whether or not that miracle is described in Scripture.

Miracle plays began to develop in the tenth century, arising within the Christian Church as dramatized parts of the liturgy. Liturgical dramas, which were written in Latin and performed by clergy during church services, featured biblical stories. Following a 1210 papal edict barring clergy from public acting, however, miracle plays became the province of towns, trade guilds, and *confréries* (brotherhoods), a shift that led to several additional changes, including: (1) use of the vernacular rather than Latin; (2) performances in halls and town squares on festival days; (3) expansion of the subject matter to nonbiblical material; (4) the organization of plays, particularly those featuring biblical stories, into cycles; and (5) a certain degree of secularization, such as the incorporation of comic elements. In England, cycles of plays were typically performed over several days, often with **scenes** or episodes staged on moveable pageant wagons drawn through a number of places in the town to make the drama available to everyone.

EXAMPLES: Jean Bodel's *Jeu de Saint Nicolas* (*Play of St. Nicholas*) and Rutebeuf's *Miracle de Théophile* (*Miracle of Theophilus*), both from the thirteenth century; the fourteenth-century French cycle *Miracles de Notre Dame; Lazarus,* from the Wakefield cycle (c. 1350); the Digby play of *Mary Magdalene* (c. 1480).

See also **mystery play.**

▶ **mirror stage:** See **psychoanalytic criticism.**

▶ *mise-en-scène:* (1) In **drama,** the **setting** of a theatrical production, including the scenery and props, and, for some critics, the arrangement of actors onstage; the term is French for "put in the scene." (2) In film criticism, the elements of the composition of a shot, i.e., everything within the camera's purview. Articulation of this cinematic space involves framing and staging, and it includes the setting (the studio set or physical locale, as well as the props); the lighting; and the actors and their appearance (costumes and makeup), performance, positioning, and movement. Some critics restrict use of the term *mise-en-scène* to what appears before the camera, whereas others include camera angles, positioning, and movement. Some critics also include sound that comes from the scene itself (not from an outside source such as a voice-over), whereas others restrict *mise-en-scène* to visual aspects.

▶ **mixed metaphor:** See **metaphor.**

▶ **mock epic, mock heroic:** A type of high **burlesque,** the *mock epic* is a lengthy **poem** about an utterly trivial subject written in the exalted manner of an **epic.** Mock epics are not generally intended to mock the epic **form** or **style,** but, rather, to mock the subject by treating it with a dignity it does not deserve. As numerous scholars and critics have pointed out, however, mock epics inevitably "cut both ways," for describing ordinary events in lofty terms using **classical conventions** highlights the amusing inappropriateness of heroic language and style.

Mock heroic is often used synonymously with *mock epic* but refers more broadly to any work in which a trivial subject is **satirized** or ridiculed by discussing it in a lofty or grandiose way. In this sense, the mock heroic is a style of writing applicable to either poetry or prose. The mock epic and mock heroic were particularly popular in the **Augustan Age.**

EXAMPLES: Alexander Pope's mock-epic poem "The Rape of the Lock" (1712, 1714), which concerns the cutting and theft of a lock of a lady's hair, begins with an **invocation** to a **muse** and later describes a card game as if it were a major military battle.

In *Joseph Andrews* (1741), Henry Fielding used the mock-heroic style to depict the battle waged by "the heroic youth" Joseph Andrews with eight hounds who set upon a minister. Challenging "those . . . that describe lions and tigers, and heroes fiercer than both" to "raise their poems or plays with the simile of Joseph Andrews, who is himself above the reach of any simile," Fielding described Joseph's dogfight in the following manner:

> Now Rockwood had laid fast hold on the parson's skirts, and stopt his flight; which Joseph no sooner perceived than he levelled his cudgel at his head, and laid him sprawling. Jowler and Ringwood then fell on his greatcoat, and had undoubtedly brought him to the ground, had not Joseph, collecting all his force, given Jowler such a rap on the back that, quitting his hold, he ran howling over the plain: A harder fate remained for thee, O Ringwood! Ringwood the best hound that ever pursued a hare, who never threw his tongue but where the scent was undoubtedly true; good at "trailing," and "sure in a highway"; no "babler," no "overrunner"; respected by the whole pack; for, whenever he opened, they knew the game was at hand. He fell by the stroke of Joseph. . . .

▶ **mode:** A manner or method of literary expression, such as **irony, pastoral,** or **satire.** While *mode* is often used synonymously with **form** and **genre,** many scholars consider this usage erroneous and distinguish the term. Some use it only to refer to the broadest, overarching literary categories, such as **comedy** and **tragedy,** whereas others use it in connection with subcategories, such as the **Gothic** and **science fiction.**

▶ **modernism:** A revolutionary movement encompassing all of the creative arts that had its roots in the 1890s (the *fin de siècle*), a transitional period during which artists and writers sought to liberate themselves from the constraints and polite **conventions** associated with **Victorianism.** Modernism exploded onto the international scene in the aftermath of World War I, a traumatic transcontinental event that physically devastated and psychologically disillusioned the West in an entirely unprecedented way. A wide variety of new and experimental techniques arose in architecture, dance, literature, music, painting, and sculpture.

As a literary movement, modernism gained prominence during and especially just after World War I, then flourished in Europe and America throughout the 1920s and 1930s. Modernist authors experimented with new literary **forms,** devices, and **styles;** incorporated the **psychoanalytic** theories of Sigmund Freud and Carl Jung; and paid particular attention to language — both how it is used and how they believed it could or ought to be used. Their works reflected the pervasive sense of loss, disillusionment, and even despair in the wake of the Great War, hence their emphasis on historical discontinuity and the alienation of humanity. Although modernist authors tended to perceive the world as fragmented, many — such as T. S. Eliot and James Joyce — believed they could help counter that disintegration through their works. Such writers viewed art as a potentially integrating, restorative force, a remedy for the uncertainty of the modern world. To this end, even while depicting disorder in their works, modernists also injected order by creating patterns of **allusion, symbol,** and **myth.** This rather exalted view of art fostered a certain elitism among modernists.

Modernism encompassed a number of literary paths, many of which became known as movements in their own right, such as **Dadaism, expressionism, formalism,** and **surrealism.** Modernist works are often called *avant-garde,* an appellation that has also been applied to more radically experimental **postmodernist** works written in the wake of World War II. Many literary scholars distinguish between "old" (or modernist) *avant-garde* works and "new" (or postmodernist) ones. A modernist surrealist work is easily differentiated from a postmodernist **Absurdist** one.

Modern and *modernist* are not synonymous. The term *modern* broadly refers to that which is contemporary, that which pertains to the present day. *Modernist* refers to the complex of characteristics shared by those who embraced or participated in the modernist movement.

EXAMPLES: Eliot's *The Waste Land* (1922), Joyce's *Ulysses* (1922), and Virginia Woolf's *To the Lighthouse* (1927) are famous modernist literary works. Modernist art includes the cubist and surrealist paintings of Pablo Picasso (such as *Three Musicians* [1921] and *Three Dancers* [1925], respectively) and the surrealist works of Salvador Dalí. Igor Stravinsky's *Le sacre du printemps* (*The Rite of Spring*) (1933) is an example of modernist music.

▶ **Modern Period (in English and American literature):** A period in English and American literary history beginning in 1914 with the outbreak of World War I and ending in 1945 with the conclusion of World War II. The term *modern* in the phrase *Modern Period* should not be confused with *modern* as it is more commonly used, that is, to refer to recent or contemporary times. The Modern Period is noted for works characterized by a transnational focus, stylistic unconventionality, or interest in repressed sub- or unconscious material; it includes works written in just about every established **genre** (as well as in new, hybrid forms) by writers such as W. H. Auden, H. D. (Hilda Doolittle), T. S. Eliot, William Faulkner, Robert Frost, James Joyce, D. H. Lawrence, Doris Lessing, Marianne Moore, Eugene O'Neill, Ezra Pound, Dorothy Richardson, George Bernard Shaw, Gertrude Stein, Wallace Stevens, William Carlos Williams, Virginia Woolf, and W. B. Yeats.

Although the beginning of the Modern Period in English literature coincides with the beginning of the **Georgian Age** in English literature, the term *Georgian* is usually used in connection with relatively traditional **pastoral** or **realistic** poems written during and after World War I by writers such as Rupert Brooke, W. H. Davies, Walter de la Mare, Ralph Hodgson, and John Masefield. A number of Georgian poets had been horrified by the tragic results of World War I and wrote poems attacking the absurdity of war in general. Many English writers not usually associated with the Georgian Age had also been deeply disturbed by the so-called Great War and, more generally, by the increasingly chaotic and absurd nature of modern life, but they expressed their alienation through radically unconventional, experimental literary forms or highly unusual subject matter rather than through traditional **styles** and realistic **representations**.

Virginia Woolf experimented with **stream of consciousness**, a style of writing reflecting a **character's** flow of perceptions, thoughts, memories, and feelings. Stream-of-consciousness **narrative** often exemplifies the way in which the modern mind attempts, consciously or, more commonly, unconsciously, to find or create coherence in a fragmented, apparently senseless world. Other writers turned to **myth** (as did Joyce) or even created their own strange visionary mythologies or **symbol** systems (as did Yeats) in order to express the psychological pain of modern life or to wrest meaning from an otherwise meaningless cosmos. In "The Second Coming" (1921), Yeats alluded to his vision of historical cycles, or "gyres":

> Turning and turning in the widening gyre
> The falcon cannot hear the falconer;
> Things fall apart; the centre cannot hold;
> Mere anarchy is loosed upon the world.

Yeats's poem ends with a combination of **apocalyptic** and mythological elements that combine to announce the advent of a dark antichrist: "And what rough beast, its hour come round at last, / Slouches towards Bethlehem to be born?"

The United States, an isolationist nation before World War I, was characterized by significant tension between political isolationism and international involvement during the postwar period. As the country in general became increasingly isolationist (as evidenced, for instance, by the Congressional defeat of American involvement in the League of Nations), American authors marched to the beat of a different drummer. They exhibited a growing interest in European authors, including the seventeenth-century English **metaphysical poets**, the **French Symbolists** of the nineteenth century, and writers of their own times (such as Joyce and French novelist Marcel Proust).

American writers of the period who felt disillusioned by the experience and aftermath of World War I quickly came to be termed the **Lost Generation**. These writers generally viewed the "traditional" American values of their youth as a sham, given the senselessness of the war and its devaluation of human life. As such, members of this group deliberately rejected American culture as hypocritical; many even moved to Europe during the 1920s, participating in movements such as **Dadaism** and **surrealism**. Expatriate members of the Lost Generation, who gathered around Gertrude Stein, included F. Scott Fitzgerald, Ernest Hemingway, e. e. cummings, Sherwood Anderson, and William Slater Brown.

The **Harlem Renaissance**, an intellectual and cultural movement that presented black life from a black point of view and was centered in Harlem, an African American area of New York City, also developed and flourished during the 1920s. For the first time in American history, African American culture was deliberately highlighted for a diverse national audience via literature, theater, music, and dance. Arna Bontemps, Countee Cullen, Langston Hughes, Zora Neale Hurston, and Jean Toomer are just a few of the figures associated with the Harlem Renaissance.

Other writers commonly associated with the Modern Period in American literature include Hart Crane, Amy Lowell, Sinclair Lewis, Edna St. Vincent Millay, Eleanor Wylie, and the **Fugitives**, a group of Southern poets best known for *The Fugitive* (1922–25), an amateur journal of poetry and criticism.

Although many English and American writers of the Modern Period rejected realism, a significant minority did not. English writers including D. H. Lawrence, E. M. Forster, and Graham Greene adapted realistic **narrative conventions** to represent new literary subjects, ranging from orgasm (Lawrence) to colonial India (Forster) to **postcolonial** Mexico (Greene). American novelist Willa Cather wrote a type of fiction often termed *genteel realism* for its effort to depict life as it really is and yet avoid vulgar or otherwise unpleasant or depressing subject matter. Cather's *My Antonia* (1918) and *Death Comes for the Archbishop* (1927) are two of her better-known works. Booth Tarkington also continued the **sentimental** vein of the realist tradition with works such as *The Magnificent Ambersons* (1918).

Works by a number of innovative English and American dramatists also appeared during the Modern Period. Of the former group, George Bernard Shaw (author of *Saint Joan* [1923]) had written plays during the preceding **Victorian** and **Edwardian** periods, and John Galsworthy (*The Skin Game* [1920], *The Forsyte Saga* [1906–21]) had become famous for realistic novels that bridged the Edwardian and Modern periods. Foremost among American playwrights of the Modern Period was Eugene O'Neill, author of *The Emperor Jones* (1920), *Mourning Becomes Electra* (1931), and *The Iceman Cometh* (1939).

The distinction between English and American writers of the Modern Period is difficult to make, as exemplified by the fact that one of the most important American writers of the period (Eliot) became a British subject, and one of the most important British writers of the period (Auden) became a U.S. citizen. It is equally difficult to distinguish between English and American writers of the Modern Period on the one hand and their Continental counterparts on the other; Proust experimented with stream of consciousness, and the German writer Thomas Mann used mythology to reveal disturbed psychic conditions. Similarly, one can compare the **themes** and formal experiments characteristic of modern literary works with those evident in musical works, paintings, and sculpture produced during the period between World War I and World War II. Like **neoclassicism** and **romanticism**, **modernism** was in fact a transnational, even transcultural movement that encompassed all of the arts.

See **modernism**.

▶ **monody:** In **classical** Greek **poetry,** an **ode** performed by one voice; now a **poem** of lamentation, sometimes intended to be sung, in which one individual grieves and mourns for another. Monody may be viewed as a type of **dirge** or, more broadly, as a type of **elegy** with one **narrator,** the mourner.

EXAMPLES: John Milton's "Lycidas" (1638), written to lament Edward King's death; Matthew Arnold's "Thyrsis" (1867), subtitled "A Monody, to Commemorate the Author's Friend . . . ," an elegy on Arthur Hugh Clough. Herman Melville's "Monody" (1891), probably written after visiting fellow writer Nathaniel Hawthorne's grave, follows:

> To have known him, to have loved him
> After loneness long;
> And then to be estranged in life,
> And neither in the wrong;
> And now for death to set his seal —
> Ease me, a little ease, my song!
>
> By wintry hills his hermit-mound
> The sheeted snow-drifts drape,
> And houseless there the snow-bird flits

Beneath the fir-trees' crape:
Glazed now with ice the cloistral vine
That hid the shyest grape.

▶ **monologic:** See **dialogic criticism.**

▶ **monologue:** An extended **narrative,** whether oral or written, delivered uninterrupted and exclusively by one person. A **dramatic monologue** is a **lyric poem** in which the speaker addresses a silent listener in the context of a situation that sheds revealing light on the speaker's character. An **interior monologue,** in its direct form, presents a **character's stream of consciousness** by approximating or mimicking his or her mental flow, plugging the reader straight into the character's thoughts, emotions, and sensations rather than having the character express them aloud. A **soliloquy** is a monologue performed onstage as part of a **play** in which a character reveals his or her inner thoughts or emotions out loud but while alone.

EXAMPLE: The following lines from Emily Brontë's *Wuthering Heights* (1847), spoken by Catherine Earnshaw to Nelly Dean:

> I cannot express it, but surely you and everybody have a notion that there is, or should be, an existence of yours beyond you. What were the use of creation if I were entirely contained here? My great miseries in this world have been Heathcliff's miseries, and I watched and felt each from the beginning; my great thought in living is himself. If all else perished, and *he* remained, I should still continue to be; and if all else remained, and he were annihilated, the Universe would turn into a mighty stranger. I should not seem a part of it. My love for Linton is like the foliage in the woods. Time will change it, I'm well aware, as winter changes the trees — my love for Heathcliff resembles the eternal rocks beneath — a source of little visible delight, but necessary. Nelly, I *am* Heathcliff — he's always, always in my mind — not as a pleasure, any more than I am always a pleasure to myself — but as my own being — so, don't talk of our separation again — it is impracticable. . . .

Tony Kushner's play *Angels in America: A Gay Fantasia on National Themes* (1992; adapted to film 2003) contains numerous monologues, including an opening monologue by a rabbi presiding over the funeral of a Jewish immigrant grandmother that introduces the **theme** of continuity versus change; eulogizing the dead woman, whose family has assimilated to America, the rabbi declares, "She fought, for the family, for the Jewish home, so that you would not grow up here, in this strange place, in the melting pot where nothing melted." Eve Ensler's *The Vagina Monologues* (1996; adapted by HBO 2002), originally a one-woman show based on Ensler's interviews with more than 200 women, consists of a series of monologues addressing topics ranging from love and sex to menstruation and birth to rape and other forms of violence against women.

▶ **monometer:** A line of **verse** consisting of one **metrical foot.**

EXAMPLES: Robert Herrick's "Upon His Departure Hence" (1648), written in **iambic** monometer, which begins "Thus I / Pass By / And die"; the anonymous **trochaic** monometer poem "Fleas," reading simply "Adam / Had'em." Many poems by William Carlos Williams contain monometer lines. "Poem" (1934) provides one example:

> As the cat
> climbed over
> the top of
>
> the jamcloset
> first the right
> forefoot
>
> carefully
> then the hind
> stepped down
>
> into the pit of
> the empty
> flowerpot

▶ **monosyllabic:** See **foot, sprung rhythm.**

▶ **montage:** From the French for "to mount," a composite of several different and typically unrelated elements that are juxtaposed and arranged to create or elicit a particular **mood,** meaning, or perception. Montage is used in various art forms, including film, music, photography, literature, and the visual arts and may thus consist of film shots, musical fragments, photographs, **texts,** or other such elements.

Montage is largely a product of **modernism,** an early-twentieth-century movement led by writers and artists seeking to break away from the constraints and **conventions** associated with **Victorianism** through experimentation with new literary **forms,** techniques, and **styles.** Following World War I, Georg Lukács, a Soviet **Marxist critic** who favored **realism** and realistic **representation,** criticized montage, which he viewed as **decadent** and concerned mainly with form rather than content. German playwright and Marxist critic Bertolt Brecht, however, countered that art is a field of production, not a container of content, and thus argued that progressive modes of expression should replace the conventional ones associated with representational art and literature. The ensuing debate between advocates of these two views came to be known as the "Brecht-Lukács" debate.

Although montage involving whole photographs, or parts thereof, manipulated to produce a design began to appear just before World War I, German artist John Heartfield is usually credited with developing *photomontage* as an art form in 1916, together with his **Dadaist** colleagues George Grosz and Hannah Höch. Heartfield, who changed his name from Helmut Herzfeld in protest against rising German nationalism, became a political activist following the war and eventually employed photomontage as propaganda to attack Hitler and the Nazi party. Photomontage is still used today as a political medium, though it is also used by visual artists and advertising designers.

Cinematic montage was pioneered during the 1920s by three Russian film directors — Lev Kuleshov, Sergei Eisenstein, and V. I. Pudovkin — following Kuleshov's discovery that viewers will interpret two unrelated shots in terms of a larger context by inferring some type of relationship, so long as those unrelated shots are shown in succession (the *Kuleshov effect*). For instance, in one of Kuleshov's editing experiments, which involved splicing shots including a waiting man, a walking woman, and a gate, viewers concluded that the man and woman met in front of the gate even though the shots were filmed at different times and places. The editing technique derived from Kuleshov's discovery involved the juxtaposition of contrasting separate shots, often in rapid succession, to suggest new and different **connotations**. Film historian David A. Cook described the process in *A History of Narrative Film* (1996) as one "whereby logically or empirically dissimilar images could be linked together synthetically to produce metaphors, to produce, that is, non-literal meaning." Eisenstein's use of the Kuleshov effect in his first film, *Strike* (1924), led to its recognition as an important cinematic editing device. Sometimes referred to in America as *dynamic cutting*, montage has been used extensively ever since, particularly in polemic documentaries and propaganda films.

Literary montage, a technique used by authors experimenting with unconventional styles of writing, was developed by the German author and Marxist critic Walter Benjamin in his drafts of the *Passagenwerk* (*Arcades Project*) (1927–39), an unfinished assemblage of quotations, illustrations, and comments regarding the cultural history of nineteenth-century Paris. Benjamin coined the term when he described his method as "literary montage. I have nothing to say only to show."

Today, photographic, cinematic, literary, and other forms of montage can all be computer-generated. Moreover, elements such as graphics, photographs, textual passages, film clips, and songs may be used to create a **hypertext** montage.

EXAMPLES: Examples of photomontage include Höch's gigantic "Cut with the Kitchen Knife DADA through the Last Weimar Beer Belly Cultural Epoch of Germany" (1919–20); the poster shown on page 314, produced by the U.S. government in 1935 to promote "Suburban Resettlement housing projects" among "typical American families with limited incomes"; photocollages in school yearbooks; and photomosaic puzzles, which consist of hundreds or thousands of pictures used to create one larger **image**.

Examples of cinematic montage based on the Kuleshov effect include the **classic** "Odessa Steps scene" in *The Battleship Potemkin* (1925), directed by Eisenstein and Grigori Aleksandrov, and the famous "shower scene" in Alfred Hitchcock's *Psycho* (1960), which was assembled from approximately one hundred different film cuts.

An example of photomontage.

Examples of literary montage include James Joyce's novel *Ulysses* (1922); **Harlem Renaissance** writer Jean Toomer's *Cane* (1923); and T. S. Eliot's poem *The Waste Land* (1920), in which Eliot combines his own poetry with lines from several **Renaissance** plays, **lyrics** from nineteenth-century opera and twentieth-century popular songs, words from the Buddha's "Fire Sermon" and a Hindu *Upanishad*, advertising slogans, and the traditional closing call used in British pubs. Christiane Paul's *Unreal City: A Hypertextual Guide to T. S. Eliot's* The Waste Land (1996) offers a hypertext montage commentary on Eliot's famous poem. Shelley Jackson's *The Patchwork Girl* (1995) is a work of **hypertext fiction** employing literary montage.

Numerous montages were created in the wake of the 9/11 terrorist attacks in 2001.

▶ **mood:** Defined by some critics as synonymous with **atmosphere,** by others as synonymous with **tone,** and by still others as synonymous with both.

Atmosphere refers to the general feeling created for the reader or audience by the work at a given point, whereas *tone* refers to the attitude of the **author** toward the reader, audience, or subject matter. The atmosphere of a work may be entirely different from the tone, although the two inevitably affect one another. Mood is probably closer to atmosphere than to tone, but, as a general term, it can correctly be applied to either. One could say that an author creates a somber mood, thereby using it as a synonym for *atmosphere*; one could also say that an author's mood is somber, thereby using it as a synonym for *tone*.

▶ **morality play:** A **medieval drama** using **allegory** to make a moral point. Morality plays, which arose in the late fourteenth century, combined the religious dramatic tradition of **mystery** and **miracle plays** with the allegorical **form**. The **genre** flourished in England in the fifteenth and early sixteenth centuries and was also popular in continental Europe, especially France and the Netherlands.

Morality plays typically were religiously oriented, with a **protagonist** who represented humanity and a cast of other **characters** including angels, demons, and **personified** vices and virtues struggling for the protagonist's soul. Intended to cultivate Christian character, morality plays **didactically** portrayed the quest for salvation and the lure of temptation. Over time, they became increasingly secular, addressing social and political issues, giving a comic face to the initially sinister characters Vice and the Devil and **influencing** the development of later **comedy** and the **interlude**. The genre began to decline in the mid-sixteenth century and largely died out by the century's end.

EXAMPLES: The anonymous morality plays *The Castle of Perseverance* (c. 1425), *Mankind* (c. 1465–70), and *Everyman* (c. 1495); John Skelton's *Magnificence* (c. 1515–16). Philip Roth's contemporary novel *Everyman* (2006) has been called a modern morality play; like his medieval analogue, the protagonist must confront death and, in so doing, reexamine his life.

▶ **morpheme:** The smallest meaningful parts of words. Morphemes are composed of **phonemes,** the smallest basic speech sounds in a language.

EXAMPLE: The word *unworthy* is composed of three morphemes: *un, worth,* and *y. Worth* is a morpheme that is also a word — and the root of the word *unworthy* — in itself. Trying to further break up the word *worth* into smaller phonemic groups would make it meaningless. *Un* is a morpheme that is a negator and *y* is a morpheme that transforms the word *unworthy* into an adjective.

▶ **morphology:** A division of **linguistics,** the study of the form of words and of **morphemes,** the smallest meaningful parts of words.

▶ **motif:** A recurrent, unifying element in an artistic work, such as an **image, symbol, character** type, action, idea, object, or phrase. A given motif may be unique to a work, or it may appear in numerous works, whether by the same **author** or different authors. In fact, a motif may be so widespread that it serves as the kernel for works typically associated with different **genres** or even different fields, such as art, music, architecture, **myth**, and **folklore**, in which hundreds of motifs including the cruel step-mother, magic carpet, perilous journey, and twin birth have been identified and even indexed.

Motif is related to but distinguished from **theme**, which refers more broadly to the statement(s) that the **text** seems to be making about its subject. A motif is a thematic element, an element that informs and casts a re-vealing light on the theme.

EXAMPLES: An egg that comes from heaven or from a woman impreg-nated by the sun is a recurring motif in founding **legends** of the three an-cient Korean kingdoms, recounted in works such as Yi Kyu-bo's *The Lay of King Tongmyông* (1193) and *The Legend of Pak Hyôkkôse*, from Iryôn's thirteenth-century compilation *Samguk Yusa* (*Memorabilia of the Three Kingdoms*). Native American **tales** draw on the trickster motif, fea-turing trickster characters such as Coyote, Rabbit, and Raven.

A **Storm and Stress** motif is woven through numerous **romantic** works, such as Mary Shelley's *Frankenstein* (1818) and Emily Brontë's *Wuthering Heights* (1847). Specific colors such as green and white serve as motifs in F. Scott Fitzgerald's *The Great Gatsby* (1925). George Bernard Shaw's play *Pygmalion* (1912) draws on the Cinderella motif, as do more recent works such as *Pretty Woman* (1990), *Ever After* (1998), Meg Cabot's *The Princess Diaries* (2000; adapted to film 2001), and *A Cinderella Story* (2004).

See also **leitmotif**.

▶ **motivation:** The combination of personality and situation that impels a **character** to behave the way he or she does. Establishing motivation is crit-ical to the plausibility of the **action**.

▶ **muckraker:** A term most often applied to American investigative jour-nalists and other writers in the early 1900s who sought to expose abuse and corruption in capitalist big business and government as well as al-liances between the two; more generally, one who investigates and publicly exposes such misconduct. The term derives from U.S. President Theodore Roosevelt's comparison of such writers in a 1906 speech to the "Man with the Muck-rake," a **character** in Paul Bunyan's *Pilgrim's Progress* (1678) who sees the filth on the floor but can neither look up nor regard the celes-tial crown he is offered in return for his muck-rake.

The muckraking movement was enabled by the advent of the mass-circulation magazine in the 1890s and flourished from about 1902 to 1912, during the **Naturalistic Period in American literature**. Muckrakers combined detailed factual description with a commitment to reform, writing exposés on topics ranging from child labor and monopolies to insurance schemes and patent medicine fraud. Lincoln Steffens is generally credited with pio-neering the **genre** with "Tweed Days in St. Louis" (1902), an article pub-lished in *McClure's Magazine* exposing political corruption, including widespread bribery, in St. Louis. Other major publishers of muckraking articles included *Collier's, Cosmopolitan,* and *Everybody's.*

FURTHER EXAMPLES: Ida Tarbell's *The History of the Standard Oil Company* (1904); Steffens's *The Shame of the Cities* (1904); Upton Sinclair's *The Jungle* (1906), a novel that exposed the disgusting conditions and rampant corruption in Chicago's meat-packing plants.

▶ **mummers' play:** See **folk drama.**

▶ **muses:** According to Greek **myth,** the nine daughters of Zeus and Mnemosyne (memory), each holding sway over a division of the arts and sciences. Poets traditionally invoked one or more of the muses for inspiration; those especially relevant to **verse** are Calliope (**epic** poetry), Erato (love poetry), Euterpe (music and **lyric** poetry), and Polyhymnia (sacred poetry). The others are Clio (history), Melpomene (**tragedy**), Terpsichore (dance), Thalia (**comedy**), and Urania (astronomy). During the sixteenth century, French poet Guillaume du Bartas transformed Urania from a pagan muse into a Christian, "Heavenly" muse. In recent times, the term *muse* has come to refer to any person, entity, or spirit — real or imaginary — invoked for guidance and inspiration.

EXAMPLES: John Milton invoked Urania at the beginning of Book 7 of his epic *Paradise Lost* (1667):

> Descend from Heav'n *Urania,* by that name
> If rightly thou art call'd, whose Voice divine
> Following, above th' *Olympian* Hill I soar,
> Above the flight of *Pegasean* wing.
> The meaning, not the Name I call: for thou
> Nor of the Muses nine, nor on the top
> Of old *Olympus* dwell'st, but Heav'nly born. . . .

Baroque poet and playwright Sor Juana Inés de la Cruz has often been called the "tenth muse," an **epithet** employed by a former patron in publishing a collection of her poetry, *The Overflowing of the Castalian Spring, by the Tenth Muse of Mexico* (1689). Puritan poet Anne Bradstreet's brother-in-law likewise adopted the epithet in publishing her first collection of poetry, *The Tenth Muse Lately Sprung Up in America* (1650).

John Fowles's erotically charged novel *Mantissa* (1982) is about an author's alternately energizing and frustrating relationship with his muse. Tracy Chevalier's imaginative **historical novel** *Girl with a Pearl Earring* (1999; adapted to film 2003) depicts a young maid as seventeenth-century Dutch painter Jan Vermeer's model and muse.

▶ **mystery fiction:** Popular fictional **narratives** with **plots** revolving around puzzles or secrets that create and even exploit a sense of uncertainty, suspense, or fear in the reader or audience. The word *mystery* has divergent **connotations,** suggesting the kind of divine or miraculous events recounted by **medieval miracle plays** and **mystery plays,** as well as baffling problems or enigmas demanding a solution or explanation. It is this latter usage of *mystery* that is operative in mystery fiction, which some scholars have traced back to Egyptian, Greek, and biblical "riddle stories" or puzzles. Mystery fiction includes *crime novels*, **detective fiction**, **Gothic literature**, *historical mysteries*, **horror** literature, *spy fiction*, *suspense fiction*, and *thrillers*. The term may therefore apply to a wide range of works, from Wilkie Collins's *The Moonstone* (1868) and Agatha Christie's *Murder on the Orient Express* (1934), novels featuring the disappearance of a valuable diamond and a murder, respectively, to David Mamet's *The Spanish Prisoner* (1997), a film revolving around a confidence game and the question of whom you can trust; M. Night Shyamalan's paranormal psychological thriller *The Sixth Sense* (1999); and the television series *Lost* (2004–), in which survivors of a plane crash are marooned on a mysterious tropical island with an equally mysterious group of "Others."

Eighteenth- and nineteenth-century Gothic **romances**, which are often set on aristocratic estates and involve relationships clouded by suspicion, fear, and danger, have had far-reaching influence on a variety of **genres** associated with mystery fiction. Works such as Ann Radcliffe's *The Mysteries of Udolpho: A Romance* (1794), Charlotte Brontë's *Jane Eyre* (1847), and Henry James's *The Turn of the Screw* (1898) are widely viewed as the forerunners of twentieth-century Gothic mystery **classics** such as Victoria Holt's *Mistress of Mellyn* (1960) and Phyllis A. Whitney's *Thunder Heights* (1960). Other descendants of Gothic fiction are the horror and suspense genres exemplified by writers such as Mary Higgins Clark (*Where Are the Children?* [1975]), Dean Koontz (*Phantoms* [1983]), Stephen King (*The Shining* [1977]), and Anne Rice (*The Witching Hour* [1990]).

With the publication of Edgar Allan Poe's "Murders in the Rue Morgue" (1841), the category of mysteries broadened to comprise detective fiction, which spawned such famous **characters** as Arthur Conan Doyle's Sherlock Holmes, Erle Stanley Gardner's Perry Mason, and Christie's Hercule Poirot and Jane Marple. Noted authors of classic *whodunits*, which feature plots in which a particular crime — usually a murder — is solved, thereby restoring order to society, include Christie, who wrote prolifically for more than five decades; Michael Innes; P. D. James; Ngaio Marsh; Ellery Queen (a **pseudonym** for two co-author cousins); and Dorothy Sayers. *Hard-boiled* detective stories, which are set in the world of the criminal underground rather than in respectable society, have been published by writers like Raymond Chandler, Dashiell Hammett, Ross Macdonald, Walter Mosley, Sara Paretsky, and Mickey Spillane. Contemporary films exemplifying these types of detective fiction include *Gosford Park* (2001) and *L.A. Confidential* (1997) (based on the 1990 novel by James Ellroy), respectively.

Crime novels have greatly influenced and, in turn, been influenced by detective fiction. Although often involving a detective, they emphasize the criminal's **motivation** and behavior rather than the detective's attempt to solve the crime. In fact, the identity of the criminal in a crime novel —

unlike that of the culprit of a detective story — is often known from the beginning. Pioneered in such works as William Godwin's *The Adventures of Caleb Williams* (1794) and Charles Brockden Brown's *Wieland* (1798), crime fiction was further developed by Wilkie Collins in *The Woman in White* (1860). Anthony Cox, who published crime novels under the pseudonym Frances Iles and detective fiction under the pseudonym Anthony Berkeley, is credited with pioneering the modern crime novel in works such as *Malice Aforethought: The Study of a Commonplace Crime* (1931).

As the crime novel became established, persistent subjects and **themes** emerged, such as criminal motivation and forensic theory and techniques. Most, if not all, crime-novel mysteries are **psychological novels,** such as Scott Turow's *Presumed Innocent* (1987) and Elizabeth George's *Deception on His Mind* (1997), and many psychological crime novels, such as Thomas Harris's *Silence of the Lambs* (1988) and Kathy Reichs's *Déjà Dead* (1997), focus specifically on fictional serial killers. Examples of novels concerned with forensic pathology include Patricia Cornwell's *Postmortem* (1990) and Jeffrey Deaver's *The Bone Collector* (1997). Jonathan Kellerman's *Alex Delaware* series (1985–), which began with *When the Bough Breaks* and features a mystery-solving child psychologist, combines elements of psychological, detective, and crime fiction, as does the film *The Usual Suspects* (1995).

Other types of mysteries include historical mysteries, spy fiction, and thrillers. Historical mysteries incorporate historical events or figures; examples include Ellis Peters's (Edith Pargeter's) *Brother Cadfael* series (1977–94), set during a period of civil war in twelfth-century England, and Andrew Taylor's *The American Boy* (2003), which includes Edgar Allan Poe as a character. Spy fiction, which focuses on intelligence and espionage, can be traced back to James Fenimore Cooper's *The Spy* (1821). It was further developed by William Le Quiex's *Guilty Bonds* (1890), which purported to offer a detailed inside account of the world of late-nineteenth-century espionage, and Rudyard Kipling's *Kim* (1901). Subsequent notable works of spy fiction include Ian Fleming's *James Bond* series (1953–65), John LeCarré's *The Spy Who Came in from the Cold* (1963), Nelson DeMille's *The Charm School* (1988), Victor O'Reilly's *Games of the Hangman* (1991), Robert Ludlum's *The Prometheus Deception* (2000), and the film *The Good Shepherd* (2006). Many thrillers — suspenseful, fast-paced, action-packed stories — are also classified as mysteries. Contemporary examples include Tom Clancy's military thriller *The Hunt for Red October* (1984); the legal thrillers *The Firm* (1991) and *Personal Injuries* (1999), by John Grisham and Turow, respectively; and Joseph Finder's corporate thriller *Killer Instinct* (2006).

See also **detective fiction; Gothic, Gothic literature.**

▶**mystery play:** As commonly defined, a **medieval** religious **drama** presenting a biblical story. *Mystery play* is sometimes used synonymously with **miracle play,** broadly defined; many scholars, however, distinguish between the two, limiting the former to plays based on Scripture and the latter to those based on nonbiblical material, such as saints' lives. Mystery plays, the most important type of medieval drama in Western Europe, generally dramatized Old Testament stories about Adam and Eve, the patriarchs, or the prophets; New Testament stories about the birth and early life of Christ; or New Testament stories about Christ's death and resurrection.

Mystery plays began to develop in the tenth century, arising within the Christian Church as dramatized parts of the liturgy. Subsequently, in the wake of a 1210 papal edict barring clergy from public acting, mystery plays became the province of towns, trade guilds, and *confréries* (brotherhoods) and were often performed on religious holidays, particularly during the festival of Corpus Christi; consequently, they are sometimes called *Corpus Christi plays*. Moreover, many mystery plays were organized into cycles depicting biblical events from the Creation to the Last Judgment. In England, where the **genre** remained popular through the sixteenth century, such cycles were typically performed over several days, often with **scenes** or episodes staged on moveable pageant wagons drawn through a number of places in the town to make the drama available to everyone. Fixed (and lavish) staging was common in France and Italy.

EXAMPLES: *The Resurrection,* from the York Pageant (1430–40); *Noah and the Ark* and *The Second Shepherds' Play,* both from the Wakefield Cycle (c. 1450).

See also **miracle play.**

▶ **mysticism:** The belief that special knowledge or awareness, particularly of ultimate reality or the divine, can be acquired only through intuitive, extrasensory means. In other words, such knowledge or awareness cannot be attained analytically or through the five senses, for it involves insight into or communion with something beyond thought or sensory perception. People have sought to achieve the mystical state (or the ecstasy that often accompanies it) in a variety of ways, ranging from ascetic deprivation (e.g., of food, sleep) to mind-altering drugs (e.g., peyote) to continuous whirling (e.g., Sufi dancing) to meditation. However induced or attained, the mystical experience is generally considered to be so intensely personal that it cannot be readily described.

Since the experience sought by mystics often involves knowledge of the divine, mysticism frequently has an explicitly spiritual or religious character. Almost every religious tradition, including Buddhism, Christianity, Islam, Judaism, and Hinduism, has a mystical branch or branches. Mysticism comes in many forms, however, not all of which are religious. Mystics may seek knowledge of "reality," for instance, a quest that may or may not involve a deity. **Transcendentalism** is a form of mysticism often said to draw on spiritual traditions even though its primary emphasis is literary, not religious, and on Nature rather than God per se.

Mysticism has two components that may seem incongruous or even conflicting to nonmystics but that mystics view as complementary. The first component is speculative, asserting the existence of a divine essence or ultimate reality that lies beyond knowledge. The second component is pragmatic, asserting that this essence can and should be known. A nonmystic might ask how people can know that which is beyond knowledge; a mystic might respond **paradoxically** by stating that what is beyond us and our traditional ways of knowing is also immanent (dwelling within us) and thus can be found through self-discovery. An ancient Hindu story positing that humanity was once divine exemplifies this point. According to the story, when other, more powerful gods decided to rob human beings of their divinity, they debated about where to hide it and, after concluding that humans would eventually travel to the tops of the highest mountains and the deepest troughs of the sea, decided to bury it where it would never be found: in the heart and soul of each individual.

Although the speculative side of mysticism has been termed its philosophical side and the practical side of mysticism its religious side, mysticism has historically been rejected by mainline philosophers and theologians. Mystics have typically acquiesced in this rejection, since they tend to position themselves outside the mainstream of philosophical and theological thought, viewing philosophical systems and religious rituals or dogmas as the petrified remains of some originally vital search for truth or a sense of divinity.

Mysticism is an ancient phenomenon in the Middle East, India, and the Far East and a more recent development in the West. A form of Christian mysticism known as **Neoplatonism** was developed in Alexandria, Egypt in the third century A.D. by the Hellenistic philosopher Plotinus. He developed the fourth-century B.C. Greek philosopher Plato's conception that things must be understood in relation to ideas — and that all ideas emanate from The One, The Good, and the Idea of Good — into a quasi-Christian, mystical philosophy / religion allowing for ecstatic coalescence with a transcendent deity, The One, through a process of self-repudiation that begins with the rejection not only of the body but also of intellectual thought. Greek Neoplatonism was further developed by an anonymous philosopher known as Pseudo-Dionysius the Areopagite and the Byzantine theologian Maximus the Confessor in the fifth and seventh centuries, respectively.

Other **medieval** versions of Christian mysticism were espoused in what is now France during the twelfth and thirteenth centuries by Bernard of Clairvaux, Hugh of St. Victor, and Bonaventura, who described union with God in terms of mystic intuition. During the fourteenth century, Christian mysticism was developed by Meister Eckhart in Germany and by Jan van Tusbrock in the Netherlands. Some Protestant theologians have treated the mystics of Germany and Holland as precursors of the Reformation, and, indeed, many of the Christian mystics who lived during the **Renaissance** did define themselves in opposition to the growing rigidity and ritualism of what we now refer to as the Catholic Church. Christian mystics, however, were not as interested in Church reform as they were in identifying a nondogmatic, meditative way that would lead outside of and beyond traditional ecclesiastical teachings. Christian mysticism typically asserts that mystical knowledge of God can be acquired by progressing not through any learnable theological system but, rather, through a difficult, disciplined, and potentially perilous journey of the individual soul, one involving cleansing self-denial; an illuminative awareness of God's love; and, ultimately, a spiritual union with or marriage to God.

The tendency of mystics, Western and Eastern, to posit the simultaneous existence of transcendent power(s) and an indwelling power to commune with such power(s) has characterized the thinking of any number of poets. Some have been consciously aware of mystical traditions; others have independently established a meditative mode aimed at communion with the ineffable through the indirection of **figurative language**. Mysticism pervades the work of William Blake; it also plays a role in works by authors such as Richard Crashaw; William Wordsworth; Samuel Taylor Coleridge; Alfred, Lord Tennyson; the American transcendentalists, especially Ralph Waldo Emerson; Herman Melville; Walt Whitman; T. S. Eliot; and D. H. Lawrence. Although **the New Critics** and other **formalists** who dominated mid-twentieth-century **literary criticism** viewed mysticism and mystical writings as unclear and imprecise, subsequent critics have taken a more favorable view of mystical **texts**, finding unusual experimentation with **form; symbolic** or other figurative language that responds to **psychoanalytic** or **poststructuralist** theory or analysis; and **mythic** or **archetypal images**, figures, and patterns that pervade the religious and secular texts of separate and diverse cultures.

FURTHER EXAMPLES: Christina Rossetti's poetry, as exemplified by her collection *Goblin Market and Other Tales* (1862), is infused with mysticism. Emerson's poems "Each and All" (1839), "Hamatreya" (1846), and "Brahma" (1857) show the **influence** of Eastern mysticism, as does Eliot's *The Waste Land* (1922), which ends with the line "Shantih shantih shantih." In a note, Eliot explained that "our equivalent" to the word *Shantih* is the phrase "The Peace which passeth understanding" and that, "repeated as here," the word forms "a formal ending to an Upanishad" (a work of Hindu theology expounding mystical knowledge). In "The Dry Salvages" (1941), a poem written after he embraced Christianity, Eliot "wonder[s] if that is what the Krishna meant" before postulating that "the way up is the way down, the way forward is the way back." But the poem, one of the *Four Quartets* (1943), comes closest to the spirit of mysticism in lines treating "the intersection of the timeless / With time":

> For most of us, there is only the unattended
> Moment, the moment in and out of time,
> The distraction fit, lost in a shaft of sunlight,
> The wild thyme unseen, or the winter lightning
> Or the waterfall, or music heard so deeply
> That it is not heard at all, but you are the music
> While the music lasts. These are only hints and guesses,
> Hints followed by guesses; and the rest
> Is prayer, observance, discipline, thought and action.

Twentieth-century works of fiction in which the influence of mysticism is pervasive include Hermann Hesse's novel *Siddhartha* (1951) and Lawrence Durrell's series of novels *The Alexandria Quartet* (1957–60).

A December 4, 2000, *Time* magazine review described singer-songwriter Erykah Badu's debut album, *Baduizm* (1997), as "blend[ing] hip-hop realism with soul-sister mysticism."

▶ **myth:** A traditional anonymous **story,** originally religious in nature, told by a particular cultural group in order to explain a natural or cosmic phenomenon. Individual myths are typically part of an interconnected collection of such **tales,** known as a culture's *mythology.* Myths generally offer supernatural explanations for the creation of the world (whether seen as the planet alone or the universe generally) and humanity, as well as for death, judgment, and the afterlife. Myths that explain the origins of humanity often focus on the cultural group telling the myth and may even portray the group, as in many Native American myths, as "the people," or the "true" people. Stories chronicling the adventures of gods and other supernatural forces, especially stories about their various feuds and encounters with mortals, are also common fare, as are tales about the fictional humans who must interact with them. The ancient Greek warrior Achilles is as much a mythic figure as Zeus, the supreme ruler of the gods in the Greek Pantheon.

Myths are distinguished from **legends,** which detail the adventures of a human cultural **hero** (such as Robin Hood or Annie Oakley) and tend to be less focused on the supernatural. Whereas a legend may exaggerate — perhaps even wildly — the exploits of its hero, it is likely to be grounded in historical fact. Myths also differ from **fables,** which have a moral, **didactic** purpose and usually feature animal **characters.**

Myths that originally served to explain mysterious natural phenomena have often been rejected as "false" as cultures have gained scientific knowledge. One does not, for instance, need to attribute winter to the months Persephone or Proserpina, in **classical** Greek and Roman mythology, respectively, unwillingly spends in the underworld if one realizes that the seasons are determined by the tilt of the earth's axis in relation to its orbit around the sun. Even when a culture no longer believes that its myths are true explanations, however, these stories often survive as receptacles of important cultural values.

A comparison of myths produced by different cultures reveals that myths are strikingly similar in the phenomena they seek to explain and the questions they address, a point that led Swiss analytical psychologist Carl Jung to argue that myths reveal a **collective unconscious,** a common inheritance among all human beings of unconscious memories dating back to the origins of human experience. Many writers have accorded myths a similarly evocative power and have either incorporated myths into their works or created their own mythic frameworks in an attempt to reach their audiences at a universal or primal level of human thought, emotion, and experience;

eighteenth-century poet William Blake and **modernist** poet William Butler Yeats are among the best known **mythopoeic** writers. Furthermore, **myth critics** have also looked beyond the idiosyncratic surfaces of individual **texts** to find mythic figures, forces, patterns, implications, and structures. Myth critics maintain that certain myths are so deeply ingrained in most cultures that literary works typically rehash the same general mythic formulas.

EXAMPLES: An ancient Babylonian creation myth elaborated in the **epic** poem *Enuma Elish* ("When on High") explains the emergence of Marduk as the chief god in tandem with the shaping of the universe. According to the myth, Marduk, originally a minor god, struck a bargain with some other gods to kill Tiamat, a fearsome dragon and salt-water god, in return for recognition as the supreme god. After killing Tiamat and defeating her husband Kingu, Marduk created the sky and waters by splitting Tiamat's body in half, then created and ordered other elements of the universe, such as the constellations. Subsequently, Marduk decided to create "Man" to serve the gods and oversaw the killing of Kingu, whose blood was used to fashion humankind.

The K'iche' (Quiché) Maya account of the creation of humankind is based on the gods' desire for beings who will remember, worship, and nourish them. As set forth in the K'iche' **narrative** *Popol Vuh* (*The Book of the People*) (c. 1550s), after creating the earth and the animals, who were condemned to a life of being killed and eaten for their inability to speak, the gods made several attempts to create men. First they tried making men out of mud, but they were too soft to be of use. Then they tried making men out of wood (and women out of rushes), but they had no minds or souls, so the gods destroyed them with a flood. Finally they tried making men out of maize (corn) but clouding their vision so they could not be gods themselves, then made women to be their wives.

▶ **myth(ic) criticism:** A type of **literary criticism** that analyzes mythic **structures** and **themes** as they are recurrently manifested in literary **genres** and individual works. A myth critic writing on John Milton's *Paradise Lost* (1667) and Joseph Conrad's *Heart of Darkness* (1899), for instance, might see both in terms of the "night journey" common to any number of **myths,** **epics,** and heroic **tales.** Myth critics argue that certain basic mythic figures and situations both permeate and transcend individual cultures; they find universal patterns in works from cultures throughout the world. Canadian critic Northrop Frye was perhaps the best-known myth critic.

Myth criticism has much in common with **archetypal criticism,** but the two approaches to literature are not identical. Myth critics focus specifically on identifying and analyzing recurrent mythic structures and themes in literary works, whereas archetypal critics approach works from a broader perspective, identifying **archetypes,** those cross-cultural **images,** figures, and story patterns manifested in a wide variety of literary works. Archetypes are often expressed in myths and in literary works using mythic structures and themes, hence the overlap between mythic and archetypal criticism.

See also **archetypal criticism, archetype, myth.**

▶ **mythology:** See **myth.**

▶ **mythopoeia (mythopoesis):** The creation or refashioning of **myths** or of a mythic framework for a literary work.

EXAMPLES: Eighteenth-century poet William Blake created a mythic framework that he wove into his poems. **Modernist** poet William Butler Yeats set forth his mythic system openly in a work entitled *A Vision* (1926). J. R. R. Tolkien sought to create an English mythology with his **tales** of Middle Earth, including the **fantasy** trilogy *The Lord of the Rings* (1954–55; adapted to film 2001–03) and *The Silmarillion*, a five-part **narrative** compiled and edited by his son Christopher and published in 1977 after Tolkien's death.

▶ **naive hero:** A **protagonist,** generally the **narrator** of a work, who cannot fully comprehend the world about him or her and who thus consistently but unwittingly misinterprets events or situations. The naive hero's naiveté often results from innocence or immaturity but may also stem from a mental defect or **disability** or a character trait such as insensitivity. A naive hero who also narrates the work is a type of **unreliable narrator,** a narrator whose opinions the reader recognizes as fallible and, therefore, untrustworthy.

Authors may use naive heroes for **comic** or **ironic** effect or to achieve **pathos,** often by having an innocent child relate horrifying events that he or she does not fully understand. Use of a naive hero is a common form of **structural irony,** creating a sustained discrepancy throughout the work between the **hero's** or **heroine's** perceptions and those of the reader or audience.

EXAMPLES: Lemuel Gulliver, the narrator of Jonathan Swift's *Gulliver's Travels* (1735), who is so impressed by the talking horses he meets in Houyhnhnmland that he can see none of their faults and, as a result, none of the virtues of humankind; the young chimney sweep in William Blake's short poem "The Chimney Sweeper" (1789), who evokes pathos. Contemporary examples of naive heroes include Forrest Gump, the decidedly obtuse narrator of Winston Groom's novel *Forrest Gump* (1986; adapted to film 1994); the doppelganger in Martin Amis's novel *Time's Arrow* (1991), who experiences the life of a former Nazi doctor who participated in the Holocaust in reverse, from death to birth; the self-absorbed English detective Christopher Banks in Kazuo Ishiguro's *When We Were Orphans* (2000), obsessed with solving the mystery of his parents' disappearance during his childhood in Shanghai; and the autistic boy in Mark Haddon's *The Curious Incident of the Dog in the Night-time* (2003).

▶ **narration:** The act or process of recounting a **story** or other **narrative.**

▶ **narrative:** A **story** or a telling of a story, or an account of a situation or event. Narratives may be **fictional** or **nonfictional.** They may be written in either **prose** or **verse.** Some critics use the term even more generally; for instance, in *The Content of the Form: Narrative Discourse and Historical Representation* (1987), **narratologist** Hayden White called narrative "a meta-code, a human universal on the basis of which transcultural messages about the nature of a shared reality can be transmitted."

EXAMPLES: A **novel** and a **biography** of a novelist are prose narratives, as are newspaper accounts and psychoanalyst Sigmund Freud's case histories. Examples of verse narratives include **ballads** and **epics.** *Amazwi Abesifazane* ("Voices of Women"), a contemporary South African project inaugurated in 2000 to recover and archive the stories of indigenous women from the apartheid era, encourages women to tell their stories visually, through the production of embroidered, appliquéd, and beaded "memory cloths" that **cathartically** detail an episode from "a day I will never forget."

▶ **narratology:** A **text**-centered, theoretical approach to the study of **narrative,** particularly in literature and film, that focuses on analysis of the **structural** components of narrative and how these components interrelate. Narratologists treat narratives as explicitly constructed systems, as **representations** that create and shape meaning. They take a neutral, non-valuative approach, seeking to identify and describe the structuring mechanics that underlie all narratives as well as particular narrative **forms,** whether comic strips, movies, novels, plays, or video games.

Major **influences** on narratology include **Russian formalism,** whose proponents focused on the form of literary works, and **structuralism,** whose proponents sought to show that all elements of human culture could be understood as parts of a system of **signs.** Russian formalists drew an important distinction between *fabula* **(story)** and *syuzhet* **(plot),** associating *fabula* with how events in a narrative would be recounted chronologically and *syuzhet* with how they are actually presented. Also influential was twentieth-century Russian theorist Vladimir Propp's *Morphology of the Folktale* (1928; translated into English 1958), an analysis of common elements in Russian **folk tales** identifying thirty-one sequential functions (e.g., **hero** leaves home, false hero exposed) and seven **character** types (e.g., **villain,** princess, helper). French structural anthropologist Claude Lévi-Strauss likewise took a systematic approach to the analysis of **myths** in his *Anthropologie structurale* (*Structural Anthropology*) (1958), identifying fundamental elements he called "mythemes."

Narratology emerged in France in the 1960s, particularly with the publication in 1966 of a special issue in the French journal *Communications* on the structural analysis of narrative. In an essay entitled "Introduction à l'analyse structurale des récits" ("Introduction to the Structural Analysis of Narratives") (1966), French **structuralist critic** Roland Barthes identified three levels of narrative — functions, actions, and **narration** — and expanded analysis of narration to include elements such as **point of view** and the role of the **narrator.** Subsequently, in *Grammaire du Décaméron* (1969), theorist Tzvetan Todorov coined the term *narratologie,* arguing that "our first task is the elaboration of a descriptive apparatus; before being able to explain the facts, we must learn to identify them." As narratology developed in the 1970s and 1980s in Europe and the U.S., practitioners incorporated concepts and techniques used by formalist and structuralist precursors as well as traditional methods of analyzing narrative fiction, such as those outlined in the "Showing as Telling" chapter of **reader-oriented critic** Wayne Booth's *The Rhetoric of Fiction* (1961). Dutch theorist Mieke Bal's *Narratology: Introduction to the Theory of Narrative* (1985, 2nd ed. 1997), first published as *De theorie van vertellen en verhalen* (1978), is a standard introduction to the approach. Other noted "classical" narratologists include Seymour Chatman, Gérard Genette, and Gerald Prince.

Narratologists distinguish among story, plot, and **discourse** (how a story is narrated), studying the **conventions** and devices that govern the transformation of stories into plots and the stylistic choices that shape narrative form. Typical narratological concerns include **characterization,** focalization (point of view, or who sees), narration (narrative voice, or who speaks), narrative tenses (use of past or present), narrative modes (e.g., showing a scene or providing a summary), and the range of entities involved in the mediation and interpretation of narratives (the real author, real reader, **implied author, implied reader,** narrator, and narratee). Many narratologists are also concerned with time; in "Discours du récit" (*Narrative Discourse*) (1972), Genette, for instance, discussed **analepsis** and **prolepsis,** forms of **anachrony,** and drew a distinction between "discourse time" (the time needed to read the narrative or a portion thereof) and "story time" (time within the world of the narrative).

Given their focus on the text, narratologists have tended to disregard readers' responses and their role in the production of meaning, leading to criticism of the approach as generating overly reductive models and ignoring contextual factors such as when and where a narrative takes place. In the last two decades, the approach has become increasingly interdisciplinary, with contemporary narratologists developing cognitive, **cultural, gender** studies, legal, and **postmodernist** branches, among others. For discussion of such "postclassical" offshoots, see, e.g., Luc Herman and Bart Vervaeck's *Handbook of Narrative Analysis* (2005).

▶ **narrator:** A speaker through whom an **author** presents a **narrative,** often but not always a **character** in the work. Every narrative has a narrator; a work may even occasionally have multiple narrators or a main narrator with subnarrators. The type of narrator used is intertwined with **point of view,** the vantage point from which the narrative is told. A work written from the **third-person** point of view may have either an **omniscient** or **limited** narrator. One written from the **first-person** may be narrated by the author, if the work is **autobiographical** or otherwise **nonfictional,** or, if **fictional,** by the **protagonist,** another character (whether major or minor), or a witness who observes but does not participate in the **action.** (Use of the **second-person** point of view is rare in prose fiction.) Furthermore, narrators may be classified as **intrusive** (opinionated) or **unintrusive** (detached), terms generally used with respect to omniscient narrators; reliable or **unreliable,** terms generally used with respect to fictional first-person narrators; or self-conscious or self-effacing, depending on whether they draw attention to their status as storytellers and to the work as a literary product. Third-person narrators (particularly omniscient ones) generally have a more authorial-seeming sound and function and are more likely to comment upon the action in addition to recounting it.

Occasionally an author will use a narrative device in lieu of a narrator. In the movie *Cast Away* (2000), for instance, Wilson, a volleyball addressed by the marooned Chuck Noland, serves as a narrative device used to inform the audience of the thoughts and feelings of the isolated, lonely protagonist.

FURTHER EXAMPLES: *The Rule of Four* (2004), a thriller coauthored by Ian Caldwell and Dustin Thomason, has a first-person narrator, who begins the story as follows:

> Strange thing, time. It weighs most on those who have it least. ....
> I can see myself now, the night it all began. I'm lying back on the old red sofa in our dorm room, wrestling with Pavlov and his dogs in my introductory psychology book, wondering why I never fulfilled my science requirement as a freshman, like everyone else.

By contrast, Dan Brown used an omniscient third-person narrator in his thriller *The Da Vinci Code* (2003; adapted to film 2006), which opens as follows:

> Renowned curator Jacques Saunière staggered through the vaulted archway of the museum's Grand Gallery. He lunged for the nearest painting he could see, a Caravaggio. Grabbing the gilded frame, the seventy-six-year-old man heaved the masterpiece toward himself until it tore from the wall and Saunière collapsed backward in a heap beneath the canvas.

Examples of works with multiple narrators include Wilkie Collins's *The Moonstone* (1868), a **mystery** composed of the written accounts of several parties; William Faulker's *As I Lay Dying* (1930), which consists of **direct interior monologues** by fifteen **characters**; and Nick Hornby's *A Long Way Down* (2005), whose four narrators first meet atop a tower block from which they each planned to jump to their death. David James Duncan's *The Brothers K* (1992), an American **epic** of sorts, is an example of a work with a main narrator, Kincaid Chance, who is the youngest of four brothers, and a subnarrator, the oldest brother, Everett.

▶ **naturalism:** With reference to the arts in general, a **mode** of **representation** that is detailed, detached, and **objective;** applied specifically to literature, a literary movement of the late nineteenth and early twentieth centuries in Europe and America that represented people in a deterministic and generally pessimistic light as products of heredity and environment. Naturalists sought to apply the scientific method to the study of humanity, using a case-study approach in literary works and portraying **characters** and situations objectively without commenting on morality or fairness. They typically focused on the poor and uneducated, the sordid and degrading, depicting life as a struggle to survive and people as being at the mercy of biological and socioeconomic forces.

Naturalism arose in France in the second half of the nineteenth century, then spread to other countries including England, Germany, Russia, and the U.S. French writer Émile Zola, the leading theorist of the movement, emphasized its scientific approach; responding to critics in the preface to the second edition of his novel *Thérèse Raquin* (1868), he explained that his "starting-point" was "the study of temperament and the profound modifications of an organism subjected to pressure of environments and circumstances":

> . . . I have chosen people completely dominated by their nerves and blood, without free will, drawn into each action of their lives by the inexorable laws of their physical nature. Thérèse and Laurent are human animals, nothing more. . . .
> . . . I simply applied to two living bodies the analytical methods that surgeons apply to corpses.

As Zola's description suggests, naturalists viewed humans as but higher-order animals, subject to their instincts, passions, and surroundings. They also believed only in the natural, physical realm and rejected religious or supernatural explanations of events. Their works accordingly expressed a deterministic philosophical viewpoint, heavily influenced by emerging **theories,** especially the English scientist Charles Darwin's theory of evolution by natural selection. Other **influences** included English political theorist Herbert Spencer's concept of the social evolution of humanity and the survival of the fittest; the economic determinism of German philosophers Karl Marx and Friedrich Engels; French **positivist** thinker Auguste Comte, who applied the scientific method to the social sciences; and French literary critic Hippolyte Taine, who advocated the impartial study of humans as products.

While some critics have viewed naturalism as an outgrowth of **realism,** particularly in light of the naturalistic emphasis on **concrete** details and the objective depiction of everyday life, others have sought to distinguish the two. George Becker, for instance, characterized naturalism in "Modern Realism as a Literary Movement" (1963) as "no more than an emphatic and explicit philosophical position taken by some realists, showing man caught in a net from which there can be no escape and degenerating under those circumstances; that is, it is pessimistic materialistic determinism." Donald Pizer, by contrast, discussing American naturalism in *Realism and Naturalism in Nineteenth-Century American Literature* (1966), distinguished naturalistic works from realistic ones based on two pervading tensions in naturalistic works that reveal "the intermingling in life of controlling force and individual worth." One tension Pizer identified lies between the **themes** of determinism and the significance of the individual, the other between the lowly subject matter and "the concept of man that emerges," namely, the discovery of the "extraordinary and excessive in human nature." From either perspective, naturalists differed from realists in their deterministic approach, with realists holding that people have at least some degree of free will that they can exercise to affect their situations and naturalists assuming humans have little if any control over what happens.

Noted naturalists aside from Zola, who more fully theorized the **genre** in *Le roman experimental* (*The Experimental Novel*) (1880), include English writers George Gissing and George Moore and American authors Stephen Crane, Theodore Dreiser, and Frank Norris.

FURTHER EXAMPLES: Zola's *Germinal* (1885); August Strindberg's *Miss Julie* (1888); Crane's "The Open Boat" (1894); Dreiser's *An American Tragedy* (1925); Ellen Glasgow's *Barren Ground* (1925); Richard Wright's *Native Son* (1940); Norman Mailer's *The Naked and the Dead* (1948).

▶ **Naturalistic Period (in American literature):** A period in American literary history commonly said to have begun around 1900 and to have ended with the outbreak of World War I in 1914. The Naturalistic Period derives its name from **naturalism,** a literary movement that **represented** people in a deterministic and generally pessimistic light as products of heredity and environment. Stephen Crane is most frequently credited with pioneering American naturalism in the 1890s with works such as *Maggie: A Girl of the Streets* (1893), which depicts life in New York's Bowery district and features a **protagonist** who commits suicide after being abandoned by a man and becoming a prostitute. Noted naturalistic novels of the period include Theodore Dreiser's *Sister Carrie* (1900), Frank Norris's *The Octopus* (1901), and Jack London's *The Call of the Wild* (1903).

Realistic novels also continued to flourish during the Naturalistic Period. Prominent practitioners included Willa Cather, Edith Wharton, William Dean Howells, and Henry James, the latter two of whom are also associated with the **Realistic Period** in American literature. Noted works include James's *The Ambassadors* (1903), Wharton's *The House of Mirth* (1905), and Cather's *O Pioneers!* (1913).

Modern American poetry is often traced to the Naturalistic Period. **Imagism,** an *avant-garde* movement emphasizing concise, direct expression and clear, precise **images,** was born in 1909, led chiefly by Ezra Pound and exemplified by the work of poets such as H. D. (Hilda Doolittle). Subsequently, in 1912, editor and critic Harriet Monroe founded *Poetry,* the first magazine to publish the Imagists and still the leading American journal devoted to poetry today. The careers of a number of other **modernist** poets such as T. S. Eliot, Robert Frost, Carl Sandburg, and William Carlos Williams also began during this period.

Furthermore, significant American drama began to emerge. The Little Theater Movement, which had arisen in France in 1887 to promote the development of plays with serious literary value, appeared in Chicago in 1906 and then spread to other American cities, bringing drama to many more people than ever before.

Finally, the rise of **muckrakers,** investigative journalists and other writers who sought to expose abuse and corruption in big business and government, which they believed were responsible for numerous social problems, also occurred during the Naturalistic Period. Noted muckrakers included Samuel Adams; Ray Stannard Baker; David Graham Phillips; Lincoln Steffens; and

Ida Tarbell, whose *The History of the Standard Oil Company* (1904) helped spur the breakup of the Standard Oil monopoly in 1911.

See **naturalism**.

▶ **nature writing:** See **ecocriticism**.

▶ **near rhyme:** See **half rhyme**.

▶ **negative capability:** A term coined by English **romantic** poet John Keats (in a December 21, 1817 letter to his brothers) to describe the capacity to be "in uncertainties, mysteries, doubts, without any irritable reaching after fact and reason." For Keats, the ability to remain open-minded — to embrace the unsure and ambiguous, to avoid the temptation to rationalize all uncertainties, to negate one's own personality and prejudices — was critical to perceiving reality in its manifold complexity. Indeed, Keats identified negative capability as the "quality [that] went to form a Man of Achievement, especially in Literature," and asserted that "with a great poet the sense of Beauty overcomes every other consideration," citing **Renaissance** poet and playwright William Shakespeare as a model of negative capability and criticizing fellow romantic poet Samuel Taylor Coleridge as "incapable of remaining content with half-knowledge." Subsequent critics have built on Keats's ideas by arguing that writers should maintain **aesthetic distance** from their subject matter and that artistic form trumps conventional standards of morality and truth.

▶ **neo-Aristotelianism:** See **Chicago school**.

▶ **Neoclassical Period (in English literature):** A period in English literary history spanning the years 1660 to 1798. The Neoclassical Period is usually divided into three literary eras: the **Restoration Age**, which ended around 1700; the **Augustan Age**, which spanned the first half of the eighteenth century; and the **Age of Johnson**, which spanned the second half of the eighteenth century.

Major writers of the period include Joseph Addison, a poet, essayist, and playwright; John Dryden, a poet, critic, and playwright; and Samuel Johnson, a poet, essayist, and **lexicographer**. Other noted writers include the novelist-playwrights Aphra Behn and Henry Fielding; William Congreve, best known for his **comedies of manners; satirical** poet Alexander Pope, and prose satirist Jonathan Swift.

See **neoclassicism**.

▶ **neoclassicism:** A style of Western literature that flourished from the mid-seventeenth century until the end of the eighteenth century and the rise of **romanticism**. The neoclassicists looked to the great **classical** writers for inspiration and guidance, considering them to have mastered every major **genre**, including the "noblest" literary forms, namely, **tragic** drama and the **epic**.

Neoclassical writers shared several beliefs. First, they thought of literature as an art, a craft requiring long and careful study. While they acknowledged the importance of individual inspiration and talent, many practiced **imitation** of the "masters" in order to perfect their work and foster proper models of expression. Second, they emphasized adherence to **form** and to the **conventions** and rules associated with given genres. Third, they thought that literature should both instruct and delight and that the proper subject of art was humanity. Unlike some of the more idealistic and expansive writers who preceded them during the **Renaissance** (and followed during the **Romantic Period**), neoclassicists started from the assumption that humanity is imperfect and limited. Nevertheless, many neoclassicists found cause for optimism, particularly in the power of reason to perfect human civilization gradually, in keeping with the **Enlightenment** thinking of the period.

The **Restoration** (of the monarchy) in 1660 marked the beginning of the *Neoclassical Period* in Great Britain, whose writers included John Dryden, Henry Fielding, Samuel Johnson, Alexander Pope, and Jonathan Swift. But neoclassicism was by no means an exclusively British phenomenon; the movement flourished throughout Europe, particularly in France and Germany. French dramatist Jean Racine's tragedy *Phèdre* (1677) exemplifies neoclassical qualities, as does Molière's satiric comedy *Tartuffe* (1667). In Germany, this movement was simply called *die Klassik,* or classicism. Notable works include Friedrich Schiller's play *Don Carlos* (1787), Johann Wolfgang von Goethe's *Iphegenie auf Tauris* (1787), and Friedrich Hölderlin's long poem *Brot und Wein* (*Bread and Wine*) (c. 1800). German classicism developed one major difference from Graeco-Roman **classicism:** the absolute, uncompromisable integrity of the human being.

Neoclassicism stressed reason, harmony, balance, restraint, order, serenity, **decorum,** and **realism** — above all, an appeal to the intellect rather than emotion. Noted statements of neoclassical principles and rules included Nicolas Boileau's *L'art poétique* (*The Art of Poetry*) (1674) and Pope's "An Essay on Criticism" (1711); preferred literary forms included the **comedy of manners, epigram, essay, fable,** letter, **ode,** and **satire.** The twentieth century witnessed a revival of neoclassical qualities in such writers as W. H. Auden, T. S. Eliot, Robert Frost, and Ezra Pound. Many critics have viewed this revival as a corrective reaction to the excesses of romanticism, whose conventions, styles, and traditions nonetheless still influence our literary landscape.

▶ **neologism:** A new word or phrase, typically coined to express economically a meaning not conveyed by any single word in the dictionary, or a new usage of an existing word or phrase. Words as common today as *intellectual* and *television* were once neologisms, as was *Cabinet* in its governmental sense. So were *Kleenex* and *Xerox,* trademarks that have entered popular parlance as synonyms for "facial tissue" and "photocopy," respectively. Indeed, at some point, every word in a language was a neologism.

Writers may invent neologisms in literary works to convey an idea or create an effect that no existing word could convey or create.

EXAMPLES: Horace Walpole invented the word *serendipity* by adding the "-ity" suffix to "Serendip," an old name for Sri Lanka, linking the word in a January 8, 1754, letter to a Persian **fairy tale** called *The Three Princes of Serendip,* who "were always making discoveries, by accidents and sagacity, of things which they were not in quest of." James Joyce's *Finnegans Wake* (1939) is rife with neologisms, including words such as *bethicket* and *funferal.* Jerry W. Ward Jr.'s poem "Jazz to Jackson to John" (1988) incorporates a neologism in the second of the following lines: "yeah, brother, it must have been something / striking you like an eargasm, / a baritone ax laid into soprano wood . . ."

The Beatles' use of "snide" as a verb in "I Am the Walrus" (1967) is neologistic, as is rapper Snoop Dogg's use of "Snoop Latin," which involves the insertion of "izz," "izzay," or other "izz-" forms to create neologisms such as *bizznatch,* a combination of "bitch" and "snatch." Other contemporary neologisms include many Internet-related terms (e.g., **blog,** *netiquette, podcast*) and *truthiness,* an old term given new meaning by mock-pundit Stephen Colbert in *The Colbert Report* debut (October 17, 2005) to describe a conception of truth based not on fact but on what one personally feels or wishes to be true. As Colbert **satirically** asserted: "I don't trust books. They're all fact, no heart. And that's exactly what's pulling our country apart today. . . . [W]e are divided between those who think with their head, and those who *know* with their *heart.*"

▶ **Neoplatonism:** A school of thought, originating in the third century A.D. in Alexandria, Egypt, and persisting until the fifth century, whose proponents believed in the superiority of mind over matter and concerned themselves with fundamental human aspirations and problems. They especially developed Plato's theory of beauty, arguing that the Absolute (the One, the Infinite Being, the source of all value and being) radiates all the beauty (and goodness and truth) that exists in this world. Neoplatonism, whose best-known proponent is the third-century philosopher Plotinus, incorporated certain elements of Christianity, gnosticism, and Oriental **mysticism** into **Platonic** thought to create a relatively optimistic, if vaguely defined, philosophical system. Later Christian thinkers were greatly influenced by the Neoplatonists, particularly by their concept of the Absolute and their understanding of beauty. Subsequently, during the **Renaissance,** Neoplatonism was revived by thinkers who stressed that the material world is a path to the spiritual realm, rather than an obstacle to or diversion from it. Writers influenced by this version of Neoplatonism often wrote about lovers practicing a version of **Platonic love** that is in fact Neoplatonic; although the lovers' ultimate goal is to apprehend Divine Beauty, they appreciate the bodily beauty of their earthly lover, believing it to signify a higher, more ethereal beauty, the experience of which will further their spiritual quest. (Neo)platonic love and lovers appear in the **courtesy books** of Baldassare

Castiglione (*The Courtier* [1528]) and in the poetry of Dante Alighieri, Petrarch (Francesco Petrarca), and Edmund Spenser.

▶ **New Criticism, the:** Named after John Crowe Ransom's book *The New Criticism* (1941), a type of **formalist literary criticism** characterized by close textual analysis that reached its height in the U.S. in the 1940s and 1950s. New Critics treated literary works, which they viewed as carefully crafted, orderly objects containing observable formal patterns, as self-contained and self-referential and thus based their interpretations on elements within the **text** rather than on external factors such as the effects of a work or biographical and historical materials. Ransom, for instance, asserted in "Criticism, Inc." (1937) that the "first law" of criticism was to "be objective, [to] cite the nature of the object rather than its effects upon the subject"; indeed, he argued that concern with the effects of a work "denies the autonomy of the artist as one who interests himself in the artistic object in his own right, and likewise the autonomy of the work as existing for its own sake." In analyzing texts, New Critics performed **close readings,** concentrating on the relationships among elements such as **images, rhythm,** and **symbols** and paying special attention to repetition. They also emphasized that the **structure** of a text should not be divorced from its meaning and praised the use of literary devices such as **irony** and **paradox** to harmonize dissimilar, even conflicting, elements.

The foundations of the New Criticism were laid in books and essays written during the 1920s and 1930s by theorists in England, notably I. A. Richards (*Practical Criticism* [1929]), William Empson (*Seven Types of Ambiguity* [1930]), and T. S. Eliot ("The Function of Criticism" [1933]). The approach was significantly developed, however, by a group of American poets and critics — with whom the term *New Critics* is most often associated — including Ransom, R. P. Blackmur, Cleanth Brooks, Allen Tate, Robert Penn Warren, and William K. Wimsatt. Generally Southern, religious, and culturally conservative, these critics argued that literature has its own mode of language, in contradistinction to the logical and scientific, such that a literary work exists in its own world and has inherent worth. As Tate asserted in "Literature as Knowledge" (1941), poetry "is neither the world of verifiable science nor a projection of ourselves; yet it is *complete.*" The New Criticism quickly gained ascendancy in American academia, with textbooks such as Brooks and Warren's *Understanding Poetry* (1938) becoming standard in college and even high school courses well into the 1970s; in their introductory "Letter to the Teacher," Brooks and Warren opened with the assertion that "if poetry is worth teaching at all it is worth teaching as poetry," emphasizing the importance of treating the poem "as a literary construct," "as an object in itself."

Given its focus on the text, the New Criticism has often been seen as an attack on **romanticism** and **impressionism,** particularly **impressionistic criticism,** which centers on the critic's **subjective** impressions of a literary work. New Critics believed that it was erroneous to interpret texts according to the psychological responses of readers, a practice they termed the **affective fallacy**. They also rejected the practice of basing interpretation on an author's **intentions,** which they called the **intentional fallacy.** By the 1970s, the New Criticism came under increasing attack with the advent of **reader-response criticism** and **poststructuralist** approaches such as **deconstruction.** Yet many of its emphases and procedures, particularly close reading and the accompanying **explication** of literary texts, have survived and thrived; as William E. Cain pointed out in "The Institutionalization of the New Criticism" (1982), "what was once the aim of a particular critical movement now defines the general aims of criticism. Close reading of literary texts is the ground that nearly all theories and methods build upon or seek to occupy."

See also **affective fallacy, intentional fallacy.**

▶ **new cultural history, the:** See **new historicism, the.**

▶ **new historicism, the:** A type of historically oriented **literary criticism** that developed during the 1980s, largely in reaction to the **text**-only approach pursued by **formalists,** including practitioners of **the New Criticism.** Pioneers of the new historicism include American literary theorists Louis Montrose and Stephen Greenblatt, whose approach transformed the field of **Renaissance** studies and influenced the study of American and English **romantic** literature.

New historicists, like formalists, acknowledge the importance of the literary text, but they analyze it with an eye to history. In this respect, the new historicism is not "new"; the majority of critics between 1920 and 1950 embraced **historicism,** focusing on a work's historical content and basing their interpretations on the interplay between the text and historical contexts (such as the **author's** life or **intentions** in writing the work). The historical criticism practiced in the 1980s, however, was not the same as that of the past. Indeed, if the word "new" still serves any useful purpose in defining contemporary historical criticism, it is in distinguishing it from such older forms of historicism.

The new historicism is informed by diverse **discourses,** including the **poststructuralist** and **reader-response** theory of the 1970s, as well as the thinking of **feminist, cultural,** and **Marxist critics.** New historicist critics assume that literary works both influence and are influenced by historical reality, and they share a belief in referentiality, that is, a belief that literature both refers to and is referred to by things outside itself. They are also less fact- and event-oriented than historical critics used to be, questioning whether the truth about what really happened can ever be **objectively** known. They are less likely to see history as linear and progressive, as something developing toward the present, and they are also less likely to think of it in terms of specific eras, each with a definite, persistent, and consistent *Zeitgeist* (spirit of the times). Hence, they are unlikely to suggest that a literary text has a single or easily identifiable historical context.

New historicists also tend to define the discipline of history more broadly than did their predecessors. They view history as a social science and the social sciences as being properly historical. In *Historical Studies and Literary Criticism* (1985), Jerome McGann spoke of the need to make sociohistorical subjects and methods central to literary studies; in *The Beauty of Inflections: Literary Investigations in Historical Method and Theory* (1985), he linked sociology and the future of historical criticism. Similarly, in "Toward a New History in Literary Study" (1984), Herbert Lindenberger found anthropology particularly useful in the new historicist analysis of literature, especially as practiced by the Scottish and American anthropologists Victor Turner and Clifford Geertz, respectively.

Geertz, who related theatrical traditions in nineteenth-century Bali to contemporaneous forms of political organization in his study *Negara: The Theatre State in Nineteenth-Century Bali* (1980), influenced many new historicists to reject the conventional distinction between literature and the history relevant to it. Unlike historicists of the past, who viewed historical contexts as "background" information necessary to appreciate fully the separate world of art, new historicists erased the line dividing historical and literary materials as well as the one separating artistic works from their creators and audiences. For instance, in "The Historical Necessity for — and Difficulties with — New Historical Analysis in Introductory Literature Courses" (1987), Brook Thomas proposed that discussion of John Keats's "Ode on a Grecian Urn" (1820) begin by considering where Keats would have seen such an urn — and how a Grecian urn came to rest in an English museum. Important historical and political realities, Thomas suggested, underlie and inform Keats's definitions of art, truth, beauty, the past, and timelessness. Moreover, new historicists have used what Geertz called **thick descriptions** to blur distinctions between history and the other social sciences, background and foreground, political and poetical events.

Indeed, new historicists have sought to **decenter** the study of literature, not only by incorporating historical studies but also by struggling to see history itself from a decentered perspective, which entails recognizing that a historian's position is historically determined and that events seldom have a single cause. New historicists remind us that it is treacherous to reconstruct the past as it really was — rather than as we have been conditioned by our own place and time to believe that it was. And they know that the job is impossible for those who are unaware of that difficulty, insensitive to the bent or bias of their own historical vantage point. Historical criticism must be "conscious of its status as interpretation," Greenblatt asserted in *Renaissance Self-Fashioning from More to Shakespeare* (1980). Hence, when new historicist critics describe a historical change, they are likely to discuss the **theory** of historical change that informs their account and to acknowledge that the changes they notice are ones that their (historically determined) theory enables them to see.

In "Keats and the Historical Method in Literary Criticism" (1979), McGann suggested that new historicists follow a set of basic, scholarly procedures, "practical derivatives of the Bakhtin school" that assume new historicist critics will study a literary work's "point of origin" via **biography** and bibliography. McGann advocated beginning with the expressed **intentions** of the author, which, if published, have modified the developing history of the work, then addressing the history of the work's reception, which has become part of the platform for studying the work at the critic's "point of reception." Finally, he advocated pointing toward the future, defining the aims and limits of the critical project, and injecting the analysis with a degree of self-consciousness to give it credibility.

By contrast, in his introduction to a collection of writings on *The New Historicism* (1989), H. Aram Veeser stressed the unity among new historicists by outlining certain "key assumptions," namely: that "expressive acts" cannot be separated from "material" conditions; that the boundary between "literary and nonliterary texts" is false; that neither "imaginative" nor "archival" (historical) discourse "gives access to unchanging truths nor expresses inalterable human nature"; that historical critiques tend to depend on the methods they condemn; and that critical discourses "adequate to describe culture under capitalism participate in the economy they describe."

These same assumptions are shared by a group of historians practicing *the new cultural history*. Influenced by *Annales*-school historians in France and post-Althusserian **Marxists,** the new cultural historians share with their new historicist counterparts an interest in anthropological and sociological subjects and methods; a creative way of weaving stories and **anecdotes** about the past into revealing thick descriptions; a tendency to focus on nontraditional, non**canonical** subjects and relations (historian Thomas Laqueur is best known for *Making Sex: Body and Gender from the Greeks to Freud* [1990]); and the tendency to invoke or engage the writings of Michel Foucault.

Foucault, a French philosophical historian who often made connections between disparate incidents and phenomena, encouraged new historicists and new cultural historicists to redefine the boundaries of historical inquiry. No historical event, he argued, has a single cause; rather, each event is tied into a vast web of economic, social, and political factors. Moreover, like Karl Marx, the German philosopher who founded **Marxism,** Foucault saw history in terms of power, but his view of power probably owed more to Friedrich Nietzsche, another nineteenth-century German philosopher. Foucault viewed power not simply as a repressive force or a tool of conspiracy but, rather, as a complex of forces that produces what happens. Not even a tyrannical aristocrat simply wields power, for the aristocrat is himself empowered by discourses and practices that constitute power.

Discipline and Punish: The Birth of the Prison (1975) illustrates some of Foucault's key ideas. The book opens with a description of the public execution of a Frenchman who had attempted to assassinate King Louis XV, then details rules that govern the daily life of modern Parisian felons. What happened to torture, to punishment as public spectacle? Foucault asked.

What network of forces made it disappear? In seeking to understand this "power," Foucault noted that, in the early years of the nineteenth century, crowds would sometimes identify with the prisoner and treat the executioner as if he were the guilty party, but he set forth other reasons for keeping prisoners alive, moving punishment indoors, and eliminating physical torture in favor of mental rehabilitation: prisoners could be used to establish colonies and trade; they could also be used as infiltrators and informers.

Greenblatt, a founding editor of the journal *Representations* and still the best known new historicist, is among the critics who have followed Foucault's lead. For instance, in *Renaissance Self-Fashioning from More to Shakespeare,* he interpreted literary devices as if they were continuous with all other **representational** devices in a culture, turning to scholars in other fields in order to better understand the workings of literature. In *Learning to Curse: Essays in Early Modern Culture* (1990), Greenblatt also acknowledged the influence of Marxist **cultural critic** Raymond Williams, who addressed topics excluded from Greenblatt's literary education at Yale. Questions about "who controlled access to the printing press, who owned the land and the factories, whose voices were being repressed as well as represented in literary texts, what social strategies were being served by the aesthetic values we constructed — came pressing back in upon the act of interpretation." Blending such concepts with poststructuralist thought about the **undecidability,** or indeterminacy, of meaning, Greenblatt developed a critical method that he has called *cultural poetics,* a term that he prefers to "the new historicism." More tentative and less overtly political than cultural criticism, it involves what Thomas called "the technique of montage" in "The New Literary Historicism" (1995): "Starting with the analysis of a particular historical event, it cuts to the analysis of a particular literary text. The point is not to show that the literary text reflects the historical event but to create a field of energy between the two so that we come to see the event as a social text and the literary text as a social event."

Not all new historicist critics are as influenced by Foucault and Williams as Greenblatt. Some, like Thomas, owe more to German Marxist Walter Benjamin, best known for essays such as "The Work of Art in the Age of Mechanical Reproduction" (1936) and "Theses on the Philosophy of History" (1940). Still others — McGann, for example — have followed the lead of twentieth-century Soviet critic Mikhail Bakhtin, who viewed literary works in terms of **polyphonic** discourses and **dialogues** between the official, legitimate voices of a society and other, more challenging or critical voices echoing popular culture.

The new historicism today remains inchoate, subject to revision as historical circumstances change. New historicists themselves advocate and even stress the need to perpetually redefine categories and boundaries — whether disciplinary, **generic,** national, or **racial** — because they are historically constructed and thus subject to change. Consequently, many new historicist critics are working at the border of other approaches, including cultural, feminist, Marxist, **postcolonial,** poststructuralist, and reader-oriented criticism.

▶ **new novel:** A term sometimes used interchangeably with **antinovel, *nouveau roman,*** or both.

See **antinovel,** *nouveau roman.*

▶ **New Wave:** See **science fiction.**

▶ **Noble Savage:** See **primitivism.**

▶ ***nom de plume:*** From the French, an author's "pen name." The term most commonly refers to *pseudonyms,* entirely fictitious names adopted by writers seeking to mask their identities or to publish works differing in kind or quality under different names. The term may also apply more broadly, however, to whatever name an author uses for publication. Thus, Mark Twain (Samuel Clemens), Dr. Seuss (Theodor Seuss Geisel), and J. K. Rowling (Joanne Rowling) may all be called *noms de plume.*

Although the term *nom de plume* is taken from the French, the French themselves use the phrase *nom de guerre.*

EXAMPLES: Benjamin Franklin wrote under the *nom de plume* Richard Saunders in his serial *Poor Richard's Almanack* (1733–58); French novelist Marie-Henri Beyle wrote under the *nom de guerre* Stendhal. Nineteenth-century female writers who adopted male pseudonyms include Amandine Aurore Lucie Dupin, Mary Ann Evans, and Charlotte and Emily Brontë, who published, respectively, as George Sand, George Eliot, and Currer and Ellis Bell. Twentieth-century Chilean poets Lucila de María del Perpetuo Socorro Godoy Alcayaga and Ricardo Eliecer Neftalí Reyes Basoalto are also better known by their *noms de plume,* Gabriela Mistral and Pablo Neruda. Contemporary novelists who have used pen names include Michael Crichton, who also writes as Jeffery Hudson and John Lange and has coauthored a book with brother Douglas Crichton under the single joint *nom de plume* of Michael Douglas, and Anne Rice, who has writen pornography under the name A. N. Roquelaure.

▶ **nonfiction:** Broadly defined, any account that is factual rather than fictional; as a literary **genre,** works of **prose** representing real people and events rather than imagined ones. Major types of nonfiction include articles, **autobiographies, biographies,** documentaries, **essays,** journals, **memoirs,** papers, and travel literature. While nonfiction is often thought of as "true" — rather than "made up," as fiction — nonfictional accounts vary in accuracy. Moreover, the boundary between fiction and nonfiction is porous. Fictional works such as **autobiographical fiction** and the **historical novel** border on fact, and nonfictional works such as *creative nonfiction* and the **nonfiction novel** make extensive use of fictional techniques. The term *faction,* a **portmanteau word** often credited to American writer Norman Mailer, refers to works that blur the boundary between fact and fiction.

▶ **nonfiction novel:** A **narrative** that uses techniques associated with **fiction** to recount factual, historical events in the form of a **novel**. American writer Truman Capote, often credited with inaugurating the **genre** with *In Cold Blood: A True Account of a Multiple Murder and Its Consequences* (1965), described the nonfiction novel in a 1966 *New York Times* interview as "a serious new art form" based on "narrative reportage" and as "a narrative form that employ[s] all the techniques of fictional art but [is] nevertheless immaculately factual." As Capote's reference to journalism indicates, nonfiction novels, which typically address recent or even contemporary events, require intensive research and often involve interviews by the **author** of those involved in the events. As novelistic narratives, however, they typically include **dialogue** and descriptions of state of mind that involve varying degrees of conjecture and may also present events out of their chronological order. Some nonfiction novels may even include **characters** who were not actually involved in the **action**.

FURTHER EXAMPLES: Norman Mailer's *Armies of the Night* (1968) and *The Executioner's Song* (1979).

▶ **nonsense verse:** A type of **light verse,** typically humorous or whimsical, that does not make conventional sense and is often written for children. Nonsense verse is characterized by an emphasis on playfulness, **rhythm,** and sound effects; use of the absurd, illogical, or unlikely; and incorporation of nonce words made up for the occasion. Although difficult if not impossible to paraphrase, nonsense verse is seldom meaningless. Noted practitioners include nineteenth-century English writers Lewis Carroll and Edward Lear, turn-of-the-century German writer Christian Morgenstern, twentieth-century Russian poet Kornei Chukovsky, and twentieth-century American poet Ogden Nash. Much nonsense verse has also been written anonymously, such as the nursery rhyme "Hey diddle diddle."

FURTHER EXAMPLES: Lear's *Book of Nonsense* (1846), a collection of **limericks** for children; D'Arcy W. Thompson's *Nursery Nonsense; or, Rhymes without Reason* (1865); Carroll's poem "Jabberwocky" (1871), the first two **stanzas** of which follow:

> 'Twas brillig, and the slithy toves
> Did gyre and gimble in the wabe;
> All mimsy were the borogoves,
> And the mome raths outgrabe.
>
> "Beware the Jabberwock, my son!
> The jaws that bite, the claws that catch!
> Beware the Jubjub bird, and shun
> The frumious Bandersnatch!"

Twentieth-century examples of nonsense verse include *An Alliterative Alphabet Aimed at Adult Abecedarians* (1947), by husband-and-wife team Huger Elliott and Elizabeth Shippen Green; the Beatles' song "I Am the Walrus" (1967); and Spike Milligan's "On the Ning Nang Nong" (1959; from his collection *Silly Verse for Kids*), which in 1998 was voted the most popular nonsense verse in England.

▶ *nouveau roman:* Literally "new novel," the French term for a type of experimental **novel**, often referred to in English as the **new novel** or **antinovel**, that subverts and violates established literary **conventions**. French literary critic Émile Henriot coined the term in 1957 in the newspaper *Le Monde* to describe Nathalie Sarraute's *Tropismes* (*Tropisms*) (1939) and Alain Robbe-Grillet's *La Jalousie* (*Jealousy*) (1957), novels that featured detailed physical description and jettisoned standard **narrative** elements such as **characterization** and **plot**.

The *nouveau roman* arose in France in the mid-twentieth century, reaching its height in the 1950s and 1960s. Sarraute and Robbe-Grillet both played leading roles in **theorizing** the genre. In "L'ère du soupçon" ("The Age of Suspicion") (1950), the title essay of her 1956 collection, Sarraute argued that the **character** had lost "the place of honor" in the novel; that **authors** and readers alike were "not only both wary of the character, but through him ... wary of each other"; and that evolution of the **protagonist** to "a being devoid of outline, ... an anonymous 'I'" enabled the author "to dispossess the reader and entice him ... into the author's territory." In *Pour un nouveau roman* (*For a New Novel*) (1963), a collection of essays on the novel, Robbe-Grillet argued that the novel had "fallen into ... a state of stagnation" and should "construct a world both more solid and more immediate," focusing on the physical presence of gestures and objects rather than on psychological, social, or functional signification ("A Future for the Novel" [1956]); he also emphasized, however, that "each novelist, each novel must invent its own form" and asserted that the term *nouveau roman* served "not to designate a school" but merely as "a convenient label applicable to all those seeking new forms for the novel" ("The Use of Theory" [1955]). Other noted *nouveaux romanciers,* or new novelists, included Maurice Blanchot, Michel Butor, Marguerite Duras, Claude Ollier, Claude Simon, and Philippe Sollers.

Rejecting the **realism** of writers such as Honoré de Balzac, *nouveaux romanciers* experimented with dislocations of time and space, repetitive descriptions or situations, and shifts or uncertainty in **point of view**, reflecting what they saw as the ambiguity and incoherence of human experience. They also tended to focus on objects rather than events or characters and to avoid or minimize **dialogue, figures of speech** such as **metaphor,** and **symbolism.** As a result, their novels often appear to be little more than a loose association of perceptions and textual fragments, and readers must take an active role in making sense of their achronological and alogical narrative sequences.

FURTHER EXAMPLES: Robbe-Grillet's *Les gommes* (*The Erasers*) (1953), Butor's *La modification* (*Second Thoughts*) (1957), Sarraute's *Le planétarium* (*The Planetarium*) (1959), Simon's *La route des Flandres* (*The Flanders Road*) (1960).

See also **antinovel.**

▶ **novel:** A lengthy **fictional prose narrative**. The novel is distinguished from the **novella**, a shorter fictional prose work that ranges from roughly fifty to one hundred pages in length. The greater length of the novel, especially as compared with even briefer prose works such as the **short story** and the **tale**, permits **authors** to develop one or more **characters**, to establish their **motivation**, and to construct intricate **plots**. Some authors and critics maintain that it is possible to write a **nonfiction novel**; novelist Norman Mailer has used the word **faction** to refer to such works. However, the stories recounted in novels are usually and perhaps essentially products of the **imagination**, despite the presence in many novels of historical facts, events, and figures.

Scholars disagree about when the novel first appeared on the literary scene. Some bestow this distinction on *The Tale of Genji* (c. A.D. 1000), a long story by Shikibu Murasaki, a Japanese court lady, about the life, particularly the love life, of a young prince. Others argue that the French writer Madame de Lafayette's *La princesse de Clèves* (1678) is the first novel fully recognizable as such, by which they mean that it contains many of the elements characteristic of the novel form as it was established in the eighteenth century, particularly in England. Still others argue that Aphra Behn, the first Englishwoman to support herself as a writer, produced the first novel when she wrote *Oroonoko* (1678), her account of the adventures of a real African prince by the same name.

Of all the candidates, however, Miguel de Cervantes's *Don Quixote de la Mancha* (part 1, 1605; part 2, 1615) is cited most often. Even scholars who do not believe that novels were written until the eighteenth century would agree that *Don Quixote* qualifies as an ancestor of the first novel. Certainly, it was the most famous and influential of the **picaresque narratives** often viewed as transitional works linking the prose tale and the novel in Western literary history. Picaresque narratives can be seen as a **framed** set of tales; **episodic** in structure, they recount a series of events linked by the presence of a single, usually roguish, **protagonist**, or main character. Although picaresque works, *Don Quixote* included, lack the sustained focus on **characterization** typical of later novels, they undeniably played a special role in the development of the novel (especially the **realistic novel**) by debunking the idealized forms of the **romance** and by legitimizing a fairly systematic examination of a specific **theme** or problem.

Scholars have identified a number of influences on the development of the novel. Some trace the **genre's** roots to **classical** times, to narrative **epics** written in **verse** that tell a sustained story and feature a single protagonist. Others have emphasized prototypical ancient Greek romances that date as far back as the second century A.D. These works, which are fairly lengthy, typically center on a pair of lovers who have to overcome various obstacles before living happily ever after. Still other scholars point to **medieval romances** and romances written during the **Renaissance**, which exhibit the length characteristic of the novel as well as an intricate plot typically featuring stories of adventure involving quests, chivalry, and the **fantastic** or supernatural. Although early examples of the medieval romance (such as Chrétien de Troye's twelfth-century *Lancelot*) were composed in verse, later examples (such as Thomas Malory's fifteenth-century *Le morte d'Arthur*) were written in prose.

The novella, though distinct from the novel, is widely viewed as an influential forerunner; it is also the form on which English writers most often drew for their subject matter. In fact, whereas the French word for novel (*roman*) associates the form with the romance, the English word *novel* derives from the Italian *novella*, itself taken from the Latin *novella narrātiō*, meaning a "new kind of story." Although *novella* is now used to refer to any fictional prose work ranging from about fifty to one hundred pages in length, it has traditionally been used to refer to **realistic**, often ribald or **satiric**, Italian and French tales written between the fourteenth and sixteenth centuries — such as those included in Giovanni Boccaccio's *Decameron* (1348–53) and Marguerite de Navarre's *Heptaméron* (1548).

Whatever its origins, the novel became established definitively as a genre in early-eighteenth-century England with the work of Daniel Defoe, Samuel Richardson, and Henry Fielding. Defoe's novels *Robinson Crusoe* (1719) and *Moll Flanders* (1722) are largely episodic in structure, but they differ both from picaresque and romance narratives and from Italian and French novellas because of the convincing solidity of their characters. Whereas Defoe emphasized the actions undertaken by his main characters, Richardson established what we have come to call the *psychological novel*. In works such as *Pamela; or, Virtue Rewarded* (1740) and *Clarissa Harlowe* (1747–48), he focused on motivation and character development, rather than the latest vagary of the plot. Like many other eighteenth-century novels, both *Pamela* and *Clarissa* employed the **epistolary** form (narratives presented and propagated through letters written by one or more characters). Fielding's *Joseph Andrews* (1742) and *Tom Jones* (1749) combined adventurous **action** with detailed characterization and are philosophically undergirded by the tenets of **neoclassicism**, whose proponents believed that the proper subject of art is humanity in the broadest sense and that literature should both instruct and delight. ("I describe not men, but manners," says the **narrator** of *Joseph Andrews*, "not an individual, but a species.")

A tremendous growth in literacy — and a related explosion in novel publication — occurred between 1750 and 1900. Reflecting evolving concerns and tastes, new generations of novelists wrote about new subjects using innovative **styles** and **structures** and published their works in new media designed to reach a growing audience. (These media included three-volume editions developed for lending libraries and the installment style of publication typical of literary periodicals and popular magazines.) In particular, the novel allowed women to break into the literary profession, which historically had been almost exclusively a male domain. Several of the best and most famous women novelists, however, fearing that their work would not be taken seriously, assumed masculine pen names, or ***noms de plume***. As a result of these changes in audience, authorship, and production, the novel took on new forms and contributed dynamically to the development of evolving literary movements.

One of the new forms that emerged during the period 1750–1800 was the **picaresque novel,** which grew out of picaresque narrative. Tobias Smollett, through works such as *Peregrine Pickle* (1751), was instrumental in developing this type of novel, in which a physically vigorous but morally imperfect **hero** gets into a series of hair-raising adventures. Through works such as *Wilhelm Meister's Apprenticeship* (1796), Johann Wolfgang von Goethe helped usher in another new form: the **bildungsroman,** a type of novel that recounts the psychological and sometimes spiritual development of an individual from childhood or adolescence to maturity. Other novelistic forms that developed during the latter half of the eighteenth century include the **sentimental novel** and the **Gothic novel.** The sentimental novel — as exemplified by Laurence Sterne's *A Sentimental Journey* (1768) — exalted the emotions, particularly those of sympathy and generosity, and portrayed their expression as the most reliable marks of human virtue. The Gothic novel — as exemplified by Horace Walpole's *The Castle of Otranto: A Gothic Story* (1764) and Ann Radcliffe's *The Italian* (1797) — also represented and relied on emotional expression. But fear and horror, rather than sympathy and generosity, were the emotions most often appealed to by these novels, which are typically set in mysterious castles full of secret passageways and supernatural occurrences.

Often associated not only with the romance but also with **romanticism** — the late-eighteenth- and early-nineteenth-century literary movement associated with writers who emphasized imagination and feeling over logical thought — the Gothic novel was further developed during the nineteenth century by writers such as Mary Shelley, author of *Frankenstein* (1818). Several nineteenth-century works commonly associated with the Gothic novel, however, do not fit neatly within the genre's confines. Jane Austen's *Northanger Abbey* (1818), for instance, is actually a gentle **parody** of Gothic fiction. Emily Brontë's *Wuthering Heights* (1847) blends Gothic and, more generally, romance elements with the emerging interests of **realism,** a nineteenth-century literary movement emphasizing the **objective** presentation of ordinary places and events.

Traditionally, literary historians have distinguished two overarching categories of novelistic prose fiction: the *realistic novel* (sometimes called *the novel proper*) and the *romance novel.* Realistic novelists strive for **verisimilitude** in their depictions of ordinary characters, situations, and **settings;** in other words, they seek to construct believable, plausible stories. Romance novelists, by contrast, generally focus on adventure, involve heroes and **villains** who are larger than life, and often feature improbable, though imaginative, situations.

The nineteenth century has often been called the age of the **realistic novel;** fiction writers whose works broadly exemplify the tenets of realism include Honoré de Balzac, Anthony Trollope, George Eliot, Gustave Flaubert, Fyodor

Dostoyevsky, William Dean Howells, and Henry James. Well-known examples of the realistic novel include Balzac's *Le père Goriot* (*Father Goriot*) (1835), Dostoyevsky's *Crime and Punishment* (1866), and James's *The Portrait of a Lady* (1881). Within the general category of realism, moreover, particular types of realistic fiction were developed. These include **local color writing,** which depicts the distinctive characteristics (**dialect,** dress, mannerisms, etc.) of a particular region; the *roman à clef,* a type of novel in which real people are represented in the guise of novelistic characters bearing fictional names; and the **historical novel,** in which historical personages (bearing their own names) and events are worked into a fictitious narrative. George Washington Cable's *The Grandissimes: A Story of Creole Life* (1880) is an example of local color writing. George Meredith's *roman à clef Diana of the Crossways* (1885) depicts the English prime minister Lord Melbourne as a character named Lord Dannisburgh. An example of the nineteenth-century historical novel is William Makepeace Thackeray's *The History of Henry Esmond* (1852), in which Queen Anne, the Pretender, and noted essayists Joseph Addison and Richard Steele appear.

Not all nineteenth-century fiction writers were realists, however. François-René de Chateaubriand, author of *Atala* (1801) and *René* (1805), is commonly classified as a romantic. Sir Walter Scott, the author of *Waverley* (1814) and *Ivanhoe* (1819), built so many romance elements into his historical settings that, despite his reputation for being the first historical novelist, scholars more commonly associate him with the romance novel than with the realistic novel. (The same may be said of Alexandre Dumas, author of *The Three Musketeers* [1844] and *The Count of Monte Cristo* [1845].) Nathaniel Hawthorne's *The Scarlet Letter* (1850), though steeped in colonial American history, was originally subtitled *A Romance.* James Fenimore Cooper's *The Deerslayer* (1841), like Herman Melville's *Moby-Dick* (1851) and *Billy Budd* (written in 1891, published posthumously in 1924), are also generally viewed as examples of the romance novel.

Some of the most acclaimed and influential novelists of the nineteenth century, however, cannot be clearly identified either with the romance novel or the realistic novel. Some of these writers, such as the Brontë sisters, combined romantic and realistic elements in their works. Others produced novels associated with a major genre (**comedy, tragedy,** or **satire**) that predates realism and, indeed, the novel itself. Charles Dickens was as much a satirist as a realistic novelist; comic and **autobiographical** early novels were followed by major works, such as *Bleak House* (1852–53) and *Our Mutual Friend* (1864–65), that contain far more **caricature, symbolism,** and **allegory** — also more absurd, fantastic, and **grotesque** elements — than are common in realistic works. Other novelists wrote works that contributed to the development of **naturalism,** a literary movement whose adherents pessimistically depicted pathetic protagonists with little if any control over their destinies. Thomas Hardy consistently employed the tragic genre but also adapted it in a naturalistic manner in novels such as *The Mayor of Casterbridge* (1886), *Tess of the d'Urbervilles* (1891), and *Jude the Ob-*

scure (1896). Other, purer examples of the naturalistic novel include Émile Zola's *Germinal* (1885), Stephen Crane's *Maggie: A Girl of the Streets* (1893), Frank Norris's *McTeague* (1899), and several novels published early in the twentieth century by Theodore Dreiser.

With the advent of the twentieth century and, shortly thereafter, the rise of **modernism,** the novel became ever more diverse in its development and increasingly difficult (if not impossible) to fit into the general categories of romance and realism. To be sure, the romance form did not die out (Daphne du Maurier's *Rebecca* [1938] is a twentieth-century romance **classic**), nor did realism. Modern writers including E. M. Forster, F. Scott Fitzgerald, D. H. Lawrence, Ernest Hemingway, and Graham Greene adapted the **conventions** of realism to represent new literary subjects ranging from colonial India (Forster, *A Passage to India* [1924]) to the "Roaring Twenties" (Fitzgerald, *The Great Gatsby* [1925]) to sexual relationships (Lawrence, *Lady Chatterley's Lover* [1928]) to World War I (Hemingway, *A Farewell to Arms* [1929]), to **postcolonial** Mexico (Greene, *The Power and the Glory* [1940]). In works such as Zora Neale Hurston's *Their Eyes Were Watching God* (1937), Richard Wright's *Native Son* (1940), and Ralph Ellison's *Invisible Man* (1947), African American authors wrote with psychological realism about the black experience in the United States.

The writers most closely associated with modernism, however, ignored both romance conventions and realism's emphasis on objectivity to carry out radical experiments with style, structure, and subject matter. In works such as *Swann's Way* (1913), *Ulysses* (1922), *To the Lighthouse* (1927), and *As I Lay Dying* (1930), Marcel Proust, James Joyce, Virginia Woolf, and William Faulkner, respectively, experimented with **stream of consciousness,** a literary technique reflecting a character's jumbled flow of perceptions, thoughts, memories, and feelings. Joyce also turned to **myth** in order both to contrast his age with heroic times past and to suggest the timeless, universal qualities of certain situations, problems, and truths. Other twentieth-century novelists used mythical contexts and structures differently; in works ranging from the novella *Death in Venice* (1912) to his novel *The Magic Mountain* (1924), Thomas Mann used mythology to reveal disturbed psychic conditions within his characters.

Following the **Modern Period,** fiction writers associated with **postmodernism** experimented even more radically with conventional literary forms and styles. While preserving the spirit and even some of the themes of modernist literature (such as the alienation of humanity and historical discontinuity), they rejected the order that a number of modernists attempted to instill in their work via mythology and other patterns of **allusion** and **symbol.** Postmodernists include William Burroughs, Donald Barthelme, John Barth, Kathy Acker, and Thomas Pynchon, the author of *V* (1963) and *Gravity's Rainbow* (1973).

Within postmodernist fiction, a special type of novel developed: the *nouveau roman,* which arose in France in the mid-twentieth century and is often called the **new novel** or **antinovel** in English. "New" or "anti" novelists featured detailed physical description and largely dispensed with standard novelistic elements such as characterization and plot, forcing the reader to struggle to make sense of a seemingly fragmented **text.** They also aimed to depict reality without recourse to a moral frame of reference and to avoid the kind of subjective narrative evaluation that creeps into realistic, naturalistic, and modernist works. Alain Robbe-Grillet's *La jalousie* (*Jealousy*) (1957) and John Hawkes's *The Blood Oranges* (1971) are commonly cited as examples of the *nouveau roman* and antinovel, respectively. Other practitioners of the *nouveau roman* include Nathalie Sarraute, Philippe Sollers, and Marguerite Duras.

Magic realism, another innovation often associated with postmodernism, also emerged, most prominently in Latin America in the late 1940s before gaining popularity worldwide. When applied to novels, the term *magic realism* refers to works characterized by a mixture of realistic and fantastic elements. Works of magic realism are set in the real world but treat the magical or supernatural as an inherent part of reality and often incorporate dreamlike sequences, **folklore,** and myths into complex, tangled plots featuring abrupt chronological shifts and distortions of time. Gabriel García Márquez's *Cien años de soledad* (*One Hundred Years of Solitude*) (1967) is an example of magic realism; Isabel Allende blended magic realism and political realism in her novel *La casa de los espiritus* (*The House of the Spirits*) (1982).

Postmodernism notwithstanding, however, most novelists in the post-World-War-II era have followed other paths; a short and eclectic list might include: Margaret Atwood, A. S. Byatt, Truman Capote, Robertson Davies, Margaret Drabble, Ernest Gaines, William Golding, John Irving, Norman Mailer, Bernard Malamud, Toni Morrison, Iris Murdoch, Vladimir Nabokov, Joyce Carol Oates, Nelida Piñon, E. Annie Proulx, Wallace Stegner, Amy Tan, Anne Tyler, John Updike, and Herman Wouk. Indeed, Capote and Mailer pioneered a new literary genre, the *nonfiction novel*, in the 1960s, using techniques associated with fiction to recount factual, historical events in the form of a novel. Also significant are a few of the novelists, such as James Clavell and James Michener, whose works are considered "popular" rather than "serious" fiction. Noted authors associated with well-defined subgenres of popular fiction include Isaac Asimov, Ray Bradbury, and Ursula Le Guin (**science fiction**); Piers Anthony, Terry Brooks, Le Guin, and Anne McCaffrey (**fantasy fiction**); and John Le Carré, Tom Clancy, and Robert Ludlum (**spy fiction**). Authors of **detective fiction** influenced by the pre-1950 work of Raymond Chandler, Agatha Christie, Dashiell Hammett, and Dorothy Sayers, include writers such as Sue Grafton, Tony Hillerman, John D. MacDonald, Ross Macdonald, and Sara Paretsky. Laura Esquivel's *La ley del amor* (*The Law of Love*) (1995) has been called the first multimedia novel, involving as it does a musical CD keyed to the plot.

▶ **novelette:** See **novella.**

▶ **novella:** As commonly used today, a **fictional prose narrative**, typically tightly structured and focusing on a single serious issue or event, that ranges from about fifty to one hundred pages in length, falling between the **short story** and the **novel.** In this sense, *novella* is synonymous with *novelette*, a term rarely used today, except disparagingly, due to the dime-store **connotations** that have grown up around it.

As traditionally understood, however, *novella* had a different meaning. Used strictly, it referred to **realistic,** often ribald or **satiric,** Italian and French **tales** written between the fourteenth and sixteenth centuries, some of which were as short as two pages. Noted examples include the prose narratives found in Giovanni Boccaccio's *Decameron* (1348–53) and Marguerite de Navarre's *Heptaméron* (1548), which contains stories ranging from approximately three hundred words to fifty pages. Used more generally, *novella* referred to later works written in other languages, provided they exhibited specific characteristics found in early Italian and French examples of the **genre.**

The traditional novella focused on a narrowly circumscribed occurrence, situation, or **conflict.** In representing the **protagonist's** reaction to a particular development in the **plot** or in working out the resolution of a particular conflict, many practitioners placed a premium on suspense and surprise. Traditional novellas, like those comprising the *Heptaméron,* were also often encompassed by a **frame story** explaining why the various "interior" stories were being recounted. Most frame stories linked novellas and their **narrators** through shared journey, disaster, refuge, or condition of exile; the story framing the *Decameron,* for instance, tells of ten young people who escape from plague-ridden Florence to a country villa, where they pass the time telling tales. Not all practitioners of the form used frame stories, however; Miguel de Cervantes, known as "the Spanish Boccaccio," dispensed with the device in *Novelas ejemplares (Exemplary Novellas)* (1613).

The traditional novella had a powerful **influence** on a variety of genres, especially the novel. Indeed, both the terms *novel* and *novella* come from the Italian word *novella,* which itself derives from the Latin *novella narrātiō,* meaning "new kind of story." Several **characters** (e.g., the betrayed husband, the corrupt clergyman) and plots (e.g., adulterous plans foiled, **wit's** triumph over force) of the traditional novella recur in novels by writers ranging from Henry Fielding, an eighteenth-century Englishman, to William Faulkner, a twentieth-century American writer, and beyond. Moreover, and more significantly, the novella's use of the frame story showed that disparate but related stories could be unified into a larger structure, paving the way not only for the novel but also for the **picaresque narrative,** itself an important influence on the development of the novel. Use of the frame story also showed that narrators could be characters and vice versa, which contributed to the development of many features of the modern novel, including the **first-person** narrator and the **unreliable narrator**. The traditional novella also influenced narrative poetry (Geoffrey Chaucer's *Canterbury Tales* [c. 1387] has been viewed as a series of novellas organized by a frame story about pilgrims on a pilgrimage) and drama (the plot of William Shakespeare's *All's Well That Ends Well* [1602–03], like that of other **Renaissance** plays, is derived from a tale in the *Decameron*).

Since the nineteenth century, the novella has thrived particularly in German literature, where its current form developed. Johann Wolfgang von Goethe, borrowing from the Italian, introduced the term *Novelle* in 1795, the year he wrote the first collection of German *Novellen*, *Unterhaltungen deutscher Ausgewanderten* (*The Recreations of the German Immigrants*). The collection includes seven stories linked by a frame story about a group of German refugees awaiting news of French army movements; typical of the traditional novella are the two stories told by a priest, one involving a man who is unexpectedly pursued by a married woman, and the other involving a man who unintentionally discovers how to open a secret compartment in his father's desk. After Goethe, nineteenth- and early-twentieth-century writers working in German adapted the form to incorporate background information, descriptions of nature, and character development, elements largely absent from the traditional novella. These modifications gave rise to the modern understanding of *novella* as applicable to lengthy, descriptive, psychologically nuanced stories such as Thomas Mann's *Death in Venice* (1912) and Franz Kafka's *The Metamorphosis* (1915).

The novella, however, has by no means been an exclusively German form since the advent of the nineteenth century. Examples from other literary traditions include French writer Amandine Aurore Lucie Dupin's *Marianne* (1876), written under the male *nom de plume* George Sand; *Notes from the Underground* (1866) and *The Death of Ivan Ilyich* (1886), Russian novellas written by Fyodor Dostoyevsky and Leo Tolstoi, respectively; and *Crónica de una muerte anunciada* (*Chronicle of a Death Foretold*) (1981) and *Amirbar* (1990), by Colombian authors Gabriel García Márquez and Álvaro Mutis, respectively. English-language examples, some of which contain elements of the traditional novella, include Henry James's *The Turn of the Screw* (1898); Joseph Conrad's *Heart of Darkness* (1899), which makes use of a frame story; Edith Wharton's *Ethan Frome* (1911), which addresses the **theme** of illicit temptation; Nella Larsen's *Passing* (1929); and Ernest Hemingway's *The Old Man and the Sea* (1952), which involves resolution of a single and simple plot conflict. More recent examples of the novella in English include Mark Helprin's *Ellis Island* (1981), A. S. Byatt's *Angels and Insects* (1991), David Leavitt's *Arkansas: Three Novellas* (1998), and Neil Gaiman's *Coraline* (2003).

O

▶ **objective correlative:** A term popularized by poet and critic T. S. Eliot in his 1919 essay "Hamlet and His Problems" to refer to actions, objects, or situations that correspond with and thus implicitly evoke a particular emotion from the audience or reader. As Eliot wrote, "The only way of expressing emotion in the form of art is by finding an 'objective correlative'; in other words, a set of objects, a situation, a chain of events which shall be the formula of that *particular* emotion; such that when the external facts, which must terminate in sensory experience, are given, the emotion is immediately evoked." Asserting that "artistic 'inevitability' lies in [the] complete adequacy of the external to the emotion," Eliot argued that "the facts as they appear" in William Shakespeare's play *Hamlet* (1602) do not justify Hamlet's depth of feeling and thus fail to provide convincing **motivation,** rendering the play "an artistic failure." *Objective correlative* was first used by the American poet and painter Washington Allston in his *Lectures on Art,* published posthumously in 1850, but it was not until Eliot redefined the term that it elicited widespread interest and debate in critical circles, especially among **the New Critics.**

▶ **objective criticism:** A type of **literary criticism** that views any given literary work as freestanding, independent of external references to its **author,** audience, or the environment in which it is written or read. That is, the work is viewed as authoritative and sufficient in and of itself, or even as a world-in-itself. Objective critics, therefore, evaluate and analyze works based on internal criteria rather than by external standards of judgment. They consider, for instance, whether a work is coherent or unified and how its various components relate to one another rather than how the work is or was received by the public. Many of the tenets of objective criticism were articulated by German philosopher Immanuel Kant in his *Critique of Aesthetic Judgment* (1790). In the twentieth century, objective criticism has evolved through the work of several groups of **practical critics,** especially those **formalists** associated with **the New Criticism.**

▶ **objective narrator:** See **unintrusive narrator.**

▶ **objectivity:** See **subjectivity.**

▶ **object-relations theory:** See **psychoanalytic criticism.**

▶ **oblique rhyme:** See **half rhyme.**

▶ **occasional verse:** **Verse** written to celebrate or commemorate a particular occasion or event. Poetry of this type may range from joyous to somber in **tone.** Occasional poems tend to have a short life span since they are written for a specific event, such as births, deaths, marriages, and military victories, but those that have unusual literary merit have survived.

EXAMPLES: Edmund Spenser's *Epithalamion* (1595), written to celebrate his marriage; Walt Whitman's "When Lilacs Last in the Dooryard Bloom'd" (1865), on the assassination of Abraham Lincoln; Maya Angelou's "On the Pulse of Morning," written for Bill Clinton's 1993 presidential inauguration; Elton John and Bernie Taupin's "Candle in the Wind 1997," sung at Princess Diana's funeral. Paul McCartney's anthem "Freedom" (2001) commemorated the terrorist attacks of September 11, 2001; "Let's Roll" (2001), by Neil Young and Booker T. Jones, more specifically memorialized the heroics of passengers on Flight 93, which crashed in a Pennsylvania field following their struggle with the hijackers. Poet Galway Kinnell's "When the Towers Fell" (2002) — containing a **pastiche** of quotations from poems by François Villon, Hart Crane, Paul Celan, Aleksander Wat, and Walt Whitman — marked the first anniversary of the September 11th tragedy.

▶ **octameter (octometer):** A line of **verse** consisting of eight **metrical feet.**

EXAMPLE: Alfred, Lord Tennyson's "Locksley Hall" (1842) written in **trochaic** octameter:

> Comrades, | leave me | here a | little, | while as | yet 'tis | early | morn;
> Leave me | here, and | when you | want me, | sound u|pon the | bugle | horn.
>
> 'Tis the | place, and | all a|round it, | as of | old, the | curlews | call,
> Dreary | gleams a|bout the | moorland | flying | over | Locksley | Hall. . . .

▶ **octave (octet):** (1) Generally, any eight-line **stanza.** (2) More specifically, the first part (the first eight lines) of an **Italian sonnet.** The octave, which follows the **rhyme scheme** *abbaabba*, precedes the **sestet** and may pose a question or dilemma that the sestet answers or resolves.

▶ **octometer:** See **octameter.**

▶ **ode:** A relatively long, serious, and usually meditative **lyric poem** that treats a noble or otherwise elevated subject in a dignified and calm manner. There are three types of odes: the *regular*, or **Pindaric,** in which the **stanzas** have a recurrent, triadic **structure;** the **Horatian,** in which every stanza has the same **rhyme scheme, meter,** and number of lines; and the **irregular,** or *Cowleyan*, with a variable stanzaic structure and form.

Originally a **classical** Greek choral poem intended for performance at a public event, odes were composed in a trifold stanzaic form involving a **strophe** sung while the **chorus** danced in one direction, an **antistrophe** sung while it moved in the opposite direction, and an **epode** sung while standing still. The strophe and antistrophe exhibited the same **meter,** the epode another. The fifth-century B.C. Greek poet Pindar, for whom the Pindaric ode is named, modeled his celebratory odes on the classical Greek choral ode. The first-century B.C. Roman poet Horace, for whom the Horatian ode is named, took a different approach, writing odes with homostrophic stanzas and a reflective **tone.** Subsequently, during the **Renaissance,** the ode was revived, and seventeenth-century English poet Abraham Cowley developed the irregular form. Composition of odes remained popular through the **Neoclassical** and **Romantic** periods but then declined; the form is rare in English today.

EXAMPLES: John Dryden's irregular ode "A Song for Saint Cecilia's Day" (1687), Thomas Gray's Pindaric ode "The Bard" (1757), John Keats's Horatian "Ode to a Nightingale" (1819). Twentieth-century examples include Allen Tate's irregular "Ode to the Confederate Dead" (1928); Robert Penn Warren's Horatian "Ode to Fear" (1944); W. H. Auden's Horatian "Ode to Gaea" (1954); Pablo Neruda's irregular *Odas Elementales* (*Elemental Odes*) (1954), which celebrate the everyday; Frank O'Hara's "Ode to Joy" (1960); and the Cranberries' song "Ode to My Family" (1994).

See also **Horatian ode, irregular ode, Pindaric ode.**

▶ **Oedipus complex:** In **psychoanalytic** theory, the desire a young child feels for the opposite-sex parent and the hostility the child correspondingly feels toward the same-sex parent. Austrian psychoanalyst Sigmund Freud, who introduced the term in his paper "A Special Type of Choice of Object Made by Men" (1910), developed the concept in the late 1800s, claiming in *The Interpretation of Dreams* (1900) that "It is as though — to put it bluntly — a sexual preference were making itself felt at an early age: as though boys regarded their fathers and girls their mothers as rivals in love, whose elimination could not fail to be to their advantage." In labeling the complex "Oedipal," Freud drew on the ancient Greek **legend** dramatized in Sophocles' play *Oedipus Rex* (c. 430 B.C.), a **tragedy** in which the **protagonist,** Oedipus, blinds himself after discovering that the man he killed years ago was his father and the woman he married is his mother.

Freud viewed manifestation of the Oedipus complex as a universal experience, a normal stage of psychosexual development occurring in children aged about three to five and ending in identification with the same-sex parent and repression of the complex. He also viewed the complex, which he associated with castration anxiety in both boys and girls, as central to the development of the **superego** and for much of his career attributed neurosis chiefly to unresolved Oedipal conflicts. For further discussion, see Peter Hartocollis's "Origins and Evolution of the Oedipus Complex as Conceptualized by Freud" (2005).

While the term *Oedipus complex* is generally applied to both sexes, it is sometimes used specifically with reference to boys. *Electra complex,* a term often attributed to Swiss analytical psychologist Carl Jung, who used it in his paper "Psychoanalysis and Neurosis" (originally titled "On Psychoanalysis") (1916), is the female counterpart; like *Oedipus complex,* it derives from an ancient Greek legend, that of Electra, who convinced her brother to kill their mother in order to avenge their father's murder.

The term *negative Oedipus complex* refers to situations in which the child's feelings are "reversed," so to speak, with desire for the same-sex parent and hostility toward the opposite-sex parent.

EXAMPLES: William Shakespeare's play *Hamlet* (1602) and D. H. Lawrence's novel *Sons and Lovers* (1913) have been said to portray protagonists with unresolved Oedipal complexes. The Brazilian film *Ele, o boto (The Dolphin)* (1987) — based on Amazonian **folklore** surrounding dolphin-man Bufeo Colorado — likewise concerns a **character** with an unresolved Oedipus complex, the son of a human female and a pink river dolphin compelled to pursue his mother. Frank O'Connor's story "My Oedipus Complex" (1950) and Frank Galati's play *Oedipus Complex* (2004), an adaptation of Sophocles' play that incorporates Freud as a character and commentator, openly address Oedipal issues and **themes**.

▶ **Old English Period (in English literature):** Also referred to as the *Anglo-Saxon Period* by historians, an era usually said to have begun in the first half of the fifth century A.D. with the migration to Britain by members of four principal Germanic tribes from the European continent: the Frisians, the Jutes, the Saxons, and the Angles (whose name, by the seventh century, was used to refer to all of the Germanic inhabitants of "Engla-land," hence, England). *Old English* refers to the synthetic, or fairly heavily inflected, language system of these peoples, once they were separated from their Germanic roots.

By the time the Germanic tribes arrived, the British Isles had been inhabited for centuries by Celtic peoples, who had been under Roman occupation for nearly four hundred years (A.D. 43–410). While some of these native British had learned Latin, their Celtic language and culture had remained intact. Christianity had also been introduced under the Roman occupation, and a British (as well as Irish) church flourished almost completely independent of Rome, helping to sustain the literate and learned traditions of the Latin West when non-Christian Germanic peoples swept into the Roman Empire.

According to Bede, a Benedictine monk often called the "father of English history" for his *Historia ecclesiastica gentis Anglorum (Ecclesiastical History of the English People)* (c. A.D. 730), the Britons, abandoned by the Romans, invited help from the Anglo-Saxons against marauding tribes to the north, only to have the mercenaries turn on them. King Arthur — if he ever existed — may have been a Romano-British war leader (perhaps nicknamed "Arcturus," Latin for "The Bear") and is credited with holding off the first waves of Germanic invader-immigrants in the early fifth century. But the Anglo-Saxons soon drove the native British into Wales and Cornwall. The invaders were themselves converted to Christianity after the arrival of Augustine (not to be confused with his famous predecessor of the same name, the fifth-century Bishop of Hippo) in 597, whose mission from Rome also included bringing the British Christian clergy into the Roman Catholic sphere. Christianity brought literacy to the orally based culture of the Anglo-Saxons; by the eighth century, Anglo-Saxon monks were prominent scholars and leading missionaries among the Germanic peoples on the Continent.

England was invaded several more times during the Old English Period by Germanic cousins of the Anglo-Saxons: Danes, Norwegians, and Swedes, all of whom were called "Vikings" by the English. These peoples were not Christianized when they arrived, beginning in the late eighth and early ninth centuries, and again in the tenth century, but eventually, like the Anglo-Saxons, they settled the lands they seized and adopted the religion of their inhabitants. The Norman conquest of England in 1066 — at the hands of still other Germanic peoples, the "Northmen" who had settled the northern area of modern France and whose language was a dialect of Old French — is generally said to have ended the Old English Period and to have inaugurated the subsequent **Middle English Period** (1100–1500).

King Alfred, often referred to by the **epithet** "Alfred the Great," is the best-known figure of the Old English Period because of his success in unifying the Anglo-Saxons against the Vikings during the ninth century. Alfred also sponsored the translation of several Latin works into Old English and inaugurated the *Anglo-Saxon Chronicle,* a record of events in England that was kept through the twelfth century. Under his influence, West Saxon, the language of almost all of the period's surviving manuscripts, emerged as a sort of "standard" among the four principal dialects.

The **epic** *Beowulf,* parts of which may have taken shape in early Germanic oral tradition but which was written down in Old English after A.D. 1000, is the period's most famous literary work and is concerned exclusively with Scandinavian peoples and events. Other notable poems, most of which were committed to writing in the eleventh century, include "Deor," "The Seafarer," "The Wanderer," and "The Dream of the Rood" (or Cross). This last poem comes from the less well-known but large body of verse that is explicitly religious in **theme,** including stories from Genesis and Exodus, as well as saints' lives and prose sermons. Although these works were put in writing in a Christianized culture, they nonetheless represent the pre-Christian Germanic past of the Anglo-Saxons. The work of a few poets, such as Cynewulf and Cædmon, was more obviously Christian in subject. Most of the writing of the period that was predominantly religious consisted of biblical **narratives** and saints' lives retold in Old English verse and homilies or sermons in Old English prose, alongside and in communication with a flourishing Latin literature.

▶ **omniscient point of view:** A **third-person point of view** in **fictional** writing that permits the **author** to present not only external details and information through an all-knowing **narrator** but also the inner thoughts and emotions of all of the **characters** of a work. The omniscient narrator is frequently described as "godlike." Authors writing from the omniscient point of view may reveal — or conceal — at their discretion. Shifts in time and place as well as shifts from the viewpoint of one character to another are common. Moreover, the omniscient point of view enables an author to comment openly upon the **action** or **theme** of the work. An omniscient narrator who makes valuative judgments is considered **intrusive,** whereas one who generally refrains from doing so is called **unintrusive.** A large number of the works that have traditionally been considered **classics** are written from the omniscient point of view — for example, Charles Dickens's *A Tale of Two Cities* (1859) and Leo Tolstoi's *War and Peace* (1864–66) (both intrusive) and Gustave Flaubert's *Madame Bovary* (1857) (unintrusive).

See also **point of view**.

▶ **onomatopoeia:** From the Greek for "name-making," wording that seems to signify meaning through sound effects. Onomatopoeic words, such as *hiss* and *sizzle*, ostensibly imitate the sounds they represent; onomatopoeic passages more broadly suggest an association between sound and meaning.

EXAMPLES: Many animal-sound words, such as *moo, purr,* and *quack*, are onomatopoeic, as are mechanical-sound words such as *beep* and *vroom*. "Suck was a queer word," the child Stephen Dedalus thinks to himself in James Joyce's *A Portrait of the Artist as a Young Man* (1916):

> The sound was ugly. Once he had washed his hands in the lavatory of the Wicklow Hotel and his father pulled the stopper up by the chain after and the dirty water went down through the hole in the basin. And when it had all gone down slowly the hole in the basin had made a sound like that: suck. Only louder.

Theodore Roethke's "The Storm" (1958) contains several onomatopoeic lines, including the following:

> While the wind whines overhead,
> Coming down from the mountain,
> Whistling between the arbors, the winding terraces . . .

Comic books often use onomatopoeia, as in *Batman* (comic book 1940– ; television series 1966–68), where words such as *bam, thwack,* and *wham* generally come accompanied by one or more exclamation points.

▶ **oppositions:** See **binary oppositions**.

▶ **oration, oratory:** *Oration* refers to a carefully crafted oral presentation, usually written with a large audience in mind and designed to emotionally move as well as intellectually persuade a body of listeners. Alternatively, it signifies the practice of writing and delivering such speeches. *Oratory* refers to the art of oration, the use of eloquent language in formal public speaking.

In **classical** Greek and Roman times, skillful orators were widely respected, and oration was a preferred mode of public **discourse**. Specific rules governed the construction of a formal oration. Corax of Syracuse (fifth century B.C.), generally considered the father of **rhetoric**, identified five parts; later rhetoricians, such as the Romans Cicero (*De oratore* [*On the Orator*] [55 B.C.]) and Quintilian (*Institutio oratoria* [*On the Education of an Orator*] [12 vols.; c. 95 A.D.]) put the number of parts at four to seven, depending on the situation. Parts included the *exordium*, an introductory segment often involving an attention-grabbing opening; the *narration*, or statement of facts regarding the issue or situation; the *proposition*, a statement of the speaker's **thesis**; the *partition*, an outline of the speaker's arguments; the *confirmation*, or proof of the proposition using logical arguments; a *refutation* of counter-arguments; and the *peroration,* or conclusion, summing up the main points and typically including an emotional appeal.

Orations are seldom heard today, and those that are delivered are rarely constructed according to classical rules. The closest thing to an oration that most of us are likely to hear would be a president's inaugural address; the closing arguments made in a highly publicized trial (such as the 1995 murder trial of O. J. Simpson); or a sermon given to tens of thousands of people attending a Billy Graham-style evangelical "crusade." Martin Luther King Jr.'s best-known address, "I Have a Dream," delivered from the Lincoln Memorial during a 1963 civil rights march in Washington, D.C., is a noted twentieth-century example.

▶ **organic form:** Form that evolves from within a work of art, growing out of an idea; the opposite of **mechanic form,** form that is externally imposed, shaped by rules and **conventions.** Organic form **privileges** the whole, emphasizing the assimilation and interdependence of component parts and the unity of form and content; mechanic form depends more heavily on tradition. Organic form is often analogized to the growth or development of a living organism; mechanic form to the use of a preconceived or preexisting mold. The concept of organic unity in art dates back to **classical** Greek times; in Plato's *Phaedrus* (c. 360 B.C.), Socrates asserts that a composition "should be like a living being, with a body of its own as it were, and neither headless nor footless, but with a middle and members adapted to each other and the whole."

Organic form and *mechanic form* are generally viewed as a contrary philosophical and linguistic pair, or **binary opposition.** The distinction was first drawn by German **romantics,** particularly A. W. Schlegel, who defended William Shakespeare against **neoclassical** critics who claimed that his plays lacked form in *Über dramatische Kunst und Literatur* (*Lectures on Dramatic Art and Literature*) (1809–11). Subsequently, English poet and critic Samuel Taylor Coleridge adopted Schlegel's characterization of organic and mechanic form in his own defense of Shakespeare, "Shakespeare's Judgment Equal to His Genius"(1818):

> The form is mechanic, when on any given material we impress a predetermined form, not necessarily arising out of the properties of the material. . . . The organic form, on the other hand, is innate; it shapes, as it develops, itself from within, and the fullness of its development is one and the same with the perfection of its outward form. Such as the life is, such is the form.

Coleridge further associated **imagination** with organic form and **fancy** with mechanic form in his *Biographia Literaria* (1817).

While organic form has been widely embraced since the advent of **romanticism,** some critics have challenged the concept or defended mechanic form (though few would use the adjective *mechanic*). In a departure from most of his colleagues, **New Critic** John Crowe Ransom, for instance, claimed that "a poem is much more like a Christmas tree than an organism" ("Art Worries the Naturalists," *Kenyon Review*, 1945). **Deconstructive** critic Paul de Man likewise questioned the concept in *Blindness and Insight* (1971), arguing that irony "can have nothing in common with the homogenous, organic form of nature: it is founded on an act of consciousness, not on the imitation of a natural object."

EXAMPLE: The contrast between Coleridge's "Kubla Khan" (1816), the structure of which reflects the struggle to recapture a drug-induced hallucination in language, and John Dryden's "Absalom and Achitophel" (1681), a political **narrative** poem written in **heroic couplets**, points up the difference between poetry with organic and mechanic form.

▶ **orientalism:** A term most closely associated with Edward Said, a **postcolonial** and **cultural critic** who, in his book *Orientalism* (1978), uses the term to refer to the historical and **ideological** process whereby false **images** of and **myths** about the Eastern or "oriental" world have been constructed in various Western **discourses,** including that of **imaginative** literature. These images and myths have sometimes involved positive idealizations and fantasies of Eastern differences (for instance, family loyalty and hospitality to strangers). Usually, however, orientalism involves denigrating fictions (for instance, deceptive "inscrutability" and loose sex). In *Orientalism,* Said demonstrated how Eastern and Middle-Eastern peoples have for centuries been stereotyped systematically by the West and how this stereotyping facilitated the colonization of vast areas of the globe by Europeans. Said has been **influenced** by the work of Michel Foucault, a French theorist often associated with **the new historicism** who examined the ways in which power is manifested and exercised through discourses.

The panel shown below, from the **classic** comic book *Scream Cheese and Jelly* (1979), which teaches children about humor and **puns**, also reinforces some of the more benign stereotypes associated with orientalism.

See also **postcolonial literature, postcolonial theory.**

▶ **Other, the:** In **psychoanalytic criticism,** that which defines and limits the subject, or self, and from which the subject seeks confirmation of its existence and agency. To put it another way, the subject only exists in relation to the Other, which both defines the self through differences and engenders a yearning for unification. Language, **ideology,** and other **symbolic** systems function as **discourses** of the Other. Twentieth-century French psychoanalytic theorist Jacques Lacan, who contended that humans have no sense of self separate from the world surrounding them until they reach the "mirror stage" of childhood, further argued in his 1955 seminar on Edgar Allan Poe's short story "The Purloined Letter" (1844) that the unconscious itself is a discourse of the Other.

Outside psychoanalytic criticism, the term *the Other* (or, sometimes, *an Other*) refers to any person or category of people seen as different from the dominant social group. Virtually any ideology involves the identification of some group as the Other, whether by virtue of ethnicity, **race, class, gender, sexuality,** or any other characteristic, a practice that often results in marginalization or oppression of that group. The emergence of **disability studies** in the 1990s increased awareness of the way in which societies construct an Other composed of persons with unrelated physical, mental, and developmental differences.

EXAMPLES: In H. G. Wells's *The Time Machine* (1895), the Time Traveller, transported to the year 802,701, finds two species of humans: the innocent, playful Eloi, whom he perceives as the **privileged,** and the shadowy, subterranean Morlocks, whom he perceives as the Other:

> [G]radually, the truth dawned on me: that Man had not remained one species, but had differentiated into two distinct animals: that my graceful children of the Upper-world were not the sole descendants of our generation, but that this bleached, obscene, nocturnal Thing, which had flashed before me, was also heir to all the ages.

In his book *Second Nature: A Gardener's Education* (1991), Michael Pollan remembers a cemetery he and his sisters built for pets and other animals who had died:

> After we interred the shoebox-caskets, we would rake and reseed the ground and plant another homemade wooden cross above the grave. I understood that crosses were for Christians. But a Star of David was beyond my carpentry skills, and anyway I was inclined to think of pets as gentiles. To a child growing up Jewish, the Other, in all its forms, was presumed to be Christian.

In the television series *Lost* (2004–), the survivors of Oceanic flight 815 refer to the members of another, threatening group living on the island as "the Others."

▶ *ottava rima:* An Italian **verse** form composed of eight-line **stanzas** with the **rhyme scheme** *abababcc*. Fourteenth-century Florentine poet Giovanni Boccaccio established *ottava rima* as the primary **form** for **epic** and **narrative** verse in Italy, most notably in *Teseide* and *Il filostrato* (both c. 1340–41); subsequently, sixteenth-century English poet Sir Thomas Wyatt introduced it into English, where **iambic pentameter** became the dominant **meter**.

FURTHER EXAMPLES: Ludovico Ariosto's *Orlando Furioso* (1516); George Gordon, Lord Byron's *Don Juan* (1819–24), a stanza from which follows:

> They looked up to the sky, whose floating glow
> Spread like a rosy ocean, vast and bright;
> They gazed upon the glittering sea below,
> Whence the broad moon rose circling into sight;
> They heard the waves splash, and the wind so low,
> And saw each other's dark eyes darting light
> Into each other — and, beholding this,
> Their lips drew near, and clung into a kiss.

Contemporary examples of *ottava rima* include Fred D'Aguiar's verse novel *Bloodlines* (2000) and Wayne Koestenbaum's lengthy poem *Model Homes* (2004), comprised of thirteen *ottava rima* **cantos**.

▶ **overdetermined:** In psychoanalysis, a term referring to the concept of multiple causation for symptoms, dreams, and behavioral or emotional reactions; in **literary criticism**, a term used to describe **texts** or textual elements involving multiple causal factors that give rise to two or more plausible, coexisting interpretations. Things that are overdetermined are hard to explain without reference to various factors, rendering meaning indeterminate in the sense that no one meaning or interpretation can be said to be definitive.

The term *overdetermined* (*überdeterminiert* or *überbestimmt*) was introduced in *Studien über Hysterie* (*Studies on Hysteria*) (1895), in which Austrian physician Josef Breuer and psychoanalyst Sigmund Freud argued that hysterical symptoms often have more than one provoking cause and that the onset of such symptoms may be delayed, triggered not by an initial traumatic event but by some later, similar trauma. Breuer attributed the term to Freud, who, describing the psychotherapy of hysteria, asserted that the genesis of neuroses such as hysteria "is as a rule overdetermined, that several factors must come together to produce this result."

Freud also applied the concept of multiple causation to dreams, arguing in *The Interpretation of Dreams* (1900) that "each of the elements of the dream's content turns out to have been 'overdetermined' — to have been represented in the dream-thoughts many times over." In the absence of a single, determinative element or source thereof, multiple interpretations "are not mutually contradictory, but cover the same ground; they are a good instance of the fact that dreams, like all other psychological structures, regularly have more than one meaning."

French **Marxist** Louis Althusser subsequently applied the term *overdetermined* to the analysis of certain historical events. In his essay "Contradiction et surdétermination" ("Contradiction and Overdetermination") (1962), Althusser argued that events resulting from multiple or conflicting factors are overdetermined and cannot be explained adequately by reference to principles of economic determinism (the belief that human events and choices result primarily from economic causes). By combining this insight with preexisting understandings of overdetermination, several post-Althusserian **Marxist critics** and **cultural critics** have analyzed, or "unpacked," textual **sites** marked by the confluence of economic, historical, literary, and psychological forces.

Other literary critics have used the term *overdetermined* primarily to discuss the nature and function of **symbols**. Symbols are overdetermined insofar as they are **metaphors** in which the **vehicle** — the **image**, activity, or concept used to describe the **tenor**, or subject — refers to a variety of things. For instance, the sea, a common symbol in literary works, may represent hope or despair; vastness, emptiness, or endless possibilities. It may be all-encompassing or isolating, the means of sustaining life or ending it, or any and all of these things at once.

FURTHER EXAMPLES: The **character** of Edgar in William Shakespeare's play *King Lear* (1606) is overdetermined. Lear's description of Edgar as a "learned Theban" suggests he is a skeptical, materialist philosopher. But seen from the perspective of English social history, he looks like a "Bedlam" or "Poor Tom" figure, a wandering beggar dispossessed by sixteenth-century laws that allowed landowners to privatize semipublic lands. And viewed in light of literary history, he exemplifies the "trickster" who turns out to be the bearer of truth.

In an essay entitled "Introduction to the *Danse Macabre:* Conrad's *Heart of Darkness*" (1989), **psychoanalytic critic** Frederick Karl treated Joseph Conrad's depiction of the jungle in his **novella** *Heart of Darkness* as overdetermined, pointing out that the jungle symbolizes both what people fear and what they destroy. Similarly, in an essay entitled "Is Morrison Also Among the Prophets?: 'Psychoanalytic' Strategies in *Beloved*" (1994), Iyunolu Osagie described Beloved, who may be a ghost-child or a flesh-and-blood escapee from a slave ship, as "an overdetermined character," arguing that her "multiple inscriptions call for a semantic layering of interpretations."

▶ **overstatement:** See **hyperbole.**

▶ **oxymoron:** From the Greek for "pointedly foolish," a **rhetorical figure** that juxtaposes two opposite or apparently contradictory words to present an emphatic and dramatic **paradox.**

EXAMPLES: Bittersweet, friendly fire, genuine imitation, open secret, virtual reality. In William Shakespeare's *Much Ado About Nothing* (1599), Claudio accuses his fiancée, Hero, of infidelity and unchastity as they stand at the altar on their wedding day: "Thou pure impiety and impious purity. . . ." In her **slave narrative** *Incidents in the Life of a Slave Girl* (1861), Harriet Jacobs defined slavery as a "living death." Serving as *Saturday Night Live*'s first host on October 11, 1975, stand-up comedian George Carlin remarked, "The term Jumbo Shrimp has always amazed me. What *is* a *Jumbo Shrimp*? I mean, it's like Military Intelligence — the words don't go together, man."

P

▶ **paeon:** See foot.

▶ **palimpsest:** From the Greek for "scraped again," a piece of parchment, papyrus, or other manuscript page from which the original **text** has been removed so the material may be reused. Since good writing surfaces were costly and often scarce in ancient and early **medieval** times, before paper became a common commodity, old ones were washed and scrubbed so they could be overwritten. In some cases, scholars have been able to recover original texts based on traces that have shown through over time or by using various technological means. In **literary criticism,** *palimpsest* has also been used **metaphorically** to refer to the multiple meanings of any word and the multiple levels of meaning in any text. With reference to the pictorial arts, the term is used to refer to a repainted canvas.

EXAMPLES: The Archimedes Palimpsest, comprised of parchment taken from several books in the thirteenth century to make a Christian prayer book, contains, *inter alia,* a tenth-century copy of various mathematical works by the third-century B.C. Sicilian mathematician Archimedes, a **Neoplatonic** philosophical text, and material by the fourth-century B.C. Athenian orator Hyperides. The idea of the palimpsest functions on several levels in Salman Rushdie's novel *The Moor's Last Sigh* (1996), which involves a painter who continually paints portraits of a woman he once loved, only to cover them over with hackneyed commercial works that he sells at extravagant prices.

▶ **palindrome:** From the Greek for "running back again," writing in which characters, such as letters or numbers, are exactly the same whether read forward or backward (ignoring punctuation and spaces). *Word palindromes* are lines or sentences that read the same way whether the words are read forward or backward. Given that the letters, numbers, or words on either side of the midpoint of a palindrome mirror one another, a palindrome is a type of **chiasmus.**

EXAMPLES: Words such as *civic, racecar,* and *radar* are palindromes, as is the sentence "Madam, I'm Adam" and the **apocryphal** line falsely attributed to Napoleon, "Able was I ere I saw Elba." Examples of numeric palindromes include 11, 202, and 3553; furthermore, adding a number (e.g., 47) to its reverse form (e.g., 74) often results in a number that is itself a palindrome (e.g., 121). An example of a word palindrome is the sentence "First ladies rule the state and state the rule 'Ladies first.'"

Adah Price, one of the **characters** and **narrators** in Barbara Kingsolver's novel *The Poisonwood Bible* (1998), makes frequent use of palindromes, such as "Amen, enema" and "Evil, all its sin is still alive."

▶ **palinode:** From the Greek for "singing again," a work written to retract a previous written statement. Generally, both the original "offensive" or "incorrect" writing and the retraction are written in **verse.** Stesichorus, a Sicilian Greek **lyric** poet of the seventh and sixth centuries B.C., is generally credited with writing the first palinode, a recantation of a prior poem blaming Helen for the Trojan War. During the **classical, Medieval,** and **Renaissance periods,** writing palinodes was fairly common.

FURTHER EXAMPLES: Geoffrey Chaucer's *The Legend of Good Women* (c. 1385), written to recant — or at least balance out — his negative presentation of women as unfaithful in *Troilus and Criseyde* (c. 1383) and other works; Gelett Burgess's "Confession: and a Portrait, Too, Upon a Background That I Rue," a rejection of his "Purple Cow: Reflections on a Mythic Beast, Who's Quite Remarkable, at Least" (1895); Ogden Nash's 1964 recantation of his 1931 **couplet** "The Bronx? / No, thonx," ending "Now I'm an older, wiser man / I cry, 'The Bronx? God / bless them!'"

▶ **pantomime:** In its purest form, acting without words. In pantomimes, the **characters** do not speak; instead, they mime stories and convey their thoughts and emotions solely through body movements, facial expressions, gestures, and posture. Costumes may also play a role, particularly in the miming of circus clowns. Pantomimes date back to **classical** times; in ancient Rome, they were usually based on a **mythological** story and featured a single actor, the *pantomimus,* who mimed all the roles and was accompanied by a **chorus.** Pantomimes featured prominently in film in the early twentieth century with the advent of the silent movie and persist today as a form of street performance. Noted twentieth-century mimes include Charlie Chaplin and Marcel Marceau.

The term *pantomime* is also often associated with the *dumb show,* a pantomimed segment of a **play.** Dumb shows, which were popular in **Elizabethan** and **Jacobean** drama and sometimes occurred as **prologues** or between **acts,** were often **allegorical** and frequently **foreshadowed** or interpreted the **action** in the play. Examples include the dumb shows in Thomas Sackville and Thomas Norton's *Gorboduc* (1562) and the regicide mimed by the players of the play-within-a-play in William Shakespeare's *Hamlet* (1602).

Pantomime may also refer to a particularly extravagant type of **drama** that emerged in eighteenth-century England combining mime with song and dance. Such pantomimes are typically based on **fairy tales** or other **folkloric** stories, such as Cinderella, Dick Whittington and his cat, and Puss in Boots, and include figures from the *commedia dell'arte.* Common elements include double entendre; jokes; numerous **scene** changes; **slapstick** humor; audience participation; and gender role reversal, with girls in boys' roles and men playing elderly women. Such pantomimes, which are still performed in Britain, Ireland, Australia, and several other countries during the Christmas season, are usually intended for the entertainment of children.

▶ **parable:** A short, **realistic,** but usually fictional **story** told to illustrate a moral or religious point or lesson; a type of **allegory.** The parable differs slightly from the **fable** and the **exemplum,** two other types of allegory also designed to make a point, insofar as a true parable is composed or told in response to a specific situation and addresses that situation, at least implicitly, in an allegorical manner. The most famous parables in Western literature are those told by Jesus and include the parables of the talents, the prodigal son, the rich man and Lazarus, the young rich ruler, and the lost sheep.

▶ **paradigm:** See *epistémé.*

▶ **paradox:** A statement that seems self-contradictory or nonsensical on the surface but that, upon closer examination, may express an underlying truth. A **rhetorical figure,** paradox provokes the reader or audience to see something in a new way. A paradox formed by the juxtaposition of two opposite or apparently contradictory words is an **oxymoron.**

The **New Critics** used the term *paradox* more broadly to refer to unexpected deviations from ordinary **discourse.** Cleanth Brooks, for instance, maintained in his essay "The Language of Poetry" (1942) that "paradox is the language appropriate and inevitable to poetry."

EXAMPLES: The zen koan, "What is the sound of one hand clapping?"; the following lines from the **classic** Taoist **text** *Tao Te Ching,* generally attributed to ancient Chinese philosopher Lao-tzu: "My words are very easy to know, and very easy to practice; but there is no one in the world who is able to know and able to practice them."

Speaking of the immense losses his forces sustained in defeating the Romans at Asculum (279 B.C.), Pyrrhus, King of Epirus, is reported to have said, "One more such victory and we are lost." By contrast, an unnamed U.S. major in Vietnam, questioned by reporter Peter Arnett about the use of heavy artillery against the provincial capital of Bến Tre, claimed, "It became necessary to destroy the town to save it" (Feb. 7, 1968).

The **metaphysical poets** made frequent use of paradox; for instance, the speaker of John Donne's poem "Lovers' Infiniteness" (1633) tells his beloved:

> Thou canst not every day give me thy heart;
> If thou canst give it, then thou never gavest it. . . .

In Richard Bach's *Jonathan Livingston Seagull* (1970), Jonathan's reproach to his friend Sullivan involves the paradoxical idea that friends can see each other "in the middle of Here and Now" by overcoming space and time:

> If our friendship depends on things like space and time, then when we finally overcome space and time, we've destroyed our own brotherhood! But overcome space, and all we have left is Here. Overcome

time, and all we have left is Now. And in the middle of Here and Now, don't you think that we might see each other once or twice?

A more recent example of paradox is the Deathstone in Piers Anthony's fantasy novel *On a Pale Horse* (1983), which the seller claims "advises the wearer of the proximity of termination, by darkening. The speed and intensity of the change notifies you of the potential circumstance of your demise — in plenty of time for you to avoid it." By contrast, Steve Martin's novella *Shopgirl* (2000; adapted to film 2005) opens with a more innocuous paradox: "When you work in the glove department at Neiman's, you are selling things that nobody buys anymore."

▶ **paralipsis:** A **rhetorical figure** involving a speaker's assertion that he or she will not discuss something that he or she in fact goes on to discuss. A variety of terms have sometimes been used synonymously with paralipsis (alternatively spelled *paralepsis* and *paraleipsis*), including *occultatio, occupatio, praeteritio,* and *preterition.*

EXAMPLES: The **narrator** of Geoffrey Chaucer's *Troilus and Criseyde* (c. 1383) regularly discusses the subject of love after refusing to discuss it, citing his own status as a failed lover and deferring to the expertise of his audience.

Marc Antony's famous speech in William Shakespeare's play *Julius Caesar* (1598) begins with a paralipsis. Declaring "Friends, Romans, countrymen, lend me your ears; / I come to bury Caesar, not to praise him," Antony proceeds to praise Caesar anyway.

▶ **parallelism:** A **rhetorical figure** used in written and oral compositions since ancient times to accentuate or emphasize ideas or **images** by using grammatically similar constructions. Words, phrases, clauses, sentences, paragraphs, and even larger structural units may be consciously organized into parallel constructions, creating a sense of balance and inviting both comparison and contrast.

Repetition often plays an important role in establishing parallelism. Sometimes a word, line, or other grammatical unit is repeated verbatim. For instance, the exact repetition of words or phrases at the beginning of successive lines or sentences is called **anaphora.** Similarly, the **refrain,** or **chorus,** of a song may be repeated word-for-word after each **stanza.** Often, however, repetition is not this strict. It may be **incremental,** as when the same basic line recurs with subtle variation throughout a poem. It may also occur when one grammatical unit reinforces another, saying the same thing but in different words. To say that a woman is lovely, then to describe her as beautiful, and then to present an **image** depicting her beauty is to use repetition of this latter sort.

Parallelism has been a particularly important device in oral composition, such as speeches and sermons, and in biblical poetry, where it often involves the restatement of the same idea in slightly different words rather than the juxtaposition of related or **antithetical** ideas.

EXAMPLES: Charles Dickens used parallelism to emphasize antithetical ideas in the opening lines of his novel *A Tale of Two Cities* (1859), where the **narrator** speaks of the year 1775:

> It was the best of times, it was the worst of times, it was the age of wisdom, it was the age of foolishness, it was the epoch of belief, it was the epoch of incredulity, it was the season of Light, it was the season of Darkness, it was the spring of hope, it was the winter of despair, we had everything before us, we had nothing before us, we were all going direct to Heaven, we were all going direct the other way.

Among the most familiar poems in India is a short one from Rabindranath Tagore's *Gitanjali* (1910), in which each line but the last begins with the word "where" in the poet's English translation:

> Where the mind is without fear and the head is held high;
> Where knowledge is free;
> Where the world has not been broken up into fragments by
>   narrow domestic walls;
> Where words come out from the depth of truth;
> Where tireless striving stretches its arms towards perfection;
> Where the clear stream of reason has not lost its way into the
>   dreary desert sand of dead habit;
> Where the mind is led forward by thee into ever-widening
>   thought and action —
> Into that heaven of freedom, my Father, let my country awake.

Likewise, in *Goodnight Moon* (1947), a **classic** children's bedtime story, Margaret Wise Brown employed parallelism first to list everything in the "great green room" and then to bid it and everything in it good night: the light, the telephone, the red balloon, a pair of mittens, the kittens, pictures of bears and a cow jumping over the moon, and so forth.

▶ **pararhyme:** See **half rhyme.**

▶ **parataxis, paratactic style:** See **style.**

▶ **Parnassians:** Originally, a group of French poets active in the latter half of the nineteenth century who sought to produce impersonal, **objective** poetry, emphasizing **form** and minimizing **authorial** presence. Influenced by French writer Théophile Gautier, who argued that art has no utilitarian value in the preface to his novel *Mademoiselle de Maupin* (1835), the Parnassians embraced **art for art's sake.** They also rejected **romanticism,** which they viewed as unduly emotional and **subjective,** and embraced **positivism,** aiming for detached description and technical precision in their works. Privileging craftsmanship, they revived complex French verse forms such as the **ballade, rondeau,** and **villanelle** and often made use of "exotic" **classical** and Oriental subjects.

Led by French poet Leconte de Lisle, Parnassianism emerged as a literary movement in the 1860s, particularly with the publication of *Le parnasse contemporain* (1866), an anthology of verse edited by Alphonse Lemerre and named for Mt. Parnassus, a sacred mountain in Greek **mythology** and home of the **muses**. Noted adherents included François Coppée; José Maria de Heredia; Catulle Mendès; Sully Prudhomme; Louis-Xavier de Ricard; and Théodore de Banville, whose *Petit traité de poésie française* (*Little Treatise on French Poetry*) (1872) was particularly influential. During the 1870s, the movement spread to England, where writers known as the English Parnassians, including Edmund Gosse, Andrew Lang, and Algernon Charles Swinburne, **imitated** the French school. Parnassianism also substantially influenced **Aestheticism** and **French Symbolism**.

▶ **parody:** From the Greek for "a song beside," a form of high **burlesque** popular since ancient times that comically **imitates** a specific, generally serious work or the **style** of an **author** or **genre**. The literary counterpart to **caricature**, which is designed to ridicule through an exaggerated depiction of an individual's features or characteristics, parody is often used to make a **satiric** (and even a political) point. Light parodies are often called *spoofs*.

EXAMPLES: J. K. Stephen parodied Walt Whitman's style in his poem "Of W. W. (Americanus)" (1891):

> The clear cool note of the cuckoo which has ousted the legitimate
>   nest-holder,
> The whistle of the railway guard dispatching the train to the inevitable
>   collision,
> The maiden's monosyllabic reply to a polysyllabic proposal,
> The fundamental note of the last trumpet, which is presumably D
>   natural;
> All these are sounds to rejoice in, yea to let your very ribs re-echo with:
> But better than them all is the absolutely last chord of the apparently
>   inexhaustible pianoforte player.

Other verse examples include Lewis Carroll's "Aged, Aged Man" (1871), which parodies William Wordsworth's "Resolution and Independence" (1807), especially the figure of the old leech-gatherer, and Algernon Charles Swinburne's "Nephelida" (1880), a good-humored self-parody of his ultrasensuous, **alliterative, anapestic** poems.

Genres are often the subject of parody. Stephen Crane parodied the "Western" in his short story "The Bride Comes to Yellow Sky" (1897), as did the Mel Brooks movie *Blazing Saddles* (1974). Likewise, *Dead Men Don't Wear Plaid* (1982) parodied **hard-boiled detective fiction**, the *Scary Movie* series (2000–06) **horror** flicks, and the *Austin Powers* trilogy (1997–2002) spy films.

Parodies may also have both general and specific targets. Woody Allen parodied the Russian **realistic novel**, and Leo Tolstoi's *War and Peace* (1869) in particular, in his movie *Love and Death* (1975). *Airplane!* (1980) parodied the television drama *Zero Hour* (1957), a remake of Arthur Hailey's play *Flight into Danger* (1956), as well as the four *Airport* movies produced during the 1970s and based on Hailey's 1968 novel of the same name. *Hot Shots!* (1991) parodied the movie *Top Gun* (1986), *Hot Shots: Part Deux* (1993) action movies, particularly *Rambo: First Blood Part II* (1985). The animated sitcom *The Simpsons* (1989– ; adapted to film 2007) regularly sends up Middle America and often focuses on more specific targets in particular episodes, such as the musical *The Best Little Whorehouse in Texas* (1978) in "Bart after Dark" (1996) and Tim LaHaye and Jerry B. Jenkins's *Left Behind* series (1995–2007) in "Thank God It's Doomsday" (2005).

Grant Wood's painting *American Gothic* (1930), featuring a severe-looking, elderly couple with a pitchfork, has been parodied many times. In music, "Weird" Al Yankovich made fun of Michael Jackson's hit song "Beat It" (1983) in his parody "Eat It" (1984). T. Coraghessan Boyle's short story "Heart of a Champion" (1974) parodied the long-running TV show *Lassie* (1954–74), *The Brady Bunch Movie* (1995) the sitcom *The Brady Bunch* (1969–74).

Other contemporary examples of parody include Alice Randall's "unauthorized" novel *The Wind Done Gone* (2001), which takes off on Margaret Mitchell's *Gone with the Wind* (1936) by exploring life at Tara and in the Old South more generally from an illegitimate mulatto slave's **point of view;** the parodic newspaper *The Onion* (1988–); and *The Colbert Report* (2005–), which parodies TV news broadcasting and punditry, especially cable shows such as *The O'Reilly Factor* (1996–).

See also **burlesque.**

▶ *parole:* See **semiotics.**

▶ **paronomasia:** See **pun.**

▶ **pastiche:** A literary, musical, or artistic work that **imitates** another's recognizable **style** or pieces together a medley of often incongruous elements from a number of existing works. Pastiche may have humorous, **satirical,** or serious intent or may simply serve as an exercise in technique. Most literary critics use the term descriptively, but some use it dismissively to describe a work that is deemed highly derivative. *Pastiche* should not be confused with *plagiarism,* in which one **author** steals a passage or idea from another, passing it off as his or her own and failing to credit the original source. Plagiarism is characterized by deceptive intent; pastiche involves open imitation or borrowing and often pays homage to its sources.

Pastiche, which may involve sustained satirical imitation of a particular author's style, is sometimes treated synonymously with **parody** but is more often distinguished from the latter by its respectful tone. In *Postmodernism, or, The Cultural Logic of Late Capitalism* (1991), **Marxist critic** Fredric Jameson characterized pastiche as "blank parody," arguing that it is "a neutral practice of such mimicry, without any of parody's ulterior motives, amputated of the satiric impulse, devoid of laughter."

EXAMPLES: Marcel Proust's *Pastiches et mélanges* (1919). Some of Carl Sandburg's poetry could be referred to as "Walt Whitman pastiche." Sherlockian pastiche has become a minor literary industry, with works such as *The Exploits of Sherlock Holmes* (1954), by Adrian Conan Doyle and John Dickson Carr, and *The Further Adventures of Sherlock Holmes* (1985), a collection edited by Richard Lancelyn Green. The Coen brothers' film *O Brother, Where Art Thou?* (2000) is also pastiche, borrowing heavily from Homer's *The Odyssey* (c. 850 B.C.), among other sources. The American Telephone and Telegraph (AT&T) headquarters building in New York City, designed by Philip Johnson and popularly known as the "Chippendale Building," has also been called pastiche, so closely does the top resemble a Chippendale cabinet.

The **anachronistic** musical score of the movie *Moulin Rouge* (2001), set in Paris at the end of the nineteenth century, is a pastiche of late-twentieth-century popular songs such as Elton John's "Your Song" (1970) and Sting's "Roxanne" (1978). Through use of the technique known as "sampling" — borrowing riffs from other, well-known songs — rap artists have also created works that involve pastiche in the sense of "medley."

▶ **pastoral:** (1) As an adjective, a term that can be applied to any work with a rural **setting** and that generally praises a rustic way of life; (2) as a noun, a term that refers to a literary **mode** historically and conventionally associated with shepherds and country living. Pastoral life has been associated by many poets (especially the ancient Greeks and Romans) with a variety of eras considered as the **golden age** of humankind. The third-century B.C. Greek poet Theocritus wrote the first pastorals, which he ostensibly based on the lives of Sicilian shepherds. The first-century B.C. Roman poet Virgil, who **imitated** Theocritus and established the pastoral as a popular literary form, set many of the **conventions** of the **genre**. Traditional pastoral verse typically involves a singing contest between two shepherds, a **monologue** praising someone or something or lamenting the loss of love, or a lament for a dead shepherd and friend.

The pastoral became so popular that it evolved into new, hybrid forms including **pastoral elegy**, pastoral **drama**, pastoral **romance**, and even the pastoral **novel**. Pastoral elements, settings, and **themes**, moreover, began to crop up in a variety of nonpastoral works (William Shakespeare's plays, for instance). The use of the term *pastoral* was extended by the critic William Empson, in *Some Versions of Pastoral* (1935), to refer to any work that cloaks complexity in simple garments (for instance, urban **characters** in a rural setting) and that praises values associated with simplicity.

FURTHER EXAMPLES: Edmund Spenser's *The Shepheardes Calendar* (1579). William Wordsworth's *Michael* (1800) is subtitled *A Pastoral Poem*. Still later examples of works containing pastoral elements include Thomas Hardy's *Far from the Madding Crowd* (1874) and Isak Dinesen's *Out of Africa* (1937; adapted to film in 1985).

See also **eclogue.**

▶ **pastoral elegy:** A serious formal **poem** in which a poet grieves the loss of a dead friend (often another poet). Composed in an elevated, dignified style, pastoral elegy, as its name implies, combines the forms and traditions of **elegy** with those of **pastoral**, specifically pastoral **eclogue**. In this type of elegy, the poet-mourner **figures** himself and the individual mourned as shepherds who have lived their lives in a simple, rural **setting**, tending their flocks. The dead shepherd is traditionally given a Greek name in recognition of the fact that the earliest examples of this **genre** were written in ancient Greece. The third-century B.C. Greek poet Theocritus is usually credited with creating the form, an early example of which is Moschus's "Lament for Bion" (c. 150 B.C.). The genre became so popular in Europe at various points during the sixteenth through nineteenth centuries that it has become common for any type of elegy on another poet to contain pastoral elements.

The pastoral elegy is highly **conventional**, generally opening with an **invocation** that is followed by a statement of the poet's great grief and a subsequent description of a procession of mourners. (In addition to people and supernatural beings, this procession may include Nature, plants and animals, and even things to which the dead poet gave imaginative existence. For instance, in "Adonais" [1821], Percy Bysshe Shelley's elegy for John Keats, the procession includes "All he had loved and moulded into thought.") The pastoral elegy also usually involves a discussion of fate, or some similarly philosophical topic, and, ultimately, a statement by the speaking poet to the effect that all is well and has turned out as it should. (In Christian elegies, such statements imply or explicitly involve affirmations of belief in an afterlife.) Expressions of bewilderment, invectives against death, belief in immortality, arrangements of flowers, and the **pathetic fallacy** are also conventional elements of the pastoral elegy.

FURTHER EXAMPLES: John Milton's "Lycidas" (1638) (for Edward King), Matthew Arnold's "Thyrsis" (1866) (for Arthur Hugh Clough).

▶ **pathetic fallacy:** A term coined by **Victorian** art critic John Ruskin in *Modern Painters* (v.3, 1856) to describe the attribution of human traits and emotions to inanimate nature. Ruskin considered such attribution a sign of artistic weakness, an "error . . . which the mind admits when affected strongly by emotion." Citing the lines "They rowed her in across the rolling foam — / The cruel, crawling foam" from Charles Kingsley's *Alton Locke* (1850) as an example, he noted that "The foam is not cruel, neither does it crawl. The state of mind which attributes to it these characters of a living creature is one in which the reason is unhinged by grief." While subsequent critics have generally used the term neutrally, modern poets have tended to avoid the device.

The pathetic fallacy is a limited form of **personification**, a **figure of speech** that bestows human characteristics upon anything nonhuman. It has a narrower scope, applying to inanimate nature rather than animals, places, synthetic objects, and so forth. Furthermore, its "humanizing" characterization is typically less sustained than that effected by personification.

FURTHER EXAMPLES: The "howling storm" in William Blake's "The Sick Rose" (1794); William Wordsworth's treatment of the moon in "Ode: Intimations of Immortality" (1807):

> The Moon doth with delight
> Look round her when the heavens are bare, . . .

Giving hurricanes human names and representing their results as purposeful exemplify a modern, journalistic use of pathetic fallacy. An August 1995 headline in the *Miami Herald* read: "Killer Storm Swirls Toward Open Seas: East Coast May Be Spared Luis's Fury." Similarly, when Katrina hit the U.S., the story aired on CNN was headlined "Hurricane Katrina Pummels Three States" (Aug. 29, 2005), with anchor Aaron Brown noting that Katrina had "spared New Orleans a direct hit."

See also **personification.**

▶ **pathos:** From the Greek for "emotion," "passion," or "suffering," a quality in a work or a portion thereof that makes the reader experience pity, sorrow, or tenderness. Pathos is distinguished from **tragedy** in that pathetic characters are generally helpless, innocent victims suffering through no fault of their own. Tragic figures, by contrast, possess a heroic grandeur and are at least partially responsible for their fates. Works involving the misuse, abuse, or death of children are almost inevitably pathetic, although an unskilled writer can easily slip into **bathos** if the effect is exaggerated or **anticlimactic.**

EXAMPLES: Charles Dickens achieves pathos in his description of the death of Paul Dombey in *Dombey and Son* (1846–48), but most critics would say he slips into bathos in describing the death of Little Nell in *The Old Curiosity Shop* (1840). Toni Morrison's *Beloved* (1987), which relates the story of a woman who deliberately kills her child to keep her from being returned to slavery, is a novel of intense emotion and immense pathos. Contemporary works filled with pathos include Rohinton Mistry's novel *A Fine Balance* (1995) and the film *Brokeback Mountain* (2005), based on E. Annie Proulx's 1997 short story. The final scenes of the movie *Million Dollar Baby* (2004), in which paralyzed former boxer Maggie Fitzgerald seeks her trainer's help in ending her suffering, evoke immense pathos.

▶ **patriarchal:** A term used by **feminist critics** to describe the structuring of society on the basis of "father-rule," or paternal authority, and the concomitant marginalization or subordination of women. Feminist critics critique patriarchal society as dominated by men promoting masculine "values" that, in turn, maintain men in positions of power — in short, as a system that perpetuates male dominance, whether in the family or in government, in the arts or in religion, and relegates women to the domestic sphere. Having been defined as **Other,** in **binary opposition** to the "superior" male and his masculine characteristics from ancient times to the present day, women have been traditionally conditioned to accept the patriarchal **ideology** that devalues them and all things labeled "feminine."

▶ **pattern poetry:** See **concrete poetry.**

▶ **pen name:** See *nom de plume.*

▶ **pentameter:** A line of **verse** consisting of five **metrical feet.** Pentameter is the predominant line length in English verse.
EXAMPLE: The last lines of Wallace Stevens's "Sunday Morning" (1915) are written in pentameter:

> Deer walk | upon | our moun|tains, and | the quail |
> Whistle | about | us their | sponta|neous cries;|
> Sweet ber|ries ri|pen in | the wil|derness;|
> And, in | the i|sola|tion of | the sky,|
> At eve|ning, cas|ual flocks | of pi|geons make|
> Ambi|guous un|dula|tions as | they sink,|
> Downward | to dark|ness, on | extend|ed wings.|

▶ **perfect rhyme:** Rhyme involving words in which the **accented** vowel sound and all subsequent sounds are identical. *Perfect rhyme* has been used as a synonym for two different types of rhyme: *true* (or *full*) *rhyme* and *rime riche* (*identical rhyme*).

When used as a synonym for true rhyme, which is the more common usage, *perfect rhyme* refers to rhyme in which the initial sound of the **stressed** syllable of the rhyming words must be different (for instance, *hit / pit* or *finger / linger*). Thus, perfect rhyme does not occur when two or more words are pronounced exactly alike. Other sounds preceding the accented vowel of the rhyming words, however, may or may not be different. Both *brim / trim* and *skim / trim* are perfect rhymes, as are *hurt, divert,* and the verb *desert.*

When used in the sense of *rime riche,* however, *perfect rhyme* refers to rhyme in which all sounds in the stressed syllable as well as all subsequent sounds are identical. Thus, words that sound exactly alike but that have different meanings — whether *doe / dough* or *dough / dough* (in the differing senses of dough for baking and money) — exemplify *rime riche,* as do pairings such as *billed / rebuild* and *compass / encompass.*

EXAMPLES: The first eight lines of John Crowe Ransom's poem "Dead Boy" (1927) contain four pairs of true rhymes:

> The little cousin is dead, by foul subtraction,
> A green bough from Virginia's aged tree,
> And none of the county kin like the transaction
> Nor some of the world of outer dark, like me.

> A boy not beautiful, nor good, nor clever,
> A black cloud full of storms too hot for keeping,
> A sword beneath his mother's heart — yet never
> Woman bewept her babe as this is weeping.

By contrast, T. S. Eliot's *Murder in the Cathedral* (1935), a play written in verse, employs *rime riche* in the following **couplet**: "And the suffering, that the wheel may turn and still / Be forever still."

▶ **performative:** A term used in opposition to *constative* by British "ordinary language" philosopher John Austin in *How to Do Things with Words* (1962) to distinguish between two classes of **locutions.** According to Austin, performative locutions are sentences that actively "do" something, such as question or admonish, whereas constative locutions are sentences that state something that can be determined to be true or false. Having established these two types of locutions, Austin went on to show that they are not mutually exclusive, that is, that a sentence can involve both elements simultaneously.

EXAMPLES: An example of a performative is the statement, "Don't touch that cookie jar!" whereas a related constative is "He didn't touch that cookie jar."

See **speech-act theory.**

▶ **periodicity:** The idea that there are distinct periods or ages within the literature of a nation or culture; the traditional framework for literary studies in English. Scholars and critics who adhere to the concept of periodicity maintain that writers within a given historical era, including those working in different **genres,** have more in common in terms of **form, style,** and **themes** than writers from other eras, even those that are chronologically adjacent.

Recently, critics of periodicity have pointed out that the parameters of literary periods are arbitrarily drawn and have little, if anything, to do with literature. For instance, the **Victorian Period** is said to span the years 1837–1901 because those are the years of Queen Victoria's reign in England, but why should we assume that Victoria's reign made Alfred, Lord Tennyson's *Poems* (1830) less like the poems of John Keats (1795–1821) and Percy Bysshe Shelley (1792–1822) than like Thomas Hardy's **fin de siècle** novel *Jude the Obscure* (1895)? Critics of periodicity also point out that many writers span periods; Hardy (1840–1928), for instance, wrote during the Victorian Period and the **Modern Period,** and William Shakespeare wrote plays during the **Elizabethan Age** and the **Jacobean Age.** To the extent that the works of writers such as Hardy and Shakespeare are **aesthetically** and thematically consistent, such consistency undermines the claims of scholars and critics who would differentiate the periods during which they were written.

Few scholars and critics today explicitly advocate periodicity. Somewhere between those who do and those who don't are somewhat traditional literary historians who argue that it is useful to think of works as falling within chronological periods loosely defined, insofar as **texts** are inevitably rooted in historical contexts, however broadly those roots may extend and however questionable our definitions of those contexts may be. Other defenders argue that periodicity promotes interdisciplinarity and **intertextuality,** providing a flexible framework for examining relationships among texts, whether literary or nonliterary, or for linking texts to the real world. Such scholars and critics thus might defend preservation of a university literature curriculum consisting of courses that group literary works under traditional chronological rubrics (e.g., "**Restoration Age** Drama"). And they undoubtedly would defend the inclusion in this glossary of entries defining the various **Periods in English literature** and **Periods in American literature.** Those most radically opposed to periodicity, on the other hand, would argue that it is misleading and thus intellectually harmful to organize a literary curriculum around periods. They might even argue that this glossary, in defining those periods traditionally, perpetuates and preserves a set of distinctions leading readers to see textual similarities — and differences — that are highly suspect and easily contradicted.

▶ **periodic sentence:** A complex sentence that is not **syntactically** complete until its very end; the opposite of a **loose sentence,** in which an independent clause is followed by one or more independent or dependent clauses. A periodic sentence includes at least one dependent clause and/or **parallel** construction (and often several of each) before the final independent clause, which completes the sentence and provides its grammatical close as well as its meaning. Periodic sentences are comparatively formal and are often used to heighten suspense by deferring the main point until the last word. Works predominantly containing periodic sentences usually exhibit **hypotactic style.**

EXAMPLES: The following sentence from Jonathan Swift's *Gulliver's Travels* (1726) is periodic:

> And it must be confessed, that from the great intercourse of trade and commerce between both realms, from the continual reception of exiles, which is mutual among them, and from the custom in each empire to send their young nobility and richer gentry to the other, in order to polish themselves, by seeing the world, and understanding men and manners, there are few persons of distinction, or merchants, or seamen, who dwell in the maritime parts, but what can hold conversation in both tongues.

So is this sentence from John Stuart Mill's *On Liberty* (1859):

> If all mankind, minus one, were of one opinion, and only one person were of the contrary opinion, mankind would be no more justified in silencing that one person than he, if he had the power, would be justified in silencing mankind.

▶ **Periods in American literature:** See **Colonial Period, Revolutionary Period, Early National Period, Romantic Period, Realistic Period, Naturalistic**

Period, Modern Period (in English and American literature), Postmodern Period (in English and American literature).

▶ **Periods in English literature:** See **Old English Period, Middle English Period, Renaissance Period** (including **Early Tudor Age, Elizabethan Age, Jacobean Age, Caroline Age,** and **Commonwealth Age**), **Neoclassical Period** (including **Augustan Age, Restoration Age,** and **Age of Johnson**), **Romantic Period, Victorian Period, Edwardian Age, Georgian Age, Modern Period** (in English and American literature), **Postmodern Period** (in English and American literature).

▶ **periphrasis:** Circumlocution, that is, a roundabout way of speaking or writing. As a **rhetorical figure,** periphrasis may be used to avoid mundane expression or for emphasis, euphemistic purposes, or comic effect. An element of **poetic diction,** periphrasis has historically been viewed as a means of elevating language and distinguishing it from **prose.** Since the eighteenth century, however, the figure has fallen out of favor, and today the term is often used pejoratively to designate the pompous or wordy.

EXAMPLES: The advertising slogan "Raid™ kills bugs dead"; the euphemistic phrase "passed away." Alexander Haig, deputy assistant to President Nixon for national security affairs, chief of staff under the Ford administration, and secretary of state under President Reagan, used periphrasis in calling a lie a "terminological inexactitude."

Alexander Pope's reference to fish as "the finny tribe" in his poem "The Rape of the Lock" (1712, 1714) both brings out the social nature of fish and calls attention to one specific characteristic ("finny"). William Shakespeare used periphrasis for comic effect in *Much Ado About Nothing* (1599), when Constable Dogberry, asked "What offense have these men done?" replies:

> Marry, sir, they have committed false report; moreover, they have spoken untruths; secondarily, they are slanders; sixth and lastly, they have belied a lady; thirdly, they have verified unjust things; and to conclude, they are lying knaves.

Although some critics have described as poetic the following passage from Joseph Conrad's *Heart of Darkness* (1899), others have found it a wordy and pompous way of saying that a jarring memory suddenly intruded upon the mysterious stillness of the present:

> There were moments when one's past came back to one, as it will sometimes when you have not a moment to spare to yourself; but it came in the shape of an unrestful and noisy dream, remembered with wonder, amongst the overwhelming realities of this strange world of plants, and water, and silence. And this stillness of life did not in the least resemble a peace. It was the stillness of an implacable force brooding over an inscrutable intention.

▶ **perlocutionary act:** A **speech act** involving a **locution,** or utterance, that affects the hearer, producing a change in his or her actions or state of mind. As introduced by British "ordinary-language" philosopher John L. Austin in *How to Do Things with Words* (1962), a perlocutionary act is "what we bring about or achieve *by* saying something, such as convincing, persuading, deterring, and even, say, surprising or misleading." Notably, the occurrence of a perlocutionary act depends not on the speaker's intent but, rather, on how the listener is affected by the statement in question.

EXAMPLE: As an **illocutionary act,** the statement "If you tell the secret, I'll kill you" could be a threat or a joke. Whether a perlocutionary act also occurs depends on whether the listener is affected by the statement, for instance, by becoming scared or deciding not to tell the secret as a result.

See **speech-act theory.**

▶ **persona:** Generally, the speaker in a literary work, often a **first-person** narrator. The term derives from the Latin word for "mask" and literally refers to that through which sound passes. Some critics equate the persona with the **narrator,** others with the **implied author.** Although the persona often serves as the "voice" of the **author,** the two should not be conflated, for the persona may not accurately reflect the author's personal opinions, feelings, or perspective on a subject.

Persona has also been used to refer to the public "face" an individual presents to others, as opposed to his private (and, by implication, true) self.

EXAMPLES: Notable literary personae include the wife-murdering Duke who speaks in Robert Browning's poem "My Last Duchess" (1842); Mr. Lockwood, the lonely invalid who tells the simmering story of Heathcliff and Cathy's love in Emily Brontë's *Wuthering Heights* (1847); Pip, the selfish young social climber who narrates Charles Dickens's novel *Great Expectations* (1861); J. Alfred Prufrock, who wonders if he "dare[s] to eat a peach" in T. S. Eliot's "The Love Song of J. Alfred Prufrock" (1917); and Tashi, who submits to genital mutilation in order to experience cultural unity with her people in Alice Walker's *Possessing the Secret of Joy* (1992).

▶ **personal criticism:** A type of **literary criticism,** often associated with **feminist criticism** and sometimes referred to as *autobiographical criticism,* in which critics incorporate their personal reactions, histories, and experience into their readings of literary **texts.** Personal critics are openly skeptical of the claims to reason, logic, and **objectivity** made by many male critics, particularly those practicing **the New Criticism** or other types of **formalist** criticism.

Personal criticism developed in the late 1980s and early 1990s, particularly in the work of feminist critics Jane Tompkins, who questioned the "public-private dichotomy, which is to say, the public-private *hierarchy* that is a founding condition of female oppression" in "Me and My Shadow" (1987), and Nancy K. Miller, who defined the approach in *Getting Personal: Feminist Occasions and Other Autobiographical Acts* (1991) as "an explicitly autobiographical performance within the act of criticism." Although personal criticism is sometimes contrasted with the politically engaged work of feminists associated with **cultural criticism** or **postcolonial theory,** the emphasis on **race, class,** and ethnicity brought to bear by these groups made personal feminist criticism possible by demonstrating that woman is not a single, monolithic, or deterministic category but rather an umbrella term covering a vast range of identities and experiences.

With the advent of more personal feminist critical styles came a new interest in women's **autobiographical** writings — and a critique of traditional autobiography, with its emphasis on action, intellectual self-discovery, and public renown, as a **gendered,** "masculinist" **genre.** Arguing that the lived experiences of men and women differ, one such critic, Leigh Gilmore, developed a **theory** of women's self-**representation** in her book *Autobiographics* (1991).

Practitioners in other areas of literary criticism have also embraced the personal approach. For instance, many **ecocritics,** influenced by the personal style of much nature writing, have employed personal criticism, as did **queer theorist** David Halperin in *Saint Foucault: Towards a Gay Hagiography* (1995). For a variety of perspectives on the place of the personal in scholarship and criticism, see "Problems with Personal Criticism" (*PLMA*, Oct. 1996).

See also **feminist criticism.**

▶ **personification:** A **figure of speech** (more specifically a **trope**) in which human characteristics are bestowed upon anything nonhuman, from an **abstract** idea to a physical force to an inanimate object to a living organism. **Prosopopoeia** is often used as a synonym for *personification.*

The term **pathetic fallacy** refers to a limited form of personification in which human traits and emotions are attributed to inanimate nature. Compared to personification in general, the pathetic fallacy is narrower in scope, since it applies only to inanimate nature rather than anything nonhuman, and its "humanizing" characterization is typically less sustained.

EXAMPLES: Examples of personification include the phrase "Father Time" and using the word *blind* to describe love; examples of the pathetic fallacy include using *kind* or *gentle* to describe a slight breeze. The following stanza from William Wordsworth's "Elegiac Stanzas Suggested by a Picture of Peele Castle, in a Storm, Painted by Sir George Beaumont" (1807) personifies the castle and uses the pathetic fallacy to characterize the storm:

> And this huge Castle, standing here sublime,
> I love to see the look with which it braves,
> Cased in the unfeeling armor of old time,
> The lightning, the fierce wind, and trampling wave.

In "The Mother Mourns" (1901), Thomas Hardy personified Nature as a parent who speaks her sad "accents" in a "dirge-like refrain":

> "My leopardine beauties are rarer,
>   My tusky ones vanish,
>   My children have aped mine own slaughters
>   To quicken my wane. . . ."

In his poem "Chicago" (1916), Carl Sandburg personified the city, directly addressing it as "you":

> They tell me you are wicked and I believe them, for I have seen your
>   painted women under the gas lamps luring the farm boys.
> And they tell me you are crooked and I answer: Yes, it is true I have seen
>   the gunman kill and go free to kill again.

Similarly, Sylvia Plath's "Mirror" (1961) personifies a mirror using the **first person,** as the poem's opening lines indicate: "I am silver and exact. / I have no preconceptions."

See also **pathetic fallacy.**

▶ **Petrarchan conceit:** A type of **conceit** that presents an exaggerated portrait of a beautiful, cruel woman and the suffering, lovestricken man who worships her. The Petrarchan conceit typically employs analogy, **hyperbole,** and **oxymoron** to figure one or both lovers and was particularly popular among **Renaissance sonneteers.** The Petrarchan conceit has been imitated both seriously and **satirically;** certain comparisons, such as that of the lover to a ship in a stormy sea, are so common that they have become **clichés.**

EXAMPLE: The fifty-fourth **sonnet** from Edmund Spenser's *Amoretti* (1595) contains a Petrarchan conceit:

> Of this world's theatre in which we stay,
> My love like the spectator ydly° sits;   *idly*
> Beholding me that all the pageants° play,   *roles*
> Disguysing diversly my troubled wits.
> Sometimes I joy when glad occasion fits,
> And mask in myrth lyke to a comedy:
> Soone after when my joy to sorrow flits,
> I waile and make my woes a tragedy.
> Yet she, beholding me with constant eye,
> Delights not in my merth nor rues° my smart: *pities*
> But when I laugh she mocks, and when I cry,
> She laughs and hardens evermore her heart.
> What then can move her? if not merth nor mone,°   *moan*
> She is no woman, but a sencelesse stone.

▶ **Petrarchan sonnet:** See **Italian sonnet.**

▶ **phallocentric: Centered** on or **privileging** the masculine, a nonnatural characteristic ascribed to institutions (including literature) and culture more generally by certain **deconstructors, feminist critics,** and **psychoanalytic critics.** When used by feminists, the term is almost synonymous with patriarchal. Psychoanalytic critics usually use the term to suggest that psychic life is conditioned by the **phallus** as understood by twentieth-century French psychoanalytic theorist Jacques Lacan. Deconstructors often prefer French **poststructuralist** theorist Jacques Derrida's term *phallogocentric,* which through the insertion of an **allusion** to the word *logos* (Greek for "word," "speech," and "reason") implies that the masculine **gender** is privileged in Western language and thought, which Derrida described as being **logocentric.**

See **phallus.** See also **deconstruction, logocentrism.**

▶ **phallus:** A **symbol** or **representation** of the penis, particularly when used to signify power. Austrian psychoanalyst Sigmund Freud identified the stage in which children become interested in their own sexual organs and in who has a penis as the phallic stage, a normal stage in the development not only of libidinal desire but also of human **subjectivity** more generally. Subsequently, twentieth-century French **psychoanalytic critic** Jacques Lacan viewed the phallus as the representative of a fraudulent power (male over female) whose "law" is a principle of psychic division (conscious / unconscious) and sexual differentiation (masculine / feminine). In works such as "La signification du phallus" ("The Signification of the Phallus") (1958), Lacan argued that the phallus is a **signifier** with no inherent meaning; rather, power and meaning are ascribed to the phallus by individual societies in which the father is the namer and lawgiver. He also argued that the phallus governs the **Symbolic order,** the repository of generally held cultural beliefs.

▶ **phenomenological criticism:** A type of **literary criticism** based upon **phenomenology,** a philosophical school of thought and method of analysis founded by German philosopher Edmund Husserl whose proponents postulate that objects attain meaning only as they are perceived in someone's consciousness. In other words, phenomenologists reject the notion that objects have inherent meaning and instead argue that objects have whatever meaning a given subject perceives in them. They also believe that all consciousness is **intentional,** that is, directed toward an object.

Roman Ingarden, a Polish thinker, was one of the first critics to incorporate phenomenology into literary theory. In *The Literary Work of Art* (1931) and *The Cognition of the Literary Work of Art* (1937), Ingarden borrowed the phenomenological concept of intentionality in arguing that a literary work: (1) has its beginnings in the intentional acts of its **author's** consciousness; and (2) represents those acts, that consciousness, so that the reader apprehends them by experiencing the work both as an object and as his or her own consciousness. According to Ingarden, readers must, however, perform "active readings" to "concretize" works; the author's perceptions are not automatically transferable — and therefore comprehensible — to the reader. Instead, the reader must engage in a "co-creative" reading that bridges **gaps** and may even resolve **ambiguities** in the work. For Ingarden, then, readers are not passive receptacles of an author's perceptions but active partners in realizing the work in their own consciousness.

Phenomenological criticism is most often associated with the **Geneva School,** a group of literary critics who approached the **text** passively, sympathetically, and meditatively in an effort to achieve an intuitive understanding of the unique consciousness of its author. Geneva critics attempted to disregard any references external to the text, including their own presuppositions and beliefs, in order to experience the author's *Weltanschauung,* or worldview, more completely and accurately.

See **Geneva School** for further explanation of this group's method of analysis.

▶ **phenomenology:** A philosophical school of thought and method of analysis founded by late-nineteenth and early-twentieth century German philosopher Edmund Husserl whose proponents postulate that objects attain meaning only as they are perceived in someone's consciousness. Husserl argued that human consciousness is **intentional** (directed toward an object) as well as unitary (in a reciprocal relationship with the object). As Husserl noted, phenomenology emphasizes the psychical realm of awareness; the phenomenologist analyzes the object as it is perceived, suspending judgments or presuppositions that are not part of the analyst's own consciousness. Husserl used the term *epochē* to refer to this suspended, or "bracketed," moment.

Phenomenologists acknowledge that objects exist in the space-time continuum, but they believe that active awareness on the part of some subject is required for an object to be intelligible. Phenomenologists thus reject any preconceived notions about epistemology or ontology (the studies of knowledge and being, respectively), since they argue that an object carries the meaning that any given subject perceives in (or for) it, rather than an inherent meaning.

Phenomenology provides the basis for **phenomenological criticism,** a form of **literary criticism** usually associated with the **Geneva School.** Geneva critics try to analyze a literary work without any external references, approaching the **text** passively, sympathetically, and meditatively to experience the unique consciousness of its **author.** Phenomenology also influenced the development of **existentialism,** particularly as expressed by German philosopher Martin Heidegger and French philosopher and writer Jean-Paul Sartre.

▶ **philology:** Broadly defined, the study of language and literature. More narrowly defined, the study of language, particularly the historical and comparative development of languages. In the twentieth century, the term **linguistics** eclipsed *philology* in **denoting** the scientific study of language, focusing on spoken rather than written language and on how language functions as a system.

▶ **phoneme:** A basic sound unit in a language. While the pronunciation of a phoneme may vary — the *p* sound, for instance, is aspirated in *pot* but not in *spot* — each phoneme is a contrastive sound unit, which means that substituting one phoneme in a word for another produces a change in meaning (or results in a nonword). Change the *f* sound in the English word *phaser* to an *l* sound, and the result is *laser;* change it to a *k* sound, and a possible — but nonexisting — word results. Phonemes may thus be seen as the building blocks of words. Each basic sound unit can be distinctly articulated, as often happens when a child is learning to read (phoneme: *f-ō-n-ē-m*), and yet one must move smoothly from one phoneme to the next to enunciate a word properly.

An alphabetic letter is not equivalent to a phoneme. For instance, *f* and *ph* represent a single phoneme in English, for the sound they signify is always the same. The letter *c* may signify the phonemic sound represented by the letters *k* or *s*, as in the words *cool* and *cereal. Ou*, when followed by *gh*, itself represents at least five phonemes, as in the following series of words: *dough, cough, through, bough, slough.* Furthermore, many letters, when followed by the letter *h* in our linguistic system, produce entirely different phonemes than those we most commonly associate with the letters themselves: *church, thanks, rough, trophy.*

The number of phonemes in any linguistic system is limited. English is often said to have about forty-five phonemes; Italian twenty-seven; and Rotokas, a language spoken in Papua New Guinea, only eleven.

▶ **phonetics:** See **phonology.**

▶ **phonocentrism:** See **logocentric, logocentrism.**

▶ **phonology:** A division of **linguistics,** the study of linguistic sound systems — that is, how speech sounds form patterns in a language. Phonology, which includes the inventory of speech sounds and the rules for combining and pronouncing them, is distinguished from *phonetics,* which refers to the study of speech sounds themselves, including their acoustic (physical) properties, how listeners perceive them (auditory phonetics), and how the vocal tract produces them (articulatory phonetics).

▶ **picaresque narrative:** See **picaresque novel.**

▶ **picaresque novel:** From the Spanish *pícaro,* meaning "rogue," a **novel** that **realistically** recounts the adventures of a carefree but engaging rascal who always manages to escape by the skin of his or her teeth. The picaresque novel is **episodic** in **structure,** its unity resulting from the near-constant presence of the central **character,** who comes from a low social class and generally lives by his or her wits rather than by honest, hard work. *Pícaros,* though adept at trickery, generally do not engage in serious criminal behavior; furthermore, they do not change, evolve, develop, or grow in the way that more conventional novelistic **protagonists** do. In general, picaresque novels are told from the **first-person point of view** and have **satiric** intent (often toward the **class** structure). True-to-life **settings** and details — many of which are coarse and bawdy — give the **genre** a realistic **texture.** Influenced by the *Satyricon* (c. A.D. 50) of the ancient Roman writer Petronius, the picaresque novel emerged as a genre in sixteenth-century Spain with the publication of the anonymous *La vida de Lazorillo de Tormes* (*The Life of Lazorillo de Tormes*) (c. 1555) and played an important role in the development of the novel through its rejection of the **romantic,** idealized depictions so popular in **medieval romances,** which featured chivalrous knights as **heroes.**

FURTHER EXAMPLES: Thomas Nashe's *The Unfortunate Traveller; or, The Life of Jack Wilton* (1594) is the first English example of the genre. The French writer Alain-René Lesage's *Gil Blas* (1715–35), Daniel Defoe's *Moll Flanders* (1722), and Mark Twain's *Adventures of Huckleberry Finn* (1884) are other **classic** examples. Twentieth-century works in which picaresque heroes and **antiheroes** appear, respectively, include Saul Bellow's *Henderson the Rain King* (1959) and John Kennedy Toole's *A Confederacy of Dunces* (1980); the works in which these heroes appear are more tightly structured than picaresque novels, strictly defined.

Television series, monthly comic books, and daily comic strips provide a continuing episodic structure hospitable to the picaresque genre. The time-travelling protagonist of the TV series *Quantum Leap* (1989–93) is an example, as is the eponymous hero of the Western spoof *Briscoe County Jr.* (1993–94). Jamie Hewlett and Alan Martin's *Tank Girl* (1988–95), who roams a bizarre postapocalyptic world accompanied by a genetically altered kangaroo, is a comic-book picaresque heroine.

▶ **Pindaric ode (regular ode):** Named for the fifth-century B.C. Greek poet Pindar, a type of **ode** that consists of **strophes, antistrophes,** and **epodes,** a triadic structure corresponding to the movement of the ancient Greek **chorus.** The strophes and antistrophes share the same **stanzaic** form, while the epodes have another. Pindaric odes, rare in English, are typically characterized by a ceremonious or even exalted **tone.**

EXAMPLE: Thomas Gray's "The Progress of Poesy" (1757).

▶ **plagiarism:** See **pastiche.**

▶ *plaisir:* See **poststructuralism.**

▶ **Platonic criticism:** A type of **literary criticism** that judges a work by its extrinsic purpose rather than by any intrinsic (artistic) value, as in Aristotelian criticism. Platonic critics determine the value of a work by assessing whether it has a useful nonartistic purpose or application, such as promoting morality.

▶ **Platonic love:** A philosophy of love set forth by the ancient Greek philosopher Plato in his *Symposium* and *Phaedrus* (c. 360 B.C.) and attributed to the female sage Diotima, who supposedly related it to the philosopher Socrates, Plato's teacher. This **theory** was further developed in the third through fifth centuries A.D. by **Neoplatonist** Roman philosophers such as Plotinus; it evolved still further during the **Renaissance,** when it informed the writings of Church fathers and love poets alike. Platonic philosophy dominated Western thinking about love until the **Medieval Period,** when the competing **courtly love** tradition emerged.

The lover of beauty, according to Platonic love philosophy, should not reserve his admiration for purely physical beauty, although appreciating an attractive body can be the first step toward worshipping beauty of a more spiritual nature. (Incidentally, the masculine pronoun has been used deliberately in the preceding sentence because the Platonic lover has traditionally been conceived of as — and specified to be — male, perhaps because in the *Phaedrus*, Socrates specifically talks about male-male relationships, asserting the superiority of nonsexual male friendships over merely physical homosexual relationships.) According to the philosophy of Platonic love — which since Plato has been applied primarily to heterosexual relationships — we should progress from contemplating physical to mental to conceptual to spiritual beauty (and so forth) until we have attained a vision of beauty at the highest level, namely, the eternal and true Ideal Beauty from which the soul is normally separated and next to which all worldly beauty pales. The Platonic lover admires the beauty in a human body as a sign of or step toward higher spiritual beauty and ultimately the absolute and perfect beauty in and of God. This doctrine also postulated that, by achieving the highest vision of beauty, the Platonic lover could actually create in his beloved a higher, more soulful beauty. Today, most people use the phrase *Platonic love* to refer to love that does not involve sexual relations, without realizing that the term has a much deeper and more complex significance.

EXAMPLES: The following lines from Percy Bysshe Shelley's "Epipsychidion" (1822) express the philosophy of Platonic love:

> Warm fragrance seems to fall from her light dress
> And her loose hair; and where some heavy tress
> The air of her own speed has disentwined,
> The sweetness seems to satiate the faint wind;
> And in the soul a wild odour is felt,
> Beyond the sense, like fiery dews that melt
> Into the bosom of a frozen bud. —
> See where she stands! a mortal shape indued
> With love and life and light and deity,
> And motion which may change but cannot die;
> An image of some bright Eternity;
> A shadow of some golden dream; a Splendour
> Leaving the third sphere pilotless; a tender
> Reflection of the eternal Moon of Love. . . .

The relationship between Jude Fawley and Sue Bridehead in Thomas Hardy's *Jude the Obscure* (1896) is essentially Platonic. Theirs was "not an ignoble, merely animal feeling" but rather "an extraordinary affinity, or sympathy...which somehow took away all flavor of grossness"; they "seem to be one person split in two."

Today's simpler use of *Platonic* is conveyed by the following joke: *He:* "Come over to my place for some scotch and sofa?" *She:* "No—but maybe a gin and platonic."

▶ **Platonism:** A body of thought associated with the fourth-century B.C. Greek philosopher Plato that includes three major doctrines concerning ideas, love, and recollection. Plato's idealistic doctrines, unlike much of his student Aristotle's thought, are not easily pinned down, for Plato did not explicitly codify his thinking; rather, he wove it (along with **antithetical** views) through his various **dialogues,** which take the form of discussions among his predecessor and teacher Socrates and other speakers on the nature of various problems.

The doctrine of ideas postulates that the materiality of the visible world (what we think of as "reality") emanates from a higher ideal realm. Plato believed that true reality lies in this invisible and universal spiritual realm and that humans should use their intellect to attempt to understand this world of ideas. For Plato, ideas were the source of everything, hence the corollary that humanity should aspire to the ideas of justice, friendship, and morality that it discovers in this unseen realm. The doctrine of love, known more commonly as **Platonic love,** equates beauty and virtue, holding that the proper appreciation and understanding of beauty can lead to a more spiritual level of being. The doctrine of recollection postulates that the soul has many incarnations and is, therefore, immortal. Although the soul "forgets" most of what it learned in higher realms during those periods in which it resides in a physical body, it does "recollect" certain ideas and **images,** which are the basis for knowledge.

Followers of Plato have so modified his doctrines over the centuries that it can be difficult to separate true Platonism (if such a thing exists) from its offshoots. Two particularly important schools of **Neoplatonism,** however, emerged from Platonic thought. The first was the Alexandrian school (associated with the Roman Plotinus), which accentuated the **mystical** elements in Platonism and which functioned nearly as a religion. The second was Italian **Renaissance** Neoplatonism (associated with Marsilio Ficino), which developed a mystical system intended to fuse Christian doctrine with Platonic thought.

See also **Neoplatonism, Platonic love.**

▶ **play:** A **story,** in **verse** or **prose,** that is generally intended to be performed onstage (in a theater and in the presence of an audience) by actors who deliver the **dialogue,** perform the actions, and follow the stage directions written by the **author.** Although *drama* is often used as a synonym for *play,* the two terms differ slightly in meaning. A play is a drama intended for performance before a theatrical audience. Although all plays are, broadly speaking, dramas, not all dramas are plays; for instance, some dramas (properly called closet dramas) are meant not to be performed but, rather, to be read as poems. The word *drama* may also be used in a narrower sense to refer to a serious play, movie, or television show.

See also **drama.**

▶ **plot:** The arrangement and interrelation of events in a **narrative** work, chosen and designed to engage the reader's attention and interest (or even to arouse suspense or anxiety) while also providing a framework for the exposition of the **author's** message, or **theme,** and for other elements such as **characterization, symbol,** and **conflict.**

Plot is distinguished from **story,** which refers to a narrative of events ordered chronologically, not selectively, and with an emphasis on establishing causality. Story is the raw material from which plot is constructed. Crafting a plot requires choosing not only which elements of a story to include — and what order to tell them in — but also relating the events of a story to one another so that causality may be established convincingly. As English writer E. M. Forster explained in *Aspects of the Novel* (1927), to say that "the king died and the queen died" is to tell a story. Adding three simple words — "The king died and then the queen died of grief" — transforms the story into a plot by including and emphasizing causality. **Russian formalists** made a similar distinction between plot and story, which they referred to as *syuzhet* and *fabula,* respectively. Unlike Forster, however, they did not emphasize causality. Rather, they argued that the literary devices (such as **rhythmic** patterns, **syntax,** and **imagery**) used by an author convert a story into a plot. More recent critics who have sought to explain this transformation from story line into plot by analyzing the "rules" that generate plot are called **narratologists.**

Plot, unlike story, frees authors from the constraints of chronology and enables them to present their chosen subjects in whatever way they see fit to elicit the desired emotional response from readers. Despite this authorial freedom (to use **flashbacks** or **anachronisms,** for instance, or to begin a narrative *in medias res*), most critics agree with the ancient Greek philosopher Aristotle's argument in the *Poetics* (c. 350 B.C.) that effective plots must have three relative parts — a beginning, a middle, and an end — that are complete in themselves. Of course, these parts need not correlate temporally with the story — for instance, when the beginning of a plot does not correspond with the chronological beginning of the story but rather begins *in medias res*. Michael Ondaatje's novel *The English Patient* (1992) begins with a nurse named Hana caring for a hideously burned, nameless man in a war-torn Italian villa. The plot subsequently tells, through interspersed flashbacks, the story of that man — Count Laszlo de Almasy, an explorer and mapmaker — and his love affair with Katherine Clifton, the wife of a colleague. At the same time, the plot includes the present story of Hana, a drifter named Caravaggio, and a Sikh bomb-disposal expert named Kip.

Aristotle's tripartite conception of plot, which he considered the primary dramatic element, still sets the parameters of discussion today. Aristotle also argued that a plot must have unity such that if any of its parts, or incidents, are removed, something seems to be missing. If a part of a work can be removed without affecting the whole, then the work is **episodic** rather than plot-based (and, according to Aristotle, inferior). This is not to say that a work must only have one story line and, thus, that subplots render a work episodic. Rather than detracting from a work's unity, a well-crafted subplot may enhance the main plot by providing a **foil** to the main plot.

Aristotle's identification of plot as a work's chief element faced increasing challenge in the nineteenth and twentieth centuries. Many critics have focused on characterization as the defining element of a literary work, viewing plot as a mere framework for showcasing character. Following this **theory**, the plot of Emily Brontë's *Wuthering Heights* (1847), composed of a carefully arranged story line, nonetheless serves primarily as a structure and spotlight for the development of Cathy Earnshaw and her volatile and brooding soul mate, Heathcliff.

Many critics and writers conceive of plot in the terms used by German writer Gustav Freytag in *Die Technik des Dramas* (*The Technique of the Drama*) (1863) to describe the structure of a typical five-act play, especially a **tragedy. Freytag's Pyramid,** his enumerated sequence of events, includes the introduction, **rising action, climax, falling action,** and **catastrophe.** Alternative and additional terms such as **crisis, resolution,** and *dénouement* have come into vogue, but Freytag's terms and sequence are still often used to describe and analyze elements of plot.

Conflict plays a central, often defining, role in plot. Some critics even maintain that plot does not exist in the absence of conflict. As the confrontation or struggle between opposing **characters** or forces, conflict usually sets the plot in motion; it is the element from which the **action** emanates and around which it revolves. In the first scene of William Shakespeare's *Romeo and Juliet* (1596), the swordfight between Benvolio, Tybalt, and their respective servants — staged in Baz Luhrman's 1996 film version as a gas-station shootout — deepens the divide between the Montague and Capulet families that turns Romeo Montague and Juliet Capulet into "star-crossed lovers."

Sometimes the word *intrigue* (which comes from the French *intrigue*, meaning "plot") is confused with *plot*. As an English literary term, however, *intrigue* refers to a type of plot in which the outcome of some scheme depends on the ignorance or credulity of its targets.

▶ **plurality:** See **heteroglossia.**

▶ **poem:** See **poetry.**

▶ **poetaster:** An unskilled or bad poet.

▶ **poetic diction:** Diction — the choice and phrasing of words — deemed suitable to **verse**. Poets and critics have long disagreed about what constitutes proper poetic diction. The ancient Greek philosopher Aristotle, for instance, argued in the *Poetics* (c. 330 B.C.) that diction should be "at once clear and not mean," using "ordinary words" for clarity and "unfamiliar terms" such as "strange words, metaphors, [and] lengthened forms" to "save the language from seeming mean and prosaic." Many subsequent theorists, however, took more extreme positions, with some maintaining that poets should speak in the ordinary language of their contemporaries.

From the **Renaissance** through the eighteenth century, elaborate and elevated poetic diction, often characterized by the use of **archaisms, epithets, periphrasis,** and unusual **syntax,** was common. As the English poet Thomas Gray remarked in a 1742 letter, "The language of the age is never the language of poetry; except among the French . . . . Our poetry . . . has a language peculiar to itself." Indeed, poetic diction reached its height in the **Neoclassical Period,** with its stress on **decorum.** With the advent of **romanticism,** however, the use of ordinary **discourse** began to gain ground, heralded by English poet William Wordsworth's effort "to bring my language near to the language of men" as well as by his derogatory characterization of poetic diction as artificial in his 1800 preface to the second edition of *Lyrical Ballads* (1798). In the twentieth century, **modernists** likewise rejected the idea of a special language for poetry, and many subsequent poets even adopted diction and discourse patterns typically associated with prose.

EXAMPLES: Words such as *ere* (for *before*), *thrice* (for *three times*), and *thou* (the formal address for *you*) are commonly associated with poetic diction. The following line from John Keats's "The Eve of St. Agnes" (1820) also exemplifies poetic diction: "Of all its wreathéd pearls her hair she frees." In ordinary discourse, the subject ("she") would precede the verb ("frees"), which would be followed by the direct object ("her hair") and its prepositional modifier ("of all its wreathéd pearls").

▶ **poetic justice:** The idea that virtuous and evil actions are ultimately dealt with justly, with virtue rewarded and evil punished. Poetic justice occurs, for instance, when a misunderstood **protagonist** is praised after a long struggle or when his or her **antagonist** is cast out from the community.

The term was coined by Thomas Rymer, an English literary critic and historiographer who viewed poetic justice as a **didactic** device conducive to furthering morality and used it specifically with reference to poetic works, including dramas, in *Tragedies of the Last Age Consider'd* (1678). Today, the term is used with reference to all types of literary works — as well as life in general—and is often applied specifically to situations in which the **hero** and **villain** get their "just deserts" at a pivotal moment for both of them, as when the villain is shot while trying to shoot the hero. Furthermore, contemporary critics almost uniformly reject Rymer's view that literature should provide moral instruction.

EXAMPLES: In Charles Dickens's *Oliver Twist* (1837), when villain Bill Sykes envisions the eyes of Nancy, the girlfriend he has viciously murdered, he accidentally hangs himself by a rope he had intended to use to escape from an angry crowd seeking vengeance for her death.

The movie *The Departed* (2006) closes with a shocking scene of poetic justice, as Sgt. Dignam shoots fellow Sgt. Colin Sullivan in the latter's own home, just as it seems that Sullivan has escaped detection as the Mafia mole in the state police force responsible for the deaths of several officers.

▶ **poetic license:** Narrowly defined, the linguistic liberty taken by poets in composing **verse**. This liberty typically involves deviations from normal patterns of speech and prose for poetic effect or to meet the demands of **versification**. Poets may use unusual **syntax, archaisms** or **neologisms, wrenched accent, eye rhymes** or **half rhymes** rather than **perfect rhymes**, and so forth. Defined more broadly, poetic license also encompasses non-linguistic liberties, such as **anachronism** or extreme coincidence, and applies to any literary form, not just poetry. Writers may thus deviate not only from virtually any rule, **convention,** or standard of **discourse** but even from logical dictates or accepted views of reality for the sake of artistic effect. When misused, poetic license is the mark of a **poetaster** or other incompetent writer.

▶ **poetics:** (1) The **theory** or principles of the nature of **poetry** or its composition. (2) Writing that expounds such theory or principles. Although the term may be used as a singular noun (critics sometimes speak of a "poetic"), this usage is uncommon. Today, *poetics* also refers to the **aesthetic** principles of any literary **genre**, including prose forms. The term has also been used occasionally to **denote** the study of **versification**.

EXAMPLE: Aristotle's *Poetics* (c. 330 B.C.).

▶ **poetry:** Literary expression characterized by particular attention to **rhythm**, sound, and the concentrated, **concrete** use of language. A major literary **genre**, poetry has been defined and described in so many different ways that one might easily argue that there are as many ways to characterize it as there are people. Take, for instance, the definitions of three American poets: Edgar Allan Poe, who called poetry "the rhythmical creation of beauty" in "The Poetic Principle" (1850); Carl Sandburg, who proclaimed it "an echo, asking a shadow to dance," in *Good Morning, America* (1928); and contemporary African American poet Rita Dove, who described it as "language at its most distilled and most powerful." However, there is general agreement about what poetry is not.

First, poetry is frequently distinguished from **verse** — broadly speaking, any rhythmical or **metrical** composition. In this view, poetry is a subset of verse, considered superior by virtue of its **imaginative** quality, intricate **structure,** serious or lofty subject matter, or noble purpose.

Second, poetry is often contrasted with **fiction**. This distinction, however, has proved more problematic because some poets and literary historians have characterized poetry *as* fiction (or even as the "supreme fiction," as in

Wallace Stevens's "A High-Toned Christian Woman" [1922]), as that which is not essentially tied to fact, to history. Seen from this angle, any imaginative artistic work might be called poetic.

Third, poetry has frequently been contrasted with **prose**. English **romantic** poet Samuel Taylor Coleridge, for instance, distinguished the two, defining prose as "words in their best order" and poetry as "the best words in their best order" (July 12, 1827, *Specimens of the Table Talk of S. T. Coleridge* [1835]). At the level of **form**, poetry emphasizes the line rather than the sentence and is organized in **stanzas** rather than paragraphs. At the level of meaning, many critics argue that prose lends itself more readily to paraphrase. While poetry can be approached intellectually, it is equally an emotional experience; one might even say that poetry is meant to be experienced rather than simply read. Poetry is rich with a suggestiveness born from the interplay of words and sounds. Other distinguishing factors between poetry and prose include auditory elements such as rhythm, **meter,** and **rhyme; diction;** and the level of concreteness. First, poetry relies on auditory elements, particularly rhythm, to a much greater extent than prose. A poem typically contains some basic rhythmic pattern, variations on which not only create auditory interest but may also introduce a new idea or viewpoint. Prose may have rhythm, but without the marked regularity and integral importance in poetry. Furthermore, poetry may use meter and rhyme, whereas prose does not. Second, poetry puts a premium on diction, the choice and phrasing of words. Although many poets have rejected the idea of a "special" **poetic diction,** particularly since the advent of **romanticism,** they must be more economical than prose authors and thus tend to pack each word with meaning, affording poetry a particular intensity. Third, poetry tends to be more concrete than prose, making particularly heavy use of **figurative language** and **symbolism** to develop specific, detailed **images** and enhance sensory impact.

Historically, poetry appears to have originated as a collective endeavor, or at least for a collective purpose, playing a major role in ceremonial events and helping preserve a group's history and traditions, which were often passed down orally from generation to generation. Many of the earliest literary (and often religious) works are poems; perhaps the oldest extant **epic** is the Babylonian *Epic of Gilgamesh* (third millennium B.C.). Over time, however, poetry became the medium for **drama,** as in **classical** Greek **tragedies,** and for individual **lyric** expression. Differing schools of thought regarding the aim of poetry also arose, with some advocating a **didactic** purpose, others viewing poetry as a source of pleasure, and still others seeing it as a medium for special, even unique, insights. Today, poetry is seen as a highly individualistic endeavor; perhaps no other form of expression is deemed so intensely personal, and therefore unique. The following lyric by Mexican poet Octavio Paz, "Entre lo que digo y veo" ("Between What I See and What I Say") (1976), written for Russian linguist Roman Jakobson, reflects one such individual take on poetry:

Between what I see and what I say,
between what I say and what I keep silent,
between what I keep silent and what I dream,
between what I dream and what I forget:
poetry.

▶ **point of view:** The vantage point from which a **narrative** is told. A narrative is typically told from a *first-person* or *third-person point of view;* the *second-person point of view* is extremely rare. Novels sometimes, but infrequently, mix points of view.

In a narrative told from a first-person perspective, the **author** tells the story through a **character** who refers to himself or herself as "I." Such a **narrator** is usually (but not always) a major participant in the **action.** This first-person narrator recounts events as he or she experiences, remembers, or hears about them. Carrie Bradshaw, one of four single women living in Manhattan whose lives and loves were chronicled by the television series *Sex and the City* (1998–2004; adapted to film 2008), serves as the voice-over, first-person narrator who provides a unifying commentary and perspective. First-person narrators are sometimes **unreliable narrators** — and they may also be **naive heroes** — who color or distort matters in ways that the reader (at least eventually) detects. Occasionally, works written from the first-person point of view contain multiple narrators, each of whom personally recounts his or her story. In Amy Tan's novel *The Joy Luck Club* (1989), several mothers and daughters convey varied perspectives on life in recounting their own histories.

Third-person narratives come in two types: **omniscient** and *limited.* In either case, the narrator is an observer who relates the story using third-person pronouns such as "he," "she," and "it." An author taking an omniscient point of view assumes the vantage point of an all-knowing narrator able not only to recount the action thoroughly and reliably but also to enter the mind of any character at any time in order to reveal his or her thoughts, feelings, and beliefs directly to the reader. (Such a narrator, it should be pointed out, can conceal as well as reveal at will.) An author using the limited point of view recounts the story through the eyes of a single character (or occasionally more than one). The reader is thus usually privy to the inner thoughts and feelings of only one character and receives the story as that character understands and experiences it, although not in that character's own **voice.**

In a narrative told from the second-person point of view, the narrator addresses a "you"; thus, a narrative that reads "If you really want to know New Orleans, you need to walk Bourbon Street at midnight . . ." would be an example of second-person narrative, as are the *Choose Your Own Adventure* books (1979–98).

FURTHER EXAMPLES: The concluding chapter of Charlotte Brontë's *Jane Eyre* (1847), a novel written from the first-person point of view, begins:

Reader, I married him. A quiet wedding we had: he and I, the parson and clerk, were alone present. When we got back from church, I went into the kitchen of the manor-house, where Mary was cooking the dinner, and John cleaning the knives, and I said —

"Mary, I have been married to Mr. Rochester this morning."

Stephen Crane's *The Red Badge of Courage* (1895), by contrast, is narrated from the omniscient point of view:

The cold passed reluctantly from the earth, and the retiring fogs revealed an army stretched out on the hills, resting. As the landscape changed from brown to green, the army awakened, and began to tremble with eagerness at the noise of rumors. It cast its eyes upon the roads, which were growing from long troughs of liquid mud to proper thoroughfares. A river, amber-tinted in the shadow of its banks, purled at the army's feet; and at night, when the stream had become of a sorrowful blackness, one could see across it the red, eyelike gleam of hostile camp fires set in the low brows of distant hills.

Katherine Mansfield's short story "Miss Brill" (1922) is written from the limited point of view:

She thought of the old invalid gentleman to whom she read the newspaper four afternoons a week while he slept in the garden. She had got quite used to the frail head on the cotton pillow, the hollowed eyes, the open mouth and the high pinched nose. If he'd been dead she mightn't have noticed for weeks; she wouldn't have minded.

Jay McInerney's *Bright Lights, Big City* (1984) is an example of a novel told from the rarely used second-person point of view:

Monday arrives on schedule. You sleep through the first ten hours. God only knows what happened to Sunday.

At the subway station you wait fifteen minutes on the platform for a train. Finally a local, enervated by graffiti, shuffles into the station. You get a seat and hoist a copy of the New York *Post*. The *Post* is the most shameful of your several addictions. You hate to support this kind of trash with your thirty cents, but you are a secret fan of Killer Bees, Hero Cops, Sex Fiends, Lottery Winners, Teenage Terrorists, Liz Taylor, Tough Tots, Sicko Creeps, Living Nightmares, Life on Other Planets, Spontaneous Human Combustion, Miracle Diets and Coma Babies. The Coma Baby is on page two: COMA BABY SIS PLEADS: SAVE MY LITTLE BROTHER.

▶ **polyphonic (polyvocalic):** Meaning "many-voiced," a term used to refer to what Soviet critic Mikhail Bakhtin called **dialogic texts,** that is, ones in which several viewpoints or **discourses** are in **dialogue** with one another. The term is closely associated with Bakhtin's **theory** of **heteroglossia**, which holds that most if not all literary works involve a multiplicity of voices that interact and compete. Discussing the concept of polyphony in *Problems of Dostoevsky's Poetics* (1929), Bakhtin contrasted two nineteenth-century

Russian novelists, Leo Tolstoi and Fyodor Dostoevsky, characterizing their respective works as **monologic** and dialogic and describing the Dostoevskian novel as "a plurality of independent and unmerged voices and consciousnesses, a genuine polyphony of fully valid voices." He also believed, however, that all novels are to some degree polyphonic since they relate the views of various **characters** as well as those of the **narrator(s)**, thereby disrupting the authoritative, **authorial** voice.

See also **dialogic criticism, heteroglossia.**

▶ **portmanteau word (blend):** A word coined by combining two other words, encompassing the original meanings of both component parts. Lewis Carroll invented the term in *Through the Looking-Glass* (1872), where Humpty Dumpty explains the **neologism** *slithy* in Carroll's poem "Jabberwocky" (1871) as follows: "Well, *'slithy'* means lithe and slimy. . . . You see it's like a portmanteau — there are two meanings packed up in one word." (A portmanteau is a suitcase that opens up into two compartments). Many portmanteau words have become commonplace in English vocabulary.

In **linguistics,** the term **blend** is generally used.

FURTHER EXAMPLES: *Smog,* coined from *smoke + fog,* has become a familiar word today, as have *brunch* (*breakfast + lunch*) and *squiggle* (*squirm + wiggle*). Contemporary portmanteau words include *spork* (a spoon and a fork combined in a single utensil), *splurchase* (a splurged-on purchase), and *Spanglish* (a "tossed salad" of Spanish and English). An extensive compilation of portmanteau words can be found in Dick Thurner's *Portmanteau Dictionary: Blend Words in the English Language, Including Trademarks and Brand Names* (1993).

Portmanteau words surface in fiction and nonfiction alike. James Joyce used them extensively in his novel *Finnegans Wake* (1939) — *ethiquetical,* for instance, combines *ethical* and *etiquette* — a practice discussed by Derek Attridge in his essay "Unpacking the Portmanteau, or Who's Afraid of *Finnegans Wake?*" (1988). Similarly, in his book *Playing the Future* (1996), Douglas Rushkoff coined the term *screenagers* to refer to teenagers raised on television, movies, and computer games.

▶ **positivism:** A philosophical school emphasizing facts and the description of phenomena. Positivists have developed a mode of empirical investigation based on that of physical scientists pursuing factual, descriptive knowledge. Positivists also reject speculation, especially about matters of "ultimate concern," arguing that philosophy and the pursuit of knowledge ought to be concerned with humanity and its condition rather than with metaphysical issues.

Positivism has its roots in the writings of the eighteenth-century Irish and Scottish philosophers George Berkeley and David Hume, but its strongest proponent was the nineteenth-century Frenchman Auguste Comte, who coined the term. The positivist philosophy is pervasive in works by John Stuart Mill, such as *On Liberty* (1859).

In the twentieth century, positivism was further redefined and refined into a philosophy known as *logical positivism,* which was championed chiefly by Austrian philosopher Ludwig Wittgenstein. Wittgenstein redefined the goal of positivism as the use of logic to elucidate human thought systematically. Logical positivism incorporates elements of experimental scientific and mathematical methods.

Although positivism has had its most direct impact on philosophical and scientific methods, critics readily acknowledge the widespread impact it has had indirectly on literature and its analysis. The development of positivism coincided with the rise of **realism** and, subsequently, **naturalism,** literary movements whose practitioners attempted to observe, organize, and present reality logically and **objectively** to readers who, in turn, were expected to approach **texts** empirically, viewing descriptions, statements made by **characters,** and **plot** developments as evidence leading to some viewpoint or interpretive conclusion. This essentially empirical approach to texts is shared by several schools of **literary criticism,** most of which require interpreters to provide evidence (textual, historical, psychological, and so forth) for their analyses. **Impressionistic criticism, personal criticism,** and **deconstruction** are among the critical schools that have resisted the influence of positivism.

▶ **postcolonial literature, postcolonial theory:** *Postcolonial literature* refers to a body of literature written by **authors** with roots in countries that were once colonies established by European nations, whereas *postcolonial theory* refers to a field of intellectual inquiry that explores and interrogates the situation of colonized peoples both during and after colonization. Postcolonial literature and theory are often, but not always, anti-imperialist in character.

The prefix *post-* in *postcolonial* implies opposition as well as chronological sequence; that is, *postcolonial* not only **denotes** the period after a former colony becomes independent but also typically **connotes** political and moral opposition to colonization. Thus, the term may cover works produced during the colonial period, such as Claude McKay's *Banjo* (1929) (Jamaica) and Chinua Achebe's *Things Fall Apart* (1959) (Nigeria), if they express resistance to colonialism and project the potential for independence, as well as works produced in the wake of independence. Moreover, the term is sometimes extended to refer to materially similar situations that do not actually involve former colonies, such as the enslavement of African Americans and English domination of the Irish. Thus, works about slavery or its aftermath, whether by African Americans or others, may express postcolonial perspectives and invite postcolonial interpretations, as may accounts addressing Ireland's status and relationship vis-à-vis England.

As a literary category, postcolonial literature has displaced narrower rubrics such as "Commonwealth literature" and "literature of the Third World" (which is usually subdivided into anglophone literature, francophone literature, and so forth). Postcolonial literature includes works by authors with cultural roots in South Asia, Africa, the Caribbean, and other places in which colonial independence movements arose and colonized peoples achieved autonomy, particularly within the twentieth century. Works by authors from so-called settler colonies with large white populations of European ancestry — such as Australia, Canada, and New Zealand — are sometimes also included. Examples of postcolonial literature include George Lamming's *In the Castle of My Skin* (1953), Kushwant Singh's *Train to Pakistan* (1956), Jean Rhys's *Wide Sargasso Sea* (1966), Gabriel García Márquez's *Cien años de soledad* (*One Hundred Years of Solitude*) (1967), V. S. Naipaul's *The Mimic Men* (1967), Wole Soyinka's play *Death and the King's Horsemen* (1975), Buchi Emecheta's *The Joys of Motherhood* (1979), Mariama Bâ's *Une si longue lettre* (*So Long a Letter*) (1980), J. M. Coetzee's *Waiting for the Barbarians* (1980), Nadine Gordimer's *July's People* (1981), Salman Rushdie's *Midnight's Children* (1981), Isabel Allende's *La casa de los espiritus* (*The House of the Spirits*) (1982), Derek Walcott's **epic** poem *Omeros* (1990), Michael Ondaatje's *The English Patient* (1992; adapted to film 1996), David Malouf's *Remembering Babylon* (1993), Doris Pilkington Garimara's *Follow the Rabbit Proof Fence* (1996; adapted to film 2002), Arundhati Roy's *The God of Small Things* (1997), Steven Frears's film *Dirty Pretty Things* (2002), and Monique Truong's *The Book of Salt* (2003).

Critical readings of postcolonial literature regularly proceed under the overt influence of postcolonial theory, which raises historical, cultural, political, and moral issues surrounding the establishment and disintegration of colonies and the empires they fueled. As an interdisciplinary field, postcolonial theory routinely crosses perceived boundaries between **literary criticism**, history, anthropology, and other subjects, in part because postcolonial theorists themselves analyze such a wide range of issues and in part because they believe that the strict division of knowledge into academic disciplines contributes to colonizing mindsets.

Postcolonial theory has been influenced strongly by thinkers primarily concerned with the Middle East and the Indian subcontinent, particularly Edward Said, a Palestinian-American scholar, and the Indian scholars Gayatri Chakravorty Spivak and Homi K. Bhabha. Said laid the groundwork for the development of postcolonial theory in *Orientalism* (1978), a study of the process by which Westerners constructed false **images** and **myths** about the "Oriental" world. Such stereotyping, he argued, contributed to establishing European domination and exploitation through colonization.

Spivak highlighted the ways in which factors such as **gender** and **class** complicate our understanding of colonial and postcolonial situations. In essays such as "Can the Subaltern Speak?" (1988), Spivak challenged postcolonial theory to address the silencing of women and other subaltern subjects, not only by and in colonial **discourses** but also in postcolonial responses to those discourses. In so doing, she expanded the meaning of *subaltern* — a British military term referring to a low-ranking, subordinate officer that in postcolonial theory designates the colonized to include voiceless groups within colonies or former colonies, such as women, migrants, and the subproletariat.

Bhabha examined how colonized peoples have co-opted and transformed various elements of the colonizing culture, a process he referred to as *hybridity*. For instance, in his essay "Of mimicry and man: The ambivalence of colonial discourse" (1987), he argued that colonized peoples turn the tables on colonizing cultures through imitation that produces a difference. Subsequently, in "DissemiNation: Time, narrative and the margins of the modern nation" (1990), he both mimicked and transformed the title of poststructuralist theorist Jacques Derrida's *Dissemination* (1972).

Important antecedents of postcolonial theorists include several writers from former colonies, particularly Achebe, Aimé Césaire, Frantz Fanon, and Edward Kamau Brathwaite. For example, in "An Image of Africa" (1977), Achebe, a Nigerian writer, characterized Joseph Conrad's **representation** of the Belgian Congo in *Heart of Darkness* (1899) as racist and condescending. Césaire, who experienced colonial life in the Caribbean and who founded the pan-national "Negritude" movement, described the barbarism of the colonizer in *Discours sur le colonialisme* (*Discourse on Colonialism*) (1950). Fanon, a West Indian psychiatrist from French Martinique who took up the cause of Algerian independence from France, analyzed the dynamics of racism and colonialism and advocated revolutionary independence movements in a series of essays. Of particular importance is the collection *Les damnés de la terre* (*The Wretched of the Earth*) (1961), including "Spontaneity," which addresses spontaneous violence and national consciousness, and "On National Culture," which describes the native intellectual's role in the development of a postcolonial national identity. Brathwaite, a Caribbean writer from Barbados, discussed *creolization,* which he defined in *The Development of Creole Society in Jamaica 1770–1820* (1971), as a "two-way process," "a way of seeing the society, not in terms of white and black, master and slave, in separate nuclear units, but as contributory parts of a whole. . . . Here, in Jamaica, fixed within the dehumanizing institution of slavery, were two cultures of people, having to adapt themselves to a new environment and to each other. The friction created by this confrontation was cruel, but it was also creative."

Postcolonial theory has also been influenced by **poststructuralist** approaches including **deconstruction**. In particular, deconstruction's challenge to hierarchical, **binary oppositions** provided postcolonial theory with conceptual strategies for undermining the ostensible difference between center and margins, between the colonizing culture and the colonized. Some postcolonial theorists, however, have criticized reliance on such abstract argumentation derived from European tradition. For example, in *Beyond Postcolonial Theory* (1998), Epifanio San Juan, Jr., a Filipino scholar, reproached postcolonial theorists whom he considered too abstract and insufficiently committed to effective political action.

Postcolonial literature and postcolonial theory continue to develop today. Neither looks the same as it did around 1990, when the terms first gained wide currency. Newer areas of study include the character and effects of diaspora — the dispersion of peoples from their homelands — and the differences among various postcolonial experiences. Notably, concepts and insights applicable to the Middle East and the Indian subcontinent often do not apply to African, Caribbean, and Hispanic or Latino contexts. Moreover, postcolonial theorists have also recognized that a given writer's angle of vision varies (as does the reader's) depending on factors such as gender, class, cultural roots, and location.

See also **orientalism**.

▶ **postmodernism:** A term referring to certain radically experimental works of literature and art produced after World War II. *Postmodernism* is distinguished from **modernism**, which generally refers to the revolution in art and literature that occurred during the period 1910 through the 1930s, particularly following the disillusioning experience of World War I. The postmodern era, with its potential for mass destruction and its shocking history of genocide, has evoked a continuing disillusionment similar to that widely experienced during the **Modern Period**. Much of postmodernist writing reveals and highlights the alienation of individuals and the meaninglessness of human existence. Postmodernists frequently stress that humans desperately (and ultimately unsuccessfully) cling to illusions of security to conceal and forget the void over which their lives are perched.

Not surprisingly, postmodernists have shared with their modernist precursors the goal of breaking away from traditions (including certain modernist traditions, which, over time, had become institutionalized and **conventional** to some degree) through experimentation with new literary devices, **forms**, and **styles**. While preserving the spirit and even some of the **themes** of modernist literature (the alienation of humanity, historical discontinuity, etc.), postmodernists have rejected the order that a number of modernists attempted to instill in their work through patterns of **allusion, symbol**, and **myth**. They have also taken some of the meanings and methods found in modernist works to extremes that most modernists would have deplored. For instance, whereas modernists such as T. S. Eliot perceived the world as fragmented and represented that fragmentation through poetic language, many also viewed art as a potentially integrating, restorative force, a hedge against the **cacophony** and chaos that postmodernist works often imitate (or even celebrate) but do not attempt to counter or correct.

Because postmodernist works frequently combine aspects of diverse **genres**, they can be difficult to classify — at least according to traditional schemes of classification. Revolting against a certain modernist tendency toward elitist "high art," postmodernists have also generally made a concerted effort to appeal to popular culture. Cartoons, music, "pop art," and television have thus become acceptable and even common media for postmodernist artistic expression. Postmodernist literary developments include such genres as **the Absurd**, the *nouveau roman,* **magic realism, Language** poetry, and other forms of *avant-garde* poetry written in **free verse** and challenging the **ideological** assumptions of contemporary society. What postmodernist theater, fiction, and poetry have in common is the view (explicit or implicit) that literary language is its own reality, not a means of **representing** reality.

Postmodernist **critical** schools include **deconstruction**, whose practitioners explore the **undecidability** of **texts**, and **cultural criticism**, which erases the boundary between "high" and "low" culture. The foremost theorist of postmodernism is French philosopher Jean-François Lyotard, best known for his book *La condition postmoderne* (*The Postmodern Condition*) (1979).

The postmodernist critique also extends to modern science. In journals such as *Social Text*, postmodernist theorists have sought to "demystify" science, arguing that it is: (1) a cultural construct whose **privileged** status among means of arriving at knowledge is undeserved; and (2) a tool of repressive ideologies that have favored the health, welfare, and interests of whites and males over people of color and females. In *The Structure of Scientific Revolutions* (1962), American historian of science Thomas Kuhn argued that what science tends to reveal is the prevailing scientific **paradigm** (which is subject to shifting). Since then, many scientists have been less attached to the idea that they are producing objectively verifiable truths and more willing to speculate about "realities," the reality of which will probably remain unprovable. Moreover, as John Horgan pointed out in a *New York Times* article entitled "Science Set Free From Truth" (1996), "some of the most prominent scientists in the world traffic in hypotheses that are remarkably postmodern in character."

Horgan cited artificial intelligence expert Marvin Minsky, who argued that computers can think; chemist Ilya Prigogine, whose work led to the development of chaos theory; and physicists such as Sidney Coleman, Andrei Linde, and John Wheeler as examples of scientists who would agree that science has reached, in Prigogine's words, "the end of certitude." Coleman and Linde suggested that our universe may be one of many, each with similar — or different — laws of physics; Wheeler, who coined the term *black hole*, argued that reality is "participatory" in nature, that it is partially the product of the questions we pose about it and thus, in some sense, "a figment of the imagination."

FURTHER EXAMPLES: Postmodernist poets include John Ashberry, Maxine Chernoff, Jori Graham, Richard Howard, James Merrill, and Maureen Owen. Harold Pinter's *The Homecoming* (1965) and Edward Albee's *Three Tall Women* (1994) are examples of postmodernist theater. Robert Wilson's *Einstein on the Beach* (1979) has been called a postmodernist opera. Postmodernist novels include William Burroughs's *Naked Lunch* (1962), Donald Barthelme's *Come Back, Dr. Caligari* (1964), John Barth's *Lost in the Funhouse* (1967), Thomas Pynchon's *Gravity's Rainbow* (1973), David Shield's *Remote* (1996), and Kathy Acker's *Empire of the Senseless* (1988), which includes the statement: "Get rid of meaning. Your mind is a nightmare that has been eating you: now eat your mind." Don DeLillo has written several postmodernist novels, including *White Noise* (1985), *Libra* (1988), and *Mao II* (1991). In a review, T. Coraghessan Boyle refers to Thomas Pynchon's *Mason & Dixon* (1997) as a postmodernist **historical novel**, explaining that "if the traditional historical novel attempts to replicate a way of life, speech and costume, the post-modernist version seeks only to be that, a version."

In 1996, *Social Text* published an article entitled "Transgressing the Boundaries: Toward a Transformative Hermeneutics of Quantum Gravity," in which physicist Alan Sokal argued that many existing laws of physics are social conventions and called for the development of an "emancipatory mathematics." Later, Sokal declared over the Internet that the article was a hoax intended to debunk postmodernist critiques of science, but some postmodernists still find more truth in the hoax than in Sokal's subsequent representation of it as "a melange of truths, half-truths, quarter-truths, falsehoods, and syntactically correct sentences that have no meaning whatsoever."

▶ **Postmodern Period (in English and American literature):** Less coherent and less well defined than many other literary eras, a period usually said to have begun in both England and North America after World War II. The Postmodern Period follows the **Modern Period** in English and American literature, which began around 1914. Both **modernist** and **postmodernist** works tend to express feelings of anxiety and alienation experienced by individuals living in the twentieth century, but postmodernist works tend to be even darker, suggesting the meaninglessness of the human condition in general through radically experimental works that defy **conventions** of literary cohesion and even coherence. Postmodernist novels fitting this description are often referred to as **antinovels**.

See **postmodernism**.

▶ **poststructuralism:** The general attempt to contest and subvert **structuralism** and to formulate new theories regarding interpretation and meaning, initiated particularly by **deconstructors** but also associated with certain aspects and practitioners of **psychoanalytic, Marxist, cultural, feminist,** and **gender criticism**. Poststructuralism, which arose in the late 1960s, includes such a wide variety of perspectives that no unified poststructuralist theory was ever identified. Rather, poststructuralists are distinguished from other contemporary critics by their opposition to structuralism and by certain concepts held in common.

Structuralism, briefly defined, is a theory of humankind that arose in France in the 1950s and whose proponents attempted to show systematically, even scientifically, that all elements of human culture, including literature, may be understood as part of a system of **signs**. Leading figures included French anthropologist Claude Lévi-Strauss and Swiss linguist Ferdinand de Saussure. Lévi-Strauss, who studied everything from the structure of villages to the structure of **myths,** looked for recurring, common elements that transcended the differences within and among cultures. Saussure, who founded **semiology,** argued that linguistic signs are composed of two parts: the **signifier** (the "sound-image") and the **signified** (the **abstract** concept **represented** by the signifier). Using Saussure's linguistic theory as a model and employing **semiotic** theory in general, structuralists claimed that it was possible to analyze a **text** or other signifying structure systematically, even scientifically, to reveal the "grammar" behind its form and meaning.

Structuralists also followed Saussure's lead in viewing sign systems in terms of **binary oppositions,** contrary pairs such as light / dark and strong / weak. For instance, in analyzing myths and texts to uncover basic structures, structuralists argued that opposite terms modulate until they are finally reconciled by some intermediary third term. They typically believed that meaning(s) in a text, as well as the meaning of a text, could be determined with reference to the system of signification — the **codes** and **conventions** that governed the text's production and that operate in its reception. Poststructuralists, by contrast, believe that signification is an interminable and intricate web of associations that continually defers a determinate assessment of meaning. The numerous possible **denotations** and **connotations** of any word lead to **contradictions** and ultimately to the dissemination of meaning itself. Thus, poststructuralists contend that texts contradict not only structuralist accounts of them but also themselves.

French theorist Jacques Derrida's 1966 paper "Structure, Sign and Play in the Discourse of the Human Sciences" inaugurated poststructuralism as a coherent challenge to structuralism. There, Derrida rejected the structuralist presupposition that texts (or other structures) have self-referential **centers** that govern their language (or signifying system) without being determined, governed, co-opted, or problematized by that language (or signifying system). Having rejected the structuralist concept of a self-referential center, Derrida also rejected its corollary: that a text's meaning is thereby rendered determinable (capable of being determined) as well as determinate (fixed and reliably correct).

Poststructuralists have suggested that structuralism rests on a number of distinctions — between signifier and signified, self and language (or text), texts and other texts, and text and world — that are overly simplistic, if not patently inaccurate, and they have made a concerted effort to discredit these oppositions. For instance, poststructuralists have viewed the self as the subject, as well as the user, of language, claiming that although we may speak through and shape language, it also shapes and speaks through us. Moreover, although poststructuralists have generally followed their structuralist predecessors in rejecting the traditional concept of the literary "work" (as the work of an individual and purposeful **author**) in favor of the impersonal "text," they have gone structuralists one better by treating texts as "intertexts": crisscrossed strands within the infinitely larger text called language, that networked system of denotation, connotation, and signification in which the individual text is inscribed and read and through which its myriad possible meanings are ascribed and assigned. (French poststructuralist psychoanalytic critic Julia Kristeva, who coined the term **intertextuality,** characterized the individual text as a "mosaic of quotations" [*Desire in Language,* 1980], an amalgam of preexisting texts whose meanings it reworks and transforms.)

Poststructuralists have even viewed the world itself as a text. This position was set forth most powerfully and controversially by the deconstructive theorist Jacques Derrida in his book *De la grammatologie* (*Of Grammatology*) (1967), where he maintained that *"there is nothing outside the text."* In order to understand what Derrida meant by that statement, consider the following: We know the world through language, and the acts and practices that constitute that "real world" (the 9/11 attacks, the decision to marry) are inseparable from the **discourses** (accepted ways of thinking, writing, and speaking) out of which they arise and as open to interpretation as any work of literature. We necessarily live, think, and act within a network of cultural discourses, within "the text." Other theorists who have deconstructed the world/text opposition include Paul de Man and Geoffrey Hartman, who claimed in *Easy Pieces* (1985) that "nothing can lift us out of language."

Jacques Lacan, a French psychoanalytic critic whose theories influenced both deconstructors and other poststructuralists, posited that the human unconscious is structured like a language. He treated dreams not as Freud treated them — as revealing symptoms of repression — but rather as forms of discourse. Lacan also argued that the **ego,** subject, or self that we think of as being necessary and natural (our individual human nature) is in fact a product of the social order and its various and often conflicting symbolic systems (especially, but not exclusively, language). The "ego-artifact," produced during what he called the "mirror stage" of human development, seems unified, consistent, and organized around a determinate center but is really a fiction. The yoking together of fragments and destructively dissimilar elements takes its psychic toll, and it is the job of the Lacanian psychoanalyst to "deconstruct," as it were, the ego, to show its continuities to be contradictions as well.

Michel Foucault, a French philosophical historian influenced by **Marxism** and most often associated with **the new historicism,** studied cultures in terms of power relationships but refused to see power in terms of simple, binary oppositions, as something exercised by a dominant **class** over a subservient class. In *Surveiller et punir: Naissance de la prison* (*Discipline and Punish: The Birth of the Prison*) (1975), he argued that power is not simply repressive power, that is, a tool of conspiracy by one individual or institution against another. Rather, power is a complex of interwoven and often contradictory forces; power produces what happens. Thus, even a tyrannical aristocrat does not simply wield power, for he is empowered by discourses and practices that embody, exercise, and amount to power.

Roland Barthes, both a structuralist and a poststructuralist over the course of his career, was one of the first to strip the author of the unique role accorded to him by Western culture and by traditional **literary criticism**. In "The Death of the Author" (1967), Barthes declared that the author as an institution (that is, the author traditionally conceived as the source of knowledge, the controller of a text's meaning, and a chief object of critical interest) was dead. Along with Foucault and de Man, Barthes viewed the author not as an original and creative master and manipulator of the linguistic system but, rather, as one of its primary vehicles, an agent through which it works out new permutations and combinations. He also elaborated on the French concepts of *plaisir* and *jouissance* (bliss), which he characterized as a binary opposition in *Le plaisir du texte* (*The Pleasure of the Text*) (1973). Furthermore, in *S/Z* (1970), he argued that texts were either *lisible* ("readerly") or *scriptible* ("writerly"). *Lisible* indicates a certain dependence on convention, which facilitates interpretation. *Scriptible* implies a significant degree of experimentation, a flouting or modification of traditional rules that makes a text difficult to interpret and, occasionally, virtually incomprehensible. Works by writers such as Jorge Luis Borges, William Burroughs, James Joyce, Gertrude Stein, and Virginia Woolf tend to be *scriptible* and *illisible* (unreaderly). In other words, works such as Borges's *Ficciones* (1956) and Burroughs's *Naked Lunch* (1962) do not make sense to readers who approach them according to standard rules of reading.

Even as poststructuralists have radically reduced the author's role, they have also diminished the role of the reader, whom they view not as a stable, coherent, and consistent subject or self but rather as the locus of competing and often contradictory discourses. They concern themselves with "reading" (*lecture*), rather than with the reader per se. Texts themselves may also be stripped of individuality, seen simply as part of writing-in-general (*écriture*). Some poststructuralist critics have gone so far as to reject the term *text* altogether, preferring *discourse*, which they broadly use to refer to any verbal structure, whether literary or not.

Poststructuralists have also radically revised the traditional concept of **theory** even as they have elevated it to a position of prime importance (so much so that poststructuralist critics who want to be taken seriously must theorize their critical practices). Theory, as poststructuralists conceive of it, is vastly different from theory as defined in more conventional literary criticism (as a general set of principles applicable to the analysis or classification of a literary work). In the view of poststructuralists, theory has to account for more than literature, since everything from the unconscious to social and cultural practices is seen as functioning like a language; thus the goal of poststructuralist theorists is to understand what controls interpretation and meaning in all possible systems of signification. Not surprisingly, this far-ranging concept has facilitated the development of theories that challenge the very underpinnings of traditional Western thought, especially the **logocentric** assumption that meaning is ultimately determinable and determinate.

Poststructuralism serves as the overall **paradigm** for many of the most prominent contemporary critical perspectives. Approaches ranging from **reader-response criticism** to the new historicism assume the "antifoundationalist" bias of poststructuralism. Many approaches also incorporate the poststructuralist position that texts lack clear and definite meanings, an argument pushed to the extreme by those poststructuralists identified with deconstruction. But unlike deconstructors, who argue that the process of signification itself produces irreconcilable contradictions, contemporary critics oriented toward other poststructuralist approaches (**discourse analysis** or Lacanian psychoanalytic theory, for instance) maintain that texts do have real, underlying meanings that poststructuralist readings can uncover. Nevertheless, of the various critical approaches associated with poststructuralism, deconstruction has had the greatest impact on the theory and practice of literary criticism, perhaps because of its emphasis on the text as **rhetoric** requiring both careful and playful **close reading**.

See also **deconstruction**.

▶ **practical criticism (applied criticism):** A type of **literary criticism** that emphasizes and responds to the characteristics of specific **texts**. Practical criticism differs from **theoretical criticism**, which emphasizes the formulation of general principles applicable to all texts rather than the **explication** of individual works. Practical critics often apply **aesthetic** principles that theoretical critics have simply postulated. But rather than elaborating on the theoretical assumptions underlying their analyses, practical critics concentrate on performing a **close reading** of the text in discussing the work and its **author**. The term *practical criticism* was first employed by **romantic** poet and critic Samuel Taylor Coleridge in his *Biographia Literaria* (1817) but given broad usage by English critic I. A. Richards, who in 1929 published a book entitled *Practical Criticism: A Study of Literary Judgment.*

Some critics distinguish between two types of practical criticism: (1) **impressionistic criticism**, which is based on the critic's **subjective** impressions and reaction to a work; and (2) **judicial criticism**, which aims to assess literary works in accordance with a set of **objective** principles and rules.

See also **impressionistic criticism, judicial criticism, theoretical criticism**.

▶ **pragmatic criticism:** A type of **literary criticism** going back to the Roman poet Horace, who in his *Ars poetica (Art of Poetry)* (c. 20 B.C.) emphasized the effect of a literary work on its audience. Pragmatic critics believe that **authors** structure works in such a way as to attain specific effects on and elicit certain responses from the reader or audience. These critics thus evaluate a work based on their perception of the success or failure of that work (or author) to achieve its objectives.

Pragmatic criticism is similar to **rhetorical criticism** in its emphasis on how — and how well — the work (or author) manages to "influence" the reader or audience (in the sense of inducing the reader or audience to respond in a particular way). Like rhetorical criticism, pragmatic criticism was practiced from **classical** times up through the eighteenth century, when its popularity declined with the rise of **expressive criticism**, which views literary works in light of their authors' thoughts and feelings. It lapsed into still deeper obscurity during the nineteenth century with the advent of **objective criticism.**

▶ **Prague Linguistic Circle:** A group of scholars centered in Prague (in the former Czechoslovakia) who continued working in the vein of the **Russian formalists** after that school was suppressed by the Soviet government in the 1930s. Leading members included Roman Jakobson (a leader of the original Russian formalist school who emigrated to Czechoslovakia from Russia) and René Wellek.

See **formalism, Russian formalism.**

▶ **Pre-Raphaelitism:** A literary movement propagated by a group of English writers of the **Victorian Period** who shared the **aesthetic** values of Pre-Raphaelite painters such as Dante Gabriel Rossetti (who was also a poet), Holman Hunt, John Everett Millais, Ford Madox Brown, and Edward Burne-Jones. What these and other members of the *Pre-Raphaelite Brotherhood* (formed in 1848) shared was the belief that European art in general and English art in particular were stuck in a rut of traditions that had dictated an increasingly tired aesthetic ever since the Italian High **Renaissance,** the birth of which they associated with the painter Raphael.

The Pre-Raphaelites greatly preferred the originality, simplicity, freshness, sharp lines, and strong colors of artists who painted before Raphael to the often idealized images and *chiaroscuro* coloration (involving the atmospheric mixture of light and shadows) characteristic of both the High Renaissance and those English painters whose work grew out of that tradition, such as Sir Joshua Reynolds (President of the Royal Academy), Sir George Beaumont, and Sir John Constable. In their own paintings, the Pre-Raphaelites strove to reveal truth through nature carefully observed and rendered brightly and precisely. Rossetti established his own version of Pre-Raphaelitism, one involving medieval **images** and **themes** and elevating beauty above all other values.

The literary tradition that emerged out of this artistic movement is noted on the one hand for its crisp descriptions and sensuous details and, on the other, for its power to suggest metaphysical states, to indicate philosophical and theological truths unobtrusively. In Pre-Raphaelite poetry, the sound of chairs being pushed back from a table, the sight of coins in a sleeping woman's hair, or the number of petals in a blossom can be **symbolically** suggestive, calling to mind the spiritual dimensions that lie behind the most commonplace objects or situations. The Pre-Raphaelite emphasis on sensuous detail led some critics to dub the movement the "fleshly school of poetry."

Major writers associated with the movement included Dante Gabriel Rossetti, Christina Rossetti, Algernon Charles Swinburne, and William

Morris, a designer now best known for his lush wallpaper patterns and the still-popular "Morris Chair." Pre-Raphaelitism had a considerable **influence** on late-Victorian **medieval** revival and also on **Aestheticism,** the movement sometimes summarized by the rallying cry **art-for-art's-sake.**

EXAMPLE: The following lines, spoken by Queen Guenevere in Morris's poem "The Defence of Guenevere" (1858), convey the spirit of Pre-Raphaelite painting and poetry. The medieval **setting,** the intensified experience of nature in the garden, the garden's subtly symbolic suggestiveness, the idea of weary thoughts giving way to sharp new perceptions, and the overriding emphasis on beauty all exemplify Pre-Raphaelitism:

> I was half mad with beauty on that day,
> And went without my ladies all alone,
> In a quiet garden walled round every way;
>
> I was right joyful of that wall of stone,
> That shut the flowers and trees up with the sky,
> And trebled all the beauty: to the bone,
>
> Yea right through to my heart, grown very shy
> With weary thoughts, it pierced, and made me glad. . . .

▶ **presence and absence:** Words given a special literary application by French theorist of **deconstruction** Jacques Derrida in *De la grammatologie* (*Of Grammatology*) (1967) when he used them to make a distinction between speech and writing. An individual speaking words must actually be present at the time they are heard, Derrida pointed out, whereas an individual writing words is absent at the time they are read. Associating presence with "logos" (the creating spoken Word of a present God who "In the beginning" said "Let there be light"), Derrida argued that the Western concept of language is **logocentric:** grounded in "the metaphysics of presence," the belief that any linguistic system has a basic foundation, or "ultimate referent," making possible an identifiable and correct meaning or meanings for any potential statement within that system. Far from supporting this logocentric view of language, however, Derrida argued that presence is not an "ultimate referent" and that it does not guarantee determinable (capable of being determined) — much less determinate (fixed and reliably correct) — meaning. He thus called into question the **privileging** of speech and presence over writing and absence in Western thought.

See also **logocentric, logocentrism.**

▶ **primitivism:** A doctrine postulating that, although humans are essentially good, they have been (and are still being) corrupted by "civilization." Primitivism emerged in the eighteenth century as a reaction against rationalistic **neoclassicism,** remained popular through the subsequent **Romantic Period,** and has persisted into the present day, though opposed by the doctrine of progress, which asserts that humanity has been improving throughout history thanks to advances in technology, science, art, and knowledge. Primitivists typically espouse a certain "back-to-nature" philosophy that has led to the glorification both of past eras and of past (and present) peoples seen as "natural" in contrast to the largely urban culture that exists today.

Primitivism is often divided into two general categories — *cultural* and *chronological*. This distinction is fairly elastic, however; as a result, the categories frequently overlap. Cultural primitivism holds that what is perceived as natural is usually preferable or superior to what is perceived as artificial. "Nature" is lauded over "culture." The simple and the instinctual are preferred to the complex and the reasoned. Cultural primitivists thus typically see the practices of still-existing tribal groups as superior to the ways of urban civilization. Advocates of chronological primitivism, by contrast, typically emphasize some golden age of humanity that supposedly existed in the past. That is to say, chronological primitivists usually claim that a particular time was the best in human history and that humanity, having subsequently lost the near-perfection it had attained during that period, has been in decline, perhaps progressive decline, ever since. Chronological primitivists have named eras as late as that of **classical** Greece as being the **golden age** of humanity.

In literary theory, primitivism has manifested itself in the belief that the best poetry is produced naturally or instinctively. Primitivists have sought to prove their theory by finding an "innate" talent for poetry in individuals who have had no formal education and among groups remote from civilization as we know it. Such searches and assertions were particularly common in eighteenth-century England and France. Jean-Jacques Rousseau, an eighteenth-century French writer who popularized primitivist concepts, also popularized the concept of the *Noble Savage*, the idea that humanity in its unspoiled, primitive state is possessed of superior intelligence, morality, and dignity.

The doctrine of primitivism has also flourished in America. In the nineteenth century, pioneers were viewed as Adamic **heroes** living off the (Edenic) land, and in the late 1960s, so-called flower children advocated escaping the military-industrial complex through drugs and what might be called the primitivism of rock 'n' roll music. (In their song "Woodstock" [1970], Crosby, Stills, Nash, and Young spoke of having to "get back to the land" to set their souls free; the song concludes with the line, "We've got to get ourselves back to the garden.") More recently, specific movements within the rock 'n' roll tradition, such as punk and grunge, have stressed directness and raw emotion, thus placing themselves in the larger, primitivistic tradition.

Primitivism has had an influence on classical as well as on popular music (Igor Stravinsky's *Le sacre du printemps* [*The Rite of Spring*] [1913] is a primitivistic, classical symphonic piece) and an even greater influence on twentieth-century novels, poems, paintings, and sculptures. Practitioners of each of these arts have made use of increasingly complex techniques and technologies to produce works that laud or mimic those produced in centuries, even millenia, past. These works, dependent upon modern methods for their creation, paradoxically reject "sophisticated" culture and civilization. Artists generally influenced by primitivist thought and expression range from the poet-novelist D. H. Lawrence to the painter Paul Gauguin (who went to Tahiti as a "missionary in reverse") to the sculptor Constantin Brancusi (*The Kiss* [1908]), who sought to capture the expressiveness of prehistoric stone carvings in his work. The English sculptor Henry Moore, a self-described "primevalist," created works suggestive of the monoliths of Stonehenge and statues of deities smoothed by centuries of weather and wear. The art of Jean-Michel Basquiat has also been associated with primitivism, as has "outsider art," a species of **folk** art, and the work of graffiti artists such as Keith Haring.

▶ **privilege:** As a verb, to address interpretively, in literary study, one set of textual or contextual issues before, and often instead of, others. Since no scholar or critic can account for all of the causes, contents, or **connotations** of even a single **text**, all interpretive acts involve some degree of privileging, which, in turn, involves priorities grounded in a hierarchy of values. For instance, **Marxist critics** privilege social **class** in analyzing texts; **reader-response critics** privilege readers' responses to literary works; and **structuralists** privilege the idea that all elements of human culture, including literature, can be understood as part of a system of **signs.**

As a noun, that status of **authors, narrators,** and **characters** which derives from information that is known — and perhaps available — to them alone. For example, **third-person omniscient** narrators (e.g., the narrator in Charles Frazier's *Cold Mountain* [1997; adapted to film 2003]) have "authorial privilege," as do characters whose **first-person narratives** are privileged by hindsight (e.g., Lily Owen in Sue Monk Kidd's *The Secret Life of Bees* [2002]).

As an adjective ("privileged"), the special status accorded to certain persons, works, ideas, or forms of expression by a given culture. Texts considered **classics** are privileged, as are Ludwig von Beethoven's nine symphonies and Julia Child's French cookbooks. In the U.S., television is privileged over radio, football over soccer, cars over public transit, the individual over the group, and so forth.

▶ **problem novel:** See **sociological novel.**

▶ **prolepsis:** The evocation in a **narrative** of scenes or events that take place at a later point in the **story.** One of the three major types of **anachrony,** *prolepsis* is sometimes equated with **flashforward,** but some **reader-response critics** have argued that it is in fact a more general term (much as its opposite, **analepsis,** is a broader term than **flashback**). For instance, prolepsis may involve an **image** that suggests something to occur in the future. More commonly, it involves a **figure of speech** in which an anticipated event or action is treated as if it has already occurred or is presently occurring, even though this is temporally impossible. Occasionally, a proleptic thought or dream disrupts the chronological flow of material being related, often manifesting itself in the conscious or subconscious thought processes of a **narrator** or of a protagonist whose mental processes are recounted by the narrative.

As a **rhetorical** device in an argument or debate, prolepsis involves anticipating an opponent's arguments or rebuttals.

EXAMPLES: The italicized clause in the following passage: "Linda had never seen such beautiful scarves. *Although she would later feel guilty having spent so much money,* she decided to buy one on the spot." Boxing manager Vic Marsillo's suggestion, during a radio interview, "Suppose we reminisce a little about tomorrow's fight?" treats the anticipated event as if it has already occurred.

A **classic** literary example of prolepsis is found in John Keats's poem "Isabella" (1820):

> So the two brothers and their murder'd man
> Rode past fair Florence . . . .

The first paragraph of Carson McCullers's *Reflections in a Golden Eye* (1941) proleptically anticipates the ending of the novel: "There is a fort in the South where a few years ago a murder was committed. The participants of this tragedy were: two officers, a soldier, two women, and a horse."

In the movie *The Empire Strikes Back* (1980), Luke Skywalker says "I'm not afraid," to which Jedi master Yoda responds "You will be." Edward P. Jones repeatedly used prolepsis in his novel *The Known World* (2003), as in the assertion "The man Loretta would eventually marry would want to know why she didn't take his last name, why she wanted no last name at all."

See also **anachrony, analepsis.**

▶ **prologue:** An introductory statement that precedes or serves as the first part of a literary work. The prologue often provides information that sets the stage for the story that follows; it may establish the **setting,** introduce the **characters,** or indicate a **theme** or moral. In a play, the prologue is usually a **monologue** delivered by one of the actors. Most prologues are written by the **author** of the work; some, however, are written by another person, often a well-known writer who has agreed to introduce and thereby commend the work.

EXAMPLES: Marie de France's "Prologue" to her collection of twelfth-century *lais,* ends with the following words:

> In your honour, noble king, you who are so worthy and courtly, you
> to whom all joy pays homage and in whose heart all true virtue has
> taken root, did I set myself to assemble lays, to compose and to relate
> them in rhyme. In my heart, lord, I thought and decided that I should
> present them to you, so if it pleased you to accept them, you would
> bring me great happiness and I should rejoice evermore. Do not con-

sider me presumptuous if I make so bold as to offer you this gift. Now
hear the beginning.

In *Plain and Simple* (1989), Sue Bender began her account of her journey
to the Amish with the following prologue: "I had an obsession with the
Amish. Plain and simple. Objectively it made no sense. I, who worked hard
at being special, fell in love with a people who valued being ordinary." In
the prologue to Michael Cunningham's *The Hours* (1998; adapted to film
2002), Virginia Woolf wades into a river to drown herself even as her husband Leonard discovers her suicide note and rushes off to try and save her.

▶ **propositional act:** A **speech act** involving a **locution,** or utterance, that
says something about something else. As introduced by American "ordinary-
language" philosopher John R. Searle in *Speech Acts: An Essay in the Philosophy of Language* (1969), a propositional act has two components: referring
to an object and predicating something upon that object. The "referring expression," according to Searle, is "any expression which serves to identify
any thing, process, event, action, or any other kind of 'individual' or 'particular'"; the object referred to in a locution may thus be the grammatical subject of that locution.

EXAMPLE: In the locution, "The house is red," the house is the object to
which the speaker refers, and the speaker predicates that it is red.

See **speech-act theory.**

▶ **proscenium:** In ancient Greek and Roman theater, the stage, a raised
area in front of the backdrop; in modern Western theater, the front part of
the stage, between the curtain and the orchestra. The *proscenium arch* is
the arch from which the curtain hangs, framing the main stage and formally separating it from the audience. While proscenium theaters remain
prevalent today, more intimate forms of staging, such as thrust stages
(open to the audience on three sides) and arena stages (theater-in-the-
round, in which the audience surrounds the stage), have become increasingly common.

▶ **prose:** From the Latin for "straightforward," ordinary written or spoken expression; as applied specifically to literature, non**poetic** expression,
that is, expression that exhibits purposeful grammatical (including **syntactic**) design but that is not characterized by deliberate or regular **rhythmic** or
metrical patterns. Major prose forms include **nonfictional** works such as **biographies** and **essays** and **fictional** works such as **novels** and **short stories.**

The development of prose has generally followed that of verse. Pioneers
of English prose include the ninth-century king Alfred the Great, who
translated several Latin works, and fourteenth-century theologian John
Wycliffe, who undertook the first complete translation of the Bible into
English (c. 1380–82). Poets tend to innovate; prose writers, by contrast,
tend to **imitate,** making belated use of those poetic innovations that can be
adapted to the prose environment. The more "artful" or "literary" the

work of prose, the more it tends to employ poetic devices, such as rhythm, **imagery**, and sonority (achieved through **alliteration, assonance, consonance,** etc.). Some creative prose writers adopt traditional poetic devices to such a great extent that the line between prose and poetry becomes blurred, hence the designation **prose poem.**

See **poetry** for discussion of some differences between prose and poetry.

▶ **prose encomium:** See **encomium, epideictic.**

▶ **prose poem:** A brief, **rhythmic** composition blending **prose** and **verse,** ranging from several lines to several pages. Prose poems are written in sentences, without the line breaks characteristic of poetry, but are heavily marked by the use of poetic devices such as **figurative language, imagery,** repetition, and even **rhyme.** The **genre** arose in France in the nineteenth century, pioneered by Aloysius Bertrand in *Gaspard de la nuit* (*Gaspard of the Night*) (1842), and subsequently gained broad currency, influencing the **Parnassians; Symbolists,** including Charles Baudelaire and Arthur Rimbaud; **Decadents,** such as Oscar Wilde; **Imagists;** and **surrealists.** Other noted practitioners of the form include German poet Rainer Maria Rilke, Mexican poet Octavio Paz, Spanish poet Ángel Crespo, and American poets Gertrude Stein and Russell Edson.

EXAMPLES: Baudelaire's *Petits poèmes en prose* (*Little Poems in Prose*) (1869); Paz's sequence of prose poems *Águila o sol?* (*Eagle or Sun?*) (1951); Geoffrey Hill's *Mercian Hymns* (1971); Charles Simic's *The World Doesn't End* (1989); Dennis Keene's *The Modern Japanese Prose Poem: An Anthology of Six Poets* (1980); Edson's *The Tunnel: Selected Poems* (1994), a collection of prose poems; Crespo's *Poemas en prosa: 1965–1994* (1998). Edson's "A Chair," from his collection *The Very Thing That Happens* (1964), follows:

> A chair has waited such a long time to be with its person. Through shadow and fly buzz and the floating dust it has waited such a long time to be with its person.
> What it remembers of the forest it forgets, and dreams of a room where it waits — Of the cup and the ceiling — Of the Animate One.

▶ **prosody:** The study of **versification,** particularly as it encompasses **meter, rhyme, rhythm,** and **stanza** form, and — to a lesser degree — sound patterns such as **alliteration.** Some say that prosody especially involves the study of **accent,** given its roles in meter, rhythm, and other poetic sound effects.

In **linguistics,** *prosody* refers to the duration (length), loudness, pitch, and **stress** of speech sounds.

▶ **prosopopoeia:** (1) A synonym for **personification.** (2) A **figure of speech** (more specifically a **trope**) in which an absent, dead, or imaginary person is given voice, typically through another person. In "Autobiography as

De-Facement" (1979), **deconstructive** theorist Paul de Man defined proso-popoeia as "the fiction of an apostrophe to an absent, deceased, or voice-less entity, which posits the possibility of the latter's reply and confers upon it the power of speech."

EXAMPLE: Jonathan Edwards's sermon "Sinners in the Hands of an Angry God" (1741) exhorts listeners to heed the voices of the damned in hell: "If it were so that we could come to speak with them, . . . we, doubtless, should hear one and another reply, 'No, I never intended to come here: . . . I in-tended to take effectual care; but it came upon me unexpectedly; . . . it came as a thief; death outwitted me.'"

See **personification** for examples of the same.

▶ **protagonist:** The main **character** in a work; usually also the **hero** or **hero-ine,** but sometimes an **antihero.** The term comes from the Greek for "first combatant" and referred to the first actor (the person with the leading role, supported by the **chorus**) in **classical** Greek **tragedy.** If the protagonist is in primary **conflict** with another character, that character is the **antagonist;** an evil antagonist is called a **villain.**

EXAMPLES: Evelina Anville is the protagonist and heroine of Fanny Bur-ney's *Evelina* (1778); Emma Woodhouse is the protagonist but dubious heroine of Jane Austen's *Emma* (1815); Becky Sharp is the unheroic — and sometimes quasi-villainous — protagonist of William Makepeace Thackeray's *Vanity Fair* (1846).

Simon Winchester's *The Professor and the Madman* (1998), a best-seller about the origins of *The Oxford English Dictionary,* begins by describing a "controversy" about whether a literary work can have more than one pro-tagonist.

▶ **proverb:** See **aphorism.** See also **folklore.**

▶ **pseudonym:** See *nom de plume.*

▶ **psychic(al) distance:** See **aesthetic distance.**

▶ **psychoanalytic criticism:** A type of **psychological criticism** that emerged in the early twentieth century and that analyzes the relationship between **au-thors** or readers and literary works, emphasizing the unconscious mind, its repressed wishes and fears, and sublimated manifestations in the **text.** Better known and more widely practiced than its "parent" approach, psychoana-lytic criticism originated in the work of Austrian psychoanalyst Sigmund Freud, who developed a **theory** of human psychology in the late nineteenth and early twentieth centuries and pioneered the technique of psychoanaly-sis, a therapeutic method that has been called the "talking cure."

Freud's theories are directly and indirectly concerned with the nature of the unconscious mind. Although Freud didn't invent the notion of the un-conscious — others before him had suggested that even the supposedly "sane" human mind was conscious and rational only at times, and even then at possibly only one level — he expanded it, suggesting that the powers motivating men and women are mainly and normally unconscious. He also identified three components of the human psyche: the **id,** the inborn, unconscious part of the psyche and the source of our instinctual physical (especially libidinal) desires; the **superego,** which internalizes the norms and mores of society and almost seems outside the self, making moral judgments and counseling sacrifice regardless of self-interest; and the **ego,** the predominantly rational, orderly, and conscious part of the psyche that mediates the often competing demands of the id and the superego. The id, insatiable and pleasure-seeking, is ruled by the pleasure principle; the ego, based on the reality principle, must choose between or balance liberation and self-gratification on one hand and censorship and conformity on the other.

Freud argued that we often repress what the id encourages us to think and do, thereby forcing these "unacceptable" wishes and desires into the unconscious. We are particularly likely to censor infantile sexual desires, which then emerge only in disguised forms: in dreams, in language (so-called Freudian slips), in creative activity that may produce art (including literature), and in neurotic behavior. One commonly repressed unconscious desire is the childhood wish to displace the parent of the same sex and take his or her place in the affections of the parent of the opposite sex, which Freud referred to as "Oedipal" (after the Greek **tragic** hero Oedipus, who unwittingly killed his father and married his mother). Notably, Freud viewed the manifestation of the Oedipus complex as a universal experience, a normal stage of psychosexual development central to the development of the superego, and for much of his career attributed neurosis chiefly to unresolved Oedipal conflicts.

Freud used dream analysis as a tool for uncovering our repressed feelings and memories. He believed that the repressed urges of the id surface in dreams, masked in **symbolic** form, and that analysis is therefore required to reveal their true meaning. Although Freud's belief in the significance of dreams was no more original than his belief that there is an unconscious side to the psyche, it was the extent to which he developed a theory of how dreams work — and the extent to which that theory helped him, by analogy, to understand far more than dreams — that made him unusual, important, and influential.

The psychoanalytic approach to literature not only rests on the theories of Freud, it may even be said to have *begun* with Freud, who believed that writers write to express their personal, repressed wishes and who was especially interested in writers who relied heavily on symbols. Such writers cloak ideas in **figures** that make sense only when interpreted, much as the unconscious mind of a neurotic disguises secret thoughts in dream stories or bizarre actions that need to be interpreted by an analyst. Freud's interest in literary artists led him to make some unfortunate generalizations about creativity; for example, in the twenty-third lecture of his *Introductory Lectures on Psycho-Analysis* (1922), he defined the artist as "one urged on by instinctive needs that are too clamorous." But it also led him to write creative literary criticism of his own, including an influential essay on "The Relation of a Poet to Daydreaming" (1908) and "The Uncanny" (1919), a provocative psychoanalytic reading of E. T. A. Hoffmann's supernatural tale "The Sand-man" (1817).

Freud's application of psychoanalytic theory to literature was imitated and then modified by numerous critics. In 1909, Austrian psychoanalyst Otto Rank, in *The Myth of the Birth of the Hero,* theorized that the artist turns a powerful, secret wish into a literary fantasy; Rank used the Oedipus complex to explain the similarities between the popular stories of so many literary **heroes.** A year later, Ernest Jones, a Welsh psychoanalyst and, later, Freud's official **biographer,** drew on the Oedipal conflict in "The Oedipus-Complex as an Explanation of *Hamlet's* Mystery: A Study in Motive" (1910), suggesting that William Skakespeare's Hamlet is a victim of strong feelings toward his mother, the queen. In the next forty years, many other critics adopted the new approach; some of the most influential included I. A. Richards, Kenneth Burke, and Edmund Wilson.

Several writers of poetry and fiction have also relied on Freudian models. For instance, Conrad Aiken, W. H. Auden, and Robert Graves applied Freudian insights when writing critical prose. Novelists William Faulkner, Henry James, James Joyce, D. H. Lawrence, Toni Morrison, and Marcel Proust have all written criticism influenced by Freud or novels that conceive of **character, conflict,** and creative writing itself in Freudian terms. The poet H. D. (Hilda Doolittle) was actually a patient of Freud's and provided an account of her analysis in her book *Tribute to Freud* (1956).

Probably because of Freud's characterization of the creative mind as "clamorous" if not ill, psychoanalytic criticism written before 1950 tended to psychoanalyze the individual author. Works were read — sometimes unconvincingly — as fantasies that allowed authors to indulge repressed wishes, to protect themselves from deep-seated anxieties, or both. For instance, in *The Life and Works of Edgar Allan Poe* (1933), Marie Bonaparte found Poe to be so fixated on his mother that his repressed longing emerges in his stories in **images** such as the white spot on a black cat's breast (said to represent mother's milk) in "The Black Cat." A later generation of psychoanalytic critics paused to analyze the characters in novels and plays before proceeding to their authors. Such critics still focused on psychoanalyzing authors, however, since they generally viewed characters (whether good or evil) as the authors' potential selves or projections of their psyches.

Some psychoanalytic critics have viewed literary works as analogous to dreams and have used Freudian analysis to help explain the nature of the minds that produced them. Such critics therefore employ Freud's dream-analysis procedures to reveal subconscious motivations. The literal surface of a work is sometimes called its "manifest content" and is treated as a Freudian analyst would treat a "manifest dream" or "dream story." Just as the analyst tries to figure out the "dream thought" behind the dream story —

that is, the latent or hidden content — so the psychoanalytic literary critic tries to expose the "latent content" of a work. Freud used the words *condensation* and *displacement* to explain two of the mental processes with which the mind disguises its wishes and fears in dream stories. Condensation involves the consolidation of several thoughts or persons into a single manifestation or image; displacement involves the projection of an anxiety, wish, or person onto the image of another. Psychoanalytic critics treat **metaphors** as dream condensations, **metonyms** as dream displacements. **Figurative language** is treated as something that evolves as the writer's conscious mind resists what the unconscious tells it to picture or describe. Daniel Weiss, for instance, defined a **symbol** — one type of figurative language — as "a meaningful concealment of truth as the truth promises to emerge as some frightening or forbidden idea" in *The Critic Agonistes: Psychology, Myth, and The Art of Fiction* (1985).

In "The 'Unconscious' of Literature" (1970), Norman Holland, an American literary critic trained in psychoanalysis, summed up the attitudes held by critics who would psychoanalyze authors, but without explicitly admitting that the author is being analyzed: "When one looks at a poem psychoanalytically, one considers it as though it were a dream or as though some ideal patient [were speaking] from the couch in iambic pentameter." One "looks for the general level or levels of fantasy associated with the language. By level I mean the familiar stages of childhood development — oral [when desires for nourishment and infantile sexual desires overlap], anal [when infants receive their primary pleasure from defecation], urethral [when urinary pleasures are the locus of sexual pleasure], phallic [when the penis or, in girls, some penis substitute is of primary interest], oedipal." Holland then analyzed Robert Frost's poem "Mending Wall" as an oral fantasy, not unique to its author, involving "breaking down the wall between the individuated self" and "some 'Other'" — including and perhaps especially the nursing mother.

While not denying the idea that the unconscious plays a role in creativity, psychoanalytic critics such as Holland began to emphasize the ways in which authors create works that appeal to readers' repressed wishes and fantasies. Consequently, they shifted their focus away from the author's psyche toward the psychology of the reader and the text. Holland's theories, which were concerned more with the reader than with the text, helped to establish **reader-response criticism.**

Freud's theoretical models have been challenged by other psychoanalytic theorists as well. Austrian psychologist Alfred Adler, for instance, argued that writers wrote out of inferiority complexes, rather than to express repressed wishes. Carl Jung, a Swiss analytic psychologist who broke with Freud over the latter's emphasis on sex, postulated a human **collective unconscious** that manifests itself in dreams, **myths,** and literature, an idea that influenced **archetypal** and **Jungian critics.** Scottish psychiatrist R. D. Laing's controversial writings about personality, repression, masks, and the double or "schizoid" self blurred the boundary between creative writing and psychoanalytic

discourse. Critics influenced by English psychoanalyst D. W. Winnicott, an *object-relations theorist,* have questioned the tendency to see reader / text as an either / or construct; instead, they have seen reader and text (or audience and play) in terms of a relationship taking place in what Winnicott called a "transitional" or "potential space" — a **site** in which **binary oppositions** like real/illusory and **objective / subjective** have little or no meaning. They see the transitional or potential reader / text (or audience / play) space as being *like* the space entered into by psychoanalyst and patient. They also see this space as similar to the space between mother and infant: a space characterized by trust in which categorizing terms such as *knowledge* and *feeling* mix and merge.

Although Freud saw the mother-son relationship in terms of the son and his repressed Oedipal complex, object-relations theorists have stressed the primacy of a still earlier relationship to the mother, one that (according to object-relations theorist Melanie Klein) dates back to the first days of infancy. And whereas Freud saw the analyst-patient relationship in terms of the patient and the repressed "truth" that the analyst could scientifically extract, object-relations theorists have viewed this relationship, like the relationship between mother and infant, as being dyadic — that is, dynamic in both directions. Consequently, they have sought to avoid the depersonalization of analysis. Contemporary literary critics who apply object-relations theory to texts go even further, refusing to categorize their interpretations as "truthful," given that interpretations are constructed from language, itself a transitional object.

Like Winnicottian critics, French psychoanalytic theorist Jacques Lacan focused on language and language-related issues. In so doing, Lacan did more than simply extend Freud's theory of dreams, literature, and their interpretation; he added the element of language to Freud's emphasis on psyche and **gender.** Lacan treated the unconscious as a language; consequently, he viewed the dream not as Freud did (that is, as a form and symptom of repression) but rather as a form of discourse. Thus we may study dreams psychoanalytically in order to learn about literature, even as we may study literature in order to learn more about the unconscious. For instance, Lacan employed a psychoanalytic technique to arrive at a reading of Poe's story "The Purloined Letter" (1845). In the process, he both used and significantly developed Freud's ideas about the Oedipal stage and complex.

Lacan pointed out that the pre-Oedipal stage, in which the child at first does not recognize its independence from its mother, is also a preverbal one in which the child communicates without the medium of language, or — if we insist on calling the child's communications "language" — in a language that can only be called *literal.* ("Coos" cannot be said to be figurative or symbolic.) While still in the pre-Oedipal stage, the child enters the mirror stage, in which it comes to view itself and its mother (and, later, other people) as independent selves. This involves projecting beyond the self and, by extension, constructing one's self (or "ego" or "I") as others view one — that is, as *another* (sometimes written as "an **Other**"). Such constructions, according to

Lacan, are just that: constructs, products, artifacts—fictions of coherence that hide what he called the "absence" or "lack" of being. The mirror stage, which Lacan associated with the **Imaginary order,** is fairly quickly succeeded by the Oedipal stage. As in Freud, this stage begins when the child, having come to view itself as self and the father and mother as separate selves, perceives gender and gender differences between its parents and between itself and one of its parents.

Lacan found significant the fact that the Oedipal stage roughly coincides with the entry of the child into language. For the linguistic order is essentially a figurative or **Symbolic order;** words are stand-ins or substitutes for things. Hence boys, who in the most critical period of their development have had to submit to what Lacan calls the "Law of the Father"—a law that prohibits direct desire for and communicative intimacy with the mother—enter more easily into the realm of language and the Symbolic order than do girls, who have never really had to renounce that which once seemed continuous with the self.

For Lacan, the father need not be present to trigger the Oedipal stage; nor does his **phallus** have to be seen to catalyze the boy's transition into the Symbolic order. Rather, Lacan argued, a child's recognition of its gender is tied up with a growing recognition of the system of names and naming, part of the larger system of substitutions we call language. A child has little doubt about who its mother is, but who is its father, and how would one know? The father's claim rests on the mother's word that he is the father; the father's relationship to the child is thus established through language and a system of marriage and kinship—names—that form the basis of rules for everything from paternity to property law.

Lacan's development of Freud's theories has influenced other contemporary critical approaches. First, his sexist-seeming association of maleness with the Symbolic order, together with his claim that women cannot enter easily into the order, prompted **feminist critics** to examine the relationship between language and gender, language and women's inequality. Some feminists have suggested that the social and political relationships between males and females will not change until language itself has been radically changed. Second, Lacan's theory proved of interest to **deconstructors** and other **poststructuralists,** in part because it holds that the ego (which Freud viewed as necessary and natural) is a product or construct. The ego-artifact, produced during the mirror stage, seems unified, consistent, and organized around a fixed center but is actually a fiction. The yoking together of fragments and destructively dissimilar elements takes its psychic toll, and it is the job of the Lacanian psychoanalyst to "deconstruct" the ego, to show its continuities to be **contradictions** as well.

Psychoanalytic theory has continued to permeate modern-day life, including popular culture. Sarah Boxer's *In the Floyd Archives: A Psychic Bestiary* (2001) at once pays homage to and sends up psychoanalysis, as in the cartoon on page 417 involving the duck Dr. (Sigmund?) Floyd and his unnamed wolf patient.

An homage to (and send-up of) psychoanalysis.

▶ **psychological criticism:** A type of **literary criticism** that emerged in the first half of the nineteenth century and that analyzes both literature in general and specific literary **texts** in terms of the creative psyche. Psychological critics generally focus on the **author** rather than the reader. Many analyze texts with an eye to their authors' personalities, using what they know about the author to understand the text. Others use literary works to reconstruct the author's personality or to get inside the author's head; **Geneva School** critics, for instance, sought to experience an author's consciousness — to become a better vessel for the author's **intentionality**, or awareness — and reflect it in their analyses. Many critics we would term psychological do not identify themselves as such, and many write in broadly untheorized terms even when using psychological techniques and methods of analysis. By contrast, practitioners of **psychoanalytic criticism,** the best-known form of psychological criticism, usually identify themselves specifically as psychoanalytic critics and structure their analyses within a relatively well-defined theoretical framework.

See **psychoanalytic criticism** for discussion of this type of psychological criticism.

▶ **psychological novel:** See **novel.**

▶ **pulp fiction:** See **science fiction.**

▶ **pun (paronomasia):** A **rhetorical figure** involving a play on words that capitalizes on a similarity in spelling and/or pronunciation between words that have different meanings. Alternatively, a pun may employ one word that has multiple meanings. Since the beginning of the eighteenth century, most puns have been used for comic effect.

EXAMPLES: William Shakespeare's *Romeo and Juliet* (1596) plays on the words *maiden, head,* and *maidenhead* (which in **Renaissance** times referred to virginity) in the following passage:

> Sampson: When I have fought with the men, I will be civil with the maids — I shall cut off their heads.
> Gregory: The heads of the maids?
> Sampson: Ay, the heads of the maids or their maidenheads. Take it in what sense thou wilt.

Dylan Thomas's poem "Do Not Go Gentle into That Good Night" (1952) puns on the word "grave" as a noun (a burial place) and an adjective (serious):

> Grave men, near death, who see with blinding sight
> Blind eyes could blaze like meteors and be gay,
> Rage, rage against the dying of the light.

The 1997 cloning of a sheep named Dolly spawned countless journalistic puns, from "When Will We See Ewe Again?" to "Will There Ever Be Another Ewe?" to "Dolly's Creators Find Wolf in Sheep's Cloning."

▶ **Puritan Interregnum:** See **Commonwealth Age (in English literature).**

▶ **purple patch:** A passage that stands out from the surrounding prose or verse by its ornate **style.** Purple patches are generally characterized by an abundance of literary devices, particularly **figurative language,** and the marked use of **rhythm.** From the Roman poet Horace's *Ars poetica (Art of Poetry)* (c. 20 B.C.), the phrase is usually derogatory, referring to an over-written passage, although it may be used descriptively.

EXAMPLES: Although full of red and green **images**, Macbeth's speech in Act 2, scene 2, of William Shakespeare's *Macbeth* (1606) is arguably a purple patch:

> Whence is that knocking?
> How is 't with me when every noise appalls me?
> What hands are here? Ha! They pluck out mine eyes!
> Will all great Neptune's ocean wash this blood
> Clean from my hand? No, this my hand will rather
> The multitudinous seas incarnadine°   *make red*
> Making the green one red.

The following passage from D. H. Lawrence's essay "Poetry of the Present" (1918) might also be considered a purple patch:

> Let me feel the mud and heavens in my lotus. Let me feel the heavy, silting, sucking mud, the spinning of sky winds. Let me feel them both in purest contact, the nakedness of sucking weight, nakedly passing radiance. Give me nothing fixed, set, static. Don't give me the infinite or the eternal: nothing of infinity, nothing of eternity. Give me the still, white seething, the incandescence and the coldness of the incarnate moment: the moment, the quick of all change and haste and opposition: the moment, the immediate present, the Now.

▶ **pyrrhic (dibrach):** A **metrical foot** in **poetry** that consists of two unstressed syllables (˘˘). Some critics do not consider the pyrrhic to be a true foot, which they maintain requires at least one **stressed** syllable. Others object on opposite grounds, arguing that the prevailing meter of a poem invariably renders one of the two syllables stronger than the other, thereby making that syllable stressed and the foot either **trochaic** or **iambic**. The pyrrhic is virtually nonexistent as the base, or predominant, foot of a poem, occurring instead as an occasional foot.

EXAMPLE: The thirty-eighth **sonnet** from Elizabeth Barrett Browning's *Sonnets from the Portuguese* (1850) begins with a pyrrhic foot:

> Ĭ hăve | bĕen próud | ănd sáid, | 'Mў lóve, | mў ówn.'

Q

▶ **quantitative verse:** See **meter.**

▶ **quatrain:** A **stanza** containing four lines. The term is also used, though less commonly, to refer to a four-line poem. No **rhyme scheme** need exist in a quatrain, but the following rhyme schemes are common: *abcb* (the **ballad stanza**), *abba*, and *abab*. The quatrain is the most common stanzaic form in English-language poetry.

EXAMPLES: Persian poet Omar Khayyám's *Rubáiyát* (c. eleventh–twelfth century), translated into English by Edward Fitzgerald and published in 1859 as the *Rubáiyát of Omar Khayyám,* contains about five hundred **epigrammatic** *rubáiyát,* or quatrains, rhyming *aaba.* Many of William Blake's *Songs of Innocence and of Experience* (1789–94) are composed in quatrains; "Infant Sorrow," for instance, has an *aabb* rhyme scheme and begins:

> My mother groan'd! my father wept.
> Into the dangerous world I leapt.
> Helpless, naked, piping loud;
> Like a fiend hid in a cloud.

Frances Cornford's humorous "Epitaph for a Reviewer" (1954) is a quatrain with an *abab* rhyme scheme:

> Whoso maintains that I am humbled now
> (Who wait the Awful Day) is still a liar;
> I hope to meet my Maker brow to brow
> And find my own the higher.

Josephine Miles often wrote in unrhyming quatrains. The following one is from her poem "Belief" (1955):

> Mother said to call her if the H-bomb exploded
> And I said I would, and it about did
> When Louis my brother robbed a service station
> And lay cursing on the oily cement in handcuffs.

▶ **queer theory:** A contemporary approach to literature and culture that assumes sexual identities are flexible, not fixed, and that critiques **gender** and **sexuality** as they are commonly conceived in Western culture. Queer theorists, like **gender critics,** take the **constructionist** position that gender is a social artifact, that masculinity and femininity are culturally constructed and determined rather than natural or innate. They further contend that sexuality, like gender, is socially constructed, arguing that the **binary opposition** heterosexual / homosexual is as much a product of culture and its institutions as the opposition masculinity / femininity. Indeed, they view sexuality as performative rather than normative, as a process involving signifying acts rather than personal identity.

The term *queer* — long used pejoratively to refer to homosexuals, especially male homosexuals — has been reclaimed and embraced by queer theorists, who apply it to both sexual relations and critical practice. With reference to sexual relations, *queer* encompasses any practice or behavior that a person engages in without reproductive aims and without regard for social or economic considerations. As a critical term, *queer* refers to writings that question generally accepted associations and identities involving sex, gender, and sexuality. As queer theorist Annamarie Jagose wrote in her book *Queer Theory* (1996), "queer is less an identity than a critique of identity." Moreover, queer theorists seek to keep the term *queer* flexible and resist the tendency to turn it into a "pride word" simply meaning homosexual. Seeking to avoid the normalization of *queer,* David Halperin asserted in *Saint Foucault: Towards a Gay Hagiography* (1995) that "Queer is by definition *whatever* is at odds with the normal, the legitimate, the dominant. *There is nothing in particular to which it necessarily refers."*

Queer theory is an outgrowth of gender criticism and, more specifically, of **gay and lesbian criticism.** In fact, the term *queer theory* is generally credited to gender theorist Teresa de Lauretis, who in 1992 edited a special issue of the journal *differences* entitled *Queer Theory: Lesbian and Gay Sexualities.* Queer theory diverges from gender criticism, however, in its emphasis on sexuality and in its broader insistence that the multifaceted and fluid character of identity negates efforts to categorize people on the basis of any one characteristic. It also diverges from gay and lesbian criticism in that its approach is more **theoretically** oriented than **text**-centered and insofar as some gay and lesbian critics advance an **essentialist** view of sexuality as biologically based. Moreover, unlike practitioners of gay and lesbian criticism, who tend to assume that sexual identity defines textual **representations,** queer theorists argue that representations define the contours of sexual identity. Like most gender, gay, and lesbian critics, however, queer theorists draw on the work of twentieth-century French philosophical historian Michel Foucault as well as that of three contemporary American theorists, poet-critic Adrienne Rich, gender critic Judith Butler, and gender critic Eve Kosofsky Sedgwick.

In his *Histoire de la sexualité* (*The History of Sexuality*) (1976), Foucault suggested that the Western conception of homosexuality was largely an invention of the nineteenth century — as was heterosexuality, its "normal" opposite. (Before that time, people spoke of "acts of sodomy" but not of homosexual *persons.*) By historicizing sexuality, Foucault made it possible to argue that all the categories and assumptions that operate when we think about sex, sexual difference, gender, and sexuality are the products of cultural **discourses** and thus social, rather than natural, artifacts.

Rich extended Foucault's theories in an essay entitled "Compulsory Heterosexuality and Lesbian Existence" (1983), in which she claimed that "heterosexuality [is] a beachhead of male dominance" that, "like motherhood, needs to be recognized and studied as a political institution." Subsequently, Butler argued in *Gender Trouble: Feminism and the Subversion of Identity* (1990) that sexual difference is also culturally produced and thus indistinguishable from gender. Sedgwick, in her book *Between Men: English Literature and Male Homosocial Desire* (1985), adapted **feminist criticism** to analyze relationships between men, between male **characters** in literary works, and, most importantly, between gender and sexuality. She later specifically critiqued the gender category "sexual orientation" in *Epistemology of the Closet* (1990), stating that "it is a rather amazing fact that, of the very many dimensions along which the genital activity of one person can be differentiated from another . . . , precisely one, the gender of object choice, emerged . . . and has remained . . . *the* dimension denoted by the now ubiquitous category of 'sexual orientation.'"

Building on these insights, queer theorists have questioned the "solidarity" and "pride" aspects of homosexual liberation movements. They argue, among other things, that lesbians and gays should not be grouped together given that their separate histories are defined by gender differences. For example, lesbians, as women, have been more affected than gay men by pay discrimination issues. Moreover, queer theorists have taken the position that liberation movements that are specifically gay or specifically lesbian ultimately encourage the development of new sets of gender-based norms that divide more than they unite.

Queer theorists are wary of identity politics, believing that identity is flexible and that categorization on the basis of a single shared characteristic is inappropriate. They question, for example, whether African American lesbians really have more in common with white, upper-middle-class lesbians than they do with heterosexual African American women. Queer theorists have also argued that identity politics tend to reinforce a web of heterosexual and heterosexist "norms." As such, some have even questioned whether it is wise to view "coming out" as the assumption of a "transformative identity."

Queer theorists, who favor coalition politics over what they view as exclusionary identity politics, seek to destabilize popular conceptions of normality and sexuality and to undermine the heterosexual / homosexual opposition. To this end, they focus attention on those who do not easily fit into the socially constructed categories of gender and sexuality (such as bisexuals, transvestites, transgendered persons, and transsexuals) and explore from a nonjudgmental perspective behaviors and practices that are often considered deviant (such as fetishes, autoeroticism, and sadomasochism). They ultimately aim to show that representations — whether in novels, movies, ads, or other media — are culturally dependent and fallible, not some sort of received or **objective** truth. By "queering the text" — by revealing within cultural representations the signs of what Rich called "compulsory heterosexuality" and by showing that meaning is the relative product of prevailing **discourses** — queer theorists seek to show that the truly "queer" thing is how quick we are to label, categorize, and judge.

The tenets of queer theory are reflected in numerous works of **literary** and **cultural criticism.** Early examples include Thomas Yingling's *Hart Crane and the Homosexual Text* (1990), Jonathan Goldberg's *Sodometries* (1992), and Michael Moon's *Disseminating Whitman* (1993). Other critics whose analyses are informed by queer theory include Lauren Berlant, Richard Bozorth, Joseph Bristow, Christopher Craft, Lisa Duggan, Elizabeth Freeman, Christopher Lane, Jeff Nunokawa, and Michael Warner. Berlant and Freeman's "Queer Nationality," which appeared in Berlant's collection *The Queen of America Goes to Washington City: Essays on Sex and Censorship* (1997), discussed the ways in which a national network of gay and lesbian affinity groups have sought to use everything from local rituals to mass-culture spectacles to alter America's self-perception as a heterosexual nation. Bozorth's book *Auden's Games of Knowledge: Poetry and the Meanings of Homosexuality* (2001) argued that Auden's poetry addresses and reflects the psychological and political meanings of same-sex desire. Some queer theorists have even suggested that the approach lends itself to the "queering" of other socially constructed categories. As Mimi Nguyen wrote in her essay "Why Queer Theory?" (1999): "It's impossible ... to imagine that 'queer' only skews gender and sexuality, and not race or class or nation, as if we might line up our social categories like cans in a cupboard."

See also **gay and lesbian criticism, gender criticism.**

▶ **quest romance:** See **romance.**

R

▶ **race (and literary studies):** A term commonly used to classify or distinguish human populations on the basis of hereditary, observable physical characteristics, particularly skin color, but now primarily considered a social or cultural construct by anthropologists, scientists, scholars, and **literary critics.** Although physical variation does exist across human populations, more variation generally exists within a given race than, on average, between racial groups. Furthermore, our conception of race often involves cultural rather than biological differences and characteristics ranging from diet to music to dress to religion. Finally, over the tens of thousands of years of human history, migration and the subsequent biological mixing of races have made racial categorization an extremely arbitrary business. For instance, states in the United States once used very different racial percentages (ratios of black-to-white ancestry, for example) in determining the racial identity of citizens for census or other purposes. An even more startling example of race as a social construct is the fact that immigrants from the Indian subcontinent are said to be "black" in Great Britain but not in North America, where the term is reserved for people of African descent.

The cultural construction of race commonly involves the practice of stereotyping as biologically "natural" or "typical" what are in fact the cultural characteristics — eating habits, attitudes toward time, and so on — of persons viewed as outside of, and therefore as **Other** by, an **ideologically** dominant group. Thus, it is hardly surprising that the constructs or fictions of race respond to, reinforce, and at some level are responsible for racism — the destructive devaluation of one cultural group by another based on supposed (but in fact nonexistent or insignificant) differences.

Literary critics, particularly those practicing **cultural criticism,** have shown that race, the social and cultural construction of race, and racism are important to the study of literature. Literary **texts,** whether written by **authors** in the racial majority or minority, attest to and may effectively critique the racial and racist attitudes prevalent in a given culture at a given time. Furthermore, literature is among the most powerful forms of **discourse** in which race is constructed and racial or racist attitudes are expressed and perpetuated. Readers also bring their own racial and racist attitudes to any work, which necessarily affect their interpretation of the text.

Finally, because racial constructs result in very different experiences for the various groups kept distinct by racial stereotyping, race — like **class** and **gender** — must be taken into account when we speak or write about literary texts, especially when discussing texts produced by writers representing different racial and cultural groups. One can hardly imagine a race-blind critical comparison of Frederick Douglass's *Narrative of the Life of Frederick Douglass, An American Slave, Written by Himself* (1845) and another famous nineteenth-century American text that deals with race and racism, Mark Twain's *Adventures of Huckleberry Finn* (1884). With regard to more recent texts, African American scholar and critic Henry Louis Gates has pointed out that black writers until recently have had to fuse black **linguistic** and cultural **conventions** and traditions with those of the white Western literary **canon** in order to reach a wide audience and avoid marginalization.

▶ **reader-oriented criticism:** See **reader-response criticism.**

▶ **reader-reception criticism:** See **reader-response criticism.**

▶ **reader-response criticism:** Generally said to have emerged in the United States in the 1970s, a type of **literary criticism** that focuses on reading as an active process and on the diversity of readers' responses to literary works. Reader-response critics raise **theoretical** questions about whether our responses to a work are the same as its meaning(s), whether a work can have as many meanings as we have responses to it, and whether some responses are more valid than others. They also provide us with models that aid our understanding of **texts** and the reading process.

Reader-response critics share not only questions but also goals and strategies. Basic goals include showing that a work gives readers something to do and describing what the reader does by way of response. Strategies, or "moves," as Steven Mailloux called them in his essay "Learning to Read: Interpretation and Reader-Response Criticism" (1979), include: (1) citing direct references to reading in the text being analyzed in order to justify the focus on reading and show that the world of the text is continuous with the reader's world; (2) showing how other nonreading situations in the text nonetheless mirror the reader's situation; and (3) demonstrating that the reader's response is analogous to the story's **action** or **conflict.**

Noted critics whose thinking anticipated reader-response criticism include I. A. Richards and Louise M. Rosenblatt. Richards, an English literary critic usually associated with **formalism,** an ostensibly **objective,** text-centered approach to literature concerned with form rather than content, nevertheless argued in *Practical Criticism* (1929) that readers' feelings and experiences provide a kind of reality check, a way of testing the authenticity of emotions and events represented in literary works. A decade later, Rosenblatt, an American literary critic, began developing a theory of reading that blurred the boundary between reader and text, subject and object, in her seminal book *Literature as Exploration* (1938). She subsequently summarized her position in an essay entitled "Toward a Transactional Theory of Reading" (1969): "a poem is what the reader lives through under the guidance of the text and experiences as relevant to the text." Recognizing that many critics — particularly formalists, who spoke of "the poem itself" and "the concrete work of art" — would reject this definition, she wrote: "The idea that a *poem* presupposes a *reader* actively involved with a *text* is particularly shocking to those seeking to emphasize the objectivity of their interpretations." Indeed, formalist **New Critics** William K. Wimsatt and Monroe C. Beardsley used the term **affective fallacy** to define as erroneous the very idea that a reader's response is relevant to the meaning of a literary work.

Stanley Fish, whose early work is seen by some as marking the true beginning of contemporary reader-response criticism, also took issue with the tenets of formalism. In "Literature in the Reader: Affective Stylistics" (1970), he argued that any school of criticism that sees a literary work as an object, claiming to describe what it is and never what it does, misconstrues the very essence of literature and reading. He suggested that literature exists and signifies when it is read; that its force is an affective force; and that reading is a temporal process, not a spatial one, contrary to the formalist practice of surveying the literary work as if it were an object spread out before them. Formalists might find elegant patterns in the texts they examined, but they failed to consider that the work appears very different to a reader in the act of reading, turning the pages and being moved, or affected, by each word.

Emphasis on how reading affects readers (and how they respond) has pervaded the work of most, if not all, reader-response critics. Moreover, reader-response critics are at least as interested in fragmentary, inconclusive, and even unfinished texts as in polished, unified ones, for it is the reader's struggle to make sense of a challenging work that reader-response critics seek to describe. For instance, in *An Essay on Shakespeare's Sonnets* (1969), Stephen Booth argued that "a Shakespeare sonnet is organized in a multitude of different coexistent and conflicting patterns" and analyzed the "reading experiences that proceed from the multiplicity of organizations in which, over the course of fourteen lines, the reader's mind participates."

German critic Wolfgang Iser also addressed the reader's struggle in his books *The Implied Reader: Patterns of Communication in Prose Fiction from Bunyan to Beckett* (1974) and *The Act of Reading: A Theory of Aesthetic Response* (1976). Iser argued that texts contain **gaps** (or *blanks*) that powerfully affect the reader, who must explain them, bridge them, and envision aspects that aren't *in* the text but that the text incites. As Iser put it in *The Implied Reader,* the "unwritten aspects" of a story "draw the reader into the action" and "lead him to shade in the many outlines suggested by the given situations."

In *Self-Consuming Artifacts: The Experience of Seventeenth-Century Literature* (1972), Fish revealed his preference for literature that makes readers work at making meaning. He contrasted two kinds of literary presentation, using the phrase *rhetorical presentation* to describe works that reflect and reinforce opinions that readers already hold, and *dialectical presentation* to refer to works that prod and provoke, challenging readers to discover truths on their own. Instead of offering a single, sustained argument, a dialectical text, or self-consuming artifact, may contain contradictory units. Rather than advancing a contorted explanation to render the units coherent, the reader-response critic describes how the reader deals with the sudden twists that characterize the dialectical text. Readers may, for instance, refer to earlier passages and see them in an entirely new light.

With the redefinition of literature as something that only exists meaningfully in the mind of the reader, with the redefinition of the literary work as a catalyst of mental events, came a concurrent redefinition of the reader. No longer was the reader the passive recipient of the ideas that an **author** plants in a text. "The reader is *active*," Rosenblatt insisted in her "Transactional Theory" essay. Fish made the same point in "Literature in the Reader": "reading is . . . something *you do*." Iser, in focusing critical interest on the gaps in texts, on what is not expressed, similarly redefined the reader as an active maker of meaning.

Elaborating on the definition of the reader, Fish argued in *Self-Consuming Artifacts* that the "informed reader" (or "the *intended* reader") is someone "sufficiently experienced as a reader to have internalized the properties of literary discourses, including everything from the most local of devices (figures of speech, etc.) to whole genres." In *The Implied Reader* (1974), Wayne Booth distinguished between the real reader and the **implied reader,** defining the latter as a "construct" of the text who "embodies all those predispositions necessary for a literary work to exercise its effect." Jonathan Culler, in *Structuralist Poetics* (1975), described the educated or "competent" reader, by which he meant the competent reader of "literature," a reader who employs the **codes** and **conventions** needed to understand the types of poems and novels studied in academia.

Subsequently, other reader-response critics pointed out that definitions of literary competence inevitably reflect the prevailing **ideology,** the beliefs of socially dominant groups and institutions. Mailloux, for instance, noted in "The Turns of Reader-Response Criticism" (1990) that the competence Culler described "was embedded within larger formations and traversed by political ideologies extending beyond the academy." He also suggested that hindsight revealed a surprising degree of similarity between **close reading** and Fish's practice of analyzing the **affective stylistics** of a text, indeed that the "reader talk of . . . Iser and Fish enabled the continuation of the formalist practice of close reading."

As the title of Mailloux's essay indicates, reader-response criticism (once commonly referred to as the "School of Fish") has morphed and diversified. Since the mid-1970s, with the rise of other critical approaches whose practitioners proved less interested in close reading than in the way literature represents, reproduces, and resists prevailing ideologies concerning **class, race, gender,** and **sexuality,** reader-response criticism has taken on a variety of new forms, some of which truly are incommensurate with formalism, with its considerable respect for the integrity and power of the text. For instance, **subjectivists** like David Bleich, Norman Holland, and Robert Crosman have viewed the reader's response not as one "guided" by the text but rather as one motivated by deep-seated, personal, psychological needs. As Holland put it, readers find their own "identity theme" in texts; in "UNITY IDENTITY TEXT SELF" (1975), he argued that as readers we use "the literary work to symbolize and finally to replicate ourselves. We work out through the text our own characteristic patterns of desire."

Meanwhile, Fish, confronted with the question of why different readers tend to read the same works in the same way, developed the concept of **interpretive communities.** In "Interpreting the Variorum" (1976), he asserted that multiple and diverse reading groups exist within any large population and that members of particular interpretive communities tend to share the same reading strategies, which "exist prior to the act of reading and therefore determine the shape of what is read." In developing this model, Fish shifted his focus away from the individual reader (and thus away from affective stylistics) and became something of a social, **structuralist** reader-response critic.

Today, reader-response criticism is often referred to as *reader-oriented criticism.* Rather than focusing on the transaction between the text and its individual reader, reader-oriented critics tend to investigate reading communities, as Janet Radway did in *Reading the Romance* (1984), her study of female readers of romance paperbacks. Reader-oriented critics also study the changing reception of literary works across time, as Mailloux did in his **pragmatic** readings of American literature in *Interpretive Conventions* (1982) and *Rhetorical Power* (1989). Some critics, including Mailloux and Jane Tompkins, have thus come to identify themselves as practitioners of *reader-reception criticism.*

An important catalyst of this gradual change and of the development of reception criticism was the **reception theory** of German critic Hans Robert Jauss. Rather than focusing on the implied, informed, or intended reader, Jauss examined actual past readers. In "Literary History as a Challenge to Literary Theory" (1967), he explored the responses of readers over time to a given literary work; in *Toward an Aesthetics of Reception* (1982), he argued that the reception of a work or author depends upon the reading public's "horizons of expectations."

Some reader-oriented **feminist critics,** such as Judith Fetterley, Patrocinio Schweickart, and Monique Wittig, have challenged the reader to become what Fetterley called "the resisting reader" in her eponymously titled 1978 book. Arguing that literature written by men tends to "immasculate" women, they adopted strategies of reading that involve substituting masculine for feminine pronouns and male for female characters in order to expose the sexism inscribed in **patriarchal** texts. Other feminists, such as Nancy K. Miller in *Subject to Change* (1988), suggested that there may be **essential** differences between the way women and men read and write.

That suggestion, however, prompted considerable controversy. A number of **gender critics** whose work is oriented toward readers and reading acknowledge that there is such a thing as reading or writing "like a woman" (or man) but also agree with Peggy Kamuf's argument in "Writing Like a Woman" (1980) that such forms of reading and writing, like gender itself, are cultural rather than natural **constructs. Gay and lesbian critics,** such as

Wayne Koestenbaum, argue that sexuality has also been socially constructed and that there is a homosexual way of reading.

Many students of contemporary critical practice would say that feminist, gender, gay, and lesbian theory have engulfed reader-oriented theory. Others, like Elizabeth Freund, have suggested that **deconstruction** has taken over the reader-oriented approach. Several critics, however, including Mailloux and Peter Rabinowitz, still define their approach as primarily reader-oriented, although their work has also been heavily influenced by **the new historicism** and **cultural criticism.**

In *Before Reading: Narrative Conventions and the Politics of Interpretation* (1987), Rabinowitz set forth four conventions or rules of reading — rules identifying which parts of a **narrative** are important, which details have a reliable secondary or special meaning, which fit into which familiar patterns, and how stories fit together as a whole. Analyzing various critical misreadings and misjudgments, he argued that politics governs the way in which those rules are applied and broken. In subsequent critical essays, Rabinowitz focused on societal assumptions about gender, race, and class, arguing that they, too, determine the way in which artistic works are perceived and evaluated. Mailloux, who called his approach "rhetorical reception theory" or "rhetorical hermeneutics," likewise described the political contexts of (mis)interpretation. In "Misreading as a Historical Act" (1993), for example, he examined a mid-nineteenth-century review by protofeminist Margaret Fuller of the *Narrative of the Life of Frederick Douglass, An American Slave, Written by Himself* (1845) — a review that seems to be a misreading until it is situated "within the cultural conversation of the 'Bible politics' of 1845." Emphasizing that reading is contingent upon history, affected by politics, and to a great extent defined and conditioned by the institutions in which texts are regularly interpreted, Mailloux reminds us that all reading is culturally situated and likely to seem like misreading someday.

▶ **Real, the:** Along with the **Imaginary** and **Symbolic orders,** one of the three orders of **subjectivity** according to twentieth-century French **psychoanalytic** theorist and critic Jacques Lacan. The Real is the intractable and substantial world that resists and exceeds interpretation. The Real cannot be imagined, **symbolized,** or known directly; it constantly eludes our efforts to name it. Death, gravity, and the physicality of objects are examples of the Real, but the words signifying these realities ultimately and utterly fail to explain or make sense of their apparent inevitability. Because the Real cannot be known, imagined, symbolized, or named, it challenges both the Imaginary and Symbolic orders. The Real is fundamentally **Other,** the mark of the divide between conscious and unconscious, and is signaled in language by **gaps,** slips, speechlessness, and the sense of the uncanny. The Real is not what we call "reality." It is the stumbling block of the Imaginary, which thinks it can "imagine" anything (including the Real), and of the Symbolic, which tries to bring the Real under its laws. The Real is frightening; we try to tame it with the law of order, language, and differentiation — that is, with the law of the **phallus,** a culturally prevalent law of referentiality that takes the male sign as its ordering principle and determines an individual's entrance into the Symbolic — and call it "reality." The Real, however, exposes the "phallacy" of the law of the phallus, revealing both the Symbolic order's reliance on the male **sign** as a referent and demonstrating the inappropriateness of such reliance in a world where meaning and comprehension rest in gaps and on the margins of what we perceive. The concept of the Real — like Lacan's schema and terminology more generally — has proven useful to psychoanalytic critics in their analyses of language, literature, and the laws governing expression and interpretation.

See also **Imaginary order, Symbolic order.**

▶ **realism:** (1) Broadly speaking, a term that can be applied to the accurate depiction in any literary work of the everyday life of a place or period. When the term *realistic* is applied to works that predate the nineteenth century, however, it usually refers more specifically to a writer's accuracy in portraying the speech and behavior of a **character** or characters from a low socioeconomic **class.** (2) A literary movement that developed in the latter half of the nineteenth century in America, England, and France in reaction to the excesses of **romanticism.** Writers associated with this movement tried to "write reality."

Realism differs from **romanticism** particularly in its emphasis on an **objective** presentation of details and events rather than a **subjective** concentration on personal feelings, perceptions, and imaginings of various characters. Realists also reject the idealized presentations, imaginative and exotic **settings,** and improbable **plot** twists characteristic of the **romance.** Realists often rely heavily on **local color,** seeking to portray faithfully the customs, speech, dress, and living and working conditions of their chosen locale. Realists also stress **characterization** as a critical (if not *the* critical) element of a literary work.

Realism should also be distinguished from **naturalism.** Although naturalists' emphasis on **concrete** details and the objective depiction of everyday life renders their fiction "realistic," naturalists differ from realists in their deterministic outlook. Naturalists view all individuals as being at the mercy of biological and socioeconomic forces, whereas realists hold that humans have a certain degree of free will that they can exercise to affect their situations.

Realists (especially nineteenth-century realists) have tended to espouse democracy and pragmatism. They have implicitly expressed these beliefs by choosing to depict lower- and middle-class subjects and characters more often than the noble ones associated with **classicism** or the fanciful ones characteristic of romanticism. Many early American realists depicted everyday life and the common person with a certain affection and respect; after the Civil War, however, a disillusioned strain developed in realistic fiction that portrayed ordinary men and women as having their share of petty vices.

Many realists, American and otherwise, have also embraced what might be termed *psychological realism* as they have turned from emphasizing the accuracy of external detail to reporting internal detail, the thought processes of the human mind or consciousness. Some authors, such as Virginia Woolf, have taken the reporting of internal detail to its extreme manifestation, using **stream-of-consciousness narration** to convey to the reader the jumble of thoughts and sensory impressions that flows unremittingly through the human mind.

Variants of realism that developed in the twentieth century include **magic realism** and **socialist realism.** Magic realists mix realistic and **fantastic** elements; in fact, magic realists arguably use such hallmarks of realism as its emphasis on detail to make their presentations of the dreamlike, **mythic,** or otherwise fantastic more plausible to readers. Socialist realists emphasized class struggle as the catalyst for historical change, employing techniques associated with nineteenth-century realism to depict the lives of average working-class citizens. In the 1930s, however, when socialist realism became the official form of the Soviet Union, it ceased to be a means of connecting with the masses and instead became chiefly a means of propagating doctrinally "correct" thinking.

Noted realists include Jane Austen, Honoré de Balzac, George Eliot, Gustave Flaubert, William Dean Howells, Henrik Ibsen, Henry James, Mark Twain, and Edith Wharton. Certain poems by Robert Browning, Walt Whitman, and Carl Sandburg can be referred to as realistic insofar as they capture real people, places, or situations by using an almost prosaic style. Pre-nineteenth-century writers who are generally realistic in their outlooks and depictions of life include Geoffrey Chaucer, William Shakespeare, and Henry Fielding.

▶ **realistic novel:** A type of **novel** that depicts **characters, settings,** and events in accordance with reality or, at least, in accordance with reality as most readers perceive it. Realistic novelists seek to write fictional **narratives** that present a plausible world. To achieve this goal, they typically include a variety of **concrete** details meant to ground their story lines in human experience.

Realistic novelists emphasize **characterization.** They typically present well-developed, **round characters** whose experiences and interactions with other characters could occur in real life and situate these characters in a specific cultural group, locale, and historical era. Perhaps most importantly, they establish convincing **motivation** for the thoughts, emotions, and actions of the characters as well as for the turns and twists of the **plot.** A realistic novel might depict the daily drudgery of a working-class girl forced to labor twelve hours a day in an English garment factory to help support her family, or it might depict the plush and lavish life of the Hungarian count who owns the factory and spends his days hosting society luncheons or playing croquet on the well-tended lawns of his English estate. Whichever scenario a realistic writer adopts, he or she will strive to plausibly present the characters, activity, and milieu therein.

The realistic novel is most often contrasted with the **romance**, which eschews realistic **verisimilitude**. Nineteenth-century **realism**, in particular, developed largely in reaction to the idealized, **conventional** subjects, **themes**, and modes of **representation** associated with **romanticism**.

EXAMPLES: George Eliot's *The Mill on the Floss* (1860), Henry James's *The Portrait of a Lady* (1881), John Steinbeck's *Tortilla Flat* (1935). More recent examples of the realistic novel include John Fowles's *Daniel Martin* (1977) and Joyce Carol Oates's *Because It Is Bitter, and Because It Is My Heart* (1990). Other contemporary authors who draw on the tradition of the realistic novel include Margaret Drabble and Naguib Mahfouz.

▶ **Realistic Period (in American literature):** A period in American literary history spanning the years 1865 through 1900. In the wake of the devastation of the Civil War, forces including capitalist industrialization; Reconstruction; northern urbanization; and rapid advances in communications, science, and transportation contributed to a great change in American literature as well as American society and politics. The work of many writers continued to exhibit a **romantic** strain throughout much of this period, but **realism** dominated the national literary scene by the epoch's end. Nevertheless, much of the work of the Realistic Period drew on both the romantic and realistic traditions. So-called romantic realists, for instance, essentially presented their subject matter accurately but wrote only about subject matter that was pleasant or positive.

Unlike romantic writers, who emphasized emotion, **imagination**, and individuality, realists aimed to present life as it really is, in its nobility as well as its banality. Although realistic authors sought to represent their subject matter in an unidealized, **unsentimentalized** way, they did not set out to emphasize the negative, the distorted, or the ugly. Rather, they sought to create truthful portraits, unlike **naturalistic** writers who depicted life with a decidedly deterministic, pessimistic bent. Novelist William Dean Howells outlined the tenets of realism in a book entitled *Criticism and Fiction* (1891).

Some realistic poets, such as Walt Whitman and Emily Dickinson, began writing during the **Romantic Period**. Others, such as Stephen Crane, Sidney Lanier, and Edwin Arlington Robinson, wrote entirely during the Realistic Period. Crane's poems, written in **free verse**, anticipate the twentieth-century experiments of Ezra Pound and the **Imagists**. Lanier experimented with **versification** by introducing musical **meter**; he is one of many writers of the Realistic Period whose romantic leanings make his work hard to categorize strictly.

The Realistic Period was also a high water mark for the novel; aside from Howells, authors include Crane, Charles W. Chesnutt, Henry James, and Mark Twain. Twain, who began his career as a Western humorist, wrote a number of popular novels, such as *Adventures of Tom Sawyer*

(1876) and *Adventures of Huckleberry Finn* (1884). He also worked with **satire,** however, disguising his merciless and cynical criticism under the guise of **historical romance** in works such as *A Connecticut Yankee in King Arthur's Court* (1889). Crane, perhaps best known for his novel *The Red Badge of Courage* (1895), pioneered American **naturalism,** a literary movement that represented people in a deterministic and generally pessimistic light as products of heredity and environment, in works such as *Maggie: A Girl of the Streets* (1893).

Local color literature, which emphasizes the **setting,** customs, **dialects,** and other features peculiar to a given region of the country, also developed and thrived during the Realistic Period. Local color writers include Bret Harte, Sarah Orne Jewett, and Kate Chopin, best known for her novel *The Awakening* (1899).

Other prose writing of the Realistic Period includes the **historical novel,** works published in mass-circulation magazines, **short stories,** and **utopian literature.** Mark Twain's "The Celebrated Jumping Frog of Calaveras County" (1867) is one of the best-known short stories in American literature. Edward Bellamy's *Looking Backward: 2000–1887* (1888) is a utopian novel. (Although the appearance of utopian **texts** during an age of realism may seem **paradoxical,** the authors of such works used some of the strategies of realism to make their depictions of the future convincing and credible.)

See **realism.**

▶ **reception theory:** A type of **reader-response criticism** that examines the reception of a literary work — namely, how that work has been viewed by readers — since its initial publication. German theorist Hans Robert Jauss is the key figure associated with reception theory. Jauss used the term **aesthetic distance** to describe the difference between how a work was viewed when it was originally published and how that same work is viewed today. In his essay "Literary History as a Challenge to Literary Theory" (1967), he added a new twist to traditional reader-response criticism by exploring the diverse responses of readers over time to a given literary work; traditional reader-response critics tended to probe the individual contemporary reader's response. Jauss later elaborated on this new approach in his book *Aesthetic Experience and Literary Hermeneutics* (1977).

Jauss concurred with other reader-response critics in rejecting the theory that a single, correct meaning can be derived from any given **text,** noting that a text can be rationally interpreted in numerous ways. He argued that readers' responses are conditioned or even determined by the confluence and interplay of their "horizon of expectations" and textual elements that confirm or challenge those expectations. Jauss readily conceded that individual readers (with all of their idiosyncratic responses) contribute to the production of meaning in a text, but also noted that the elements of the text itself serve to limit and shape readers' interpretations. He thus struck a balance between the contribution of the reader and that of the text in establishing meaning.

Unlike some traditional reader-response critics, however, Jauss emphasized that readers' expectations change with the passage of time. These changing expectations, coupled with knowledge of (and reaction to) past readers' responses, combine to produce for each literary work a critical "tradition" that is continuously enriched and modified as new generations of readers emphasize different points or see old ones in a new light. Ultimately, Jauss proposed the existence of an active and evolving **dialogue** between texts and the continuous flow of readers over the course of time.

▶ **refrain:** A phrase, line, or lines that recur(s) throughout a **poem** or song. The refrain may vary slightly — for instance, through **incremental repetition** — but is generally exactly the same. It usually occurs at the end of a **stanza** or section but need not do so. When a refrain is intended to be repeated or sung by a group of people, it is called a **chorus.**

EXAMPLES: Every stanza but the last in Alfred, Lord Tennyson's "Mariana" (1830) concludes with the following two-line refrain:

> She said, "I am aweary, aweary,
> I would that I were dead."

The last stanza ends with an incremental repetition in the second line of the refrain: " 'O God, that I were dead!' "

The refrain of Robert Burns's poem "Auld Lang Syne" (1896) is an entire stanza, a chorus meant to be repeated after every subsequent stanza:

> For auld lang syne, my dear,
> For auld lang syne,
> We'll take a cup o' kindness yet,
> For auld lang syne.

The four-line chorus from the popular song "It's a Small World" (1963) by Richard and Robert Sherman **anaphoristically** repeats the song title three times. The theme song of the TV show *Friends* (1994–2004) — The Rembrandts' "I'll Be There for You" (1994) — similarly repeats the title in the refrain.

▶ **regular ode:** See **Pindaric ode.**

▶ **Renaissance:** French for "rebirth," a term referring to a transformation of Western culture that followed the **Medieval Period,** the so-called Dark Ages of European history. A transitional period, bridging the **Middle Ages** and the beginnings of the modern world, the Renaissance began in fourteenth-century Italy and spread throughout Europe during the fifteenth century. Most scholars agree that the Renaissance ended during the seventeenth century; in England, the ensuing **Neoclassical Period** is often said to have begun in 1660, with the **Restoration** of the monarchy.

The changes associated with the Renaissance were both sweeping and revolutionary, transcending national boundaries within Europe as well as altering the way in which life was lived and understood at least as profoundly as life has been altered in modern times by the development of nuclear physics and the invention of the computer. The most important of these changes was a **paradigm** shift from a predominantly theocentric, Christian perspective to an increasingly secular, anthropocentric one, as humankind rather than God became the center of human interest. Other significant changes included: a cosmological revolution during which the Ptolemaic theory of an earth-centered universe, a theory dating from the second century A.D., was abandoned in favor of the Copernican understanding that the earth revolves around the sun; a dramatic schism within Western Christendom that led to the Reformation and the rise of Protestantism; the discovery of the so-called New World; the emergence of nationalism and international commerce as we now know them; the rise of an imperialism that would culminate with Europe dominating the globe in the nineteenth century; and German printer Johann Gutenberg's invention of the printing press, whose movable type greatly facilitated book production and thus made possible an unprecedented explosion of communication, knowledge, and scholarship.

Beginning with the Italian poet Petrarch (Francesco Petrarca, 1304–74), **classical** scholars (later referred to as humanists) revitalized interest in the pagan **authors** and **texts** of ancient Greece and Rome. By 1500, the works of the Greek philosophers Plato and Aristotle had been translated; within decades, Aristotle's ideas about biology, like Plato's philosophies of politics and love, were published in book form. Plato's writings about love in the *Symposium* (c. 360 B.C.), together with the **Platonic love** philosophies developed by subsequent **Neoplatonist** Roman philosophers such as Plotinus, gave rise to a Renaissance Neoplatonism that colored a variety of works, including Baldassare Castiglione's *Il cortegiano* (*The Courtier*) (1528), an early and extremely influential *courtesy book*. Courtesy books — published first in Italy, then in France, and finally in England — set forth rules governing cultivated behavior in royal and noble courts as well as the relationships between aristocratic men and women. They also extolled the accomplished, well-rounded gentleman, counseling aspiring courtiers to cultivate a wide range of artistic, athletic, conversational, intellectual, and romantic capabilities.

The focus on the developing individual evident in courtesy books was also characteristic of Renaissance art and religious **discourse**. For instance, in art, there was more variation among the Madonnas depicted in Renaissance paintings than among their **medieval** counterparts. In his book *Renaissance Self-Fashioning: From More to Shakespeare* (1980), **new historicist** Stephen Greenblatt proposed a provocative corollary to the view that Renaissance art tended to represent individuals, not types, suggesting that during the Renaissance the human individual came to be seen *as* a work of art. In religion, the Reformation — which was instigated by German monk

Martin Luther in 1517 as an effort to reform the Roman Catholic Church and ended in schism — also elevated the individual. Central to the Reformation was the idea that although ecclesiastical intermediaries may provide comfort and guidance, they are neither necessary nor sufficient for an individual's salvation. Protestant reformers insisted that believers were their own priests, capable of a direct personal relationship with God; consequently, they were empowered to confess their own sins, read scripture on their own, and interpret God's word in light of their own experience.

As exemplified by the Reformation's challenge to the authority of the Church in Rome, the spirit of questioning was as characteristic of the Renaissance as was the focus on the individual. The tendency to question received "truth" also lay behind the Copernican revolution in astronomy and, more broadly, led to a growing skepticism regarding supernatural and occult explanations for everyday occurrences and behaviors. Increasingly, scientists and nonscientists alike argued that all of known reality could be explained in accordance with natural laws, some of which were not yet known or understood but all of which were potentially knowable and provable.

As a result of this new attitude and outlook — and following famous early experiments by scientists such as Nicolaus Cusanus, a fifteenth-century German cardinal generally credited with proving that air has weight by showing that plants derive some of their own weight from the atmosphere — the Renaissance became an age of scientific testing. The printing press, which had itself developed through scientific advances, in turn advanced science by enabling the publication of experimental results. Over time, scientific discourse entered the language of literature; in his **epic** *Paradise Lost* (1667), the Puritan poet John Milton acknowledged recent scientific discoveries and theories even as he questioned the ultimate wisdom of the scientific ambition to know and understand everything.

Other artists of the Renaissance welcomed scientific advances and, more important, the spirit of scientific discovery, seen as akin to the artistic spirit of the age. Indeed, the Renaissance was a period in which the arts and sciences developed in tandem, reinforcing one another. (By contrast, since the rise of **romanticism** in the late eighteenth century, the arts have tended to critique scientific and technological approaches to life.) Particularly important in establishing this link was Italian artist and scientist Leonardo da Vinci, who introduced the idea that visual representations should reflect correct geometric perspective. Significantly, Leonardo's emphasis on accurate perspective inspired more careful study of living and nonliving things, which in turn led to new levels of geometric sophistication that laid the groundwork for technological illustration and design as we now know them. Scholars have argued, for instance, that the design and development of the internal combustion engine would have been impossible without Leonardo's emphasis on perspective. Meanwhile, perspective in the visual arts allowed for the development of **realistic** representation, which remained a generally accepted **convention** of artistic representation until the rise of **modernism** in the twentieth century. Although art remained heavily dependent upon Church funding, artists were increasingly freed of religious restraints as secular painting — especially portraiture — became more acceptable and even embraced.

As the example of Leonardo suggests, the Renaissance — with its emphasis on the individual and discovery — produced a number of individual geniuses, "Renaissance men" who had a profound impact not only on the arts and sciences but also on how humanity conceived of itself, its capabilities, and its place in the universe. Nicolaus Copernicus (1473–1543), whose treatise *De revolutionibus orbium coelestium* (*On the Revolutions of the Celestial Spheres*) (1543) revolutionized astronomy, was also a cleric, doctor, mathematician, and diplomat. Michelangelo Buonarroti (1475–1564), perhaps the best-known painter of the Renaissance, was also an architect, engineer, poet, and sculptor whose impact on sculpture is now generally recognized as being even greater than his influence on painting. Raphael (1483–1520), a student of Michelangelo's, not only produced what many art critics have described as the world's greatest painting (the Sistine Madonna) but also served as chief architect of Saint Peter's Church in Rome. Galileo Galilei (1564–1642), imprisoned by the Church for supporting the Copernican view that the earth revolves around the sun, was a painter, writer, musician, and scientist who is now considered the founder of modern experimental science due to his work in astronomy and physics. His ideas paved the way for German mathematician and astronomer Johannes Kepler (1571–1630), who discovered the laws of planetary motion, and Sir Isaac Newton (1642–1727), the English mathematician and philosopher best known for describing gravitational laws. French thinker René Descartes (1596–1650), perhaps most famous for the statement *Cogito, ergo sum* ("I think, therefore I am"), also invented analytic geometry and subsequently had as great an impact on the evolution of mathematics as he did on the future of philosophy. The English physician William Harvey (1578–1657), who explained the workings of the heart and the circulation of human blood, is credited with having profoundly altered the course of Western medicine, much as William Shakespeare (1564–1616) — actor, director, playwright, and poet — is generally acknowledged to have had an unparalleled influence on Western literature ever since the seventeenth century.

In addition to Castiglione, Milton, and Shakespeare, notable Renaissance writers and their works include: Desiderius Erasmus (*In Praise of Folly* [1509]), Ludovico Ariosto (*Orlando furioso* [c. 1513]), Sir Thomas More (*Utopia* [1516]), Niccolò Machiavelli (*The Prince* [1532]), François Rabelais (*Pantagruel* [1532]), Michel de Montaigne (*Essais* [1580]), Edmund Spenser (*The Faerie Queene* [1590–96]), and Miguel de Cervantes (*Don Quixote* [1605, 1615]).

▶ **Renaissance Period (in English literature):** A period in English literary history spanning the years 1500 to 1660. The Renaissance Period, conceived broadly, is usually divided into five literary eras: the **Early Tudor Age** (1550–58); the **Elizabethan Age** (1558–1603); the **Jacobean Age** (1603–25); the **Caroline Age** (1625–49); and the **Commonwealth Age,** or *Puritan Interregnum* (1649–60).

Major poets of the period include John Donne, John Milton, Sir Philip Sidney, and Edmund Spenser. Notable prose writers include Sir Thomas More and Francis Bacon. William Shakespeare, poet and dramatist, has probably had the greatest impact on Western literature, profoundly influencing its course up to the present day.

See **Renaissance.**

▶ **renga:** See **haiku.**

▶ **representation:** Generally speaking, the use of one thing to stand for another through some **signifying** medium. A representation of an event is not the event itself but rather a statement about or rendition of that event. An artistic representation is an **image** or likeness of something achieved through a medium such as language, paint, stone, film, etc.

New historicists use the term *representation* to refer to the **symbolic** constructions of a given society in a specific era. These constructions are predominantly but not exclusively verbal; for instance, the placing of a criminal on public view in "the stocks" could be viewed as a representation of the New England Puritan belief in the communal implications of individual sin and the consequent importance of public penance. New historicists view representations as instruments that maintain the status of the dominant **class** by reflecting and propagating the culture's prevailing **ideologies** and power relations.

FURTHER EXAMPLES: William Shakespeare's play *Hamlet* (1602) and the coronation of Queen Elizabeth I may both be referred to as **Renaissance** representations because they served as elaborate, highly **figurative,** and powerfully significant (re)statements of their culture's predominant ideological thinking about power and hierarchy, **gender** and primogeniture, and law and order.

▶ **resolution:** When used generally, the culmination of a fictional **plot;** when used specifically with reference to **tragic drama,** the concluding action, or **catastrophe,** one of five structural elements associated with **Freytag's Pyramid,** a model developed by nineteenth-century German writer Gustav Freytag for analyzing five-act plays, and tragedies in particular.

▶ **Restoration Age (in English literature):** The first of three literary eras within the **Neoclassical Period** in English literature, generally characterized by **satire, wit,** and a reaction against Puritanism. The Restoration Age began in 1660, when the House of Stuart (via Charles II) was restored to the English throne after the eleven-year **Commonwealth Age,** or **Puritan Interregnum** (which means, literally, "between reigns"). It is generally, if arbitrarily, said to have ended in 1700. The libertine spirit of Restoration

Age literature — which focused on the royal court, aristocratic intrigues, and clever repartee — starkly contrasts with that of the preceding, Puritan-dominated era, during which public dancing was virtually eliminated and public theaters closed. With the reopening of theaters and the support of the king, drama flourished during the Restoration Age. Particularly popular was Restoration comedy, a type of **comedy of manners** influenced by **neoclassical** French playwright Molière (Jean-Baptiste Poquelin); noted examples include William Wycherley's *The Country Wife* (1675), Sir George Etheredge's *The Man of Mode* (1676), and William Congreve's *The Way of the World* (1700). Major forms of **tragedy** included the *heroic drama*, exemplified by John Dryden's *The Conquest of Granada* (1670), and the *she-tragedy*, exemplified by Thomas Otway's *The Orphan* (1680), which centered on the unjust suffering of a virtuous woman.

In poetry, the **heroic couplet** was the dominant form, advocated by Dryden, the most noted critic of the age and the writer whose works most fully reflect the priorities and values associated with neoclassicism, such as reason, balance, **decorum,** and order. Samuel Butler inaugurated a tradition of humorous, typically **satiric** verse with his **mock-heroic** poem *Hudibras* (1662–77), intentional **doggerel** ridiculing the Puritans. John Milton, a poet who published his greatest works during this literary epoch, was a Puritan; as such, he is never referred to as a Restoration Age writer even though he was arguably the foremost writer of the time.

In prose, leading figures included Aphra Behn, also a popular playwright and poet and the first Englishwoman to support herself as a writer; religious writer John Bunyan; philosopher John Locke; and diarist Samuel Pepys. Noted works include Bunyan's **allegory** *Pilgrim's Progress* (1678) and Behn's *Oroonoko* (1688), often identified as the first **novel**. Also new in the Restoration Age was the development of professional journalism, in newspapers such as Henry Muddiman's *London Gazette,* which premiered as the *Oxford Gazette* in 1665 and is still published today.

See **neoclassicism.**

▶ **revenge tragedy:** A type of **tragedy**, particularly popular in the **Elizabethan** and **Jacobean Ages,** modeled loosely on the plays of first-century A.D. Roman playwright Seneca and centered on the pursuit of vengeance. Revenge tragedies (the most extreme of which are sometimes referred to as *tragedies of blood*) generally deal with a son's quest to avenge his father's murder or vice versa. English dramatist Thomas Kyd is credited with establishing the **genre** in his play *The Spanish Tragedy* (c. 1586).

A typical revenge tragedy is characterized by intrigue and bloodshed and includes the following elements: (1) the ghost of the murdered man who seeks revenge and implores or orders the **protagonist** to act; (2) hesitation on the part of the protagonist seeking revenge; (3) other delays that retard the accomplishment of the act of revenge; (4) dissimulation, such as feigned insanity to deceive the murderer; (5) dramatic scenes of gore and horror, especially during the showdown between the protagonist and the **villain;**

(6) the use of devices such as plays-within-a-play and **soliloquies;** and (7) a **catastrophic** end for all involved.

Although fashioned in the **Senecan tragic** tradition, particularly insofar as they involve considerable violence and an occasional ghost, revenge tragedies diverge from Seneca's plays in bringing violent events onstage for the audience to see and experience in the most graphic and **cathartic** and way possible.

FURTHER EXAMPLES: William Shakespeare's *Hamlet* (1602), the best-known revenge tragedy written in English; *The Revenger's Tragedy* (1906), generally attributed to either Cyril Tourneur or Thomas Middleton.

▶ **Revolutionary Period (in American literature):** A period in American literary history spanning the years 1765 to 1790. In 1765, the English Parliament passed the Stamp Act, igniting the first serious opposition in the American colonies to English rule. For the next twenty-five years, until the implementation of the United States Constitution in 1789, the majority of American writing was politically motivated, whether supportive of English rule or revolutionary in character.

Most of the poetry of the Revolutionary Period was **neoclassical** in style and used forms such as the **burlesque, satire,** and **epic** for patriotic political ends. The *Hartford Wits*, a literary society comprised of poets associated with Yale University, imitated neoclassical models such as English poet Alexander Pope, embraced federalism, and sought to establish a national literature; noted members included Timothy Dwight; John Trumbull, whose **mock epic** *M'Fingal* (1776, 1782) was modeled on Samuel Butler's *Hudibras* (1663); and Joel Barlow, whose epic *The Vision of Columbus* (1787) aimed to inspire "the love of national liberty." Philip Freneau, known as the "Poet of the American Revolution," wrote both political works, such as "The British Prison-Ship" (1781), and lyrical pieces, such as "The Wild Honey Suckle" (1786), that anticipated American **romanticism.** Poets writing in the tradition of the **Graveyard School** and emphasizing an appreciation of nature also **foreshadowed** romanticism.

Revolutionary prose was often polemical, written to encourage and even inspire the movement for political independence from England and to promote national unification. Thomas Paine championed an absolute break with England in his revolutionary tract *Common Sense* (1776). Alexander Hamilton and James Madison contributed the majority of the essays making up *The Federalist Papers* (1787–88), a collection setting forth much of the political theory underlying the U.S. Constitution and advocating its ratification. Other major politically oriented prose authors of the period include Benjamin Franklin, who began to write his *Autobiography* in 1771, and Thomas Jefferson, who authored the Declaration of Independence (1776). By contrast, the first American novel, William Hill Brown's *The Power of Sympathy* (1789), was a **sentimental, epistolary novel** supposedly based on the true story of a woman who was seduced by her brother-in-law, became pregnant as a result, and committed suicide after the birth of her illegitimate child.

The African American literary tradition, inaugurated late in the **Colonial Period,** also developed. In poetry, Phillis Wheatley, an American slave, published *Poems on Various Subjects* (1773). In prose, Jupiter Hammon, a slave in New York, expressed his views on slavery and Christianity in *An Address to the Negroes of the State of New-York* (1786), and Olaudah Equiano's **slave narrative** *The Interesting Narrative of the Life of Olaudah Equiano, or Gustavus Vassa, the African, Written by Himself* (1789), became a sensation in both England and America, fueling the nascent antislavery movement.

Drama also entered the American literary arena during the Revolutionary Period. The first professionally staged American play was Thomas Godfrey's tragedy *The Prince of Parthia* (1767), the first professionally staged American comedy Royall Tyler's *The Contrast* (1787). Throughout the period, drama was most influential and widespread outside of New England, where the Puritan suspicion of the medium remained strong. Philadelphia, New York, and Charleston became magnets for playwrights, who modelled their works largely after those of neoclassical English dramatists Oliver Goldsmith and Richard Brinsley Sheridan. American drama was distinguished from the English, however, by its subject matter, which was chiefly historical, **didactic,** and patriotic in nature. Mercy Otis Warren, for instance, wrote satiric anti-British plays, such as *The Group* (1775), which were intended for publication rather than performance.

▶ **rhetoric:** The art of persuasion through speaking and writing; one of the seven major **medieval** subjects of study (and, more specifically, part of the trivium, the other two members of which were logic and grammar). Such well-known **classical** writers as Aristotle stressed the importance of the rhetorical arts, which in ancient times were seen as essential to effective argumentation and **oratory.** Classical theorists identified five components of rhetoric: (1) *invention* (the argument itself or its supporting evidence); (2) *disposition* (the arrangement of that evidence); (3) **style (diction,** patterns, **images, rhythms** of speech, etc.); (4) *memory;* and (5) *delivery.* They also identified three types of rhetoric: (1) *deliberative* (to persuade toward a course of action regarding public policy); (2) **epideictic** (to praise or blame, thereby demonstrating the rhetorical skill of the orator); and (3) *forensic* (to establish through a forum-like setting — such as a court of law — either a positive or negative opinion of someone's actions).

Since classical and medieval times, rhetoric has acquired negative **connotations,** most of which are associated with its inherent neutrality toward truth and falsehood and the ensuing possibility that it may be used to promote lies or immorality. Used pejoratively, *rhetoric* connotes empty rhetoric — language that sounds good but is at best insubstantial and, at worst, a deliberately distorting medium.

▶ **rhetorical accent:** See **accent.**

▶ **rhetorical criticism:** A type of **literary criticism** emphasizing examination of the **rhetorical** strategies and devices **authors** use to get readers to interpret their works in certain ways. Practitioners of rhetorical criticism identify and analyze the devices of persuasion present in a work that are designed to elicit or even impose a particular interpretation or response. Rhetorical critics also study the interaction of author and reader and view the **text** as a means of communication between the two.

Rhetorical criticism is similar to **pragmatic criticism** in its emphasis on how — and how well — a work (or author) manages to guide or influence the audience's response. Like pragmatic criticism, rhetorical criticism was practiced from **classical** times up through the eighteenth century, when its popularity declined with the rise of *expressive criticism,* which views literary works in light of their authors' thoughts and feelings. It fell into still deeper obscurity during the nineteenth century with the advent of **objective criticism.** More recently, however, rhetorical criticism has been resurrected and revamped, in the work of critics associated with **reader-response** and **reader-oriented criticism.**

For an introduction to rhetorical criticism, see Sonja Foss's *Rhetorical Criticism: Explanation and Practice* (3rd ed. 2004). For noted examples of rhetorical criticism, see Wayne Booth's *The Rhetoric of Fiction* (1961) and Thomas Benson's *Landmark Essays on Rhetorical Criticism* (1993), including Herbert Wicheln's influential essay "The Literary Criticism of Oratory" (1925).

▶ **rhetorical figures (schemes):** One of the two major divisions of **figures of speech,** the other being **tropes.** Unlike tropes, which turn one word or phrase into a **representation** of something else, rhetorical figures involve a less radical use of language to achieve special effects. **Antithesis, apostrophe, chiasmus, oxymoron, paradox, parallelism,** *rhetorical questions,* **syllepsis,** and **zeugma** are considered to be the major rhetorical figures. Other rhetorical figures include **amplification, anaphora, antonomasia, aposiopesis, asyndeton, hyperbaton, hysteron proteron, paralipsis, periphrasis,** and **pun (paranomasia).**

▶ **rhetorical irony (verbal irony):** See **irony.**

▶ **rhyme:** Broadly, a correspondence or echoing of similar sounds in words; more specifically, the repetition of identical vowel sounds in the **stressed** syllables of two or more words, as well as of all subsequent sounds. When most people speak of words as rhyming, they are referring to a specific type of rhyme — **perfect rhyme** — and, indeed, to a specific type of perfect rhyme — *true,* or *full, rhyme,* in which the initial sound of the stressed syllable in the rhyming words differs. Seventeenth-century English poet John Milton's definition of rhyme as "the jingling sound of like endings" describes rhyme of this sort. Thus, *bard / lard / shard / marred* are true rhymes, as are *thinking / drinking / shrinking.* But *bard / barred* and *board / bored* are not; nor are *bard / hoard* or even *bard / beard / board.* These latter word sets are examples of *rime riche* and **half rhyme,** respectively. In *rime riche,* the second type of perfect rhyme, all sounds in the stressed syllable as well as all subsequent sounds are identical. In half rhyme, words contain similar sounds but do not rhyme exactly. Half rhyme typically results from **consonance** or **assonance,** similarities in consonant and vowel sounds, respectively. When words appear to rhyme based on their spelling but sound completely different when pronounced — as in *dough / tough* — no rhyme exists; rather, this phenomenon is labeled **eye rhyme.**

Perfect rhyme may further be classified as **masculine** or **feminine.** A masculine rhyme involves one stressed syllable, as in the pair *low / blow* or *toe / below.* A feminine rhyme has one stressed syllable followed by one or more identical unstressed syllables, as in the double rhyme *shatter / splatter* or the **triple rhyme** *clattering / flattering.* Some critics would argue that, although perfect rhyme may be masculine, not all masculine rhyme is perfect; masculine rhyme, they would maintain, may involve half rhyme (*care / core*) or even eye rhyme (*how / low*).

Finally, rhyme may be classified according to its placement within a poetic line or lines. Rhyme can occur at the end of two or more lines (**end rhyme**), within a line (**internal rhyme,** including **leonine rhyme**), or at the beginning of two or more lines (**beginning rhyme**).

Rhyme should be distinguished from **rhythm,** which refers generally to the measured flow of words in a passage or work and signifies a basic (though often varied) beat or pattern in language established by pauses and stressed and unstressed syllables. First, rhyme is generally limited to poetic works, whereas rhythm is a feature of both prose and poetry. Second, critics generally agree that rhythm, unlike rhyme, is an indispensable element of poetry. Of course, poets often use rhyme to establish or intensify the rhythm of a poem and to help structure a given passage or work. A poet's **rhyme scheme,** or pattern of rhymes, for instance, may delineate **stanzas** and unify the poem as a whole through its recurrent regularity. To emphasize the distinction between rhyme and rhythm, some critics have suggested returning to an older spelling of *rhyme: rime.*

Rhyme has long been a popular poetic tool, especially of Romance- and English-language poets. It does not, however, usually appear in ancient poetic works; while it was used in Chinese poetry such as the *Shi Jing (Classic of Poetry),* it does not generally appear in the works of **classical** Greece or Rome or those written in Sanskrit or Hebrew. Some scholars have theorized that the absence of rhyme can be traced to the nature of the ancient languages of these cultures. The fewer syllables that follow a word's final, accented syllable, the easier rhyming becomes. *Can,* for instance, is more easily rhymed than *canister.* Many ancient languages tended to be suffixal rather than prefixal — that is, to follow the root with numerous syllables rather than preceding it — hence making rhyming more difficult. English, by contrast, is a prefixal language, which may account for the greater development of rhyme in English-language poetry. Romance languages such as Italian and Spanish rhyme even more readily.

Some scholars have suggested that the origin of rhyme as we know it lies in the early Christian Church and, more specifically, in the African church Latin that developed after the time of the theologian Tertullian (c. A.D. 160–230). Later, priests throughout Europe began introducing rhyme in order to make long passages of liturgy easier to listen to and remember. By the fourth century A.D., key liturgical readings and responses had evolved into rhymed poems; some of these, such as the "Stabat Mater" and "Dies Irae," are familiar to churchgoers today. During the **Middle Ages,** **hymns** were composed that combined assonance and consonance, **alliteration** and end rhyme, and during the **Middle English Period** more specifically, rhymed verse came to prevail over the alliterative pattern characteristic of **Old English** poetry.

The trend in the twentieth century was toward dispensing with rhyme, or at least minimizing its use. Notably, unrhymed verse written in English dates at least as far back as the sixteenth century, when **blank verse** (broadly defined, any unrhymed verse, but usually referring to unrhymed **iambic pentameter**) first appeared. As the use of true rhyme declined, forms such as half rhyme became increasingly popular but were also eclipsed as nonrhyming **free verse** became the dominant means of poetic expression. Today, few poets compose using rhyme, at least of the conventional kind.

▶ **rhyme royal (rime royal):** Introduced by fourteenth-century English poet Geoffrey Chaucer, a seven-line poetic **stanza** written in **iambic pentameter** with the **rhyme scheme** *ababbcc.* Rhyme royal, often said to be named for James I's use of the form in his **dream vision** *The Kingis Quair* (*The King's Book*) (c. 1424), became a standard, even dominant form of English verse during the fifteenth century and continued to be used periodically thereafter. Poets who have used the form include William Shakespeare, William Wordsworth, and W. H. Auden.

FURTHER EXAMPLE: The following stanza from Chaucer's *Troilus and Criseyde* (c. 1383):

> And whoso seith that for to love is vice,
> Or thraldom, though he feele it in destresse,
> He outher° is envyous, or right nyce°   *either; foolish*
> Or is unmyghty, for his shrewedness,°   *impotent because*
> To loven; for swich manere folk, I gesse,   *of his nastiness*
> Defamen Love, as nothing of him knowe.
> They speken, but thei benten nevere his bowe!

▶ **rhyme scheme:** The pattern of **rhyme** in a **poem** or **stanza,** typically described by assigning a lower case letter to each new rhyming sound. Certain poetic forms, such as the **sonnet, triolet,** and **villanelle** — as well as stanza types, such as the **Spenserian stanza** — are **conventionally** composed in accordance with a specific rhyme scheme. Thus the rhyme scheme of an

Italian sonnet is generally *abbaabbacdecde,* whereas that of a ballad stanza is *abcb.*

▶ **rhythm:** From the Greek for "flow," a term referring to a measured flow of words and signifying the basic (though often varied) beat or pattern in language that is established by **stressed** syllables, un**stressed** syllables, and pauses. Rhythm is a feature of both **prose** and **verse.**

Rhythm is distinguished from **meter,** which involves the organization of syllables and pauses into a more formal, regular pattern of stress units with a dominant **foot** (what in music would be called a "beat"). Rhythm is also distinguished from **rhyme.** In verse, rhythm is often accompanied by rhyme but need not be; while rhyme intensifies rhythmic patterns, it is not an essential element of poetry. In prose, where rhyme is uncommon, rhythm is generally established by imitating the cadences of everyday speech and through the use of devices such as **euphony, parallelism,** and repetition.

▶ *rime riche* **(identical rhyme):** See **perfect rhyme.**

▶ **rime royal:** See **rhyme royal.**

▶ **rising action:** The part of a **drama** that follows the inciting moment (the event that gives rise to the **conflict**) and precedes the **climax** or the **crisis.** During the rising action, the **plot** becomes more complicated and the **conflict** intensifies. Rising action is one of five structural elements associated with **Freytag's Pyramid,** a model developed by nineteenth-century German writer Gustav Freytag for analyzing five-act plays, and **tragedies** in particular.

▶ *roman à clef:* French for "novel with a key," a **novel** that **represents** real people in the guise of fictional **characters.** Usually the **author** makes the identities of the characters readily apparent, at least to contemporary readers. This is particularly true when the novelist has written a *roman à clef* to **satirize** an individual or individuals, or some associated event. The **genre** dates to seventeenth-century France, where it was developed in works such as Madeleine de Scudéry's *Clélie* (1654).

FURTHER EXAMPLES: Lady Caroline Lamb's *Glenarvon* (1816) is a *roman à clef* about the poet George Gordon, Lord Byron, thinly disguised as the character Clarence de Ruthven, Lord Glenarvon. In Mary Shelley's **apocalyptic** novel *The Last Man* (1826), the characters of Adrian, Earl of Windsor, and Lord Raymond are portraits of Percy Bysshe Shelley (Mary Shelley's husband) and Byron, respectively. **Harlem Renaissance** writer Wallace Thurman portrayed a variety of contemporaries in his *roman à clef Infants of the Spring* (1932), including Alain Locke (Dr. Parkes), a key leader of the movement; the poet Countee Cullen (De Witt Clinton); writer and folklorist Zora Neale Hurston (Sweetie May Carr); the artist Richard Bruce Nugent (Paul Arbian, of whom the author wrote "Since he can't be white, he will be a most unusual Negro"); and the writer Langston Hughes (Tony Crews, said to have "no depth whatsoever, or else he was too deep for plumbing by ordinary mortals").

Joe Klein's novel *Primary Colors* (1996; adapted to film 1998), initially published anonymously, was based on Bill Clinton's first campaign for the White House, portraying Clinton as aspiring candidate Jack Stanton; adviser George Stephanopoulous as political operative Henry Burton; and campaign director James Carville as Richard Jemmons, "a hyperactive redneck from outer space."

▶ **romance:** A term that has been used at different times to refer to a variety of **fictional** works involving some combination of the following: high adventure, thwarted love, mysterious circumstances, arduous quests, and improbable triumphs. Although some scholars during and since the **Renaissance** have maintained that romances were first written in ancient Greece (Homer's *The Odyssey* [c. 850 B.C.] has been called a prototypical romance), most literary historians maintain that the romance originated in twelfth-century France. The term *romance* derives from the French word *roman* and was first used exclusively to refer to **medieval romances** (sometimes called *chivalric romances*) written in French and composed in verse. These **narratives** were concerned with knightly adventure, **courtly love,** and chivalric ideals. By the seventeenth century, the term was used to refer to any medieval romance, whether in verse or prose and regardless of country of origin.

Unlike the **epic,** a narrative form that exalts the struggles associated with a heroic era of tribal warfare, the romance pertains to a courtly era associated with chivalry. Romances represent the supernatural as characteristic of this world rather than of the gods or their will. They also tend to have what we would describe as a psychological interest or component; the landscapes of romance are often outward manifestations of the **hero's** or **heroine's** inner state. Thus, a despairing character is likely to stumble into a cave, and temptation is likely to be encountered in a deep forest rather than on a broad, sunny plain. The *quest romance* was adapted and internalized by **Romantic** and **Victorian Period** poets, who in works like Percy Bysshe Shelley's "Alastor" (1816), John Keats's "La belle dame sans merci" (1820), and Robert Browning's "Childe Roland to the Dark Tower Came" (1855) turned the search for the Grail (or Girl) common in medieval and Renaissance romances into an often frustrated psychological quest for some ideal, forbidden, lost, or otherwise unreachable state or condition.

The meaning of *romance* broadened considerably over time, especially in the twentieth century. The term has been used to refer to any fictional work that features the supernatural, some sort of quest or "impossible dream," intense love, and unusual subjects and events. Today, *romance* is usually understood to refer to a fictional account of passionate love prevailing against social, economic, or psychological odds, but any **plot** that revolves around love can now be characterized as a romance. (*Romance* may even be used as a synonym for love, as in the sentence "Our romance had to end.") Love stories whose **characters**, situations, or events are given a historical **setting** are often referred to as *historical romances*. When romance **conventions** are overlaid, as is often the case, with the emotionally and supernaturally charged features of **Gothic** literature, the resulting works may be called *Gothic romances*. In a further broadening of this term's meaning, *romance* has been recently used to signify any work whose author rejects **realistic verisimilitude** in favor of fanciful or **fantastic** depictions.

Romance is also used in the phrase *Romance languages*. The five principal Romance languages, all of which are derived primarily from the Roman language Latin, are French, Italian, Portuguese, Romanian, and Spanish.

FURTHER EXAMPLES: *Le roman de la rose* (*The Romance of the Rose*), initially composed by Guillaume de Lorris around 1230 and expanded by Jean de Meung around 1270, and Edmund Spenser's *The Faerie Queene* (1590, 1596) are romances in the original sense of the term, which, with varying levels of laxity and generality, may be used to describe Emily Brontë's *Wuthering Heights* (1847), Nathaniel Hawthorne's *The Scarlet Letter* (1850), William Morris's poem "Rapunzel" (1858), Margaret Mitchell's *Gone With the Wind* (1936), Erich Segal's *Love Story* (1970), any Harlequin paperback, Danielle Steel's books, and films like *Sleepless in Seattle* (1993), *My Big Fat Greek Wedding* (2002), and *Hitch* (2005). The latter three works are examples of a hybrid **genre**, the **romantic comedy**.

▶ **romantic:** A term with an array of meanings, first used to characterize **narratives** called **romances** that arose in **medieval** times and featured improbable **plots**, hence its often pejorative **connotation** as "implausible." Later, in seventeenth-century France, the term was used more sympathetically to signify the tender or sad, a usage that spread to England and Germany in the eighteenth century, when it was often applied to melancholy works with exotic **settings**. Some critics viewed these works as imaginative, others as patently silly. Nineteenth-century German philosopher Friedrich Schlegel was the first to apply the term to a literary movement that arose in opposition to **neoclassicism**, which emphasized qualities such as reason, order, restraint, balance, and **decorum** in emulation of **classical** literature; subsequently, Swiss writer Madame de Staël popularized this usage in *De l'Allemagne* (1810), her study of Germany and German culture, including its philosophy and literature. The movement, which became known as **romanticism**, is generally said to have extended from the end of the eighteenth century through much of the nineteenth, depending on the country in question; for instance, England's **Romantic Period** spanned the years 1798–1837, America's 1828–65. Today the terms *classic(al)* and *romantic* are still used in **binary opposition**, with *classic(al)* designating the rational, unified, orderly, stately, enduring, and finite and *romantic* referring to the emotional, changing, chaotic, improbable, visionary, and infinite.

▶ **romantic comedy:** See comedy.

▶ **romantic irony:** See **irony.**

▶ **romanticism:** A broad and general term (like **classicism,** with which it is often contrasted) referring to a set of beliefs, attitudes, and values associated with a shift in Western culture that was characterized by a reaction against **Enlightenment** rationalism and an emphasis on emotion, innovation, nature, the individual, and **subjective** experience; more specifically, a literary movement in Europe, Russia, and America generally said to have extended from the end of the eighteenth century through much of the nineteenth, depending on the country in question.

Most critics agree that romanticism arose first in Germany and England, followed by America and other European countries such as France. For instance, England's **Romantic Period** spanned the years 1798–1837, America's 1828–65. William Blake, William Wordsworth, Samuel Taylor Coleridge, John Keats, Percy Bysshe Shelley, Mary Shelley, and Emily Brontë were among the foremost romantic writers in England; prominent American romantics included Emily Dickinson, Ralph Waldo Emerson, Nathaniel Hawthorne, Herman Melville, Edgar Allan Poe, Henry David Thoreau, and Walt Whitman. Johann Wolfgang von Goethe, Victor Hugo, and Alexander Pushkin were noted romantic writers in Germany, France, and Russia, respectively.

Romantics rejected many of the artistic **forms** and **conventions** associated with classicism and **neoclassicism,** considering them to be overly constricting and detrimental to the artistic mission. They differed, however, in their interests and emphases. Some urged a revival of **medievalism** (an interest in emulating certain aspects of the **Middle Ages**); others emphasized the importance of freedom from all traditions. Some tended to turn literature into a vehicle for the **fancy,** a mode of escapism; still others, such as Coleridge and Wordsworth, drew a distinction between fancy and **imagination, privileging** the latter as the source of creativity. But they generally shared the view that spontaneous writing was essential to a true **representation** of **subjective** experience and thus put a premium on original expression as well as the use of everyday language rather than **poetic diction.**

Romantics also embraced **primitivism,** which postulates that people are good by nature but corrupted by civilization. Closely related to the belief in humanity's original goodness was the romantic esteem, even reverence, for childhood and emotions, the most "natural" of human manifestations. In fact, romantics often regarded emotions as more reliable than reason, which they tended to view as a negative product of civilization, unlike the eighteenth-century Enlightenment philosophers who celebrated reason as the vehicle furthering and expanding human capabilities. The conception of civilization as a corrupting influence also led romantics to glorify nature, which they tended to view as the **antithesis** of materialism and artifice and to which they often imputed a **mystical** or even **sublime** quality. Finally, looking outward, and believing in the essential goodness of human beings, many romantics demanded political and social change. Some looked to the

French Revolution of 1789 as a political blueprint for improvement, at least before the excesses of the Reign of Terror became widely known; others focused on the unparalleled (if unfulfilled) possibilities for beneficial social change that the revolution engendered.

As the foregoing discussion suggests, romantics also prized individualism and the sanctity of individual self-expression. They considered self-analysis especially constructive, particularly as it pertained to personal development, and brought the review of and focus on self into the realm of literature. Observations on nature frequently served as an occasion for self-reflection or meditation on the human condition and the individual human self.

Romantic writers frequently perceived themselves as both sensitive and unappreciated. (In fact, the romantics may be chiefly responsible for popularizing, and even glorifying, the **theme** of the suffering artist — the lonely, misunderstood artistic genius.) Although romantics recognized the potential represented by the new machinery and scientific developments so prized in the industrial era, they also felt undervalued (or even rejected) by a world increasingly fixated on progress and what Wordsworth called "getting and spending" in his **sonnet** "The World Is Too Much with Us" (1807). The intensity of personal self-assessment and the pursuit of the spiritual or otherwise **fantastic** often seemed to create an unbridgeable chasm between the susceptible romantic poet and an increasingly commercial and technologically oriented society. Not surprisingly, the **heroes** and **heroines** of romantic literature often share their creators' perceptions of alienation and difference from the society at large.

Many romantics also felt an affinity with the **Gothic** and the **grotesque.** Gothic literature is typically characterized by a general **mood** of decay, suspense, and terror; **action** that is dramatic and generally violent; loves that are destructively passionate (like that of Cathy and Heathcliff in Emily Brontë's *Wuthering Heights* [1847]); and grandiose yet gloomy settings. The grotesque, which Gothic literature often invokes, involves artistic representations that are always strange — even bizarre or unnatural — and often disturbing. Unlike the neoclassicists, who viewed the Gothic as crude or even barbaric, romantics celebrated its freedom of spirit, mystery, and instinctual authenticity, which meshed well with their own emphasis on individuality, imagination, and sublimity.

As with all other literary movements, a reaction against romanticism eventually set in. **Realism,** an effort to "write reality" that emerged in the latter half of the nineteenth century, emphasized the **objective** presentation of details and events rather than personal feelings or perceptions. At the same time, romanticism became the target of increasing (and increasingly vitriolic) criticism. The self-centeredness, **sentimentalism,** and improbability of many romantic works incited some of the harshest attacks, many of which came from **Victorian** writers and critics. In *Appreciations, With an Essay on Style* (1889), Walter Pater called Wordsworth a "brain-sick ... mystic" and described Coleridge's work as "represent[ing] that inexhaustible discontent, languor, and homesickness, that endless regret, the chords of which ring all through our modern literature." In *Essays on Criticism* (1865), Matthew Arnold argued that Percy Bysshe Shelley suffered from "the incurable want . . . of a sound subject-matter," characterizing him as an "ineffectual angel beating in the void his luminous wings in vain." In *Fiction, Fair and Foul* (1880–81), John Ruskin attacked Shelley's lyrics as "false, forced, foul"; he not only criticized such poems as Shelley's "The Sensitive Plant" (1820) on the scientific grounds that "Sensitive plants can't grow in gardens! . . . Dew with a breeze is impossible" but also mounted a more personal attack on the poet, calling him a "blockhead — and he thinks himself wiser than God though he doesn't know the commonest law of evaporation!" Nonetheless, regardless of the ferocity of Victorian criticism, romantic elements continued to pervade nineteenth-century works and still play a major role in literature today, especially the emphasis on individual perspective and artistic originality.

▶ **Romantic Period (in American literature):** A period in American literary history spanning the years 1828, when Andrew Jackson was elected to the presidency, to 1865, the year the Civil War ended. The limits of American unity were tested during this period, due to the rapid rate of westward expansion and, more importantly, the issue of slavery, which increasingly divided the nation. During this turbulent and often contentious time, the first truly American literature was produced, independent of English models, with significant works appearing in all areas except for drama, thereby giving rise to the appellation *American Renaissance*.

The Romantic Period has also been called the *Age of Transcendentalism*. Adherents of **transcendentalism,** an idealistic philosophical and literary movement that arose in New England, maintained that each person is innately divine, with the intuitive ability to discover higher truths. They rejected dogmatic religious doctrines, praised self-reliance, and gloried in the natural goodness of the individual. Transcendentalism is most closely associated with the poet and essayist Ralph Waldo Emerson, who outlined the movement in an essay entitled "The Transcendentalist" (1842). Other members of the movement included Amos Bronson Alcott; early feminist Margaret Fuller; and Henry David Thoreau, best known for his essay "Civil Disobedience" (first published in 1849 as "Resistance to Civil Government") and his book *Walden* (1854). Members of the Transcendental Club contributed writings to *The Dial* (1840–44), the group's quarterly periodical.

Romantic writers generally emphasized emotion over intellect; the individual over society; inspiration, **imagination,** and intuition over logic, discipline, and order; the wild and natural over the tamed. In poetry, Edgar Allan Poe took the novel step of formulating his own **theory** of poetry, based on which he produced a **symbolist** verse that would heavily **influence** post-Civil War poetry and the **Symbolist movement** in France. "The Raven" (1845) and "Annabel Lee" (1849) are perhaps his most famous poems. Subsequently, Walt Whitman challenged poetic **conventions** with the radically personal and informal **lyrics** he published in *Leaves of Grass* (1855), a collection of poems composed in **free verse** addressing subject matter deemed highly taboo at the time, such as sex. In a letter to Whitman (July 21, 1855), Emerson called the collection "the most extraordinary piece of wit and wisdom that America has yet contributed," praising Whitman for his "free and brave thought" and "large perception." Other romantic poets included William Cullen Bryant, Emily Dickinson, Frances Ellen Watkins Harper, Paul Hamilton Hayne, Henry Wadsworth Longfellow, James Russell Lowell, Henry Timrod, and John Greenleaf Whittier.

Washington Irving and James Fenimore Cooper, novelists whose careers had begun during the preceding **Early National Period**, produced some of their best works during the Romantic Period. But it was writers like Nathaniel Hawthorne and Herman Melville who more truly exemplified novelistic **romanticism**. Hawthorne's *The Scarlet Letter* (1850) and Melville's *Moby-Dick* (1852) are among the most well-known American works. Louisa May Alcott, William Brown, William Gilmore Simms, and Harriet Beecher Stowe are other notable writers of the period. Stowe's *Uncle Tom's Cabin* (1852) is not only credited with being America's first **sociological novel**, it is also often said to have instigated the Civil War by its depiction of slavery.

Other types of prose were also common in the Romantic Period. On one hand, a group of Southern writers including John Pendleton Kennedy and William Alexander Caruthers developed a plantation tradition idealizing plantation life through **historical romances** and sketches. On the other, **slave narratives** and **autobiographies** became increasingly popular in the North, even as they were banned in the South. Frederick Douglass's *Narrative of the Life of Frederick Douglass* (1845) and Harriet Jacobs's *Incidents in the Life of a Slave Girl* (1861) are two of the most well-known examples of the **genre**. Furthermore, Western writers such as Davy Crockett chronicled frontier life, and essayists including Oliver Wendell Holmes, Emerson, and Thoreau were widely read. Short stories such as Hawthorne's "Young Goodman Brown" (1835) and Poe's "The Fall of the House of Usher" (1843) and "The Tell-Tale Heart" (1843) captivated readers. Poe also pioneered **detective fiction** through works such as "Murders in the Rue Morgue" (1841).

A number of new periodicals, which often reflected the sectional divisions that were tearing the country apart, were founded during the Romantic Period. The *Southern Literary Messenger* (1834–64) represented the views of the South; in the North, the *Atlantic Monthly* (1857–) and *Harper's Magazine* (1850–) joined the *North American Review* (1815–1940, 1964–), which was established during the Early National Period. Abolitionist newspapers and pamphlets also sprang up, even though many of their editors and authors were persecuted. For instance, William Lloyd Garrison, editor of the *Liberator,* was attacked and dragged through the streets of Boston by a mob in 1835.

American **literary criticism** also began during the Romantic Period. Poe, who developed an analytical approach to literary criticism, is usually credited as being America's first real critic. Simms and Lowell are other noted critics of the time.

Drama, unlike other forms of literary expression, did not produce very distinctive works. Most dramatists continued to **imitate** English spectacles and romantic **tragedies** modelled on William Shakespeare's plays. Of particular interest were stage adaptations of well-known novels (such as *Uncle Tom's Cabin*) and short stories (such as Irving's "Rip Van Winkle" [1819]). Also popular was the star system, which, as its name suggests, subordinated both play and actors to one "star," one name actor.

See **romanticism.**

▶ **Romantic Period (in English literature):** A watershed era in the history of English literature usually said to have commenced with the 1798 publication of Samuel Taylor Coleridge and William Wordsworth's *Lyrical Ballads,* a volume that included such well-known poems as Coleridge's "The Rime of the Ancient Mariner" and Wordsworth's "Lines Written a Few Miles Above Tintern Abbey." Some scholars, however, maintain that the Romantic Period began before 1798, arguing that certain works published before that date — such as Robert Burns's *Poems* (1786); William Blake's *Songs of Innocence* (1789); Mary Wollstonecraft's *A Vindication of the Rights of Woman* (1792); and various **Gothic** works published by writers including Ann Radcliffe, William Godwin, and Horace Walpole — exemplify the radical changes in political thought and literary expression commonly associated with English **romanticism.** The period is generally said to have ended in 1832, with the passage of a major electoral reform bill, or in 1837, with the coronation of Queen Victoria, after whom the subsequent **Victorian Period** is named.

In addition to Coleridge, Wordsworth, and Blake, critic Charles Lamb and novelists Jane Austen and Sir Walter Scott are generally viewed as early or "first generation" romantics. Noted works include Austen's *Sense and Sensibility* (1811) and *Emma* (1815), which critics have pointed out reflect the priorities and values of the preceding **Neoclassical Period** as fully as those of romanticism, and Scott's **historical novel** *Waverley* (1814). Austen also adapted — and **parodied** — the **conventions** of the Gothic romance in *Northanger Abbey* (written c. 1798, published 1818). Major "second generation" English romantic poets, who published their most important work after 1815, include George Gordon, Lord Byron (*Don Juan* [1819–24]); John Keats ("Ode on a Grecian Urn" [1820]); and Percy Bysshe Shelley ("Adonais" [1820]). Prose writers of this second phase of English romanticism include Mary Shelley, whose novel *Frankenstein* (1818) shows the clear influence of the late-eighteenth-century Gothic tradition; Thomas de Quincey, best known for his provocatively titled **autobiographical** novel *Confessions of an English Opium-Eater* (1821); essayist and literary critic William Hazlitt, whose *Spirit of the Age* (1825) presented portraits of his

Other science fiction authors who wrote dur[ing]
include American authors Hal Clement, Philip J[osé Farmer]
(best known for his *Dune* series [1965–85]), Wa[lter]
Silverberg. Edgar Rice Burroughs, best known
who had begun writing space stories — includi[ng]
Venus series — several decades earlier, also cor
fiction. In addition, several authors otherwise u[n]
produced notable science fiction works, as exem[plified by]
Nevil Shute's *On the Beach* (1957; adapted to
novelist Daniel Keys's *Flowers for Algernon* (19
as *Charly* (1968).

In the 1960s, a new type of science fiction call
peared on the scene. The phrase "New Wave" –
French phrase used in criticism — was adopted i[n]
cock, a respected British science fiction author,
by the British science fiction magazine *New W*
cock, who drew on the unconventional science
Burroughs in formulating his ideas and who la
New Worlds, encouraged science fiction writers t
tional science fiction and to experiment. Among
recommended avoiding the themes of space trave
fare and concentrating instead on the mysterie
essence, "inner space," rather than outer space, b
"soft" science fiction, with its emphasis on huma
tion, challenged the "hard," which "soft" practi
step with the turbulent times.

Moorcock handpicked several authors to adva
J. G. Ballard, who wrote *The Four-Dimensional*
The Terminal Beach (1964); John Brunner, autho
(1968); and E. C. Tubb, who in 1997 published *T*
in his "Dumarest Saga." Brian Aldiss also wrote
though he expressed reservations about the tende
de-emphasize plot. American authors who wrote
stories included Samuel R. Delaney, Philip K. D[ick]
Harlan Ellison, John Sladek, Norman Spinrad, a
The film *Minority Report* (2002), which is set in W
year 2054 and which involves a "precrime" departr
humans called "precogs" to predict murders befor
on Dick's short story "Minority Report," first pu
magazine *Fantastic Universe.*

While Moorcock was promoting his ideas, Ame
their own version of New Wave writing under the i
rill, a science fiction author, reviewer, and anthrop
until 1966 published an annual collection of scienc
Year's Best SF. Merrill, like Moorcock, sought to
by encouraging writers to incorporate contempor

the id
(1930
N
twent
the R
the G
in 19
most
Maur
of Jap
Fukus
It v
fiction
tion,
produ
named
were
charac
subma
ity of
the inv
printed
lishing
Witl
grew n
or in J
which
magazi
ish autl
non Ha
and Art
continu
writers
science
may ex
tual sci
for any
ton Boc
more va
strong
minded'
essential
value on
The
tion was
the edita

breaks in the **action** and **dialogue** and by the lowering and raising of the curtain in a conventional **proscenium** theater. In the **classical** French tradition, the entrances and exits of **characters** delineate the scenes in a play, but English theater has been less consistent in this regard. Reconfigured scenery, a change of **setting**, or (especially) indications that time has passed may indicate the commencement of a new scene in English drama. Distinguishing between scenes in modern works is often difficult and subject to critical debate.

▶ **scheme:** See **figure of speech, rhetorical figures.**

▶ **science fiction:** A type of **fiction** that is grounded in scientific or pseudo-scientific concepts and that, whether set on Earth or in an alternate or parallel world, employs both **realistic** and **fantastic** elements in exploring the question "What if?" As British novelist Kingsley Amis explained in *New Maps of Hell* (1964), science fiction deals with a situation that "could not arise in the world we know, but which is hypothesized on the basis of some innovation in science or technology, or pseudo-science or pseudo-technology, whether human or extraterrestrial in origin." Such situations may entail either wonders or disasters. Other topics and **themes** typical of the **genre** include **utopian** or **dystopian** societies, fantastic journeys to unknown worlds, time travel, alien invasions and encounters, wars involving mass destruction, the destruction or assimilation of cultures, questions of identity, and the (d)evolution of humanity.

The term *science fiction,* which was coined in 1851 by British author William Wilson and popularized in the late 1920s by science fiction novelist and publisher Hugo Gernsback (who coined the term *scientifiction*), encompasses such a wide variety of works that many have claimed it defies definition. Science fiction writer and editor Damon Knight, for instance, asserted in *In Search of Wonder* (1956) that *science fiction* "means what we point to when we say it." Ursula K. Le Guin, a leading author and theorist of both science fiction and **fantasy fiction,** wondered in her 1993 introduction to *The Norton Book of Science Fiction* whether "the non-definability of science fiction [is] perhaps an essential element of it."

Forerunners of science fiction typically recount **tales** of adventurers who have travelled to unknown worlds. For instance, *Vera historia* (*True History*), written around A.D. 150 by Lucian of Samosata, included a journey to the sun and the moon. **Dream visions** of the **Medieval Period** were religious in nature, describing journeys to heaven, hell, and the limbo called purgatory. By the beginning of the sixteenth century, several authors had imaginatively written about flights into space, where utopian societies were sometimes discovered. Thomas More's *Utopia* (1516), in which a sailor speaks of an **idyllic** land beyond the sea, is an early example of utopian literature said to anticipate science fiction. Other early works about fantastic journeys include Bishop Francis Godwin's *The Man in the Moone* (1638), John Wilkins's *Discovery of a New World in the Moone* (1638), Cyrano

de Berg
(c. 1640
berg's N
ground)
Most
major w
first scie
horrifica
human c
of scienc
books.
The n
science fi
into shor
(1850). J
els such a
(1864) ar
der the S
jects for s
(1894) ar
ward: 20
both Eng
capitalist
tice. Anot
Shelley's 7
Other not
include R
Althoug
first scien
having en
Wells not
eties, and
concept of
chine (189
The War
broadcast
caused pan
tually inva
Followir
ing the inte
became par
themes incl
Wright's tr
[1932], Poi
dystopian s
Brave New

Analog Science Fiction and Fact) (1930–). Campbe
ence fiction stories should involve predictions based
and principles and provide inspiration for future sc
lished an influential story in *Astounding* entitled "W.
that was adapted to film as *The Thing* (1951, 1982
thors for the magazine including Canadian A. E. Var
alized in 1940) inspired science fiction readers to
Isaac Asimov, perhaps best known for his *Found*
1982), who contended that "modern science fiction is
ture that consistently considers the nature of the chan
sible consequences, and the possible solutions"; and F
1947 set forth five principles for science fiction writin
tial and prolific author, argued that science fiction sho
world; (2) make this faraway environment an integra
feature a human problem or dilemma that is the focu
that the developing problem relates to and results fr
and, most importantly, (5) rely on accurate scientifi
who wrote for Campbell include Ray Bradbury (w
novel *Fahrenheit 451* [1953]); Lester Del Rey; L. Ron
Dianetics: The Modern Science of Mental Health [195
tology); Henry Kuttner; Catherine L. Moore (who w
Clifford D. Simak; and E. E. Smith, Ph.D. (known as "

Another influential and independent group of An
writers and fans known as the Futurians emerged in t
which was based in New York and active from 1938
ence fiction fans "should be forward-looking ('futu
tive." Members included James Blish, Damon Knig
Robert A. W. Lowndes, Frederik Pohl, and Donald
considered the group's leader in the 1930s). Asimov
with the group.

In 1949 and 1950, respectively, two important new
azines appeared: *The Magazine of Fantasy and Scie*
and *Galaxy* (1950–80). *Galaxy,* edited by Pohl and H
a number of works in serial form that became partic
cluding Heinlein's *The Puppet Masters* (1951), Pohl a
Space Merchants (1952), and Asimov's *The Caves of*
to film 1984).

Hollywood's popularization of several recurring th
tion further contributed to the popularity of the ger
include *The Day the Earth Stood Still* (1951), a mov
the end of civilization; *Forbidden Planet* (1956), wh
speare's play *The Tempest* (1611) into a cautionary ta
of scientists; and the cult favorite *Invasion of the Bod*
which, through its depictions of "pod creatures" taki
ings, has been said by some to reflect fears of commur
individual freedom.

into their works. The American authors she most influenced tended to be already established writers such as Roger Zelazny, perhaps best known for *He Who Shapes* (1966); Kurt Vonnegut, whose *Slaughterhouse-Five* (1969) boosted science fiction's standing in the academic world; and Silverberg, the author of *Dying Inside* (1972).

While British and American New Wave writers such as Ballard, Brunner, Delaney, Ellison, and Silverberg remained popular throughout the 1970s, hard science fiction began to make a comeback. Writers like Clement, Fred Hoyle, Larry Niven, and others who had published in *Analog* resisted Moorcock and Merrill's philosophy. Although the New Wave movement eventually lost some of its influence, both in England and America, its guiding principles have continued to inspire new science fiction incorporating sophisticated literary techniques and topics related to the world's emerging political and moral problems.

The 1970s also marked a turning point for science fiction in terms of two other influences on the genre. First, many authors began to mix fantasy fiction — which generally differs from science fiction in featuring magic and the supernatural — and science fiction. Second, new themes such as the evolution of **gender** relations and gender roles emerged when female authors such as Le Guin, Marion Zimmer Bradley, Anne McCaffrey, Alice Sheldon, and Kate Wilhelm began contributing to a genre that had previously been dominated by men.

Toward the end of the twentieth century, a group of younger American authors influenced by William Gibson's novel *Neuromancer* (1984) started writing a new type of science fiction called **cyberpunk,** a mix of hard and soft science fiction that reflected the ideas and attitudes of the rebellious counterculture "punk" movement. Cyberpunk authors Rudy Rucker, Neal Stephenson, and Bruce Sterling write about future worlds populated by "cyborgs" — hybrid beings that are part human and part machine — living in societies dependent upon technology for their daily existence. But more traditional science fiction, now a blend of various influences of the past century, is still written and published in magazines like *Isaac Asimov's Science Fiction Magazine* (1977–).

Contemporary science fiction authors include Samuel R. Delaney (*Dahlgren* [1975]), Orson Scott Card (*Ender's Game* [1986]); Lucius Shepard (*Life During Wartime* [1987]); Lois McMaster Bujold (*Falling Free* [1989]); Kim Stanley Robinson (*Red Mars* [1992]); Paul J. McAuley (*Red Dust* [1993]), and Octavia E. Butler, who is best known for *The Xenogenesis Trilogy,* comprising *Dawn* (1987), *Adulthood Rites* (1988), and *Imago* (1989) and reissued as *Lilith's Brood* in 2000. Authors who are not typically classified as science fiction writers but who have made significant contributions to the genre include Stephen King, author of *The Dead Zone* (1979); Doris Lessing, whose four-novel *Canopus in Argos* series (1979–83) considers the possibilities presented by a feminist utopia; Carl Sagan, whose novel *Contact* (1985) was adapted into a 1997 film starring Jodie Foster; and Michael Crichton, whose *Jurassic Park* (1990) became a blockbuster movie in 1993. Other popular science fiction movies from the past few decades include *Close Encounters of the Third Kind* (1977), *E.T.* (1982), and the *Star Wars* movies (1977–2005).

▶ *scriptible* **(writerly):** See **poststructuralism, text.**

▶ **second-person point of view:** See **point of view.**

▶ **semantics:** See **linguistics.**

▶ **semiology:** Another word for **semiotics.** The term *semiology* was coined by Swiss linguist Ferdinand de Saussure, whose theory is set forth in the *Cours de linguistique générale* (*Course in General Linguistics*), published posthumously in 1916 and based on student notes of his lectures.
See **semiotics.**

▶ **semiotics:** A term coined by American philosopher Charles Sanders Peirce to refer to the study of **signs,** sign systems, and the way meaning is derived from them. **Structuralist** anthropologists, psychoanalysts, and **literary critics** developed semiotics during the decades following 1950, but much of the pioneering work had been done at the turn of the last century by Peirce and by the founder of modern **linguistics,** Ferdinand de Saussure.

To a semiotician, a sign is not simply a direct means of communication, such as a stop sign or a restaurant sign or language itself. Rather, signs encompass body language (crossed arms, slouching), ways of greeting and parting (handshakes, hugs, waves), artifacts, and even articles of clothing. A sign is anything that conveys information to others who understand it based upon a system of **codes** and **conventions** that they have consciously learned or unconsciously internalized as members of a certain culture. Semioticians have often used concepts derived from linguistics, which focuses on language, to analyze all types of signs.

Although Saussure viewed linguistics as a division of semiotics, much semiotic theory rests on Saussure's linguistic terms, concepts, and distinctions. Semioticians subscribe to Saussure's basic concept of the linguistic sign as containing a **signifier** (a linguistic "sound image" used to represent some more **abstract** concept) and **signified** (the abstract concept being represented). They have also found generally useful his notion that the relationship between signifiers and signified is arbitrary; that is, no intrinsic or natural relationship exists between them, and meanings we derive from signifiers are grounded in the differences *among* signifiers themselves. Particularly useful are Saussure's concept of the **phoneme** (the smallest basic speech sound or unit of pronunciation) and his idea that phonemes exist in two kinds of relationships: **diachronic** and *synchronic.*

A phoneme has a diachronic, or "horizontal," relationship with those other phonemes that precede and follow it (as the words appear, left to right, on this page) in a particular usage, utterance, or **narrative** — what Saussure called *parole* (French for "word"). A phoneme has a synchronic, or "vertical," relationship with the entire system of language within which individual usages, utterances, or narratives have meaning — what Saussure called *langue* (French for "tongue," as in "native tongue," meaning language). *Up* means what it means in English because those of us who speak the language are plugged into the same system (think of it as a computer network where different individuals access the same information in the same way at a given time). A principal tenet of semiotics is that signs, like words, are not significant in themselves but instead have meaning only in relation to other signs and the entire system of signs, or *langue*.

Given that semiotic theory underlies structuralism, it is not surprising that many semioticians have taken a broad, structuralist approach to signs, studying a variety of phenomena — ranging from rites of passage to methods of preparing and consuming food — in order to understand the cultural codes and conventions they reveal. Furthermore, because of the broad-based applicability of semiotics (including the emphasis on *langue*, or system), structuralist anthropologists (such as Claude Lévi-Strauss), **psychoanalytic theorists** (such as Jacques Lacan and Julia Kristeva), and literary critics (such as Roland Barthes, before his turn to **poststructuralism**) have made use of semiotic theories and practices.

See also **structuralism, structuralist criticism.**

▶ **Senecan tragedy:** A term used to refer both to (1) **tragedies** written by Seneca, a first-century A.D. Roman playwright (who modelled his own work on that of the fifth-century B.C. Greek playwright Euripides); and (2) **Renaissance** tragedies written during the **Elizabethan Age** that were modelled on Seneca's **classical** tragedies.

Seneca composed tragedies in five **acts**, a structure used more or less consistently by playwrights until the nineteenth century. He frequently employed **bombast**, a **chorus**, and a ghost; his plays showcased drastically conflicting emotions, emphasized violence and revenge, and inevitably ended in **catastrophe**. Seneca's emphasis on highly charged human emotion has been cited by many critics as crucial to the development of English drama, which had previously been used merely to portray events in an **allegorical** or **symbolic** manner.

Elizabethan playwrights **imitating** Seneca used these same basic elements but changed the character of Seneca's tragedies in two crucial ways. First, Elizabethan playwrights such as Thomas Kyd (*Spanish Tragedy* [1586]) deliberately brought violence *on*stage; in Seneca's tragedies, **characters** merely reported violent acts, which occurred offstage. Second, ignorant of the fact that Seneca's tragedies were **closet dramas** (plays meant to be read or recited, not performed), they presented their plays using actors. Elizabethan playwrights also employed an even more **rhetorical** style than Seneca, who was himself noted for his bombastic language. Aside from bombast, Elizabethans favored such devices as **hyperbole**, intensely dramatic and drawn-out **soliloquies**, and **stichomythia**. Thomas Sackville and Thomas Norton's

Gorboduc (1562), commonly recognized as the first Elizabethan tragedy, was just such a Senecan tragedy.

As the Elizabethan Age progressed, two distinct forms of Senecan tragedy began to emerge. One, exemplified by *Gorboduc*, closely parallels Seneca's tragedies and is learned, even pedantic, in spirit. The other, pitched at a broad audience and noted for its extreme emotion, blood, and gore, proved far more influential in the development of English literature and of English tragedy more specifically. This latter form, known as the **revenge tragedy** (or, in its most extreme manifestation, the *tragedy of blood*) mixed English **medieval** tragic tradition with classical Senecan tragedy, as exemplified by William Shakespeare's *Hamlet* (1602).

See also **revenge tragedy.**

▶ **sensibility:** A receptiveness or susceptibility to emotions and sentiments (rather than logic, reason, and thought). Sensibility is generally associated with delicacy of feeling, **empathy** with others, and sensitivity to beauty. A whole **literature of sensibility**, including the **sentimental comedy** and the **sentimental novel**, developed and flourished during the eighteenth century, drawing on the thought of philosophers such as Anthony Ashley Cooper, the third earl of Shaftesbury, who asserted the natural benevolence of humankind in *Characteristicks of Men, Manners, Opinions, Times* (1711), and reacting against two seventeenth-century philosophical currents, Stoic rationalism and Thomas Hobbes's characterization of humanity in *Leviathan* (1651) as inherently selfish and self-interested. Today the term **sentimentalism** is often used to derogate works containing what we would view as an overabundance of sensibility.

Sensibility has a second application in modern critical **discourse**, one referring to an individual's sensitivity (both intellectual and emotional) to **aesthetics** and sensory experience. Thus, one might speak of a writer — or, for that matter, of a friend — as having a romantic or poetic sensibility. T. S. Eliot used the phrase **dissociation of sensibility** to refer to authors whose works reveal a divergence of thought and feeling.

See also **Age of Johnson, dissociation of sensibility, literature of sensibility.**

▶ *sententia:* See **aphorism.**

▶ **sentimental comedy (drama of sensibility):** One of the literary manifestations of **sentimentalism** and the **literature of sensibility** in the eighteenth century, a type of **drama** featuring virtuous but beleaguered middle-class characters who ultimately triumph over evil, immorality, or injustice. Sentimental comedies arose in reaction to what was viewed as the excess, impropriety, and debauchery of **Restoration Age** drama, which English bishop Jeremy Collier attacked in his *Short View of the Immorality and Profaneness of the English Stage* (1698). Irish writer Richard Steele is generally credited with inaugurating the **genre,** which was geared toward a growing middle class that prided itself on respectability and which tended to flatly represent **characters** as either completely good or completely bad.

While termed **comedies,** sentimental comedies were intended to engage the audience's sympathy, to evoke tears rather than laughter. (Indeed, the French counterpart was called the *comédie larmoyante,* or "tearful comedy.") The **genre** began to decline in the latter half of the eighteenth century, although sentimental dramas continued to be written — and to be popular in some quarters — well into the nineteenth century. Due to the **caricatures** — and also the jarring **plot** twists — that tend to accompany works designed to teach moral lessons, sentimental comedies almost invariably strike modern audiences as unconvincing and unrealistic.

EXAMPLES: Steele's *The Conscious Lovers* (1722), Hugh Kelly's *False Delicacy* (1768), Richard Cumberland's *The West Indian* (1771).

▶ **sentimentalism:** A term usually used pejoratively today to refer to works that play excessively and unconvincingly on the audience's emotions, particularly those of pity and sympathy. Authors are open to the charge of sentimentalism when, having failed to establish adequate **motivation,** they elicit those emotions through fast-acting, artificial means (for example, **scenes** involving drawn-out, tearful goodbyes and the use of saccharine romantic music). Literature is also labeled *sentimental* when an author exploits and exaggerates **sensibility,** i.e., susceptibility to feeling rather than reason.

What is viewed as sentimental in one era may not seem so in another; furthermore, what strikes one person as unvarnished sentimentalism may seem compelling and moving to another. Although contemporary critics and readers find incredibly exaggerated and "hokey" the types of death-bed scenes common in eighteenth- and nineteenth-century **sentimental novels** and **comedies,** many critics and readers of those eras were impressed by the power of such works to express and evoke genuine emotion.

EXAMPLES: Harriet Beecher Stowe's *Uncle Tom's Cabin* (1852) is a nineteenth-century example of a work steeped in sentimentalism, as reflected in the scenes in which a young slave mother, carrying her child, leaps from ice floe to ice floe across the Ohio River in a desperate attempt to escape a slave trader, and the death of the angelic Evangeline, who gives each of her family's slaves a lock of her hair, having preached to them the value of living a good Christian life:

> It is impossible to describe the scene, as, with tears and sobs, they gathered round the little creature, and took from her hands what seemed to them a last mark of her love. They fell on their knees; they sobbed, and prayed, and kissed the hem of her garment; and the elder ones poured forth words of endearment, mingled in prayers and blessings, after the manner of their susceptible race.

The musical *Annie* (1977; adapted to film 1982) and the television series *Lassie* (1954–74) are seen by many modern audiences as extremely — and sometimes excessively — sentimental; critically acclaimed films noted for

fabli...
Chau...
tamé...
in sh...
write...
Rue ...
in an...
empl...
the v...
denc...
ninet...
an a...
Hon...
Gerr...
story...
as Sl...
Erne...
Mar...
Jean...

F...
Aml...
"Th...
"Th...
Hav...
(197...
(199...
the ...

▶ si...
or ...
(*sh...*

E...
nar...
mer...
"H...
"st...
rea...

▶ s...
exi...
sig...
sor...
are ...
lar...
it ...
pr...

The Seven Cardinal V...
Virtues, considered the co...

▶ **Seven Deadly Sins:** Th...
Christian church believed ...
on the part of the sinner. ...
the sins of the Devil, wh...
sins of the world, which i...
which included lust, glutt...
fact more similar to what...
sins, pride was considere...
Satan's original fall from g...
ject matter for medieval (i...
ture, especially **allegories**.

Countering each of the...
gether, the Seven Contrar...
(wrath), kindness (envy), ...
(gluttony), and diligence (sl...

EXAMPLES: In very differ...
Tale," one of the *Canterbu*...
first book of Edmund Spen...
and characterize each of the...

▶ **sextet:** See **sestet**.

▶ **sexualities criticism:** See g...

▶ **sexuality:** A term referenc...
mosexual, bisexual, transgen...

Queer theorists, as well as...
ics, take a **constructionist** vie...
uct of prevailing social and ...
Drawing on gender theory, w...
with the **gender** designations ...
innate, such critics argue tha...
homosexuality and heterosex...
over, they tend to reject the s...
sexual, instead viewing sexual...
sexual orientation as well as ...
to transvestism.

Other gender, gay, and les...
taining that sexuality, like sex ...
is innate (genetically determin...
and heterosexuals are different ...
ics believe men and women to ...
tend that there are distinct hor...
and writing.

their sentimental power include *West Side Story* (1961), *Field of Dreams* (1989), *Braveheart* (1995), and *Million Dollar Baby* (2004).

▶ **sentimental novel:** One of the literary manifestations of **sentimentalism** and the **literature of sensibility** in the eighteenth century, a type of **novel** that typically appealed to the middle class in its emphasis on the importance of good conduct and rewards for adhering to moral standards. Sentimental novels also exalted emotion, portraying its expression as the mark of the virtuous. English novelist Samuel Richardson is generally credited with pioneering the **genre** in his **epistolary novel** *Pamela, or Virtue Rewarded* (1740).

FURTHER EXAMPLES: Oliver Goldsmith's *The Vicar of Wakefield* (1766); *Emma: Or, the Unfortunate Attachment: A Sentimental Novel* (1773), attributed to Georgiana Cavendish, Duchess of Devonshire; Johann Wolfgang von Goethe's *The Sorrows of Young Werther* (1774); William Hill Brown's *The Power of Sympathy* (1789). In the nineteenth century, Jane Austen's *Sense and Sensibility* (1811) **satirized** the genre and the concept of **sensibility** more generally, but many works continued in the sentimental vein, such as Susan Warner's *The Wide, Wide World* (1850). Harriet Jacobs likewise drew on the techniques and **conventions** of the sentimental novel in her **slave narrative** *Incidents in the Life of a Slave Girl* (1861) in order to represent her vulnerability to the sexual advances of white men and thereby evoke readers' sympathy.

▶ **septenary:** See **heptameter**.

▶ **sestet (sextet):** (1) Generally speaking, any six-line poem or **stanza**. (2) More specifically, the second part (the last six lines) of an **Italian sonnet**. The sestet succeeds the **octave**, which may pose a question or dilemma that the sestet answers or resolves, and usually follows the **rhyme scheme** *cdecde*, although variations occur.

▶ **sestina:** A tightly structured French **verse** form consisting of six **sestets** (six-line **stanzas**) and a three-line **envoy**. Widely acknowledged to be one of the most complicated verse forms, the sestina originated in **medieval** Provence. The six terminal words of the first stanza (1-2-3-4-5-6) are repeated in a specific and complex pattern as the terminal words in each of the succeeding stanzas (6-1-5-2-4-3; 3-6-4-1-2-5; 5-3-2-6-1-4; 4-5-1-3-6-2; and 2-4-6-5-3-1). They are also repeated in the envoy, at the end of the three lines (5-3-1) and in the middle (2-4-6). Early practitioners include Arnaut Daniel, a Provençal **troubadour** generally credited with inventing the form, and Italian poets Dante Alighieri and Petrarch (Francesco Petrarca). Noted practitioners in English range from the **Elizabethan** Sir Philip Sidney to the **Victorian** Algernon Charles Swinburne to the **modernist** Ezra Pound.

EXAMPLES: Rudyard Kipling's regular "Sestina of the Tramp-Royal" (1896), which ends "Gawd bless this world! Whatever she 'ath done — /

Excep' when awful long —
liked it all!'" Examples of
"Altaforte" (1909), which ι
rejoicing as its terminal woι
and Elizabeth Bishop's "Seι
land Sestina" (1988) adherι
stanzas and the envoy follоι

> There's somethι
> No other meets
> of walking on a
> and skipping stο
> The solitude is sι
> and heard in whι

> The kingbird anc
> bring music to th
> and chipmunks o
> The flight of gullι
> The flowers in thι
> and daisies spring

> The dune is but a
> Its borders are mι
> The green appearι
> to compliment duι
> The dune crest, plι
> gives way in gentlι

> The mood of peacι
> The water, tranquι
> as songs from whiι

▶ **setting:** That combination of
provides the general backgrouι
work. The general setting of a w
individual scene or event; noneι
tribute to the overall setting. Iι
backdrop of the play, that is, thι
ting frequently plays a crucial roι

▶ **Seven Cardinal Virtues:** The
tian theologians as being of parι
charity (love), faith, hope, fortι
Biblical teachings (1 Cor. 13:13
as such, they have often been caι
virtues, emphasized by ancient ι
natural virtues.

Whe
agree tl
and ma

▶ **Shakι

▶ **shapι

▶ **she-ι

▶ **shorι
rhymeι
ten in
often ι
EXAι
Timot

Many
folloι

▶ **shι
word
storiι
as O
(the ι
**novι
The
forrι
shipι
simι
or cl
shor
reve
war
subι
chaι
ber

T
froι

Sanders Peirce contended that **symbols** are also signs. Calling the symbol a "sign proper," he argued that symbols do not involve natural or inherent relationships to what they suggest but, rather, arbitrary socially and culturally determined relationships. For instance, when flown by ships, monochromatic flags of certain colors are internationally understood to represent specific conditions; red signifies danger or revolution, yellow quarantine, black death or protest, white truce or surrender, green proceed, and orange distress.

Swiss linguist Ferdinand de Saussure defined the "linguistic sign" as composed of a **signifier**, a linguistic "sound-image" used to represent some comparatively **abstract** concept, and a **signified**, the concept being represented. As set forth in the *Cours de linguistique générale* (*Course in General Linguistics*), published posthumously in 1916 and based on student notes of his lectures, Saussure argued that a "linguistic sign is not a link between a thing and a name, but between a concept and a sound pattern," and characterized a "linguistic system" as "a series of differences of sound combined with a series of differences of ideas." He also argued that the relationship between signifier and signified is arbitrary, that is, that no intrinsic or natural relationship exists between them. For instance, French speakers regard the signifier *pour* as meaning "for," whereas to English speakers the same signifier means "cause to flow in a continuous stream" or "rain heavily." Saussure further argued that the meaning of any given sign arises from the difference between it and other signs in the same linguistic system.

Differences in language make meanings recognizable; the word *pour* means what it does in English because it is distinct from other words (such as *four* and *peer*) with which it can be compared and contrasted. Differences in meaning — including differences in the meaning of a given word in different verbal contexts — are learned **conventions** that speakers understand *as if* they were positive qualities, givens of Nature.

▶ **significance:** A term used in **hermeneutics** to designate how readers relate the *verbal meaning* of a work to other elements in their lives, such as personal experiences, values, beliefs, and general cultural mores. Significance is typically distinguished from verbal meaning, which refers to the **author's** intended meaning. Hermeneutic theory, whose best-known proponent is twentieth-century American critic E. D. Hirsch, postulates that verbal meaning can be determined but that significance cannot, since various readers bring different beliefs, values, and experiences to a **text**. Whereas verbal meaning can be construed as constant, significance changes from reader to reader; thus, no one significance is more right or wrong than any other. Hirsch therefore argued that significance is not the proper subject of hermeneutic analysis.

▶ **signified:** See **signifier**.

▶ **signifier:** In **linguistics**, the "sound-image," or word, used to **represent** a comparatively **abstract** concept, the **signified**. For example, the word *flag* is a signifier that calls up the idea of a flag, the signified, in the mind of an English-speaking person. According to Swiss linguist Ferdinand de Saussure, the relationship between signifier and signified is arbitrary — there is no intrinsic reason, for instance, why the word *flag* calls up the idea of a flag rather than a flea or a flood — and established by **convention,** such that the signifier and signified together constitute a **sign** understood by members of the same linguistic system. Indeed, one signifier may have many signifieds (*eye* may refer to the center of a hurricane, the hole in a needle, or the organ of sight), and one signified may have many signifiers (as is the case with synonyms such as *big* and *large*).

While Saussure **privileged** sound and speech in his analysis — set forth in the *Cours de linguistique générale* (*Course in General Linguistics*), published posthumously in 1916 and based on student notes of his lectures — contemporary theorists apply the term *signifier* equally to spoken and written forms of words. The term is also used in the field of **semiotics** (or **semiology**), the study of signs more generally, to refer to the material or physical form of a sign; for example, a thumb's up gesture is a signifier of approval in some cultures, the color orange a signifier of construction.

Poststructuralists have pointed out that every signified is also a signifier, creating an endless chain of signification. For instance, while the signifier *flag* calls up the idea of a flag, the idea of a flag in turn evokes other signifieds, such as country and patriotism, which themselves evoke still more signifieds, such as courage and sacrifice.

▶ **simile:** A **figure of speech** (more specifically a **trope**) that compares two distinct things by using words such as *like* or *as* to link the **vehicle** and the **tenor.** Simile is distinguished from **metaphor,** another trope that associates two distinct things, but without the use of a connective word. To say "That child is like a cyclone" is to use a simile, whereas to say "That child is a cyclone" is to use a metaphor. In either case, the cyclone is the vehicle, the **image** used to represent the child, which is the tenor, or subject of the figure.

An **epic,** or **Homeric, simile** is an extended and elaborate simile in which the vehicle is described at such length that it nearly obscures the tenor.

EXAMPLES: Percy Bysshe Shelley's "Adonais" (1821) uses a simile to figure life:

> Life, like a dome of many-coloured glass,
> Stains the white radiance of Eternity
> Until Death tramples it to fragments. . . .

Twentieth-century Indian sage Ramana Maharshi made use of a simile in imparting philosophical advice:

> Wanting to reform the world without discovering one's true self is like trying to cover the world with leather to avoid the pain of walking on stones and thorns. It is much simpler to wear shoes.

Where literature is concerned, American poet Robert Frost asserted that "writing free verse is like playing tennis with the net down"; Yiddish novelist Isaac Bashevis Singer declared, "The short story is like a room to be furnished; the novel is like a warehouse."

The following **alliterative** passage from Jane Urquhart's *Away* (1993) concludes with a simile involving *as* rather than *like:*

> In this vibrant September he remembered the terror of late summer storms that had darkened noon and thundered at the door while lightning tore at the tops of thrashing pines, and because most of his previous life had been erased he played with these memories and even the fear connected to them as if they were bright new toys.

Hip-hop artists routinely employ similes. In the Fugees' "How Many Mics" (1996), Lauryn Hill compared being without a microphone to a beat that lacks a snare. In "We Got the Beat" (2004), Talib Kweli used six similes in the opening stanza alone, using *like* to make comparisons to things as different as college radio, a cockpit, a French kiss, and Loch Ness.

▶ **site:** A nongeographic "space," or place, where identity or meaning is formed or determined, largely by external forces such as those of history, language, or **ideology**. Characterizing a **text** as a site — an approach taken primarily by **poststructuralist** critics — diminishes the creative role of the **author**. Similarly, when the human subject, or self, is viewed as a site — whether influenced by what certain **psychoanalytic critics** term **the Other** or by the social and economic forces **privileged** by **Marxist critics** — the status of the individual is reduced.

▶ **situational irony:** See **irony**.

▶ **situation comedy (sitcom):** See **comedy**.

▶ **slant rhyme:** See **half rhyme**.

▶ **slapstick:** See **comedy**.

▶ **slave narrative:** A type of **narrative** written by a former slave that typically recounts his or her life as a slave and escape from slavery. Slave narratives written by Africans or African Americans in America in the eighteenth and nineteenth centuries generally focused on the hardships of slavery (particularly the cruelty and hypocrisy of slave owners, the abuse and suffering of slaves, and the separation of slave families), the slave's yearning for education and freedom, and Christian beliefs and virtues. The narratives were **didactic,** chiefly intended to convince the reader that slavery, the so-called "peculiar institution," needed to be abolished. As such, scholars have debated the extent to which they were strictly **autobiographical;** events might be relayed out of chronological order, **dialogue** might be fictionalized, and **characters** might be composites or even based on stereotypes. The first American slave narrative, *A Narrative of the Uncommon Sufferings, and Surprizing Deliverance of Briton*

Hammon, A Negro Man, was published in 1760, but the **genre** was most prominent in the thirty years leading up to the Civil War (1861–65), after which slavery was abolished by the Thirteenth Amendment.

While slave narratives from America (or the Caribbean) are best-known, others exist, too. Several slave narratives from the eighteenth and early nineteenth centuries recount the experience of enslaved whites in North Africa, such as *The History of the Long Captivity and Adventures of Thomas Pellow, in South Barbary* (1740), written by a Cornish man captured by Barbary pirates and sold into slavery as a boy. There are also modern slave narratives, such as Francis Bok's account of his enslavement as a child in Sudan, *Escape from Slavery: The True Story of My Ten Years in Captivity — and My Journey to Freedom in America* (2004).

FURTHER EXAMPLES: Frederick Douglass's *Narrative of the Life of Frederick Douglass* (1845) is the best-known American slave narrative. Other examples include Olaudah Equiano's *The Interesting Narrative of the Life of Olaudah Equiano* (1789) and Harriet Jacobs's *Incidents in the Life of a Slave Girl* (1861).

▶ **socialist realism:** A **mode** of **representation** characterized by a **Marxist** emphasis on **class** struggle as the catalyst for historical change and employing the techniques of nineteenth-century Russian **realism**. The term was likely coined in 1932, the year the *Literary Gazette,* the official publication of the Union of Soviet Writers, published an article asserting that "the masses demand of an artist honesty, truthfulness, and a revolutionary socialist realism in the representation of this proletarian revolution." It was used with reference to all of the arts, from literature and film to painting and sculpture, as well as architecture and music.

Socialist realism became the official literary **form** of the former Soviet Union in the 1930s, adopted by the Communist regime's Party Central Committee in 1932 and by the First Congress of the Union of Soviet Writers in 1934, which described it as "the truthful, historically concrete representation of reality in its revolutionary development" and further asserted that such representation "must be linked with the task of ideological transformation and education of workers in the spirit of socialism." All works were to be consonant with Marxist-Leninist **ideology,** class-conscious, Party-minded, and accessible to and reflective of the people's interests and values; they were to glorify communism and present a **didactic,** optimistic view of the proletarian struggle against bourgeois capitalism and toward social consciousness. Writers and artists were viewed as agents of the state whose principal role was to reinforce and advance doctrinally "correct" thinking. Key figures in the adoption and promulgation of the form included the USSR's dictatorial leader Joseph Stalin, who in 1932 called writers "the engineers of human souls"; Russian writer Maxim Gorky, who authored an essay "On Socialist Realism" (1933); and Soviet politician Andrei Zhdanov, who formulated "Zhdanovism," an anti-Western cultural policy of strict, ideologically-based control of the arts.

Socialist realism persisted until the collapse of the Soviet Union in 1991, though strictures were somewhat relaxed following Stalin's death in 1953 and in the 1980s under the reform policies of Mikhail Gorbachev. It had minimal impact in the Western world, where it was roundly criticized for state censorship and propagandistic aims, but became an important form in Eastern European countries under Soviet domination during the twentieth century.

EXAMPLES: Socialist realist novels include Gorky's *Mother* (1906), Fyodor Gladkov's *Cement* (1925), Alexander Fadeyev's *The Rout* (1927), and Nikolai Ostrovsky's *How the Steel Was Tempered* (1936). Examples of socialist realist art include Karp Trokhimenko's painting "Stalin as an Organizer of the October Revolution," done in the 1940s, and Boris Eremeevich Vladimirski's painting "Roses for Stalin" (1949).

▶ **sociological novel:** A **novel** detailing the prevailing societal — economic, political, and social — conditions during the period in which the work is set. Sometimes called *problem novels, social novels,* or *thesis novels,* sociological novels are often **didactic** and usually advocate social or political change.

EXAMPLES: Elizabeth Gaskell's *Mary Barton* (1848), Charles Dickens's *Hard Times* (1854), Upton Sinclair's *The Jungle* (1906), John Steinbeck's *The Grapes of Wrath* (1939). More recent examples include T. Coraghessan Boyle's *The Tortilla Curtain* (1995); *The Swallows of Kabul* (2005), written by Algerian army officer Mohammed Moulessehoul under the *nom de plume* Yasmina Khadra; and Walter Mosley's *Easy Rawlins* **mystery** series (1990–), which documents life in the Watts neighborhood of South Central L.A.

▶ **Socratic irony:** See **irony.**

▶ **soliloquy:** In a **play,** a **monologue** delivered by a **character** while alone on stage that reveals inner thoughts, emotions, or other information that the audience needs to know.

EXAMPLES: William Shakespeare's *Hamlet* (1602) contains perhaps the most famous soliloquy in English literature: "To be, or not to be: that is the question . . . . " In Peter Shaffer's 1973 play *Equus*, psychiatrist Martin Dysart muses about the "normalizing" goal of professional therapy; his speech is effectively a soliloquy since the only other character onstage is his deeply disturbed patient Alan Strang, whom he has hypnotized:

> The Normal is the good smile in a child's eyes — all right. It is also the dead stare in a million adults. It both sustains and kills — like a God. It is the Ordinary made beautiful; it is also the Average made lethal. The Normal is the indispensable, murderous God of Health, and I am his Priest. . . . Sacrifices to Zeus took at the most, surely, sixty seconds each. Sacrifices to the Normal can take as long as sixty months.

John Guare's play *Six Degrees of Separation* (1990; adapted to film 1993) includes soliloquies by several characters, including the **protagonist,** Louisa

Kittredge, who, having been conned by a young man pretending to be Sidney Poitier's son, marvels that "everybody on this planet is separated by only six other people. Six degrees of separation . . . ."

▶ **sonnet:** From the Italian word for "little song," a **lyric poem** that typically consists of fourteen lines (usually printed as a single **stanza**) and that typically follows one of several **conventional rhyme schemes**. Sonnets may address a range of issues or **themes**, but love, the original subject of the sonnet, is perhaps still the most common.

Two major types of sonnets exist: the **Italian**, or *Petrarchan*, **sonnet** and the **English**, or *Shakespearean*, **sonnet**. (*Petrarchan* and *Shakespearean* refer, respectively, to the most famous practitioners of these forms: Francesco Petrarca and William Shakespeare.) The Italian sonnet has two parts: the **octave**, eight lines with the rhyme scheme *abbaabba*, and the **sestet**, six lines usually **rhyming** *cdecde* or *cdcdcd*. The English sonnet is divided into three **quatrains** and a **couplet**, rhyming *abab cdcd efef gg*. The **Spenserian sonnet**, which follows the same basic stanza **form** as the English sonnet, consists of three quatrains rhyming *abab bcbc cdcd*, to link the quatrains together, and a couplet rhyming *ee*. **Iambic pentameter** is the most common **meter** for all three forms.

The sonnet originated in Italy in the thirteenth century, developed by Sicilian poet Giacomo da Lentini and Tuscan poet Guittone d'Arezzo. The form eventually spread to other European countries, flourishing during the **Renaissance** and reaching England in the early sixteenth century. Sir Thomas Wyatt, who translated and **imitated** Italian sonnets, is generally credited with introducing the form into England; Henry Howard, Earl of Surrey, is generally credited with developing the English sonnet form specifically. Subsequently, during the **Neoclassical Period**, the sonnet declined throughout Europe before being revived by **romantic** poets in the nineteenth century.

Over time, various poets have experimented with the sonnet form. George Meredith, an English novelist and poet, wrote sixteen-line poems with an *abba cddc effe ghhg* rhyme scheme in his sequence *Modern Love* (1862). **Victorian** poet Gerard Manley Hopkins developed the *curtal sonnet*, a short, ten-line form divided into a six-line stanza followed by a four-line stanza with a half-line tail. Nineteenth-century French poet Paul Verlaine and twentieth-century English poet Rupert Brooke tried "inverting" sonnets; Verlaine flipped the parts of the Italian sonnet in "Sappho," the last sonnet in his collection *Les amies (The Girlfriends)* (1868), opening with the sestet, and Brooke inverted the English form, beginning with a couplet in "Sonnet Reversed" (1911). *Terza rima sonnets* follow the linking rhyme scheme *aba bcb cdc ded ee*. Many twentieth-century and contemporary sonneteers have experimented even more radically with the form, dispensing with meter and/or rhyme altogether.

Noted sonneteers writing in English include Sir Philip Sidney, John Milton, John Keats, William Wordsworth, Elizabeth Barrett Browning, Dante Gabriel Rossetti, Robert Frost, Edna St. Vincent Millay, W. H. Auden, and

Robert Lowell. Other noted sonneteers include Joachim du Bellay, Pierre de Ronsard, and Charles Baudelaire, writing in French; in German, Georg Rudolf Weckherlin, Gottfried Bürger, August Graf von Platen, and Rainer Maria Rilke; in Italian, Dante Alighieri and Michelangelo; and, in Spanish, Garcilaso de la Vega.

FURTHER EXAMPLES: Sidney's **sonnet sequence** *Astrophel and Stella* (1591); Donne's *Holy Sonnets* (c. 1607–13). Oscar Wilde included "Hélas," an Italian sonnet about his career as a writer, as an **epigraph** to his *Poems* (1881):

> To drift with every passion till my soul
> Is a stringed lute on which all winds can play,
> Is it for this that I have given away
> Mine ancient wisdom, and austere control? —
> Methinks my life is a twice-written scroll
> Scrawled over on some boyish holiday
> With idle songs for pipe and virelay°   *jingle*
> Which do but mar the secret of the whole.
> Surely there was a time I might have trod
> The sunlit heights, and from life's dissonance
> Struck one clear chord to reach the ears of God:
> Is that time dead? lo! with a little rod
> I did but touch the honey of romance —
> And must I lose a soul's inheritance?

Twentieth-century examples include Claude McKay's "If We Must Die" (1919), Pablo Neruda's *Cien sonetos de amor* (*100 Love Sonnets*) (1960), Ted Berrigan's *The Sonnets* (1964), Seamus Heaney's sonnet sequence "Clearances" (1987), Bernadette Mayer's *Sonnets* (1989), and Wanda Coleman's *American Sonnets* (1994). Marilyn Hacker's verse novel *Love, Death, and the Changing of the Seasons* (1986) is composed of sonnets and **villanelles**.

See **sonnet sequence** for further examples.

▶ **sonnet redoublé:** See **sonnet sequence.**

▶ **sonnet sequence (sonnet cycle):** A series or group of **sonnets** interconnected by subject and written by one poet. The sonnet sequence frequently explores the **theme** of love and the poet's fluctuating attitudes toward it.

Form may also be used to heighten the unity of the sequence. In a *corona,* or *crown of sonnets,* the last line of each sonnet serves as the first line of the next, and the last line of the final sonnet echoes the first line of the opening one, thereby coming full circle. An even more demanding form, the *sonnet redoublé,* consists of a corona of fourteen sonnets succeeded by a final, fifteenth sonnet in which all of the prior linking lines are repeated, in order.

EXAMPLES: William Shakespeare's 154 sonnets, first published as *Shake-Speares Sonnets* (1609); Elizabeth Barrett Browning's *Sonnets from the Portuguese* (1850); Dante Gabriel Rossetti's *The House of Life* (1881); Rupert Brooke's *1914* (1915).

▶ **speech-act theory:** A theory of language, originally developed by British "ordinary-language" philosopher John L. Austin, that emphasizes the contextual, performative nature of speech and views utterances as acts governed by rules. Speech-act theorists contest the traditional assumptions that: (1) all possible sentences are either *kernel* (basic) sentences or variations of them; and (2) these kernel sentences declare something that can be determined to be either true or false.

In his most influential work, *How to Do Things with Words* (1962), Austin classified **locutions** (utterances) as **constatives** or **performatives.** Constative locutions are sentences that state something that can be determined to be true or false. Performative locutions, by contrast, are sentences that actively "do" something, such as question, admonish, or plead. Some performatives, which Austin called "explicit performatives," actually create the result they intend when they are uttered, as when a minister pronounces, "I baptize you in the name of the Father, the Son, and the Holy Ghost," or when the dealer in a card game states, "Deuces are wild." Having made the distinction between constatives and performatives, however, Austin then demonstrated that the two categories are not mutually exclusive. For instance, "You are in trouble" is a constative insofar as it asserts a state of affairs and a performative insofar as it makes a threat. Austin also identified three major types of speech acts: (1) the **locutionary act,** which he defined as "an act *of* saying something" (with a meaning); (2) the **illocutionary act,** which he characterized as the "performance of an act *in* saying something" (e.g., informing, ordering, warning); and (3) the **perlocutionary act,** "what we bring about or achieve *by* saying something" (e.g., persuading, surprising, misleading). He emphasized the need to distinguish between illocutionary acts, which perform a particular function, and perlocutionary acts, the occurrence of which depends on whether the utterance actually affects the hearer's actions or state of mind.

Subsequently, in *Speech Acts: An Essay in the Philosophy of Language* (1969), John R. Searle, an Austin disciple, further developed speech-act theory, arguing that "talking is performing acts according to rules" and identifying four types of speech acts. The **utterance act,** which Searle defined simply as "uttering words," occurs whenever someone speaks, regardless of whether the utterance makes sense. The **propositional act,** defined as "referring and predicating" — referring to an object and predicating something upon that object — involves saying something about something else. For instance, in Searle's example "Sam smokes habitually," Sam is the object referred to, and "smokes habitually" is the predicating expression. Searle also adopted two of Austin's speech acts, the illocutionary and perlocutionary acts, noting that illocutionary acts need not have perlocutionary effects and that perlocutionary effects need not depend on the speaker's intent.

H. P. Grice, another ordinary-language philosopher, also made significant contributions to speech-act theory in essays such as "Logic and Conversation" (1975), where he developed his concept of the *communicative presumption,* a set of assumptions that he claims are shared by speakers of any given language.

Many of the tenets of speech-act theory have been incorporated into contemporary approaches to **literary criticism.** Grice's concept of the communicative presumption, for instance, played a major role in the development of **discourse analysis.** Austin's and Searle's speech acts have provided a conceptual model for critics from a variety of approaches for the systematic analysis of **discourse.** Certain speech-act theorists have revised **mimetic criticism,** arguing that literature — rather than offering a **representation** or **mimesis** of real places, things, people, and their utterances — is instead "mimetic discourse," language that **represents** the language through which we represent ourselves in the real world. Other critics using speech-act theory to revise traditional concepts of literature and, more specifically, prose **fiction** have proposed that readers and **authors** alike share the assumption that the overall framework set up by the author in a work may violate ordinary standards of **verisimilitude.** However, *within* that framework, illocutionary statements made by characters must be taken at face value — that is, assumed to be reliable and to rest on a commitment to truth of assertion, just as if they were illocutionary statements made in the real world. **Deconstructors,** who view **texts** as **rhetoric** (rather than as a picture window through which a fixed and reliably correct meaning or truth may be glimpsed), have used speech-act theory to suggest that the performative nature of language leads readers to interpretive impasses, points at which they must choose between contradictory interpretive possibilities and accede to the **undecidability** of the text's meaning.

See **illocutionary act, locutionary act, perlocutionary act, propositional act,** and **utterance act** for further discussion of these types of speech acts.

▶ **Spenserian sonnet:** A type of **sonnet** developed by sixteenth-century English poet Edmund Spenser that follows the same basic **stanza** form as the **English,** or *Shakespearean,* **sonnet** — three **quatrains** followed by a **couplet** — but whose **rhyme scheme** — *abab bcbc cdcd ee* — links the three quatrains together. The **form** is rare.

EXAMPLE: The seventy-fifth sonnet from Spenser's **sonnet sequence** *Amoretti* (1595):

> One day I wrote her name upon the strand,
> But came the waves and washéd it away:
> Agayne I wrote it with a second hand,
> But came the tyde, and made my paynes his prey.
> "Vayne man," sayd she, "that doest in vaine assay,
> A mortall thing so to immortalize,
> For I my selve shall lyke to this decay,
> And eek my name bee wypéd out lykewize."
> "Not so," quod I, "let baser things devize
> To dy in dust, but you shall live by fame:
> My verse your vertues rare shall eternize,
> And in the heavens write your glorious name.

> Where whenas death shall all the world subdew,
> Our love shall live, and later life renew."

Richard Wilbur's "Praise in Summer" (1947) is a twentieth-century example of the form.

▶ **Spenserian stanza:** A complex **stanza** form developed by sixteenth-century English poet Edmund Spenser for his long **narrative** poem, *The Faerie Queene* (1590, 1596). A Spenserian stanza has nine lines with the **rhyme scheme** *ababbcbcc*. The first eight lines are written in **iambic pentameter,** and the final line is an **Alexandrine** (iambic **hexameter**). Other poets who have used the form include the **romantics** George Gordon, Lord Byron; John Keats; and Percy Bysshe Shelley.

EXAMPLES: The opening stanza of the first **canto** of Spenser's *The Faerie Queene:*

> A gentle Knight was pricking on the plaine,
> Ycladd in mightie armes and silver shielde,
> Wherein old dints of deepe woundes did remaine,
> The cruel markes of many' a bloody fielde;
> Yet armes till that time did he never wield:
> His angry steede did chide his foming bitt,
> As much disdayning to the curbe to yield:
> Full jolly knight he seemed, and faire did sitt,
> As one for knightly giusts and fierce encounters fitt.

Keats employed the Spenserian stanza form in "The Eve of St. Agnes" (1820):

> Anon his heart revives: Her vespers done,
> Of all its wreathéd pearls her hair she frees;
> Unclasps her warméd jewels one by one;
> Loosens her fragrant bodice; by degrees
> Her rich attire creeps rustling to her knees:
> Half-hidden, like a mermaid in sea-weed,
> Pensive awhile she dreams awake, and sees,
> In fancy, fair St. Agnes in her bed,
> But dares not look behind, or all the charm is fled.

▶ **spondee:** A **metrical foot** in **poetry** that consists of two **stressed** syllables (´´). The use of the spondee as the base, or predominant, foot of a poem is rare.

EXAMPLES: bést-knówn, fúll móon, séa bréeze. The first half of the nursery rhyme "One, two, buckle my shoe," is heavily spondaic, as is the first **stanza** of Dylan Thomas's poem "Do Not Go Gentle into That Good Night" (1952):

> Dó nót gó géntle into that góod níght,
>
> Óld áge should búrn and rave at close of day;
>
> Ráge, ráge against the dying of the light.

▶ **spoof:** See **parody.**

▶ **sprung rhythm:** A type of **meter,** developed by nineteenth-century English poet Gerard Manley Hopkins to imitate the **rhythm** of speech, in which the number of **stressed** syllables in a line is constant but the number of unstressed syllables varies. In sprung rhythm, each of the stressed syllables must occur as the first syllable of a **foot,** with each foot typically containing a total of one to four syllables. Accordingly, sprung rhythm may have four types of feet: the **monosyllabic** (´), **trochee** (´ ˘), **dactyl** (´ ˘ ˘), and first **paeon** (´ ˘ ˘ ˘).

Hopkins, who described his system of **prosody** in an "Author's Preface" (1883) posthumously published in *Poems* (1918), considered himself more the **theorist** than the inventor of sprung rhythm. Indeed, he deemed sprung rhythm "the most natural of things . . . the rhythm of common speech and of written prose," reflected in works ranging from William Langland's *Piers Plowman* (1366–87) to **choruses,** nursery rhymes, and "weather saws." Some critics, however, have disagreed, as Paull F. Baum did in "Sprung Rhythm" (1959), viewing it "not [as] a modification or extension of conventional verse" but as a "new creation," Hopkins's "own blend of the freedom of prose and the ordered patterns of verse."

EXAMPLE: Hopkins's "The Windhover" (1918) (the marks identifying stressed syllables are the poet's own):

> I caught this morning morning's minion, king-
>
> dom of daylight's dauphin, dapple-dawn-drawn Falcon, in his riding
>
> Of the rolling level underneath him steady air, and striding. . . .

▶ **spy fiction, spy novel:** See **mystery fiction.**

▶ **stanza:** A grouped set of lines in a **poem,** usually physically separated from other such clusters by a blank line. Stanzas often have a recurrent **form:** a constant number of lines; a constant number of **feet** per line; and a set **meter** and **rhyme scheme.**

Some critics use the term **strophe** synonymously with *stanza;* others draw a distinction between the two, using *stanza* for the regular, **rhymed** divisions of a poem and *strophe* for irregular, unrhymed divisions.

▶ **stichomythia:** A form of dramatic **dialogue,** also called "cut-and-parry" or "cut-and-thrust" dialogue, in which two actors alternately exchange barbed and pregnant one-liners. Stichomythia is characterized by the use of **antithesis** and repetition, particularly in turning an opponent's words to one's own advantage in argument or repartee. It originated in **classical** Greek **drama** and features prominently in **tragedies** by Aeschylus and Sophocles, such as *Agamemnon* (c. 458 B.C.) and *Antigone* (c. 441 B.C.), respectively. First-century A.D. Roman playwright Seneca also used the device, as did **Elizabethan** playwrights, particularly in **Senecan tragedies** but also in **comedies** such as William Shakespeare's *Love's Labour's Lost* (c. 1597–98).

EXAMPLE: The following lines from act IV, scene IV, of Shakespeare's *Richard III* (1597), in which King Richard attempts to convince his sister-in-law Queen Elizabeth, whose sons he murdered to ascend to the throne, to help him woo her daughter:

> King Richard: Say, I, her sovereign, am her subject love.
> Queen Elizabeth: But she, your subject, loathes such sovereignty.
> King Richard: Be eloquent in my behalf to her.
> Queen Elizabeth: An honest tale speeds best being plainly told.
> King Richard: Then, plainly to her tell my loving tale.
> Queen Elizabeth: Plain and not honest is too harsh a style.
> King Richard: Your reasons are too shallow and too quick.
> Queen Elizabeth: O, no, my reasons are too deep and dead; —
>   Too deep and dead, poor infants, in their graves.
> King Richard: Harp not on that string, madam; that is past.
> Queen Elizabeth: Harp on it still shall I till heart-strings break.

▶ **stock character:** An established, instantly recognizable **character** type to whom the audience or reader ascribes specific characteristics by virtue of **convention.** Some stock characters recur within a particular **genre,** whereas others regularly appear in a variety of genres. Stock characters are often, but not always, stereotyped or **flat;** many are **caricatures** drawn simply and defined by a single idea or quality, but some are more fully developed, or **round.**

EXAMPLES: In **fairy tales,** the wicked stepmother and her intended victim, a beautiful, innocent young girl; the **villain** with an oily-looking "handlebar" mustache in **Victorian melodramas** and early movies; the strong, silent, gun-toting macho cowboy in American Westerns. The braggart soldier appears in works ranging from ancient Roman **comedies** such as Plautus's *Miles Gloriosus* (c. 205 B.C.) to William Shakespeare's plays to *commedia dell'arte* (a form of improvisational comedy in which the braggart soldier is called "il Capitano") to the musical *A Funny Thing Happened on the Way to the Forum* (1962; adapted to film 1966). Contemporary Disney productions often include wise-cracking sidekicks: the crab Sebastian in *The Little Mermaid* (1989); the green, one-eyed monster Mike Wazowski in *Monsters, Inc.* (with Pixar, 2001); the title character's friend Lilly Truscott in *Hannah Montana* (Disney Channel; 2006–).

▶ **stock response:** An uncritical, automatic, "knee-jerk" response to a given situation from the audience or reader; a response according to **convention** rather than true feeling or appropriate judgment.

EXAMPLES: The death of a child typically elicits sadness; soldiers going into battle carrying the flag evoke a feeling of patriotism.

▶ **Storm and Stress:** See *Sturm und Drang.*

▶ **story:** A **narrative** of events ordered chronologically.
See **plot** for the distinction between plot and story.

▶ **stream of consciousness:** In psychology, the continuous flow of past and present experience through the conscious mind; in literature, a narrative cause a particular social group to view those texts as meaningful. They are especially indebted to Barthes, who in works such as "The Death of the Author" (1967) and *S/Z* (1970) pronounced the death of the author, emphasized the role of the reader (or, more precisely, *lecture,* or reading), and differentiated the *lisible* (readerly) text (one that would provide the reader with a world replete with fixed meanings) from the more open, *scriptible* (writerly) text (one that invites readers to create meaning).

Structuralism and structuralist criticism began to wane in the late 1960s, when they came under vigorous attack by **poststructuralists.** Poststructuralists rejected the structuralist claim to scientific analysis. More importantly, they argued that meaning could not be definitively determined, maintaining that all systems of signification endlessly defer meaning through a chain of **signifiers.** Each word, according to poststructuralists, evokes a number of possible significations, which in turn evoke other significations in an interminable sequence so that no single meaning can ever be positively ascertained to be the true and correct one. In fact, some significations may even be contradictory, making an absolute determination of meaning impossible.

▶ **structure:** Often equated with **form,** the arrangement of material in a work, that is, the ordering of its component parts or the design devised by the **author** to convey content and meaning. In a poem, for instance, structure encompasses the division of the material into **stanzas.** Some critics extend the use of the term to include the arrangement of ideas or **images.** In a play, structure refers to the division of the material into **acts** and **scenes** as well as to the logical progression of the **action.** (**Freytag's Pyramid** provides one model for analyzing the sequence of events in a **tragedy:** introduction, **rising action, climax, falling action, catastrophe.**) In discussing novels, critics typically use the term to refer to **plot** (the ordering of the events that make up the **story**).

Some critics, such as those associated with the **Chicago school,** have distinguished between structure and form, arguing that form is the emotional force or shaping principle that gives rise to the mechanics of structure. For instance, in *The Idea of the Humanities and Other Essays* (1967), Chicago school theorist R. S. Crane described form as the "principle of construction, from which [the artist] infers, however instantaneously, what he must do in constituting and ordering the parts."

Other critics, particularly **the New Critics,** have distinguished between structure and **texture.** In *The New Criticism* (1941), for instance, John Crowe Ransom used *structure* to refer to the general intellectual content of a poem, that is, whatever can be paraphrased, and *texture* to refer to the surface details of a work, such as **imagery, meter,** and **rhyme.** He also argued that structure and texture together yield the poem's ontology, its utterly unique quality of being.

▶ ***Sturm und Drang* (Storm and Stress):** A late-eighteenth-century German literary movement in which **drama** was the **genre** of choice and whose adherents emphasized inspiration, emotion, passion, and individualism. The term is taken from the title of Friedrich Maximilian von Klinger's play *Der Wirrwarr, oder Sturm und Drang* (*Confusion, or Storm and Stress*) (1776). Led primarily by German poet and philosopher Johann Gottfried von Herder, the *Sturm und Drang* movement was characterized by rebellion against the **Enlightenment** preoccupation with reason and the strict tenets of French **neoclassicism**, such as the three **unities**. Proponents **privileged subjectivity**, exalted nature, and embraced the **folk**, or common people; their works tended to be extremely nationalistic and typically featured **conflicts** between the individual and society, particularly the **tragic** struggle of a solitary young genius against societal strictures.

Significant influences included folk traditions; the ancient Greek **epic** poet Homer; eighteenth-century Swiss philosopher Jean-Jacques Rousseau, who popularized **primitivist** concepts; and English **Renaissance** poet and playwright William Shakespeare, whom proponents of the movement considered liberated from **classical** conventions and whose works had recently been translated into German by Christoph Martin Wieland (8 vols.; 1762–66). Other writers associated with the movement included Johann Wolfgang von Goethe, Jakob Michael Reinhold (J. M. R.) Lenz, Friedrich Müller, and Friedrich Schiller. Certain English novels, such as Emily Brontë's *Wuthering Heights* (1847), show the influence of the German Storm and Stress movement.

FURTHER EXAMPLES: Goethe's play *Götz von Berlichingen* (1773) and **epistolary novel** *Die leiden des jungen Werthers* (*The Sorrows of Young Werther*) (1774). Other noted plays include Lenz's *Die Soldaten* (*The Soldiers*) (1775), Heinrich Leopold Wagner's *Die Kindermörderin* (*The Child-murderess*) (1776), and Schiller's *Die Räuber* (*The Robbers*) (1781).

▶ **style:** Used generally, the way in which a literary work is written. The message or material that the **author** communicates to the reader, along with how the author chooses to present it, produce an author's individual style. Critics who analyze literary works on the basis of style are called stylisticians and are said to practice **stylistics**.

Style can be investigated from a number of vantage points. It has traditionally been divided into three major categories — *high* (grand), *middle* (mean), and *low* (base, plain) — all generally associated with the subject matter of the work. Thus, for instance, a high style was considered appropriate to lofty works, such as **epics**, a middle style to love poems, and a low style to comedies. Accord between style and subject matter was a key element of literary **decorum**, an important **convention** in **Renaissance** and **neoclassical** times, as was compatibility between the style of a work and its **action, characters**, and **setting**. Style has also been broadly divided, however, based on the **binary oppositions classic(al)/romantic** and **poetry/prose,** with some advocating a special **poetic diction** distinct from ordinary **discourse**. Furthermore, in the twentieth century, Canadian **archetypal critic** Northrop Frye formulated a new stylistic distinction based on whether a work employs the language of everyday speech or makes use of formal advancement . . . made up of mediocrity, hate, and dull conceit." Attacking rationalism and logic in favor of **imagination**, he advocated "a new mode of pure expression," which he called surrealism, defined as "Psychic automatism in its pure state, by which one proposes to express — verbally, by means of the written word, or in any other manner — the actual functioning of thought. Dictated by thought, in the absence of any control exercised by reason, exempt from any aesthetic or moral concern." He further described surrealism as "based on the belief in the superior reality of certain forms of previously neglected associations, in the omnipotence of dream, in the disinterested play of thought." Subsequently, in 1929, Breton published a second surrealist manifesto in the final issue of the movement's flagship journal, *La révolution surréaliste* (*The Surrealist Revolution*) (1924–29).

As Breton's manifestos suggest, surrealists aim to transcend the reality to which we are accustomed, to enter the realm of the "super-real," and to unify the conscious and unconscious. As such, they **privilege** dreams, hallucinations, and the sleep/wake boundary and seek to tap into the unconscious through techniques such as "automatic writing" and "automatic drawing," spontaneous expression said to be given over to and guided by unconscious impulses. Other common techniques include collage and "exquisite corpse," in which individuals collaborate in the production of a **text** or visual image through cumulative additions, typically in accordance with some rule or after seeing the prior segment.

Surrealism has also had significant sociopolitical dimensions. Indeed, it was founded as a revolutionary movement, geared toward achieving social change by freeing society from false rationality and social strictures. Many members embraced communism, and its second journal, *Le surréalisme au service de la révolution* (*Surrealism in the Service of the Revolution*) (1930–33), was even more political than the first. However, the more mainstream journal *Minotaure* (1933–39), which featured surrealist art and literature, brought the movement more recognition.

Significant influences on surrealism aside from Dadaism and Freudian thought include the fifteenth- and sixteenth-century Dutch painter Hieronymus Bosch; two nineteenth-century French poets, Charles Baudelaire and Arthur Rimbaud; and the twentieth-century Greek-Italian painter Giorgio de Chirico. Surrealism in turn significantly influenced a variety of literary **genres** as well as film and art. **Absurdist** playwrights Eugène Ionesco and Samuel Beckett are indebted to the movement, as are many **magic realists**; **Beat writers** such as William Burroughs and Allen Ginsberg; and Caribbean writer Aimé Césaire, a founder of the *négritude* movement. Moreover, while surrealism reached its height as a movement between the first and second world wars — and while various scholars have argued that the movement ended with World War II, Breton's death (1966), or the death of Spanish surrealist painter Salvador Dalí (1989) — surrealist works continue to be produced today, particularly in the visual arts. Indeed, Terrance Lindall, an artist and author of the *New International Surrealist Manifesto*

(2003), has asserted that "Surrealism Isn't Dead, It's Dreaming," the subtitle of an essay entitled "What's New in the Surreal World" (2006).

Noted surrealist writers aside from Breton include Louis Aragon, Jean Cocteau, René Char, Paul Éluard, Benjamin Péret, and Philippe Soupault. Surrealist artists include Jean Arp; Max Ernst; René Magritte; André Masson; Joan Miró; Man Ray; and Salvador Dalí, who, in prototypical surrealist fashion, once declared, "There is only one difference between a madman and me. I am not mad."

EXAMPLES: Breton's novel *Nadja* (1928), which begins, "Who am I? If this once I were to rely on a proverb, then perhaps everything would amount to knowing whom I 'haunt.'" Other noted surrealist literary works include *Les champs magnétiques* (*The Magnetic Fields*) (1920), coauthored by Breton and Soupault using the automatic writing technique; Robert Desnos's *La liberté ou l'amour!* (*Liberty or Love!*) (1927), a collection of poems; and Leonora Carrington's short story "Down Below" (1944), recounting the author's experiences "on the other side of the mirror" following her mental breakdown.

Examples of surrealistic artwork include Ernst's painting *Le baiser* (*The Kiss*) (1927); Dalí's painting *The Persistence of Memory* (1931), shown on page 501; Alberto Giacometti's sculpture *Woman with Her Throat Cut* (1932); and Dorothea Tanning's painting *Eine kleine nachtmusik* (*A Little Night-music*) (1943).

Surrealist films include *Un chien andalou* (*An Andalusian Dog*) (1929), a sixteen-minute short by Luis Buñuel and Dalí that begins with a woman's eye being slit open; *L'âge d'or* (1930), a collaborative Buñuel/Dalí feature film; and *Meshes of the Afternoon* (1943), a film short by Maya Deren and Alexander Hammid filled with dreamscapes and Freudian overtones.

More recent surrealist literary works include Joseph Jablonski's poetry collection *In a Moth's Wing* (1974) and Franklin Rosemont's essay collection *An Open Entrance to the Shut Palace of Wrong Numbers* (2003). Contemporary surrealist artwork was exhibited at the *Brave Destiny* show at New York's Williamsburg Art & Historical Center (2003). Other contemporary works permeated by surrealism include *Twin Peaks* (television show 1990–91, film 1992), created by Mark Frost and David Lynch, and Lynch's film *Mulholland Drive* (2001).

▶ **suspense fiction, suspense novel:** See **mystery fiction.**

▶ **suspension of disbelief:** Temporary acquiescence in the premises of a **fictional** work, regardless of reality or probability. **Romantic** poet Samuel Taylor Coleridge coined the phrase in his *Biographia Literaria* (1817), referring to "willing suspension of disbelief for the moment" as "poetic faith." Some **genres,** such as **fantasy** and **science fiction,** routinely require suspension of disbelief, whereas other genres are more realistic. Generally speaking, audiences and readers are more willing to suspend disbelief when a story is internally is used to represent a part. In synecdoche, the **vehicle** (the **image** used to represent something else) is part of the **tenor** (the thing being represented) or vice versa. Synecdoche is distinguished from **metonymy**, a trope in which one thing is represented by another that is commonly and often physically associated with it. Referring to a boat as a "sail" involves synecdoche, whereas referring to a monarch as "the crown" involves metonymy.

EXAMPLES: Examples of synecdoche in which a part represents the whole include referring to a car as "wheels" and to the violins, violas, cellos, and basses in an orchestra as the "strings." Likewise, in William Shakespeare's play *Romeo and Juliet* (1596), Capulet has "two more years" in mind when he hopes that "two more summers" will "wither in their pride" before his daughter Juliet is thought "ripe to be a bride." The **narrator** in Elie Wiesel's **autobiographical** novel *Night* (1958), interned in Nazi concentration camps where he is terribly underfed and overworked, speaks of himself as "a body. Perhaps less than that even: a starved stomach."

By contrast, use of "society" to mean "high society," as in Jane Austen's *Mansfield Park* (1814) and many other nineteenth-century novels, involves synecdoche in which the whole represents a part.

▶ **synesthesia:** See synaesthesia.

▶ **syntax:** The arrangement—the ordering, grouping, and placement—of words within a phrase, clause, or sentence; the study of the rules governing such arrangement. Some critics extend the meaning of the term to encompass such things as the complexity or completeness of these arrangements. Syntax is a component of grammar, though it is often used—incorrectly—as a synonym for grammar.

Syntax has also been viewed as one of the two components of **diction** (the other being vocabulary), the general character of language used by a speaker or **author**. The sentences "I rode across the meadow" and "Across the meadow rode I" exhibit different syntax but identical vocabulary. To replace "meadow" with "sea of grass" is to alter the vocabulary but not the syntax. And to say "Rode I across the sea of grass" is to use diction very different from "I rode across the meadow." The combination of unusual syntax and vocabulary is a feature that often differentiates **poetic diction** from that of prose.

▶ *syuzhet:* See **fable, Russian formalism**.

T

▶ **tail-rhyme stanza:** A **stanza** ending with a short line that **rhymes** with one or more earlier, similarly short lines and in which each short line serves as a "tail" to one or more preceding, longer lines with a different rhyme. Tail-rhyme stanzas often follow the **rhyme scheme** *aabaab* or *aabccb-ddbeeb*, with *b* representing the tail-rhymes. The French term for tail-rhyme is *rime couée*.

EXAMPLE: Geoffrey Chaucer's "The Tale of Sir Topas" (c. 1387) is written in tail-rhyme stanzas, the first of which follows:

> Listeth, lordes, in good entent,
> And I wold telle verrayment°   *verily*
> Of myrth and of solas;°   *solace*
> Al of a knyght was fair and gent
> In bataille and in tourneyment,
> His name was sire Thopas.

▶ **tale:** A comparatively simple **narrative,** either **fictional** or **nonfictional,** written or related orally in **prose** or **verse.** A tale often recounts a strange event, focusing on something or someone exotic, marvelous, or even supernatural. Tales may be attributable to a particular **author,** whether known or anonymous, or may simply be part of the **folklore** of a given culture. While tales tend to be relatively short, the term is broad enough to apply to longer works ranging up to full-length **novels.**

Tale is sometimes used interchangeably with **short story,** or even as a general term encompassing the short story, among other literary forms, but modern critics typically distinguish between the two. The tale places more emphasis on actions and results than on **character,** which is the chief focus of the short story. Furthermore, tales are more casually constructed — and, consequently, far looser in terms of **plot** and **structure** — than short stories, which bear the mark of an author's careful and conscious fashioning.

EXAMPLES: Traditional "short" fictional tales include *The Canterbury Tales* (c. 1387), a collection of tales by Geoffrey Chaucer such as "The Miller's Tale" and "The Wife of Bath's Tale"; *The Thousand and One Nights* (also called *The Arabian Nights*) (c. 1450), an anonymous collection of Arabic tales such as the stories of Aladdin and Sinbad; Jonathan Swift's *A Tale of a Tub* (1704); and a variety of **folk tales** (e.g., the story of Chicken Little), **fairy tales** (e.g., Rapunzel, Cinderella, and Hansel and Gretel), and tall tales (e.g., Pecos Bill and his bouncing bride, Mark Twain's "The Celebrated Jumping Frog of Calaveras County" [1865]). A modern example of a relatively short tale is José Saramago's *O conto da ilha desconhecida* (*The Tale of the Unknown Island*) (1998). Examples of broader use of the term *tale* to encompass longer works include Lady Shikibu Murasaki's *The Tale of*

Genji (c. A.D. 1000), Charles Dickens's novel *A Tale of Two Cities* (1859), and Margaret Atwood's novel *The Handmaid's Tale* (1985).

Examples of nonfiction tales include Michael Allin's *Zarafa: A Giraffe's True Story, From Deep in Africa to the Heart of Paris* (1998), a 224-page, sometimes fairy-tale-like account of a giraffe given to the French king Charles X in 1826 by the Ottoman viceroy of Egypt, and Paul Collins's *Banvard's Folly: Thirteen Tales of Renowned Obscurity, Famous Anonymity, and Rotten Luck* (2002), brief accounts of thirteen people famous in their time but virtually unknown today.

▶ **tenor:** The subject of a **trope**. Every trope has a tenor and a **vehicle;** the vehicle is the **image,** activity, or concept used to illustrate or **represent** the tenor. For instance, in Emily Dickinson's "Fame is a bee" (*Collected Poems*, #1673), *fame* is the tenor, illustrated by the vehicle *bee.*

The terms *tenor* and *vehicle* were first used by English critic I. A. Richards, who introduced them with reference to **metaphor,** one of the principal tropes, in a book entitled *The Philosophy of Rhetoric* (1936). According to Richards, both tenor and vehicle typically undergo change in the metaphorical process, hence his definition of metaphor as "a transaction between contexts." Richards also viewed tenor and vehicle as the two equivalent parts of a metaphor, unlike prior critics, who commonly viewed what we now call the vehicle as mere ornament, less important than what we now call the tenor.

FURTHER EXAMPLES: Instead of saying, "Last night I read a book," you might say "Last night I plowed through a book." *Plowed through* (or the activity of plowing) is the vehicle of the metaphor; *read* (or the act of reading) is the tenor, the thing being figured. In the moment in which reading and plowing are metaphorically associated, intellectual activity is suddenly placed in an agricultural context (and vice versa), thereby altering slightly the significance of each of the metaphor's two terms.

The opening lines of Langston Hughes's poem "Long Trip" (1926) employ two vehicles — "wilderness of waves" and "desert of water" — to metaphorically illustrate one tenor, the sea: "The sea is a wilderness of waves, / A desert of water." Likewise, in *The Blind Assassin* (2000), Margaret Atwood's **narrator** uses two vehicles to describe herself: "I was sand, I was snow — written on, rewritten, smoothed over."

▶ **tension:** (1) Generally, the balance or equilibrium between opposing elements in a literary work, especially a **poem,** that give it stability and wholeness. (2) As used by **New Critic** Allen Tate in "Tension in Poetry" (1938), the totality of, or interrelation between, what he defined as the two types of meaning in a poem: "extension" (**concrete, denotative** meaning) and "intension" (**abstract, metaphorical** meaning). Tate deemed tension the "central achievement in poetry," arguing that "good poetry is a unity of all the meanings from the furthest extremes of intension and extension." Examining the use of gold as an **image** in John Donne's "A Valediction: Forbidding Mourning" (1640), for instance, Tate argued that while the denotative conception of gold as finite logically contradicts its connotation of infinity, the two meanings enrich rather than invalidate one another.

In a distinct but related usage, New Critics as well as other types of critics applied the term *tension* to "conflict structures," that is, **binary oppositions,** or contrary pairs of qualities, such as abstract/concrete, general/particular, and **structure/texture.** New Critics in particular tended to evaluate poems in part based on the manifestation of such oppositions, particularly as they involved **irony** and **paradox.** Some critics maintained that the tension itself gives a work its **form** and even its **cohesiveness.**

▶ **tercet:** Broadly speaking, a group of three lines of **verse.** So used, *tercet* may apply to a **poem,** a **stanza,** or a part of a stanza, and it may also apply regardless of **rhyme scheme.** Thus, the term may encompass a wide variety of forms, including the **haiku,** an unrhymed, three-line poem; the closing, usually unrhymed three-line stanza of the **sestina;** the *aba* stanzas of the **villanelle;** the interlocking stanzas of *terza rima,* which **rhyme** *aba bcb* etc.; and the two three-line components of the **sestet,** which often rhyme *cdecde,* in the **Italian sonnet.** A tercet in which all three lines rhyme (*aaa*) is often called a **triplet.**

EXAMPLE: The following stanza, one of six tercets in Trumbull Stickney's "Mnemosyne" (1902):

> I had a sister lovely in my sight:
> Her hair was dark, her eyes were very sombre;
> We sang together in the woods at night.

Adrienne Rich's "Terza Rima" (2000) contains thirteen numbered sections written almost entirely in tercets.

▶ *terza rima:* An Italian **verse** form composed of three-line (**tercet**) **stanzas,** often **iambic** meter, with an interlocking **rhyme scheme.** In *terza rima,* the final words of the first and last lines of each tercet **rhyme,** and the final word of the middle line of each tercet rhymes with the final words of the first and last lines of the following tercet, creating a linking rhyme pattern typically closed by a single line or **couplet** whose final word rhymes with the final word of the middle line of the last tercet, hence the rhyme scheme *aba bcb cdc* etc., ending *yzy z* or *yzy zz.* The form, generally attributed to Florentine **epic** poet Dante Alighieri, who used it in his *Divina commedia* (*The Divine Comedy*) (1321), was imported into English by Geoffrey Chaucer in "A Complaint to His Lady" (1374).

The term *terza rima sonnet* refers to a fourteen-line poem or section of a poem following the rhyme scheme *aba bcb cdc ded ee.*

FURTHER EXAMPLES: Percy Bysshe Shelley's "Ode to the West Wind" (1820), which begins:

> O wild West Wind, thou breath of Autumn's being,
> Thou, from whose unseen presence the leaves dead
> Are driven, like ghosts from an enchanter fleeing,

> Yellow, and black, and pale, and hectic red,
> Pestilence-stricken multitudes: O thou,
> Who chariotest to their dark wintry bed
>
> The wingèd seeds, where they lie cold and low,
> Each like a corpse within its grave, until
> Thine azure sister of the Spring shall blow . . . .

Twentieth-century uses or adaptations of the form include Robert Frost's *terza rima* sonnet "Acquainted with the Night" (1928), Archibald MacLeish's "Conquistador" (1932), W. H. Auden's *The Sea and the Mirror* (1944), and Sylvia Plath's "The Sow" (1957).

▶ **tetrameter:** A line of **verse** consisting of four **metrical feet**.

EXAMPLE: In Thomas Hardy's "Channel Firing" (1914), written in **iambic** tetrameter, skeletons resting in a churchyard are momentarily disturbed by the noise of gunnery practice on the English Channel:

> That night | your great | guns, un|awares,
> Shook all | our cof|fins as | we lay,
> And broke | the chan|cel win|dow-squares,
> We thought | it was | the Judge|ment-day
>
> And sat | upright. | While drear|isome
> Arose | the howl | of wa|kened hounds:
> The mouse | let fall | the al|tar-crumb,
> The worms | drew back | into | the mounds . . . .

Much of Dr. Seuss's (Theodor Seuss Geisel) verse for children was written in **anapestic** tetrameter, including his first children's book *And to Think That I Saw It on Mulberry Street* (1937).

▶ **text:** From the Latin "to weave," a term commonly used to refer to a written work or passage thereof. When used in this manner, *text* may be applied to objects ranging from a poem or book to a biblical passage or written transcript of an oral interview. Other critics include nonwritten material, such as **images** or music, in the designation *text*, as long as that material has been isolated for analysis.

In the 1960s, **structuralist critics** took issue with the traditional view of literary compositions as authoritative, personalized works constructed by individual, purposeful **authors** who orchestrated both **form** and meaning. Maintaining that all literature is subject to a set of **codes**, they identified literary compositions as texts, the essentially impersonal products of a social institution they called *écriture* (writing). They also argued for interpretation of texts based on an impersonal *lecture* (reading) involving awareness of how the **linguistic** system functions and reference to **conventions** and rules governing understanding of the text.

Roland Barthes, a French **theorist** who transitioned from structuralism to **poststructuralism,** distinguished *text* from *work* in a different way, characterizing a text as open and a work as closed in his essay "De l'oeuvre au texte" ("From Work to Text") (1971). According to Barthes, who described the work as "a fragment of substance" and the text as "a methodological field," works are bounded entities, conventionally classified in **genres**, with a determinable and determinate meaning, whereas texts are paradoxical, resist classification, and defer and multiply meaning; works are thus experienced as objects of consumption, texts as activities of production that call for reader collaboration. In *S/Z* (1970), Barthes divided texts into two categories: *lisible* (readerly) and *scriptible* (writerly). Texts that are *lisible* depend more heavily on convention, making their interpretation easier and more predictable. Texts that are *scriptible* are generally experimental, flouting or seriously modifying traditional rules — indeed to the point of becoming *illisible*, or unreaderly. Ultimately, texts that are *lisible* restrict reader participation more than those that are *scriptible*, which encourage or even demand cocreative involvement and effort.

Like structuralist critics, **poststructuralists** have rejected the traditional concept of the work in favor of the impersonal text. Unlike structuralists, however, they deny the possibility of determinable and determinate meaning, viewing the text as an endless chain of **signifiers** with no fixed meaning. Furthermore, they treat texts as "intertexts," interconnected, crisscrossed strands within language, an infinitely larger text in which individual texts are inscribed and read. Indeed, they even see the world itself — the network of cultural **discourses** in which we live and think — as a text, a view perhaps most famously expressed by French **deconstructive** theorist Jacques Derrida, who declared in *De la grammatologie* (*Of Grammatology*) (1967) that *"there is nothing outside the text."* Some poststructuralists, however, have rejected the term *text* in favor of *discourse*, which they apply broadly to any verbal structure, whether literary or not.

▶ **textual criticism:** The scholarly attempt to ascertain the original or authoritative version of a **text**, eliminating any alterations, whether accidental or intentional, made over time. Textual critics seek to find or identify the original or authoritative version; if it is unavailable, lost, or destroyed, as is commonly the case, they aim to reconstruct or restore it as precisely as possible from extant variants.

Textual critics typically examine all available printed versions of the text as well as any manuscripts or parts thereof (such as rough drafts) that have survived. They then compare these versions to examine the evolution of the work, to find and rectify copying or publishing errors, and to find and (if possible) emend intentional changes, such as corruptions to the text made by the addition of material. In examining textual variants, textual critics produce a stemma, or family tree, of versions, identifying common ancestors and the relationships among versions. While textual critics employ different methodologies, they ultimately aim to produce an edited version of the text that accords as closely as possible to that intended by the **author**. Some, for instance, select a base text, such as the oldest manuscript or best surviving text, and use variants to identify and emend errors;

others eclectically assemble the text using parts deemed authentic from a variety of versions.

Textual criticism dates back to ancient times and has been applied to works ranging from **classical** Greece to the present day. Major areas of study include classical texts, such as Plato's *Republic* (c. 360 B.C.); Biblical texts, particularly from the New Testament; and the works of the **Elizabethan** poet and playwright William Shakespeare. Noted textual critics include Johann Albrecht Bengel, who prepared an edition of the Greek New Testament published in 1734 and established an influential canon of textual criticism — preferring harder readings to easier ones — in his essay "Forerunner of a New Testament to Be Settled Rightly and Carefully" (1725); Karl Lachmann, who took a scientific approach to textual criticism, as reflected in his edition of Lucretius's first-century A.D. philosophical poem *De rerum natura* (*On the Nature of Things*) (1850); Ronald B. McKerrow, who advocated using "copy-texts" as base texts and produced an edition of the *Works of Thomas Nashe* (5 vol., 1904–10); W. W. Greg, who denied the copy-text authority over "substantive readings" in "The Rationale of Copy-Text" (1950–51); and Fredson Bowers, who argued that textual and **literary criticism** are interdependent in his book *Textual and Literary Criticism* (1959).

▶ **texture:** A term referring to the surface details or elements of a work (especially a **poem**) apart from its basic **structure**, argument, or meaning. Texture includes **imagery, meter, rhyme,** and other sound patterns such as **alliteration** and **euphony,** the sensuous and **concrete** aspects of a poem as opposed to its intellectual content. The **connotations** of words may also be viewed as part of a work's texture; the **denotative** meanings of those same words may not. **New Critics,** such as John Crowe Ransom, used *texture* in opposition to *structure* in analyzing a poem.

▶ **theater of the absurd:** See Absurd, the.

▶ **theme:** The statement(s), express or implied, that a **text** seems to be making about its subject. The theme of a work on suffering, for instance, might be that suffering is in God's plan and should therefore be accepted. The term *theme* is generally applied to the main idea or message in a text but is sometimes applied more broadly to include secondary ideas or messages, hence the characterization of themes as "major" or "minor." A theme can be moral, or even *a* moral or lesson, as was common in older works, or it may emanate from an unmoralized, or less obviously moral, perspective, such as an **archetypal** or philosophical one.

Theme is related to but distinguished from **motif,** a recurrent, unifying element in a work such as an **image, symbol,** or **character** type that informs and casts a revealing light on the theme.

FURTHER EXAMPLES: The theme in George Orwell's *Animal Farm* (1945) is that power corrupts — and that absolute power corrupts absolutely. In an interview with Padma Viswanathan ("Travels with My Tiger," *Montreal*

Review of Books [Fall & Winter 2001–2002]), author Yann Martel asserted that the theme of his novel *Life of Pi* (2001) "can be summarized in three lines. Life is a story. You can choose your story. And a story with an imaginative overlay is the better story."

▶ **theoretical criticism:** A type of **literary criticism** that emphasizes the formulation of general principles for all **texts** rather than the **explication** of individual works, as in **practical criticism.** Theoretical critics postulate a set of **aesthetic** principles that can be used to analyze and evaluate literary works in general. Aristotle's *Poetics* (c. 330 B.C.) is perhaps the best-known example of theoretical criticism; other noted examples include I. A. Richards's *Principles of Literary Criticism* (1924) and Wayne Booth's *The Rhetoric of Fiction* (1961).

American critics by and large engaged in practical rather than theoretical criticism during the first half of the twentieth century. However, with the advent of the **Chicago school,** which emphasized **theory** and method, theoretical criticism came into vogue. Theoretical criticism has since been written by practitioners of approaches ranging from **formalism** and **structuralism** to **cultural criticism, feminist criticism, the new historicism,** and **queer theory. Poststructuralists** in particular have placed a premium on theory, insisting that critics theorize their critical practices.

See also **practical criticism.**

▶ **theory:** A term variously used to refer to: (1) a set of principles used to explain or make predictions about a particular phenomenon; (2) the generally accepted principles and methods in a given field of study; and (3) **abstract** reasoning or hypothesizing. In scientific circles, however, *theory* is distinguished from *hypothesis,* the latter being a supposition (e.g., that flatworms can survive in acidic environments) subject to verification through observation and experimentation, the former being a generally accepted model or framework that has so far withstood the test of time and experimentation. Nevertheless, as British philosopher A. J. Ayer noted in *Philosophy in the Twentieth Century* (1982), "There never comes a point where a theory can be said to be true. The most that one can claim for any theory is that it has shared the successes of all its rivals and that it has passed at least one test which they have failed."

In **literary criticism,** *theory* has traditionally referred to a set of general principles applicable to the classification, analysis, and evaluation of literary works. Whether or not critics openly draw on particular theories of literary interpretation, their readings are usually informed by some theory about literature that provides a basis for their questions and conclusions. Critics who operate without a theoretical framework are vulnerable to the charge of making arbitrary, idiosyncratic, or **impressionistic** judgments.

Numerous types of literary criticism, generally grounded in theories of literary criticism, have arisen over the centuries, ranging from the **mimetic criticism** of the fourth-century B.C. Greek philosopher Plato to contemporary

postcolonial theory. Within each of these approaches are narrower critical principles, which have also been called theories. Hence *écriture féminine* — the idea, advocated by a group of **feminist critics,** that there is such a thing as women's writing — may itself be called a theory.

Moreover, **poststructuralists,** who have sought to formulate new theories of interpretation and meaning, have both elevated and revised the concept of theory. In their view, theory must account for more than literature, since everything from the unconscious to social and cultural practices is seen as functioning like a language; it must explain what controls interpretation and meaning in all possible systems of signification. Not surprisingly, this far-ranging concept has facilitated the development of theories that challenge the very underpinnings of traditional Western thought, especially the **logocentric** assumption that meaning is ultimately determinable and determinate.

▶ **thesis:** A term with several distinct meanings but perhaps most commonly used in universities to refer to one of two things: a paper or monograph written by a degree-seeking candidate in fulfillment of academic requirements; and the position taken by someone expostulating on a particular topic with the intent of proving that position plausible or correct. The term is sometimes also equated with **theme,** particularly the main idea advanced by an **author** in a **text.** Finally, in **prosody** (the study of **versification**), *thesis* is used by those who follow the original Greek usage to refer to a **stressed** syllable in a **foot** of verse (as opposed to the **arsis,** or unstressed syllable). In the later Latin usage — in which the terms became reversed — *thesis* refers to an unstressed syllable (and *arsis* refers to a stressed syllable). According to Greek usage, the thesis of the word *thesis* falls on the first (the stressed) syllable, whereas under the Latin usage, the thesis of the word *thesis* falls on the second (the unstressed) syllable.

See also **accent.**

▶ **thesis novel:** See **sociological novel.**

▶ **thick descriptions:** A term used by twentieth-century American anthropologist Clifford Geertz in *The Interpretation of Cultures* (1973) to refer to contextual descriptions of cultural products or events. Geertz, whose work greatly influenced contemporary **literary criticism,** followed British philosopher Gilbert Ryle in distinguishing between "thin" descriptions, which merely describe an action or behavior, and "thick" descriptions, which address context and meaning; for instance, "the difference, however unphotographable, between a twitch and a wink is vast" — as is the difference between a wink and a parody of the same action. The goal of thick description is to reveal the interlocking **conventions** or **discourses** that cause a production (like William Shakespeare's *Hamlet* [1602]) or event (such as the coronation of Queen Elizabeth I) to have a particular meaning or meanings for people within a given culture (such as that of **Renaissance** England). In conducting **close readings** of literary works, **new historicists** have used thick descriptions to relate **representational** devices within the **text** to historical, economic, and **symbolic** (and often non**linguistic**) structures operative outside it in the culture at large.

▶ **third-person point of view:** See **point of view.**

▶ **three unities:** See **unities.**

▶ **threnody:** In the original Greek usage, a **dirge** in the form of a **choral ode.** Today, any type of dirge.

EXAMPLES: Ralph Waldo Emerson's "Threnody" (1846), written on the death of his young son; Depeche Mode's song "Blasphemous Rumours" (1987). Samuel Barber's *Adagio for Strings* (1936), often referred to as a musical threnody, was performed by a number of symphony orchestras throughout the United States during the weekend following September 11, 2001.

▶ **thriller:** See **mystery fiction.**

▶ **tone:** The attitude of the **author** toward the reader, audience, or subject matter of a literary work. An author's tone may be serious, playful, mocking, and so forth. The term is now often used to mean "tone of voice," a difficult-to-determine characteristic of **discourse** through which writers (and each of us in our daily conversations) reveal a range of attitudes toward everything from the subject at hand to those being addressed.

Although the terms *tone* and **atmosphere** may both be equated with **mood,** their meanings differ. Unlike *tone,* which refers to the author's attitude, *atmosphere* refers to the general feeling created for the reader or audience by a work at a given point. Tone is sometimes also equated with **voice,** particularly in the sense of a creative authorial voice that pervades and underlies literary work.

▶ **tone color:** A phrase used by American poet Sidney Lanier in *The Science of English Verse* (1880) to compare the musicality of the sounds of words to timbre in music.

▶ **trace:** A term used by twentieth-century French theorist of **deconstruction** Jacques Derrida in works such as *De la grammatologie* (*Of Grammatology*) (1967) to refer to any and all possible meanings that differ from the one a spoken or written utterance is deemed to have, that is, the "definitive" meaning established and constituted by its very difference from innumerable, nonpresent meanings. Such meanings (the trace), which Derrida viewed as features of any utterance, are neither fully **present** nor wholly **absent.** They are not exactly present, for they differ from what the utterance is deemed to signify, yet they are not entirely absent, for they remind us of and lend import to the meaning we assign to that utterance by virtue of their difference. The significance of any utterance thus depends just as surely on those potential meanings that are rejected as on the single meaning bringing horrifying events onstage for the audience to see and experience. William Shakespeare's *Hamlet* (1602) is the most famous example of this tradition.

Elizabethan tragedians were responsible for a number of other innovations. They modified the classical tragic protagonist; unlike Aristotelian tragic heroes, who could not be characterized as being unusually good or bad, Elizabethan protagonists were often predominantly ruthless people. Elizabethan tragedies also differed from their ancient counterparts insofar as they tended to present, in order, the events leading up to the tragedy instead of beginning *in medias res* and relying on **flashbacks** to explain how the disaster came to pass. In addition, Elizabethan tragedians introduced the element of humor; the gravediggers in *Hamlet,* for instance, provide a level of **comic relief** that is usually absent from classical tragedies. Elizabethan dramatists were also responsible for the development of **tragicomedy,** a new genre that blended the essential elements of tragedy and **comedy.** Subsequently, during the **Restoration Age,** another blended genre called the *heroic tragedy,* or *heroic drama,* developed.

Classical tragedy exerted a particularly strong influence in seventeenth-century Europe, particularly France, where dramatists such as Jean Racine and Pierre Corneille systematically studied and imitated classical tragedians. Corneille wrote his own *Médée* (1635), although he also immortalized heroes from other national traditions, such as the Spaniard El Cid in his play, *Le Cid* (1636). Racine, too, drew on Greek lore in *Andromaque* (1667) and *Phèdre* (1677), but, like Corneille, also told the stories of nonclassical heroines, such as *Esther* (1689) and *Athalie* (1691). So strong was the classical influence that both playwrights, like their contemporaries, also tried to follow the so-called classical **unities** for fear of incurring critical condemnation. Playwrights in Spain and Germany likewise relied heavily on the classical tragic tradition. German poet and playwright Andreas Gryphius, for instance, modelled his dramas on Senecan tragedy.

During the eighteenth century, several writers of tragedy broke with tradition, replacing noble protagonists with middle-class characters as the tragic heroes of so-called **domestic** (or *bourgeois*) **tragedies.** Prose also became the dominant mode of expression for tragedy. Verse never recovered its prominence, although it remained a vehicle for tragic expression throughout the nineteenth and twentieth centuries.

In the nineteenth century, the **novel** became the main tragic form. In his influential critical study *Mimesis: The Representation of Reality in Western Literature* (1946), Erich Auerbach posited that the **realistic novel** was the culmination of Western literary expression because it treats ordinary characters in a serious and tragic way. Drama, however, did not disappear. On the contrary, Scandinavian playwrights Henrik Ibsen and August Strindberg expanded the boundaries of what was previously considered tragedy by introducing disease, psychological imbalance, and personal quirkiness as tragic subjects. For instance, in Ibsen's play *A Doll's House* (1879), the protagonist, Nora, becomes increasingly dissatisfied with the traditional female role of wife and mother. Strindberg's *Dance of Death* (1901) portrays an even more horribly destructive marriage.

Few modern works may be called tragedies, at least if we use the term as it has been developed to describe and define classical, medieval, or even Elizabethan versions of the genre. Today's "tragic" heroes are apt to be **antiheroes,** thoroughly ordinary, middle-class or proletarian, even down-and-out individuals whose downfall is likely to be attributable to society or to a psychological abnormality, rather than to fate or a moral flaw. Tennessee Williams's unstable Southern belle, Blanche, from *A Streetcar Named Desire* (1947), is just one example of the twentieth-century tragic hero, as is Arthur Miller's pathetic salesman, Willy Loman, in *Death of a Salesman* (1949).

Some modern playwrights have stretched the boundaries of the tragic genre by incorporating **the Absurd** and **black humor** into their works. Others have imported classical elements (such as the chorus); still others have injected **psychoanalytic theory** and analysis into "ancient" stories. Despite these variations, a number of plays are generally said to be tragedies; among them are Eugene O'Neill's *Mourning Becomes Electra* (1931), Federico García Lorca's *Blood Wedding* (1935), Miller's *A View from the Bridge* (1955), Jean Anouilh's *Becket* (1960), and David Henry Hwang's *M. Butterfly* (1988).

Contemporary television series that likewise stretch the boundaries of tragedy include *The Sopranos* (1999–2007), in which mob boss Tony Soprano wreaks violent havoc even as he pursues psychoanalytic therapy, and *The Wire* (2002–08), both of which have been compared to Greek tragedy. Indeed, *The Wire* co-creator David Simon openly acknowledged his debt to classical Greek tragedy in an interview given to *The FADER* magazine ("The Left Behind," Aug. 12, 2006), explaining that what "spoke to me was the Greek drama in which fated and doomed protagonists are confronted by a system that is indifferent to their heroism, to their individuality, to their morality. But instead of Olympian gods, . . . we have post-modern institutions. The police department is the god, the drug trade is the god, . . . Capitalism is the ultimate god in *The Wire*. Capitalism is Zeus."

▶ **tragedy of blood:** See **revenge tragedy.**

▶ **tragic flaw:** A character trait in a **tragic hero** or **heroine** that brings about his or her downfall. Traits like arrogance or **hubris** (excessive pride) are common tragic flaws, but a **protagonist's** tragic flaw need not be "negative"; rather, it is simply the characteristic from which a reversal of fortune ensues. Thus, courage or generosity may equally be the trait whose expression leads to the direst of consequences.

The term *tragic flaw* is often used as a synonym for **hamartia,** but this usage is not strictly correct. *Hamartia* is more general, applicable to any error in judgment that brings about the protagonist's downfall; *tragic flaw* refers specifically to an inherent character trait. Hamartia may result from a **character's** tragic flaw but is not, technically speaking, the flaw itself. Rather, hamartia is the misstep or mistake that engenders the protagonist's poem "Mottoes" (1844) capture something of the spirit and the ideas of the movement:

> The rounded world is fair to see,
> Nine times folded in mystery:
> Though baffled seers cannot impart
> The secret of its laboring heart,
> Throb thine with Nature's throbbing breast,
> And all is clear from east to west.
> Spirit that lurks each form within
> Beckons to spirit of its kin;
> Self-kindled every atom glows
> And hints the future which it owes.

▶ **transformational linguistics:** One of the two components of Noam Chomsky's **theory** of **linguistics**, which he postulated in *Syntactic Structures* (1957). Chomsky's theory is termed *transformational* in its belief that a certain set of transformative rules produces numerous variations on "kernel sentences" (basic sentences) in the "deep structure" of any given language. In English, such a kernel sentence might be "Tom chased Jerry." Various transformative rules in English allow us to take this basic sentence and modify it. For example, we might use a passive construction ("Jerry was chased by Tom") or a question ("Was Tom chasing Jerry?" or "Was Jerry being chased by Tom?") or an imperative form ("Tom, chase Jerry!"), and so forth.

See also **generative linguistics.**

▶ **travesty:** A type of low **burlesque** that treats a dignified subject in an especially undignified, even debased, way. Travesty ridicules a topic, literary **convention,** or specific work by employing a grossly low **style.**

EXAMPLES: In *Henry IV* (c. 1599), William Shakespeare uses the **character** Ancient Pistol, a commoner and friend from Henry's wild youth, to ridicule heroic speech, as in the following lines:

> O braggart vile and damned furious wight!
> The grave doth gape, and doting death is near;
> Therefore exhale.

Twentieth-century examples of travesty include the film comedy *Bananas* (1971), in which hapless **protagonist** Fielding Mellish sets off for a fictional banana republic to impress his activist girlfriend, is catapulted to the presidency, and is tried for treason upon returning to the U.S. (only to object, after cross-examining himself, "This trial is a travesty. It's a travesty of a mockery of a sham of a mockery of a travesty of two mockeries of a sham. I move for a mistrial."); playwright Tom Stoppard's *Travesties* (1974), a metatravesty, or travesty of travesties; and the television sitcom *Married with Children* (1987–97), which *Newsweek* writer Rick Marin described as making "nuclear waste of the nuclear family" ("Nuking the Nuclear Family," Apr. 29, 1996). The contemporary television comedy *South Park*

(1997–) also frequently employs travesty; death, for instance, is routinely trivialized, as with Kenny's recurring demise, in various absurd and grotesque ways, in most episodes of the first five seasons.

See also **burlesque**.

▶ **trimeter:** A line of **verse** consisting of three **metrical feet.**

EXAMPLE: The **hymn** "Amazing Grace" (1779), written by John Newton, in which **iambic tetrameter** and iambic trimeter lines alternate throughout:

> Amaz|ing grace! | (how sweet | the sound)
> That sav'd | a wretch | like me! . . .

The opening lines, written in **trochaic** trimeter, of Robert Browning's "Home Thoughts, from Abroad" (1845):

> Oh to | be in | England
> Now that | April's | there. . . .

▶ **triolet:** A **medieval** French **verse** form consisting of an eight-line **stanza** with the **rhyme scheme** *abaaabab*. The first two lines are repeated verbatim in the last two, and the fourth line is the same as the first.

EXAMPLES: Thomas Hardy's "The Puzzled Game-Birds" (1901):

> They are not those who used to feed us
> When we were young — they cannot be —
> These shapes that now bereave and bleed us?
> They are not those who used to feed us,
> For did we then cry, they would heed us.
> — If hearts can house such treachery
> They are not those who used to feed us
> When we were young — they cannot be!

Other examples of triolets include Robert Bridges's "Triolet" (1873), Frances Cornford's "To a Fat Lady Seen from the Train" (1910), Sandra McPherson's "Triolet" (1973), and Sophie Hannah's "The Guest Speaker" (2003).

▶ **triple rhyme:** See **feminine rhyme, rhyme.**

▶ **triplet:** A **tercet** (a group of three lines of **verse**) in which all three lines rhyme (*aaa*).

EXAMPLE: Alfred, Lord Tennyson's "The Eagle: A Fragment" (1851) is composed of two triplets:

> He clasps the crag with crooked hands;
> Close to the sun in lonely lands,
> Ringed with the azure world, he stands.
>
> The wrinkled sea beneath him crawls:
> He watches from his mountain walls,
> And like a thunderbolt he falls.

▶ **trochee:** A **metrical foot** in **poetry** that consists of one **stressed** syllable followed by one unstressed syllable (´˘).

EXAMPLES: tróchĕe, tércĕt, búmmĕr, líttlĕ, pártў; the adage "April showers bring May flowers." The speaker in Robert Browning's "Soliloquy of the Spanish Cloister" (1842) uses trochaic **tetrameter** when he says "Twénty-|nĭne dĭs|tínct dăm|nátiŏns . . . ." Theodor Seuss Geisel, better known as Dr. Seuss, also often wrote in trochaic tetrameter, as reflected in the title of *One Fish Two Fish Red Fish Blue Fish* (1960) and in the **dialogue** of Sam-I-Am in *Green Eggs and Ham* (1960).

▶ **trope (figure of thought):** One of the two major divisions of **figures of speech** (the other being **rhetorical figures**). *Trope* comes from a word that literally means "turning"; to trope (with figures of speech) is, figuratively speaking, to turn or twist some word or phrase to make it mean something else. **Metaphor, metonymy, personification, simile,** and **synecdoche** are sometimes referred to as the principal tropes. Other tropes include **hyperbole, litotes,** and **meiosis.**

▶ **troubadour:** A medieval **lyric** poet, associated with the Provence region of southern France, who composed songs in **verse** in *provençal* (known as the *langue d'oc*). Troubadours, active between the late eleventh and early fourteenth centuries, created many new verse forms and were instrumental in the development of the ideal of **courtly love.**

EXAMPLES: Guillaume d'Aquitaine (1071–1127), Arnaut Daniel (fl. 1180–1200).

▶ **true rhyme:** See **perfect rhyme.**

▶ **truncation:** See **catalexis.**

▶ **turning point:** See **crisis.**

U

▶ *ubi sunt:* From the Latin for "where are," a common literary **motif** that laments the passage of time by asking what has happened to beloved people, things, or ideas of the past. This motif is often repeated throughout a work, particularly one written in **verse**, as a **refrain.**

EXAMPLES: In François Villon's "Ballade des dames du temps jadis" (1489), the *ubi sunt* motif appears in the refrain, "Mais où sont les neiges d'antan?" Translated into English by Dante Gabriel Rossetti as "The Ballad of Dead Ladies" (1870), the corresponding refrain is "But where are the snows of yester-year?" A twentieth-century example is "Where Have All the Flowers Gone?," a **folk song** written by Pete Seeger in the mid-1950s but popularized during the Vietnam War era in versions recorded in 1962 by The Kingston Trio and Peter, Paul, and Mary.

▶ **undecidability:** See **deconstruction.** See also **aporia.**

▶ **understatement:** See **meiosis.** See also **litotes.**

▶ **unintrusive narrator:** An **omniscient, third-person narrator** who relates a **story** without (or with a minimum of) personal commentary. Also called an *objective* or *impersonal narrator,* an unintrusive narrator "states the facts" and, as far as possible, leaves matters of judgment up to the reader. The most drastic examples of unintrusive narrators are those who do not even relate the **characters'** feelings, motives, or states of mind. Many contemporary critics question the very concept of the unintrusive narrator, arguing that a self-effacing **voice** does not and probably cannot exist.

EXAMPLES: The following **realistic** works feature unintrusive narrators: Stendhal's *The Red and the Black* (1830), Gustave Flaubert's *Madame Bovary* (1857), and the novels in Anthony Trollope's *Barsetshire* series (1855–67) and *Palliser* series (1864–80). Unintrusively narrated short stories include Ernest Hemingway's "The Killers" (1927) and Paul Theroux's "Clapham Junction" (1980). The narration in the movie *March of the Penguins* (2005) was generally unintrusive, particularly compared to the original French version, *La marche de l'empereur* (2005).

▶ **unities:** A set of three **structural** principles for **drama** calling for unity of **action,** time, and place. Unity of action was a rule of **plot** requiring that the work present a single, continuous action without extraneous subplots. Unity of time mandated that the action occur within a single day, unity of place that it occur within one location. The three unities were intended as devices to assure **verisimilitude;** literary critics claimed that a **play,** performed of necessity in one place over a few hours, could not seem realistic if its action took place in a number of **settings** over long periods of time.

Although the unities are often ascribed to the ancient Greek philosopher Aristotle, particularly to his *Poetics* (c. 330 B.C.), Aristotle emphasized only unity of action, writing that "the plot, being an imitation of an action, must imitate one action and that a whole, the structural union of the parts being such that, if any one of them is displaced or removed, the whole will be disjointed and disturbed." With regard to time, he observed that "Tragedy endeavors . . . to confine itself to a single revolution of the sun, or but slightly to exceed this limit" but did not prescribe such a limit. He did not discuss unity of place.

It was Italian and French critics of the sixteenth and seventeenth centuries who, expanding on — or misreading — Aristotle, developed the unities of time of place and established all three unities as prescriptive rules. In Italy, **Renaissance** critic Lodovico Castelvetro formulated the unities in 1570 in translating and analyzing the *Poetics*. In France, **neoclassical** playwright Jean Mairet is generally credited with introducing the unities, which he strictly observed in his play *Sophonisbe* (1634). Unity of time was often interpreted as requiring that the action take place over a period of no more than twenty-four hours; some critics, however, limited the period to twelve hours or even to the length of time needed to perform the play itself. Unity of place, narrowly interpreted, meant confining the action to one specific place; more broadly interpreted, to one city.

A dramatist failing to adhere to the unities risked not only critical condemnation but even the banishment of the "offending" play from the stage. So seriously was the requirement taken that when rivals accused French playwright Pierre Corneille of violating these rules in *Le Cid* (1636), Cardinal Richelieu ordered the Académie Française (the French Academy of Letters) to settle the bitter quarrel. After prolonged deliberation, the Académie concluded that Corneille had in fact violated the putatively **classical** rules, although it conceded that the passion, force, and charm of the play garnered for it both public adulation and a considerable place in French theater.

In England, a few seventeenth-century dramatists (such as Francis Beaumont and John Fletcher) attempted to adopt or, at least, adapt the unities, but, unlike the French and the Italians, the English generally ignored them. Subsequently, in all three countries, the unities — save perhaps unity of action — were largely abandoned with the waning of **neoclassicism** and the rise of **romanticism**.

▶ **unreliable narrator:** A **narrator** who, intentionally or unintentionally, fails to provide an accurate report of events or situations and whose credibility is therefore compromised. Unreliability may result from a wide range of causes, such as innocence or immaturity, lack of information, mental **disabilities** or other impairments, bias or prejudice, or deliberate lying. **Authors** using unreliable narrators generally provide the reader with sufficient information to assess the narrator's reliability and correct misinterpretations; some, however, leave the narrator's reliability open to question.

EXAMPLES: Charlie Marlow in Joseph Conrad's *Heart of Darkness* (1899) and *Lord Jim* (1900); Nick Carraway in F. Scott Fitzgerald's *The Great Gatsby* (1925). Examples of unreliable narrators whose fallibility is not revealed to the reader or audience until late in the **narrative** include the easily-deceived John Dowell in Ford Madox Ford's *The Good Soldier* (1927) and Verbal Kint, who spins an elaborate web of deception in the film *The Usual Suspects* (1995) to conceal his identity as the ruthless criminal mastermind Keyser Soze.

Contemporary examples of unreliable narrators include the unnamed narrator of Chuck Palahniuk's *Fight Club* (1996; adapted to film 1999), who suffers from multiple personality disorder; Leonard, the memory-impaired **protagonist** of the movie *Memento* (2001); and Joey Ice Cream, a hustler and pathological liar from the television series *The Black Donnellys* (2007).

▶ **urban legend (urban myth):** A type of contemporary **folklore** typically involving an **apocryphal,** often cautionary **tale** that varies locally and is frequently circulated widely on the Internet. Urban legends need not be set in the city, though many are. Stories about potentially plausible but generally nonexistent dangers are common, as are tales of misinformation, such as the claim that a college student whose roommate commits suicide automatically receives straight As for the semester. The stories are often couched as having happened to a "friend of a friend" to lend credibility but are commonly either entirely fabricated or only partially true. Jan Brunvand, an American folklorist who has compiled numerous collections of urban legends, succinctly defined the **genre** through the title of one of his books, *Too Good to Be True: The Colossal Book of Urban Legends* (1999). Numerous websites have sprung up to investigate and debunk urban legends, including <www.snopes.com>.

FURTHER EXAMPLES: The story of baby pet alligators being flushed down toilets in New York and subsequently thriving in the city's sewer system; the story of a man who, drugged at a party, awakens naked in a bathtub filled with ice and finds a note (sometimes scrawled in lipstick on a mirror) warning him that one of his kidneys has been removed for sale on the black market. Another urban legend is the assertion that author Kurt Vonnegut gave a commencement speech at MIT advising new graduates to "wear sunscreen." In reality, Vonnegut neither gave nor wrote any such address; rather, the text attributed to him, widely circulated on the Internet as an email "forward" and made into a popular song by filmmaker Baz Luhrmann, was written by Mary Schmich as a column published by the *Chicago Tribune* in 1997.

▶ **utopia:** (1) An ideal place that does not exist in reality. (2) A work describing such a place. The word *utopia,* which evokes the Greek for both *outopia,* meaning "no place," and *eutopia,* meaning "good place," is itself a **pun** referring to a nonexistent good place. English writer Sir Thomas

More coined the term in 1516, using it as the name of his model society as well as the title of his book *Utopia*.

Utopian literature, which reached its height in Anglo-American literature in the nineteenth century, describes, but does not necessarily promote, an **author's** vision of the ideal place. Utopias are frequently depicted as distant and delightful lands lost, forgotten, or unknown to the rest of the world until their (re)discovery by an adventurous traveller who returns to tell the tale. Some utopian **texts** subtly **satirize** the specific utopia described; others satirize humanity's yearning for utopia in general. **Dystopias,** by contrast, are horrific places, usually characterized by degenerate or oppressive societies.

EXAMPLES: Plato's *The Republic* (c. 360 B.C.); Francis Bacon's *The New Atlantis* (1627); Edward Bellamy's *Looking Backward: 2000–1887* (1888); William Morris's *News from Nowhere* (1890); H. G. Wells's *A Modern Utopia* (1905); and James Hilton's *Lost Horizon* (1933), which describes the Tibetan paradise of Shangri-La. Contemporary examples of utopian literature include James Redfield's *The Celestine Prophecy* (1993) and Garrett Jones's *Ourtopia* (2004).

Samuel Butler's *Erewhon* (1672) is a utopian satire. Lois Lowry's *The Giver* (1993) depicts a false utopia; so, in a way, does the movie *The Matrix* (1999), in which Agent Smith characterizes the original matrix — which humans rejected — as "designed to be a perfect human world."

See also **dystopia.**

▶ **utterance act:** The utterance of words; a type of **speech act.** Introducing the term in *Speech Acts: An Essay in the Philosophy of Language* (1969), American "ordinary-language" philosopher John R. Searle maintained that utterance acts "consist simply in uttering strings of words," noting that "[o]ne can utter words without saying anything." Thus, an utterance act occurs whenever someone says something, regardless of whether or not it makes sense.

See **speech-act theory.**

▶ **Varronian satire:** See **Menippean satire.**

▶ **vehicle:** The **image**, activity, or concept used to illustrate or represent the **tenor**, or subject, of any **figure of speech.**

See **tenor** for further discussion of the relationship between tenor and vehicle and the critical origins of these terms.

▶ **verbal irony:** See **irony.**

▶ **verbal meaning:** See **significance.**

▶ **verisimilitude:** The apparent truthfulness and credibility of a **fictional** literary work. Works that achieve verisimilitude seem believable to the reader or audience, whether because they mesh with human experience or accord with **conventions** that enable the **suspension of disbelief.**

▶ *vers de société:* French for "society verse," a type of **light verse** directed at polite society and its concerns. *Vers de société* frequently makes use of elaborate French **forms** such as the **rondeau** and the **villanelle.** Though characterized by **wit** or mild **satire**, *vers de société* is always polished, elegant, and graceful.

EXAMPLES: Frederick Locker-Lampson's collection *London Lyrics* (1857); Walter Learned's "Time's Revenge" (1889):

> When I was ten and she fifteen —
>   Ah me, how fair I thought her!
> She treated with disdainful mien
>   The homage that I brought her,
> And, in a patronizing way
> Would of my shy advances say:
>   "It's really quite absurd, you see;
>   He's very much too young for me."
>
> I'm twenty now; she, twenty-five —
>   Well, well, how old she's growing!
> I fancy that my suit might thrive
>   If pressed again; but, owing
> To great discrepancy in age,
> Her marked attentions don't engage
>   My young affections, for, you see,
>   She's really quite too old for me.

▶ **verse:** Broadly defined, **rhythmical** or **metrical** composition, whether **poetry** in general or an individual poem; more narrowly, an individual line of poetry or a **stanza** of a poem or song. For example, William Wordsworth's poem "I Wandered Lonely as a Cloud" (1807) can properly be referred to as verse, whereas its eponymous first line is *a* verse. Some critics distinguish between poetry and verse, noting that all poetry is verse, but that not all verse is poetry. Many of those who make this distinction argue that verse is a lower form of expression than poetry; verse, they suggest, is notable mainly for its rhythmic and metrical form, whereas poetry is characterized by **imagination**, a less obvious and more intricate **structure**, and a lofty purpose. Other scholars simply claim that verse is the more inclusive term, covering **forms** such as **light verse** that are typically not classified as poetry. Of course, even this distinction implies a certain hierarchy in which poetry is valued more highly than "mere" verse.

▶ **versification:** A term referring to: (1) the art of composing **verse**; (2) the **form** or **metrical** structure of a particular **poem**; (3) the adaptation of a **text** from **prose** to verse. The study of versification is called **prosody**.

▶ *vers libre:* The French term for **free verse**.
See **free verse**.

▶ **Victorian Period (in English literature):** An era in English literary history generally said to span Queen Victoria's reign (1837–1901) but sometimes dated back to the Reform Act of 1832, the first of three major electoral reform bills. The period is often divided into two parts: early Victorian, ending around 1870, and late Victorian. Major literary movements during the Victorian Period included **realism, Pre-Raphaelitism,** and **Aestheticism.**

During the Victorian Period, England reached the height of its power and influence, as reflected by the phrase "the sun never sets on the British Empire." The period was marked by rapid political, socioeconomic, and technological change stemming from industrialization and urbanization and spawned pressure for reform on issues ranging from **class** divisions to Irish autonomy to women's rights. Science became a discipline, and new ideas, such as Charles Darwin's theory of evolution by natural selection, set forth in *On the Origin of Species* (1859), posed a challenge to long-standing religious ideas and institutions.

The literature of the Victorian Period comes in virtually all **forms** and **genres** and was written in **styles** ranging from the **romantic** to the realistic, the **satirical** to the **decadent**. Noted nonfiction prose writers included essayist and historian Thomas Carlyle, utilitarian philosopher John Stuart Mill, religious thinker and writer John Henry (Cardinal) Newman, and art critic John Ruskin. Among the major novelists and short story writers were Charlotte Brontë, Charles Dickens, George Eliot, Thomas Hardy, Rudyard Kipling, Robert Louis Stevenson, William Makepeace Thackeray, and Anthony Trollope. Noted playwrights included Arthur Wing Pinero, George Bernard Shaw, and Oscar Wilde. In poetry, leading figures included Matthew Arnold, Elizabeth Barrett Browning, Robert Browning, Christina Rossetti, Dante Gabriel Rossetti, and Alfred, Lord Tennyson, whose **elegy** for Arthur Henry Hallam, entitled "In Memoriam A. H. H." (1850), is sometimes singled out as the quintessential Victorian poem, perhaps because the **theme** most common in Victorian poetry is that of loss with its attendant uncertainty. This is not to say that Victorian poets never celebrated life or the present; Robert Browning's "Rabbi Ben Ezra" (1864) begins "Grow old along with me! / The best is yet to be, / The last of life, for which the first was made." But Arnold's characterization, in "Stanzas from the Grande Chartreuse" (1867), of a generation "Wandering between two worlds, one dead, / The other powerless to be born" better conveys the generally wistful, elegiac **mood** of Victorian poetry.

The common conception we now have of the Victorians as prudish, hypo-critical, stuffy, narrow-minded, and complacent is not entirely accurate, al-though it is true that: (1) segments of English society, particularly the growing middle class, did espouse many moralistic views that led to this conception; and (2) a number of Victorian writers euphemistically dance around certain subjects (notably sex) that are dealt with more directly in previous as well as subsequent periods. Still, the stereotype of Victorianism—bound up as it is with the identity of a pious, proper, and beloved queen who allegedly advised her daughter to "Lie back and think of England" on her wedding night— disregards the richness of the period, which also produced a number of out-landishly comic writers, such as Lewis Carroll and Edward Lear, both writers of **nonsense verse,** and W. S. Gilbert, the whimsical humorist, poet, and play-wright best known for the comic operas he wrote with Sir Arthur Sullivan. Moreover, the unattractive characteristics of Victorian thinking, behavior, and character were recognized and condemned by Victorians themselves, many of whom rebelled against the "spirit" of the era or engaged in critical self-examination.

▶ **villain:** See **antagonist.**

▶ **villanelle:** A French **verse** form consisting of nineteen lines grouped in five **tercets** followed by a **quatrain** and involving only two **rhymes,** with the **rhyme** scheme *aba aba aba aba aba abaa.* The first line of the first tercet is repeated as the last line of the second and fourth tercets while the third line of the first tercet is repeated as the last line of the third and fifth tercets. Furthermore, both lines are repeated as a **couplet** in the last two lines of the quatrain. Sixteenth-century French poet Jean Passerat is generally credited with estab-lishing the fixed form of the villanelle, which initially developed from Italian **folk songs** and entered English literature in the nineteenth century.

EXAMPLES: W. E. Henley's "Villanelle" (1888); Edwin Arlington Robin-son's "The House on the Hill" (1894), which follows:

> They are all gone away,
> The House is shut and still,
> There is nothing more to say.

Through broken walls and gray
  The winds blow bleak and shrill.
They are all gone away.

Nor is there one to-day
  To speak them good or ill:
There is nothing more to say.

Why is it then we stray
  Around the sunken sill?
They are all gone away,

And our poor fancy-play
  For them is wasted skill:
There is nothing more to say.

There is ruin and decay
  In the House on the Hill:
They are all gone away,
There is nothing more to say.

Twentieth-century villanelles include Dylan Thomas's "Do Not Go Gentle into That Good Night" (1951); Sylvia Plath's "Mad Girl's Love Song" (1954); Elizabeth Bishop's "One Art" (1976); Martha Collins's "The Story We Know" (1980), which employs **incremental repetition** in both repeated lines; and Stephen Cramer's "Villanelle After a Burial" (1997).

▶ **vocabulary:** See **diction.**

▶ **voice:** A term referring to: (1) the manner of expression of the speaker in a literary work (particularly the **narrator**) or of a **character** in the work (e.g., Huck Finn's "voice"); (2) the **style** of a given **author** (e.g., the "voice" of American poet Walt Whitman); or (3) the unique and pervasive human presence that the reader or audience senses is the driving force behind a literary work and the source of its ethical norms and values. This creative authorial voice, which **reader-response critic** Wayne C. Booth called the **implied author** in *The Rhetoric of Fiction* (1961), underlies every element of the work (**characterization, imagery, plot, theme,** etc.), whether written in an **objective** or **subjective** manner.

W

▶ **weak ending:** The final syllable of a line of **verse** that is **stressed** to conform to the **meter** but would be unstressed in ordinary speech. So defined, the term *weak ending* is distinguished from **feminine ending,** in which a line of verse ends with an unstressed, **extrametrical** syllable. Some critics, however, use the term as a synonym for feminine ending.

EXAMPLE: The following **stanza** from Samuel Taylor Coleridge's "The Rime of the Ancient Mariner" (1798) concludes with a weak ending, given the **wrenched accent** in the word *countree:*

> Oh! dream of joy! is this indeed
> The lighthouse top I see?
> Is this the hill? is this the kirk?
> Is this mine own countree?

▶ **whodunit:** See **detective fiction.** See also **mystery fiction.**

▶ **wit:** Derived from the **Old English** *witan,* meaning "to know," a term whose meaning has changed several times over the centuries. In the late **Middle Ages,** *wit* referred to intellect and intelligence as opposed to knowledge. During the **Renaissance,** it came to signify wisdom. In the seventeenth century, when it began to suggest creativity or **fancy,** the term was frequently associated with a group we now call the **metaphysical poets,** writers prized for the originality and agility of their poetic expression. In the eighteenth century, during the **Neoclassical Period,** a reaction against this definition set in, and wit came to be associated not with ingenious twists and turns of fancy but rather with judgment, reason, and the ability to articulate commonly held truths in an original and persuasive manner. English writer Joseph Addison distinguished between true and false wit according to its focus; true wit, he claimed, revealed similarities between apparently unlike ideas, whereas false wit associated unlike words through ornamental devices such as **puns.**

Today, the meaning of *wit* is closest to the seventeenth-century definition, although we are likely to associate the term with **comedy** and laughter in addition to creativity. Wit is now most commonly thought of as clever expression. We also tend to think of wit as being characterized by a mocking or **paradoxical** quality, evoking laughter through apt phrasing (**epigrammatic** writings are common vehicles for wit, for instance). Even today, however, wit retains the **medieval** sense of intelligence, insofar as it is viewed as an intellectual form of humor.

EXAMPLES: Writers often cited for their wit include Aphra Behn, John Donne, Alexander Pope, Jane Austen, Oscar Wilde, George Bernard Shaw, Dorothy Parker, and Stephen Fry. Witty remarks on marriage include

Nancy, Lady Astor's statement "I married beneath me. All women do," and French novelist Colette's remark "Among all the forms of absurd courage, the courage of girls is outstanding. Otherwise there would be fewer marriages." Flannery O'Connor, best known for her short stories, once said: "Everywhere I go I'm asked if I think the university stifles writers. My opinion is that they don't stifle enough of them. There's many a bestseller that could have been prevented by a good teacher."

▶ **wonder tale:** See fairy tale.

▶ **word accent:** See accent.

▶ **wrenched accent:** In a line of **verse**, the **stress** imposed on a syllable to conform to the **meter**, contrary to the stress in everyday speech. **Accent** is "wrenched" when the **metrical accent** trumps the **word accent**, forcing stress onto a syllable that would normally go unstressed. When a wrenched accent occurs at the end of a line of verse, the line is said to have a **weak ending.**

EXAMPLES: The accent in *morning* in the following **stanza** from Christopher Marlowe's "The Passionate Shepherd to His Love" (1599) is wrenched, falling on the second syllable rather than the first and creating a weak ending:

> The shepherd swains shall dance and sing
> For thy delight each May morning:
> If these delights thy mind may move,
> Then live with me and be my love.

Likewise, the following line from Samuel Taylor Coleridge's "The Rime of the Ancient Mariner" (1798) contains two instances of wrenched accent, with the metrical shifting of stress to *roar* in the word *uproar* and to *from* in the phrase *bursts from*:

> What loud uproar bursts from that door!

Z

▶ **zeugma:** Broadly defined, a **rhetorical figure,** from the Greek for "yoking," in which one word or phrase governs or modifies two or more words or phrases. Zeugma usually involves a single verb that governs multiple nouns or prepositional phrases, as in the Biblical verse beginning "And rend your heart, and not your garments" (Joel 2:13), but may involve other constructions, such as the use of one noun to govern various verbs or the use of one adjective to modify various nouns. The device may suggest parallels between things commonly differentiated or differences between things commonly equated; alternatively, it is often used for the comic effect created by deploying the same word in very different contexts, as in the movie *So I Married an Axe Murderer* (1993), where **protagonist** Charlie MacKenzie declares, "She was a thief, you gotta believe, she stole my heart and my cat."

Definitions of *zeugma* and its relationship to *syllepsis* have varied from ancient Greek times to the present day. Some scholars have used the terms synonymously, a common practice today. Others have defined syllepsis as a type of zeugma in which the yoked words or phrases manifest a grammatical or **semantic** disparity. For example, in the sentence "The car was stolen, the bicycles left untouched," the verb "was" is grammatically correct with respect to the car but incorrect with respect to the bicycles. By contrast, in the line from Alanis Morissette's song "Head over Feet" (1995) referring to a man who held his breath and the door for her, the verb pairings are grammatically correct but discordant in meaning, with *held* applying to each noun object in a very different way. Still other scholars distinguish the terms entirely. For instance, in *The Arte of English Poesie* (1589), a treatise often attributed to George Puttenham, the author differentiates zeugma from syllepsis on the basis of congruity, associating zeugma with a yoking word that applies in a similar sense to others and syllepsis with a yoking word that applies in a different sense to others.

FURTHER EXAMPLES: The line from Cicero's "Pro Cluentio" speech (66 B.C.) "Lust conquered shame, boldness fear, madness reason" exemplifies zeugma broadly defined, with the single word "conquered" governing "shame," "fear," and "reason." The lines from Alexander Pope's poem "The Rape of the Lock" (1712, 1714) in which the **narrator** muses that the **heroine** will "stain her Honour, or her new Brocade, / . . . Or lose her Heart, or Necklace, at a Ball" use syllepsis to illustrate how "society types" often equate the significant and insignificant, valuing material goods as highly as moral or spiritual ones.

More contemporary examples of zeugma appear in Gore Vidal's **historical novel** *1876* (1976), in which the **protagonist** Charles Schuyler reports that his daughter Emma has given newspaperman Jamie Bennett "her

Medusa gaze, causing him to turn if not to stone to me"; Amy Tan's novel *The Hundred Secret Senses* (1995), in which protagonist Olivia Laguni, who is sitting in a half-empty restaurant with her husband Simon, muses "We were partners, not soul mates, two separate people who happened to be sharing a menu and a life"; and Catie Curtis's song "Kiss That Counted" (2001), in which the singer-songwriter shuts her windows and her eyes in a futile attempt to guard against the kiss she realizes will leave her undone.

Acknowledgments

W. H. Auden. "About the House" (3 lines), "Heavy Date" (4 lines), "Musée des Beaux Arts," "Postscript" (8 lines) to "Prologue: The Birth of Architecture," "The Cave of Nakedness" (3 line epigram). From W. H. *Auden: The Collected Poems* by W. H. Auden. Copyright © 1976 by Edward Mendelson, William Meredith, and Monroe K. Spears, executors of the estate of W. H. Auden. Used by permission of Random House, Inc. and Faber and Faber Ltd.

Amiri Baraka. "An Agony, As Now" (6 lines). From *The Dead Lecture*r by Imamu Amiri Baraka. Copyright © 1964 by Amiri Baraka. Excerpt (5) lines from *Return of Native* by Amiri Baraka. Copyright © 1969 by Amiri Baraka. Reprinted by permission of SII/Sterling Lord Literistic, Inc.

Matsuo Bashō. "the old pond–" (3 lines). From *Bashō and His Interpreters: Selected Hokku with Commentary*, compiled, translated, and with an Introduction by Makoto Ueda. Copyright © 1992 by the Board of Trustees of the Leland Stanford Junior University. Used by permission of Stanford University Press, www.sup.org. All rights reserved.

John Berryman. Dream Song #23 "The Lay of Ike." From *The Dream Songs* by John Berryman. Copyright © 1969 by John Berryman and renewed 1997 by Kate Donahue Berryman. Reprinted by permission of Farrar, Straus & Giroux, LLC and Faber & Faber Ltd.

Elizabeth Bishop. "The Fish" (9 lines). From *The Complete Poems 1927–1979* by Elizabeth Bishop. Copyright © 1979, 1983 by Alice Helen Methfessel. Reprinted by permission of Farrar, Straus & Giroux, LLC.

Frances Cornford. "Epitaph for a Reviewer" (4 lines). From *Selected Poems* by Frances Cornford. Copyright © 1954 by the Cresset Press. Reproduced by permission of Enitharmon Press/Enitharmon Editions Limited.

Countee Cullen. "Yet Do I Marvel" (2 lines). From *Color* by Countee Cullen. Copyright 1925 by Harper & Brothers. Copyright renewed 1952 by Ida M. Cullen. Copyrights held by Amistad Research Center, Tulane University, administered by Thompson and Thomson, New York, NY. Reprinted with permission.

E. E. Cummings. "l(a." From *Complete Poems: 1904–1962* by E. E. Cummings, edited by George J. Firmage. Copyright © 1958, 1986, 1991 by the Trustees for the E. E. Cummings Trust. Used by permission of Liveright Publishing Corporation.

Emily Dickinson. "A bird came down the walk" (4 lines), "Faith is a fine invention" (4 lines), "I dwell in possibility" (12 lines), "I taste a liquor never brewed" (4 lines), and "In Winter in my Room" (3 lines). From *The Poems of Emily Dickinson*, edited by Thomas H. Johnson, Mass.: The Belknap Press of Harvard University Press. Copyright © 1951, 1955, 1979, 1983 by the President and Fellows of Harvard College. Reprinted by permission of the publishers and Trustees of Amherst College.

George Dillon. "The World Goes Turning" (5 lines). From *Boy in the Wind* by George Dillon. Copyright © 1927 by Viking Press and renewed 1955 by George Dillon. Reprinted by permission of Nan Sherman Sussman.

H. D. (Hilda Doolittle). "Oread" (6 lines). From *Collected Poems 1912–1944* by H. D. Copyright © 1982 by the estate of Hilda Doolittle. Reprinted by permission of New Directions Publishing and Carcanet Press Limited (UK/ Commonwealth).

Russell Edson. "A Chair." Excerpt from a prose poem. From *The Very Thing That Happens, Fables and Drawings* by Russell Edson. Copyright © 1960, 1961, 1962, 1963, 1964 by Russell Edson. Reprinted by permission of New Directions Publishing Corp.

T. S. Eliot. "The Waste Land" (2 lines). From Collected Poems *1909–1962* by T. S. Eliot. Reprinted by permission of Faber & Faber, Ltd. Excerpt from "The Dry Salvages." From *Four Quartets*. Copyright © 1943 by T. S. Eliot and renewed 1971 by Esme Valerie Eliot. Reprinted by permission of Houghton Mifflin Harcourt Publishing Company.

Bob Englehart. Excerpt from Bob Englehart's blog, September 27, 2006. http:// blogs.courant.com/bob_englehart/2006/09/september_27_20.html#more. Reproduced by permission of the author.

Kathleen Craker Firestone. "Island Sestina" (21 lines). From *The Fox Islands, North and South* by Kathleen Craker Firestone. Copyright © 1996 by Kathleen Craker Firestone. Reprinted by permission of the author.

Allen Ginsberg. "Howl" (3 lines). From *Collected Poems 1947–1980* by Allen Ginsberg. Copyright © 1955 by Allen Ginsberg. Reprinted by permission of The Wylie Agency.

Theodor Seuss Geisel (Dr. Seuss). "How did it get so late . . ." (5 lines). From *Ode on the Subject of Septuagenarianism* by Dr. Seuss. Copyright © 2003 by Dr. Seuss Enterprises, L.P. All rights reserved.

Thom Gunn. "Considering the Snail" (8 lines). From *My Sad Captains* by Thom Gunn. Copyright © 1994 by Thom Gunn. Reprinted by permission of Farrar, Straus & Giroux, LLC and Faber & Faber Ltd.

Carla Harryman. "For She" (8 lines). Excerpt from prose poem, "For She," which appeared in *Under the Bridge* by Carla Harryman. Copyright © 1982 by Carla Harryman. Published by This Press in 1982. Used by permission of the author.

Langston Hughes. "Harlem (2)" and "Long Trip" (2 lines). From *The Collected Poems of Langston Hughes* by Langston Hughes, edited by Arnold Rampersad with David Roessel, Associate Editor. Copyright © 1994 by the estate of Langston Hughes. Used by permission of Alfred A. Knopf, a division of Random House, Inc., and Harold Ober Associates, Inc.

Jane Kenyon. "Having It Out with Melancholy" (5 lines). From *Constance* by Jane Kenyon. Copyright © 1993 by the estate of Jane Kenyon. Reprinted by permission of Greywolf Press, Saint Paul, Minnesota.

Philip Larkin. "Toads" (4 lines). From *The Less Deceived* by Philip Larkin. Copyright © 1955 by The Marvell Press. Reprinted by permission of The Marvell Press, England and Australia.

D.H. Lawrence. "Fish" (4 lines), "Love on the Farm" (4 lines) and "Poetry of the Present" (1 paragraph). From *The Complete Poems of D. H. Lawrence* edited by V. de Sola Pinto & F. W. Roberts. Copyright © 1964, 1971 by Angelo Ravagli and C. M. Weekley, executors of the estate of Frieda Lawrence Ravagli. Used by permission of Viking Penguin, a division of Penguin Group (USA) Inc., Pollinger Limited, and the estate of Frieda Lawrence Ravagli.

Robert Lowell. "Waking Early Sunday Morning" (stanza). From *Selected Poems* by Robert Lowell. Copyright © 1976 by Robert Lowell. Reprinted by permission of Farrar, Straus & Giroux, LLC.

Michael McClintock. Haiku (3 lines) from *Tundra: The Journal of the Short Poem*, issue no. 2, 2001. Reprinted with permission of the poet.

Josephine Miles. "Belief" (4 lines). From *Collected Poems 1930–1983* by Josephine Miles. Copyright © 1983 by Josephine Miles. Used with permission of the poet and the University of Illinois Press.

Ogden Nash. "Reflections on Ice-Breaking." From *Verses from 1929 On* by Ogden Nash. Copyright © 1930 by Ogden Nash. First appeared in *The New Yorker*. Reprinted with permission. (update to follow)

Dorothy Parker. "Résumé." From *The Portable Dorothy Parker* by Dorothy Parker, edited by Marion Meade. Copyright © 1926, 1928 and renewed 1954, 1956 by Dorothy Parker. Used by permission of Viking Penguin, a division of Penguin Group (USA) Inc. and Gerald Duckworth and Company Ltd.

Octavio Paz. "Between What I. . . ." (5 lines) and "Writing" (4 lines). From *The Collected Poems of Octavio Paz 1957–1987*, edited and translated by Eliot Weinberger. With additional translations by Elizabeth Bishop, Paul Blackburn, Lysander Kemp, Denise Levertov, John Frederick Nims, Mark Strand, and Charlies Tomlinson. Copyright © 1971 by New Directions Publishing Corp. Copyright © 1972, 1973, 1978, 1979, 1986 by Octavio Paz and Eliot Weinberger. Reprinted with permission of New Directions Publishing Corp.

Sylvia Plath. "Daddy" (9 lines). From Ariel by Sylvia Plath. "Mirror." Copyright © 1963 by Ted Hughes. Reprinted by permission of HarperCollins Publishers, Inc. and Faber and Faber Ltd.

John Crowe Ransom. "Dead Boy" (8 lines). From *Selected Poems, Third Edition, Revised and Enlarged* by John Crowe Ransom. Copyright © 1924, 1927 by Alfred A. Knopf and renewed 1952, 1955 by John Crowe Ransom. Used by permission of Alfred A. Knopf, a division of Random House, Inc. and Carcanet Press Limited (UK/Commonwealth).

Adrienne Rich. "Toward the Solstice" (1 line). From *The Dream of a Common Language: Poems 1974–1977* by Adrienne Rich. Copyright © 1978 by W. W. Norton & Company, Inc. Reprinted by permission of the author and W. W. Norton & Company, Inc.

Theodore Roethke. "The Storm (Forio D'Ischia)" (3 lines). From *The Collected Poems of Theodore Roethke* by Theodore Roethke. Copyright © 1961 by Beatrice Roethke. Used by permission of Doubleday, a division of Random House, Inc.

Robert B. Shaw. "Renovations" (2 lines). Copyright © 1977 by Robert B. Shaw. Reprinted with permission.

Edith Sitwell. "Trio for Two Cats and a Trombone" (2 lines). From *Façade and Other Poems 1920–1935* by Edith Sitwell. Copyright © 1950 by Edith Sitwell. Reprinted by permission of David Higham Associates Limited.

Stevie Smith. "Our Bog is Dood" (stanza). From *Collected Poems of Stevie Smith*. Copyright © 1972 by Stevie Smith. Reprinted by permission of New Directions Publishing Corp. and Hamish MacGibbon, James & James (Publishers) Ltd.

Wallace Stevens. "Study of Two Pears" (2 lines) and "Sunday Morning" (7 lines). From *The Collected Poems of Wallace Stevens* by Wallace Stevens. Copyright © 1954 by Wallace Stevens and renewed 1982 by Holly Stevens. Used by permission of Alfred A. Knopf, a division of Random House, Inc. "Of Mere Being" (1 line). From *Opus Posthumous* by Wallace Stevens, edited by Milton J. Bates. Copyright © 1989 by Holly Stevens. Preface and Selection copyright © 1989 by Alfred A. Knopf. Copyright © 1957 by Elsie Stevens and Holly Stevens and renewed 1985 by Holly Stevens. Used by permission of Vintage Books, a division of Random House, Inc. and Faber & Faber Ltd. (UK).

Rabindranath Tagore. "Gitanjali, poem #35" (10 lines). From *Gitanjali* by Rabindranath Tagore. Copyright © 1956 by Rabindranath Tagore. Published by Macmillan and Co. Ltd. Reprinted by permission of Visva-Bharati.

Don Taylor. Excerpt from translation of *Iphigenia at Aulis* by Euripides. From *Euripides: The War Plays*, Metheun Drama Series, 1990. Copyright © 1990 by Don Taylor. Reprinted by permission of Random House, UK.

The Onion. "EPA to Drop 'E,' 'P' from Name." Published by *The Onion*, March 23, 2005, and appeared at http://www.theonion.com. Copyright © 2005 by *The Onion*. Reprinted by permission of The Onion, Inc. All rights reserved.

Dylan Thomas. "A Refusal to Mourn the Death, by Fire, of a Child in London (6 lines)" and "Do Not Go Gentle Into That Good Night" (6 lines). From *The Poems of Dylan Thomas* by Dylan Thomas. Copyright © 1952 by Dylan

Thomas. Reprinted by permission of New Directions Publishing Corp. and David Higham Associates Limited.

Derek Walcott. "A Far Cry from Africa" (stanza). From *Collected Poems 1948–1984* by Derek Walcott. Copyright © 1986 by Derek Walcott. Reprinted by permission of Farrar, Straus and Giroux LLC and Faber & Faber Ltd.

Jerry W. Ward. "Jazz to Jackson to John" (13 opening lines, plus 3 other lines). Copyright © 1988 by Jerry W. Ward, Jr. Reprinted by permission of the author.

Rachel Wetzsteon. "Stage Directions for a Short Play." From *Other Stars* by Rachel Wetzsteon. Copyright © 1994 by Rachel Wetzsteon. Used by permission of Penguin, a division of Penguin Group (USA) Inc.

C. Webster Wheelock. "Arrogant paragon" (2 double dactyls), "History, Gistory" (2 lines), and "Monocle-bonocle." From *History Gistory* (unpublished). Reprinted by permission of the author.

William Carlos Williams. "Poem (As the cat)" and "The Red Wheelbarrow" (8 lines). From *Collected Poems: 1909–1939*, Volume 1. Copyright © 1938 by New Directions Publishing Corp. Reprinted by permission of New Directions Publishing Corp. and Carcanet Press Limited (UK/Commonwealth).

W. B. Yeats. "The Lake Isle of Innisfree" (2 lines), "The Second Coming" (4 lines), "The Wild Swans at Coole" (2 lines). From *The Collected Works of W. B. Yeats: Volume 1: The Poems, Revised*, by Richard J. Finneran. Copyright © 1924 by The Macmillan Company and renewed 1952 by Bertha Georgie Yeats and A. P. Watt Ltd. on behalf of Michael B. Yeats.

Art

Garry Trudeau, *Doonesbury* Snoopy doghouse cartoon. DOONESBURY © 1997 G. B. Trudeau. Reprinted with permission of UNIVERSAL PRESS SYNDICATE. All rights reserved.

Gary Larson, "Edgar attacked by a werewolf" cartoon. The Far Side ® by Gary Larson © 1994 FarWorks, Inc. All Rights Reserved. The Far Side ® and the Larson ® signature are registered trademarks of FarWorks, Inc. Used with permission.

Gary Larson, "Has a bun in the oven" cartoon. The Far Side ® by Gary Larson © 1990 FarWorks, Inc. All Rights Reserved. The Far Side ® and the Larson ® signature are registered trademarks of FarWorks, Inc. Used with permission.

Hieronymus Bosch, "Hell" panel from *The Garden of Earthly Delights*. *The Garden of Earthly Delights*: "Hell," right wing of triptych, c. 1500 (oil on panel) by Hieronymus Bosch (c. 1450–1516) © Prado, Madrid, Spain/The Bridgeman Art Library.

Index of Authors
and Titles

About the Authors

Ross Murfin, E. A. Lilly Distinguished Professor of English and former provost at Southern Methodist University, has also taught at the University of Virginia; Yale University; and the University of Miami, where he was the dean of the College of Arts and Sciences until 1996. He is the author of *Swinburne, Lawrence, Hardy, and the Burden of Belief* (1978); *The Poetry of D. H. Lawrence: Texts and Contexts* (1983); *Sons and Lovers: A Novel of Division and Desire* (1987); and *Lord Jim: After the Truth* (1992); and the editor of *Conrad Revisited: Essays for the Eighties* (1983). The series editor of Bedford/St. Martin's popular Case Studies in Contemporary Criticism, he has also edited two volumes in the series, Joseph Conrad's *Heart of Darkness* (second edition 1996) and Nathaniel Hawthorne's *The Scarlet Letter* (second edition 2006).

Supryia M. Ray is a writer, editor, and English teacher. A summa cum laude graduate of the University of Miami, she has assisted Ross Murfin in the research and preparation of more than a dozen volumes in the Case Studies in Contemporary Criticism series and authored "Contextual Documents and Illustrations" for the second edition of *The Scarlet Letter*. She graduated magna cum laude from Harvard Law School in 1998, served as a law clerk on the U.S. District Court and the U.S. Court of Appeals, entered private practice as a litigator, and then performed public-interest environmental advocacy in Washington, D.C. She also served for two years with Literacy AmeriCorps, teaching adult learners a variety of subjects including English, reading, writing, and public speaking. She now divides her time between teaching and writing.